# Prison Reform in Lancashire, 1700-1850

"Those darling bygone times, Mr. Carker," said
Cleopatra, "with their delicious fortresses, and their dear
old dungeons, and their delightful places of torture, and
their romantic vengeances, and their picturesque assaults
and sieges, and everything that makes life truly
charming! How dreadfully we have degenerated!"

Charles Dickens, *Dombey and Son*

# Prison Reform in Lancashire, 1700-1850

## A STUDY IN LOCAL ADMINISTRATION

*Margaret DeLacy*

STANFORD UNIVERSITY PRESS
*Stanford, California 1986*

Stanford University Press
Stanford, California

© 1986 by the Board of Trustees of the
Leland Stanford Junior University

Printed in the United States of America

CIP data appear at the end of the book

Published with the assistance of
the Andrew W. Mellon Foundation

*To my parents*

# Acknowledgments

I would like to thank, in addition to the libraries listed in the Document Sources, the following institutions for giving me access to numerous secondary works and for other assistance: in Oregon, the Clackamas County Library, the Multnomah County Library, the Oregon Health Sciences University, Reed College, and the University of Oregon; in Washington, D.C., the Library of Congress and the National Library of Medicine; in London, the Institute of Historical Research and the Society of Friends' Library; and in England, the Essex, Oxford, and West Yorkshire County Record Offices.

I would also like to thank the following librarians and archivists for their time and patience in giving me personal assistance: Ms. Gaddes at the Lancaster City Library; Mr. David Jones, Mr. David Smith, Ms. Janet Parkinson, and Mr. George Fisher at the Lancaster County Record Office; Ms. Glenise Matheson at the John Rylands University Library in Manchester; Ms. Margaret DeMotte at the Manchester Central Library; Ms. Nancy Hanks at the National Library of Medicine; and Ms. Alice Prochaska at the Public Record Office.

Mr. Kenneth Neale, Mr. M. Butters, and Colonel J. S. Haywood of the Home Office made it possible for me to visit Lancaster and Preston Prisons and helped me track down Lancashire records that had not been deposited in government archives. I would like to thank Mr. Fall, the governor at Lancaster, Mr. G. W. Morrall, the deputy governor at Preston, and the staff at each prison for giving me tours of their respective prisons and answering numerous questions. I would also like to thank the Governor of HM Prison, Bedford, for his assistance.

I will always be grateful to the numerous scholars working in this field who very generously shared both their own work and their sources with me. They include Dr. Marguerite Dupree, Dr. Robin Evans, Dr. Tony Howe, Dr. Walter Joseph King, Ms. Valerie Johnston, Dr. Sean Mc-Conville, Mr. Malcolm Ramsey, Dr. Wayne Joseph Sheehan, Judge Eric Stockdale, Dr. Heather Tomlinson, Dr. Richard Trainor, Dr. John Styles, and Dr. John Walton.

Finally, I am especially grateful to those scholars who not only shared their own work with me but also read and criticized portions of this book. They include Dr. Victor Bailey, Dr. John Dinwiddy, Mr. Michael Collinge, Dr. V. A. C. Gatrell, Dr. Michael Ignatieff, Ms. Joanna Innes, Dr. Margaret Pelling, Sir Leon Radzinowicz, and Dr. David Smith. Dr. Lawrence Stone and Dr. Robert Darnton, who served as advisers for the thesis that formed the basis for this book, also provided valuable editorial advice, as did the anonymous readers for Stanford University Press, who undertook an often unrewarding task with patience and understanding.

Margaret DeLacy

# Contents

# Tables and Figures

# Prison Reform in Lancashire, 1700-1850

# Introduction

There are several reasons for the recent scholarly interest in the history of prisons. First, like asylums, workhouses, and reformatory schools, prisons are examples of what Erving Goffman has called "total institutions."[1] Sociologists have become interested in the effect that these closed institutions have on their inmates, both by separating them from the outside world and by creating a different sort of community inside. These institutions all attained their modern form within the past hundred years.

Second, the subject has contemporary political importance. In both England and America the prison system is now under severe strain, as a rapidly rising crime rate crams more and more prisoners into old, deteriorating buildings. The resulting prison revolts and riots have attracted widespread attention and become political issues in their own right, as has the treatment of political prisoners both at home and abroad. At such a time it seems useful to try to understand how the modern prison system developed, how we treated our own prisoners in the past, and how previous generations coped with their own rising crime rates and political prisoners.

Third, developments within historiography have encouraged a renewed interest in the administrative history of prisons. Ever since Dicey's lectures on law and public opinion, but more especially within the past generation, historians have debated the origin of the "welfare state" and the reasons for the legislation of the "Age of Reform" in the first half of the nineteenth century.[2] Prison reform was part of this movement and shared the characteristics of other reforms: a gradual shift of initiative from local to central power, the establishment of a central commission and of a national inspectorate to enforce and superintend governmental decisions, and support from a small group of "middle-class" agitators. Unlike the New Poor Law, the Victorian prison system is still alive; very few English prisons were built after 1877, and the discipline that the old buildings still dictate would still be recognizable to the man of 1840. If the continued existence of the English prison system gives the English some reason to be interested in its past, it concerns Americans for another reason: the United States is now debating whether to continue along a path similar to that taken by England a century ago. By giving the central government increasing power to intervene in local administration and by turning to it for revenue, Americans are gradually shifting control from local to national government.

Like many of the other reforms of the past century, prison reform has evoked mixed feelings among historians. The more traditional see the story as one of progress. This, in general, has been the attitude of local historians and of the biographers of such great reformers as John Howard and Elizabeth Fry. The most important historians of the subject, Sidney and Beatrice Webb, also adopted this view, at least for the period before 1877, although they tempered it with sharp criticism of certain decisions and concluded that "it is probably quite impossible to make a good job of the deliberate incarceration of a human being in the most enlightened of dungeons."[3]

To radical writers—such as Bernard Shaw, who wrote a lengthy preface to the Webbs' book—imprisonment was a fundamental mistake: an institution best abandoned entirely. Among certain recent authors, imprisonment symbolizes everything that is most detestable in the modern state; it is a "totalitarian" instrument of power, used to hammer men into a new image when they are inside and to maintain a repressive structure of power among those outside. To these thinkers, every innovation of the Age of Reform simply put more nails into a coffin built round living men.

This attitude toward the institutions of the modern state in general and toward the prison in particular is by no means new:[4] books expressing this view have always had a relatively wide circulation among the reading public. They did not have much effect on working historians, however, until the appearance of a series of specialized works written for an academic audience. The first of these was Gertrude Himmelfarb's essay, "The Haunted House of Jeremy Bentham" (1965). This account of the failure of Bentham's Panopticon largely amounted to an attack on its author. The Panopticon, Himmelfarb argued, began as an apparently liberal innovation in prison discipline but rapidly degenerated into an exercise in cost-cutting exploitation, as Bentham was carried away by the beautiful image of himself as the all-powerful and enriched Contractor.[5]

Especially important was Himmelfarb's use of the Panopticon as a departure point for a total reevaluation of "philosophical radicalism." Bentham, she argued, elevated the "greatest happiness of the greatest number" above all other social desiderata, including rights, liberty, and the guarantees provided by common law. With Bentham, she wrote, "There was no question of the 'rights' of prisoners and paupers, for there was no such thing as rights at all. There were only interests, and the interests of the majority had to prevail. The greatest happiness of the greatest number might thus require the greatest misery of the few." She added that Bentham was as uninterested in the idea of liberty as he was in that of fundamental rights, because they "obscured the real issues, which were happiness, security and good government."[6]

Himmelfarb's disquiet about the effect of utilitarian beliefs on social policy had a great impact on the authors who followed her. Her view of Bentham as a self-interested manipulator of the poor, a "spider in his web," has been echoed by other writers on the Panopticon and extended to other reformers, such as Howard. It has become common to assume that prison reformers were motivated by self- or class-interest in the furtherance of "social control"—an assumption that Himmelfarb herself might not endorse.[7]

This article was also important because of the strength of its imagery. For the historians who have followed Himmelfarb, the Panopticon—that "machine" for "grinding men good" with its "big brother" inspection system, its exploitative work, its codified rules, its fertile inventions for manipulating both body and soul—has entirely eclipsed as a cautionary symbol those two great "gothic" monuments to royal caprice and official neglect, the Bastille and Newgate. For many, the squalor of early modern life is preferable to the automated management of 1984. Himmelfarb has provided thinkers such as Foucault with an appropriate symbol for the modern state. It may be important to remember, therefore, that whatever the Panopticon represents, English society persistently balked at adopting it.

Six years after Himmelfarb's article appeared, David Rothman published a complete reevaluation of the history of American custodial institutions in *The Discovery of the Asylum*. In this wide-ranging intellectual history, Rothman described the transition from the small, familial institutions of the Colonial period to the large, highly regimented institutions of the early nineteenth century, which were organized on a military model. According to Rothman, reformers in Jacksonian America attempted to compensate for the family's perceived failure to act as a stabilizing force by providing institutional discipline for the mad, the poor, the criminal, and the young. "The reformers' original doctrines," he concludes, "were especially liable to abuse, their emphasis on authority, obedience, and regularity turning all too predictably into a mechanical application of discipline. And by incarcerating the deviant and dependent, . . . they discouraged—really eliminated—the search for other solutions that might have been less susceptible to abuse." Rothman ends with a call to avoid institutional responses to social problems because "proposals that promise the most grandiose consequences often legitimate the most unsatisfactory developments."[8]

This is also the position taken by Michel Foucault, whose book *Discipline and Punish* appeared in 1975, following his earlier *Madness and Civilization*. *Discipline and Punish* centers on the transition from a society based on representative torture in the name of the monarch to one of systematic incarceration in the name of public order. When Foucault speaks of incarceration he refers not merely to prisons but also to all modern residential institutions, from reform schools and insane asylums to schools and hospitals. These "carcerals" all maintain order by systematically manipulating their residents. To this end, they make regular divisions and classifications not only in space (e.g., cells) and time but also in the character of their inmates. Foucault considers this last division of particular importance, because it employs the methods on which such modern disciplines as medicine, psychiatry, and sociology are based: a preliminary "examination" and a continuing and inescapable observation or surveillance. The information gained thereby is used to establish standards of normality and deviancy: concepts that were unknown before these institutional methods appeared. Carcerals actually create deviancy and deviants, both by labeling them as such and by separating the deviants from the rest of society.[9]

Foucault argues that the creation of deviancy is a deliberate ploy on the part of the bourgeoisie: first, because it separates the more active and intelligent malefactors from their natural sympathizers among the lower classes; second, because it diverts attention from the greater illegalities perpetrated by the middle and upper classes; and third, because the dependent and easily controlled deviants can be turned into informers and make useful tools for spying on the lower classes. By these means, political radicalism and social unrest are controlled. The high recidivism rate of prisons, therefore, is not an accident or a sign of failure, but the very purpose of their existence.

Prison reform was built into the prison system from the start; it serves the prisons rather than changing them. Far from failing, prison reform has succeeded in keeping the prison firmly rooted in our society. It was never intended to change the way prisons function, but to make them more "corrective" and more "rigorous." "For a century and a half," Foucault writes, "the prison had always been offered as its own remedy: the reactivation of the penitentiary techniques as the only means of overcoming their perpetual failure."[10]

Foucault's arguments have served as the starting point for several young historians. Especially important is a recent book by Michael Ignatieff, *A Just Measure of Pain: The Penitentiary in the Industrial Revolution, 1750-1850*, which applies many of Foucault's theories to an account of a specific era in English penal history. Ignatieff's conclusion contains deliberate echoes of Foucault. Foucault had asked, "Is it surprising that the cellular prison, with its regular chronologies, forced labour, its authorities of surveillance and registration, its experts in normality, who continue and multiply the functions of the judge, should have become the modern instrument of penality? Is it surprising that prisons resemble factories, schools, barracks, hospitals, which all resemble prisons?"[11] Ignatieff in turn concludes, "Humanitarianism was inextricably linked to the practice of domination. . . . It was no accident that penitentiaries, asylums, workhouses, monitorial schools, night refuges, and reformatories looked alike, or that their charges marched to the same disciplinary cadence. Since they made up a complementary and interdependent structure of control, it was essential that their diets and deprivations be calibrated on an ascending scale, school—workhouse—asylum—prison, with the pain of the last serving to undergird the pain of the first. Nor was it accidental that these state institutions so closely resembled the factory."[12]

Ignatieff agrees with Foucault that prison reform and incarceration served each other in a complicated way: "To interpret the history of reform as a cycle of good intentions confounded by unintended consequences is to see it as a history of failure. But reform was a success. . . .

Yet . . . it is a success full of paradox. The movement . . . established among a skeptical, middle-class public the ideal that prisons ought to reform, without ever having to convince them that penitentiaries actually did so. . . . Typically, few reformers ever bothered to torture the recidivism rates into a validation of the penitentiary."[13]

Ignatieff supports his conclusion with an account of the initial development of the penitentiary and of the motives that underlay the reformers' efforts. He fixes this development firmly in its specific historical context: economic (the Industrial Revolution), social (changes in the crime rate and in the behavior of crowds), legal (changes in the jurisdiction of justices of the peace), military (the disruption of penal transportation overseas), political (the battle between Whigs, Tories, and Radicals), and intellectual (the development of "materialist" psychology). He leans toward Rothman's thesis that the reformers were motivated by concern over the apparent disintegration of the social order and by their desire for "a social order based on deferential reconciliation." These factors combined with a sense of guilt (produced by the feeling that "the rich bore some responsibility for the social genesis of crime"), political interests, and religious beliefs to produce a special blend of attitudes affecting penal policies. The end result of these interlinked changes was the experimental national prison at Pentonville, and Ignatieff vividly describes the harsh and solitary regime enforced there. Ignatieff's argument has been echoed by several other radical historians and has been widely accepted by historians in general.[14]

The present book was designed as a test of the radical view, to which it is heavily indebted. I have several objections, however, to the radicals' attempt to explain complex events as merely the history of the domination of one group by another. The first objection is that the approach is based on a theory of "social control"—a phrase that is, unfortunately, so highly charged and yet so vague that it obscures more than it reveals. Many authors who use it really mean "socialization," that is, the way a society acculturates its members. Others use it as a rough synonym for "discipline," so that, for example, the discipline exercised in a school is seen as a form of "social control." Lurking behind the phrase, and all the more potent because tacit, is a more or less Marxist class theory. "Social control" is useless as a tool unless one knows who is being controlled and who is doing the controlling. The usual, although often unproven, assumption is that it is the lower, or working, class that is being controlled, and the aristocracy, the upper class, the middle class, or the bourgeoisie that is doing the controlling. Although authors vary in the care with which they delineate the parties to this relationship, many radical writers assume that any system that furthers the stability of an unequal society necessarily benefits those toward the top, and was, therefore, deliberately created for this purpose. This assumption may make sense when the right to exercise power is clearly at issue, and when the two sides to a conflict are well delineated, as in debates over politics or the right to vote. It becomes more dubious when the identities of the parties to the conflict are unclear. Anyone who lives in society is subject to communal controls, but not all controls, even those that apply differentially to members of different status groups, are "social controls" in the generally accepted sense of the phrase. An example would be the control exercised by guilds or trade unions over the right to work and over working practices. Another would be the control exercised by the old over the young in establishing minimum drinking, driving, and voting ages. If the theory of social control is shorn of its basis in class theory, it loses its bite and its meaning: to say that a school exercises "social control" in this sense is not an explanation but a tautology. If by social control we mean that an upper class is engaged in controlling a lower one, then the classes must be carefully specified and the divergence in their interests demonstrated. This is particularly important when cultural values rather than material goods are in question. Such values may percolate up and down without any proselytizing by the class that holds them—often, indeed, to its dismay.

In a recent review article, Michael Ignatieff has conceded this point. As he eloquently wrote:

The "social control" model of the prison's function which informed my own work assumed that capitalist society was systematically incapable of reproducing itself without the constant interposition of state agencies of control and repression. . . . Important as the penal sanction may have been in sustaining discipline in pauperized labor markets, or in constituting wage discipline itself in the face of worker resistance, we ought not to take these instances as typical of the role of state force once the wage bargain has been widely accepted. . . . Even in objectively exploitative . . . conditions of labor, one can conceive of men and women voluntarily coming to work. . . . By describing all social relations as relations of domination, Foucault neglects the large aspects of human sociability, in the family and in civil society generally, which are conducted by the norms of cooperation, reciprocity, and the "gift relationship."[15]

This is not to say that a theory based on cultural consensus or imitation is necessarily more appropriate than one based on social conflict, but merely that there are circumstances in which one or the other may be the more plausible alternative. Ideally, we will search for a reasonable balance between the consensual and the coercive while recognizing that this balance is constantly changing.

The problem becomes particularly acute in the case of the penal system, because the admitted purpose of this institution is control. Radical writers have tended to assume that the Victorian habit of distinguishing between the respectable and unrespectable poor was disingenuous, that it served the wish to divide and conquer. They have, therefore, tended to associate the poor and the criminal in order to place them in opposition to the middle or upper classes, feeling that both could only gain from an overthrow of the established order. For example, Peter Linebaugh has suggested that in imposing especially severe penalties on murderers, the members of Parliament who passed the Murder Act were expressing their class hatred.[16]

A class-based approach to penal law is not necessarily incorrect, but it requires demonstration in every specific case. A consensual model may be equally useful in understanding a particular series of decisions, as may a theory based on social conflicts that have other dividing points than those of class. As much as anything, prison, like war, is an institution created by the old but experienced by the young.

Even laws governing property crimes, such as larceny, met with a generally favorable response, even from the poor, who, after all, were the most frequent victims as well as the most frequently imprisoned perpetrators of such crimes. David Philips, in an investigation of criminal prosecution in the Black Country in the mid-nineteenth century, has pointed out that

large numbers of workingmen prosecuted other workingmen for thefts . . . from themselves; they did not simply exact informal retribution from them, but invoked the whole formal and cumbersome process of the law. . . . This suggests two things. First, they must have believed that the system of law had at least some element of justice and fairness about it. . . . Secondly, whatever their feelings about the law and its agents, they cannot have been totally opposed to the idea of invoking the law to prosecute thefts of private property. . . . By making use of the law in this way, they showed an acceptance of its basic legitimacy as applied to themselves and their affairs.[17]

As is quite evident from even the most skeptical reading of their comments, criminals themselves often accepted most of the premises of the ethical system that surrounded them, however much they may have resented heavy-handed attempts to drive the message home.

If the poor were not always antagonistic toward the rules that created the prison, they were also often ambivalent about the rules that were introduced within it. Perhaps the most unpleasant and frightening aspect of imprisonment is the imposition of an unavoidable and unprotected intimacy with serious and often dangerous criminals. Prisoners are afraid of each other. They are also frightened by the possibility of brutality from the staff and, in the early nineteenth century, they were afraid of dying from hunger or disease. The Hulks gained their reputation for brutality partly because of their appalling disease rate, but also because the staff battened down the hatches at the end of the day and left the convicts within to their own devices. While prison reform received a mixed response from prisoners, many welcomed at least moderate controls on behavior, which offered them a measure of protection from each other. Among them were the rules governing general cleanliness and hygiene, rules preventing extortion of food, and rules providing for classification of prisoners according to their sex, age, and offense. How consistently these rules were enforced is open to some doubt. It also seems clear in retrospect that the silent and separate systems went too far in preventing mutual "contamination."

Nevertheless, prisoners themselves often invoked the rules governing classification and strongly resented being confined with more serious offenders. They also expected a degree of protection from prison staff and were increasingly likely to protest if they felt a turnkey had failed to intervene in a fight or had responded too slowly to an illness. Though many prisoners probably welcomed the improved provisions for their health and comfort, some bitterly regretted the loss of freedom and autonomy this necessarily entailed. There was an inevitable trade-off between freedom and protection, and though historians may decide for themselves which they would prefer, they cannot do so with assurance for others.

The story of prison reform, therefore, is not simply the story of the repression of one group, consisting of prisoners, by another group, consisting of administrators. Prisoners themselves were deeply divided over the issue of prison reform as a whole and over the desirability of any particular reform. Even politically radical prisoners like Henry Hunt, John Knight, and John Doherty not only accepted the need for penal imprisonment for (nonpolitical) criminal offenses but also insisted that the authorities enforce a division between them and other convicts. They wished to remove themselves from prison and to control the corruption of prison officers that prevented the system from working "properly"—but not to eliminate imprisonment as an institution. Indeed, they were often strong proponents of the belief that imprisonment ought to be reformative.[18]

The radical argument also raises a problem in ethics. Some authors claim that the solution to the dilemma of choosing between dangerous freedom and corrupting control is to abandon imprisonment entirely. The worst thing about prison reform, for them, is not its content but the fact that it legitimizes imprisonment. If prisons were allowed to decay, without the constant investment of effort, money, and good intentions, perhaps they would be used less often, thus producing a clear benefit to those thousands of potential inmates no longer jailed. This theory applies a deterrent to the judge, who is prevented from sentencing offenders to prison by the absolute wretchedness of those already there. This rather backward deterrent is subject to the same objections originally raised against the eighteenth-century defenders of the "bloody code" of exemplary capital punishment: is it just to punish one man beyond his deserts in order to affect the behavior of someone else? Although the convict population is rising rapidly, both the English and the Americans have deliberately avoided building new prisons, at least partly from a desire to encourage alternatives to incarceration. This is all very well for the convicted robber who now receives a year's probation, but what of the convicted burglar or rapist who is serving out his time jammed into a Victorian cell with three other men, unable even to take a shower for weeks on end? In any case, it is by no means evident that excess prison capacity produces excessive convictions, as the declining conviction rate in England after 1855 suggests. In the late nineteenth century, prisons all over England were shut down for want of inmates.

Moreover, it is doubtful whether even the most appalling prison conditions, even when accompanied by riots, would do much to interest the public in an alternative "decarceration" policy. What evidence there is suggests the opposite. If imprisonment can be changed only if our social structure changes fundamentally, then there seems no reason why we should not make what improvements we can while awaiting that (surely distant) event. Rothman has suggested that reformed institutions are particularly liable to abuse; this may be true, but there were plenty of abuses in the more casual administration of the eighteenth century as well. Furthermore, I cannot help wondering what sort of institutions we will end up with if we make it clear that we will do nothing at all to improve them and really do not care how they are run.

A final objection is purely practical. We do not, in fact, know to what extent the reforms discussed by Ignatieff, Foucault, and others were actually carried out in the prisons. Foucault pays no attention whatever to this problem. Ignatieff concentrates on the "national" prisons, Pentonville and Millbank. Yet these institutions are by no means typical English prisons; from the start they were designed as special experimental places for particularly dangerous offenders. Life in even the largest of the provincial prisons was a world apart. Is it useful to write about how the middle classes were preoccupied with maintaining social order, if they never did much about it? There is a parallel between this controversy and the one about the effects of the New Poor Law; recently some researchers, such as Eric Midwinter, have pointed out that in many regions of England this controversial reform largely amounted to cosmetic changes in the titles of poor law officers. As Midwinter has written, "The continuum between old and new in the country's Poor Law management comes as no surprise. Nevertheless, it must be demonstrated, or the general significance attached to a dramatic Act of Parliament may be allowed to conceal the character of its humdrum practice at the local level."[19]

If we are ever to weigh the costs of prison reform against its benefits, we must know what both were. Despite lengthy arguments, we still know very little about what English prisons were actually like. Many scholars have written about reforms, but we do not know what it was that was being reformed. It is easy to find prison scandals but less easy to reach an understanding of day-to-day life. The only way to uncover the character of the "humdrum practice" of prison administration at a local level is through patient case studies based on archival research in local records. This book undertakes such a case study of a single county prison system, bearing in mind the radical picture of nineteenth-century prisons as sterile, highly regimented institutions that imposed a strict regime on their cowed inmates. We will follow a single county prison system over a long period in order to determine what the system was like before it was reformed; what led local administrators to embark on reform; just what reforms were in fact made; the political, economic, and social context that defined the reforms; and what sort of prison system they created.

One result of a molehill view of history is that many variations appear in a terrain that, viewed from the mountain, might look like a smooth plain. Prisons that might seem quite similar when encompassed in a study of national penal policy based on central records emerge as very diverse when viewed separately, just as the statistically similar families of the demographer take on individuality as the subjects of biography. Historians need both approaches, even though the angle of view may help determine the final conclusion. Certainly, one of the chief conclusions of this study is that though policy choices and new ideas played an important role in the character and quality of the English prison system, on the whole it was impossible for anyone to control that system by making comprehensive policy decisions at the top. Even within a single county, prisons were diverse. Lancashire alone had four prisons, each of which differed radically from the others. They ranged from Lancaster Castle, which was more or less a model of the "unreformed" system, to Preston, as close to a model of the new system as any county prison, to Salford, reformed but embodying all the abuses of the old system—corrupt, crowded and brutal—to Kirkdale, brand-new but nearly ungoverned.

The overall character of these institutions was determined chiefly by three factors: the nature and number of their inmates, the quality of their staff, and the extent of their day-to-day administrative supervision. English prison staffs were comparatively small, and interference by overseers like the justices or the inspectors was comparatively infrequent, so even after the Age of Reform had broken the autonomy of prisoners, the general character of the inmates and of the culture they brought with them into the prison determined many facets of daily life, such as the extent of violence. The level of serious violence in nineteenth-century English prisons was comparatively low because most of the prisoners were not violent and had not been committed for serious, violent offenses—and because mid-nineteenth-century England was a comparatively nonviolent society.

The prison administrators had little control over the character of the inmates, but they exercised some indirect control over their numbers. Though the question of prosecution rates is at the edge of this study, the size of prison populations was a critical element in the quality of prison life. Even more important, however, was the direct control that administrators exercised over the quality of the prison staff, and particularly over the governor. The choice of governor was the single most important decision that could consciously be made in prison affairs, and one made even more significant by prison reform. Eighteenth-century reformers emphasized the need to choose good gaolers, and success in this area was far more important for the realization of their ambitions than were the disciplinary codes they drew up or the buildings they created. While Lancashire's records do not reveal how gaolers were chosen, they do, as this book shows, reveal how the character of particular gaolers affected their prisons. In many ways prison reform made controlling the behavior of the gaoler even more difficult than it had been before.

Unlike Foucault and other radical authors, I do not see the proliferation of institutions in the modern period as in itself a matter for concern. Institutions unavoidably circumscribe freedom, but so do many other dispositions; a cruel "foster family" may be as confining as stone walls and iron bars for the involuntary resident. Though the quality of a prison's food, shelter, and medical care is important, the overall quality of prison life and of the penal system in general depends far more on humane administration than on the adoption of any particular scheme for reform.

Nevertheless, Foucault and Ignatieff are correct in maintaining that the "reformative" prison of the nineteenth century survived despite its complete failure to fulfill its ostensible goal of rehabilitation. Nothing can force people to reform. They can change, but only if they themselves wish to. We can sometimes make it to their advantage to change, or remove barriers in the way of change, but no kindly counseling or carceral "archipelago" can produce true conversion. Most prisoners do indeed reform, because most wish to. John Clay found that about two-thirds of his prisoners did not return to gaol within a reasonable period; today, after a further century and a half of constant dedicated effort, in almost any prison about two-thirds of a typical assortment of prisoners will not return. Certain sorts of offenders may have a higher or lower propensity to repeat their offense, but there is no evidence that any system, any program, any effort, will change the propensity of any given offender to return by more than a marginal amount. Reformation and "rehabilitation" can take place—indeed, they take place more often than not—but it is beyond our power to impose them, as it was beyond the power of earlier reformers. We cannot wrest grace from providence.

Like their inmates, prisons have a life of their own, and they can also prove to be remarkably resistant to reformation imposed from outside. The history of prison reform is far more complicated than a simple history of ideologies or of the dominance of one class by another could suggest. It is a story of mixed motives, intractable problems, and unintended consequences. The Lancashire prison system, as this book shows, was produced by the interaction of many factors: political events, such as the Luddite disturbances; economic problems, such as the postwar inflation; contemporary preoccupations with such issues as the value of free speech, representative government, and reformative punishment; scientific theories, such as a contagionist model of disease; technical constraints, such as prison architecture; particular personalities, such as individual gaolers; and a shifting balance of power between the people of the county, the justices, the inspectors, the prison staff, and Parliament. It seems likely that a similarly complex interaction characterizes all prison systems and that all prison administrators must juggle with the conflicting demands of limited financial resources, administrative inertia, corruption, political conflict, and recalcitrant inmates—indeed, with all the problems of government in an imperfect world.

# CHAPTER I

# The Eighteenth-Century Gaol

To most authors of general histories, English prison history begins with John Howard. Before that, despite a few flickering ideas, prisons were sunk in Gothic darkness, ruled by cruelty and corruption. With the exception of Pugh's book on medieval imprisonment and a few recent monographs, many still unpublished, most writing on the subject has dismissed the first millennium of English prison life as a single unchanged and unchanging world of squalor, violence, and disease. The Webbs set the tone by devoting seventeen pages of their history of local prisons to the institutions of the sixteenth, seventeenth, and eighteenth centuries, and a further fourteen pages to the period from 1700 to 1773, under such headings as "filth and stench," "cruelty," "licentiousness," and "public apathy." They concluded that "the state of prisons seemed an evil for which there was no remedy," before turning with relief to "John Howard," "his character," "his journeys," and "his policy."[1]

Several recent works have followed the same pattern. W. L. Burn, in the *Age of Equipoise*—until recently the only widely read general history to examine seriously the subject of prison reform—wrote that "the reforms in the management of prisons ought not, in fairness, to start with Howard," but then devoted only half a sentence to the SPCK and Oglethorpe before returning to Howard.[2] Although Ursula Henriques, in her textbook, *Before the Welfare State*, devotes an entire section to a discussion of prison reform based on recent research, she still closely follows the Webbs, seeing the eighteenth-century gaol as a place of unrelieved squalor, extortion, and endemic gaol fever. She attributes these conditions to the prevalence of the fee system, claiming that "the eighteenth-century collapse in administration was nowhere more apparent than in the management of prisons."[3] In another recent book, Bryan Keith-Lucas, while acknowledging the central place of penal institutions in county budgets, confines himself to emphasizing the "appalling" condition of many gaols, the herding together of prisoners, and the fee system. There is no suggestion that any change took place in the years before Howard.[4]

A few young radical historians have attacked this view on two fronts. First, they show that Howard was by no means unique. Robin Evans's recent monograph provides an extensive account of the intellectual history of prison architecture and of *encellulement* in particular. Michael Ignatieff has emphasized the role of some of Howard's contemporaries, especially Jonas Hanway and the mid-century medical reformers whom Howard knew in London and whose advice on the prevention of gaol fever was the key element in the early reforms.[5]

Second, after identifying a larger group of reformers and conceding that they did bring about substantial changes, these critics have gone on to question the value of those so-called reforms. Gertrude Himmelfarb and several followers have succeeded in depicting Bentham as a greedy, power-hungry, and totalitarian "manipulator." Other historians have portrayed Howard and his "circle" (e.g., Paul, Hanway, Whitbread, and Neild) as bourgeois dissenters who wanted above all to control the lower classes—to bring criminals' behavior into conformity with the sanctimonious dictates of middle-class morality. In doing so they built "total institutions," destroyed the prison community, and created "machines" far less humane than the casual residences they had found. As Rod Morgan recently wrote: "In the eighteenth century the prison was transformed from being a mere container . . . to a carefully planned environment for the moral reconstitution of the convicted and sentenced. If the prison was to deter and reform, prisoners had to be separated from those community influences which had been productive of crime. Prisoners were to be stripped of their social identities, all traces of individuality systematically eradicated, normality suppressed. . . . The reformist vision with which Howard's name has been inextricably linked has . . . been productive of as much cruelty, misery and vice as it prevented."[6]

The logic of this argument should entail a more sympathetic attitude toward the eighteenth-century gaol, but this has in fact been lacking, even though recent monographs in local history have provided material that might sustain such an interpretation.* Local prison administration in the eighteenth century has continued to be largely neglected. In fact, the earlier eighteenth century presents serious difficulties for the radical historians because they tend to accept the radical class-based interpretation of eighteenth-century law advanced by the followers of E. P. Thompson. According to this view, the criminal law of the eighteenth century was wielded by the aristocracy, which used it as a weapon to maintain its power in the countryside.[7] This negative view of the aristocracy that was responsible for local administration has impeded what would otherwise be a natural tendency among those protesting nineteenth-century changes to paint the eighteenth-century gaol in rosy colors. In general, the radicals have accepted the contention of earlier historians that the late eighteenth century marked a radical break from what had gone before, without themselves engaging in the sort of local research that could show what the institutions had been like before they changed or how great the change was.

No one would deny that the Age of Reform saw a significant break with the past, nor that the growth of large residential "total" institutions is an important feature of the modern world. Nevertheless, the argument can be overdone. By neglecting the fact that the unreformed prison has its own history of reform and by concentrating heavily on certain types of sources—particularly those that are national in scope, such as the memoirs of reformers and the *Parliamentary Papers*—historians have distorted if not entirely misdrawn the picture.

First, this approach has exaggerated the problem of the inception of

---

*See, for example, Eric Stockdale, "John Howard and Bedford Gaol," in John C. Freeman, ed., *Prisons Past and Future* (papers given at the Howard Bicentenary Conference; London, 1978), pp. 15-24: "It would . . . be a mistake to think that Howard was the first Sheriff to interest himself in the prison building itself. . . . Various minor modifications and improvements had been made in earlier years [and] many sick prisoners received a degree of sympathetic consideration from the magistrates. There are many references to extra food being provided for such prisoners. . . . The documents relating to the appointment of the gaoler are relatively few, but they demonstrate once again that the gaol was important in the community; and that the identity of the man appointed and his qualifications for office were matters of concern to magistrates and other citizens, as well as to the High Sheriff himself" (pp. 19-21). See also Wayne Joseph Sheehan, "The London Prison System, 1666-1795" (Ph.D. dissertation, University of Maryland, 1975); Robin Evans, "A Rational Plan for Softening the Mind: Prison Design, 1750-1842" (Ph.D. dissertation, University of Essex, 1975).

Information on the major manuscript collections and parliamentary papers consulted by the author, together with the abbreviations used in citing documents, can be found in Document Sources, pp. 255-59. For dating, see p. 231.

reform in the late eighteenth century. Jennifer Hart's question—Why did abuses suddenly appear "intolerable" to certain groups in the early nineteenth century?—becomes especially difficult to answer if one begins by assuming that these abuses had existed and been widely tolerated for many centuries.[8] The events associated with the Industrial Revolution obviously affected the severity of the problems involved, yet that fact does not explain the emergence of a wholly new sensitivity to social problems among some members of local elites. To explain that sensitivity, as Ursula Henriques has conceded, one must turn to such "special circumstances" as personal suffering, a "violent shock to the consciousness," and "participation in a conflicting sub-culture." In addition, she hypothesizes a complete change in culture, from a "traditional" to a "forward-looking" outlook within the nation at large.[9]

The problem becomes less severe if it can be shown that by the end of the eighteenth century a well-established tradition of social concern and of responsible and relatively humane administration already existed. In that case, one might assume that exceptional situations, such as the size of London or the rise of a market economy, could have caused a breakdown in the administrative system and eventually necessitated drastic new solutions, without any sudden and independent change in culture, consciousness, or sense of responsibility among the landed gentry. This hypothesis accords more closely with what we know of the best-documented branch of local administration, the Poor Laws. In that area a tradition of relatively humane administration continued throughout the eighteenth century—including the "Speenhamland years"—before it began to disintegrate and was replaced by the stringencies of the New Poor Law. For both prisons and Poor Laws, by the early nineteenth century a new response had emerged that included a new reliance on large institutions—but this response did not necessarily require a sudden and unprecedented sensitivity to the problems themselves.

A second and related effect of the distorted view of prison reform is that it has led historians to place an undue emphasis on the thoughts and activities of "middle-class" reformers, and on their London-based pressure groups. This bias is shared by the traditional writers and the radicals, for whom it fits neatly into a class-based theory of social control. To quote Ursula Henriques again: "Most reforms were pre-empted by middle-class activists," who were "members of middle-class minority groups."[10]

This approach has led to the neglect of the institutions of local, particularly county, government, in which "middle-class" and largely urban "minority group" reformers played a small part. (Evangelicals in particular are notable only for their complete absence from any role in Lancashire prison reform during the entire period covered by this study.) This approach has also led to an implicit but bewildering discontinuity in the radical argument, by which that well-entrenched landed aristocracy that had been manipulating the legal system with such success suddenly and inexplicably disappears, to be replaced—both in its concern for social control and in its ability to manipulate the system—by an urban bourgeoisie. In fact, throughout the early nineteenth century it was the aristocratic, Anglican, and often Tory county bench that bore the responsibility for running the prisons and for implementing any reforms. An understanding of the attitude, problems, and administrative traditions of the eighteenth-century bench, therefore, is vital to an understanding of the implementation of reforms in the Howardian period. It can, moreover, provide an element of continuity lacking in most historical accounts.

This chapter will examine some of these administrative traditions to see what effect they had on prison life. Did the justices, in fact, simply abandon prisoners to the tender mercies of cruel and extortionate gaolers, to die of disease, neglect, and starvation? Or were prisons administered along the lines of the old Poor Law: often rough, capricious, and inadequate but offering real safeguards in a dangerous and unreliable world? Did the unreformed prison remain forever unchanged?

## Prisons and County Government

Lancashire is one of England's largest and most remote counties. Because of its great size the county was divided into six hundreds: West Derby (which included Liverpool), Amonderness (which included Preston), Salford (which included Manchester and several other large textile towns), Leyland, Blackburn, and Lonsdale (which included Lancaster, the county town). These hundreds were further divided into divisions, each with its own high constable. The divisions were split into parishes, and, because Lancashire parishes also tended to be very large, the parishes were further subdivided into townships, the basic unit of county administration.

The Lancashire justices, like their colleagues in Yorkshire, had evolved a system to deal with the county's large size. The Quarter Sessions, the chief judicial and administrative body, met every quarter at

Lancaster and then followed a fixed series of adjournments to Preston, to Ormskirk or Wigan, and to Manchester. Each adjournment administered the business of its own hundreds and was usually, although not invariably, attended by its own set of justices. Unless a special adjournment was called in an emergency, there were, therefore, sixteen Quarter Sessions meetings each year. The names of each quarter's session varied somewhat; I have reduced this to four standard seasonal names: Easter, Trinity, Michaelmas, and Epiphany.

At the beginning of the eighteenth century, Lancashire was a very poor county; isolated and lawless, it was distinguished by a long history of rebellion and recusancy. The county contained a great variety of terrains, but much of the countryside was rough and hilly, making communication difficult. Agriculture was inefficient and unproductive. For centuries one of the poorest and most backward counties in England, and then, suddenly, one of the most developed, wealthy, and densely populated, Lancashire cannot claim to be "typical." It can, however, claim to be entirely different from London, the source of most of our information on prisons, and to be important in its own right. By the middle of the nineteenth century its municipal and county prisons contained nearly one-fifth of all the prisoners in England and Wales. Its four county prisons were among the largest in the country. The criminal classes of Manchester, Liverpool, and the smaller textile towns were attracting national attention—as were the methods used in the county prisons to deter and, it was hoped, to "reform" criminals. Moreover, from the time of the Industrial Revolution, Lancashire experienced in magnified form all the difficulties and dislocations caused by industrial development. It thus provides a graphic example of problems that the rest of England would confront more gradually.*

Prisons appeared before justices and Sessions. They are among the oldest local institutions in England, going back to Anglo-Saxon times. By the later Middle Ages there were many different sorts of prisons, corresponding roughly to the large number of different courts entitled to use imprisonment as a sanction. The county gaols may be seen as a product of the Norman legal system: they were used by the king's judges for breaches of the king's law. The king's civil representative in the county,

---

*The only municipal prison of any significance in Lancashire during this period was the Liverpool borough gaol. For some time after its incorporation, Manchester sent its borough prisoners to the New Bailey under contract. Municipal prisons and local police or village lockups are not considered in this study.

the sheriff, was responsible for the gaols' administration; justices of the peace had little legal authority in prison affairs. It was the sheriff who, legally, acted as gaoler, appointed prison officers, had custody of the prisoners, was responsible for bail and escapes, and answered for any breaches of discipline.

The sheriff's jurisdiction, an artifact of the system's antiquity, was unfortunate. After 1340, sheriffs held office for only one year; after 1377, they could be reappointed only after the lapse of three years. The result was that sheriffs had little opportunity to become familiar with their responsibilities and lacked the experience to administer prisons effectively. Ordinarily, they appointed a deputy to act as the real gaoler, sometimes paying him a salary. But since each sheriff could appoint whom he pleased, the gaoler's tenure of office was insecure, and the practice of bribing successive sheriffs to retain the office became common, although it was strictly prohibited by law.[11]

As justices of the peace took on more responsibility for the financial, legal, and civil administration of the counties, the sheriff increasingly became a figurehead, with little interest in day-to-day duties. He continued to be responsible for the collection of certain revenues due the Crown and for certain expenditures, including the building of gaols, the maintenance of condemned prisoners awaiting transportation or execution, and the costs of execution. Occasionally, conscientious sheriffs such as John Howard and John Wilkes took a serious interest in the prisons under their charge, but these men seem to have been exceptional.

Despite the erosion of the sheriff's role, one important shrieval institution survived in Lancashire long after it had disappeared from other counties. This was the Sheriff's Court or Tourn, known in Lancashire as the Sheriff's Board, a local parliament attended by county dignitaries in town for the Assizes. The justices used this body to make joint decisions that would be binding on all the adjourned sessions. In the late seventeenth and early eighteenth centuries this was the chief administrative body of the county; unfortunately, most of its records for this period have been lost.[12]

One other person also exercised important authority over prison administration, although he possessed few official powers. This was the Assize judge. The judge made twice-yearly circuits to "deliver" the county gaol; unlike the justices, who often sent prisoners to the houses of correction, he committed to the gaol alone. When the county prison required major renovation, a grand jury "presented" the gaol to the judge at Assizes. The judges felt a proprietary interest in the gaols and successfully intervened in their management. Long before the nineteenth-century act that empowered them to review the legality of prison regulations made by the justices, judges in open court were hearing the complaints of prisoners about their accommodations and demanding that conditions be improved.[13]

Nevertheless, by the eighteenth century the justices were the real rulers of the counties. Whether or not they had a legal mandate in prison affairs, they were the only group in a position to exercise authority over prison management on a regular basis. It was the justices who committed offenders to gaol to await trial, and it was the justices who levied the county rates. The evidence shows that by the eighteenth century they were prepared to intervene in a wide range of prison problems.

Until the late eighteenth century, the main use of imprisonment was to hold persons who might be needed for trial. Laws permitting courts to use it as a penalty in itself dated as far back as the Middle Ages, but its expense always discouraged its use. Although many petty offenders found themselves in gaol because they could not or would not pay fines, debts, or recognizances, imprisonment as an initial penalty in criminal cases was usually reserved for serious offenders whom the government was reluctant to execute: the powerful who had committed political offenses, the knowing who might betray others under pressure, and the religious, who might be considered martyrs. Most prisoners, however, were awaiting some event rather than serving fixed terms.

Over the years, a large body of statute law, common law, ordinance, and custom had grown up to protect prisoners from extortion, cruelty, and neglect. On the whole, these laws defined the rights of prisoners rather than prescribed the conduct of the gaoler. Instead of providing for the supervision of administrators, the laws granted prisoners rights to redress in the courts and rewards for successful prosecution. Most important were the attempts to control extortion. Though some gaolers received salaries, most of their income came from fees. A long series of statutes set strict limits on admission fees, though gaolers were free to provide extra goods and services at any price they chose. Municipal corporations, such as Coventry and Bristol, sometimes issued special regulations fixing the prices of commodities for sale in the prison and requiring good conduct from the gaoler. The London prisons were regulated especially closely; in the late seventeenth century zealous aldermen went so far as to prohibit unauthorized female visitors, misbehavior in chapel, gambling, and drinking.[14]

Tudor legislation permitted justices of the peace to collect rates for building gaols and to provide financial support for prisoners. Especially important was the legislation passed under Edward VI that for the first time created separate institutions for penal incarceration after conviction.[15] The new houses of correction (Lancashire's were erected by the early seventeenth century) were intended to serve as real prisons in the modern sense of the word: places for the deterrence, punishment, and rehabilitation of inmates after trial. While the distinction between gaols and houses of correction was not observed in practice, it is important to note that the houses of correction were under the superintendence of the justices, not of the sheriffs. Historians who speak of "prisons" run by irresponsible fee-taking gaolers are entirely neglecting those institutions that were actually intended for post-trial custody. In this context the relaxed regime of the gaols that were intended to provide pre-trial detention is more understandable.

In Lancashire, geography frustrated the intent of this legislation; it was so expensive and time-consuming to arrest, convey, and prosecute petty offenders that rural townships seldom considered compliance worthwhile. The distance between the houses at Preston and Manchester and the gaol at Lancaster led Lancashire's justices to commit to the nearest institution whenever legally possible, thus blurring the distinction between them. The county houses of correction remained very small until the nearby population exploded in the late eighteenth century.[16]

There is evidence that prison conditions deteriorated in the later seventeenth century, leaving some inmates to face starvation unassisted either by the abundant private charity of the Middle Ages or the experimental public support of the Tudors. There is also evidence of corruption and of political jobbery in prison administration, paralleling a similar degeneration in national and local government. Nevertheless, this period also saw a national effort to improve prison conditions, including new legislation, new financing, and new building. Probably the most important achievement of the Restoration period was the act of 1670 that established a procedure for the release of insolvent debtors and that protected imprisoned debtors from extortion and contact with felons.[17]

In the few counties that have been studied, such as Oxfordshire, Yorkshire, and Lancashire, the last two decades of the century saw a flood of petitions from prisoners, suggesting a decline in conditions, a raising of expectations, or a change of administrative procedures. Possibly all three were involved. In Lancashire, the hard years that came at the end of the century increased the strain on the gaol, resulting in complaints and outbreaks of sickness. But this period also saw a slow but steady and, ultimately, successful effort by the justices to bring the situation under control.

## The Buildings

By the end of the seventeenth century, all three of Lancashire's county institutions were well established. During the Civil War, Lancaster Castle was occupied and damaged, but most of its medieval towers, joined by the curtain wall in a rough ring around the keep, survived. The Quaker leader George Fox, imprisoned in the Castle in the late seventeenth century, complained about conditions there to the Assize judge, who ordered that extensive repairs be made.[18] The Dungeon Tower was torn down during construction of a women's prison in the early nineteenth century, but most of the rest of the Castle, including the curtain wall, keep, well tower, court complex, gatehouse, and one other ancient round tower, still stands. As a prison, the Castle had serious deficiencies. Parts were extremely old. Moreover, it had not been intended for the custody of miscreants, and its rambling design made the separation of prisoners difficult, security fragile, and supervision almost impossible. With their small deep windows (in the case of the lower cells, no windows at all) and their stone-flagged floors, the cells could be cold, dark, and uncomfortable. Few of the rooms had originally possessed fireplaces.[19]

By the standards of London prisons of the same time, however, Lancaster had many advantages. By 1703, after extensive repair work, only one debtors' room in the Castle lacked a fireplace. Overcrowding in the 1720's led to further complaints by the debtors about smoky chimneys, the housing of prisoners in rooms without fireplaces, and leaking roofs, but these problems were rapidly repaired by the justices. Moreover, the Castle could claim a large and attractive courtyard, a clean water supply from its own wells, and many large rooms. The worst off were the penniless convicted felons; they were often lodged in subterranean rooms under the Dungeon and Well towers that were large and dry but unheated, unventilated, and windowless.

The history of the Salford house of correction is obscure, partly because its administration was largely left to the Salford justices while the other three sessions decided jointly on any changes made at Preston. The bridewell opened in Manchester in 1657, but the building itself may have served as a prison for recusants in the sixteenth century. A surviving picture shows a small house with a pitched roof and cells overlooking the street. From the windows of these, inmates lower bags to passersby for charity. The house and its outbuildings received extensive repairs in 1700, 1720, 1746-47, and 1757. It was completely rebuilt once more in 1774.[20] John Howard visited Manchester shortly after this last transformation and described it as follows: "Separate Court-yards and Apartments for Men and Women. The former have Work-rooms, over which are Chambers. Their Night-rooms or Dungeons, in a passage or long room forty-five feet by six are close; eleven feet by eight; eleven steps below the yard; but not properly under ground being on the declivity of a hill. —Women have three rooms on the ground-floor, and three chambers: here is also a dungeon, down nine steps, fourteen feet by thirteen; but women are not put there."[21]

Preston's history is a little clearer. Located a little out of town on the banks of the Ribble, it had been a convent of the Grey Friars until the dissolution of the monasteries. In 1618, after years of steady pressure from the government, the Lancashire justices finally agreed to purchase this property for the county house of correction. They appropriated £700 for erecting and finishing the house and for furnishing it with working implements and gardens.[22] Like Manchester, Preston underwent major renovation in the 1740's. Expenditures of £40 or more are also recorded in 1724, 1762, 1768, 1772, and 1774, and at frequent intervals thereafter. Howard wrote that no water was available to prisoners, although there is evidence of a pump in earlier years. He found a large room on the ground floor, "in which are eleven Closets, called *Boxes*, to sleep in; and another Room, the Dungeon." Above it was a large workroom for the men and a smaller one for the women. All the rooms were dirty at the time of his visit and the prison was in disrepair.[23]

The frequency of repairs at all three of these institutions makes it clear that the eighteenth-century justices did not neglect them. Although the keeper was responsible for minor repairs, Quarter Sessions frequently raised money for improvements. For example, the justices ordered the collection of rolls for more than £5 for repairs at the Castle twenty-eight times between 1704 and 1769. These rolls were often for more than £100.[24]

The comfort of prisoners, however, depended as much on the quality of the original buildings as on the frequency of repairs. On the whole, prisoners in the Castle were fortunate, although the felons must frequently have been wretched. Preston, however, despite frequent repairs, was probably uncomfortable from the beginning. With only four rooms, it was ill equipped for any significant expansion in the number of prisoners. There can be no question that the bridewells needed attention even more urgently than the gaols.

## Prison Life

Since the raison d'être of the gaols was to restrict the liberty of their inmates, the first question for a study of prison life is the extent to which prisoners were confined. Some so-called prisoners were not imprisoned at all, or were frequently let out. While "imprisoned" in the Castle in the late seventeenth century, the Quaker Roger Haydock visited churches in Westmoreland and attended two debates in Cheshire.[25] Roger Kenyon, the clerk of the peace, admitted to the Earl of Derby in 1683 that of sixteen Quaker and Catholic prisoners officially in the Castle, eleven were lodging elsewhere.[26]

Prisoners of conscience, who were rare after 1700, were not the only ones to gain a measure of liberty. Some debtors enjoyed a similar freedom. In London the practice of freeing debtors for a fee became well established; in Lancashire ordinary debtors normally remained within the Castle walls, but late-seventeenth-century evidence suggests that the many mesne-process debtors were allowed the liberty of the town and could even work outside the gaol. (These were people arrested on mesne process for failing to provide bail for their appearance at the hearing that would officially establish their debt. Until this hearing was held, they were not "in execution.") Thomas Fell, a perennial and irascible prisoner, complained to Quarter Sessions in 1693 that debtors working in the town were coming up to the Castle on Saturday morning and collecting prison allowances.*

---

*For a more detailed description of arrest on mesne process, see Wayne Joseph Sheehan, "The London Prison System, 1666-1795" (Ph.D. dissertation, University of Maryland, 1975), pp. 7-8, and the *House of Commons Journals* 47 (1792): 640-52. See also LCRO, QSP, Lanc. M 1693, no. 15. Thomas Fell was imprisoned in 1692 and could not gain release because he refused to make his property over to his creditors and was, therefore, not insolvent. In 1693 he applied for an allowance of 3s. per week, stating that the entire income from his estate was going to his creditors. He was refused, but received an allowance in 1702. He died in the Castle in 1722. He may be the same man as the Thomas Fell, yeoman, of Aughton (near Hindpull) who was presented in 1687 for riotous assembly and for throwing a man into the river Lune.

Lax or venal keepers of the houses of correction may also have granted some liberty, although the justices did not approve. One of the terms imposed on the keeper when the Preston house first opened was that the master would see that "the prisoners goe not abroade to the charge or trouble of the towne or cuntrie where they are, or to converse abroade or have anie meetings but to bee kept close to their worke."[27] Among the articles against the corrupt keeper of Preston in 1703 was one complaining that he had allowed some prisoners to escape without pursuit and "others to goe abroad at their free will and pleasure."[28] A prisoner supposedly confined in Salford witnessed a murder in another house in 1749.[29]

Though keepers may have been rather lax from time to time, gaolers could not afford to allow convicted felons or debtors in execution to escape. Escapes did take place at rare intervals, but they were attended with very high penalties for the gaoler, particularly if the fugitive was not recaptured. Lancashire's most corrupt gaoler, John Ellitson, allowed at least five prisoners to escape. At least one, Robert Arrowsmith, was recaptured and punished by being chained to a post during the day.[30]

The mid-century gaoler Edward Styth also suffered an escape. A group of debtors had sued for release under an insolvency act and had been granted their discharge in court when a technicality came up about the indemnification of the sheriff against actions of escape by creditors. When the Quarter Sessions refused to free the debtors, a group of them broke prison. All but two were recaptured, but Styth found it necessary to post an armed guard around the gaol for six months, "the Debtors being very Riotous having knocked down the Turn Key and threatening to Murder him and the Gaoler and to make their Escapes apprehending they were detained there Contrary to the sence of the Legislator."[31]

To prevent escapes and to identify prisoners for the guards, felons were usually placed in irons, although a wealthy criminal could avoid irons by paying a fee to compensate the gaoler for the greater risk. Critics of eighteenth-century prisons maintain that gaolers often loaded new prisoners with especially heavy fetters in order to extort greater fees. John Ellitson did attempt this, but he was clearly an exceptionally cruel and extortionate gaoler. After Ellitson's reign, no complaints on this issue have been found; in fact, there are few complaints of any sort of extortion. Judging from the prisoners' readiness to petition about other matters, it seems likely either that gaolers were not in fact ironing prisoners unreasonably or that the practice was so widely accepted that no one thought to complain. Ordinary ironing was both practiced and accepted; to this day the popular image of the convict endows him with a ball and chain.

Despite public acceptance of irons and the real need for them, they were unpleasant and sometimes dangerous to the wearer. Gaolers knew this well. Heavy fetters impeded movement, although prisoners managed to shuffle around with the chain held up by a string under their clothes. More important, if the irons were too tight or too heavy they could cut off circulation and cause severe swelling, "mortification" (gangrene), loss of a limb, and even death. At the end of the century, partly through the efforts of a liberal gaoler, John Higgin, the Castle became one of the first prisons in England to abandon the use of irons except as a combined punishment and safety measure for recaptured escapees. Higgin believed that ironing could produce "conduct which I could not effect by solitary confinement" among refractory prisoners, but he also went to some length and considerable risk to avoid fettering the insane.[32]

Little evidence has survived about the general health of prisoners in this period. In the late seventeenth century, when the gaols were crowded, times hard, and conditions poor, mention of sickness and epidemic disease is common. In the hard year of 1699, forty debtors who had been imprisoned for two years or more petitioned the Wigan Sessions. Many debtors, they claimed, had starved to death despite "the charities of many honourable persons," and many were now suffering from "a strange disease which immediately deprives them of theire reason amd sences, noe other reason whereoff can be given but theire unwholesome fare and bad lodging." Only the kindness of their gaoler, Henry Bracken, had prevented the "contagious distempers" from spreading even further. The parish register records an unusually high number of deaths among prisoners for that year.[33]

This is the last reference to epidemic disease in the Lancashire records until 1775, when the Lancaster Sessions ordered a special payment to a local apothecary who had saved the lives and restored the health of several prisoners.[34] Although there was some increase of disease in the 1720's, Lancaster apparently survived the first three-quarters of the eighteenth century without experiencing a serious epidemic. Though there were occasional and usually well-publicized epidemics in other eighteenth-century gaols, it seems likely that the picture of fever-ridden gaols beset with epidemic typhus has been overdrawn. It was at the end of the century, when serious overcrowding accompanied an increase in the number of long imprisonments and a fall in the value of allowances, that the problem became severe.*

Prisoner deaths were usually noted in the register of the parish of St. Mary's, which included the Castle. Use of this source is open to technical objections, but it does provide a rough estimate of the absolute numbers dying during a period about which other information is lacking. The number of deaths is remarkably steady: in only eight years of the eighteenth century did more than five Castle prisoners die (not counting wives, children, and staff). Excluding 1715—when the Castle was filled with wounded "rebels," eleven of whom died—in only two years, 1728 and 1729, did more than ten prisoners die. According to the registers, an average of 2.36 prisoners died per year between 1690 and 1755, and an average of 1.88 between 1756 and 1820. A little more than three persons of all sorts residing in the Castle died annually between 1691 and 1755. This rate fell to a little more than two from 1756 to 1820.[35]

For those confined within its walls, life in the Castle bore a closer resemblance to that in an unreformed university than it did to a modern prison. The educational metaphor was frequently used for prisons, which were called "schools," "seminaries," and "colleges" of crime. The similarity did not lie only in the educational opportunities offered by each. Lancaster and many other gaols resembled colleges in physical layout, demography, controls on entry, and social customs. Lancaster was a residential building constructed around a central courtyard with a gatehouse, open at certain set hours, through which visitors had to pass. Its residents were largely young men, though a number of prisoners' families were permitted to live within the walls; of those listed in the parish registers as dying within the Castle, about one in six was not a prisoner. Gaols, of course, also contained female prisoners, whose numbers rose considerably toward the end of the eighteenth century; we do not know to what extent they were separated from the men before the Age of Reform.

---

*Joanna Innes has found evidence of several outbreaks of gaol fever in the eighteenth century in other provincial prisons, as have I. In many cases, however, these were due to exceptional circumstances, particularly to sudden overcrowding. There is no evidence that typhus epidemics were common. Mr. Sheehan has informed me that he has found a similar shortage of epidemics in the London prisons during most of the century (with the obvious exception of the notorious Newgate epidemic). Even a hundred documented instances of gaol fever in the eighteenth century would mean that any particular prison was likely to see only one outbreak in the course of the century. For the rising incidence after 1770, see below.

Some of the inhabitants acted as servitors for their wealthier companions. A small shop and a tap provided popular gathering-places for men whose social life was otherwise restricted, as well as a lucrative source of income for the gaoler. The prisoners dined together and shared common rooms, enlivening the monotony of viewing the same faces day after day by indulging in regular banquets and celebrations at night, and by playing games such as skittles, bowls, and draughts during the day. Some men took well to this institutional life while others hated it, but it had not been designed to be unpleasant.

Life in the eighteenth-century gaol, therefore, had many compensations lacking in the nineteenth-century prison—although debtors continued to enjoy great license long after the lives of other inmates had been more closely regulated. Nevertheless, the prison life of the period had its darker side. The Castle was always haunted by a handful of poor prisoners who had been convicted and sentenced to death, a penalty often commuted to transportation. While a rich felon could obtain a fair degree of comfort, those who could not afford extra fees slept on straw on the lower floors of the Dungeon and Well towers. Even the most optimistic account must note the description provided by one of Higgin's descendants, who wrote that the crowded Dungeon cells became so hot and were filled with "noxious exhalations so deadly" that the turnkeys each morning would leave the doors open for some time before they dared to enter.[36]

Though the communal nature of prison life offered important benefits to prisoners, it also had its drawbacks. The herding together of all sorts of prisoners without supervision was perhaps preferable to solitary confinement, but it created its own difficulties. By law, the gaoler had to provide debtors and criminals with separate sleeping quarters; though this provision seems to have been better enforced in the eighteenth century than it had been at the end of the seventeenth, felons and debtors continued to mix by day. Among them were the insane and the "weak-minded." Upon occasion these people could present a danger to their companions, and the more harmless ones were sometimes teased unmercifully.

Although drunken brawls were common in the Castle, evidence of systematic victimization is rare. In 1693 Thomas Fell complained that a prisoner acting as warder had maliciously beaten him "with un-Reasonabell bllowes," but the court rejected his complaint.[37] In 1703 another prisoner complained that his chambermates had pushed and threatened him for refusing to subscribe to an "unjust and unreasonable" information against the gaoler when the justices came to inquire into his conduct.[38] Life-threatening assaults seem to have been comparatively rare, but when a nineteenth-century parliamentary commission collected evidence on several prisons' experimental separation of prisoners, many witnesses testified that they were relieved to be protected from regular harassment by their fellows. The commission was biased, but there can be no question that constant, unavoidable, and unsupervised contact between prisoners was a mixed blessing.

The prison was not, or not always, a Hobbesian jungle, however. Ample evidence survives of strong and well-organized prisoner self-government in London; it seems likely that similar organizations existed in the larger provincial prisons, especially among the debtors. The earliest evidence of such a system in Lancashire appears in a rule book compiled shortly after 1772. Most of the rules themselves were, apparently, somewhat older. Ironically, the greatest part of the book is concerned with the establishment of an orderly mechanism for enabling debtors to collect debts owed to them by their fellows, including provisions for distraint and for the auction of belongings.[39]

According to this book, all the debtors met in a monthly "court" to hear cases and settle their accounts. Every three months the majority elected a constable and a judge. A sheriff, selected by "juniority," empaneled a jury who could hear cases of debt up to £5 and punish minor offenses. The court paid the constable either 2s. 6d. or 3s. a month, and also employed a person to fetch letters from town at 3s. a month. A "clerk" was permitted to charge fees for copying out "court" writs and for furnishing a copy of the orders that debtors needed the justices to sign in order to obtain allowances. Debtors could also hire court-approved counsel for 6d.

The court collected 7s. 2d. in "garnish" (a traditional entrance fee) from every new debtor. If the debtor refused to pay, it could collect the money by distraint. The 2d. went to the clerk, and 1s. went to ale. The rest of the money went to the court, which paid all its own expenses and salaries and distributed whatever remained equally to all the debtors except to any women, who paid half as much garnish and received a comparable proportion in return. The court also provided newspapers and a copy of Burn's *Justice of the Peace* for debtors to use. It punished infractions, including petty theft; fouling of the pump area, bowling green, or privy; drinking with Crown prisoners; emptying chamber pots out of windows; "abusing, aspersing or vilifying" another debtor; and swearing. Merchants from the town and Crown prisoners were allowed to plead cases by proxy. Finally, the court oversaw the organization of the chambers, ruling that members of each chamber were to subscribe jointly for fuel, that each chamber might collect a 1s. entrance fee after a trial period of three nights, and that the foreman of the jury and the constable were to examine each room for cleanliness once a month.

A petition of 1704, in a hand resembling that of Thomas Fell, suggests that this formal system of debtor self-government extended back at least to the beginning of the century. It complains that prison officers had appropriated the garnish money of 2s. 4d. a head and requests that it be returned to "such Constabell as the debtters in Lancaster Castell shall Apoynt According to the Ansshent Costoms."[40]

Prisoners also helped each other in informal ways. In 1737 the Quarter Sessions, apparently inadvertently, cut off the allowances of a number of "poor, necessitous" prisoners. According to a subsequent court order, these men "must inevitably have starved" without charity from the citizens of the town. Elizabeth Dickenson, the wife of one of the starving debtors, however, managed to find 2s. 3½d. to buy porridge, oatcakes, cheese, and small beer for Thomas Waring, a lunatic Crown prisoner whose allowance had been reduced. The justices later repaid her.[41] Another well-intentioned prisoner was Samuel Short, a gentleman debtor who, like the vicar of Wakefield, read the services of the *Book of Common Prayer* to his fellow prisoners on Sunday mornings and evenings. On two occasions Quarter Sessions noted its approval and voted him 40s. as a reward.[42]

It was not just the world within the walls that provided support for prisoners. The community outside was vital to their existence. Although most prisoners could not leave the gaol, a constant stream of townspeople wandered back and forth through its gates. The wives and children of debtors were free to come and go during the day. Debtors under mesne process also walked around the town or saw friends, creditors, and attorneys within the Castle. Many debtors worked in the gaol and were visited by employers, suppliers, and potential customers. Tradesmen came in seeking customers, delivering food and drink, and bringing supplies to the prison market, the tap, and the gaoler's house. Family and friends of the prisoners came, bringing with them small comforts.

The prison provided employment for the inhabitants of the town, while many prisoners relied on the town's charity. The Castle employed artisans such as masons, blacksmiths, glaziers, roofers, and carpenters as well as permanent staff such as night guards. It was the Castle that brought the Assizes to Lancaster, providing income for innkeepers, taverners, stablers, and anyone with a spare room to rent; for lawyers, solicitors, and clerks; and even for the tailors, dressmakers, milliners, and dealers in luxury goods who traded with the wives and daughters of gentlemen attracted by the festivities of Assize week. During the rest of the year townspeople could gain a small income by renting beds and furnishings to prisoners and by lodging and feeding their families and friends.*

In return, the townspeople gave charity to impoverished prisoners. Their help was particularly important when a financial emergency arose, since prisoners often had to wait until the next Quarter Session to remedy a mistake, enforce payment of overdue allowances, or gain consideration for special problems. Crown prisoners took turns begging in the town, while the charity box at the entrance to the Castle provided those permitted to beg at the grating with a fairly regular income. In addition there were charitable gifts and bequests; in 1770 debtors received £22 15s. annually from endowments.[43]

Under the act of 1670, debtors had the right to purchase food and drink from the town. This prevented the gaoler from enjoying a monopoly that would enable him to charge extortionate prices. Debtors knew their rights, valued them, and were quick to complain when they were infringed. In 1711 they complained to Quarter Sessions about a prisoner serving as turnkey who had interfered with their access to goods from the town and had charged fees to visitors, apparently against the gaoler's orders. When Quarter Sessions rejected their petition, they persevered and obtained a true bill at the Assizes; the final outcome is unknown. Debtors submitted a similar petition against a turnkey in 1748. Gaolers disliked the constant admission of goods, since the open gate was an obvious hazard to security, but they had little choice.[44]

The greatest advantage of this continuous coming and going from prison lay in the measure of protection it gave prisoners from systematic brutality or extortion. The justices of the peace, their clerk, and various officers of the court frequently visited the Castle on business, while most

---

*Joanna Innes has pointed out that the Assizes were not necessarily held in the same town as the county gaol. Nevertheless, this was by far the most common arrangement and in Lancashire was almost necessitated by rough terrain. When the south part of the county built a new prison in the nineteenth century, a new Assize soon followed.

inmates of the prison had family, friends, or associates in the town who could be counted on to protest any flagrant ill-treatment. That brutality occurred then as now there can be no question, but the openness of the prison made it more difficult for the gaoler to engage in actions of which the community disapproved.

## Gaolers and Keepers

In the introduction to *State of the Prisons*, Howard wrote that he had originally begun visiting prisons in the hope of finding a precedent for paying gaolers salaries instead of permitting them to collect fees and profits from a prison tap. Following Howard's lead, prison historians have often emphasized the venality and corruption of the eighteenth-century gaoler and have suggested that the substitution of salaries for fees was one of the most important reforms of the late eighteenth century. The Webbs, for example, wrote that

So long as the keeper of the gaol was permitted to make a profit out of the prisoners committed to his charge, it was quite impracticable to secure conditions of health or decency, or even of common humanity. . . . The absence of an adequate salary and the opportunities for exaction had attracted to the office of gaoler, as was bitterly remarked, none but "low-bred, mercenary and oppressive, barbarous fellows, who think of nothing but enriching themselves by the most cruel extortion, and who have less regard for the life of a poor prisoner than for the life of a brute."[45]

This contention, however, is open to challenge. Wayne Joseph Sheehan's recent research on London gaols has shown that, though gaolers were very corrupt in the late seventeenth and early eighteenth centuries, a period of reform occurred between 1729 and 1732, and for the rest of the century the City aldermen succeeded in appointing gaolers who were generally honest, competent, and humane. "There are enough tributes to their good behavior and humanity," Sheehan comments, "to suggest that the popular stereotype of the cruel and oppressive gaoler no longer applied to the City keepers. Surely, the gaolers' improved conduct must rank as the most satisfying transformation in the City prison system during the eighteenth century."[46]

The Lancashire evidence also suggests that, though often venal, county gaolers were rarely cruel or barbarous. An examination of the differences between gaolers and keepers of county houses of correction suggests that the fee system did create serious inconveniences but that payment by salary was by no means the most critical factor in shaping the conduct of prison staff or in bringing about the changes associated with the Age of Reform.

Strictly speaking, the gaoler was the governor of the county gaol alone, while the keeper presided over the house of correction and other institutions such as lockups. In common speech the difference was often ignored. In some counties, the gaol and the house of correction were either under a single roof or near one another; in such places, particularly when the combined prison population was small, one man was often appointed to superintend both.

Even when held by a single man, however, the offices remained quite distinct. The houses of correction were governed entirely by the justices of the peace, who paid for the houses' erection, sentenced offenders to custody, and appointed keepers, fixed their salaries, and dismissed them at will. The justices thus exercised over keepers that complete control that reformers wished to place over gaolers at the end of the century. The county gaol, on the other hand, was still technically the province of the sheriff, who, even in Lancashire, retained the right to appoint its gaoler.

Whereas the keeper was legally entitled to a salary fixed by the justices and collected from the county rates, the gaoler usually maintained himself and his family by collecting fees. Sheriffs could and on occasion did provide salaries—in fact, between 1752 and 1770, sheriffs regularly paid £31 a year to Lancaster gaolers—but they had no power to collect money for that purpose from the ratepayers. Instead, they claimed their expenses directly from the Crown. Even when he received a salary, the gaoler relied on fees for the greater part of his income.

Though the difference in methods of remuneration was accidental, it nevertheless makes sense if the difference between the two prison populations is considered. There were always some gaol prisoners who could afford to pay for luxuries, but most of the inmates of the house of correction had been committed because of their destitution. Vagrants, vagabonds, men unable to support their bastards, and men who had left their families on the parish were almost by definition insolvent, while petty thieves and prostitutes had often turned to crime because of poverty. Moreover, most of the inhabitants of the gaol, in legal theory at least, were not undergoing punishment but merely being kept in a safe place until punishment could be enforced. Inmates of the house of correction were actually supposed to be undergoing "correction": they were not only to support themselves by hard labor but also to lead a spartan life.

Since the comforts that the gaoler supplied at a profit would have undercut the purpose of the house of correction, the keeper was forbidden to provide them. For example, when the keeper of the Preston house was dismissed for misconduct in 1703, one of the articles against him was "that he does not set to worke Correct or punish such as have been Committed to him but entertains some at his owne table like boarders takeing . . . what he can get from every one."[47]

Since the keeper was expected to augment his income by acting as a taskmaster for his prisoners and since he sometimes continued to own a business, the salary attached to his post was only a part of his total income. At the beginning of the eighteenth century the keeper of Salford received only £14 10s. a year, which was raised in 1732 to £25. This, however, may have been considered a part-time job. The keeper of Preston, who was expected to live in, received £60 a year throughout the century—a relatively generous wage. The gaoler at the Castle, however, earned much more in fees; in 1783 John Higgin estimated his income from fees at £360 a year. During most of the century the gaolership was a very lucrative post.[48]

Because the post of keeper involved constant intimate contact with prisoners as a taskmaster, as well as commercial dealings, a lower level of earnings, and the supervision of a much humbler class of inmates, there was often a distinct difference between the status of the gaoler and that of the keepers. The gaoler of Lancaster was a very important man in the community. He was also, usually, a well-educated one. Bare literacy did not suffice for a position requiring a good deal of legal expertise; the gaoler had to decide whether a great variety of writs, warrants, and releases, particularly those involving actions for debt, were in order. Because of the seriousness of the crimes for which some prisoners were committed to the Castle, the post was a dangerous and responsible one; it was also financially hazardous.

In law, the sheriff, as custodian of the gaol, was responsible to the county for all prisoners within it. If a felon escaped, the sheriff could be fined, and if a debtor escaped, even if for only half an hour, the sheriff was liable to the creditor for the full amount of the debt. Sheriffs passed their responsibilities on to the gaolers by requiring them to sign a bond indemnifying the sheriff against any expenses caused by the gaoler's negligence. By the early nineteenth century, this bond was £10,000. Despair after the escape of a debtor who was being taken to London on a writ of habeas corpus allegedly caused one gaoler to commit suicide. Even before their appointment, therefore, gaolers needed to be, and usually were, well born, well connected, and reasonably well off. Though not aristocrats, they belonged to respectable landed and professional families, while keepers tended to be men of lower social status and to enjoy fewer opportunities for advancement and gain.* William Tomlinson, the keeper of Preston from 1685 to 1696, had "little estate of his own" but married a widow with £40 a year. He had been a quartermaster in the militia and the deputy bailiff of the Earl of Derby before becoming keeper. His success as a bailiff in dealing with malefactors was one of the reasons for his appointment.[49] Thomas Whitlow, the keeper of Manchester from 1763 to 1790, was a chandler who employed the inmates in spinning wicks. Only one eighteenth-century gaoler (John Birdsworth) and one nineteenth-century keeper (William Liddell) are known to have been publicans, although in Bedfordshire men of this trade monopolized the office. Birdsworth was also the farmer of the vicarage lands. His son-in-law, Henry Bracken, who served briefly as gaoler, was a prominent local physician, educated at Leyden, who became mayor of Lancaster. One nineteenth-century keeper (Liddell) had been a sergeant in the army, while two gaolers (Higgin and Hansbrow) had been captains in the militia.[50] Three gaolers (John Ellitson and the two Higgins) were cousins of justices. Two gaolers founded gentry families, while the Higgins, father and son, inherited the estate of Wood Hey near Bury. John Junior's eldest son, William, became bishop of Limerick and Londonderry, while his third son, also called John, was a successful attorney and the town clerk of Lancaster. Another son, Thomas, who assisted his father but failed to replace him, was a cotton manufacturer and became mayor of Lancaster.[51]

One thing united the gaolers and the keepers. For both, keeping a prison was a family business. Edward and James Styth served as gaolers for most of the period between 1744 and 1771, while the father-and-son pairs of the Higgins and the Hansbrows governed Lancaster continuously from 1781 to 1867. At Manchester the Ouldhams and Walkers together governed the house of correction from before 1690 until 1755. William Dunstan and his two sons, Thomas and Richard, served as keepers from 1794 until 1841, while two more sons, George and Henry,

---

*John Higgin wrote that he had once held in custody two debtors whose joint debts totaled £59,000 and that two actions for recovery of debts had been brought against him (LCL, D 6351, no. 24). Cf. Eric Stockdale, *A Study of Bedford Prison, 1660–1877* (London, 1977), pp. 170-71.

served as deputy governors of the Salford New Bailey. The Stanleys at Preston seem to have been father, son, and grandson; with the Cowburnes they ran Preston from about 1703 until 1793, except for a single year. An undergaoler at Lancaster named James Birdsworth was probably a relative of the gaoler John, while John Higgin, Jr., employed two of his sons as assistants.

If such nepotism was an abuse, it was one that certainly continued unchanged into the nineteenth century. It also, however, reflected the value of experience in managing a prison. It was almost inevitable that the sons (and often the wives) of gaolers should assist them; the family lived in the prison, the gaoler was often away on business, and he had to have someone whom he could trust absolutely on the spot for twenty-four hours a day. Even the reformers emphasized the value of experience; they often recommended the hiring of army men, who had at least learned how to command others and how to administer. Essentially, therefore, both gaols and houses of correction tended to be family businesses with a fairly stable management. This continuity of management could make prisons resistant to major changes in penal philosophy.

Lancashire gaolers were frequently venal: happy to extend special privileges or to provide special goods for a price. John Higgin's recollections of his father's predecessor probably describe a typical eighteenth-century governor:

Mr. Dean was an intemperate Man, and encouraged drinking and Gambling in the Gaol, to benefit the Taps which were the perquisite of the governor[.] The two Miss Deans presided at the Wine Tap which was Kept in the Room now called the Snug. Beer was brewed in the Prison and sold in the Room still called "the Tap." The conducting of the Prison was a good deal left to the Head Turnkey, Robinson, who remitted punishment and granted favors to the Prisoners. One Gentleman paid as much as £20 for various indulgences he was committed for Forgery. [H]e wore no irons and in the end was allowed to sit in Miss Deans room.[52]

There is, however, only one case of habitual cruelty by a Lancashire gaoler: in the 1690's John Ellitson prompted a torrent of complaint from prisoners, who alleged that he extorted money from them, beat them without cause, chained them unreasonably, locked them up in disagreeable places, prevented free access to visitors, and engaged in various forms of corrupt behavior, including selling the lead off the roof and granting and receiving bribes.[53] Ellitson, however, both preceded and followed humane gaolers who were praised by their charges. His predecessor, James Melling, helped prisoners find room to work and lent them money to buy supplies, and his successor, Henry Bracken, sometimes forgave the fees owed him by poor prisoners and was credited by petitioners in 1699 with saving them from death by hunger and disease.[54]

Moreover, the prisoners' vigorous complaints against Ellitson's behavior suggests that they neither expected nor tolerated abusive or excessively corrupt behavior by gaolers. Scattered complaints in the course of the eighteenth century suggest that turnkeys—who were themselves often debtors—occasionally extorted money for admitting goods or prisoners to the debtors' side of the gaol. In one further case, a man held for sureties on charges of breaking and entering and attempted rape complained that the gaoler had confined him in the Condemned Hole. Because of this "intolerable" treatment, for which the gaoler had already been reproved by justices, the prisoner was discharged with a small fine.[55]

Little evidence about the conduct of keepers has survived. In the 1680's there were complaints about the failure of two successive keepers of Preston to live in the house. The choice of the next keeper, William Tomlinson, who had married the widow of a recusant, became a subject of a bitter political battle because of suspicions that he was a Jacobite. At one point a maidservant accused him of saying to some of his Irish prisoners, "I hate my very Christne name for the sake of the orringe pill," and then sitting down to drink with them.[56] Tomlinson's successor, John Bannister, proved even worse. Two towns preferred an indictment against him, and the Sheriff's Board dismissed him on charges of "extortion oppression neglect of duty wilfull and negligent escapes debauchery despiseing and affronting the Justices of the peace [and] contemning and disobeying their orders."[57] No evidence has been found of further complaints until the Cowburne affair in 1781. Howard observed that at one time the Preston keeper had become too old to manage his charges—a chronic problem throughout the period.

Though it remains sketchy, therefore, the Lancashire evidence tends to support Sheehan's contention that the conduct of prison officers improved after 1720 and provides no support for the widely held belief, repeated regularly in textbooks and histories, that eighteenth-century gaolers were cruel, oppressive, and barbaric. These contentions may be proved correct by further close investigation in other counties, but until they can be documented it is better to admit ignorance than to accept assumptions made without evidence.

It seems evident that the favorite panacea of the reformers and of later historians, conversion from fees to salaries, could by itself have had little effect on the penal system, since keepers were paid in this manner throughout the eighteenth century, with little effect on their conduct or on their responsiveness to the justices. If anything, the houses of correction were probably less well governed, less orderly, dirtier, more uncomfortable, and more licentious than the gaols, if only because their small size and powerless inmates aroused less interest among the justices and the public.

Furthermore, despite the Webbs' assertions, opportunities for improper profiteering did not occur only in institutions on a fee system. The gaoler made most of his profit by providing services that were, theoretically, in free competition with those available from the town. When he charged fees or provided drinks, prisoners knew what they were paying, and illegitimate exactions were difficult to conceal. The prohibition of alcohol and later of tobacco, like all such prohibitions, merely drove up the price of these goods and transferred the profits into even less reputable hands.

In fact, the adoption of a system of state provision of such commodities as food, furniture, and clothing offered the corrupt gaoler and his staff almost unlimited opportunities for peculation and for fraudulent dealings with contractors, at the expense both of prisoners (who received inferior goods) and of ratepayers. The justices had as much difficulty in preventing such activities as they had in eliminating direct extortion; William Liddell of Preston was accused of peculation in 1828, while the radical printer John Doherty, imprisoned for a few days in the New Bailey in 1832, claimed that its keeper was using the prisoners' bread to feed his horse, dogs, and pigs.[58] The question is not whether corruption was possible (it always is) but whether it was permitted; changes over the century in the standards by which men were chosen and by which they judged themselves were more important than an alteration in the method by which they were paid.

Nevertheless, the justices' anxiety to replace independent fee-collecting gaolers with salaried men who would be more firmly under their control is an important symbol of the justices' increased readiness to assume responsibility for prison administration and of their willingness to intervene directly if necessary. It was closely linked to other and far more important changes, of which the most important was, perhaps, the effort (often unsuccessful) to find "new men" to serve as gaolers and keepers, men who displayed the humaneness tempered with firmness that the reformers valued. Other changes were intended to make prison government more professional, more consistent, and more directly answerable to the justices and, as far as possible, to invest this newly responsible government with many powers previously exercised by the prisoners. The changes (sometimes unintended) in the role of the gaoler that these efforts entailed were probably the most important single feature of the prison reforms of the late eighteenth and early nineteenth centuries.

## County Rates and Prison Allowances, 1690-1776

The amount that justices raised to build or repair prisons and to aid prisoners could mean the difference between life and death for their charges. On the other hand, since the maintenance of law and order in general and of prisons in particular accounted for a significant part of a rate that was both outmoded and inequitable, even well-intentioned justices had to balance the welfare of prisoners against the resentment of ratepayers. The quality of their decisions was critical both to their prisoners and to their own standing in the countryside.

Lancashire's rating system descended from assessments made in 1334 for the "tenth and fifteenth," and continued in the same general form until the nineteenth century. Rates were assessed from the top down rather than from the bottom up. That is, instead of sending men around to look at every piece of property in the county and then working out what a given percentage of the total assessment would bring, the justices started with the given amount they needed to raise from a new rate. Then, meeting at the Sheriff's Board, they agreed among themselves how the burden should be divided among the six hundreds. The amount each hundred owed was then further divided among the parishes and townships, often in the same proportions that they had originally paid to the tenth and fifteenth. The constables of each township then collected the money and paid it to the high constables for their hundreds.[59]

Fresh assessments were sometimes made within each township to distribute the burden more fairly among the ratepayers, but the town still had to come up with its fixed amount. Despite the original intent of Parliament, assessments were made only on real estate, and once the assessment had been made for a particular rate the proportions by which the hundreds contributed were never changed.

This system was relatively efficient and inexpensive to run, and it was reasonably flexible in dealing with changes in the fortunes of individual taxpayers. It was, however, ill adapted to absorb long-term changes in the prosperity of one region as compared with others, and it was extremely inefficient in tapping new or commercial wealth. The fact that each tax had its own assessment also meant that certain areas paid disproportionately more for certain projects and less for others.

Many other rates were collected from a smaller base than the whole county. Every parish paid for its own poor. Other responsibilities, such as highways and bridges, were paid for by a variety of authorities. Salford hundred alone paid for the Salford house of correction, while the other five hundreds jointly paid for Preston; for this reason, in Lancashire the costs of the houses of correction, although they were legally "county" houses, were not a part of the county budget as they were elsewhere. Even in the nineteenth century they always had separate accounts and separately appointed treasurers.

By the beginning of the seventeenth century, five taxes, or "leys," each with its own assessment, were regularly levied on the whole county: the subsidy, the [tenth and] fifteenth, the ox ley, the maimed soldiers and Marshalsea ley, and the soldiers' ley. The most important was the soldiers' ley, which was first assessed in 1588 to provide money for soldiers injured in the war with Spain.[60] This was a revision of the fifteenth, in which West Derby's liability was reduced and that of Leyland increased. In 1624 the Sheriff's Board decided that the fifteenth, which by then was three centuries old, had become too inequitable for regular use and agreed to make the soldiers' ley the basis for all general county rates.[61] It was this tax that usually paid for repairs to the Castle. The hundreds probably collected rates for the houses of correction on the same assessments. From the consolidation of the rates in 1739 until 1815, the soldiers' ley was used for all county expenditures, including ones previously financed from other leys.

By the late eighteenth century these rates completely failed to correspond with the actual wealth of the areas taxed. This is especially evident at the township level. Until 1815 Liverpool paid £4 9s. 5d. to a county roll of £1,000, while in the same hundred (West Derby), Ashton paid £7 11s. and Wigan £9 5s. 10d. Ulverston in Lonsdale paid £15 7s. 9d. for the same rate, although in 1801 Liverpool contained 5,322 taxed houses and Ulverston only 248.[62]

In 1637 a sixth rate was added. Called the prisoners' ley, it was levied in accordance with an act of 1572 that authorized justices to tax every parish up to 6d. or 8d. a week to provide support for the prisoners in the county gaols. The churchwardens were to collect the money each week and pay it to a special treasurer living near the gaol, who was to distribute it to the prisoners. The wording of the original statute is vague; the Webbs say that it was "originally in all cases confined to convicted felons," but the statute refers only to "prisoners."[63] Lancashire gave it to debtors as well. The prisoners' ley was always collected for a single fixed amount: £43 6s. 8d. (originally £43 15s. 4d.), which represented what the justices considered to be a reasonable weekly taxation of each parish as provided by the act. The money was paid to the high constables, who then paid the appointed joint treasurers, one of whom was always the mayor of Lancaster.[64]

By the late seventeenth century, Lancashire apparently collected the prisoners' ley between two and four times a year, spending between £80 and £180 annually. At a conservative estimate, spending at this level would provide allowances for about forty debtors at the usual rate of 1s. a week each, or for eighty felons at 6d. a week. The significance of such expenditures depends on what assumptions are made about the size and composition of the prison population, but it seems evident that a substantial proportion of all prisoners did receive county support.

In 1739 an act of Parliament consolidated the county rates, making it possible to collect them all together on the basis of a single assessment. In Lancashire the rate chosen was the soldiers' ley first established in 1588. A single treasurer for the county stock was also appointed, and the special prisoners' fund was merged with the others. Since the treasurer occasionally submitted his accounts to the Quarter Sessions, it is possible to gain some sense of the size and composition of the county budget and of the place of prisons within that budget, although the figures are only approximate. A five-year set of such budgets is shown in Table 1. The period from July 1745 to March of the following year is missing. Since the budgets cover the period of the '45, it is likely that certain expenditures, particularly that for troops, were unusually high.

"Vagrants" took over half of all expenditure. The main expense was probably the cost of removing vagrants to their place of settlement. Lancashire's expenditure on vagrants was disproportionately large because other counties often "passed" their Irish vagrants to Liverpool and left Lancashire to pay the fare for their voyage home. Lancaster Castle and its prisoners took about a fourth of the total (26 percent), with support for prisoners accounting for about a tenth. In less disturbed years, prisoners would probably have taken a slightly larger proportion of the

## TABLE I
### Lancashire's Treasurer's Accounts, 1743/4-1749

| Period[a] | No. of months | Vagrants | Troops | Bridges | Repairs to Lanc. Castle | Prisoners' support | Misc. | Total | Approx. avg. per month |
|---|---|---|---|---|---|---|---|---|---|
| 13 Mar 1743/4-15 Jly 1745 | 16 | £640.16.4 | £30.9.2 | £4.2.3½ | £45.5.8 | £187.15.9 | — | £908.9.2½ | £57 |
| 13 Mar 1745/6-28 Apr 1747 | 13 | 1,011.0.5½ | 423.19.9 | 73.6.4 | 215.10.6 | 94.7.9 | — | 1,818.4.9½ | 140 |
| 28 Apr 1747-23 Jly 1747 | 3 | 71.8.6 | 6.15.2 | 5.5.2 | 129.7.11½ | 31.4.0 | — | 244.0.9½ | 81 |
| 23 Jly 1747-18 Apr 1748 | 9 | 410.6.0 | 68.10.3 | 60.3.0 | 31.14.8 | 82.18.5 | £40.14.5[b] | 694.6.9 | 77 |
| 20 Apr 1748-4 Apr 1749 | 11 | 390.10.11 | 37.2.0 | 30.5.1 | 335.6.9 | 108.15.3 | 234.2.6[c] | 1,136.2.6 | 103 |
| TOTAL | 52 | £2,524.2.2½ | £566.16.4 | £173.1.10½ | £757.5.6½ | £505.1.2 | £274.16.11 | £4,801.4.½ | £92 |
| Percent of total | | 52% | 12% | 4% | 16% | 10% | 6% | 100% | |

[a] Note that the financial and civil New Year began on March 25.
[b] For guarding bridges during cattle epidemic.
[c] Special work on bridges.

whole. Total county expenditure averaged a little under £100 a month or a little over £1,000 a year, a level at which it apparently remained until the last quarter of the century. Prisoners' allowances averaged a little under £10 a month, or £116 a year, an amount similar to that collected under the earlier ley. In other counties, the costs of the house of correction would also appear in the budget. In order to estimate the total cost of county imprisonment, therefore, we must add at least £100 a year for the two houses at Preston and Manchester, since after 1732 the salaries of the two keepers alone amounted to £85. In other counties, where the houses were included in the budget and conveyance of vagrants was often less expensive, imprisonment would probably have accounted for a larger proportion of the whole, but even in Lancashire it was always significant. In England as a whole in 1792, maintenance of prison buildings took nearly one-third of the total county spending (29.2 percent), by far the largest single category of expenditure. Support for prisoners took an additional 14.5 percent. Together with prosecutions (10.8 percent), these costs of controlling crime took over half of the aggregate county expenditure.[65]

Many of the costs of law enforcement were not borne by the county but were distributed in an unpredictable way between the offender, his family, his prosecutor, and his parish. In theory, the offender paid his own conveyance fees, which could reach £4. The constable escorting him paid traveling expenses from his own pocket and then obtained an order for reimbursement from the offender. If the offender could not pay, his property was distrained. If that was insufficient, his parish had to pay. Constables often experienced a good deal of difficulty in gaining reimbursement, which did something to dampen their zeal. It also meant that it was more expensive for outlying areas to prosecute offenses than it was for those near Lancaster or the sessional towns. Conveyance to one of the five locations where the Quarter Sessions met was often expensive enough to discourage prosecution; conveyance to the Assizes was even more costly.[66]

Though constables "presented" and prosecuted petty offenses against public order, more serious crimes such as larceny, burglary, rape, or assault were usually prosecuted by the victim. Until 1752 all prosecutors and witnesses paid their own expenses, and for most prosecutors the process was both expensive and time-consuming. After 1752 poor prosecutors, and after 1754 poor witnesses in any felony prosecution, could receive compensation from the county rate if the offender was convicted of a felony. An act of 1770 authorized payment to prosecutors if the grand jury found a true bill, and to witnesses in any felony prosecution, but until Peel's Act (1826) this included only costs incurred after the indictment was drawn up and covered only felony prosecutions. Despite the limitations, these acts encouraged prosecution, while the repayments to prosecutors and their attorneys took a rapidly increasing proportion of county expenditure.[67]

Since Assize prosecutions were far more expensive than similar actions before petty or Quarter Sessions, many offenders apparently benefited from a reduction of charges to bring cases before lesser tribunals, as well as from a general reluctance to prosecute at all. On the other hand, prosecutions before the Assizes were usually for the more serious crimes, in which the costs of prosecution weighed less in the decision to press charges. It seems likely that the increasing compensation for felony prosecutions, therefore, led to disproportionate increases in the number of prosecutions for minor felonies (e.g., petty theft) as opposed to those for serious felonies (e.g., murder) or misdemeanors (e.g., assault). This factor, along with changes in sentencing laws, helps explain the rapid growth in the houses of correction toward the end of the eighteenth century.

One outlay not itemized in the treasurer's accounts is transportation of convicted offenders. It was an expensive undertaking. A standard minimum for one prisoner was £8 10s. 2d., but costs could rise to £12. Gaolers, who received a set fee per mile for each prisoner no matter how many convicts they took at a time, could make a good profit by conveying prisoners in groups. Because of the complexity of the transaction, the dependence of overseas voyages on good weather, and the financial advantages of delaying until there was a sizable group to be transported, felons often spent long periods in gaol after conviction. Women, and men in poor health, often never left at all, since the county did not transport those thought unable to support the rigors of the voyage or unlikely to find employment at its destination. Lancaster Castle thus contained a permanent population of convicts, although the county preferred to transport them.

There were always some prisoners, debtors and felons alike, who possessed the means to support themselves in comfort during their stay. Felons often managed to shelter their assets from the law. Debtors were not necessarily bankrupt. As long as a debtor remained in prison, his creditor could not recover from his estate. Debtors arrested on friendly process to clear other obligations and farmers, yeomen, or gentlemen who went to prison rather than sell their holdings probably began with enough to keep them in prison for some time. Many debtors were small businessmen caught in a temporary liquidity crisis, unable to collect from their creditors to pay their own debts. A long imprisonment, however, could reduce most prisoners to penury.

Many prisoners received financial help from their families and their friends. Families that could afford it were expected to support their black sheep; if they failed to do so, the justices would issue orders requiring them to provide adequate maintenance. For example, when a Lancaster apothecary, Thomas Whalley, had his wife, Priscilla, arrested in 1699—on the grounds that she had disturbed the peace, threatened his life, annoyed his tenants, drank, and was unfaithful—the Sessions ordered him to pay her the comparatively large allowance of 5s. per week.[68] Most families, however, would not have required a court order to persuade them to contribute to the needs of close relatives. The crucial factor was how far prisoners had come from home; in their petitions they sometimes pointed out that they were far from their friends, while Irish prisoners received special consideration because they had no local assistance.

Many prisoners could pursue their trade in gaol. In 1707 there was a short-lived attempt to establish a "Woollen Manufactory" in the Castle. Forty-seven debtors (including Thomas Fell) signed a petition to the Sessions saying that their allowances had been reduced because they were employed in the work but that since the scheme had fallen through, they were "ready to perrish for want of bread."[69] In 1722 a debtor named John Exton wrote that he had supported himself in prison for two years by weaving until prevented by the gaoler, John Birdsworth. There is little evidence about felons' work, but in 1767 their allowances were raised on the grounds that they were suffering from bad weather and unemployment.[70]

A few prison jobs were also available. Aside from those employed by the debtors' court or the individual rooms, one or more of the debtors always served as turnkey, a role that did not necessarily endear them to their companions, and others served as wardsmen or warders. A document of 1711 lists several prison workers, including three "bum bailiffs," a daily laborer, a turnkey at £12 a year, and a tapster at £10 a year. Two women were listed: one minded the prisoners' children and the other probably ran errands for a commission. All of these were also receiving the county allowance. Some casual work was occasionally available, particularly nursing for the women.[71]

Debtors who had demonstrated their insolvency at a hearing under one of the acts were in law entitled to an allowance of 4*d*. a day, or 2*s*. 4*d*. a week, from their creditors (this had been raised in 1728 from 18*d*. a week). Howard maintained that very few of the debtors he saw had actually succeeded in obtaining this money. This seems likely, since most debtors were released after insolvency hearings; few creditors were persistent enough to keep a demonstrably insolvent man in gaol at their own expense. Convicted felons awaiting transportation were in law entitled to the "king's allowance" of 2*s*. 6*d*. a week. Howard wrote that no felons were receiving this allowance at the time of his visits, although at least one sheriff recorded such payments to seven felons, in accounts submitted in 1773.[72]

The county allowance was intended to cover the needs of each prisoner alone. If his family was poor, it received relief from its parish. There are examples of family members imprisoned together receiving separate allowances. At the end of the seventeenth century, allowances varied greatly. On occasion, Quarter Sessions granted as much as 2*s*. 6*d*. a week. Other prisoners received much less; in 1695 a debtor named Richard Croser complained that his four small children were being maintained by their parish and that he himself was "liable to perish with hunger" on 6*d*. a week.[73]

The last five years of the seventeenth century saw a determined effort by the justices to regulate the system more closely. By this time the annual cost of the allowances far exceeded the amount the justices had originally provided, and the treasurer of the fund was making regular appeals for additional money. In 1695 the court forbade him to pay more than 1*s*. to any prisoner without an order from the Quarter Sessions. The justices had been issuing private orders, "3ˢ to some and 1ˢ 6ᵈ to others which is a great . . . oppresion to the County."[74] In the hard year of 1699, the court resolved that it would not allow any debtor more than 1*s*. unless he was sick. A petition by 49 debtors to the same session suggests that a "ratepayers' revolt" may have lain behind these efforts at retrenchment. The prisoners, "sore visited with strange diseases of long continuance," said that they were in danger of starving because the high constables had failed to pay the treasurer of their fund. The court ordered the constables to pay within two weeks or be fined £5 each.[75]

A further crisis arose in the 1720's, probably because of the sharp increase in the number of debtors. In the summer of 1721 the Sheriff's Board resolved that all debtors not under execution be cut off from their allowances. At Michaelmas the Lancaster Sessions accordingly ordered the treasurer to stop the allowances of 39 prisoners. That winter six prisoners wrote the Lancaster Sessions that the board had reduced them "to the greatest Extremity." They had appealed the board's order and been told to apply to their own Quarter Sessions for relief orders. Five more debtors signed a similar petition in the spring. At least four were reinstated, but the months of delay between the meetings must have reduced some at least to starvation. In 1724 the Manchester Sessions, without explanation, cut off thirteen debtors, and the Lancaster Sessions did the same to eight prisoners the next year.[76]

The greatest crisis came in 1737, when the Lancaster Michaelmas Sessions suddenly came to the conclusion that allowances for debtors were illegal and that the justices had no power to charge the inhabitants of the county with the cost. They ordered the treasurer to cease payment of allowances to debtors. The results were disastrous. Fourteen debtors nearly starved to death. The Epiphany Sessions, unable to tolerate this result, simply ignored the legal issue and ordered that the allowances be resumed, on the grounds that the prisoners were poor and necessitous. Thereafter, the justices continued the traditional practice and no further objection was raised until 1822, when an expenditure committee of the Annual General Session reported that the weekly shilling, now supplemented by ten pounds of potatoes, "may have proceeded from motives of humanity" but was not legally chargeable to the county rate.[77]

Although the justices had agreed to limit the allowances to 6*d*. a week for felons and 1*s*. a week for debtors, they had some difficulty in enforcing the limit, particularly in years of dearth and high prices. They also had difficulty in keeping people who did not need the allowances off the rolls. Orders on the treasurer could be made by single or "double" justices as well as by Quarter Sessions, and prisoners naturally sent to the most generous justice in their area. The Quarter Sessions, therefore, was engaged in a constant battle to restrain its more prodigal members. In 1733, for example, it reduced three orders and also dealt with a debtor who was receiving 2*s*. 4*d*. from his creditor but had repeatedly succeeded in obtaining allowance orders from single justices. In 1742 the court again ordered the treasurer to reduce excessive allowances. Six years later the Manchester Sessions ordered that all allowances be made by Quarter Sessions, but Lancaster amended the order to permit two justices to sign orders.[78] On the whole, the limits were fairly well maintained, but by the 1760's, as prices began to rise, it became increasingly evident that they were insufficient. In 1767 the Lancaster Sessions increased the allowances of felons to 1s. The order was meant to be temporary but it was repeated in 1768, 1769, and 1770. By the time of Howard's visits, 1s. was the standard rate. The shilling allowance, which provided less than two pennyworth of bread a day, also became increasingly inadequate and was gradually replaced by the provision of goods in kind, until in the nineteenth century a prison dietary was established.

It is difficult to assess the adequacy of these allowances for eighteenth-century prisoners. According to the Webbs, 1s. a week was common by the end of the century, although some prisons were lower and many higher. Lancashire, however, may have been unusual in giving any allowance to debtors. Furthermore, the cost of living varied from area to area and year to year. All that can be said is that Lancashire overseers offered similar sums to their poor and that debtors' allowances were actually somewhat higher per capita than those given to many poor families. The crucial question is, How much of their allowances did the prisoners have to pay in fees? Prisoners arrested on criminal process paid two sets of fees, at the beginning and end of their imprisonment (providing they were released). The fees at their entry paid the cost of their conveyance, admission, and "garnish," amounting to several shillings. At their release felons paid the gaoler's fees and a variety of legal fees—until 1774, when the court was permitted to order the county to pay as much as 13s. 4d. for every acquitted or discharged prisoner. Felons might pay other fees, to avoid irons, for example, or they might purchase extra comforts like washing, but in law they were not compelled to do so.

An extortionate gaoler could make felons so uncomfortable that they were forced to buy indulgence, but most felons were probably so poor that it was not worth his while to do so. Felons were not charged for their usual housing, in the worst cells in the prison, but wealthy felons sometimes rented more luxurious quarters. The county provided them with straw to sleep on, but some rented bedding. Once his entrance and exit fees were allowed for, a felon had nearly the whole of his allowance to spend on food, provided he was willing to endure the squalor that the justices considered good enough for criminals.

Debtors paid about 8s. for admission and discharge as well as a garnish of 7s. 2d. (Female debtors paid half as much garnish.) Theoretically, once in prison debtors could live as cheaply as felons if they lodged in the "common room" and either slept on straw or provided their own bedding. In practice, however, many debtors paid an initial fee and a weekly rent to inhabit one of the more comfortable rooms. Even the poorest debtors felt entitled to proper bedding rather than straw; if they lived too far away to transport their own, they rented a bed either from the gaoler or from townspeople. Debtors who claimed the utmost destitution sometimes mentioned that they had been reduced to selling their beds, while others included the cost of bedding in petitions asserting that their allowances were inadequate. The justices seem to have agreed that debtors, even when wholly supported by the county, were entitled to beds. By statute the gaoler could charge 7*d*. per person per week for a bed, whether single or shared, but many debtors paid 3*d*. to 4*d*. a week to townspeople for bedding and sometimes for washing as well.[79]

Although prisoners in receipt of a substantial income did not, by the middle of the eighteenth century, receive county allowances, the allowance was considered the bare minimum, to be supplemented by other means. It seems probable that nearly all poor debtors received occasional supplements to their weekly shillings. Although prisoners in the gaol were not required to work, they frequently did so without losing their allowances, and it seems likely that by mid-century they were expected to do so. In the rare cases of serious infirmity that kept prisoners in their cells, a supplement was offered; for example, in 1772 the court ordered an extra shilling a week for Sarah Shelfox, an aged transportee. Insane prisoners also received larger allowances. Prisoners who fell ill were provided with nursing, special food, and treatment by an apothecary at county expense. Though the gaoler probably earned more each year in fees and perquisites than all the prisoners together received in support from the county, after 1699 prisoners already on the allowance submitted very few petitions complaining of its inadequacy. This fact, together with evidence of the amounts paid in poor relief and the apparent absence of epidemic disease, suggests that the allowance was sufficient for most prisoners over most of the century, though it was by no means a liberal maintenance.

By the 1770's, however, inflation had made these allowances increasingly inadequate. Howard noted in 1777 that prisoners received about half as much bread as they had when the allowances were originally fixed, the penny loaf weighing about half a pound. As he wrote, "Many criminals are half-starved; such of them as at their commitment were in health, come out almost famished, scarce able to move, and for weeks incapable of any labour."[80] Fourteen years later, Jeremy Bentham was outraged on hearing that the dietary at Wymondham was 2*d.* worth of bread a day, along with some unspecified amounts of other foods. He commented that "under a regimen like this a prison must be a scene of perpetual famine. . . . I should speak honestly and call it *torture.*"[81]

For poor prisoners, and particularly for poor debtors, the steadily decreasing value of the shilling allowance was probably the single most important factor affecting their welfare, and certainly helps to account for much of the misery and disease apparent in the prisons of Howard's day. Since Parliament failed to pass any insolvency acts between 1781 and 1793, debtors were unable to apply for their "groats" and were also spending longer terms in gaol, increasing their dependence on their allowances. Felons were also spending longer spells in gaol, after the disruption of transportation.

The justices were hampered in their ability to deal with these problems by legal restrictions and by the extremely antiquated and inefficient rating system. The rates had failed to keep pace with economic changes, and most of the judges, because they were rural landed proprietors, came from over-rated areas. Prison expenditure was a sufficiently large part of the budget to require careful control.

Under these conditions it is no wonder that the justices made every effort to keep the costs of prison administration to a minimum. The evidence shows, however, that a large proportion of all prisoners did receive assistance from the county and that this assistance was adequate if not generous through most of the eighteenth century. If the evidence does not support a very optimistic view of prison life, it also suggests that justices were not merely leaving prisoners to starve. Given the inadequate base of the county rates, the real question is not why the justices were anxious to control spending but how they managed to finance the enormous expenditures of the next age of reform.

The appalling conditions of mid-eighteenth-century English prisons have become a cliché, but one that so far lacks documentary support. The large London prisons, which usually furnish historians with their more sensational examples, were not necessarily typical; London evidence should not be extrapolated to the provinces, nor the rule of city corporations to that of rural justices. Even in the case of London, new research shows that the picture requires considerable modification and suggests that historians have been insensitive to major changes in prison life and governance that occurred before the Age of Reform. The unreformed prison has its own history of reform. Over the centuries a marked pattern of change is apparent in every aspect of prison life. Prison conditions often mirror social stresses, and those periods when many factors interacted to cause a partial breakdown in prison conditions and administration have stood out particularly clearly. Such a period seems to have occurred during the hard years at the end of the sixteenth century. Similar difficulties arose during the political and religious controversies at the end of the seventeenth century, when hunger and disease reappeared together in prisons crowded with large numbers of prisoners of conscience. Signs of strain also accompanied a large increase in the numbers of gaoled debtors in the 1720's, at the time of the economic collapse that followed the South Sea Bubble.

Nevertheless, the mid-eighteenth century seems to have been a time of relative stability. Complaints from prisoners died down. The prison population remained stable or dropped. The problem of a corrupt, brutal, and extortionate prison staff had been dealt with in the early years of the century; following the departure of Lancaster gaoler John Ellitson in 1699 and of the keeper of the Preston house of correction in 1703 there were no further scandals for almost a century. The number of deaths dropped, though perhaps only because the population also dropped. Low, relatively stable prices meant that the fixed allowances were, if not ample, at least adequate. National legislation regulated prison fees. It is certainly still possible that many or most prisons in the mid-eighteenth century were places of terror and death, but if so, the onus of proof must rest on those who make the contention. Too many historians have relied on speculation, and it is as important to recognize what we do not know as to describe what we do. While this study cannot show conclusively that the horrors of eighteenth-century prison life have been exaggerated, it does reveal several factors that deserve consideration.

First, Lancashire's justices did intervene in prison affairs. They were attentive to the need to keep prison buildings in a tolerable state of repair and they were reasonably responsive to petitions from prisoners about this subject. They also provided a minimal level of financial support for insolvent prisoners. They occasionally investigated when prisoners complained of mistreatment. The eighteenth-century history of Lancashire's prisons suggests that the justices were usually well intentioned, although it also shows that they lacked energy and zeal, waited until they received petitions instead of initiating comprehensive changes on their own, and on occasion permitted errors and inefficiency to cause real hardship. Nevertheless, their general conduct compares favorably with that of many local governments today.

Second, prisoners, particularly debtors, knew their legal rights and were prepared to exercise them, either by petitioning the Quarter Sessions or by prosecuting delinquent prison officers—although it is true that most prison officers successfully escaped the criminal penalties attached to misconduct, at most suffering dismissal from office. In view of the notorious litigiousness of Englishmen, the prisoners' determination to defend their rights should not be surprising. The collections of signatures and marks at the bottom of petitions show that prisoners joined together to invoke the formal mechanisms of the national legal establishment that, in other ways, was being used against them. The riot and escape of 1755 shows that debtors who ordinarily accepted their lot were capable of a collective sense of grievance and concerted action when they believed they were being held illegally.

Third, though the prison death rate may well have been high, there is little evidence, before the last quarter of the century, that eighteenth-century Lancashire's gaols harbored the epidemic fevers that have become such a fixture of prison literature. Typhus is a disease of overcrowding as well as of dirt and hunger; there is no reason to believe that any of the three county prisons was frequently overcrowded in this period. When prisons did become crowded, at the end of the sixteenth, seventeenth, and eighteenth centuries, fevers apparently returned.

Fourth, prisoners received support from communities both within and outside the walls. The constant going and coming from the prison had a few disadvantages; it weakened security, enabled prisoners to consult with their partners in crime, and made it easy for prostitutes to ply their trade. On the whole, however, it was undoubtedly beneficial for the prisoners. Whether the community life within the walls was equally beneficial is a matter of opinion. It was certainly necessary; prisoners clubbed together to perform functions that no other authority was at that time prepared to fulfill, such as arranging for cooking, cleaning, and heating in their rooms. They administered justice and revenged misdeeds. They provided each other with entertainment, support in times of need, scribes and advisers, employers and servants. Though it was not exceptionally violent, however, the eighteenth-century prison community did not live in utopian peace. It contained bitterness, feuding, and intimidation. Some prisoners petitioned against the privileges of others. Prisoners who served as warders and turnkeys often behaved badly and were resented. Constant drunkenness and gambling created endless brawls. The justice of the prisoners' "kangaroo courts" was not necessarily either fairer or more lenient than that of the gaolers who would replace them. The gaolers themselves were often absent and, when present, apparently exercised little control over the behavior of either the prisoners or the turnkeys. Weak or unjustly treated prisoners had no recourse and no hope of protection from the relentless persecution of their fellows. Most obvious of all is the mixture of fear and contempt with which the debtors regarded the felons. Debtors not only approved of the separation between themselves and the felons, they demanded it.

In the absence of any adequate studies, it is difficult to date the onset of the next period of trouble with any precision, but it began perhaps as early as 1765. In that year prices rose, although they would rise more sharply later. In 1764 Lancaster Castle was presented at the Assizes for repairs; it was presented for a second time in 1775. In that same year, major rebuilding began at Manchester. In 1779 a gaoler committed suicide; four years later his successor died in the first major epidemic to sweep the Castle in the course of the century. By the time of John Howard's visits, Lancashire's prisons were undergoing what seemed to be yet another in a long series of periodic crises involving rising prison populations and prices. Lancashire was not unique in this regard. During his early visits, before the publication of *State of the Prisons*, Howard found several counties planning additions to their prisons or completely new buildings. What initially seemed merely one more episode in a long series of short-lived crises, however, began to take on an entirely different character as years passed and no relief came into sight. Instead of being a temporary aberration, the wretched state of England's penal institutions was becoming a permanent affront to an established tradition of rough but relatively humane administration. Moreover, prison crowding and hunger were beginning to threaten not only the sensibilities but also the lives of the county justices who administered them, as epidemics of typhus appeared. As the magnitude of the problem became evident, as new theories on crime and disease began to emerge, and as new resources became available, the response of the justices began to take on a completely new character. Under the guidance of a few energetic reformers, this response was to amount to a comprehensive attack on the communal life of the prison.

CHAPTER 2

# Prison Populations

## The Eighteenth-Century Stasis

Changes in the size and composition of the prison population are a vital key to the events of the Age of Reform, but the causal relationship is complex. The size of the prison population directly reflected the rate of prosecution (the crime rate), but this rate was not an independent variable. It reflected social and economic changes that may have actually increased the number of offenses, but it also reflected changes in the willingness of victims to prosecute, which in turn was conditioned by their fear that crime was increasing, by new government policies, and by their sense of the resources available for punishing offenders.

The changes in prison populations, moreover, did not merely reflect external events but themselves affected the nature and quality of prison life. A large institution cannot be run in the same way as a small one; incarceration in a room with twenty others is not the same as incarceration in solitude; a prison filled with short-term offenders is not the same as a prison filled with men serving life sentences; and populations that fluctuate or grow rapidly will not have the same effect as populations that reach the same levels over a longer period.

In sentencing, no clear distinction was made between the house of correction and the county gaol. Felons and misdemeanants went to both. The two institutions were not, however, completely interchangeable. Vagrants rarely went to the Castle (and then probably because they had originally been charged with another offense). Debtors never went to the houses of correction (except for a few who appeared at Preston in the nineteenth century). In general, since the Castle was by far the most secure prison and since the Assizes sat in Lancaster, prisoners charged with serious crimes, including nonclergyable felonies, went to the Castle, as did most prisoners held for failure to pay fines. The remaining prisoners went to whatever institution was most convenient at the time. The gaols, therefore, held only part of all prisoners, and punitive imprisonment in some penal institution was a common experience for offenders.

In the unreformed prison, fluctuations of prison population were common, and large changes could lead to serious crises. Over the years a complex of events recurred. Periods of rising population, rising prices, and social stresses are loosely coordinated with periods of new prison building and legislation. Common sense suggests how these factors might be linked, though the links are not necessarily direct. Research in a few counties has suggested that in early modern England, prosecutions, particularly prosecutions for property crimes, tended to rise in years of dearth.[1] Gaols that contained a large proportion of debtors were particularly vulnerable to periods of economic collapse.

Aside from the effect that rising prices and economic instability may have had on the crime rate and, hence, on the number of prisoners, they also had a direct effect on the conditions of prison life. Their impact was especially pronounced in the unreformed prison, because prisoners there depended on fixed monetary allowances. The substitution of provision in kind for money payments, though it had disadvantages, did at least provide a cushion against the total erosion of the value of support.

Though Lancashire enjoyed relative stability during most of the eighteenth century, in very bad years problems could interact to cause a vicious cycle. Dearth sent more debtors and possibly more criminals to the prisons, where they pressed on prison allowances at the very time that those who were already in prison needed more just to stay alive. Because the rating system was cumbersome and inequitable, it was difficult for the county to increase rates, especially at a moment when ratepayers themselves were suffering financial difficulties. Hunger and overcrowding raised the death rate. The timing of petitions and the evidence of mortality statistics suggest that the most serious suffering among prisoners was caused by these sudden crises and not by chronic neglect.

## The Rising Numbers

Prison populations seem to have been relatively stable during the mid-eighteenth century, but at the end of the eighteenth century a new pattern emerged. Though it seemed initially that the prisons were experiencing yet another short-lived surge in numbers, that surge was, in fact, part of a much more extensive and rapidly accelerating trend. Beginning at some point in the late eighteenth century, prison populations rapidly reached crisis levels and then continued to rise throughout the first half of the nineteenth century. There is no question that this rise occurred. The difficulty is to determine its causes and to explain the effect it had on prison life and organization.

Traditional histories have limited their discussion of prison populations largely to the immediate Howardian period—that is, to the last two decades of the eighteenth century following publication of *The State of the Prisons* in 1777. The historians have attributed the sudden and dramatic increase in new prison construction (42 new penal institutions were begun in 1789 alone) to two factors: the revulsion aroused by Howard's revelations and a sharp increase in prison populations resulting from the disruption of overseas transportation of convicts during the American Revolution.

Howard was certainly interested in encouraging new building; he published several plans and was a close friend of the prison architect William Blackburn. Nevertheless, there is no evidence that Howard's efforts were decisive. For one thing, enormous sums were spent; it is incredible that one man's influence, however great, could have persuaded the frugal justices and the notoriously tight-fisted corporations to make such commitments. For another, given a stable prison population, many of Howard's suggestions could have been adopted without such large-scale building. Occasionally he commented that the "situation" of a prison was unhealthy and should be changed, but most magistrates could have brought their prisons to an acceptable level of cleanliness and comfort without tearing them down entirely. About Lancaster Castle, for example, he wrote that it would "be a good gaol" if a new infirmary were built.[2] Instead of basking in Howard's approval, however, the Lancaster justices embarked on a massive program of building and repair that involved presenting the Castle for the second time in ten years and the construction of new courts, a new gaoler's house, new debtors' rooms, and a whole new felons' prison, all before 1794. Just about the only thing they did not build was a new infirmary.

It seems likely that such massive building was related to major changes in the size and composition of the prison population, but the rise caused by the disruption of transportation overseas was probably smaller and more gradual than many historians have realized. First, even at the best of times there were often delays in transporting convicts. Second, some felons had never been transported. Third, although the national total of convicted felons may have seemed large, there were not very many in any given provincial gaol. In 1779, after transportation had ended, London held nearly 200 felons, but Howard found only 16 felons in York, England's largest provincial gaol, and only 11 in Lancaster. Finally, what the war gave with one hand it took away with another; less serious criminals could now be impressed into the armed services. The immediate effect of the American war, therefore, was as much a change in quality as in quantity. As Michael Ignatieff has recently pointed out, it was the return of peace in the early 1780's that marked the real crisis, as the number of convicts began to mount and the Home Office became more and more dilatory in arranging for their removal.[3]

Factors other than the disruption of transportation contributed to the rising number of felons. As Sir Leon Radzinowicz has shown, the number of offenses designated as felonies grew rapidly in the eighteenth century, at the same time as the percentage of convicted felons executed for their crimes dropped.[4] In most provincial prisons the absolute numbers of convicted felons remained relatively small in the 1780's: in 1783 Stafford gaol had 15 convicts out of a total prison population of 90, and Warwick only 7 out of a total of 91. The lack of facilities for keeping felons, however, and their relatively long stays made the problem a serious one; the fears expressed by county sheriffs and gaolers about mutinies and outbreaks of epidemic disease proved well justified.[5] Moreover, the problem accelerated at the end of the century. The number of criminals who remained at Lancaster from an earlier Assize had reached 72 by the March Assize of 1801. This increase probably resulted from the use of imprisonment as a substitute for execution or removal, since the number of prisoners for trial apparently remained relatively steady between 1767 and 1806, with a spike in 1801. Between 1806 and 1817, however, the number of prisoners for trial at the Assize also increased rapidly. After 1806, not only were fewer felons removed but more were prosecuted as well, and the two trends together raised the number of criminals in the Castle who were serving sentences or awaiting transportation from 33 in 1806 to 232 in 1817. The number dipped again briefly after the peace (see Table 2).[6]

Felons were only a part of the increasing prison population. Toward the end of the eighteenth century, the number of prisoners in all cate-

TABLE 2

*Prisoners Listed in Lancaster Assize Calendars,*
*Selected Years, 1767–1822*

| Year | March | | August | |
|------|-------|-------|--------|--------|
| | No. in calendar | No. up for trial | No. in calendar | No. up for trial |
| 1767 | — | — | — | 28 |
| 1775 | — | 25 | — | — |
| 1776 | — | 21 | — | — |
| 1782 | — | 31 | — | — |
| 1783 | — | 25 | — | — |
| 1792 | — | 27 | — | — |
| 1793 | — | — | — | 14 |
| 1794 | — | 21 | — | — |
| 1801 | 173 | 101 | 177 | 71 |
| 1802 | 130 | 39 | 118 | 41 |
| 1803 | 110 | 32 | 127 | 36 |
| 1804 | 115 | 39 | 101 | 39 |
| 1805 | 97 | 33 | 58 | 18 |
| 1806 | 60 | 27 | 112 | 59 |
| 1807 | 115 | 62 | 106 | 37 |
| 1808 | 115 | 38 | 115 | 53 |
| 1809 | 117 | 46 | 126 | 58 |
| 1810 | 130 | 55 | 124 | 63 |
| 1811 | 130 | 53 | 126 | 49 |
| 1812[a] | 129 | 55 | 182 | 90 |
| 1813 | 154 | 75 | 137 | 53 |
| 1814 | 134 | 57 | 137 | 67 |
| 1815 | 184 | 91 | 161 | 21 |
| 1816 | 216 | 74 | 265 | 94 |
| 1817 | 352 | 120 | 348 | 101 |
| 1818 | 328 | 128 | 270 | 47 |
| 1819 | 256 | 112 | 183 | 75 |
| 1820 | 227 | 123 | 246 | 85 |
| 1821 | 258 | 105 | 221 | 56 |
| 1822 | 221 | 77 | — | — |

[a]In May 67 prisoners were up for trial in special Luddite Assizes.

gories, including debtors, began a steady rise that would last until the mid-nineteenth century. At the moment, we cannot pinpoint the starting point of this trend; in some counties it might have been under way as early as 1760. In Lancashire, it was evident by the 1780's. Though eighteenth-century figures on debtor populations are poor, a count of the number of debtors filing insolvency papers reveals a slight rise in the 1770's and a more sustained increase beginning in the 1790's. What hap-

TABLE 3
*Debtors Committed to Lancaster Castle, 1798-1818*

| Year | Number committed | Discharged as insolvent | | Year | Number committed | Discharged as insolvent | |
|---|---|---|---|---|---|---|---|
| | | No. | Pct. | | | No. | Pct. |
| 1798 | 162 | 22 | 14% | 1809 | 309 | 52 | 17% |
| 1799 | 175 | 33 | 19 | 1810 | 306 | 75 | 24 |
| 1800 | 190 | 51 | 27 | 1811 | 366 | 107 | 29 |
| 1801 | 247 | 59 | 24 | 1812 | 303 | 115 | 38 |
| 1802 | 206 | 38 | 18 | 1813 | 343 | 141 | 41 |
| 1803 | 207 | 54 | 26 | 1814 | 272 | 122 | 45 |
| 1804 | 202 | 31 | 15 | 1815 | 282 | 128 | 45 |
| 1805 | 203 | 62 | 30 | 1816 | 441 | 181 | 41 |
| 1806 | 266 | 41 | 15 | 1817 | 576 | 250 | 43 |
| 1807 | 267 | 47 | 18 | 1818 | 526 | 221 | 42 |
| 1808 | 319 | 59 | 18 | | | | |

SOURCE: *Parliamentary Papers.*
NOTE: A letter of John Higgin gives the following total numbers of debtors committed to Lancaster Castle: 1815, 238; 1820, 546; 1826, 734; 1828, 551; 1829, 590; 1830, 643.

pened in the 1780's is unclear, because between 1781 and 1794 Parliament failed to pass any insolvency acts, but it seems likely that this inaction increased the number of debtors remaining in prison for long periods.[7]

Figures collected by Parliament reveal that the number of debtors committed to Lancaster Castle continued to rise rapidly in the first two decades of the nineteenth century (see Table 3); other sources show that their numbers reached a peak in 1827 and then remained at a high but relatively stable level.[8] Total committals of debtors rose from 162 in 1798 to about 734 in 1826. Parliament tried to reduce the severe overcrowding among debtors by easing their release under the insolvency acts and making these acts permanent, but even these measures were not enough to compensate for the increasing flood of committals. Indeed, they may have made the problem worse, since they led debtors to seek committal on friendly process in order to clear their debts. Increasing crowding among the debtors drove Lancaster's gaoler, John Higgin, almost to desperation and led to several outbreaks of unrest on the debtors' side of the gaol.

The population rise in the houses of correction was equally dramatic. Evidence from calendars suggests that in the mid-eighteenth century two or three dozen offenders came before the Preston and Salford ses-

TABLE 4

*Prisoners Listed in Calendars, Preston and Manchester Houses of Correction,*
*Selected Years, 1756-1790*

| | | | | | Manchester | |
| | | | | | | No. in |
| Year | Preston | Manchester | Year | Preston | Total | custody |
|------|---------|------------|------|---------|-------|---------|
| 1756 | 3 | 10 | 1778 | 39 | 43 | — |
| 1759 | 8(Ep) | 16(Ep) | 1779 | 24 | 54 | — |
| 1760 | 4 | 26(E) | 1780 | 23 | 49 | 17 |
| 1765 | 34 | 13 | 1781 | 32 | 55 | 23 |
| 1766 | — | 30(Ep) | 1782 | 39 | 49 | 17 |
| 1770 | 22 | 39 | 1783 | 39 | 72 | 31 |
| 1771 | 24 | 39 | 1784 | 65 | 84 | 26 |
| 1772 | 20 | 30 | 1785 | 56 | 82 | 26 |
| 1773 | — | 38 | 1786 | 72 | 88 | 44 |
| 1774 | 35(E) | — | 1787 | 57 | 88 | 38 |
| 1775 | 29 | 30(T) | 1788 | 70 | 112 | 42 |
| 1776 | 25 | 49 | 1789 | 58 | 111 | 44 |
| 1777 | 31 | 48 | 1790 | 106 | 175 | — |

NOTE: Ep indicates Epiphany Sessions, E Easter Sessions, T Summer Sessions. All others are Michaelmas Sessions.

sions. The Preston and Salford houses probably held between five and twenty offenders each between sessions; Howard found as few as six and as many as 21 in Manchester. In the mid-1780's, however, the numbers listed for trial at both houses approximately doubled (Table 4). By 1790, 175 prisoners appeared in the calendar for a single Manchester Session. Committal statistics collected by Henry Fielding, the Salford chaplain, show that there were 685 committals in 1801. This figure would rise to a high of 4,034 in 1827. By 1801 there were already 243 felons committed to Manchester and the number continued to rise steadily, nearly quadrupling by 1826. Equally important, however, was the number of misdemeanants. Starting at 360 in 1801, the committal rate had risen to 1,365 in 1825 and 1,772 in 1827, nearly five times its level at the beginning of the century. The number of petty offenders, such as vagrants, also rose sharply (see Table 5).[9]

For the period between 1820 and 1842, we at last have both total criminal committals and daily average populations for all Lancashire's prisons, including the new house of correction at Kirkdale, near Liverpool, which opened in 1820. Though the pattern varied slightly from prison to prison, total committals at the four institutions combined continued

TABLE 5

*Total Committals to the Salford New Bailey, 1801 and 1811-1827*

| Year | Vagrants | Nonpayment of bastardy orders | Uttering base coin | Lewd women | Offenses against game laws | Misdemeanors | Felons | Total |
|------|------|------|------|------|------|------|------|------|
| 1801 | 24 | 46 | 6 | 5 | 1 | 360 | 243 | 685 |
| 1811 | 49 | 136 | 14 | 9 | 2 | 324 | 219 | 753 |
| 1812 | 87 | 172 | 20 | 8 | 4 | 328 | 257 | 876 |
| 1813 | 69 | 144 | 13 | 8 | 7 | 456 | 306 | 1,003 |
| 1814 | 98 | 109 | 4 | 16 | 6 | 480 | 327 | 1,040 |
| 1815 | 210 | 168 | 5 | 23 | 4 | 631 | 425 | 1,466 |
| 1816 | 253 | 330 | 10 | 28 | 16 | 888 | 454 | 1,979 |
| 1817 | 485 | 516 | 21 | 33 | 13 | 1,034 | 792 | 2,894 |
| 1818 | 329 | 331 | 16 | 23 | 9 | 875 | 746 | 2,329 |
| 1819 | 725 | 431 | 19 | 30 | 22 | 1,077 | 737 | 3,041 |
| 1820 | 961 | 403 | 14 | 18 | 18 | 1,070 | 853 | 3,337 |
| 1821 | 783 | 336 | 9 | 27 | 8 | 1,136 | 706 | 3,005 |
| 1822 | 374 | 271 | 13 | 19 | 6 | 1,204 | 725 | 2,612 |
| 1823 | 289 | 344 | 10 | 19 | 6 | 1,110 | 712 | 2,490 |
| 1824 | 405 | 318 | 7 | 15 | 7 | 1,321 | 893 | 2,966 |
| 1825 | 220 | 320 | 10 | 21 | 10 | 1,365 | 933 | 2,879 |
| 1826 | 369 | 610 | 32 | 20 | 37 | 1,161 | 937 | 3,166[a] |
| 1827 | 780 | 532 | 16 | 24 | 21 | 1,772 | 889 | 4,034 |

SOURCE: Manchester Central Library, Henry Fielding, "Tables Showing the Total Number of Prisoners Committed to the New Bailey, Salford, under the Several Charges Specified . . ." (paper read to the Manchester Statistical Society, 1834-35).
[a]Corrected from the original.

to climb until 1842.[10] The daily average population, however, began to fall after 1834, suggesting a drop in the length of sentences. The combined daily average population rose by 600 prisoners, from about 1,440 in 1820 to 2,040 in 1834, before falling briefly to its earlier level in 1837. The number of prisoners in individual prisons continued to fluctuate throughout the middle of the century, but the worst strain seems to have come in the period between the 1780's and the 1830's, whose unprecedented problems took administrators by surprise (see Table 6).[11]

This trend may explain why the steady efforts at prison reform throughout the period from Howard to the accession of Victoria seemed to have borne so little fruit. Reform did take place, but it was often overwhelmed by the increasing numbers of bodies. This steady and rapid increase in prison populations is the single most important fact underlying all the changes in early-nineteenth-century prison administration.

TABLE 6
*Daily Average Population, Lancashire Prisons, 1823-1842*

| Year | Lancaster | Preston | Kirkdale | Salford | Total |
|------|-----------|---------|----------|---------|-------|
| 1823 | 271 | 143 | 507 | 517 | 1,438 |
| 1824 | 280 | 148 | 529 | 603 | 1,560 |
| 1825 | 313 | 125 | 489 | 601 | 1,528 |
| 1826 | 368 | 166 | 580 | 609 | 1,723 |
| 1827 | 457 | 251 | 613 | 674 | 1,995 |
| 1828 | 427 | 191 | 560 | 529 | 1,707 |
| 1829 | 358 | 183 | 533 | 469 | 1,543 |
| 1830 | 406 | 211 | 539 | 504 | 1,660 |
| 1831 | 437 | 204 | 522 | 480 | 1,643 |
| 1832 | 424 | 206 | 588 | 543 | 1,761 |
| 1833 | 408 | 226 | 574 | 524 | 1,732 |
| 1834 | 427 | 528 | 573 | 512 | 2,040 |
| 1835 | 450 | 160 | 627 | 552 | 1,789 |
| 1836 | 437 | 175 | 615 | 530 | 1,757 |
| 1837 | 341 | 174 | 337 | 572 | 1,424 |
| 1838 | 455 | 183 | 368 | 653 | 1,659 |
| 1839 | 451 | 174 | 315 | 586 | 1,526 |
| 1840 | 460 | 214 | 344 | 641 | 1,659 |
| 1841 | 516 | 216 | 417 | 685 | 1,834 |
| 1842 | 515 | 234 | 494 | 719 | 1,962 |

## Some Causes of the Rise

Though the rising tide of inmates both caused and complicated efforts at prison reform, it would be a mistake to simplify the relationship between these factors. The increase in prisoners may have led to prison reform, but prison reform may also have contributed to the increase in prisoners. The rising number of petty offenders in penal institutions suggests not only a higher crime rate but also a greater willingness to take formal legal action over conflicts previously solved less formally. Enlarged prison capacity made this decision possible in cases where it had not been so before. The Manchester house of correction, for example, was rebuilt in 1774 and again in the late 1780's, opening on a new site in 1790. Preston reopened on a new site in 1789. In all three cases, the number of names in prison calendars rose sharply immediately *after* the new prison opened.

In a sense, therefore, the prison reformers who built larger prisons may have helped to create the problem they wished to solve. Some reformers of the time understood this dilemma. Sir George Onesiphorus Paul, for example, was very concerned about the increased readiness of Gloucester justices to commit previously tolerated offenders to the new prison built by his efforts.[12] This discretionary element in the system of justice affected petty offenders to a much greater extent than it did those who had committed graver crimes; murderers were always prosecuted, but lewd women were not. The knowledge that felons were likely to be imprisoned rather than executed may also have encouraged the upgrading of certain offenses to felonies and made convictions easier to obtain.

Michael Ignatieff and others have argued that the economic and social strains of the late eighteenth century encouraged those in authority to send more and more offenders to gaol. Along with recent historians of crime, they have pointed to specific new laws related to the needs of a market economy: laws designed to increase the control that masters exercised over their workers. Other laws, such as those permitting summary committals, encouraging prosecution of certain offenders, and allowing manipulation of the powers to condemn and reprieve, more generally enhanced both the actual and the symbolic power of a class that felt itself threatened by social change. The effect of these changes was to increase the number of those imprisoned not only for felonies but for petty offenses as well.

These scholars have also pointed out that the rising number of prisoners in the late eighteenth century was only part of an increasing resort to institutionalization. For example, Andrew Scull has claimed that in this period the English abandoned their traditional family-centered response to insanity and, indeed, to all forms of deviance. He attributes this change to the development of a mature market economy and to an increasing commercialization that made the "ruling class" receptive to the idea of institutionalization for "problem populations." Another factor was that the proportion of the population directly dependent on poor relief had increased "at precisely the point in time when the growing power of the bourgeoisie and their increasing dominance of intellectual life was reducing the inclination to tolerate such a state of affairs." Simultaneously, new theories were portraying insanity, for the first time, as "a condition existing more pervasively among the lower classes of the community—a distinct species of pathology which could not be considered as just one more case of poverty and dependency."[13]

As an explanation of the rise of institutions, this emphasis on broad social changes is more satisfying than the traditional emphasis on political events such as the disruption of transportation. Nevertheless, such models often conflate the "bourgeoisie" with the "ruling classes" and assume that though social changes might take place at the bottom of the pyramid, intellectual changes occurred only at the top. It was the "ruling class" that changed its "receptivity" and the "bourgeoisie"—which has somehow replaced the aristocracy—that lost its "tolerance." Ignatieff is more careful in identifying the reformers he has in mind as a group associated by politics and religion as well as by class, but he too writes as if the decision to resort to institutional solutions for social problems was made wholly by a small elite group of "Whig" reformers, with the rest of the nation merely reacting to their lead.

At no time during the Age of Reform did the bourgeoisie play a significant part in county prison administration, though its role began to grow toward the middle of the nineteenth century. It is true that some members of the traditional professions, particularly doctors and clergymen, and some gentlemen who had inherited mercantile wealth did participate in the administrative decisions of this period, but in Lancashire, at least, the traditional landed gentry remained firmly in control of county administration. It was they who raised the rates, ran the prisons, and presided over the courts.

Both the landed gentry and the bourgeoisie certainly exercised an important influence over the rate of prosecution. Each group could and did initiate prosecution. Gentlemen could prosecute in their own right and, acting as justices, could put pressure on constables to enforce the laws against alehouse keepers, prostitutes, and similar petty offenders. Masters could prosecute their workers, tradesmen could imprison debtors, and members of the trading classes could and did form societies to finance and encourage prosecutions.

There is no reason, however, to assume out of hand that the upper classes—however defined—were the only group to respond positively to the social changes of this period or to the accompanying growth of institutions. Many other groups participated in the expansion of the system of justice. Petty juries could veto the sentences of those charged with indictable crimes by finding them "not guilty" or by committing "pious perjury" if they felt the legal penalty was too severe, and they did not hesitate to use this power. The minimum property qualification to sit on such a jury was a £10 freehold or copyhold, a lifetime leasehold of £20, or the possession of £20 worth of property.

Furthermore, most crimes in England were prosecuted by the victim;

though government officers and gentlemen initiated some prosecutions, there was also a growing stream of complaints, informations, depositions, and prosecutions from workmen whose pockets were picked in public houses, women whose linen was stolen from clotheslines, husbandmen who had lost their poultry, wives beaten by their husbands, drinkers assaulted in alehouses, and quarreling neighbors, as well as from those who simply objected to nuisances or to immoral activities in their neighborhood.

For such people, the expansion of local institutions offering justice, and the growing concentration of population in areas near these institutions, presented a new opportunity as well as a new form of oppression. In the English system of justice, which depended on citizen participation for prosecution, the power to decide to prosecute was diffused throughout the population and was much less amenable to deliberate policy decisions than it was in Europe or the United States.

It seems likely that the enormous social and political changes under way by the end of the eighteenth century would have affected the willingness of the lower social groups as well as of the "ruling classes" to prosecute. Increases in the mobility of the population and the growing size of towns did not have to amount to actual urbanization before the delicate links binding village communities could be strained. The behavior of villagers was finely balanced between their desire to maintain "neighborliness" and the need to control the behavior of their more aggressive or obstreperous members; as towns became bigger and their citizens began to encounter more and more strangers, neighborliness ceased to exercise such a strong claim on their patience. At the same time, other traditional mediating institutions, such as the church, lost much of their power.

The destruction of these links also compelled Englishmen to turn to different, more formal and institutional modes of punishment. Methods intended to invoke community censure and eventual reconciliation, such as pillories, processions, and public confessions, began to lose meaning. There was little point in issuing a stern warning or binding a misdemeanant to keep the peace when the offender was a stranger who could easily melt away to commit further offenses elsewhere. The rich were not the only ones to be disturbed by the way that economic disruption and the growing market economy had undermined traditional communal controls over behavior; the poor, though they often committed offenses, were also far more vulnerable to the dangers and losses caused by a breakdown of order.

Even apparently simple reforms could acquire a momentum of their own and contribute to the rising numbers of inmates. Such reforms affected members of different groups in ways that were completely unintended, and often unanticipated, by their original proponents. For example, one important contributor to rising prison populations was the steady effort of the central government to compel counties to assist with a wide range of legal costs. Parliament passed a long series of acts to this end, beginning in 1752 and culminating in Peel's Criminal Justice Act of 1826. The first of these acts permitted courts to award compensation for expenses to poor prosecutors, and later poor witnesses, in a gradually increasing number of cases. Other acts repaid constables for conveyance and paid the clerk's fees of acquitted felons.[14] These acts were particularly important in counties such as Lancashire, where the high cost of conveyance and of travel to trials acted as a significant brake on prosecutions.

These acts extended the protection of the law more fully and fairly to the poor—particularly to the working poor, who under the old system were frequently unable to prosecute crimes committed against them because of the cost and the loss of time involved. Reimbursement for time and out-of-pocket expenses made it possible for the poor as well as the rich to use the process of law to redress personal injuries and, in that sense, made the law more egalitarian. These acts also helped correct the serious inequities experienced by poor people accused of crimes. Their estates were no longer subject to distraint for conveyance and, if found not guilty, they were less likely to be held in prison for legal fees.

Indivisible from the increasing equality of access to the law was the increased encouragement to prosecute. Indeed, these amount to the same thing. An increasing reliance on the courts, however, caused unprecedented and unanticipated changes in local administration. The new acts, which greatly benefited some poor people and liberated others, sent ever more offenders—a disproportionate number of whom were also poor—to gaol. The rapidly increasing populations of convicted offenders in local prisons eventually contributed to national intervention in prison administration, which altered the balance of relations between the prisons and the communities that surrounded them. That change, in turn, often disconcerted the local justices who had encouraged prosecution in the first place. Equally disconcerting to the justices was the fact that the rising demand for judicial services, which were often needed most in urban areas that had few suitable landed gentlemen, eventually compelled them to accept some changes in the social composition of the county bench.

Moreover, these acts imposed new and extremely heavy financial burdens on the counties, which now had to pay most of the cost of what had previously been private prosecutions. These costs rapidly became the single largest item in county budgets, and the counties demanded that the national government assume some of the burden. When it did, however, the inevitable result was a partial loss of local autonomy and the increasing integration of localities into a more uniform national network. Counties began to lose control over their own rates and expenditures, which again caused changes in the role of local government.

Finally, an inability to quantify the "actual" increase in the incidence of crime does not constitute proof that no increase occurred at all. Indeed, it seems reasonable to assume, with earlier historians, that the intense political, social, and economic turmoil of the years of war and Industrial Revolution did increase the incidence of "real" crime. There is also some merit in the eighteenth-century argument that more trade led to more opportunities for criminals. Finally, demographic change may have increased the number of youths "at risk." The balance of the evidence still suggests that eighteenth-century fears had some foundation in fact, even if the reaction was sometimes excessive: increasing prosecution accompanied rather than counterfeited an increased rate of crime.

However complex the causes, the result was unambiguous: a rising tide of prisoners. Their unprecedented numbers posed a formidable challenge to a society that had tried to maintain a tradition of relatively humane administration. In Lancashire the rise in prison populations was especially dramatic, and the social stresses particularly acute. Even if social anxiety lay behind both the increased committal rate and the demand for a more vigorous prison discipline, these two results to some extent canceled each other out. It was simply not possible for Lancashire's prisons to cope in any coherent way with the constant and constantly increasing flood of humanity. Moreover, the increasing reliance on imprisonment to punish petty offenses eventually led to extremely short average terms of confinement. These short terms made nonsense of the reformers' ambitious plans. The growth of large institutions contained within itself enough contradictory tendencies to frustrate most systematic attempts at change and to ensure that those changes that were made would have unexpected results.

# CHAPTER 3

# The Decision to Reform

## Changing Attitudes: Thomas Butterworth Bayley
*and the Salford Bench*

The surge of prison populations at the end of the eighteenth century and the growing misery of long-term prisoners as a result of rising prices would probably have evoked some response from the justices.* Two critical factors ensured that the solution chosen was the incarceration of substantial numbers of offenders in large institutions built on a plan that encouraged classification (or at the extreme, separation) of prisoners—institutions governed by a new sort of staff and guided by a new system of discipline. The first factor was the threat of gaol fever. The second was the appearance of a small but influential group of leaders among the county gentry dedicated to an active policy of reform: men like Sir George Paul in Gloucestershire, Samuel Whitbread in Bedfordshire, the Duke of Richmond in Sussex, and Thomas Butterworth Bayley in Lancashire. Bayley's character and convictions left an indelible stamp on Lancashire's prison system.

Bayley was born in 1744 of a respectable Nonconformist Manchester

---

*The mention of long-term prisoners may surprise some readers, since average prison terms were very short in the nineteenth century. In the late eighteenth century, however, gaols held two groups for longer terms than was common during the mid-eighteenth century: debtors, because there were no insolvency acts, and felons, because there was no transportation and there were fewer executions. These long-staying groups were especially vulnerable to worsening conditions. It is true that as the nineteenth century progressed, the *average* term became shorter because of the increasing percentage of petty offenders. This average, however, conceals changing proportions at both extremes, as imprisonment replaced both whippings and executions.

family. His father, Daniel, was a deputy lieutenant for the county. Both Daniel and his father-in-law, Thomas Butterworth, were trustees of the Cross Street Chapel in Manchester. Thomas also became a trustee, while another of his colleagues on the bench, Dorning Rasbotham, was the son of a trustee. As with Howard, it is difficult to gauge the extent of Bayley's religious conviction; the Webbs describe him as an occasional conformist, while one of his sons was to become an archdeacon of Stow and a canon of Westminster.[1] Like so many of England's legal reformers, Bayley was educated at Edinburgh. In accordance with his Presbyterian/ Unitarian upbringing, he seems to have been a rather radical young man; he corresponded with Wilkes and joined the Society of the Supporters of the Bill of Rights. In fact, he even offered to marry Wilkes's daughter. He was also a founding member of the Whig Club.[2]

Throughout his life, Bayley remained faithful to the Wilkite principles of his youth. John Brewer has recently written that the Wilkite views of the law rested on four main principles: first, that public officials should be accountable to the people for their actions; second, that justice should be impartial, providing equal access to the law for everyone, giving no special protection to those in high places, and preventing the abuse of the law for gain by corrupt officials (including prison officers); third, that every accused offender should receive due process without intervention by the Crown or by those in power; and finally, that all officials should govern by the consent of the governed, without relying on military sanctions.[3] Along with Beccaria, the Wilkites believed that the law must be clear and unambiguous, publicly known, and consistently applied in order to maintain both justice and deterrence. They also held strong views on the duties of the magistrate. They loathed "trading justices," and when they themselves obtained office, they tried to set a high—and highly public—example of good conduct. Brewer concludes that although Wilkites wished to improve the lot of the poor and expose abuses, they did not accept the "paternalism of the moral economy," since several of their leaders advocated a free market economy.[4]

Bayley's career exemplifies these preoccupations and ambivalences. A devoted reader of Adam Smith, he believed that the problem of hunger in the countryside could only be solved by improved methods of tillage, including the enclosure of common lands—not by the enactment of Corn Laws.[5] (His agricultural experiments, conducted on his own estate, Hope, led to his becoming an F.R.S.) He applied similar beliefs to the industrial world that was growing up around him, writing in 1802 that the weavers who were petitioning for regulation of their trade were "deluded by cunning Democrats to solicit what they cannot obtain, or which if obtained would materially injure themselves."[6] Yet his attitude was not completely unsympathetic; in 1798 he had urged Pitt to adopt a minimum wage bill "to keep quiet the lower Orders and conciliate their good Will."[7] He is said to have personally dispersed at least one riot. Moreover, he was one of the chief influences behind the 1802 bill to regulate children's work in factories.[8]

As a judge, Bayley adamantly refused to seek pardons for those whom he had convicted (since justice should be consistent and determinate), but he showed continuing concern for the welfare of convicts, frequently writing to the Home Office to protest conditions in the prisons and the Hulks. A strong opponent of trading justices, he was ready to resign over an obnoxious appointment to the Salford bench but remained in the hope of furthering plans for a police "which I have endeavoured to establish for 25 years of laborious service."[9] Like Howard, he bitterly opposed the fee system in prisons.

Bayley soon became a leading member of the Unitarian "establishment" in Manchester and also an important figure in its scientific community. He served as a trustee of the Warrington Academy. Together with Thomas Percival, his closest friend, he founded the Manchester Literary and Philosophical Society. With Percival and the Society's secretary, John Ferriar, he founded Manchester's Board of Health in 1796. Like many Manchester Nonconformists, he emphasized the importance of education. He was a founder of Manchester's unsuccessful College of Arts and Sciences, and encouraged the establishment of Sunday schools, "to counteract the causes of increasing vice and misery, by promoting the moral and religious instruction of the rising generation amongst the poor." Such activities reveal his consistent adherence to the principles of his youth.[10]

This Unitarian "Whig of the old school" succeeded not only in the liberal city but in the Tory county. He joined the Salford bench shortly after leaving Edinburgh and became perpetual chairman of the Quarter Sessions. During the war with France he joined the militia and became lieutenant-colonel-commander of the Manchester Volunteer Corps. He was one of Lord Liverpool's chief local advisers and recommended to him (as chancellor of the duchy) suitable candidates for the bench. He also became receiver-general of the duchy quitrents and served as high sheriff and constable of Lancaster Castle.[11]

Bayley was, therefore, peculiarly well placed. To local projects he could lend his power and prestige as a justice, at a time when very few of Manchester's ablest men could attain that office, while to his work on the bench he brought a Nonconformist zeal for good works combined with a knowledge (as a friend of Percival's and a member of the scientific community) of the latest developments in public health and social thought. He was an extremely active justice at a time when Salford, as a result of Lancashire's custom of banning manufacturers from the bench and of Lord Liverpool's distaste for Nonconformists, was chronically short of magistrates. Manchester, which was still governed by a court leet, had no Quarter Sessions of its own, so the Salford justices determined all the city's criminal cases.

It is difficult to measure the extent of Bayley's influence on the Salford bench. Dorning Rasbotham was clearly a strong ally, as was Samuel Clowes, who joined with Bayley to report on the Salford house of correction, but the attitude of the other justices remains obscure. Bayley, however, was undoubtedly the strongest force on the bench, and he probably framed most of its decisions. For whatever reasons, the Salford bench in these years displayed a distinctive style and showed a particular preoccupation with the maintenance of godliness and public order.

For example, when the Lord's Day Proclamation appeared in 1781, it was entered in the order books of the different sessions, with a list of signatory justices. Five justices signed in Lancaster, two in Preston, six in Ormskirk, and thirteen of the relatively small Manchester bench. When the proclamation "for preventing Vice, Profaneness and Immorality" appeared in 1787, the Salford Sessions, including Rasbotham, Bayley, and Clowes, was the only one to take special notice of the event, "being convinced of the propriety and Necessity of a strict Compliance with it." It was the Manchester justices who alone repeatedly emphasized the need for "humane confinement" in the prisons.[12]

These conflicting impulses shaped the new prisons: a traditional hatred of disorder and particularly of license; a new severity and rigor of enforcement, resting on the hope that the consistent application of the law would increase deterrence and reduce offenses; an emphasis on individual moral regeneration; and a concern for the welfare of the disadvantaged as well as a more fundamental concern with the protection of the public and the maintenance of order. The same impulse that imprisoned drunkards abolished the prison taps. The knowledge that the taps had been abolished increased the readiness to imprison. The increasing disarray of England's prisons and the anxiety to reform them were indivisible from an increasing anxiety to restore order to the outside world.

## County Institutions on the Eve of Reform

Lancashire had already begun to rebuild its penal institutions before Howard's visits and before the end of transportation to America. The Salford house of correction was presented by a grand jury and rebuilt between 1770 and 1775 at a cost of £1,671. Lancaster Castle had been presented in 1764 but apparently only for the purpose of carrying out repairs.[13]

Meanwhile, Parliament passed several important acts governing prisons. In 1759 it authorized justices to make rules for the governance of prisons, which would be hung up and displayed to the prisoners. In 1773 it ordered the justices to appoint chaplains for the gaols; although the Webbs maintain that this act was neglected, Lancaster complied with it, appointing a regular chaplain in 1774. In the same year (1774), Alexander Popham successfully sponsored two parliamentary bills. One of them ordered the release of acquitted prisoners in open court so that they could not be held for nonpayment of fees. The other, known as the Gaol Fever Bill, required regular cleaning, annual whitewashing, ventilation, the appointment of a regular doctor, and the provision of separate sickrooms.[14]

The Hulk Act of 1776 permitted the use of the Hulks for prisoners originally sentenced to transportation (or sentenced to death and pardoned on condition of transportation), while William Eden and William Blackstone attempted to find a more permanent solution to the problem by drawing up regulations for national penitentiaries to hold convicts. Their plan, passed as the Penitentiary Act in 1779, was greatly admired by Bayley, who lamented the government's dilatoriness in establishing "the most effectual Mode of Punishment, both to *prevent* Offences, and to *reform Criminals*."[15] Another act of the same year attempted to reduce the number of imprisoned debtors by forbidding imprisonment for debts less than £10.

Although Lancashire apparently complied with all these acts, they affected prison life only indirectly, by causing a slight reduction in the total number of inmates. Because the Castle was already relatively clean, for example, the main effect of the Gaol Fever Act was to cause the justices to set aside two rooms in the Dungeon Tower for the sick and to give a new title to the man who already served as apothecary to the prisoners.

Acts passed in the following years were to have a more profound effect. The first of these resulted from the efforts of Thomas Gilbert, who reverted to the seventeenth-century vision of the houses of correction as institutions for disciplining the idle poor. (This act passed in the same session as another with the same author. "Gilbert's Act" provided for the union of parishes to build workhouses and to improve the relief of the poor; its passage encouraged justices to intervene more actively in the parochial administration of poor relief.) Gilbert pointed out that few bridewell prisoners actually performed useful labor. His act of 1782 required the separation of bridewell prisoners by age and sex, the banning of alcohol, the provision of workrooms, and the enforcement of productive labor (up to twelve hours a day). Its embargoes on contact between the sexes and its requirement for classification according to crime to avoid the "contamination" of the less guilty meant that many houses of correction had to add extra rooms. Again, both Manchester and Preston had already anticipated some of these provisions; both already separated the sexes and encouraged their inmates to work. The act did finally compel Preston to raise its keeper's salary to £80 and to abandon its tap, something Manchester had done in 1777.[16]

The final, and most important, acts concerning prisons were passed in 1784. These established committees of justices to authorize expenditures. For the first time Parliament explicitly permitted the complete destruction, removal, and rebuilding of county gaols, and authorized justices to borrow for this purpose on the security of the county rates, a device developed by Paul in Gloucestershire. The acts prohibited the use of dungeons (i.e., below-ground cells) for imprisonment. They extended to the county gaols the provisions for classification followed in the houses of correction (under Gilbert's Act) and to the houses of correction the provisions for cleanliness previously applied to gaols. It was after passage of these acts that Lancaster, Preston, and Manchester gaols were all rebuilt.[17]

Though Lancashire complied with these acts relatively promptly, they really permitted change more than they caused it. Parliament passed such acts because the members, themselves country gentlemen, wanted the power to carry out reforms in their own counties. The justices of the more liberal counties waited for new laws that would entitle them to take action that cost the ratepayers money; they were not reluctantly forced into activity by a powerful Parliament. Less liberal counties could and did simply ignore these acts. That many justices wished to rebuild their gaols is shown by the large number of private acts passed to expedite the process. Prison acts to some extent governed the chronology of certain reforms, since the justices waited for their passage, but it was other, underlying changes that really forced reconstruction.

Manchester, with its reform-minded bench, perhaps provides the clearest example of this process. In 1777, only two years after they had finished rebuilding the house of correction, the Salford Sessions resolved to inquire into the condition and management of the prison.[18] Immediately after the passage of Gilbert's 1782 act, the Sessions nominated Clowes and Bayley to inspect the house in accordance with that act's provisions. Their report, which appeared in 1783, showed that even in new prisons traditional problems remained and that the rising population was already causing crowding, filth, and indiscipline. Their recommendations epitomized the goals of the eighteenth-century reform movement.

Clowes and Bayley had found the prison in the charge of the turnkey's wife. Although the prisoners had no complaints about the keeper, the rooms and the inmates were crowded, dirty, and offensive. Most of the prisoners were idle, others were spinning wicks for candles—"a very unprofitable sort of labour." There was no tap and no fees, and the surgeon visited regularly, but there was no chaplain, no religious instruction, and no allowance for food or clothing. Because of the rising population of "this trading County," the practice of confining felons for trial at the Sessions in Salford rather than at Lancaster, and the substitution of imprisonment for transportation, the prison was crowded "beyond what was possible to be conceived" when it opened in 1774.[19]

Clowes and Bayley recommended that the hundred buy additional land and erect a new courthouse, offices, chapel, workrooms, and a separate court to divide petty offenders from felons. "For want of *such Separation*," they pointed out, "most Gaols are wretched *Schools* of Wickedness, where many Persons, (especially of tender Years, as yet not hardened or profligate,) are *nominally* sent for Correction for trifling Crimes, but in *fact* are doomed to *Destruction*."

Second, they urged that the prisoners should be set to work. "It is reasonable," they wrote, "that Prisoners should labour for their own Subsistence; this will tend to preserve their Health and Chearfulness, and it is well known that constant and laborious Employment is most friendly to the Principles and Habits of Virtue." Moreover, they added in a note, "Hard Labour and Confinement are admirable Punishments also for many Sorts of Crimes, which are the offspring of *Idleness* and *Dissipation.*" The main object of work, therefore, was to make the prisoners into better men and women; earnings were a secondary consideration. Nevertheless, like so many others, the two justices believed that prisoners, if industrious, could earn enough to offset nearly the whole expense of the prison. Even in Lancashire, this hope was to prove overly optimistic.

Finally, Clowes and Bayley urged that the whole prison be swept and washed regularly and that the windows of every room be opened daily. Two rooms were to be set aside for an infirmary. Each room was to have clean towels twice a week and every prisoner a clean shirt once a week. Iron bedsteads were to be provided, along with straw and blankets, in order that each prisoner might sleep in a separate bed in the night rooms—except the felons and the refractory, who were to be confined in cells but change partners nightly. All prisoners were to wash their hands and face every day before receiving their food. The inspectors established a fixed diet and ordered that irons, which they considered to be unnecessary because of the strength of the building, be removed from all prisoners. They also recommended that any new night rooms be small enough to allow prisoners to sleep alone and suggested a corridor plan. All of these regulations closely accorded with Howard's proposals in the preface to the *State of the Prisons.*

The report suggests that the reason for rebuilding was a large increase in population. The form recommended for the new building, however, was determined by a combination of moral and sanitary considerations. The prisoners were to be separated by sex and crime for moral reasons, but the cellular plan, the separation by night (particularly the rule that prisoners could not share beds), and the goal of having one prisoner in each night cell all seem to have been prompted by a desire to avoid physical as much as moral contamination. Similarly, they promoted work, first, because it improved health, second, because it was ethically desirable, and finally, because it saved money—in that order. Acts of Parliament seem to have been only an auxiliary reason for making changes that were desirable on other grounds.

In Bayley's eyes, Preston's problems were even more pressing than those of Manchester, because Preston, unlike Manchester, still maintained the traditional fee system and prison tap. In 1781 he suggested to a Preston justice that the persistence of these practices had created a corrupt and brutal regime. He said that he had recently examined a Preston prisoner named Ellen Gregson about a felony committed by William Collier. In the course of her examination, Gregson alleged that Edward Cowburne, the keeper, had loaded her with heavy clogs and irons, which had caused dangerous wounds in her legs, that he often locked her in a dungeon and beat her, that he made the prisoners work for him at low wages, that he took one ounce of every pound of flour brought into the prison, that he supplied prisoners with necessities at high prices, that he punished complainants by striking them with a clog, and that he had extorted 7s. 6d. as a fee from departing prisoners.[20]

As proof of these charges, Bayley included a letter found on William Collier in which he asked his wife to send him 7s. 6d. for his discharge fee, along with a "dasent pare of Brichas to put on and Somthing to ty A Bout my Neack and a Hat to put on for you No that I have none to Cover my Hed." "It appears to me shocking," commented Bayley, "that 7s. should be demanded from a *naked* Man. . . . Mr. Howard has some noble Observations on this Subject of extorting Fees from poor Prisoners: I doubt not you have his excellent Book."

Bayley felt obliged to offer a little advice to the Preston justices:

> I will just hint to you, That the Justices here very frequently visit and examine our House of Correction without the Gaoler; That he has a fixed Salary of £60 per annum, and is not allowed on any Pretence to take Fees . . . nor to sell Ale, Beer—or any other Thing to the Prisoners. He is a Chandler and employs many of them in Spinning *Wick*, but We take care That He gives the usual Prices for it. Since We discontinued the Tap in the Prison—The Change in the Regularity of it is amazingly great, And I would rather double our Governors Salary, Than suffer him again to sell Liquors in it.

This is a rather different picture of the Manchester prison from the one Bayley was to provide two years later; the latter leaves the reader with the impression that the prison had been neglected by the justices and that many of the prisoners were left idle.

When the Preston justices examined Cowburne, he denied all the charges. His deposition reveals a half-reformed institution, run in a benevolent way but lacking Manchester's rectitude. He stated that Gregson arrived at Preston with sores on her legs, attributed variously by the doctors attending her (whom he paid) to venereal disease and scrofula. He denied locking her in the dungeon but admitted that he had put her in a "dark box" (probably one of the sleeping cells seen by Howard) to punish her after she had disrupted the prison by declaring that "whilst there was a man in the House she would have him." She had broken down part of the prison to get to Collier, costing the county £16 in repairs, and had torn the prison blankets and bedding. Her "Allurements and Enticements" had forced him to discharge a turnkey.[21]

Cowburne absolutely denied the charges relating to provisions, a denial confirmed by the woman who fetched goods for the prisoners. He admitted that he employed some of the prisoners but said that Gregson had worked for other prisoners, reeling worsted. Twice he had given her 9s. 3d. when she was sick and he had given 5s. 11d. to Collier, from a bequest augmented from his own pocket. He also provided poor prisoners with meat from his own table "to prevent them from absolutely being starved." He conceded that he charged fees and kept a tap but pointed out that both were perfectly legal and that Manchester was the only prison in the country without a tap. He denied holding any prisoner for failure to pay fees. To support his contentions, he called a servant and the surgeon, who had unsuccessfully treated Gregson for scrofula and was paid two guineas by Cowburne.

Cowburne's testimony shows that Preston was by no means a model prison. The walls could be broken down. Turnkeys slept with prisoners. Prisoners hired one another. Sick prisoners depended on the charity of the keeper to avoid starvation. If Cowburne did not actually detain prisoners for his fees, he probably gave them the impression that he would. To men like Bayley, such a regime seemed corrupt and licentious. Nevertheless, if this testimony is to be believed, Preston was run in accordance with old-fashioned standards of management and with a certain benevolence. Prisoners chose their employers and their work; they were paid directly in money and could send a servant down to purchase whatever they wished with their earnings. Prisoners were by now receiving blankets and bedding. Charitable funds were distributed to the sick, who also received prompt medical attendance. The prison was still very small, but the justices kept an eye on its affairs. By midcentury standards, Preston was quite acceptable, and gaolers were sometimes slow to adjust to the expectations of reformers. Nor was the Preston bench filled with reformers. Despite Bayley's urgings, they failed to abolish the tap or to take further action. Lancaster also made no major changes until after the great epidemic of 1783.

## The Decision to Rebuild

Clowes and Bayley submitted their report on Salford in May of 1783. In July a special adjournment of the Manchester Sessions approved the report but postponed consideration until the next sessions. It also approved the recommendation made by a grand jury at the Assizes that a special adjournment of the Preston Sessions be held to consider the state of the Castle and of the houses of correction.

That summer, gaol fever struck Lancashire. Already endemic in Liverpool, it had spread to Manchester and Preston. A prisoner from Manchester brought it to Lancaster Castle, where it killed several people, including the gaoler. At Michaelmas, fear of fever drove the justices out of Preston to Chorley. There a bench that included Bayley, Rasbotham, and Clowes from Salford resolved that Preston also needed a new house of correction and that Lancaster needed a house for the gaoler, rooms for debtors, and separate rooms and courts for the male and female felons.

At Epiphany, with fever still raging, the Lancaster Sessions proposed a spring meeting of the Sheriff's Board to discuss the problem. The Manchester Sessions, considering that the houses of correction were "crowded with very great numbers of unhappy Wretches, many of whom are dangerously Sick of a putrid fever," concurred, adding in its own didactic style that the prisons should provide "Humane confinement, wise correction and exemplary Punishment and that they may be constructed so as to prevent the dreadful public Calamities which may be occasioned by the Increase of the said distemper among the poor Prisoners and from them spreading itself [*sic*] abroad."

Preston was presented in the summer of 1785. In the fall, the Lancaster Sessions appointed a committee to report on improvements to the Castle. Howard's friend William Blackburn provided the initial plans. The Michaelmas Sessions of 1786 chose Thomas Harrison of Chester, a distinguished local architect, to produce the final design. In the winter of 1785 Manchester again resolved to rebuild its own house of correction in order to add workrooms and allow prisoners to be classified and housed in separate cells, as well as to gain enough space for a total of 100 prisoners. Blackburn (who died at Preston in 1790) was again the architect. Construction began at Manchester in 1787 and at Preston in 1788. Liverpool borough also rebuilt its gaol, on a radial plan of Blackburn's, and its house of correction in 1786.[22]

The timing of the decision to rebuild suggests that neither Howard nor parliamentary legislation played a decisive role. Lancaster and Manchester had already taken some steps toward reform before Howard's first visit, although these measures later proved inadequate. The initial moves in the second and much more important wave of reform in the 1780's, at both Manchester and Lancaster, again antedated the important legislation of 1782 and 1784. In 1784, in fact, the county was eagerly awaiting new legislation.

Though certain local leaders constantly agitated for reform, the immediate precipitant of the decision to rebuild the gaols was the fear of fever. The rising prison population, which helped breed fever, would probably have compelled rebuilding eventually, but the close correlation between the arrival of the epidemic and the universal decision to go ahead with massive reconstruction suggests that the threat of fever won the more cautious justices over to the recommendations of the activists. Without that threat, the justices might have been less willing to give men such as Bayley a free hand to rebuild entirely instead of making a few judicious alterations. The content of the reforms—the design of the buildings, the supervision of officers, the rules, dietary, and so on—was determined by the reformers, because no one else had much interest in the subject. But had it not been for crowding and disease, they might have agitated indefinitely. Bayley himself wrote in 1785 that "many of the Judges, and the greater part of the Magistrates—have had no *other* Object in view—than to prevent the Contagion of the *Gaol* Fever; Fear, and the selfish ideas of personal Safety carry them so far; the other great Points of Policy and Humanity in the plan of the Penitentiary House, Solitary Imprisonment etc. have been treated as chimerical—and expensive *Experiments*."[23] This argument gains further strength from the fact that the Hulks, which were almost certainly far worse than the unreformed gaols and which had been intended only as a temporary expedient, survived eighty years of continuous and bitter criticism from men such as Howard himself. The final decision to abandon them was attributed by at least one contemporary observer to the cholera epidemic of 1849.[24]

Historians have failed to appreciate the role of typhus for two reasons.* First, they have always assumed, following the Webbs, that epidemics of gaol fever were so common in the eighteenth century as to be unremarkable. Thus they neglected to realize the significance of the epidemic of the 1780's. Though gaol fever may have been endemic, however, it seems unlikely that epidemics were frequent. Even in London such events were not taken lightly. Moreover, the renewed emphasis that

---

*Robin Evans and Michael Ignatieff are exceptions. Evans lists two major causes for prison rebuilding, the American war and gaol fever. He discusses the analogy between fear of contagion from fever and fear of contagion from vice and points out that prisons were rebuilt in courtyards on airy sites to prevent fever.

physicians such as Percival placed, in the 1780's, on the efficacy of environmental "public health" measures led to a new willingness to turn to rebuilding and increased separation as a cure.

Second, because of their reliance on national sources such as debates on bills, historians have failed to stress the fact that Howard's visits came at the beginning, not the end, of a period of accelerating crisis. The smooth progress of parliamentary legislation should not conceal this fact. Writers frequently suggest that after Howard's visits, the cessation of transportation in 1775, and the publication of *State of the Prisons* in 1777, new ideas gathered momentum and conditions grew steadily better. In fact, however, in the 1780's many prisoners were still dependent on fixed money allowances, which were being severely eroded by rising prices. Not only untransported felons but also many more misdemeanants and offenders judged under summary process crammed the gaols.

To make these points is not to take a materialistic view of reform. Gaol fever frightened the justices, but they would not have chosen rebuilding as a remedy unless doctors had begun to suggest that this was the best preventative. If the reformers were beginning to speak of an equation between physical contagion and moral contamination, it was the physicians who supplied them with the idea of separation as a preventative for disease.

## The Challenge of Gaol Fever

Bayley's background enabled him to act as a bridge between the conservative bench and a more radical group of Manchester thinkers who were interested in a new approach to social problems. It was this group that set the agenda for the coming age of social reform in the north of England. Most of them were physicians, and the reappearance of epidemic typhus gave them the leverage they needed to press for a comprehensive program of reform. In turn, this program depended on changes in the traditional models of disease transmission. These changes were to have a profound effect on all of Lancashire's social institutions, including its prisons, which were for the first time explicitly designed to prevent both physical and moral contagion.

These doctors formed part of a closely knit circle of friends who were linked by political and religious sympathies as well as by a general interest in scientific progress and social reform. In general they were Nonconformists (usually Unitarians who called themselves Presbyterians) who had received their education in provincial dissenting academies before proceeding to Edinburgh. With little prospect of advancement in London, many chose to remain in the provinces, where they established a network of provincial scientific societies. Among those who remained in the north were Dr. John Heysham of Carlisle, developer of the "Carlisle Life Table" and author of a book on typhus; Dr. John Heygarth of Chester and later Bath, a close adviser of Howard's and the inventor of fever hospitals; Dr. John Aikin, son of the head of the Warrington Academy and biographer of Howard; and Drs. Matthew Dobson and James Currie of Liverpool.[25]

The Manchester members, who were all closely associated with Bayley in the founding of the Literary and Philosophical Society and other city institutions, included Thomas Percival, John Ferriar, and Charles White, a prominent local obstetrician, son-in-law of a local justice and sheriff. They shared a strong interest in public health stemming from personal experience, a belief that public health problems were closely linked to other social problems, and the hope that they could develop statistical methods that could guide a rational policy to control and reduce the incidence of disease. They were closely connected to French reformers such as d'Alembert, Voltaire, Lavoisier, Diderot, and Pinel and to the Americans Thomas Jefferson, Benjamin Franklin, and Benjamin Rush, as well as to Joseph Priestley, who had taught at the Warrington Academy. Howard himself stayed at Warrington while publishing *State of the Prisons* at the press of William Eyres and formed close friendships with the circle around the Academy.[26]

To understand the role these men played in the creation of Lancashire's social institutions, one must first understand the development of disease theory in the eighteenth century. As the century opened, two equally plausible and apparently incompatible models of disease transmission held sway: contagionism and anticontagionism, or miasmatism. In practice, nearly all physicians adopted a compromise, but the different formulations of that compromise resulted in bitter divisions within the medical community. They also proved critical in determining the direction taken by reformers late in the century.

Though contagionism had a long history, it could not account for some of the most puzzling features of the epidemic diseases. It could not explain why they *were* epidemic—that is, why their incidence varied so dramatically from year to year and also from season to season. Moreover, observation proved clearly that many who had frequent and direct contact with sufferers nevertheless escaped infection themselves. For this reason, medical writers from Hippocrates on had recourse to atmospheric explanations, based on the "epidemic constitution" of the atmosphere, that is, on the specific combination of temperature, moisture, season, elevation, and local peculiarities.[27]

In the mid-eighteenth century attention began to shift from the temperature or moisture of the air to the role of filth as a cause of air pollution and, therefore, of disease. According to this theory, decay or putrefaction, generated in organic materials such as excrement or marshy bogs or even produced as a result of ordinary breathing, released poisonous particles into the air. When these reached a certain concentration disease resulted. The revival of miasmatism, or the "filth theory of disease," in the early nineteenth century by men like Chadwick fueled the first national public health movement.

Contagionists, on the other hand, believed that though filth contributed to the spread of disease, epidemic diseases could not arise spontaneously out of conditions in the environment. Rather, these diseases were brought into a community by infected persons or goods and could spread only by direct contact with others. This contact did not have to be by touch; clothing or air, particularly polluted air, could carry particles of disease emitted by a sick person, but only across a few feet at most. Thus, isolation of the victim, particularly in a well-ventilated room, and efforts by the attendants to avoid contact and to cleanse themselves of any lingering particles on their bodies or clothing could prevent the spread of disease.

Contagionism and miasmatism stood at opposite ends of a spectrum that permitted many shades of opinion in between, but the extent to which doctors emphasized one or the other had a crucial effect on their choice of preventive measures. If the natural conclusion of miasmatists was that health rested on the control of sources of atmospheric pollution, such as open sewers, the natural conclusion of contagionists was that the first line of defense against epidemics must be quarantine. Both groups believed in cleanliness, but the contagionist cleansed from the inside out—first the person, then the room, then the street—while the miasmatist cleansed from the outside in—first public spaces, then private.[28]

The emphasis that contagionists placed on direct contact also led them to stress the discrete nature of epidemic diseases and thus to classify the wide array of symptoms seen by the physician into syndromes characteristic of specific diseases. They relied on an analogy with smallpox: inoculation could exactly reproduce one case of smallpox in a second subject.

The first bundle of symptoms exactly resembled the next. Miasmatists, on the other hand, believing that diffused atmospheric conditions caused disease, were less interested in sorting symptoms into groups of specific diseases. A particular state of the atmosphere affected everyone and caused symptoms that should appear in all victims. Many miasmatists believed that though there were different diseases, in any particular season sufferers from all diseases would exhibit certain common tendencies. Thus, when conditions favored digestive diseases, victims of both influenza and scarlet fever would exhibit symptoms of digestive disease.[29]

By the early eighteenth century these two "scientific" views of disease had prevailed over the earlier models, which had been based on divine intervention, astrology, or the humors. Over the next two centuries the emphasis kept swinging between the two views, while each was progressively refined. The first landmark was the publication of Richard Mead's *A Short Discourse Concerning Pestilential Contagion and the Methods to Be Used to Prevent It* in 1720. Mead was largely concerned with the plague, which had appeared in France and was menacing England, but his remarks applied to all contagious fevers. He admitted the theory of humors enough to argue that a body in which they were not properly balanced was more susceptible to infection. He therefore recommended a healthy life, free of depression or passion, a good diet, and "cooling" or "acid" foods such as citrus fruit and vinegar, to "keep the blood from inflaming."

The main part of this short book, however, was devoted to the assertion that contagion was actually spread by three agents: air, diseased persons, and goods transported from infected places. To control the first, Mead recommended greater cleanliness, including street cleaning. He suggested that houses be strewn with "cooling herbs" and washed with water and vinegar: "As *Nastiness* is a great Source of *Infection*, so *Cleanliness* is the greatest Preservative."[30] To control the other two agents he suggested that goods and persons entering the country from abroad be quarantined and that the attendants of the sick be careful not to inhale near them.

Mead specifically mentioned prisons in his book, pointing out that gaol fever was "always attended with a Degree of Malignity in proportion to the *Closeness* and *Stench* of the Place: and it would certainly very well become the Wisdom of the Government, as well with Regard to the health of the *Town*, as in Compassion to the *Prisoners* to take Care, that all Houses of Confinement should be kept as Airy and Clean, as is consistent with the Use, to which they are designed."[31]

Mead carefully evaluated the relative usefulness of contagionist and miasmatic models. He concluded that "a corrupted state of Air is without doubt necessary to give these Contagious Atoms their full Force," but "it is evident that *Infection* is not received from the Air itself, however predisposed, without the Concurrence of something emitted from Infected persons."[32] Mead, therefore, accepted the contagionists' emphasis on the specificity of epidemic diseases but also the miasmatists' argument that disease could be transmitted over a distance by corrupted air. It should be remembered that Mead was writing about plague, which, since it is carried by rats, has an incidence that cannot be explained by direct physical contact between victims.

The generation of physicians who flourished at mid-century was able to make important contributions to public health based on Mead's compromise. Nevertheless, their interpretations of his work often seriously circumscribed their efforts. Doctors never entirely lost sight of the need for cleanliness—which, if pursued single-mindedly, could have helped reduce the incidence of disease—but, presented with a multicausal theory of disease, they tried to achieve prevention by concentrating on the most easily controlled causes. Though they accepted elements of both explanations, they thus tended to lean toward miasmatism. For example, Sir John Pringle, president of the Royal Society and the leading expert on prison medicine of his time, developed an elaborate causal theory dependent on the climate, the air, and the humors. It led him to recommend, among other things, that fever patients be scattered in many small hospitals with those ill of other diseases or injuries, instead of being isolated in a single place.[33]

The best example of the drawbacks of this approach is the famous outbreak of gaol fever at Newgate in 1750, when the terrified authorities brought in the best available consultants, Pringle and Stephen Hales, a specialist in disease in the navy. Discovering that Newgate was very dirty and unbearably offensive, the two concluded that the solution lay in an enormous ventilator (Hales's own invention) that could expel the noxious miasma. The prison was first cleaned by the sheriff and some assistants, but there is no evidence that they washed any of the prisoners.[34] Belief in the efficacy of the ventilator may have led the authorities to overlook more traditional remedies, such as whitewashing and the burning of clothing and bedding. When the epidemic appeared at Bedford, the justices there also erected a large ventilator.[35] Miasmatism, as it was practiced in the middle of the eighteenth century, therefore, encouraged a reliance on palliatives that removed or masked unpleasant odors without destroying the causes of disease.

By the late eighteenth century, medical thinkers had developed a third approach to disease. This view, which has been called sensualism or Hartleian materialism, rested on Locke's contention that all knowledge depended on sense impressions. Because the physician also attained knowledge through his direct experience of his patients, the first state of sensualism encouraged empiricism: a reliance on clinical experience rather than on medical theory, on symptoms rather than on causes, and on the symptomatic classification of disease. It thus assisted the development of both statistical and clinical medicine.[36]

The second stage of materialism, however, had a more complex effect, because it stressed the divorce between the outside world and the sensate individual, dependent on his sense impressions and his physical integrity for all his information. Where traditional philosophy had assumed a split between a faulty body and an eternal immaterial spirit, materialists emphasized the unity of body and spirit and hence the close identification between psychic and somatic health. Because the spirit was part of the brain and the brain was merely a physical organ, a part of the body, anything that disrupted the body might affect the brain and its perceptions, and an injury to the brain could cause a disorder of the intellect or even of the conscience. It followed that moral failures, such as crime, and mental failures, such as madness, might result from physical diseases. Healing the body might cure the spirit. Medicine, therefore, might be considered a "moral science." Conversely, if the sense impressions of the victim mediated all knowledge of disease, perhaps what seemed to be objective diseases were merely the products of a disordered nervous system.[37]

Michael Ignatieff has recently suggested that the rise of materialism led doctors to espouse the curative value of institutional care for the poor and, thus, encouraged the development of large social institutions. He argues that the identification between body and mind fostered by "Hartleian materialism" led Lancashire physicians such as Thomas Percival to emphasize the role of mental problems, such as depression and remorse, in causing illness. Disproportionate illness among the poor, therefore, could signify moral failures such as lack of discipline. This theory could easily lead medical thinkers to use "the language of social and moral condemnation veiled as the language of medicine."[38] In this way, the use of "Hartleian categories provided 'scientific' legitimacy . . . for medical condemnation of the indiscipline of the poor" and "led doctors to be confident that once the bodies of the poor were subjected to regulation, their minds would acquire a taste for order." For this reason, medical reformers such as Percival "insisted that institutional confinement was the sole way to change the poor. The sick could not be cured in their homes; they had to be given moral therapy in the hygienic asceticism of an institutional quarantine."[39] Early prison reformers like Hanway merely borrowed this conceptual framework in arguing that crime was also a disease.

Unfortunately for this argument, the Lancashire physicians who were especially fertile in creating medical institutions, such as Percival and Ferriar, were contagionists who explicitly rejected materialism.[40] They did, however, accept the materialists' view of the importance of direct clinical experience and also their interest in, although not their explanation for, the connection between psychic and somatic disorders. They founded insane asylums, wrote extensively on insanity, hypochondria, and hysteria, and maintained close connections with lunacy reformers such as Rush and Pinel.

In general, although they, unlike the materialists, held that diseases were objective entities that came from outside the sufferer and were transmitted by contact, the Lancashire doctors also believed that the resistance any individual could offer to invasion by a disease was affected by his or her general physical and mental health. Thus, Howard explained the susceptibility of robust young convicts to gaol fever by the sudden shock to their spirits caused by their being ironed and thrust into close, offensive dungeons. Ferriar argued that the general debility among the poor caused by inadequate diet and night work rendered them especially vulnerable to epidemics. Both the physical and the mental debilitation of the poor increased their liability to disease.[41]

Though this approach sometimes led physicians into class-based moral strictures, it also left them in a rather ambivalent position with regard to society as a whole. It suggested that the first line of defense against disease might be quarantine but that prevention of widespread debility would involve fundamental changes in society. It also suggested that the sudden resurgence of fever might be the result of social failure. This line of thought helps to explain the generally radical political views held by this generation of physicians and their uneasy attitude toward the rise of the factory. Bayley, Percival, and Ferriar were leading advocates of factory reform, and several medical reformers were widely suspected of Jacobinism.[42]

These reformers were by no means unhesitating proponents of institutional confinement for the poor. In general, they preferred to treat the poor at home. The new dispensaries that appeared in this period were specifically designed to enable the poor to receive medical aid without being admitted to hospitals, and some institutions, such as the Manchester Infirmary, also experimented with "home patient" schemes. White, his protégé Aikin, and Percival all wrote extensively on hospital management. They warned doctors to ensure that hospitals did not spread disease instead of curing it and to take great care to avoid admitting unsuitable cases. Percival, for example, urged that hospitals keep complete records of their patients so that doctors could compare the outcome of institutional cases with those they saw at home in order to avoid admitting patients who would have a lower risk at home. "The discretionary power of the physician or surgeon, in the admission of patients," he wrote, "could not be exerted with more justice or humanity than in refusing to consign to lingering suffering, and almost certain death, a numerous class of patients, inadvertently recommended as objects of these charitable institutions."[43]

Their disease theory led these doctors to believe that all large buildings in which many people were gathered—particularly those whose inmates were debilitated—posed a serious threat to public health, whether these buildings were hospitals, factories, or lodging houses. Percival warned that "no precautions relative to the reception of patients, who labour under maladies incapable of relief, contagious in their nature, or liable to be aggravated by confinement in an impure atmosphere, can obviate the evils, arising from *close wards* and the false economy of crowding a number of persons into the least possible space."[44]

Because disease resulted from contact or close proximity and not merely from poisoned air, however, contagionist physicians believed it was possible to design buildings that could reduce or eliminate the dangers of cross-infection and institutional epidemics. Moreover, they believed that the use of such structures to quarantine the sick could prevent epidemic fevers from spreading among the population at large. This goal, however, could be achieved only with close attention to the institutions' design and administration.

Like prisons, hospitals face a dilemma: how to ensure close supervision of patients and, simultaneously, provide patients with privacy and separation? The two are at odds: if patients are placed in single rooms, nurses cannot observe all of them constantly. Moreover, single rooms are more difficult to keep clean and demand more space, requiring nurses to walk long distances. They are also more difficult to ventilate effectively.

The theory of disease transmission that any particular writer espoused helped determine his choice of plan. Miasmatists urged that all fever hospitals be removed to the country, where the air was purer and there was less danger that the miasma emanating from the hospital would infect surrounding communities. If people spread contagion, their ingress and egress could be controlled, but if contagion was spread in the air, no one could prevent it from escaping. Moreover, in the country, buildings could be scattered over a site, thus providing free ventilation and avoiding the dangerous buildup of poisons in the air. If this plan was not followed, patients could not be grouped together by disease because the increased concentration of poison in the air would increase the severity and contagiousness of their disease. Miasmatists such as Florence Nightingale campaigned for long wards that could be constantly supervised by a single nurse, that could be thoroughly and easily cleansed, and, most important, that could be thoroughly and constantly ventilated.[45]

The contagionists, on the other hand, argued that patients should be separated from each other as far as possible, preferably in small single rooms but if necessary in rooms holding only two or three patients. As with the prisons, this plan proved impossible to implement. The contagionists next urged that all patients suffering from similar ailments be grouped together in separate areas or institutions. They also encouraged hygienic controls on traffic in and out of the hospital; the hospital, they felt, should be quarantined from the surrounding community. The poor were discouraged from visiting sick friends, patients' clothing and possessions were to be purified on entry, and nurses were to take precautionary measures on entering and leaving. Measures designed to prevent people from transmitting disease by direct contract were more important than the removal of the hospital to an isolated site; indeed, these reformers preferred urban sites as both more accessible and less threatening to the poor.[46]

There was a strong resemblance between these new hospitals and the new prisons. Percival, in fact, when asked about the design of a new county hospital and later the new House of Recovery, recommended the plan of the New Bailey.[47] This resemblance was not due merely to an unconscious or metaphoric association between moral and physical contagion but also to the fact that in the late eighteenth century the need to control physical contagion was paramount in both institutions. With a partial remedy at hand, the threat of disease, and particularly of typhus, was increasing rapidly.

Typhus, or gaol fever, is caused by a microorganism called *Rickettsia prowazeki*, which is carried by body lice. It is traditionally known as a hardship disease, because to take hold it requires a combination of dirt (to support the lice) and malnutrition or stress (to lower resistance). Since lice do not fly and since they die rapidly once infected with typhus, they cannot carry the disease very far; close contact, therefore, is necessary to spread the disease and overcrowding is necessary to support a large epidemic. A certain degree of dirt and privation in the population at large provides the reservoir of lice and endemic disease that enable epidemics to break out in crowded institutions. Small gaols could foster endemic or occasional cases of typhus, but it seems unlikely that most of them could have experienced frequent epidemics in the relatively uncrowded conditions of the early eighteenth century. The most notorious cases in early modern England were the "black Assizes," when the disease spread in packed courtrooms; similarly, the great Newgate epidemic of 1750 followed overcrowding resulting from postwar demobilization.[48]

At the end of the century, at about the time of Howard's visits, there was a resurgence of the disease. Howard himself found some record of gaol fever within the past decade or so at about 20 of the 105 prisons he visited. Liverpool borough gaol suffered in 1775, and in the same year some sort of illness affected the Castle. The epidemic of 1783 hit Lancaster, Liverpool, Manchester, and many other local prisons along with towns throughout England. It was followed by further epidemics in the succeeding decades.[49]

These prison epidemics had two main causes. The first was a growing incidence of typhus among the population at large. This was the natural result of all the changes associated with urbanization: a rising population, domestic crowding, and filth. The war may also have helped generate these outbreaks; armies and navies, like gaols and hospitals, were always particularly susceptible to typhus, and soldiers and sailors had enough contact with the general population to spread it. Though it is probably true that prisoners infected others with typhus, it is also true that new prisoners had carried it into the gaols from infected towns.

Gaolers and justices perennially claimed—along with generals, captains, and corporations—that the disease had not originated in their prisons but had been brought from somewhere else. Their protestations held some truth, for conditions in some of the northern towns were far worse than they were in the houses of correction. Even Carlisle, which was, comparatively speaking, a model of cleanliness, suffered from an epidemic in 1781. Liverpool suffered from an estimated 3,000 cases of typhus annually in the years between 1787 and 1796.[50] Endemic and epidemic typhus was also common in Manchester. Engels, writing in 1844, stated that it had never been wholly stamped out in Manchester's worst slums. Between 1846 and 1848 there were still more than a million cases of typhus and typhoid in England as a whole.[51]

The second reason for the rising incidence of typhus was that the gaols themselves were becoming more crowded, especially with felons who— because they often came from the poorer parts of the population, because they were the worst-treated class in the prisons, and because they tended to spend longer periods in confinement—were especially susceptible to disease. Under such conditions, no matter how clean the gaol was usually kept, typhus often broke out. Even today, it is difficult to control lice when large numbers of people live together in a single area, although we know how typhus is transmitted and have more effective disinfectants. Not even conscientious cleaning could have eradicated the disease. Dirty conditions among the felons probably promoted the Lancaster Castle epidemic of 1783, but we know that John Higgin, who succeeded his father in that year, was always extremely anxious to keep the prison clean. Everyone who visited it (except Henry Hunt) commented on its cleanliness. Yet Higgin himself wrote that it was impossible to prevent disease when the prison was crowded. Nor was he the only gaoler who noted the connection between typhus and overcrowding. The Home Office papers from 1783 to 1786 are full of urgent pleas from local authorities for the removal of the growing number of long-stay transportees because their presence increased the chances of disease.[52]

The rise of typhus in the late eighteenth century contributed to the rise of contagionism, and contagionist theory led doctors to understand that typhus was a specific disease and thus to identify the group of symptoms that characterized it. Because of its emphasis on discrete diseases, contagionism encouraged the effort to sort different "fevers" into distinct diseases. In turn, the prevalence of typhus led to the adoption of contagionist models, because the model of disease transmission suggested by contagionism applies well to the way typhus actually spreads; although it is an insect-vector disease it can only spread in close proximity. The incidence of other insect-borne diseases, such as plague and yellow fever, and of such water-borne diseases as cholera is much harder to explain by direct personal contact between victims. Thus other disease models prevailed in America, where yellow fever was the greatest threat, and in nineteenth-century England, which was obsessed with the fear of cholera.

Typhus was a frightening, dramatic, and dangerous disease, and the new understanding of its transmission and spread was likely to cause both fear and guilt among local administrators. As doctors accumulated evidence, they were able to show that the disease flourished in conditions of overcrowding and squalor, often in places such as army barracks, ships, hospitals, gaols, factories, and the new urban slums. The revival of typhus in these areas suggested that certain social failures were responsible for the miserable conditions that bred it. Though comprehensive social reform was desirable to eliminate the underlying cause, however, contagionist theory suggested that the first and most immediate line of defense against typhus was the establishment of institutional quarantine in buildings that not only isolated sufferers from the outside world but also circumscribed their contact with each other.

The fear of fever prodded men into action, and the new insights of medical theory determined the direction of that action. Justices felt that the existing state of affairs directly threatened their own well-being and that of the general public. They believed that they could avert the danger by constructing new prisons. Having accepted this reasoning, they saw many additional advantages to better-located buildings laid out in small rooms rather than open wards. The prisoners themselves could now be protected (it was hoped) from epidemics of gaol fever by the rigorous imposition of cleanliness and by the construction of their own lazarettos in the form of separate infirmaries. Moreover, the use of plans like those recommended for the new hospitals would bring greater security and reformation as well as better control of disease. If the majority of justices were interested only in preserving their personal safety, the few reformers such as Bayley who played an active role in planning and administering the gaols were prepared to take a longer view and to ensure that the new buildings were designed to promote moral and spiritual as well as physical integrity. The new prisons owed their existence to overcrowding and disease, but they owed their design and their discipline to a small group of dedicated reformers who were determined to exploit this opportunity to fashion a new model of correction.

It was the growing fear of typhus that was the decisive factor in determining the timing of new prison construction. It was the Gloucester epidemic that enabled Sir George Onesiphorus Paul to persuade his reluctant fellow-justices to construct a new gaol at enormous expense. The chronology of the rebuilding in Lancashire shows a similar conjunction of a great man and a great fear.

# CHAPTER 4

# The New Discipline

## The Establishment of Fixed Rules

Lancaster Castle was the first prison in the county to have fixed rules; a committee consisting of Bayley, Rasbotham, and four other justices drew up a suggested code for the criminal prisoners in 1785. Rules were drawn up for Preston in 1792 and for Salford in 1794, after the new buildings had opened. A second set of rules, applicable only to Crown prisoners, was established for Lancaster in 1795 and approved by the Assize judge.[1]

It was natural that as the prisons grew bigger and more complex, administration would have to become more formal, but as Michael Ignatieff has pointed out, the establishment of written rules was also a deliberate measure intended to increase the rationality and accountability of the system. Prisoners would know what was expected of them and where they stood. They would know how they must behave and also how the gaoler ought to behave toward them. Prisoners would be accountable to the gaoler for their behavior and the gaoler would be accountable to the justices for his. The mere existence of this rational environment was supposed to aid in the reform of the deviant.[2] English reformers, from the Levellers to the Wilkites and Benthamites, had urged the creation of a fixed, rational, comprehensible, and written code of law, believing that good laws in themselves might help make good men. It is perhaps ironic that their dreams came to fruition only in the world of the prison—a world that in other ways represented the antithesis of that society of consenting, independent, and free citizens that so many of them had envisioned—and that these very rules helped strip prisoners of the last vestiges of self-government by mutual consent.

Although they controlled the behavior of both the prisoners and the gaoler, the written codes had a more radical effect on the prisoners than on their keepers. Gaolers had already been subject to a long list of regulations in common and statute law; the new rules simply added the further requirements of recent legislation. Although measures were taken to make gaolers more accountable for their adherence to the new rules, such as the appointment of visitors and the requirement that books be kept, no new sanctions were added. If a gaoler persistently misbehaved or broke the rules, the justices could in most cases do nothing but attempt to have the sheriff dismiss him. The only criminal sanctions were those provided by much older laws.

For the prisoners, however, these rules marked a distinct change. Although Puritans had attempted to enforce a "reformation of manners" in certain city prisons at the beginning of the seventeenth century, these efforts had had little permanent effect. In every area except escape, laws concerning gaol prisoners had been permissive rather than restrictive; they had established rights such as free access but said nothing about prisoners' behavior. Bridewell prisoners seem to have been similarly unrestricted in practice, although in law they were supposed to work. With the establishment of fixed rules, however, came a specific set of punishments for their infringement, to be enforced either by the gaoler himself or, if the breach was serious, by the justices. The mere establishment of written rules, therefore, marked a transition from an informal justice administered in many cases by the prisoners themselves to a formal justice administered by the gaoler and magistrates.

What the gaolers lost in autonomy, they gained in authority and responsibility. This development may have been unpopular with lazy gaolers who wished to be left in peace to neglect their charges, but reform-minded gaolers welcomed their increasing power to interfere in the daily lives of their prisoners. The difference such a code could make is clear in Lancaster Castle, where, because of problems in obtaining the approval of the Assize judges, the debtors were still without rules in 1812, although rules had governed the Crown prisoners since 1795. Even allowing for the greater license always permitted to debtors, the difference this disparity created in their respective positions was enormous. John Higgin had little power to prevent drunkenness, theft, quarreling, or even violence among the debtors. Unless they appealed to the usual processes of law (e.g., having an assailant bound over to keep the peace), all that he could do was persuade the justices to withdraw the offenders' allowances. The formal rules cost the prisoners a good deal of freedom, particularly at Manchester, where the zealous magistrates expected repentance and reform, not merely the good behavior accepted at Preston and Lancaster. On the other hand, the prisoners did gain a measure of protection both from each other and from the exactions of mercenary gaolers. This same process is apparent in many other areas of reform.

## Accountability

The reformers were extremely anxious to increase the accountability of the entire prison staff. This was to be achieved in three ways. First, the gaoler's income was to come from the justices rather than the prisoners. His financial interest in the conduct of the prison was consistently and steadily reduced. This movement began very early: the prevention of extortion was one of the first objects of prison law. Prohibitions on the sale of office, for example, were enacted in 1421 and 1623 as well as 1718. An act of 1729 had required that a table of fees be fixed and publicly displayed and had set up a machinery for hearing complaints of extortion. Beginning with the abolition of prison taps so strongly urged by Bayley, a series of steps substituted a fixed salary for a variety of fees; the final act came in 1815.[3] Some gaolers supported this change; at Lancaster John Higgin took the initiative in persuading the justices to replace his fees with a salary.[4]

More important in controlling corruption was the use of paid professional subordinate officers in jobs traditionally held by prisoners. The new turnkeys were strictly forbidden to accept any payment from prisoners, although in many gaols, including Lancaster, they could still accept gratuities for showing visitors around. At the beginning of the nineteenth century, Lancaster turnkeys still collected money from prisoners to purchase goods in the town and to convey mailed parcels from the station to the prison, but Higgin eventually put a stop to this service, although he still allowed them to traffic in bread. By 1812 it was a very serious thing to accuse a turnkey of accepting bribes or gratuities.[5]

A second way of gaining oversight over prison staff was the requirement that they keep a full set of written records, open to inspection by the local magistrates. This meant a journal for both the chaplain and the surgeon. The gaoler, aside from his own journal, was expected to keep separate registers recording admissions and releases, punishments, financial transactions, and prisoners' daily conduct. Apparently, this rule was frequently neglected; in 1812 none of the Castle officers kept a journal although financial accounts, a punishment book, and a register of prisoners did exist.[6] Following the strong recommendation of the commission of 1812, compliance became more regular. Such record keeping, as the commission pointed out, not only made officers more accountable but also offered them some protection against malicious accusations by prisoners.

Finally, there was the increased supervision of the justices. Visiting justices were first authorized by an act of 1785. Lancashire lost no time in appointing them, but they varied in their zeal. Bayley, inevitably, seems to have been very active, not only in visiting Salford and later the New Bailey but also as a member of the building and finance committee for Lancaster. James Fenton, the recorder of Lancaster, whom Howard praised for his humanity, was probably another conscientious appointee. After the deaths of the reformers, however, and the ebbing of the initial excitement, the justices became more lax.

Boards of visitors, often including all the justices in the division, continued to be regularly appointed, but they did not take a very active interest in the good government of the prisons. Justices were quite ready to attend when the gaoler asked them to strengthen his discipline by ordering additional punishment or by binding disputants over to keep the peace. Their main effect, therefore, was to increase control over the behavior of the prisoners, not to correct excesses by the gaoler. Any improvement in the gaolers' conduct, therefore, probably came from greater care in making the original appointment, or a different moral climate, rather than extensive on-the-job supervision.

## Chapel

Lancaster Castle had no professional clergyman until one was required by an act of 1773. Having appointed the chaplain and agreed to pay £36 toward his salary of £50, the local justices naturally wished to see his services utilized, but chapel services were not popular with the prisoners. In 1777 John Dane complained to the Sessions that some prisoners were avoiding chapel or misbehaving during services. The justices immediately ruled that all Anglican prisoners were to attend services and to behave themselves or lose their allowance. Dane could simply give the county treasurer a list of miscreants and their names would be removed from his list of recipients.[7]

This is another example of the way in which a "reform" undoubtedly beneficial in intention became a means of greater control over prisoners. Originally, the intention was to provide a service, but the justices, having paid for the service and being increasingly worried about the spiritual welfare of their charges, decided to compel them to use it.

Furthermore, the actual decision was made on the initiative of the gaoler, not the justices. John Dane, who later hanged himself and whose administration was deplored by the Higgins, hardly qualifies as a reformer, but even he, in one way, was seeking greater order in the gaol. Instead of seeing the period as one in which zealous and high-minded justices gradually imposed their vision on callous, brutal, and ignorant gaolers, one might equally well see the position as reversed, with gaolers asking largely uninterested magistrates for greater power to regulate their charges.

Several of these themes reappear in a petition John Higgin sent to the Preston bench in the summer of 1785. Higgin complained that since the abolition of the prison tap prisoners were sending for liquor from the town at unreasonable hours. He added that persons from the town were causing inconvenience by attending the Sunday services at the Castle and requested the direction of the court for his future conduct. The court resolved that he had "a right and ought in the faithful discharge of his Duty to Exercise his Authority Discretionary in all matters that may tend to the good and better Regulation of the said gaol and prevent Intemperance." It also affirmed his right to ban visitors from chapel.[8]

Again, in this case, it was the gaoler who initiated the action by asking for advice from the bench. (In 1786, when the rules had been established, the committee had recorded that Higgin approved of the regulations, being "above all things desirous to have as little as possible left to his Will or discretion in the management of his prisoners.")[9] The decision of the bench, however, was to confirm his own regulatory powers. Instead of being a mere security officer, paid to keep inmates from escaping, the gaoler was becoming an active pastor—a governor rather than a keeper. Moreover, the net result of the decision was to restrict the access of outsiders to the prison, whether they were publicans, whose hours were to be limited, or would-be chapelgoers.

A subsequent entry in Higgin's journal, made more than thirty years after his original request, sheds some light on his motives for seeking to exclude outsiders from the chapel. On April 18, 1817, a Mr. Ripley of Lancaster presented himself at the Castle gate, armed with a letter of admission from R. Atkinson, Jr., a local justice. The previous week, Thomas Higgin had refused to let him in. Atkinson, John Higgin wrote angrily, "I would gladly suppose, must have been imposed upon otherwise he would not have thought his Interference necessary. —If he had given himself time to Reflect, I presume he would not have given an order for the admission of a Drunkard, who is become Bankrupt . . . to gratify his Curiosity in gazing at the unhappy Men under sentence of Death."[10]

Higgin combined a moral disapproval of Ripley with a humanitarian distaste for the idea that condemned men should be regarded as interesting exhibits. Such voyeurism was a popular eighteenth-century recreation. Higgin, whom his chaplain believed to have "feelings of humanity too great for the situation he holds" because he found public executions so distressing, was clearly revolted by this custom.[11]

After so many years of autocratic power, however, and because he disliked the justice in question, Higgin also bitterly resented such interference with his authority. In his journal, which the justices were supposed to read, he wrote:

This is not the first time of the improper interference of this young Magistrate. . . . After 35 years Service in a very arduous and responsible situation I ought to be able to judge as to the propriety of admitting persons into the prison. The manner in which this Note was sent bespeaks the Hostility and Enmity of this Gentleman. . . . However willing I may be to accompany Mr. Atkinson Junior, or any other Magistrate, through the Gaol, yet I must say, that it is not decorous to grant orders of this Nature which can only be done to annoy me in the Execution of my Duty.

By this time, instead of pleading for greater regulation of the prison by the justices, being "desirous to have as little as possible left to his Will," Higgin had come to feel that they were interfering with his authority to run the gaol along reforming lines. This evolution is partly due to the changes of time; Higgin himself was growing older and more crotchety, while the justices with whom he had cooperated were dying and being replaced by lesser men. It was also, however, part of a real transition in the role of the gaoler.

## Prison Clothing

Originally, there were two humanitarian reasons for providing prisoners with clothing. First, many prisoners either arrived in rags or were soon reduced to raggedness. Not only was this state uncomfortable and unhealthy, but it made it more difficult for the prisoner to find work after his release. Second, dirty clothing was well known to cause infection. Filthy clothes harbored parasites, encouraging typhus and skin ailments. Reformers soon realized that a complete change of clothes had other advantages, including increased security. If the county provided clothing it was almost inevitable that buying in bulk would result in a uniform, which also guaranteed fair distribution and made it possible to clean and return clothing without complicated sorting. Uniforms, in turn, made criminals easily recognizable at a time when fetters, the traditional means of distinguishing them, were falling into disuse. Recognizable clothing at least complicated escapes. Bentham, always ingenious, went so far as to suggest that prison uniforms be made with one sleeve long and one short; prisoners would then acquire a distinctive tan that would brand them even without their clothes.

An additional advantage of a prison uniform was the humiliation it imposed on the wearer. Fetters had also served this purpose; their abandonment perhaps made reformers more conscious of this effect. The adoption of uniforms addressed the "lesser eligibility" problem confronting reformers; as they increased the physical comforts of prisons they had to find compensatory psychological discomforts in order to discourage criminals. Uniforms did both at once; they were cleaner, better, and more comfortable than the prisoners' own clothing and yet were still humiliating to wear.

Exactly the same process went on inside the prison: different classes of prisoner were distinguished from each other by different clothing or badges, making it easier for prison officers to tell at once where they belonged and painting the felon with a deeper dye (at least in official eyes) than the misdemeanant. Uniforms were, therefore, part of the process of institutionalization, which marked prisoners as members of a community apart. They were also part of the process of classification, which sought to segregate different groups of prisoners from each other to protect women, the young, and the relatively innocent from "hardened felons." (The ultimate conclusion of this process was solitary confinement.)

This argument can be carried too far, however. Most magistrates, more concerned with bricks and mortar than with "chimerical" ideas about transforming prisoners' minds, were not particularly anxious to introduce uniforms, provided that other measures could be taken to safeguard health. The Lancaster rules called for cheap and useful uniforms, "so contrived as to prevent escapes," the Preston rules included the provision of white flannel clothes suitable for the season, and the Manchester rules, as usual the most ideological, mentioned a uniform and, for the worst felons, shaven heads and "Certain Marks or Badges of Disgrace . . . as well to humiliate the Wearer, as facilitate Discovery in case of Escape." Nevertheless, we have no evidence that any of these prisons actually adopted uniforms at the time. Lancaster was still without uniforms 26 years later, when John Higgin explained to the commission of 1812 that the justices had balked at the expense. Instead, the clothes of incoming prisoners were baked in an oven, thus satisfying the concern for health if not for moral suasion.[12]

Again, Higgin himself seems to have been the chief supporter of the proposed reform, arguing that the cost of providing clothing for the most ragged was taking a large proportion of the Charity Fund. In 1816 his son was finally able to report that he had clothed fourteen condemned men for the first time in the new uniform of blue and yellow. In 1820 Gurney wrote that the Castle prisoners were manufacturing all their own clothing.[13] Preston, meanwhile, seems to have bought clothing piecemeal for such prisoners as needed it.

On the whole, although the eventual introduction of prison clothing contributed greatly to the health and comfort of the poorer prisoners, it to some extent restricted their freedom and certainly branded them as members of an outcast tribe. In this area as in many others, what seemed initially to be a humanitarian measure and a real benefit to many extremely ragged prisoners was to prove a mixed blessing.

## Prison Labor

Prisoners in the houses of correction had always been expected to work. Stuart legislation had required the counties to provide the necessary implements. Eighteenth-century writers frequently complained that the bridewells had completely failed to comply with this requirement, but it seems likely that Lancashire had a relatively good record in this respect. Occasional inventories and bills mention such implements as cards and looms, while other sources suggest that prisoners usually depended on the proceeds of their labor. Many prisoners in Lancaster Castle also worked for their keep, although the gaolers were occasionally hostile to the practice and the prisoners had to find their own materials and tools.

During this period two changes took place in the nature of prison labor. First, it became more strictly regulated. Originally, prisoners were paid directly in money for what they did, on a piecework basis. Though the master of the house of correction was supposed to "set the prisoners to work," the real constraint, in the bridewells as in the gaol, was economic. Just as in the world outside, in prison one could work or starve. Prisoners with means apparently were not otherwise compelled to work in either institution, nor, apparently, were the hours, sort, or amount of work specified.

The many improvements in the prisons essentially achieved a more democratic provision of goods in kind rather than money. The state undertook to guarantee a minimum supply of food, staff income, accommodation, heat, cleaning, and (eventually) clothing. In order to repay itself for these benefits in at least a symbolic manner, the state confiscated the profits from prisoners' labor, leaving them only a very small percentage of the wages they had earned, and controlling the use of even that remnant.

Since the prisoners no longer received a full reward for their labor, and since their necessities would be supplied whether or not they actually applied themselves to their tasks, the authorities had to substitute indirect compulsion, that is, statutory punishment, for the earlier direct economic compulsion. At the same time, the county, rather than the prisoners, became the judge of what they should do, what they should produce, how long they should work, and what they should consume. The keeper, from being one employer among several, became the person authorized to punish prisoners if they refused to work for the county, and the gaoler, for the first time, enforced labor in return for prison allowances. This development in some ways paralleled the development of the factory system outside, where the need for machines to work constantly, the difficulty in controlling quality, and the impossibility of estimating each person's production on a piecework basis led employers to regulate the hours their employees worked, to punish lapses or misbehavior, and to establish regulations for conduct.

The second change was the transformation of prison labor from a primarily reformative activity to a more punitive one. The increasing benefits of imprisonment had created, in the minds of reformers at least, a problem of "lesser eligibility," of making the prisons disagreeable enough to deter crime. Among those now confined in the bridewells were convicted felons, who deserved severer treatment than petty offenders, but prisoners could not simply be made to work more than people outside. Many laborers already worked to the limits of their strength and beyond, while legislators would not force inmates to work to the point of damaging their health. Moreover, hours had to suit the capacities of the weakest, not the strongest. The act of 1782, therefore, established a maximum of twelve hours' labor, of which two hours were allowed for meals, bringing the total down to ten. The need to allow the prisoners air and exercise, as well as security considerations, brought the average down even further, since the prisoners were most safely locked up, unlocked, and counted by daylight. The winter workday was only about eight hours in all, with time out for meals, exercise, and other routines. In fact, the net result of the new regulations was, probably, that many prisoners worked less than they had when left alone to earn their own keep.

For petty offenders such a regime might be acceptable, but legislators felt it was inadequate for the increasing number of felons. For this reason the Hulk Act of 1776 ordered that convicts be set to hard labor, presumably something more arduous than common prison work. There was a fundamental conflict between the attempt to provide particularly odious labor for felons and the desire to encourage reformation. By making work itself a punishment, hard labor was unlikely to establish a positive attitude among inmates. In fact, however, prisons found it difficult to provide unpleasant labor. Tasks such as stone breaking posed obvious security problems, although some gaols did introduce stone sawing. The workhouse occupation of oakum picking was sometimes used, and Lancaster Castle punished rule breakers by setting them to wind bobbins for the weavers, but these were hardly the laborious, physically demanding occupations Parliament had in mind. Sexual bias relegated the most arduous job, the laundry, to women. Eventually, therefore, either the prisoners sentenced to hard labor ended up doing the same work as everyone else, which was the most profitable arrangement, or the justices and gaolers exercised their ingenuity in developing completely useless tasks merely to "torment" the prisoners. (The word is Bentham's; he bitterly opposed the practice.)

Cubitt's treadmill, introduced in the 1820's, was the logical result of this process, but "shot-drill" also proved popular. The latter required men to carry heavy balls of shot from one pile to another and back again. Such Sisyphean labors had certainly not been envisaged by the more progressive reformers; Bayley had urged, with Howard, that the primary purpose of prison labor was to make prisoners better men and to preserve their health and "cheerfulness." Punitive labor was, however, the inevitable concomitant of improving prison conditions to the point that administrators feared imprisonment was becoming attractive.

Although many reformers of this period saw the imposition of labor as the sine qua non of their schemes, it was rarely carried off with success. This failure stemmed partly from the reformers' own fatal ambivalence about whether prisons were reformative or deterrent, but still more from their inability to create institutions that could be penal while providing labor with substantial rewards. In the end, labor was split into two parts. One part was purely punitive. Though it may have done something to keep inmates healthy, hard labor produced little of value and made no pretense of redeeming the mind. The other part became something close to occupational therapy. Only in rare cases were prisoners productive. The new rules made it difficult to avoid work entirely, but since the prisoners had little real incentive, it took a herculean effort to persuade them to work very hard. Despite all the reformers' hopes, few inmates can have found prison labor either satisfying or reformative.

### Drink

Throughout most of the eighteenth century, Lancashire prisoners, whether debtors or felons, bridewell or Castle inmates, received their allowances and earnings in money and purchased their own food and drink (with the exception of spirits, which were prohibited by an act of 1750). For such prisoners, a prison shop and tap was an obvious convenience, provided it did not become an instrument of extortion. Legally guaranteed access to similar goods in the town provided an automatic control over the price and quality of the goods offered. John Higgin mentioned that he had made a large profit from the Lancaster tap, selling good wine at a reasonable price.[14]

Zealous magistrates would have liked to abolish all alehouses and prison taps. Not only did the latter offer opportunities for extortion and bad conduct by the gaoler but they also led to tippling, drunkenness, and rowdiness. Aldermen in seventeenth-century London attempted to ban strong beer and ale, and in 1729 a parliamentary committee reminded members of the numerous inconveniences of prison taps.[15]

Beer, however, if not vital to life, was at least important to it. Poor felons could be left to drink water from the Castle well. Debtors, however, were legally entitled to beer and considered having to drink water instead a severe hardship. Many houses of correction did not have an adequate supply of drinking water; Howard wrote that at Preston the prisoners had no water all all. Beer, therefore, along with internal taps, remained a feature of all three Lancashire institutions for most of the century.

The attack on drink in the 1770's and early 1780's was at least expedited by the fact that the improvements of buildings and the measures necessary to improve health greatly increased the amount of water regularly available and used in the prisons. The new buildings included pumps, cisterns, baths, and sewers. Obedience to the provisions of the Gaol Fever Act required a fairly large and regular supply of water for filling baths and washing the rooms. The towns themselves were slowly improving their water supplies, though they lagged far behind the needs of their growing populations.

Although much of the prison water came either from wells or rainwater, it was still a health hazard, as the frequent epidemics of bowel disease show. By forcing prisoners to abandon beer for water, the reformers may have unintentionally done something to counteract the other benefits of greater cleanliness. One advantage of using old castles for gaols was their deep and separate wells.

Thomas Butterworth Bayley's energetic campaign to abolish taps made Manchester one of the first dry prisons in the country. The Salford justices saw all alehouses as breeding grounds of crime and disorder, but it was easier to impose their distaste on institutions they controlled. Their hostility also implied a hardening attitude toward criminals: while providing for the prisoners' necessities, they also demanded greater discipline and the abolition of all unnecessary comfort or cheer. The justices, being virtuous, certainly thought that prisoners should have no more cakes and ale. For this reason, they did not merely forbid the keeper to sell alcohol, they forbade prisoners to have it at all unless ordered by a surgeon. At Lancaster, where the bench was less zealous but still reformist and influenced by Bayley, the prison tap remained until abolished by law in 1783. Although the 1786 rules allowed all prisoners to bring in three pints of ale a day, this was forbidden to criminals by the 1795 rules. At Preston, where Bayley had little influence, the justices also permitted Cowburne to keep his tap until 1783. Moreover, the Preston rules of 1792 specifically permitted prisoners to have both milk and small beer occasionally, presumably at county expense since no one was allowed to bring it in or sell it.[16]

Although Higgin had persuaded the justices in 1785 to allow him to limit the purchasing times of liquor for the debtors, no one ever succeeded in controlling their alcoholic consumption. Poor debtors would order their permitted ration of three pints of beer and then sell it to the wealthy. Stronger liquor was regularly smuggled in. The records of the early nineteenth century are full of the resulting drunken brawls, which make it easy to understand why the authorities were so anxious to control drinking.

Aside from a simple dislike of drinking and drunkenness, reformers abolished taps because they wanted to end the gaoler's dependence on the prisoners for his income, with its tendency to encourage extortion and improper favoritism. The reformers were concerned not merely to improve the lot of the poor prisoners but also to increase the severity meted out to the better-off. The abolition of the gaoler's chief source of income, moreover, and its replacement by a salary controlled by the justices increased (at least in theory) their ability to make the gaoler answerable to them. Howard made many of these points in *The State of the Prisons*; the Manchester bench merely echoed him when they explained in 1777 that "it is Highly requisite that no Gaoler or other Servant be suffered to hold the Tap. . . . Gaolers who hold or let the Tap, find their Account in not only Conniving at but promoting Drunkenness, besides the Gaolers Interest in the Sale of Liquors, may prompt him to be partial in his behavior to his prisoners, and to treat at least with neglect those who are poor and have nothing to Spend."[17]

The abolition of the tap and other measures drove such transactions underground but did not by any means eliminate them. It removed one important source of favoritism, corruption, and violence, but there were many others. All three houses of correction suffered from abuses that were ignored or disregarded by the justices. Without continuous and energetic action by the prison governors it was impossible to control corruption and bribery among the turnkeys, and without continuous superintendence by the justices many governors continued to make corrupt profits and to play favorites among the prisoners. Though the abolition of the prison taps was a definite step forward in the battle against corruption, it was by no means the end of the war.

## Diet

In the 1770's both debtors and felons at Lancaster received a shilling a week, most of which they spent on food, while bridewell prisoners pur-

TABLE 7

*Approximate Weekly Dietaries of Lancashire Prisons from Rules*

| Lancaster Castle (1786) | Salford (1794) |
|---|---|
| Felons: | 10½ lbs. bread |
| 10½ lbs. bread | 4 lbs. potatoes |
| 7*d*. worth of cheese, butter, | 1 lb. beef |
| peas, potatoes, turnips, etc. | 3¼ oz. salt |
| ½ lb. beef | 1 pt. peas |
| 1 qt. broth | 12 oz. oatmeal |
| 4 oz. salt (1812) | 3 oz. cheese |
| (Approximate cost, 2*s*. 7*d*.) | 1½ oz. rice |
| Debtors: | |
| 1*s*. worth of bread | |
| 10 lbs. potatoes | |
| | |
| *Preston (1792)* | |
| 10½ lbs. bread | |
| 10½*d*. worth of | |
| peas, potatoes, etc. | |
| ½ lb. beef | |
| 1 qt. broth | |

chased food with their earnings. As inflation ate into the value of the fixed county allowances, reformers urged that food be provided in kind, both to guarantee prisoners a minimum level of support and to prevent them from spending an undue proportion of their county money on drink or other nonessentials. Manchester, however, was the only prison that decided to specify the entire diet in weight rather than value; both Preston and Lancaster established a weight for bread but set a money value for accompanying vegetables and dairy food. Debtors received ten pounds of potatoes each week along with a shilling's worth of bread.

The establishment of fixed dietaries, like all the other reforms we have examined, had the double purpose of providing a reliable minimum level of maintenance, which was desperately needed by the poorer prisoners, and at the same time of making imprisonment more severe by reducing freedom of choice, imposing a bland diet, and outlawing small luxuries. For the prisoners who, lacking friends, family, money, or work, had occasionally been in danger of starvation in years of dearth and high prices, the new dietary offered a real advantage. This advantage was achieved, however, at a severe cost for everyone else, since the fixed diets were inadequate (see Table 7).[18]

There are two standards against which this diet can be judged. By a modern standard, it was seriously deficient in calories and many nutrients, although the Lancashire habit of substituting potatoes for bread or gruel explains why scurvy was a less serious problem there than in the south. To judge it by the standard of the times, two questions must be answered. How did the prisoner's diet compare with that of some comparable person outside? And, given a certain per capita allowance of money, was its content a reasonable choice? It is hazardous to make any firm statements about the diet of the free poor, but Drummond and Wilbraham have collected some useful evidence. Among other things, they estimated the cost of some of the budgets from Frederic Eden's *State of the Poor*. For example, a laborer, his wife, and three children living in Kendal in Westmoreland spent, according to their estimates, about £20 2s. out of a total income of just under £30. Counting the three children as two adults, this represents an annual per capita expenditure of £5, or about 2s. per week. In 1786 the cost of a similar diet at Lancaster was 2s. 7d.[19]

Prison diets can also be compared to those of other large institutions, such as the army and navy. The military diets, like those of the prisons, made little allowance for fresh fruit or vegetables (except potatoes), but they provided much more protein and were more expensive, although still inadequate calorically. The army allowed a pound of bread and a pound of meat per soldier per day. The navy spent 9s. 2¼d. per sailor per week in 1811. Even by contemporary standards, therefore, prison diets were at a low level, although probably somewhat better than those of the worst-paid urban workers or country dwellers in years of dearth.*

Most important, however, is the question of what sorts of change these dietaries imposed on prison standards. The mere drawing up of the dietaries did not result in their enforcement. It took a long time to establish these dietaries as the unalterable and single sources of food. The evidence from this period shows that given the choice, prisoners spent the same allowances on a greater variety of food and strongly resisted the imposition of the high-starch diet.

---

*Sir Noel Curtis-Bennet, *The Food of the People* (London, 1946), pp. 179-80. See also J. C. Drummond and Anne Wilbraham, *The Englishman's Food: Five Centuries of English Diet* (London, 1958), appendix, p. 563, which includes a rough estimate of the nutritional value of this and other dietaries. The Poor Law Commission, however, published diets purporting to show that the independent agricultural laborer was the worst fed and the convicted or transported thief the best off. See W. E. Passey, "Houses of Correction in England and Wales" (M.A. thesis, University of Liverpool, 1936), appendix 1, pp. 116-17.

In the beginning, although food was now provided in kind, it was easily converted back into cash. Prisoners received their entire daily allotment every morning. They could then sell or barter unwanted items (especially bread) to local traders, who came up to the Castle with food, for items they preferred. By 1812 there was a common kitchen for the felons, but it does not seem to have been much used, and the debtors always did their own cooking at the fireplace in their rooms. At some point before 1812, John Higgin stopped the direct trade between criminals and townspeople because "some remarks had been made in Lancaster, that the prisoners in the Castle had more bread than they could eat." He therefore ordered that the criminals were to sell their bread only to the debtors, through the medium of the turnkeys (since the criminals and debtors were not allowed to communicate); but the criminals were still free to spend money they gained in this way on other food. A little later Higgin forbade the women to buy coffee and tea because they were injuring their health by selling too much bread in exchange for these "innutritious" beverages.

When the commission of 1812 asked Higgin why he did not prohibit the sale of bread rather than the purchase of tea, he explained that the women substituted cheaper oatmeal and potato cakes for their bread and used the extra money to buy "milk, vegetables, and other nutritive food . . . and I considered the cakes . . . as wholesome as bread, and therefore not improper to be substituted . . . if the women liked it better."[20] This is evidence that when left to themselves, prisoners sometimes chose a more nutritious diet than that offered at the same cost by a fixed dietary. Even the despised coffee and tea were not wholly useless beverages since they were safer than water and were usually taken with sugar and milk, supplying badly needed protein and calories. The commission, however, unmoved by Higgin's arguments, urged that the sale of bread be prohibited.

Four years later, the twin problems of increasing population and the resulting disorder led Thomas Higgin, then acting as his father's deputy, to impose further controls on food. This action aroused the hostility of the prisoners and led to a bitter confrontation. The porridge war began on August 30, 1816, when Thomas recorded in his journal that "owing to the very crowded state of the Gaol, the prisoners have some difficulty in cooking their victuals. I observe that this is a source of frequent quarrelling amongst them—and this added to the difficulty of their paying Rooms Money—are the causes of almost endless dispute and inconvenience—so much so—that I think of putting the prisoners upon a dietary system—this will certainly deprive them of many little comforts, but upon the whole will I trust be productive of much good."[21]

On November 25 Thomas began making porridge in the kitchen boilers. That night the prisoners in the first yard sent a message to all the others, telling them to reject the porridge and refuse to go to work in the morning. Higgin also made a tactical error: fearing that it would take too long to cook the porridge in the morning, he ordered it to be made in the evening and reheated the next day. "Altho the Porridge was excellent last Evening," he wrote, "yet I find it impoverished by standing all night and not so well flavoured." Understandably, prisoners in two yards rejected their gruel in the morning and refused to work. Higgin took their food away, locked them in their cells, and told them they would have nothing else. He commented angrily that "it is lamentable to see such insolence within the walls of a prison, when thousands of the industrious and labouring poor, cannot get bread." There were further disturbances that afternoon and the next day, providing Thomas with "proof of the Spirit of insurrection . . . that prevails in the Gaol." At one point he and his father were attacked by a group of prisoners, forcing him to draw his pistol, but he eventually prevailed, putting the ringleaders in solitary and rewarding the well-behaved with a quart of soup paid for from the Charity Fund.

Although Thomas's imperious temperament, so different from that of his father, doubtless exacerbated the situation, it is easy to understand why the prisoners resisted a change that deprived them of "many little comforts." Not only had they to some extent lost the privilege of preparing their own food, but the porridge itself was unappetizing and unsalable. The change, therefore, meant a reduction in both the variety and the quality of their diet. Though nineteenth-century gaolers continued to substitute gruel or potatoes in times of dearth, bread remained a staple of the prison diet. In the middle of the century, prisoners still "trafficked" in bread despite the gaoler's best efforts to prevent the practice. By now, however, criminals could not obtain food from outside and bartered or sold their rations to their fellows, at some cost to their health.

The gradual introduction of fixed dietaries lessened the prisoners' freedom of choice and, while saving a few from hunger or starvation, caused malnutrition for many. Here again it was the gaoler, not the justices, who made many of the decisions about when and to what extent a reform would be introduced.

\*

Many writers have maintained that the new prison discipline resulted from the disruption of transportation during the war with America, which caused an intellectual revolution by forcing reformers to develop a "punitive" rather than a merely custodial institution in order to deal with all the convicted felons who had previously been shipped out. Though this argument does contain an element of truth, it is still a serious overstatement. First, the increasing number of felons who could not be transported represented only a part of the changing size and composition of the prison population. Far from being central to the new prisons, the most serious class of "transportees" was treated in the local prisons as an embarrassing appendage.

Second, this argument is too narrow because it looks only at England. The problem of maintaining offenders at home had existed for a long time on the Continent, where transportation was uncommon, though not unknown. Most educated Englishmen must have known something about penal policies in Europe, particularly in Holland, France, and Germany. Even the Hulks were by no means an English innovation; French convicts had for many years done "galley service" in stationary old ships, working at the same sort of dredging and dockwork ashore that the English were later to introduce. Moreover, many continental countries (including Russia) were at this time reconsidering the uses of imprisonment and prison discipline, as the campaign by Beccaria and others forced them to develop alternatives to the death penalty. The United States also developed a new and highly experimental prison discipline during this period. The disruption of transportation was a uniquely British problem, but the changes that followed it appeared, for one reason or another, in many other countries as well.

What seems to have underlain these changes in both population and regime throughout Europe was an increasingly severe and "legalistic" or formal attitude toward offenses, which combined with a rising population and economic hardship to increase both formal prosecutions and total convictions. Meanwhile, a growing respect for the value of human life inspired measures to reduce prisoner mortality, both directly (by reducing the number of executions) and indirectly (by reducing hardship and disease). People were valued more highly and judged by a higher standard. Both this new severity and this new benevolence affected not only the total numbers of prisoners (more were going in and fewer leaving) but also the quality of the discipline imposed on the small world within the walls. Population growth alone would have necessitated many of the changes—such as new buildings, improved measures for public health, increasingly formal regulation, and more responsible officers—but this influence was undeniably accompanied by changes in attitudes and, in fact, partly caused by them.

Another way in which the established argument is too narrow is that it tends to ignore the houses of correction, the traditional penal institutions. This period did not so much foster a new idea of punitive imprisonment as simply mark a final stage in the gradual but steady assimilation between the gaols and the bridewells. County gaols already provided secure custody for dangerous offenders and were accustomed to hold long-stay inmates. Houses of correction were accustomed to provide penal imprisonment, though usually for relatively short terms—up to about three years. In this period the houses of correction expanded rapidly and, in the process, adopted the greater security and more formal regulation of the gaols, while the gaols kept their increasing numbers of sentenced offenders busy by imposing the labor previously required by the houses of correction. Lancaster Castle, in fact, began officially to accept "bridewell prisoners" from Manchester, while Manchester held nearly all its own felons. In a sense, we can say that prisoners began to be classified on a regional basis, rather than by the gravity of their crime. Exactly the same process has taken place in England since the Radzinowicz report of 1968 and the development of "dispersal prisons" to deal with a similar problem of rising population, and it appears to have resulted in similar changes in discipline.*

If these are the possible underlying explanations of the reforms, what was the nature of the reforms themselves? Looking at them in one way, we could say that these reforms created an embryonic welfare state incorporating many advances that would be introduced only haltingly in the world outside. Prisons guaranteed subsistence, housing, and medical care, provided water, cleaning, and lighting, and offered free social services such as schooling and counseling. This gain, however, was achieved only at the cost of introducing many more regulations and petty restrictions and by virtually confiscating wages. Seen in another way, the reforms represented the systematic imposition of a puritanical code that was hostile to even the most innocent pleasures and that tried to impose continuous penitential drudgery in place of drinking, smoking, playing,

---

*See Roy D. King and Kenneth W. Elliott, *Albany: Birth of a Prison, End of an Era* (London, 1978). The "dispersal" policy and the arrival of serious offenders at Albany forced an increasingly rigid and formal regime onto an initially informal prison.

free speech, and good cheer. All the senses were "mortified"; cells were even designed to prevent the prisoner from seeing out the window. Food was deliberately made bland, clothing ugly, and beds hard.

Perhaps the fairest summary of the reforms would be to say that they systematically sacrificed liberty to equity and security. Many basic needs were supplied, but at the expense of freedom of choice and self-determination. In some cases, such as diet, this loss was so great that it actually undermined the ostensible purpose of the reform, which was to improve the inmates' health. In other cases, such as the imposition of cleanliness, the benefits far outweighed the cost.

In most of these cases, the reformers knew what they were doing; the effects were intended. They wanted to humiliate prisoners and to compensate for greater physical comfort with increased mental distress. They also wanted to reduce the power of the prison community. Equally important, however, was an unintended and paradoxical result of their efforts. The reformers had meant to protect the prisoners and to increase the supervision and accountability of the gaoler. In fact, the day-to-day administration of the reforms created a bureaucracy far more powerful than anything that had gone before. Everything the reformers did increased the presence, the responsibility, and the power of the gaoler. It is not surprising, therefore, that many reforms were actually made on his initiative. It was the gaoler who chose the diet, found the uniforms, and classified the prisoners. It was the gaoler who gained the legal right to administer formal justice and to enforce with a wide range of penalties the increasing number of prison rules. His greater powers were almost entirely gained at the expense of prisoners' rights or by the forfeiture of their responsibilities. An anarchic democracy became an autocracy.

The loss of prisoners' rights in turn brought the growing isolation of the prison community, impeding the effectiveness of magisterial supervision. As the institution began to provide basic commodities such as food and clothing, as the gaoler gained the legal right to punish prisoners and the power to control what they said and did, he exerted more control over what outsiders, including his nominal supervisors, could discover about the prison. Most gaolers did not seriously abuse the power they were given, while the increase in their responsibilities encouraged the development of a professional attitude and attracted many able administrators. Nevertheless, this development does explain why the very worst prison scandals (cases not of neglect and indifference but of positive and systematic brutality—of deliberate starvation, whippings, beatings, and other tortures) occur after, not before, this period of reform, which enabled gaolers to clamp the lid down on simmering gaols until they exploded.

This increase in the gaoler's power, however, like all the other reforms we have discussed, took place very slowly; it was barely beginning in the late eighteenth century. Although most of the reforms had already been required by the prison rules, many were not actually adopted for decades. In the next chapter we will examine the position of John Higgin in the early nineteenth century to see how this gradual change affected life in Lancaster Castle.

## CHAPTER 5

# The Reforming Gaoler

### Was It Murder? The Commission of 1812

After Howard's death in 1790, his work was taken up by James Neild, treasurer of the Society for the Relief and Discharge of Persons Imprisoned for Small Debts. By the turn of the century, Neild was becoming concerned about the lagging pace of reform; legislation had been passed but was not enforced and the prisons were in many cases as bad as they had been before Howard. In order to publicize the problem he made a second survey of English penal institutions, visiting Lancaster at least three times—in 1802, 1805, and 1809. Neild had nothing but praise for Higgin's general method of administration:

In the excellent management of this Prison . . . there is the most clear and demonstrative proof of how much more *Humanity* and *Firmness* operate to produce penitence and reformation, than *Harshness* and *Severity*; which . . . tend rather to harden the heart than reform the manners. . . . They were all usefully and peaceably at work; . . . no Criminal was ever fettered at any time when I have been here. . . . Such is the force of well-tempered authority, the influence of example, and the impressive weight of steady, calm, and active attention to duty.[1]

Nevertheless, signs of strain were just below the surface. The prison's population was rising rapidly. In 1802 Neild found a total of 166 prisoners. By 1809 the total was 218; most of the increase was due to an additional 40 debtors. Neild commented that the debtors' wards were overcrowded. When there were no more than seventy or eighty debtors, many could have their own beds, but on his last visit there were only three single beds in the whole debtors' wing. From January to August of 1812, the average number of prisoners was 291, and on August 12 the total was 340. Political tension was also evident. "A spirit of restlessness" had led the debtors to form a "committee of *Association*, or *Secrecy*," and "by correspondence with others, equally misadvised, . . . they were led to believe that a Gaoler had no controul, and might even be set at defiance." For this essay in independence they were disciplined by the county.[2]

Neild expressed particular disquiet over the treatment of the handful of lunatics in the Castle. Lunatics could be sent to Lancaster under the vagrancy laws, but usually they had committed a serious crime (often murder) and had been declared insane by a jury. They thus tended to be violent and intractable. Legislation passed in 1809 provided for the establishment of county lunatic asylums, but these could not be built immediately, and it was not until 1816 that most lunatics were removed from the Castle.

In many regards, the lunatics in the Castle were better off than their counterparts in asylums. They were kept separate in a new tower that had a kitchen, a dayroom with a fireplace, pump, and privy, and sleeping cells above. They were fettered and chained only as a last resort, although sometimes this restraint extended to chaining them to their beds or seats. Thomas Higgin had visited the Manchester Asylum to study methods of treating the insane, and later entries in the gaoler's journal suggest that the Higgins gave these inmates a good deal of compassionate attention.

Frequently violent, often dangerous, and always enigmatic, the lunatics posed a serious threat to prison order. Neild strongly recommended that a special "recess" be set aside for them, saying that he had found "*five Maniacs*, two of whom were furiously frantick" in 1805. He warned that the lack of proper facilities personally endangered the gaoler and the staff, and suggested that the lunatics be removed to a hospital or "some retired seclusion."[*]

Neild's warning went unheeded, but his fear was justified. Seven years later the treatment of a lunatic, combined with the other tensions Neild

---

*James Neild, *State of the Prisons in England, Scotland and Wales* (London, 1812), p. 329. Though lunatics had occasionally been committed to the Castle in the eighteenth century, the problem really dated from the act of 39 and 40 Geo. III, c. 94 (1799). Passed in a panic after an assassination attempt on the king, this act provided for the detention of criminals acquitted of serious crimes because of insanity.

had seen in the prison, were to produce the greatest storm in the Castle's history and lead to a full-scale investigation of Higgin's administration by a parliamentary commission. Its report shows how the room system of self-government among the debtors functioned under the stress caused by political divisions, overcrowding, and aggressive or drunken members. It also shows how a reforming gaoler exercised his authority.

On May 4, 1812, a Lancaster debtor named John Unthank wrote a letter to Sir Francis Burdett, asking him to say something in the House of Commons about the confinement of lunatics in county gaols. He suggested that if lunatics could not be removed entirely, they should at least be in the care of a civilian. As it was, not only the lunatics suffered but also the debtors, who, being nearby, were "subject . . . to the *Screams of the unfortunate People which is really excruciating* to the feelings to hear."[3]

As Unthank wrote, the screams of one of the lunatics were echoing through the prison. James Rawlinson had been convicted at the 1809 March Assizes of killing a man "in a fit of frenzy," and was found insane by a jury. He had once attempted to hang himself in prison, but was cut down just in time. In late April 1812 he became very violent and agitated and began screaming "Murder! Kill me! Kill me!" On the morning of Friday, May 1, he was, with some effort, put into a separate cell.[4] On Saturday night, May 2, Thomas Birch, an elderly turnkey in charge of the lunatics, took his grandson, Thomas Wright, and a Crown prisoner, Thomas Lee, up to Rawlinson's cell to give him his dinner. Birch was afraid of Rawlinson, who had often torn his clothes and assaulted him. As they opened the door, Rawlinson rushed out of the cell and grabbed Birch. Birch managed to push him back into his cell and then sent for John Cooper, another turnkey.

What happened after that was a matter of some controversy. Everyone agreed that there were blows. Cooper stated that when they opened the cell to remove Rawlinson's heavy clogs, Rawlinson rushed out, grabbed at Lee's genitals and got his trousers, and kicked violently. Cooper then hit him a few strokes with a light switch to make him loose his hold. Rawlinson was wearing heavy fustian trousers and all four testified that the blows were only as hard as were needed to loosen his hold and had done no damage.

Seven debtors—Jacob Wilson Wardell, George Tengatt, George Collier, James and William Mallalieu, Joseph Dickinson, and William Goulden—later testified that they heard shouts and the sound of blows. A Crown prisoner named Thomas Griffith said that Lee had told him he had kicked Rawlinson in the ribs with his clogs, and that Birch and Cooper had beaten Rawlinson with "the bull's pizzle . . . at one end as big as my fist."[5] Lee, however, who had since been discharged, vehemently denied most of these statements. The whip in question was a gentleman's light riding switch, "about the thickness of my finger." The beating was not violent and he had not told Griffith it was. Elijah Major, a Crown prisoner named by Griffith as present at this conversation, denied it ever took place.[6]

The beating may have been more severe than any of the four participants was willing to admit, but Rawlinson's subsequent conduct suggests that he cannot have been seriously injured. The next day another turnkey, John Clark, went with Birch and a Crown prisoner named John Dewsnip to give Rawlinson his breakfast. They discovered that he had managed to break his figure-of-eight handcuffs. When they opened the door, Rawlinson rushed out screaming, spat in Clark's face, and said, "I wish I had my bloody knife." Dewsnip, who had had no part in the events of the previous day, testified that Rawlinson was in good health. Clark said that Rawlinson had no breeches on. He saw his body up to the hips and there was no mark on it. The men decided to put a stronger pair of handcuffs on the lunatic: two bracelets joined by a short chain. On Wednesday, May 5, Rawlinson's screams ceased. When Birch, Wright, and Lee came up to his cell with breakfast, they found him dead. They stated that he had managed to take his stockings off, twist them into a rope, and wind them around his neck in such a way as to strangle himself.

In the meantime, Unthank was having troubles of his own. In the autumn of 1811 he had engaged in a series of drunken brawls with two debtors named Spencer and Drummond. When Higgin heard that Spencer had broken his leg fighting Unthank, he had written to the justices, declaring both men guilty of riotous and disorderly conduct. The justices had promptly suspended Spencer's and Unthank's county allowances. When Unthank received Burdett's answer to his letter on May 15, he began to gloat in a manner that several of his fellows found offensive. One of them heard him say, "We have laid a scheme for the old villain, we'll teach him for taking my bread and potatoes away, blast him." Drummond took exception to Unthank's words and got into another altercation with him.[7]

The next day Drummond sued the articles of the peace against Unthank before James Stainbank, a Lancaster justice. Stainbank ordered

Unthank to find sureties to keep the peace, but the Lancaster tradesmen refused to provide bonds, "on account of Mr. Higgin." Unthank was, therefore, imprisoned on the Crown side of the gaol from May 16 to May 18, when he was able to find mitigated bail. On his release, his old room-mates threw him out and he had to find a new room.[8]

Shortly thereafter, Unthank was involved in yet another dispute, this time with turnkey John Clark, and was again bound to keep the peace. When he could not find bail, Higgin interceded to have his bail excused, saving him from further confinement. Unthank complained, however, that Higgin had refused to send for his friend, Jacob Wilson Wardell, as a witness on his behalf. Wardell consoled him by agreeing that it was very bad conduct toward him but that they "should set all to rights by and by."[9]

Wardell then took up the correspondence with Burdett himself. Unthank, he wrote, "seems funked from an Idea that he shall be further persecuted by the Gaoler," but Wardell was prepared to continue the correspondence for him. "My Motto is nec cupio, nec metuo," he wrote. Wardell briefly sketched his own character—"I am perfectly independent in my principles; . . . *intentionally* it is not in my Nature to exaggerate anything"—and went on to inform Burdett of Rawlinson's death. He hinted that Rawlinson had been murdered after "an unmerciful flogging." The coroner's inquest had been extremely perfunctory and he, Wardell, had heard two Crown prisoners, Richard Smith and Thomas Lee, say that when they laid out Rawlinson's body it was "a Mass of congealed Blood and disfiguration." He warned that Smith and Lee might not tell the truth until their discharge because they were in Higgin's custody, adding that many debtors were afraid of Higgin because he had two brothers-in-law on the bench and could prevent their discharge.*

Wardell wrote several more letters to Burdett but made little progress in his attempt to have Rawlinson's death discussed in Parliament. Although he complained that the scandal could not be considered fairly in Lancashire because the justices were biased, he did succeed in gaining a local inquiry into other possible abuses. On May 26 he wrote to the sheriff of the county charging that Higgin had failed to remove ordure from the Castle, that he refused to open the prison gates for shipments of coal

---

*PRO, HO 42/125, May 24, 1812. The sister of a third justice, Col. Bradshaw, was married to another of Higgin's brothers-in-law.

weighing less than ten hundredweight, that he failed to visit debtors' rooms, and that he had prevented two poor debtors named Hayes and Goulden from receiving charitable funds for their legal expenses because they had not hired Higgin's son John, a local attorney.*

Within two weeks the justices held a special hearing on Wardell's charges. Nothing in Wardell's letter or the recorded testimony before the magistrates referred to Rawlinson, although the justices seem to have looked into the matter privately later that summer. Meanwhile, another group of Castle debtors set up a committee to defend Higgin. One hundred fourteen debtors out of an approximate total of 146 then in the Castle signed a petition to the justices expressing indignation at the "dark, silent, insidious and assassin-like" behavior of Wardell.[10]

The hearing first considered the matter of the ordure. It turned out that it came from the twice-yearly emptying of the Castle cesspool and had remained for a day or two longer than usual because the carters were celebrating the Whitsun holidays. Higgin admitted that he restricted small coal deliveries but explained that this applied only to deliveries by horse and cart, since they required that the entire gate be opened, endangering security at a time of serious overcrowding. Several debtors testified that they customarily demanded a load of coals as room-money from new entrants and that the ten hundredweight then supplied was usually adequate. If it was not, they made a collective subscription for a new load. A debtor whom Higgin paid to keep the passages clean testified that Higgin himself often provided coals for prisoners who could not afford them. The only complainant for this charge was William Mallalieu; since he and his son had successfully prevented between twelve and twenty debtors from entering their room they may have had more difficulty than most in procuring coal.

Higgin admitted that he did not visit the debtors' rooms daily, but the debtors wrote that they preferred the existing arrangements. He denied absolutely the charge that he was involved in improper dealings with Hayes and Goulden. His son John stated that he had obtained the release of Hayes and of another debtor named Chapman gratis but had refused

---

*PRO, HO 42/125, May 31, 1812. See also *PP* 1812-13 V, Report of the Commissioners on the State of Lancaster Prison, and the Treatment of Prisoners Therein, pp. 82-83. Thomas Higgin described Goulden as "a bad character," with some justification. Goulden himself admitted to the commission that the members of his room had expelled him twice within the past year for being drunk and disorderly. At the time the commission met he was reduced to living in a cell.

to act for Goulden because his brother Thomas Higgin gave him a bad character. He was able to submit the letter he had sent his agents saying that Hayes and Chapman were very poor, requesting them to obtain their release "as an act of charity," and offering to pay their stamp duties from his own pocket. It is difficult to disentangle what happened in Goulden's case because Goulden was illiterate (Higgin wrote his letters for him), but apparently his plaintiff refused the £5 offered by the Thatched House Society to compound for his debt. Later, when he became supersedable (eligible for release by the courts rather than his creditor), Higgin told him that he himself would have to find the money for his legal fees.

At the end of the hearing, the five justices decided that the charges were "wicked, malicious and without foundation." As a punishment for bringing malicious charges they withdrew the allowances of seven debtors: Wardell, the Mallalieus, Goulden, John Hankin, William Rideal, and George Tengatt. With a single trivial exception, this list comprised all those who had given any evidence, however unimportant, for the complainants. Five of those seven were later to be among the seven who testified to hearing blows on the night of May 2. The Annual General Session, meeting two weeks later, seconded the justices' conclusions. The prisoners in the Castle celebrated Higgin's discharge by wearing oak leaves in their hats; Wardell was later to charge Thomas Higgin with distributing these and so encouraging a spirit of "party."

Wardell remained determined to press his case. On June 17 he sent four petitions to Burdett: one each from Tengatt, Hankin, and Goulden, and the fourth from a newcomer named Samuel Scuffum, a former actor. Wardell ended a long account of the hearing with a bitter attack on the conduct of the justices who were trying to "impress a *Terror amongst* the *Debtors* . . . to frustrate the possibility of any future Accusation. . . . The Gaoler has much Reason to *dread* future Evidence . . . by the Criminality of Conduct of his Turnkeys in flogging the Felon to Death I wrote to you some time ago."[11] Three days later he anxiously wrote again, accusing Higgin of bribing his witnesses, by giving "12 of the greatest Blackguards 5 *Shillings each* which he said was the *benefaction* of some Person. . . . I cannot but disbelieve that any one would give a benefaction under such restrictions."[12]

It seems strange that Wardell should profess ignorance of the source of this money, since both Howard and Neild refer to a list of benefactions at Lancaster that included one of £3 from Henrietta Rigby's estate to provide 5s. each to "twelve of the most necessitous and well-behaved prisoners."[13] It is only fair to Wardell to add that two of the recipients of the benefaction testified in Higgin's favor at the hearing and that two served on the committee that produced the petition of the 114 debtors against Wardell. Three of the twelve were also among the six debtors who sat on the coroner's inquest over Rawlinson. Another three had, along with Goulden, recently lost their allowances for being party to the sale of beer, but the three former were restored after making an apology that Goulden failed to second. Because of overlaps, seven of the Rigby beneficiaries had nothing to do with subsequent events. Although there is no evidence that Higgin did anything but distribute the money to those he found most "deserving," Wardell's complaint does light up a certain moral ambiguity in the role of the reforming gaoler, who had simultaneously to act as impartial arbiter and selective benefactor for those he lived among, in order to encourage "reformation" and "good behavior." When to this dual role was added laxness on the part of the superintending authorities and bitter political divisions within both gaol and county, it was almost inevitable that some prisoners would feel aggrieved.

On July 3 Burdett presented the four petitions to the House of Commons. The three from Goulden, Tengatt, and Hankin complained that they had lost their allowances after giving evidence at the magistrates' hearing and that such action must tend to discourage complaints in the future. The fourth, from the actor Scuffum, alleged that he had been unjustly confined in a punishment cell without a bed, fire, candles, pen, ink, paper, or clean linen, and that the laundress and a Mr. Stanton, a "comedian," were refused access to him.[14]

None of the petitions referred to Rawlinson, but in the course of the debate Burdett read one of Wardell's letters suggesting that Rawlinson had come to his death by foul means. He also read a letter from John Spencer complaining that when "by mere accident I slipped off a Stone in the yard and most unfortunately broke my leg," his surgeon had not been allowed in to set it properly, as a result of which he was still lame.[15] Burdett, though dubious about the charges because he had so often heard Higgin praised, felt the debtors' petitions should be pursued. It seems likely that the petitions would have received little attention if the suspicious circumstances surrounding Rawlinson's death had not loomed in the background. The Commons finally decided against a parliamentary inquiry (which would have been limited to the charges in the petitions) after Castlereigh promised that the government would make its own investigation into the conduct of the gaol. Meanwhile, Higgin and the justices collected their evidence and assumed a united front.

The government's investigation took the form of a royal commission of three men: Benjamin Hobhouse, Thomas Macdonald, and William Roberts. It was empowered to hear all complaints and charges, written and spoken, not merely those that had been the subject of the petitions to Parliament. The commission's report began by dismissing the complaints made before the justices in June, using the depositions made then as proof that they were unfounded. It also dismissed three further complaints from Wardell but found that Thomas Higgin had in fact told Wardell that he had been "horsewhipped and horseponded at York" and had later threatened to pull his nose if they ever met outside the prison. Higgin claimed provocation and escaped with a reprimand.[16]

The commission then commented with some asperity on the characters of Wardell, Unthank, and the Mallalieus. Wardell had revealed his "temper of mind" in a letter to the justices' clerk boasting of the fortune he had spent, including estates worth £30,000—"a history," wrote the commission, "which, it is evident, he considered as calculated to give impressions the direct reverse of those to which they seem to be entitled."[17] The report went on to speak of evidence showing that Wardell had sworn revenge on the gaoler with the Mallalieus' support, and that Unthank and Wardell had "laid a scheme" against Higgin. Unthank himself, from his own evidence, was frequently drunk and quarrelsome, while James Mallalieu "showed the spirit of his character, by declaring, when asked if they had requested to have it [their allowance] back, that they could not 'cringe' to the magistrates who had decided against them."[18]

Next, the commission considered the four petitions one by one. Several witnesses testified that Samuel Scuffum had sworn to escape, and that his confinement was thus a fair punishment. Moreover, Scuffum's own statements before the commission directly contradicted many of the complaints in the petition. Most important was his testimony about the conduct of Cooper, the turnkey who had locked him up, since Cooper was also the man accused of beating Rawlinson. Scuffum said that Cooper had behaved "very politely," and his account suggested that

Cooper had displayed considerable patience.[19] Scuffum also related how Higgin had interceded for him after his fellow debtors had "hooted" him out of his room for petitioning Parliament and had accused him of theft. The commission thus dismissed his petition.

The commission dismissed the other three petitioners as well, pointing out that there was evidence that they had conspired against Higgin and that in any case they could have regained their allowances by writing an apology in the customary manner. The commission then considered a more serious charge made by John Spencer in a letter to Burdett. Spencer was the debtor whose leg had been broken when Unthank knocked him down. He was treated by the prison surgeon's apprentice, who turned out to be Robert Higgin, yet another son. Higgin did not splint the leg but only bandaged it. Spencer suspected that the leg was not properly set, but when the surgeon, Mr. Baxendale, came, he left it as it was. Spencer then sent his wife to John Higgin to ask for another doctor, but the gaoler said, "He has had Mr. Baxendale, has not he; what does he want?" and turned away.[20] After trying for nearly a week to obtain a second visit from Baxendale, Spencer decided to hire a private surgeon, a Mr. Howitt, but he arrived late in the day and was turned away at the gates.

More than a week after the accident, Spencer consulted Cooper, the turnkey, who agreed that the leg was not set correctly and sent for the surgeon. Again Robert Higgin turned up, and again he failed to reset the leg. On Monday Baxendale arrived and finally splinted the leg, but when the splints were taken off, the leg was not set properly and the bones overlapped. Spencer again sent for Mr. Howitt, who finally arrived and agreed that the leg had been badly handled, but advised against having it broken again.

Baxendale's testimony amounted to a simple denial. His "senior pupil" Robert had attended to the leg properly, so he had merely continued the treatment. Spencer was very intemperate and subject to gout; the inflammation this disease caused in his leg had interfered with the cure, but his pupil had made no mistakes. Howitt, however, stated uncompromisingly that in his opinion the job had been botched.

Faced with this professional disagreement, the commission retreated precipitately. It simply accepted Baxendale's assertion that the healing of the leg was hampered by gout and intemperance, and dismissed the complaint. The commissioners even failed to examine other possible witnesses on the subject, such as Cooper or Robert Higgin himself. Nor did they call in a third doctor to examine the leg. Although Spencer's charges touched John Higgin's own conduct only marginally, the commission's reluctance to investigate them thoroughly leaves it open to accusations of bias and must stand as its greatest failure.

After considering several minor matters, the commission finally turned to its real raison d'être, Rawlinson's death. It immediately became clear that, as Wardell had charged, the coroner's inquest and the whole manner of dealing with the body after death had been utterly inadequate. The coroner, having been told that Rawlinson committed suicide by strangling himself, had treated the inquest as a mere pro forma proceeding. He did not call in a surgeon to examine the body, nor did he do any more himself than glance at the mark around Rawlinson's neck and the "upper part" of his body. The jury he called consisted of six debtors and six stonemasons working on the Castle. Higgin told the commission that it was customary to choose the jury from people employed on the Castle works, "though I can't say I quite approve of it."[21] The jury was simply left in the room with the body, which was covered by a sheet, and informed that anyone who wished could have it uncovered. Not unnaturally, no one did. For this reason, neither the coroner nor the jury could testify as to whether the body bore marks of ill-treatment. They rapidly came to the conclusion that Rawlinson had committed suicide and disbanded. The coroner did not even keep minutes.

Nevertheless, in the end there was not much doubt about how Rawlinson died. Wardell had suggested that no one ironed as the lunatic had been could have strangled himself, but the commission put a man in the same irons, equipped him with the rough knife found on the body, and found that it was possible for him to cut up his stockings and strangle himself. Wardell's hint that Rawlinson died from the beating he had received and that his suicide was a fabrication seems extremely unlikely, since by all accounts he was in rude health for several days after being beaten. Wardell's suggestion that Rawlinson was not really a lunatic at all was patently absurd; he had been found insane by a jury and his behavior was extremely erratic. Any vestiges of credibility that Wardell retained were destroyed when Hankin stated that Wardell had intended to bribe the two discharged prisoners who had laid out the body, Thomas Lee and Richard Smith, to testify against Higgin. This claim is borne out by the fact that Wardell named Smith to Burdett as a possible witness, although when they were called, both men strongly defended Higgin.

After the hearing had ended, a former turnkey submitted a letter he had received from Wardell. "The commissioners," he wrote, "spoke to me *confidentially*, and I had four interviews. . . . You lived as turnkey some time here; I have *an authority* to offer you a very *considerable sum*, if you will disclose certain communications touching the Crown side, and which will be remitted you at a moment's notice, and an additional assurance of *Government*, indemnifying you from any *inconvenience*. I speak *officially*; and as the sum would be an object to your family, I think it is worthy of your best consideration."[22]

The commission described this letter as "totally destitute of truth," and it must be said that in writing it Wardell convicted himself of dishonesty and of attempting to suborn witnesses.

The only remaining question is how severely Rawlinson was beaten on the evening of May 2. No one denied that he was beaten; some degree of physical force was both inevitable and acceptable in the days before the insane could be controlled by medication. In fact, the beating resulted from Higgin's desire to permit as much freedom as possible to his charges. If, according to the traditional practice with lunatics, Rawlinson had been so heavily ironed as to preclude free movement or had been chained to the wall of his cell, he could not have been so active or posed such a threat to the turnkeys.

This, at least, was the opinion Higgin expressed, in his only real comment on the case. In a letter he wrote to Edward Wilbraham Bootle in July, he said:

I am aware that Lunatics may be kept like wild Beasts chained fast to a Wall, or to the Floor, without the use of a Whip, but with such a filthy mode of Treatment their Health is soon injured. The Turnkey cannot let out a madman with any degree of safety unless he is master of him. Rawlinson had not received the slightest degree of correction during several preceeding months, but he was then in frenzy and striving to conquer the Turnkeys, which for his own comfort could not be allowed. My directions to Birch . . . is never to whip them on the body however unruly. I have now one Lunatic, viz. Richard Coleman, who has been here *10* years, another James Mort 8 years, and another Martha Whewell 8 years. If they had been vigorously treated they would not have been in existence at this moment, especially when we take into Consideration that the place . . . in which they are confined is not calculated for their Health and Comfort, but merely for their safe custody. . . . I am not ashamed to acknowledge to you that I cannot attend to them in a manner consonant with my own feelings, or desire, if I did, more important matters would be neglected and I should be ruined. . . . It would be a great relief to my mind if Government would direct that these unhappy Objects should be removed to St. Luke's, or to one of the Lunatic Asylums at Liverpool, or Manchester, where they could have medical aid.[23]

Until May 2 Rawlinson was not handcuffed and enjoyed considerable freedom of movement. The question is whether the force used to subdue him was excessive. Although the evidence does not offer an unequivocal answer, it favors the turnkeys. The prosecution could not find a single person able to testify to seeing any bruises on the body, while the defense found at least six witnesses ready to swear that they had seen Rawlinson unmarked. No one outside the small circle of Wardell's intimates was willing to suggest that Rawlinson could have been ill treated, and Wardell never formally charged such treatment. It seems likely that if the debtors really believed that Rawlinson had been brutally beaten, a few independent men would have been willing to give evidence.

The commission's report cleared Higgin of all the charges against him, although it did criticize minor aspects of the prison regime. The officers came in for censure for their failure to keep adequate books. The commission approved the justices' conduct of the June hearing as well as their decision to cut off the allowances of the seven witnesses, although it did not approve the decision of the Annual General Session to advertise publicly the names of the recalcitrant debtors. The coroner was criticized for his carelessness. The commission commented on Higgin's "inadvertency" in moving Rawlinson's body but also gave him almost fulsome praise:

He has passed through the trial in a manner which cannot but confirm the good character he had before acquired. . . . Every circumstance which came under our observation has evinced his disposition to administer relief to those who were suffering under the pressure of sickness or extreme indigence, or of that frequent cause of mortification and misery among prisoners of debt, the ill-treatment they receive from those with whom they are forced to live; his readiness to give assistance and advice for the settlement of differences among them; . . . and the correct and proper application of such charities as are distributed under his recommendation. . . . A succession of debtors in the gaol . . . presented themselves with great earnestness to bear their testimony to the humane and generous conduct of their gaoler, whom they represented as the father and the friend of the indigent debtor.[24]

No disciplinary action resulted from the commission's report. Cooper had sued Unthank and Wardell for slander at the September Assizes and won damages, but the hearing was well over before the report appeared. The commission showed some bias in favor of Higgin from the start and tended throughout to judge witnesses on the basis of their "appearance and demeanor," but there seems no reason to dismiss their report as a whitewash. Whatever the rights and wrongs of its findings, however, the report is valuable for its detailed picture of an administrative system in the process of reform. It offers a graphic example of the paradoxical effect of this period of change, which left the gaoler both extraordinarily powerful and extremely vulnerable.

Higgin and his staff were vulnerable for three reasons. First, they lived in an age of great political tension, tension that was reflected in the prison and made it difficult to govern harmoniously. Political disputes were common among debtors; Unthank and Drummond fought over politics while the majority of the pro-Higgin debtors taunted Wardell and his allies with cries of "Burdett's men!" This was the summer of the Luddites; political activists were trickling in to join the criminal prisoners and more were to arrive in the fall. Since Burdett and his allies found it politically advantageous as well as morally desirable to campaign against prison abuses and to air prison scandals, even a conscientious man could find himself caught up in a whirlwind of party enmity.

Second, the gaol staff were vulnerable simply because of overcrowding in the prison. In 1812 the Castle was at bursting point. Among the debtors this crowding caused stress and endless quarreling. It caused disputes about the admission of debtors to rooms on their arrival; the occupants of whatever room the newly incarcerated debtors entered were likely to resent the newcomers for taking up space. Overcrowding made it difficult for inmates to cook their food properly and to eat their meals. It forced them to share beds. The admission of wives and children became a cause for dispute, especially when the wives wished to sleep with their husbands in rooms full of other men.

Higgin tried to avoid the petty disputes and to be impartial in judging the more serious ones, but inevitably some of his decisions displeased one of the parties. Most of the leading anti-Higginites had a particular outstanding grievance: Wardell because Higgin had refused to send for a magistrate to decide his dispute with another debtor, the Mallalieus because of disputes over the admission of debtors to their room, Spencer and Unthank because they had lost their allowances for fighting, William Rideal (another June witness) because he had previously been cut off for writing "spiritedly" about the admission of a debtor to his room, Goulden because he had been cut off for selling ale and had failed to apologize.

Third, the staff were vulnerable because standards of conduct were changing, leaving them without a straightforward code of behavior. They were in the same position as Trollope's Warden of a generation later: accustomed to the old ways, publicly judged by the new, and uncertain themselves of how they should act. Higgin wished to maintain a high standard of personal conduct, yet, with the full approval of the justices, he built a family empire that seemed indefensible to radicals such as Hunt. Cooper returned ostensible bribes but carried on a little "agency" in bread for the debtors. The coroner and the prison officers kept records in a perfunctory manner that suited the magistrates but appalled the commissioners. Higgin found it necessary to assist the debtors with their financial and legal affairs, if only to help them get out and so relieve the congestion, but this role naturally placed him in an equivocal position. Everyone, in dealing with the prisoners, had difficulty in drawing the proper line between informal friendliness and a starchy, impersonal professionalism.

Even more evident than Higgin's vulnerability, however, was his enormous personal and official power. It is important to realize that he did not gain this power by enforcing a reign of terror, but though his methods were relatively gentle, his authority was extensive. Part of this authority certainly resulted from his nepotism. He had relatives both above and below him in the prison. Although his Houseman brothers-in-law took no part in the inquiries into his conduct, the relationship could only have added to the reluctance of their colleagues to pry too closely into Higgin's affairs. Higgin could also claim a rather tenuous relationship with Justice Bradshaw, who gave strong testimony in his defense and took an active role in the administration of the gaol; however insignificant the connection may have seemed to Bradshaw, it offered aggrieved prisoners reasonable grounds for doubting his impartiality. One of the problems, in fact, with appointing "gentleman" gaolers in the provincial towns of this period was that they were almost bound to have such connections with the local gentry.

It was natural that Higgin, a man with a number of sons, living in a country town, would take one as his own assistant and apprentice the others to respectable professional men whom he knew in the course of business. When he sent one son to the school run by the prison chaplain it made little difference, but the results in three other cases were unfortunate. The first was the use of his son as a deputy, a practice so common in this period as to be unremarkable. The second was the apprenticeship of Robert Higgin to the Castle surgeon. This meant that prisoners were treated by the gaoler's son, who was hardly likely to preserve an independent attitude toward possible medical hazards. Nor, if he made a mistake, did prisoners find it easy to appeal. The third was John Higgin's entry into the law and his agreement to act as solicitor for some of the prisoners. John maintained, and provided evidence to prove, that he took on many cases for poor debtors gratis, from charitable motives, and that his relationship with the gaoler only helped the debtors. Even if he never took a fee from a prisoner, however, John's willingness to get prisoners freed on his father's or brother's recommendation can only have increased both their power over their charges and the resentment of the less favored. The distribution of alms can support as real a power as the use of menaces.

Higgin II could control not only his son John's services but also many similar benefits. To some extent the reformers intended to provide gaolers with this power; in their anxiety to encourage the prisoners' reformation they allowed the gaoler to make little discretionary rewards for good behavior. Charitable bequests further enabled the gaoler to reward the well-behaved. Reforming magistrates had tried to make the debtors' allowances another means of controlling behavior, resolving that these should be withdrawn in certain cases, such as drunken or irreligious conduct.

In theory the gaoler himself had no authority to withdraw or grant allowances. The commission report frequently pointed out that three of the petitioners had no quarrel against Higgin, since it was the magistrates, not he, who had withdrawn their allowances. In fact, however, the magistrates could only assess the behavior of prisoners according to the gaoler's information, and ordinarily they accepted his recommendations as a matter of course. Higgin himself, to his credit, distributed charity lavishly, both from the Charity Fund and from his own pocket. When Wardell wrote of the 114 debtors who had signed the petition in Higgin's defense, he added that they all owed the gaoler money! Even Wardell was in his debt. From the testimony of other debtors we know that Higgin often paid the room entrance fees of poor debtors, gave coal to the poorer rooms in winter, and supplied clothing and cots, sometimes from his own house, for the destitute. It is clear that his good will made all the difference to the lives of the poor debtors. Higgin had become the only source of the funds that prisoners had previously collected and administered themselves.

However just was the dismissal of Wardell's charges, there was some truth to his complaint that no one in Lancashire could obtain a fair hearing against Higgin. The commission's report shows that the checks, both traditional and reformist, on the gaoler's conduct were extremely weak. The coroner's duty to hold an inquest on every prisoner who died in the gaol was one such check, but this had clearly become a perfunctory matter and the jury, consisting of debtors and Castle workmen, was not disinterested. It is no wonder that some prisoners, seeing such laxity, became suspicious or apprehensive.

The justices should have offered another check, but their attitude toward Higgin is summed up by the fact that they ascribed their failure to inspect the prison or require written journals to "that perfect confidence which their knowledge of the gaoler and the high character he has acquired during his long course of service had led them to repose in him."[25] In fact, the justices' anxiety to scotch criticism of Higgin led them to publish three separate vindications of his character after the June hearing and to publicize the names of the debtors who had "by Effrontery and Intimidation" interfered with his duty, as well as to suspend their allowances. Although Higgin seems to have deserved their trust, such partisanship, however well intended, was likely, as one of the protesting debtors wrote, to "deter any witness from giving evidence upon any subject that may hereafter be brought forward against the said gaoler, and there can be no safety in a place where such authority is exercised."[26]

## Demagogue Radicals and the "Black Catalogue of Traitors": Politics and the Prison, 1812-1832

The commission's exoneration of Higgin and his fellow officers, however welcome to them, did nothing to alleviate the underlying tensions caused by overcrowding and the bitter political rivalries of the Napoleonic period. The population of the Lancashire prisons continued to rise steadily for a generation. The opening of a third house of correction, Kirkdale, near Liverpool, in 1820 offered only a temporary alleviation of the problem. When overcrowding was combined with the public events that took place in Lancashire during this period, the tension in the prison could only increase.*

During Higgin's tenure of office there were four main waves of political agitation in Lancashire, each of which left a flotsam of captives in the local prisons. The first came in the already tense year of 1812, the year of the Luddite disturbances. The spring of that year brought a rash of food riots, arson, and illegal organization. During May and June a special commission in Lancaster tried 58 people, imprisoning 7, transporting 17, and executing 8. In June 38 men were arrested for administering an unlawful oath to Samuel Fleming, a government spy. Their leader was John Knight, a Saddleworth manufacturer, described by John Foster as a "determined Jacobin."† Knight was first imprisoned in 1794 and lived just long enough to become a Chartist in 1838; he was probably the most important of the local radical leaders. To the disgust of the authorities, the "38," ably defended by James Scarlett, John Williams, and Henry (later Lord) Brougham, were acquitted after a ten-week imprisonment.

The next wave came during the unrest of 1817. After the abortive march of the "Blanketeers," 29 men were arrested. Most were hastily released, but 9 were committed for trial, including John Bagguley and Samuel Drummond, reputedly the most violent and hotheaded of the radical leaders.[27] They were held for five months in extreme discomfort because of the severe overcrowding at the Salford New Bailey. One of the justices admitted to the Home Office that since no free beds were avail-

---

*In 1816 Higgin was so concerned about overcrowding that he begged the undersheriff to send a military force to guard the prison, claiming that he was having great difficulty keeping the prisoners under control and was "obliged to go armed into the prison. We are at a loss to know how we are to get over this winter. . . . Should an insurrection take place you must be well aware that our lives and assistants would have little or no chance amongst such a set of desperate fellows" (PRO, HO 6/1, Dec. 12, 1816). I am grateful to Judge Eric Stockdale for sending me this reference.

†John Foster, *Class Struggle and the Industrial Revolution* (London, 1974), p. 139. According to Foster, Knight, born in 1763, was first imprisoned in 1794 for two years. In 1801 he was on the county executive of the United Englishmen. He edited the *Manchester Political Register* in 1816 and the *Manchester Spectator* in 1818; in both cases his work ended in his arrest under the act suspending habeas corpus. In the 1830's he worked for the Trade Union movement, particularly for Doherty's spinners, and in 1831 he became secretary of the Oldham Political Union. Shortly before his death he became the Oldham treasurer for poor relief. For different stages of Knight's career, see also J. L. Hammond and Barbara Hammond, *The Skilled Labourer, 1760-1832* (New York, 1967; orig. ed. 1919); Donald Read, *Peterloo: The "Massacre" and Its Background* (Clifton, N.J., 1973; orig. ed. 1958); and Robert Walmsley, *Peterloo: The Case Reopened* (Manchester, 1969).

able, the prisoners had been put in a storeroom and given fresh straw. Eventually they were released without trial because the justices could not substantiate any of the charges against them.

Parliament, meanwhile, had passed an emergency act suspending the provisions of habeas corpus. The government took advantage of this act to rearrest Bagguley on suspicion of high treason, along with John Knight, Samuel Bamford (another well-known local radical), and fifteen other Lancashire men. In all, 37 men were arrested throughout England. The prisoners were taken to London for a brief hearing and then scattered in prisons all over the country. Their presence often unnerved local officials, who were well aware that any slip would be attended with publicity and who knew that the state prisoners would be disruptive. In Gloucestershire, the Whig justice Sir George Onesiphorus Paul protested the heavy use of certain "model" county prisons for these men, "thereby making the county of that prison a party in the war with printers; in which it has no particular concern."[28] The Tory Higgin was equally disconcerted when he learned that he was again to receive John Bagguley. Although he received exceptionally privileged treatment, Bagguley later tried to arouse a scandal over his imprisonment.

A third group of prisoners came in 1819. A spinners' strike of 1818 led in January to the imprisonment of their leader, John Doherty, in Lancaster Castle, where he immediately began to petition Peel on behalf of the misdemeanants there. In August he was joined by the leaders of the meeting that ended in the Peterloo massacre. They included "Orator" Hunt, the day's speaker, and James Moorhouse, his host; Joseph Johnson, a sponsor of the meeting; John Knight; John Thacker Saxton, a reporter for the radical *Manchester Observer*; Samuel Bamford; Bamford's friend "Dr." Healey, an illiterate apothecary; and three other local radicals. As they arrived at Lancaster, the debtors greeted them with handshakes, "a shout and many good wishes," according to Bamford.*

Hunt and Knight were released on bail the next evening, while John-

---

*Samuel Bamford, *Passages in the Life of a Radical*, ed. W. H. Chaloner, vol. 2 (London, 1967; orig. ed. 1844), p. 3. According to one local historian, the inmates collected stones in one of the gateway turrets as part of an attempt to rescue Hunt, but there is no record of any actual disturbance. Perhaps Hunt's release on bail forestalled the intended riot (William Oliver Roper, "Materials for the History of Lancashire, II" [Chetham Society, 1907], p. 240).

The Peterloo massacre took place when a committee of Lancashire justices, headed by Hulton, ordered first the amateur yeomanry and then the professional hussars to charge a largely peaceful crowd gathered to hear Hunt speak. Eleven people were killed.

son and Moorhouse had obtained release in Manchester, but the other prisoners seem to have remained in the Castle until their trial seven months later. At the trial in York, with Scarlett this time prosecuting, Hunt, Johnson, Knight, Healey, and Bamford were all convicted and sentenced to imprisonment; the other five were acquitted. The convicted prisoners were again scattered among different provincial gaols.

Hunt, however, did not drop from public view. He soon sent a characteristic letter from Ilchester to Johnson, Bamford, and Healey at Lincoln. He was querulous about their luck: "your time will pass pleasantly away, it is a mere nominal imprisonment." He himself, on the other hand, was suffering in the two best rooms in the gaol, having a "very good Bed Room and a very good sitting Room" to himself but a yard only ten paces square. A prisoner was sent in daily to act as his servant but "*mine is literally solitary confinement.*"[29]

The government soon had reason to regret sending Hunt to what it believed was a model prison but that he described as "the worst Jail in England." From what he persisted in calling his "dungeon" he sent sharp attacks on the gaol and its "reforming" governor, William Bridle. Eventually, his charges were pressed in Parliament. A royal commission verified many of Hunt's allegations of insanitary conditions, flogging, and torture, much to the embarrassment of the government and the Somerset magistrates. The scandal over the "Ilchester Bastille" probably helped bring about the Prison Act of 1823. At the same time another Peterloo participant, Richard Carlile, sent to Dorchester for publishing the work of Tom Paine, was producing a journal, *The Republican*. His charges that prisoners were frequently flogged in Dorchester provoked an investigation that confirmed his allegations.[30] Although John Knight also stood trial with the Peterloo defendants, he was sentenced to Lancaster with five other men—Nathan Broadhurst, George Dewhurst, John Berry, William Fletcher, and John Adamson—on reduced charges of unlawful assembly, stemming from a different meeting.

The final wave of political imprisonments came in the early 1830's, with the initial defeat of the Reform Bill. In 1830 Hunt, after a disgraceful campaign on both sides, defeated the Whig E. G. Stanley at Preston, then a unique borough with universal male suffrage. Soon afterward, Nathan Broadhurst returned to Lancaster Castle, charged, along with several others, with seditious conspiracy and attendance at an illegal meeting. The men were convicted on reduced charges of unlawful assembly and sentenced to a year in Lancaster. In 1832 John Doherty, now the publisher of a radical newspaper, *The Poor Man's Advocate*, also returned to Lancaster after a local clergyman sued him for libel.[31]

Once inside the walls of Lancaster, each of these four waves of prisoners, which in some cases comprised the same men, succeeded in raising fundamental questions about the way in which the prison was administered and the prisoners treated. Their radical activism, combined with John Higgin's Tory sympathies, aroused a storm of controversy, renewed with each new wave of prisoners, that was to last a generation. In the course of the controversy, two issues became inextricably entwined. The first was the question of whether political prisoners were entitled to special treatment. The second, although raised by the political prisoners, was over what rights, if any, were possessed by all prisoners, and in particular over their right to free communication as a safeguard against abusive treatment.

Until the end of the eighteenth century, the question of how political prisoners were to be treated did not emerge as a major problem, because no rules prescribed special treatment for any prisoners save debtors. Prisoners had certain legally established rights, such as the right not to be tortured, but the conduct of their daily lives was left to their own determination. Many fewer restrictions were placed on ordinary activities such as seeing visitors, corresponding, speaking with other prisoners, working, and idling. Some restrictions were imposed for security reasons, but what privileges there were, such as special rooms, were allocated to those who could pay for them. Prisoners were not distinguished in any but the roughest fashion by the crime they had committed, and the man of means, whatever his crime, could live like a lord.

The Howardian reforms, however, established classes of prisoners based on the seriousness of the crime they had committed. To some extent the different groups were treated differently; some felons, for example, were sentenced to "hard labor," while each class was lodged separately. Many activities that had formerly been permitted to everyone were now either prohibited or allowed only as privileges for certain classes. It was not until all prisoners were classified in this way that the issue of how to class political prisoners could arise. It was standardization that created the demand for differentiation.

The question of whether political prisoners are entitled to special treatment has caused controversy ever since, partly because it is so difficult to determine just who is a political prisoner. Although by this time in England people were rarely imprisoned for their religious beliefs (apart from some prosecutions for blasphemy and a few other miscellaneous cases), there were several sorts of political prisoners.*

The first group consisted of those held by executive fiat. These were political prisoners pure and simple. With habeas corpus suspended, these men were held on a warrant from the home secretary on suspicion alone, without trial. They were not formally charged with any specific illegal acts, nor were they informed of the grounds on which they were held. The only long-staying Lancashire prisoner in this category, during this period, was John Bagguley, the Blanketeer leader arrested in 1817. There can be no question that he received special and highly privileged treatment.

The second group consisted of those who were publicly tried and convicted of specific acts that were widely acknowledged to be political crimes—in general, the nonviolent expression of opinions dangerous or inimical to the state, such as criminal libel against persons in power, sedition, and seditious conspiracy. (High treason might qualify, but traitors were singled out for special execration.) The Peterloo prisoners, who were held on a bewildering collection of charges—which were reduced at intervals until the men were finally convicted of conspiring to hold an unlawful and seditious assembly—were in this category. They experienced varied but on the whole moderately privileged treatment. This group would later include many Chartists.

The third group, then as now, was the one that caused the most difficulty, because it included those who broke ordinary nonpolitical sanctions in pursuit of political ends. These crimes included nearly all violent acts, such as assault and murder, and more importantly, such illegal acts as riot, unlawful assembly, and tumultuous petitioning. There was also a gray area of activities that were more economically than politically motivated, such as attempting to form a trade union, plug pulling, "turning out" factories, arson, or extortion. Depending on the motive of the perpetrator, these might or might not be called political crimes. The man who quarreled with his neighbor and burned his ricks out of malice, or who joined with friends to throw his enemy in a river, might

---

*The last prisoner of conscience I have found in Lancashire was George Connard, an Oldham painter and Owenite who had been arrested for debt. At his insolvency hearing he was remanded to the Castle because he stated that he did not believe in a future state of punishment (PRO, HO 20/8 pt. 2, Joseph Hume to John Russell, Aug. 27, 1839). This claim, according to legal tradition, rendered Connard's sworn statements useless, because they were not made in the fear of God.

be charged with arson, assault, riot, conspiracy, illegal arming, and even unlawful assembly—but he had clearly not committed a "political" crime.

Everyone seems to have agreed that prisoners in the first two groups— state prisoners committed under the Habeas Corpus Suspension Act and prisoners committed for purely political crimes such as sedition—deserved special treatment. The controversy arose over the third, borderline group, to which the vast majority of "political" prisoners belonged. The radicals held stubbornly to the conviction that such prisoners deserved special treatment, but in general, the authorities disagreed. In their eyes the prisoners were being held not for their opinions but for specific illegal acts and ought to be treated in the same way as everyone else convicted for committing the same acts, with whatever motive.

A list printed in the *Parliamentary Papers* in the summer of 1840 of all prisoners being held for offenses such as libel, sedition, and riot makes it clear that by the early Chartist era prison authorities were drawing a firm line between the comparatively few people sentenced for the "political" offense of seditious conspiracy and the much larger number sentenced for the more common crimes of riot, riotous assembly, or riotous assault. The Kirkdale house of correction held nearly eighty prisoners charged with riot, not counting those released either before or just after trial. With two exceptions (one man convicted of an aggravated offense went to Lancaster, another was in poor health), all these prisoners were treated as ordinary misdemeanants, while six of the seven seditious conspiracy prisoners held in Lancaster and Kirkdale received special privileges, being permitted to purchase whatever they wanted. The one remaining Lancaster prisoner and four more at Preston were probably too poor to take advantage of this and engaged in prison work in return for an allowance.[32]

Along with the issue of the status of political activists, the radicals' presence in the gaols aroused a second debate about the rights of all prisoners. The radicals themselves were often ambivalent about the issues raised by prison reform and "model prisons." The only major figure to question imprisonment as such was William Godwin. Carlile's *Republican* argued that prisons were so poorly run that they were not meeting the standards set for them by Parliament and expected by the public. Hunt testified before a select committee on county rates in 1825 that spending on county gaols could and should be cut by more than half, but he expected the savings to come from the elimination of jobbery and corruption in the provision of food and clothing for prisoners, not from the reduction of commitment rates or a complete overhaul of penal policy. Rather than questioning the idea that prisons could reform their inmates through a well-administered regime, the radicals concentrated on arguing that local corruption was preventing such institutions from doing their job properly.[33]

Despite their ambivalence, the radicals' own prison experiences led them to challenge many of the changes in prison life promulgated by the reformers. In particular, they contested the increasing regimentation of prison life, the requirement that all prisoners work, the use of hard labor, and the introduction of separate confinement. "Have not these unhappy wretches been vitiated in youth, and brought up and educated as culprits?" John Doherty asked himself and his readers. "Will hunger enlarge their minds or the tread-mill purify their morals? What pains have been taken to improve these men's minds? What has been done to convince them that their previous pursuits were injurious to society, disgraceful to themselves, and offensive to God?"[34]

Though the Lancashire radicals frequently complained of the conditions of confinement, the center of the debate was the rights of prisoners to communicate freely: to send and receive information without censorship, interference, or oversight by the gaoler and his staff. Without this right, they argued, the petty corruption and misbehavior of local officials could never be brought to light and poor prison conditions would never have a permanent remedy.

It was inevitable that the political prisoners would be the ones to force this issue. They were, almost by definition, disproportionately anxious to communicate with others, while the content of their communications was especially likely to be obnoxious to the authorities and to seem unlawful and dangerous. Finally, because of their abilities and the fact that they had friends in high places, the radicals were better placed than most prisoners to bring their grievances into public view. In the end, though they won a final battle, they lost the war. Yet their conflict reveals some of the underlying divisions, both local and national, of this period and raises important questions about the balance between freedom and security.

The conflict began in 1812, at a time when Lancaster Castle was already experiencing overcrowding and political disputes among the prisoners. John Higgin himself, like most of the justices who had appointed him, was probably a staunch Tory although not an extreme one. The Rawlinson affair in the summer of 1812—when the self-proclaimed "Burdettites" in the gaol obtained support from radicals in Parliament to publicize scandalous allegations about his administration of the prison—can have done nothing to increase his tolerance for either the radicals or Burdett. Meanwhile, throughout the late spring, summer, and fall, Luddites trickled into the prison. Higgin loathed their opinions and made his feelings clear to them. Moreover, he enthusiastically undertook the role of government informer. In the summer of 1812 he passed a number of "communications" from a prisoner named Smith to W. R. Hay, chairman of the Salford Quarter Sessions, a great collector of information who was later to be the chief adviser to the Peterloo committee of justices.[35]

In November Higgin wrote the Home Office directly, saying that he had discovered a "union" among the Luddites that had led him to watch their correspondence closely. He enclosed extracts from their letters that revealed "a Connexion with persons raised above poverty though perhaps not placed in very affluent Circumstances, but possessing fair Education. . . . No doubt remains on my mind that Sir F. Burdett and Major Cartwright were well aware what was going on in the Neighbourhood of Manchester etc. and the various information which my official station has enabled me to connect has impressed on my mind a firm conviction that the late rebellious state of this county and of Yorkshire etc. may chiefly be attributed to the written addresses and inflammatory Harangues of those Persons."[36]

Among the passages Higgin enclosed were several written by John Knight. One of them, to his wife, suggests the way in which Higgin spoke to his charges: "Soon after our arrival here we had the audacity to petition to be indulged with a Newspaper at our own Expence—on which occasion our Governour told us the Bible would suit us better and be more useful to us and with which our Dayroom was furnished."[37] At the time, Knight accepted this rebuff, consoling himself by citing biblical condemnation of the oppression of the poor, but in the future this question of newspaper reading would be a perpetual bone of contention.

It was one of Knight's co-conspirators in 1820, John Adamson, who unintentionally precipitated a major conflict over the issue in Lancaster Castle when he sent an indignant letter to his sister about their trial.

"Look how the Iseralits was oppressed," he wrote, "but nothing to the Oppression of the Presant day—Look at our workhouses Look at our Goals—look at our streets—Rags and wretchedness is the industrious Poor mans Companion—O God when wilt thou hear the Crys of the oppressed. . . . Exodus 2 Ch. 23 to 25 and it came to Pass, In Process of time that the King died and the People sighed by reason of their Bondage."[38]

Despite the evidence that Adamson had been applying himself to the Bible provided for him, Higgin found his letter disturbing enough to take it to the Lonsdale magistrates. The justices, after stating that several such "Letters of seditious, inflammatory and blasphemous tendency" had been written by the prisoners to their friends and then made public, resolved to order the gaoler to prohibit all such correspondence. They also inquired of the Home Office to what extent the magistrates ought to allow letters from political prisoners on misdemeanor charges. Sidmouth's answer apparently favored the magistrates, as Higgin thereafter became even more energetic in censuring and censoring the correspondence of the men whose opinions he detested and whose letters sometimes contained invidious references to himself.[39]

Meanwhile, the radicals began to complain bitterly about their treatment. They objected to being compelled to work on pain of starvation. The Quarter Sessions had authorized the gaoler to punish all felons and misdemeanants before or after trial who refused to work or who worked in a "slovenly or improper manner" by placing them in solitary confinement, withdrawing their allowance of food, or deducting a part of their earnings (although in practice no prisoners were compelled to work before trial). Convicted prisoners who refused to work lost part of their allowances unless they could afford to maintain themselves, in which case the whole allowance was withdrawn.[40] The political prisoners objected to this rule, claiming they had special status. They further complained that Higgin had banned radical newspapers from the gaol.

The man to whom they complained was George Williams, a former soldier and a dedicated radical who had somehow been appointed to the West Derby bench in 1809 and who remained persistently out of tune with his fellow magistrates. The mayor of Liverpool, where Williams three times ran for Parliament with a complete lack of success, described him with disgust as one of those "who are always gratified in having . . . opportunities of making inflammatory speeches to the lower Orders."

He finally entered Parliament in 1832, sitting for three years as the Liberal MP for Ashton under Lyme.*

On June 10, 1820, Williams wrote Higgin that he had received a letter from Nathan Broadhurst complaining that the political misdemeanants were being forced to work and that their newspapers had been confiscated. He claimed that both practices were illegal and added that he was himself sending a newspaper to Broadhurst. Higgin confiscated the paper and cut off the allowances of those prisoners who refused to work, asking his son to write Williams announcing his actions. On June 17 Williams sent an angrier letter to Higgin. Thomas Higgin, he wrote, had pointed out that the stoppage of the newspaper was common in many prisons. Williams, however, would "look to no Precedent or Example, those things complained of are either lawful or unlawful, and right or wrong accordingly—if any Act of Parliament confers a Power on Justices to make Regulations for Prisons, those Regulations I conceive must be in the *spirit of English Law*, or they are not justified in making them, or who knows what solitary Confinement, Fetters or Torture, may not become with some persons, and towards certain offences, wholesome discipline."[41]

Williams was mistaken about what the "spirit of English law" would permit. The censoring of prisoners' mail was an ancient practice. Moreover, the justices of the peace submitted regulations to Assize judges in order to make sure that they were in conformity with the law. Although torture was illegal, both fettering and solitary confinement were accepted, both by law and by precedent, as "wholesome discipline." The "spirit of English law" was not, in fact, heavily weighted in favor of prisoners; once convicted of a crime, inmates, in legal theory, lost most of their rights, while convicted felons lost even their right to life. One can-

*PRO, HO 42/167, John Wright, mayor of Liverpool, to Sidmouth, June 18, 1817. For Williams see William Wardell Bean, *The Parliamentary Representation of the Six Northern Counties of England, 1603-1886* (Hull, 1890). Williams joined the army under Burgoyne at the age of twelve, leaving in 1800 after 25 years of service all over the world. In August 1803 Williams was "drafted" as lieutenant-colonel-commander of the Second Liverpool Volunteers. He was a member of the radical Liverpool Concentric Society. In his 1818 campaign for Parliament he gained only two votes, while the two winners received over fourteen thousand each. He was always active on the bench. A teetotaler, he served on the "Drunken Committee" in Parliament. He was still on the bench in 1848. See Robert Walmsley, *Peterloo: The Case Reopened* (Manchester, 1969); Barbara Wittingham-Jones, "Liverpool's Political Clubs, 1812-1830," *Transactions of the Lancashire and Cheshire Historical Society* 111 (1959): 117-38; Brian Harrison, "Two Roads to Social Reform: Francis Place and the 'Drunken Committee' of 1834," *Historical Journal* 11 (1968): 272-300.

not easily argue that the legal trend in this period was toward increasing prisoners' rights.

Williams was assuming the old radical position that something in the spirit of the constitution protected the subjects' rights against infringement, even when that infringement was permitted by Parliament. It is not clear, however, that prisoners counted as subjects since, like children, madmen, and married women, they suffered special restrictions in their legal rights. In any case, by the time Williams wrote his letter, concern that civil rights be extended to prisoners was being replaced by the desire for more effective prison discipline.

Goaded by Williams's attacks, the justices submitted the case to two northern circuit barristers: Scarlett and Starkie. Both men had helped prosecute Broadhurst and Knight; Scarlett had also led the prosecution against the Peterloo speakers, for which Hunt never forgave him. Scarlett was, however, a liberal who had joined with Henry Brougham and John Williams to defend the Luddites in 1812. He had been a close friend of Romilly's and had supported his campaign to abolish many capital statutes. Many of his associates were prison, as well as law, reformers. He was, therefore, well qualified to judge the magistrates' case. Although Starkie's answers were lost, William Hulton preserved Scarlett's.[42]

The justices had set three questions: could they withdraw food and clothing from convicted persons refusing to work? Could they ban newspapers and political publications from prisons? And, did the gaoler have the power to read prisoners' correspondence? Scarlett's advice was such as might have been expected from a liberal barrister. He agreed that the magistrates had all these powers—although in the case of newspapers his agreement was very grudging. He strongly advised that the justices act with restraint and discretion. Starkie's opinion was apparently more favorable, for Thomas Higgin lost no time in putting it into Williams's hands.

Williams immediately wrote again to Broadhurst, stating that he placed no reliance on the opinions of counsel. Although there was little he could do to alter the situation, he hoped that "the Reformers, who with the Courage of Martyrs, devote themselves to their Country," might someday see how " 'Seat Sellers,' and 'Seat Buyers' in adversity, may be trusted in a solitary cell," and how "the black Catalogue of Traitors, under the several Denominations of Spies, Instigators, Blood-money Men, and their Employers, how Murderers who have hitherto eluded Justice—may deport themselves in Solitude and Imprisonment, *begnawn* by their Consciences."[43]

To Williams's dismay, Higgin, availing himself of his newly confirmed powers, promptly impounded this letter. At about the same time, he brought suit against Williams for a libel contained in another letter, no longer extant, to John Doherty. Considering the violence of Williams's language, and particularly the veiled reference to the Peterloo officers in "Murderers who have hitherto eluded Justice," it is no wonder that relations between Williams and his brother justices were somewhat strained.

On August 8 the Annual General Session met in Preston. It provided Higgin with retroactive vindication, ordering him to withhold all newspapers and political publications sent to the Crown side of the gaol. Higgin was also ordered to open and read all letters to or from the Crown prisoners, except for letters between prisoners awaiting trial and their attorneys, and to detain those that seemed improper. The court then heard Williams's letters but deferred consideration of them until he was present. It also ordered that the letters be printed and that copies be sent to Williams and to every other justice in the county. William Hulton seems to have been chiefly responsible for the court's actions. Perhaps he was stung by Williams's contemptuous reference to Peterloo, since Hulton had initiated the attack of the military.

On August 22 the Session again met to consider the issue. Attendance was unusually high—37 justices from all over the county—though the size of the meeting may have been due to the fact that the court was also making appointments for the Kirkdale house of correction; meetings for choosing officers always drew large numbers. Five members of the Peterloo Committee of Nine were present, as well as W. R. Hay, who had advised them. Edward Bootle Wilbraham, a Tory MP and the chief defender of Peterloo in the House of Commons, was also there, but he was a frequent attender and would have come in any case to represent the Kirkdale justices. The court issued and printed a unanimous resolution that Williams's letters to Broadhurst were "peculiarly calculated to destroy all Discipline . . . and are insulting to the Magistrates of the County." Higgin, they said, "exercised a sound and commendable Discretion in withholding" them.[44]

The irrepressible Williams, however, decided to carry the war into a new arena. After an unsuccessful attempt to interest Sidmouth at the Home Office in his case, he brought his son-in-law, W. James, MP for

Liverpool, into the act. In January 1822 James wrote Broadhurst that he believed he, Broadhurst, had been "very harshly and cruelly treated, if I may not say unjustly." He enclosed £5 as a token of his sympathy and wrote a cover letter to Higgin ordering him not to open the letter to Broadhurst since it was a breach of parliamentary privilege to open members' letters.[45] Higgin did open the letter, and James announced a motion in the House of Commons relative to a breach of privilege. The news elicited a small flurry of anxious letters from Lancashire to the Home Office. Among them was a letter from Thomas Higgin pointing out that the rule permitting the opening of letters was in Justice Bayley's own hand and had been drawn up after consultation with the lord chief justice and the lord chief baron. He explained that the rule had been made in the first place in order to have other means of maintaining security than putting the prisoners in irons. Thomas enclosed a letter from his father, who had lost his temper completely:

The practice of inspecting the Letters of persons confined on the criminal side of the Gaol had been uniformly enforced to his knowledge, upwards of forty three years, especially against suspicious persons. . . . No Complaint was ever made to any of the Judges, or Magistrates, before the Demagogue Radicals came here. They have been no little annoyed by the *wholesome restrictions*, because they have not had free scope for their seditious and almost treasonable Expressions used in their Correspondence, even with some Members who, ought to be ashamed of the Encouragement given to desperate Characters, who, under the pretence of Reform seek to Ruin their Country.[46]

James's motion was debated in the House of Commons on February 25. The debate centered on two issues. The first was the magistrates' power to make regulations for prisons. Could they control every aspect of prison life, or only such areas as food and clothing? Did the approval of two Assize judges establish the presumptive legality of the regulations? If the regulations were legal, yet clashed with parliamentary privilege, which ought to prevail? Several members expressed a fear that, in James's words, the House would recognize "two different legislatures; one composed of both Houses of parliament, with the king at their head, and the other composed of judges, magistrates and gaolers."[47]

The second issue was whether Parliament needed to provide prisoners with direct recourse to members. Several speakers brought up the case of Ilchester, expressing a good deal of mistrust about the willingness of justices to deal with prison abuses. They argued that if prisoners had complaints to make, they were entitled to appeal to MPs. If the gaoler could read every letter and if parliamentary privilege could not protect letters to members from censorship, then the gaoler could effectively stifle all public criticism, while the justices could not be trusted to remove the grievance. Brougham spoke in support of James's motion while three Lancashire men—Lord Stanley, Peel, and Samuel Horrocks—spoke against it. When the question was put, it was defeated by a vote of 167 to 60. Although he had raised serious issues, Williams had not succeeded in making Lancaster into a second Ilchester.

Meanwhile, Williams was arrested on the libel charge brought by Higgin. He stood trial at the Lent Assizes on March 23, 1822, and was acquitted.[48] There the matter lay, with the honors roughly divided. The issue, however, and the resentments it had created, did not die. Neither the magistrates nor the radicals forgot the battle. In 1826 the Annual General Session ruled that prisoners might see friends only once in three months. The court also repeated its order that the gaolers prohibit "immoral, seditious, indecent or blasphemous publications," or any others that were "grossly libellous or exciting prisoners to Insubordination or wicked or immoral conduct." It ordered the gaoler to read all letters to and from prisoners, except those of debtors, and to hold back any letter containing improper material. With the chaplain's approval, the gaoler might read the unobjectionable parts of the letter to the prisoner, or explain the objections so that another might be written.

The practice of the prison had withstood every attack. In fact, it had become even more restrictive; henceforth, the gaoler was to bowdlerize mail in accordance with the most fastidious moral code, as well as engage in political censorship. Higgin's successor, for example, confiscated letters from common-law wives. Moreover, similar censorship was being exercised in Lancashire's other prisons, although newspapers soon reappeared. The political attacks of the radicals merely entrenched the prison administrators in a sort of defensive severity that, combined with Victorian censoriousness, resulted in a substantial loss of free speech and expression for the prisoners.

The issue revived in the tense year of 1832, when Nathan Broadhurst, Knight's co-defendant of 1819, returned to the Castle, charged with seditious conspiracy and attendance at an illegal meeting. He had been arrested in London, where he had gone to testify for Henry Hunt, now MP for Preston, in a libel case Hunt had brought against the *Times*. Ten days after the Assizes, on March 27, Hunt presented a petition to Parliament from Broadhurst and three fellow prisoners complaining of their treatment in the Castle. At first they had been given the gaol allowance, but "in consequence of their being unable to do the work assigned to them," they were ordered to find their own food and fuel.[49] Hunt himself complained that Higgin had opened his letters.

As is so often the case in the field of penal policy, the debaters proceeded in complete ignorance of what had been said and done in the past. This time, however, the conflict ended in an indirect victory for the radicals, when a complaint from the debtors paralleled the ones made by the Crown prisoners. On April 4, only a week after the first petition, Hunt presented one from the debtors complaining of Higgin's nonresidence in the Castle. Higgin was, indeed, not living in the Castle and by this time had handed over many of his duties to his son Thomas, although Thomas also had a cotton manufacturing business to oversee. John Higgin had tried but failed to persuade the justices to make Thomas gaoler in his place. He then attempted to bring Thomas in through the back door: John remained the nominal gaoler, but it was Thomas who did much of the work.

However reluctant the justices were to appoint Thomas as gaoler, they winked at the arrangement by which he carried out most of the routine duties at the Castle with his father's advice. When, however, the gaoler's nonresidence was publicly brought to the justices' attention, a committee headed by Edmund Hornby concluded that he ought to live in the Castle. Higgin promised to do so, but while he slept in the Castle, he continued to maintain another house in his son's name. The debtors, led by S. G. Anderton, concluded that they could get no satisfaction from the visiting justices and petitioned Parliament, complaining not only of the nonresidence but also that Thomas had a conflict of interest since his business was a creditor of some of the gaoled debtors. Anderton added that Thomas was embezzling bread shipments and illegally confining complaining debtors in solitary. Commons ordered that the petition be printed, and when the Annual General Session met in September, it agreed that Anderton should send his charges in writing to the visiting justices.[50]

One week later, the *Preston Chronicle* published an open letter from Anderton to John Higgin containing twenty charges. In January Higgin, admitting at least some of the charges by default, resigned. Even the Whiggish *Preston Chronicle* proved sympathetic to him, quoting with approval the comment in the *Lancaster Gazette* that "in no gaol in England has there been better order and regularity observed than this, . . .

owing to the judicious and excellent arrangements of Mr. Higgin and his son."[51] Since John was at this time about 72, he would probably have had to resign soon in any case, although he lived until 1847. He may have resigned simply because he was too old and weary to endure yet another confrontation. A new gaoler, James Hansbrow—like John Higgin a captain in the militia—was soon appointed, apparently without much disagreement.

Although Higgin was forced out of office, it was clear that by mid-century the political prisoners had lost the greater war. By then it had become regular practice to treat political activists charged with such "ordinary" crimes as riot like ordinary prisoners, although prisoners held for sedition still received special treatment. Even they were to some extent hampered by the increasing number of prison regulations. During the controversy, however, the radicals had raised important questions about the lawfulness of prison administration and about the "inalienable" rights of the prisoner that applied to all gaoled criminals.

The parliamentary debates over these issues centered on two questions. First, could prisoners who refused to work be deprived of their food allowances? Second, could the gaoler, with the permission of the magistrates, read and censor correspondence? Neither question applied to political prisoners alone, and ordinarily such problems, though important, would have been normal issues of prison administration to be settled in a routine way. However, because of the extraordinary political bitterness of the period, because those who raised these issues were political prisoners, and because those who supported them in Parliament stood to gain a great deal if the government could be embarrassed over its treatment of prisoners, they became political issues. Time and again they were confused with the question of whether the political prisoners should ever have been arrested at all, or whether, once convicted, they were entitled to special treatment. No one ever forgot that the fall of a Paris prison had symbolized a revolution.

Two of the "ex-cons" in the House, Hunt and Burdett, were especially successful in questioning the treatment of all prisoners, whatever their crimes. These two men had been convicted for political crimes, but once in gaol, they soon became concerned about the whole system of legal coercion and about what they saw as repressive administration. Both men, at various times in the parliamentary debates, drew attention to the unchecked supremacy of the magistrates, claiming that the justices systematically violated fundamental rights of the prisoners under their care. The focus of the debate, therefore, kept shifting between the wisdom of trusting a politically biased magistracy to safeguard the rights of political prisoners and the wisdom of entrusting a socially biased magistracy with prisoners at all.

During this period there were some checks on the conduct of the magistracy. The Assize judges passed on the legality of their regulations for the prisons, a duty that the judges took very seriously, and from time to time they used this power to control general policy. The Home Office, although it snubbed Williams, did exercise a general supervision of the justices' conduct, often demanding reports or explanations about particular charges. Finally, Parliament also debated the justices' conduct and sometimes ordered investigations if it suspected that they were not doing their job.

Moreover, all these issues were debated in the open, in the full glare of intense publicity both in London and in the county. John Higgin, who repeatedly found himself sucked into political controversy, became bitter about the constant inquisitions he endured. A mild, quietly disposed, and sensitive man who disliked quarrels, he spent most of his official life in a storm. That it was often only a tempest in a teacup did nothing to allay his dislike of the men who had conjured it up.

Though the radicals used the openness of the system to stir up controversy, it was that very openness that they were struggling to preserve. Step by step, the prison was withdrawing from the community. Prisoners were more and more isolated not only from each other but from the world outside the walls. Visits were restricted and wives banished. The introduction of prison food and prison dress cut down on contacts with the outside world, as prisoners ceased to barter for supplies and became increasingly identifiable by diet and dress as a race apart. The development of prison labor eliminated commercial contacts.

Partly for their own purposes, the radicals fought to keep the prisons open. They wished prisoners to be free not only to read and write as they pleased but also to complain about their treatment without fear of intimidation. In many other fields the radicals had battled over freedom of speech, of the press, and of petition, so it is not surprising that, when convicted, they carried the battle into the prisons. In the case of prisons, however, the trend was against them and they were repeatedly defeated. Gaolers gained complete control over every point of contact between the inmates and the outside world. This development, in turn, deprived the prisoners of an important protection against mistreatment. "How are we to make our complaint known to the magistrates?" New Bailey prisoners asked John Doherty when he heard that the keeper was cheating them of bread and refusing them writing paper. "Suppose he refuses to inform the magistrates that we want them, what then, will he be punished? . . . How is it to become known?"[52]

In a sense, the radicals were defeated by their own success at agitation. The rules permitting the Lancaster gaoler to superintend correspondence were well established. They might, however, have been relaxed in time if the radicals had not produced papers that simultaneously complained of the restrictions on their speech and criticized the conduct of the magistrates in the most violent terms. The justices, who naturally saw no reason to relax the regulations in order to promote criticism of themselves, dug in their heels and passed increasingly restrictive rules. As a result, censorship in all the prisons increased. Although enforcement varied, the precedent was established. To this day, British prison letters are censored, or their delivery stopped, for the most trivial reasons. Not even petitions to members of Parliament can pass through the prisons unread. Letters to the press, though often smuggled out, are still officially prohibited.

There was another paradoxical reason for the ultimate failure of the radicals. This was their success in using prison affairs as a weapon against the magistracy as an administrative body. The successive investigations into prison management conducted by or for Parliament began to erode public confidence in the county justices, and subsequent events did little to restore it. The radicals were particularly effective in drawing attention to the justices' financial maladministration. Meanwhile, the "philosophic radicals" undermined confidence in the justices' commitment to administrative reform. The combined attack proved devastating and, over the next half-century, the justices lost more and more power to the Home Office. It is questionable whether this process resulted in either more efficiency or more "reform" in the county prisons, although the first step, the appointment of inspectors, was an undeniable improvement. Ultimately, centralization meant a loss of local accountability. The magistrates were guilty of many sins, but at least they often met in public and saw their decisions debated publicly in the local press. Moreover, although they themselves were often remote, they were still less likely than were civil servants in London to be entirely cut off from personal contact with their charges, or from personal experience of the practical problems of running individual prisons.

When Anderton petitioned the visiting justices, he could print his charges in the local press and force Higgin to resign. No such scrutiny could be turned on the secretive Home Office. As the power to make decisions was removed to a central office, local people lost their sense that they had a special interest in local prisons run by a resident gentry. The national newspapers, though continuing to cover issues of prison policy as well as the great scandals, could not pay the sort of constant attention to small administrative problems that the local press provided, while hundreds of local newspapers could not be regularly read and consulted in London, where the decisions were now made.

When people lose the power to discuss and influence decisions made about an institution, they often lose interest in the institution altogether. English prisons are unique in the extent to which administrative decisions are made by the central government. When the prison administrators ceased to be accountable to their own communities, an important check was lost on their activities. Though the prison inspectors continued to issue reports, the reports were probably read less widely. Moreover, through an accident of British law, the central government obtained powers of stifling criticism that the local rulers had never possessed; under the Official Secrets Act it became illegal for civil servants, including the humblest prison guard, to discuss any aspect of their work. As a result, English prisons have never again been as open to scrutiny, or as subject to debate, as they were in the early nineteenth century.

Many prison officials would argue that the restriction of free speech is a good thing; prison staff need some protection against disruption and false or malicious public accusations. Without such protection, able candidates would be deterred from entering the prison service and good officers might be unjustly pilloried by the press.

The experience of the Napoleonic period, however, suggests that a more open policy holds real advantages. The political prisoners of that period were certainly disruptive in the extreme. They did everything in their power to make life difficult in the prisons. They refused to cooperate, sometimes to the extent of staying in bed, slung accusations with great enthusiasm, and frequently used slanderous language to infuriate and provoke. They created constant uproar in the prisons and promoted innumerable inquisitions into the conduct of gaol officers for their own political ends. They also, however, forced debate on issues that desperately needed airing. They questioned the whole basis of authority in the countryside and cast doubt on the justices' competence and fairness. They brought up fundamental questions of penal theory and personal rights; at this time they were almost the only group to question the use of solitary confinement or to maintain that the "spirit of English law" prohibited not merely cruelty but also the infringement of prisoners' rights. They compelled magistrates to account for their actions in Parliament, and in many prisons, such as Coldbath Fields, Ilchester, and Dorchester, they brought about the correction of very serious abuses, such as the use of frequent floggings. Although the cards were stacked in favor of the authorities, the radicals succeeded in discrediting several cruel or incompetent men. Doherty was as good as his word when he promised complaining prisoners in the New Bailey that "the system should at any rate be exposed, if it could not be mitigated."[53] Despite the trouble their relentless criticism caused, the radicals served as badly needed prisoners' advocates behind an iron curtain maintained by increasingly autocratic governors.

# CHAPTER 6

# Paying for Prisons: County Finance and Administration, 1776-1850

*The Rising Rates, 1776-1830*

The pace of prison reform depended on the willingness of ratepayers to accept its cost, a factor that could not be taken for granted. One of the great unsolved questions of the history of this period is how the English government, at all levels, managed to raise the revenue to cover rapidly increasing expenditure in a period of generally straitened circumstances. The story of the French fiscal crisis and the role it played in the fall of the ancien régime is well known, but the fact that England faced similar financial problems has not received sufficient attention, although Peter Mathias has found that English taxation was high compared with that of France, and during the Napoleonic wars was three times the French level.[1]

At the same time that Cobbett was writing that "the *cause* of our present miseries . . . is the *enormous amount of the taxes,* which the government compels us to pay for the support of its army, its placemen, its pensioners etc. and for the payment of the interest of its debt," that Orator Hunt was proclaiming that "everything they ate, drank, wore, and even said, [was] taxed," and that Bamford was explaining to the Privy Council that land taxes hurt the poor by raising the price of bread, county rates were also rocketing.[2] This movement was largely concealed behind the growth of the poor rates; under the provisions of the County Rate Consolidation Act of 1739, the churchwardens and overseers of the poor collected the county and poor rates together, handing the county's share to the high constables. In their collections they merely demanded

AMOUNT (000 POUNDS)

1785    1790    1795    1800    1805    1810    1815

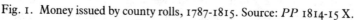

Fig. 1. Money issued by county rolls, 1787-1815. Source: *PP* 1814-15 X.

the total sum owed, without distinguishing to the taxpayers how much went to the poor and how much to other local expenditure.[3]

Because the poor rates were so large, ratepayers took many years to realize that the county budgets were rising much faster than even the poor rates, although the justices who superintended the spending of the money were well aware of the problem. After 1800 the increase accelerated. By 1825 national concern had led to the formation of a parliamentary Select Committee on the Expenditure of County Rates. The committee found that the rates were rising chiefly because of a combination of increased prosecution rates and new prison building to hold the growing number of convicts. In the counties making returns to the committee, prosecution costs had risen from £3,977 in 1792 to £76,647 in 1823.[4]

TABLE 8

Percentage Cost of Categories of Expenditure, County Only,
Selected Periods, 1744-1850

| Object of expenditure | 1744-49 | 1787-88 | 1800-1801 | 1810-11 | 1821 | 1841-50 |
|---|---|---|---|---|---|---|
| L.C. repairs | 16% | — | 0.2% | 2.8% | 11.0% | 16.3% |
| L.C. improvements | — | 11.7% | 16.0 | 4.6 | — | — |
| L.C. prisoners | 10 | 28.9 | 11.0 | 9.2 | 6.9 | — |
| L.C. salaries (incl. county treas.) | — | 5.4 | 3.8 | 6.3 | 5.0 | 1.8 |
| Taking offenders to gaol | — | 6.4 | 11.2 | 7.3 | 10.2 | 5.5 |
| Vagrants | 52 | 21.1 | 8.8 | 6.9 | 12.3 | 2.0 |
| Coroners | — | 7.0 | 2.9 | 3.6 | 3.3 | 7.3 |
| Corn inspectors, etc. | — | 0.4 | 1.2 | 0.4 | 1.8 | 3.6 |
| Bridges | 4 | 0.3 | 4.2 | 1.5 | — | — |
| Militia, etc. | 12 | — | — | — | 0.8 | — |
| Militia families | — | — | 14.4 | 32.3 | — | — |
| Riots | — | — | — | — | 4.8 | — |
| Prosecution of felons | — | 13.2 | 22.3 | 22.2 | 38.0 | 40.2 |
| Lunatics' maintenance | — | — | — | — | 1.7 | 6.3 |
| Crown prisoners in Kirkdale | — | — | — | — | — | 6.8 |
| Misc. | 6 | 2.5 | 3.9 | 2.5 | 3.8 | 10.1 |
| TOTAL | 100% | 96.9% | 99.9% | 99.6% | 99.6% | 99.9% |
| Total for Lancaster Castle, including salaries | 26% | 46.0% | 31.0% | 22.9% | 22.9% | 18.1% |

Because of Lancashire's rapid growth during this period, these developments were even more pronounced there than in England as a whole. The amount collected by county rolls went from about £1,000 a year in the mid-eighteenth century to more than £4,000 by 1787 and £30,000 by 1815 (see Fig. 1). Five years later it had risen to £47,000. Expenditure on the Castle and its prisoners rarely took less than a fifth of the total collected by county rolls; in 1787 repairs, improvements, prisoners, and county salaries (most of which went to the Castle gaoler, chaplain, and surgeon) took nearly half (46 percent) of the total. In only one year of those listed in Table 8 did the combined costs of the Castle and the prosecution of offenders take less than half the total. By 1796, according to the deputy county clerk, about £26,000 had been spent on the Castle construction.[5] A second spurt of building at the gaol between 1814 and

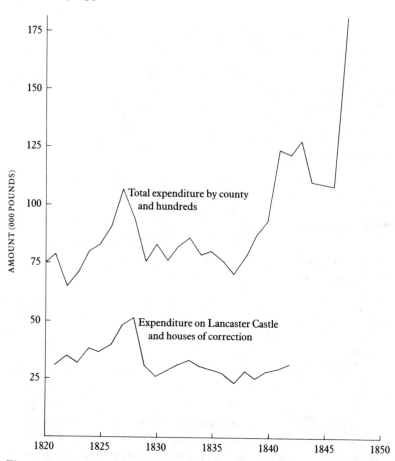

Fig. 2. Total county and hundred expenditure compared with expenditure on Lancaster Castle and the hundred houses of correction, 1820-1847. Sources: *PP* 1850 XIII; Robert Hindle, *An Account of the Expenditure of the County Palatine of Lancaster for a Period of 23 Years . . . with Remarks* (London, 1843).

1823 helped account for part, but not all, of the great rise in expenditure in those years. After that, as new items such as the care of lunatics and the county constabulary appeared on the budget, the Castle took a smaller proportion.

This, however, is only a small part of the story. Because of Lanca-

TABLE 9

*Expenditures of County and Hundreds, 1820-1842*

| Object of expenditure | Percent of total expenditure | Amount (000) |
|---|---|---|
| Prisons | 38.7% | £763.9 |
| Prosecutions | 19.6 | 387.4 |
| County and private lunatic asylums | 11.1 | 219.4 |
| Bridges | 10.2 | 202.0 |
| Conducting offenders to prison | 4.3 | 85.9 |
| County constabulary | 3.5 | 70.0 |
| Coroners | 2.4 | 47.8 |
| Passing vagrants | 2.4 | 47.7 |
| Law expenses | 1.3 | 24.9 |
| Inspectors of weights and measures | 1.0 | 20.7 |
| Riots | 1.0 | 19.3 |
| Miscellaneous | 4.3 | 84.5 |
| TOTAL | 99.8% | £1,973.5 |

shire's peculiar method of allocating expenditure among the hundreds, many items that were included in the budgets of other counties, such as the houses of correction, were accounted for separately and did not appear in the county budget. By 1820 total county and hundred spending on items usually included in county budgets elsewhere had reached £75,000 a year. It would rise to £180,000 a year in 1847 (see Fig. 2). The county houses of correction and Lancaster Castle combined took between a quarter and a half annually of this larger sum (see Table 9). This sum, in turn, was roughly a quarter of the gross total collected for the poor rates, which had risen from about £80,000 a year in 1785 to a peak of about £560,000 in 1818. After 1818 the amount spent on the poor fell, while total county and hundred expenditure continued to rise.[6] In 1828, a peak year of prison spending, the cost of the Castle and the houses of correction alone amounted to over £50,000, or more than a tenth of the total Poor Law assessment of just under £500,000.

Although the county officers and the justices of the peace must have known what was happening, the county budget was not widely publicized and ratepayers for the most part remained ignorant of this element in their poor rate assessments until a few radical critics, assisted by the *Preston Chronicle*, began to campaign about this issue in the 1830's.

## The Incidence of Rates and the Reassessments

By the end of the eighteenth century, the greater responsibility and work entailed by the rapid increase in prosecutions and the expansion of county expenditure were creating serious strains in Lancashire's government. Amateur justices began to find it difficult to cope even with routine business, particularly in those areas where there were few gentlemen qualified to serve and a rapidly rising industrial population. Tradition forbade the appointment to the bench of anyone connected with "trade," and the work was so arduous that the few gentlemen living nearby were reluctant to act.[7]

The turn of the century saw a serious crisis in Lancashire's government. The first casualty of the rise in prosecutions was the Sheriff's Board, which the growing business of the Assizes made impossible. Deprived of a central decision-making body at just the time when their need of it was increasing, and harassed by their growing responsibilities, the justices fell to quarreling among themselves. The overworked magistrates of the southern half of the county, who had always resented having to make the long trip up to Lancaster, demanded an annual meeting in Preston to debate and settle all general county business. The Lonsdale justices, jealous of Lancaster's privileges as the county town, resisted fiercely.[8]

In 1795 the Lancaster justices finally forced the issue by dismissing the county treasurer. After an attempt at reconciliation failed, the three southern benches agreed to bring a bill into Parliament providing for an annual meeting to transact county business at Preston. Despite the efforts of the Lonsdale justices, the bill became law in 1798 as the Lancashire Sessions Act. Thereafter, county business was transacted at Preston by the Annual General Session, attended by all the Lancashire justices who chose to come. A formal meeting in June received reports and accounts; these were then published and a second meeting in September discussed them and made resolutions.[9]

The crisis did not end with the passage of the Sessions Act. The regional divisiveness that had developed during the bitter struggle over its passage made the rural justices especially sensitive to the way county expenditure was rising and to the unequal way the rates were apportioned. In the hard year of 1801, when spending reached a sharp peak, the justices went so far as to prepare a case in support of an act of Parliament to reassess the entire county, but then times improved, spending declined again, and the discontent temporarily subsided.[10]

It is no wonder that ratepayers were dissatisfied with an assessment unchanged for nearly two hundred years; the question is why widespread resistance did not appear earlier. By 1800 the incidence of rates had become extremely capricious; the thinly populated rural areas of the north were paying many times the assessment of the large industrial complexes that had grown up in the south. Several Lancashire parishes had become so small in the intervening years that they regularly paid more to the county rate than they did to support their own poor.[11]

Local observers agreed that the rates fell on the land, although it was the cities that were responsible for many of the problems that created expenditure, particularly a high crime rate. In this period the bench overwhelmingly represented landowning rather than mercantile or professional interests, and the overtaxed, lightly populated rural areas were disproportionately represented since they were more suitable for gentlemen's seats. Although the precise incidence of the rates cannot be determined, it seems that the great expansion of the county rates at the turn of the century and the extensive building programs were supported by the very men whose estates bore a disproportionate part of the costs, paid either from their own pockets or from those of their tenants. Until 1815 the antiquated rating system prevented any attempt to tap the new industrial and commercial wealth springing up around them. It is difficult to understand how the county managed to sustain the increase of services and facilities provided during these years, particularly since the wars, the income tax, and the poor rates were placing taxpayers under considerable strain.[12]

Part of the answer no doubt lies in the fact that landlords also benefited from the Industrial Revolution. Several Lancashire estates developed profitable collieries, while many were able to market their produce to the large new urban markets. The price of corn more or less kept pace with the rises in money wages. It is also true that inflation made the real rises in the rates a good deal smaller than their pound totals. Nevertheless, many Lancashire estates were ill placed to take advantage of such opportunities; in general, Lancashire's farms were small, unproductive, and inefficiently run. As a result, throughout the period, Lancashire became more and more dependent on imported corn. The harvests were extremely poor in 1792 and 1795 and from 1798 to 1800. Because of the

TABLE 10

*Percentages Paid by the Hundreds to a County Rate, 1739-1841*

| Hundred | 1739, Pct. | 1815 Amount (000) | 1815 Pct. | 1829 Amount (000) | 1829 Pct. | 1841 Amount (000) | 1841 Pct. |
|---|---|---|---|---|---|---|---|
| Lonsdale | 16% | £278.2 | 9% | £282.4 | 7% | £302.0 | 5% |
| Amonderness | 19 | 258.1 | 8 | 295.0 | 7 | 364.5 | 6 |
| Blackburn | 18 | 278.9 | 9 | 373.9 | 9 | 497.5 | 8 |
| Leyland | 9 | 171.1 | 5 | 172.3 | 4 | 199.9 | 3 |
| Salford | 14 | 918.4 | 30 | 1,554.3 | 37 | 2,703.3 | 44 |
| West Derby | 24 | 1,201.4 | 39 | 1,536.7 | 36 | 2,124.9 | 34 |
| TOTAL | 100% | £3,106.1 | 100% | £4,214.6 | 100% | £6,192.1 | 100% |

wet climate and poor soil, oats, never popular with urban workers, were the largest crop. Farm labor was scarce and became scarcer as the war and industrial opportunities pulled men away.[13]

Though it is easy to understand why the rural justices and the ratepayers they represented might have felt aggrieved by the beginning of the nineteenth century, it seems odd that Liverpool—by common consent the most under-rated community in Lancashire—was the place that chose to force the issue. Whatever the reason, in 1807 the borough refused to contribute to the county rate on the grounds that the county assessments were unequal.[14] Prodded into action at last, the county again resolved to bring a bill into Parliament for a new county assessment. It was forestalled, however, by a national act of 1815 establishing a pound rating system.[15] Almost immediately, Lancashire carried out its first general assessment in nearly two hundred years, basing it on receipts and rents from 1812. This assessment greatly increased the contribution of the industrial south. By 1827 Liverpool was protesting that it had been over-rated, and its appeal forced a second valuation in 1829. The further valuations that took place in 1840 and 1852 steadily increased the contribution of Salford and lowered that of the northern hundreds (see Table 10).[16]

The southern manufacturers who were beginning to trickle onto the bench in some numbers by the 1830's, as the exclusionary policy of the government broke down under pressure, never looked favorably on these new rates.[17] Owing to a legislative anomaly, the act establishing the county rate assessment required that valuations be based on the full, or gross, income of the properties concerned, while the assessments for the poor rate were made upon net income, after insurance, repairs, and depreciation. Moreover, assessors rated urban property at 8 percent of its cost and rural property at 3 percent. The fact that the city property owner had to devote a larger proportion of his income to costs was recognized by the poor rate assessors but not by the county rate assessors. To some extent this inequity was counterbalanced by the fact that only real property, not machinery or stock in trade, was assessed, but the mill owners ignored this consideration.[18]

Aside from the irritation it caused year in and year out, the difference in the rating systems had serious repercussions in bad years. The county rate was reassessed only rarely, but the poor rate, being a strictly local tax, was assessed annually. Between new assessments for the county rate the system worked just as it had in the past; that is, every section of the county paid a fixed proportion of the amount to be levied, according to its share at the last general assessment. The rate was actually collected, however, as a percentage of the poor rate and along with it. In bad years, many large enterprises gained reductions in their poor rate assessments, since their net income had fallen. The area as a whole, however, still owed the same amount to the county rate. In years of real hardship, when enterprises gained reductions in their poor rate assessments and many buildings were simply abandoned, the remaining solvent ratepayers had to find not only the money for an increased expenditure on their own poor (because of the hard times) but also to pay an increased percentage toward the county rate. Except in very bad years, however, it is difficult to believe that the urban areas were seriously over-rated; the four northern hundreds contained 26 percent of the population in 1831 and, under the assessment of 1829, paid 27 percent of the rates.[19]

Prices were in general dropping throughout this period. The price for manufactured goods fell especially sharply during the "hungry forties" immediately after the last assessment of 1841, which had been based on 1840 prices. The fact that county spending failed to follow suit was a further irritant to angry ratepayers. After reaching a sharp peak in the 1820's, by the mid-thirties spending had fallen back only to the level of the earlier 1820's, and after 1838 it again began to shoot up. By the early 1830's an organized pressure for fiscal reform had appeared.

## The Attack on the Rates

The years after Peterloo saw the development of a sustained radical attack on county government. When the radicals turned to the subject of the rates, they found natural allies among the disgruntled ratepayers of the large industrial conurbations. Although the two groups often failed to agree about purely local issues, it was easy for them to unite in hostility toward an unrepresentative and repressive rural oligarchy that was flinging away hard-earned money on unpopular causes while sheltering behind the bounty of the Corn Laws. Even the radicals accepted the mounting county expenditure on prosecutions as unavoidable, so they concentrated their attack on the less easily defensible expenditure on local prisons and prison salaries. Their leader was George Williams, who took the county to court three times with appeals against the misapplication of the rates. In one case the money had been intended for the erection of army barracks, a particularly obnoxious allocation for the veterans of Peterloo. According to Williams he won at King's Bench each time, but the county refused to reimburse his legal costs, and the expense finally forced him to drop this method of compelling economy.[20]

By this time Williams was convinced that the only way to force the justices to be more responsible financially was to make the position of justice an elected post. He wrote to the Commission for Enquiring into County Rates in 1835 that this "ancient and constitutional right of the people" to elect their justices was now even more necessary, since the revenue had grown in Lancashire from £1,000 in 1770 to nearly £100,000.[21] His campaign in favor of elected justices received support from the radical MP for Middlesex, Joseph Hume, who introduced a bill for the establishment of separate elected boards to administer county expenditure. The bill foundered after several members pointed out that it was virtually impossible to separate the judicial and executive functions of the justices; few Englishmen were prepared to accept an elective judiciary. Lancashire was to take the lead in reviving this issue in the late 1840's.[22]

One of the county's problems was that it had made several long-term commitments—particularly for salaries—at a time when prices had been higher. These salaries, most of which went to prison personnel such as the governor, chaplain, taskmasters, matron, and surgeon at all four institutions, now seemed excessive to the man in the street. Many justices, however, were reluctant to lower the amount paid to people who had served the county well for many years and who had in many cases taken on more obligations to suit their anticipated incomes. Although by the 1830's such salaries represented a relatively small proportion of total expenditure (for example, payments to the Lancaster staff and the county treasurer combined took between 2 percent and 5 percent of the county rolls), the reformers returned again and again to the extravagance of the sums involved.

On this issue the bench was divided, with the most liberal and active justices favoring reduction while the conservatives, such as W. R. Hay and William Hulton, opposed it. In 1829 a committee of five justices, including Thomas D. Hesketh and Thomas Batty Addison, both long-serving chairmen of the Annual General Session, proposed a reduction in most county salaries that would have saved about £1,700 a year, out of a gross county and hundred expenditure of about £76,000 a year. The committee's report was printed, but the Session resolved to debate each salary separately as positions became vacant. For some time it seemed as if the committee's suggestions would be brushed aside; when the chaplaincy of the New Bailey became vacant shortly afterwards, Henry Fielding was appointed at the old salary.[23]

In the spring of 1831, however, the *Preston Chronicle* revived the issue. In March a letter from "Rusticus" appeared, supporting the committee and complaining bitterly about the profligate spending on prison salaries: "I am convinced no satisfactory reason can be adduced, why the salaries of Chaplains of Gaols should have been fixed so high; for most of the men with whom they pass away their time are very ignorant;—their learning, therefore, need not of necessity be *profound*; nor is there any demand for their dress to be very expensive. Why, then, should salaries be allowed which make it very desirable for a clergyman to have the *privilege* of labouring all his life-time within the walls of a prison?"[24] On April 9 Rusticus returned to the attack. He begged the justices to abolish the office of county treasurer entirely and in that way save the £600 a year his salary cost. Even greater savings would come from reducing payment to "the family firm of Messrs, the Gaolers of Lancaster Castle. Who would ever imagine that these persons, good gaolers no doubt, ought to be paid 1300 pounds annually?"[25]

Although most ratepayers probably agreed with Rusticus, Addison and his committee were generally unsuccessful in persuading the justices to reduce salaries when making new appointments. Despite the appearance in 1833 of a book entitled *Remarks on the County Expenditure* by an angry Preston accountant named Robert Hindle, which was warmly praised by George Williams, agitation over the county rates was temporarily subsumed by local debate on the incorporation of Manchester and by more pressing national issues, such as the Reform Bill. Meanwhile,

Parliament took some of the pressure off the justices by following the recommendation of the Commission for Enquiring into County Rates that the national government undertake to pay half the costs of county prosecutions. These costs continued to be listed in the county budgets but were no longer raised on the county rates.[26]

At the end of the 1830's the rates again began to rise, although not nearly as rapidly as total county expenditure, since the national funds took an increasing share of the burden. In 1839 the Annual General Session voted to raise the salary of John Clay, the chaplain at Preston, by £100 to £350, though not without a battle and claims that the vote was miscounted. In the same year, Lancashire decided to establish a police force; this expense was to become a bitterly contested issue until the justices divided the county into several police districts and permitted each to determine the size of its force. In 1840 a third county assessment increased Salford's share by 7 percent.

In 1843 Robert Hindle produced a second book, *An Account of the Expenditure of the County Palatine of Lancaster for a Period of Twenty-three Years . . . with Remarks*. The "remarks" were extremely scathing, while the "account" itself contained many damaging quotations from such authorities as the inspectors of prisons. As a whole, it amounted to a complete indictment of magisterial government. The book received wide publicity and circulation, not least among the justices themselves. Partly because of its influence, they decided in 1844 to establish a permanent finance committee in order to keep a closer watch on expenditure.

Meanwhile, the prison buildings were becoming older and more dilapidated, prison committals were still rising, and penal theory was changing. The combined and strenuous efforts of the prison chaplains and the inspectors finally overcame the determined prevarication of the justices, who agreed to build new ranges of cells at Preston and Kirkdale. In 1846 a committee of magistrates met with Captain William John Williams, the inspector, and Joshua Jebb, the surveyor general, and concluded that further drastic alterations would be necessary, including the conversion of Lancaster Castle into a women's prison. The justices managed to put off further action for several years, partly on the grounds of expense; the ratepayers were already complaining bitterly about the cost of the new wings at Preston and Kirkdale. According to rumor (which in this case was nearly accurate), the justices had spent almost £8,000 on the Kirkdale chapel alone.[27]

The final explosion came in 1847 and 1848, when the county found itself embarked on several building schemes. The rates, which did not even represent the entire cost of the projects concerned, shot up dramatically. From £59,617 in 1845-46 they rose to £95,613 in 1846-47 and £103,739 in 1847-48. Though expenditure for general purposes rose about £10,000 during this interval, most of the increase came from the Preston/Kirkdale building (£12,000 in 1846-47 and £21,000 in 1847-48) and from the two new lunatic asylums necessitated by recent legislation (£31,000 in 1846-47 and £11,600 in 1847-48). In 1847-48 the Poor Law Union of West Derby paid £3,517 for its poor rate and £5,439 for the county rate. The general finance committee reported to the Annual General Session in 1848 that total spending for the past year, including amounts contributed by the national government, had been nearly £180,000.[28]

In January 1849 the guardians of the Poor Law unions, who were responsible for collecting the county money along with the poor rates and who thus bore much of the odium caused by the increases, held an indignation meeting at Newton. They eventually agreed to bring a bill into Parliament establishing a county financial board. Justices would make up one-third of the board, and the other two-thirds would consist of representatives elected by the Poor Law unions.[29] Despite initial enthusiasm, the bill, introduced first by Hume and a second time with changes by Thomas Milner Gibson, failed for several reasons.[30] Many members shared the contempt of the Poor Law guardians that the Rev. J. S. Birley of Bolton expressed before the committee on the bill:

Elected guardians may be respectable men, but many of our boards of guardians are composed of persons who were overseers under the old system of the Poor Law; they are persons of very narrow-minded views; and I know one or two cases in Lancashire where their very rough manner and their proceedings have driven some of the magistrates away from the board; very few of the magistrates . . . do attend the boards of guardians. . . . I am afraid that instead of taking an enlarged view of any matter or question, we should be led away just by the opinion of the hour, and that they would be very often penny wise and pound foolish. My opinion of the judgment exercised by the Poor Law guardians in Lancashire is not very exalted.[31]

By this time also, the Lancashire justices were putting their own house in order. In 1850 they compelled their incompetent treasurer, William Hulton, to resign.[32] Social, economic, and political tensions eased, and interest in the bill dropped. Perhaps the most important influence within Parliament was Sir John Packington's shrewd cross-examination of the witnesses before the committee on the act. Packington succeeded in showing that rates in Lancashire were actually lower than they had been in the 1820's, both on a poundage and a per capita basis. He demonstrated, to the satisfaction of a majority of the committee reporting on the bill, that the justices had had little choice but to authorize the building program that had forced the rates up. Several justices also testified that they had tried but failed to obtain government loans that would have spread the costs more gently over several years. In its report the committee stated that the justices had conducted their financial affairs "with proper attention to economy, with just regard to the public interests, and with all the publicity required by law."[33] It found that discontent arose either from the adoption of police, in which case experience had mitigated complaints, or from the costs of gaols and asylums, in which case the justices had no choice but to approve spending to comply with acts of Parliament. Parliament rejected the bill and, the economy having improved, for the time being the "ratepayers' revolt" was stifled.

There can be no question that the Lancashire justices spent money with a relatively liberal hand. Lancashire's prison staff earned more than any other in England, except for the staffs of York Castle and of London-area prisons such as Newgate and Coldbath Fields.[34] When Higgin was drawing £1,000 a year he was probably the most highly paid gaoler in England, although the gaolers of some of the larger urban prisons, especially in London, may well have earned similar sums in fees. Higgin's huge salary was to some extent an accident of geography: it had been settled in lieu of conveyance fees and other perquisites and, because of Lancashire's position and terrain, conveyance fees had always been extraordinarily large. County chaplains, however, were also very well paid. Though Lancashire's justices avoided the extravagance of the Yorkshire justices, who spent over £100,000 at Wakefield and about £200,000 at York Castle within a short period at the end of the 1840's (enough to buy a separate mansion for each prisoner), they spent more on one complex of buildings at Kirkdale than the Poor Law guardians did for whole workhouses designed for several hundred inmates.[35]

To some, even this expenditure seemed niggardly. John Clay always felt that his salary was inadequate, and he criticized the parsimony that made the magistrates hesitate to build additional separate cells in the early 1850's. The refusal of the justices to make large outlays persistently hindered attempts at wholesale prison reform. Although Frederic Hill objected to the costs of the separate system, the inspectors in general, and the Home Office as well, complained constantly about the dilapidated state into which the local prisons were allowed to fall. Even Hill at one point said that the New Bailey was not fit to hold a single prisoner.[36] Inevitably, the justices were caught between the united force of the chaplains, governors, surgeons, prison inspectors, and the government, on the one hand, and the irate ratepayers, on the other.

In many cases the justices got good value for their money. The Lancaster Castle gaolers, Higgin and Hansbrow, were both outstanding for their humanity. The bench's greatest failings were the uncritical loyalty it displayed toward those it appointed and its leaning toward nepotism. For able and well-connected gaolers this support could be an invaluable source of strength, permitting them to exercise a firm and consistent discipline in an uncertain world, but incompetent or cruel officials were also able to shelter both themselves and their sons beneath this dispensation. A related problem was the lack of adequate provision for superannuated staff, which made the justices reluctant to discharge officers who were too old to fulfill their duties adequately. Although difficulties cropped up at all three houses of correction, serious scandals were rare, in marked contrast to the borough prisons at Liverpool and Manchester. Lancashire also succeeded in finding prison chaplains of exceptional energy and ability, including not only Clay, who achieved a national reputation, but also Fielding at Salford and Appleton and Horner at Kirkdale.

It seems certain that if the guardians and the urban ratepayers had had their way, outlay would have been drastically cut. In the similar Poor Law institutions, almost every item of expenditure was smaller. The cost of the buildings was lower (though this was to some extent due to the greater need for security at the prisons and to the development of cellular confinement), staff salaries were considerably smaller (the highest salary on record for a workhouse master was £150), and expenditure per inmate was less.[37] A letter in the *Liverpool Courier* in 1837 pointed out that the weekly per capita expenditure on food at Kirkdale was 5s. and in the Liverpool workhouse, 2s. ½d.[38] As a result of such economy, the workhouses were largely staffed with incompetent and sometimes cruel men and women, both in Lancashire and throughout the country. As one historian has written recently, "on the whole, . . . the Poor Law service did not attract men and women who were well-qualified, much less dedicated, largely because the rates of pay were from the first ridiculously low."[39]

Where city councils ran the gaols, they often tried to practice a similar frugality. Heather Tomlinson described such a state of affairs in Yorkshire, where a committee appointed by the York city council refused to accept the justices' recommendations on the expenditure for the gaol and "took refuge in instituting cheeseparing and petty measures" such as limiting inmates to bread and gruel for the first fourteen days of confinement. According to Tomlinson, "they did not merely fail in their attempt, but also succeeded in creating greater problems which eventually led to the prison's closure."[40] Lancashire's justices had a good case for their greater liberality.

This story contrasts with the usual model of social reform, employed both by conservative and radical historians, in which a "rising middle class" seizes the initiative from the aristocracy in order to achieve reform. In the traditional version, the middle class is inspired by its increasing self-confidence and the need to overthrow "old corruption" and to reform corrupt institutions. In the radical version, it acts upon its anxiety over the mounting threat of social disorder from the lower classes, and the result is the creation of repressive social institutions. What this model overlooks, however, is the fact that these institutions could not exist at all unless someone paid for them, that control of their finances meant control of the number and quality of the institutions, and that such control remained firmly in the hands of the gentry. Although the gentry was far better able than the urban middle class to insulate itself from the dangers of crime and disorder, it continued, however reluctantly, to create these institutions and to provide them with the level of financial support necessary, although the cost of prison reform aroused protest against the rates and ultimately against the gentry's authority. It was the urban middle class, personified by local accountants, Poor Law guardians, and ratepayers, that bitterly opposed all new prison building or expenditure.

A bench that contained both Hulton and Williams obviously contained a wide spectrum of opinion on the value of social institutions and on the way they should be managed, but the justices were constrained in their activities by the weight of their responsibilities. Whatever individual justices might think, the bench as a whole had to come to some sort of consensus in order to make day-to-day administrative decisions. Fur-

TABLE II
*Amount Raised by Rates (County and Hundred),*
*Five-Year Averages, 1829-1849*

| Period | Amount |
| --- | --- |
| 1829/30 to 1833/34 | £71,255 |
| 1834/35 to 1838/39 | 58,220 |
| 1839/40 to 1843/44 | 88,977 |
| 1844/45 to 1848/49 | 78,454 |

thermore, the range of their decisions was circumscribed by the law; when acting as judges they had little choice but to commit certain offenders to prison even if they were apprehensive about the growth of penal institutions. Similarly, they were constrained by Parliament to create asylums, which placed a heavy burden on the rates. Once these institutions had appeared, the justices tried to maintain a certain minimal standard of decency in their administration.

In general, they were successful in controlling expenditure after 1815, and there is no evidence that the rates themselves were unreasonable, nor that they fell most heavily on the middle classes.[41] In Lancashire between 1821 and 1841, the population rose by two-thirds, from a little over one million to 1,667,054. During the period from 1815 to 1841 the total assessed wealth of the county doubled from about three million to about six million pounds.[42] During this period, the county expanded the services it provided, introducing, in particular, the rural police and enormously improved provision for lunatics. Because of greater national government contributions, however, the total actually levied by county and hundred rates did not rise appreciably on average, even including the special rates for the constabulary divisions (see Table 11). Because of the rises in assessed value, the pound rate actually dropped considerably. Even when gross expenditure is used, accepting the complainants' argument that what they received from the nation in one hand they paid back with the other, total expenditure went from an average of £92,926 in the period 1824-28 to £128,472 in 1844-48—an increase of one-third, or less than the increase in either population or assessment.[43] Even allowing for a drop in prices, the burden cannot have become significantly heavier.

If this is the case, then we are left with a paradox. In the first period of building, the 25 years between 1790 and 1815, rates multiplied tenfold.

The payments unquestionably were allocated unequally and did not benefit from industrial growth. The men on whom the rates fell most heavily sat on the bench and approved the increases. Aside from proposing a reassessment in 1801, a proposal that came to nothing, these men made no attempt to alter the situation until the most under-rated community in the county protested. In the second period of building, from about 1821 to 1859, expenditure rose more slowly and its effect was largely dissipated by industrial development and national contributions. At the same time, several other taxes, particularly the poor rate, were falling, thus easing the pressure on taxpayers. Yet throughout this second period there was continuous bitter criticism of the rates.

Part of the explanation for this paradox lies in the fact of representation. Whatever may have been the actual incidence of the rates toward the end of the eighteenth century, the landowners and gentlemen sitting on the bench believed that they themselves were paying the lion's share. This belief helped justify their claim to rule, since it was the payment of taxes that determined the "stake" one had in government. At the beginning of the next century, they successfully redistributed what was becoming an intolerable burden, but only at the cost of undermining their exclusive claim to authority. As the nation moved to broaden the suffrage, the existence of a body of appointed but hereditary rulers in the counties—a "rural House of Lords" without even a balancing House of Commons—became increasingly unacceptable to the urban ratepayers, who were now paying their full share of county costs. The presence on the bench of a handful of the wealthiest and most successful mill owners did little to allay this discontent. Together the radicals and the ratepayers launched an attack against the justices on the points where they seemed most vulnerable: the way they ran their prisons and the way they spent the county rates. Far from increasing the power of the "ruling class," the heavy cost of prison reform and other social institutions proved both politically and socially disruptive. By the end of the nineteenth century the effort of the justices, under pressure from Parliament, to provide new services and new institutions for the inhabitants of their counties would cost them their local power.

# CHAPTER 7

# The Nineteenth-Century Prisons

Though historians are divided over the effects of the reforms of the late eighteenth century, there is a more general consensus on those of the nineteenth century. Peel's Act of 1823, which abolished all fees, provided for prison instruction and religious services, and established a formal classification system, is usually seen as a step forward. The act sponsored by the Duke of Richmond's committee in 1835, which increased central control over the prisons—providing in particular for appointed prison inspectors—is also seen as beneficial. In general, however, from the introduction of the treadmill in the early 1820's, and especially after the development of the theories of separate and solitary confinement in the mid-1830's, the historians' picture is of an ever-growing repressiveness in which the chief concern of prison officials was to come up with more effective ways to "break the spirit" of their charges.

This interpretation rests on these writers' generally hostile attitude toward Benthamite radicalism, at least as revealed in its prison policies, and on a distaste for middle-class Evangelicalism. To Michel Foucault, "le panoptisme"—the "endless interrogation" made possible by the new form of Benthamite prison—was simply another instrument of social control, like factories, schools, or hospitals, in fact, like all the institutions of the welfare state.[1] To Gertrude Himmelfarb, Bentham's "haunted house" was a vehicle for a fantasy of personal aggrandizement.[2] To Ursula Henriques, the reformative efforts of earnest Evangelicals "might nowadays be called brain-washing." "There was indeed," she writes, "a flavour of self-deception, if not of deliberate hypocrisy, about much of the propaganda for the separate system. . . . For many nineteenth-century reformers religion was an instrument of social discipline, for application to other people, especially the lower orders, not to themselves. . . . Their stock adjectives for inflicted suffering were 'wholesome' and 'salutary' and the stench of unctuous sanctimony still rises from their pages." Even Bentham, she explains, was willing to employ the religious sanction, because "he had been frightened by the French Revolution."[3] This picture has some truth, but it overestimates the extent to which prisons were run by ideas rather than by men and underestimates the problems with which the administrators were grappling. It dismisses the reformers' good intentions as a mere screen for class oppression, while it greatly overestimates their success in attaining their disciplinary goals. In concentrating on the writings of nationally important reformers, it ignores those men, such as the county justices, who were actually implementing and administering the reforms. These men have sometimes been portrayed as mere agents of the parliamentary, inspectional, or bureaucratic will. More often, they are depicted as playing a purely reactionary role. Both these views are misleading. The county bench had a mind of its own. Its members sat in Parliament and enjoyed both power and patronage. Their decisions were as significant and as representative of English intentions as were the writings of the middle-class reformers. The justices were often willing, sometimes even anxious, to implement reform, but under their guidance the counties rarely adopted the radical measures of control suggested by the more zealous national campaigners.

The standard historical view also neglects a second group that had a critical role in the decision to adopt reforms, in the day-to-day administration of the gaols, and in the strictness or kindliness of their regime: the individual prison governors. Finally, it underestimates the success that the prisoners themselves often had in forcing compromises on administrators or in undermining their efforts. The influence of these groups, along with the inevitable compromises imposed by problems of finance, overcrowding, and administration, meant that nineteenth-century prisons were profoundly different not only from their eighteenth-century predecessors but also from the stringent penal fantasies of idealistic reformers.

## The Buildings, 1816-1845

During the war years little prison building had gone on, but construction resumed again in 1816. Under the pressure of an increasing number of inmates, Salford more than doubled in size, and Lancaster, which had already constructed a new felons' prison, added an entire women's prison within its walls.[4] Although Preston had been presented in 1816, work did not get under way there until the 1820's. In 1817 the Ormskirk and Wigan Sessions moved to Liverpool, and in 1818 the justices decided to construct an entirely new house of correction at Kirkdale, a nearby suburb. Eventually, South Lancashire received a separate Assize as well.

Although the cells built at the end of the eighteenth century were hailed at the time as a great advance, they had many deficiencies. The new buildings often followed a "contagionist" plan, with small groups of separate cells arranged in squares around a central yard, corridor, or workroom. These were much harder for staff to supervise than either the old-fashioned large wards or the panopticon and radial cell wings of the future. Although the cells were intended to house single prisoners, the pressure of rising numbers filled them with up to five inmates each.

The felons' prison at Lancaster proved especially inconvenient. It consisted of two towers, each containing eight sleeping cells to a floor. The cells were built back to back, four on each side, around a thick masonry core and opened onto a corridor going around the circumference of the tower. Since they were on the inside of the tower, with the corridor between them and the outer wall, they had no windows at all, only a small ventilation hole over the door to the corridor outside. Since the towers consisted of ten very small floors surrounded by extremely thick stone walls, it was difficult to provide moving air, either for ventilation or for heat. It was impossible for a prison officer to see into a cell unless he mounted the stairs and looked through its door; nor, if he was on one floor, could he easily hear anything at all on other floors.[5]

Samuel Bamford, who was imprisoned in Lancaster after Peterloo, graphically described his experience of these cells in his memoirs:

During the day . . . I had imbibed a favourable opinion of this prison. The day-room and yard were clean and airy, and whilst the attendant was sweeping out the cells and making the beds, I had gone in, and found them with their doors all open, lighted with the forenoon sun, and as white and sweet as a constant application of quick lime could make them. . . . At the head of the cell was an iron slab, full of perforations, and resting on the projections from the wall; a sack with straw in, a couple of blankets or so, and a good horse-rug, made up our bed, and the whole being apparently clean, I promised myself a sleep as sound as a king could enjoy. . . . A capital prison thought I. . . . Besides, I had heard that these felon-dungeons were constructed under the direction of the celebrated "humane Howard." . . .

We turned in, and . . . I began to feel as if I were being smothered. My old complaint on the lungs had gone with me to this place. . . . I now began to feel as if I was closed up in a coffin, and not a breath of air above and around me. How dreadful were my sensations! . . . My chest heaved for air . . . and I stood leaning on my bed, pumping and gasping, in the close suffocating den.[6]

Henry Hunt also commented that his cell was "most infamously close" and that "I thought I should have been suffocated for some time after I entered it."[7]

Even in successful designs, eighteenth-century reforms created a number of intractable architectural problems. The open wards of the "unreformed prison" were often close, dark, and difficult of access, but these problems were relatively simple to remedy. It was not too difficult to break through walls to let in light and air. A single officer could take in a room full of twenty or more persons at a glance; locking up, unlocking, and delivering food were all relatively rapid operations. The commitment to nightly cellular confinement complicated these activities, even before there was any interest in the complete separation of prisoners. It was the eighteenth-century development of cellular confinement that provoked a corresponding emphasis on the need for "inspection," since previously this had been a less difficult procedure.

Bentham believed his Panopticon solved this difficulty. Along with the innovative plan itself, Bentham introduced many novelties to make it function properly. For instance, he replaced solid masonry with structural iron and provided duct heating, running water, and water closets in every cell—refinements that are still missing in many English prisons today.[8] In many ways, the Panopticon represented a revolt against what Bentham considered a cruel system, and particularly against the sensual deprivations and discomforts imposed in the reformed prison. He objected to the meagerness of the diet, the dark cold cells with their tiny, high gratings, the monotony and unhealthiness of prison labor, the multiplication of petty rules, the solitude, and the enforcement of unprofitable activities merely to harass the prisoners. A design that made it easier to observe the prisoners, he felt, would enable him to increase their comfort without endangering security.[9]

The more humane elements of Bentham's plan, however, were ignored. No one ever paid much attention to his bitter criticism of such reformed prisons as Wymondham. The two disciplinary elements of his scheme, inspection and industrial labor, were simply added on to the existing reformed prisons. Most of the new building carried out in Lancashire during the early 1820's followed his plan of a circle of cells arranged around a central inspection station. Kirkdale opened with two semicircular wings enclosing airing courts. At Salford the male felons' wards followed a similar plan, as did the treadwheel yards, the male misdemeanants' airing yards, and the female felons' cells.[10] At Lancaster the women's penitentiary and the male felons' dayrooms were built closely around a central station, a plan that won the grudging approval of the Society for the Improvement of Prison Discipline.[11]

In general, however, the SIPD preferred the "new" radial prison plans, where cells were built along long corridors radiating out from the center. Though officers sitting in the center could not see into each room, it was possible to arrange large numbers of cells, along with dayrooms and workrooms, in such a way that they could be easily superintended from the center. Radial plans had been common in hospitals since the Middle Ages, when religious foundations adopted cross-shaped plans to increase the number of patients while still permitting views of the central chapel. With the revival of miasmatism in the early nineteenth century, this layout again became popular, since it promoted ventilation while permitting good supervision and avoided the need for patients and nurses to travel outside in the cold between buildings.[12] Blackburn experimented with this design in his plans for the National Penitentiary in 1782 and for the Liverpool borough prison built between 1795 and 1797, but apparently without much success.[13] By the 1840's, however, it had become the standard prison plan. Lancashire was slow to adopt it, although Preston gradually extended its wings and added new ones to become a radial prison. A radial plan was also chosen for the rebuilding of Kirkdale in the late 1840's.

Though Lancashire adopted the panopticon plan, however, it did not follow Bentham's suggestion that rooms be made large enough to hold several prisoners comfortably. Prisons, like hospitals, had partially retreated from the insistence of the reformers of Howard's generation that inmates be separated completely at night, and Peel's Act merely enjoined classification of prisoners into groups, not cellular separation. In designing prisons, however, reformers were still dominated by the fear of moral if not physical contamination and built single night cells. As a result, the nineteenth-century cells were nearly as uncomfortable as their predecessors. Being designed for only one person, the cells were quite small and were usually built of stone. They were too small to heat individually (until the development of efficient gas fires), and the early Victorians did not have a technology adequate to heat them collectively, particularly when the development of the theory of separate confinement made acoustical isolation desirable; this precluded the introduction of hot air ducts and pipes.[14] Some prisoners complained that their cells were "close," but most complained of the cold. At Salford there was a constant battle between the administration, which was determined to maintain ventilation for health, and the prisoners, who were equally determined to stop uncomfortable drafts by stuffing their unglazed windows with rags. The small, cold, dark, and rather clammy cells can only have exacerbated the symptoms of lung disease, especially tuberculosis, though the partial separation of prisoners may have impeded its spread. On the whole, the provision of an acceptable level of comfort in single cells arranged so that their inmates could not communicate with each other required a level of technology that was not available in the early nineteenth century.

Lancashire's prison capacity frequently lagged behind the population of prisoners; when by necessity the cells were stuffed with extra men they became hot, noisome, cramped, and claustrophobic. In 1813 Higgin wrote that the Castle was holding 325 prisoners and "there is not room for another."[15] The parliamentary return of 1818 showed that the Castle, which by then had an estimated capacity of 390 prisoners, maintained a daily average of 466. The opening of the women's penitentiary with a suggested capacity of 120 prisoners temporarily eased the pressure. In 1823 the Castle reported a capacity of 136 separately housed prisoners, an absolute capacity of 495 with several prisoners to a cell, and a prison population of 286, well within its span. In 1827, however, the population rose to 457. The greatest number at one time in 1826 was 578 and in 1827, 545, well beyond the capacity of the gaol even when several prisoners were crammed into a single cell.[16]

For the next decade, the total population of the Castle remained relatively stable. Except for a drop in 1837, the criminal population rose steadily from the time of Peterloo to the hungry forties, but a slight reduction in the number of debtors helped smooth out the overall change. This was only a limited advantage, because criminals could not be assigned to debtors' rooms. In the depression after 1837, the population again began to rise rapidly; by 1841-42, the *average* population was 515, well above the official capacity, and at one time in 1842 there were 629 prisoners. At some time during every year between 1830 and 1843, Lancaster held 495 prisoners or more.

Though none of the other three county prisons regularly exceeded its official capacity, the number of prisoners rarely dropped below the total number of single cells. For example, Kirkdale had between 334 and 384 single cells seven feet four inches wide at one end, six feet eleven inches at the other end, and six feet nine inches long. On the day that the prisoners were counted for the annual returns to the secretary of state, there were frequently over 600 prisoners and the total once reached 737.[17] Attempts at classification only exacerbated the shortage of space, since fluctuating populations meant that some classes had too many cells while others went short. For example, the 23 vagrant boys at Salford in 1837 must have been reasonably comfortable in 29 double-bedded cells, but what of the 60 female vagrants sharing 10 such cells? Although the massive construction efforts of the postwar years made it just possible for Lancashire's buildings to contain their inmates, their numbers placed an obvious strain on the county's institutions and administrators. Lancashire was not the only county to experience overcrowding: the Duke of Richmond's committee reported in 1835 that of the 136 supposedly reformed prisons covered by the act of 1823, only 36 (possibly only 24) could separate prisoners at night.[18]

Yet though many people went to prison, few stayed for long. The average term of confinement in the 36 largest English county prisons between 1838 and 1842 was 46 days. Salford was slightly below the national average, the other three Lancashire gaols a little above.[19] It was difficult for the staff even to visit the prisoners and learn their names, let alone "reform" or "institutionalize" them. It is no wonder that Salford, once a model for the nation, rapidly became notorious for its discomfort and disorder, or that its beleaguered administration eventually abandoned any pretense of classification (except to separate men from women). A county that had counted its committals by tens in the eighteenth century saw them regularly exceed ten thousand by the 1830's and rise to over forty thousand by 1858, the first year for which complete figures have survived. Under such constant stress, it is no wonder that the prisons and their administrators often failed to justify the reformers' hopes.

## Diet

Because prisons were self-contained and because imprisonment was widely thought to pose a special threat of disease, the better-run prisons rigorously enforced such protective measures as washing the floors, liming the walls, fumigating clothes, bathing new arrivals, and separating the sick, long before similar measures appeared in the poorer quarters of the cities that surrounded them. Moreover, prison surgeons tended to rely on relatively simple remedies, particularly food and bed rest; on the whole this treatment probably benefited their patients.

On the other hand, precisely because they were controlled, crowded, and isolated communities, prisons were subject to special hazards. The diet of five hundred prisoners could be suddenly altered, almost at the stroke of a pen. Such control made mistakes disastrous. Prison communities were now large enough to foster epidemics. Gastroenteritis posed a special problem, not only because infected cooks in a central kitchen could spread the disease but also because there was little knowledge of the special hazards involved in the preparation of very large quantities of food. The substitution of cellular confinement for the large wards where prisoners had prepared their own food increased this hazard.

The essential constituents of a healthy diet had not yet been established. Even the connection between diet and scurvy was not universally accepted. In 1822 the committee administering Millbank prison cut the inmates' diet severely, yet the resulting outbreak of scurvy was attributed by many to Millbank's unhealthy location; it took some time for doctors to persuade the committee to introduce oranges, and even then the doctors' opponents were not convinced.[20] Serious scurvy was rare in Lancashire until after the adoption of the government dietary of 1843, which reduced the allowance of potatoes. In 1847-48 the Kirkdale surgeon reported between twenty and thirty cases of scurvy, "a disease we never knew before."[21] Nutritional deficiency also contributed to other diseases, either by lowering resistance or by creating specific symptoms such as cirrhosis of the liver, "debility" or "exhaustion," anemia, and, possibly, "fits." It certainly increased the irritability of the prisoners, though Victorians believed that a "low" diet decreased "animal spirits" and made prisoners more tractable.

Some prisoners were malnourished on arrival. In 1847 Millbank sent nine boys to Preston. Their average age was nearly sixteen, their average height was four feet eight and two-thirds inches, and their average weight was eighty-three and one-half pounds. They gained an average of six and two-thirds pounds each in eight months of imprisonment. The surgeon reported to the prison inspector Frederic Hill that these boys were deficient in energy, rickety, and scrofulous, but all he gained for his effort was a rebuke from the Home Office for failing to enter their condition in his journal and to use the proper channels (the visiting justices) to report their condition.[22] Prisons also held many diseased prostitutes and emaciated alcoholics along with the unsturdy poor.

However inadequate it may have been by modern standards, the prison diet, combined with the medical services available there and the short average term, was good enough to attract many of the poor. This assertion sounds like a piece of Chadwickian propaganda in favor of lesser eligibility, but it is so well documented as to be beyond doubt. There were occasional cases of deliberate entry in the eighteenth century, but these were generally men who had themselves committed for debt to avoid other obligations, such as service in the army. By the 1830's, however, deliberate entry had become very common. Every county prison saw such cases. One woman had been committed to the New Bailey more than two hundred times; she came there "generally to recruit her health."[23]

John Clay, at Preston, attended a dying woman who, "sinking under disease, and recollecting the attention she had received, some years before, in the hospital of the prison, . . . committed a trifling theft in order to obtain admission to it again."[24] Captain Hansbrow recorded many similar cases, such as the woman committed for being drunk and disorderly who, the day before her release, "exclaimed in a passion of tears, 'Oh! Sir, if I only had such food outside as I have here, you would never see me in a prison.'"[25] In 1843 he discharged an epileptic who "wept bitterly *at being put out of gaol*, having no prospect before him but that of the workhouse."[26] In 1847 he reported on Bridget Campbell, who had been sentenced to transportation but remained at Lancaster because she was unfit for removal. "I have more than once asked her if she wished to petition the Magistrates . . . for her liberation; but she answered she was better off where she was."[27]

Vagrants knew perfectly well that many prisons were more comfortable than the workhouse, and in the fall the prisons filled with men who had chosen their offense to provide them with a winter's lodgings. It was also common for young men in the workhouse to break its windows or commit other petty vandalism in order to move to the prison. "One of the most serious and increasing obstacles to good discipline," complained inspector William John Williams in 1837, "is the common practice of tramps and prostitutes, when infected with foul diseases, (not admitted into the public infirmaries), committing some slight offence for the purpose of obtaining medical treatment in prisons. Their committals are generally for one or two months to hard labour, which they seldom or never undergo, oftentimes passing the entire of the term in hospital; and many of the females are scarcely discharged a month, ere they return again for surgical care. Such prisoners are more disorderly in behaviour, more pernicious in example, and more difficult to control, than any other class."[28]

Throughout the period there was a constant seesaw between the desire of the authorities, both central and local, to cut the diet in the interest of making imprisonment less attractive and their need to keep prisoners in good health. In the 1820's the prisoners found a strong ally in John Smith, the Lancaster surgeon. In 1829 he reported to the visiting justices that recent cuts in the diet had more than quadrupled the number of deaths. Between 1822 and 1824, he pointed out, only four inmates had died. At that time the weekly diet for working prisoners had included seven pounds of bread, two and a half pounds of oatmeal, ten pounds of potatoes, four ounces of cheese, four ounces of salt, a half pound of boned beef, one quart of broth, and one quart of stew. Women also received a pint of milk daily. Prisoners could spend part of their earnings on food or receive gifts from friends. The Prison Act of 1823, however, contained a section that the justices interpreted to mean that prisoners should be confined strictly to the prison diet. According to Smith, the ban on gifts and purchases of food had visibly damaged the prisoners' health. Moreover, in 1826 the justices themselves decided to reduce the Lancaster diet in an attempt to make the four county prisons more uniform.

The death rate rose immediately. In 1825 there had been only one death per 123.5 prisoners. In the four and a half years after the reduction, the average was one per 39.75. The surgeon concluded that "insufficiency of food is the principal if not only cause of all the mischief which has ensued."[29] His efforts finally persuaded the justices to improve the dietary. After two successive increases, by 1829 working prisoners received a diet similar to that of 1822, while prisoners who refused to work received seven pounds of bread, two and a half pounds of oatmeal, four and a half ounces of salt, and ten pounds of potatoes per week (see Table 12).[30] For several classes of prisoner this final version was a much more generous diet than the one the government introduced after 1843. This "Graham dietary" divided prisoners into classes according to their length of stay, ranging from one week to four months and over. Since most prisoners stayed for a relatively short term, this system considerably reduced the total provision of food at many institutions.[31]

After the diet was increased in 1828-29, the Castle death rate dropped. From eleven deaths a year in 1829 it fell to eight in 1830 and then to five in 1831. It averaged a little under four and a half per year from 1830 to

TABLE 12
*Weekly Dietaries for Lancashire Prisons, 1835*

*Lancaster*
Convicted male prisoners:
  7 lbs. bread
  2½ lbs. oatmeal
  10 lbs. potatoes
  1½ lbs. beef
  5 oz. rice
  1½ gills of peas (3/8 pint)
  4 oz. cheese
  2 oz. onions
  3½ oz. salt
Convicted female prisoners:
  7 lbs. bread
  2½ lbs. oatmeal
  5 lbs. potatoes
  1 lb. beef
  5 oz. rice
  1½ gills of peas
  3½ oz. salt

*Preston*
  8¾ lbs. bread
  2 lbs. oatmeal
  5 lbs. potatoes
  1 lb. beef
  3 gills of peas
  4 oz. cheese
  4 oz. salt
  ¾ lb. stew

*Salford*
Male prisoners:
  8¾ lbs. bread
  31½ oz. dry oatmeal
    (for 14 qts. cooked)
  5 lbs. potatoes
  1 lb. beef
  2 qts. pea soup
  3½ oz. salt
  1 qt. stew
Female prisoners:
  7 lbs. bread
  3½ oz. salt
  7 pts. stew
  14 qts. gruel

*Kirkdale* (for six days)
  7 lbs. bread
  3 lbs. potatoes
  3 pts. stew with 3 lbs. potatoes,
    meat, salt, and pepper
  12 pts. gruel
  2 qts. broth
  4 oz. bacon

1843.[32] A comparison of the incidence of disease in the two periods before and after 1829 does not, however, suggest that a poor diet played a role in the incidence of any one disease. The late 1820's were bad years at other institutions as well, and it is difficult to relate this fact to any dietary changes. The surgeon of Kirkdale wrote in 1827 that more inmates had died there in the past year than in any other year since the opening. A miasmatist, he explained that this death rate did "not arise from disease generated in the Prison but has been the effect of a particular state of the atmosphere from which cause all the Hospitals and publick institutions for the relief of sick persons have suffered more severely than at any previous period for a number of years."[33] His list of the causes of death does not suggest any single cause: dysentery (two cases), typhus, gradual decay (someone aged 75), exhaustion, diseased knee,

smallpox, cancer of the womb, apoplexy, venereal disease, peritoneal inflammation, inflammation of the lungs, and "mortification."

It is not evident in Lancashire, therefore, as it is at Millbank, that a
single decision to reduce the diet resulted in an outbreak of disease. Yet
though the changes in diet may not have had an obvious effect, it does
seem clear that the diet as a whole, both before and after the change, was
lacking in variety and balance, and that the increasing strictness with
which prisoners were confined to the gaol diet was not to their advantage. Many prisoners stayed in gaol for such short periods that the effect
was not serious, but it was still there. It also seems clear in this instance
that though increasing central supervision benefited prisoners in marginal institutions, it also harmed many others.

The story of prison diets in the nineteenth century is complex. There
is no single trend but a series of backward and forward movements, the
product of three interacting and sometimes conflicting trends: the con-
tinuation of eighteenth-century policies to equalize the condition of all
prisoners by outlawing the purchase of special comforts and by attempting to make different prisons more similar by state regulation; the limi-
tation set by administrative frugality and a need for lesser eligibility; and
an increasing scientific understanding of human nutritional needs.

### Health

Concern for the health of prisoners had been the chief precipitant of
the prison rebuilding undertaken in the Age of Reform. How well did
the prisons fulfill the hopes of reformers? It is difficult to extract useful
information from the raw data that are available. When the surgeon of
Millbank, William Baly, tried to collect data for an article on prison mortality in 1844, he could obtain adequate information (from the *Parliamentary Papers*) for only about five years, between 1838 and 1842.[34] (Captain Hansbrow, however, sent him a complete return of Lancaster
deaths, causes of death, and average population for the entire period
from 1825 to 1843. Lancaster and Millbank, where Baly himself kept
records, were the only two prisons in England with such complete records.) I have been more fortunate than Baly in obtaining average daily
populations for all of Lancashire's prisons, which were published in
1843 by Robert Hindle for the period from 1820 to 1842.[35] These averages can be compared with the number of deaths in each prison in each
year after 1823, which were published in the schedule B returns in the

TABLE 13

*Lancashire Prison Death Rates by Period, 1823-1846*

(Avg. death rate per 1,000 prisoners)

| Period | Lancaster | Preston | Kirkdale | Salford | Total |
|---|---|---|---|---|---|
| 1823-42[a] | 17.64 | 7.55 | 15.73 | 13.41 | 13.58 |
| 1823-42 | 17.94 | 7.67 | 17.92 | 14.76 | 14.57 |
| 1823-31 | 20.30 | 7.08 | 15.45 | 11.96 | 13.61 |
| 1833-42 | 15.24 | 7.92 | 15.99 | 14.72 | 13.47 |
| 1838-42 | 14.43 | 6.22 | 17.16 | 17.68 | 13.87 |
| 1838-42[b] | 15.94 | 5.39 | 16.96 | 16.86 | — |
| 1840-46[c] | 8.46 | 3.10 | 14.92 | 10.83 | 9.33 |

NOTE: All data are mine except as indicated.
  [a]Excludes 1832.  [b]Baly's data.  [c]*Parliamentary Papers.*

*Parliamentary Papers.*[36] Unfortunately, Hindle's averages run from June to June while the returns were calculated from Michaelmas to Michaelmas, but the yearly fluctuation in population was probably small enough to be insignificant when the results are averaged over several years. For the period between 1840 and 1846, calculations of the death rate appear in the *Parliamentary Papers* for three Lancashire prisons and can be estimated for the fourth (Preston), but these figures are not strictly comparable with those from 1823 to 1842. For the years that Baly also covered, I was able to compare my calculations with his and found that mine were about one death per thousand higher; I am unable to account for the discrepancy. Unless otherwise noted, the rates given in Table 13 are based on my calculations.

Several additional technical problems arise in using these figures. The first is the use of a yearly average of daily populations. In other words, the deaths are compared with total "prisoner-days" divided by 365. This is an appropriate basis, but it is not the only appropriate basis. Another possibility would be a comparison based on total committals. Since the average term served was falling during this period, the number of committals was rising even when the average yearly population stayed more or less steady. The effect of this on death rates is difficult to gauge. This problem of using yearly average populations to calculate institutional death rates aroused heated debates in the nineteenth century, but it probably did not create serious distortions in prison death rates.

The second problem is the question of infants. One prison, Salford, listed infant deaths separately in its returns from 1833 to 1841. The other three did not, and it is impossible to estimate their number. After some hesitation, I have decided to exclude the Salford infant deaths. This may cause Salford's death rate to be artificially low compared with that of other prisons. Many women bore children in prison or brought them in with them, and infant deaths could form a significant fraction of the whole: there were two infant deaths out of a total of eight at Salford in 1836, five out of a total of seventeen in 1840, and three out of a total of fourteen in 1841.

A third problem is the question of whether to separate criminals from debtors. Baly attempted to do this, but the schedule B returns do not list debtors' deaths separately. Since I wished to evaluate the administration of the prison as a whole, the health of the entire population seemed an appropriate base. Criminal death rates were higher in the gaols than in the houses of correction because the gaols contained some convicts sentenced to very long terms.

A fourth problem is the treatment of deaths from cholera. Cholera was a disease whose incidence was more or less out of the control of prison administrators and physicians; its causes were not understood at this time and few treatments were effective. If the cholera deaths of 1832 are included in averages they may skew the final results, making a prison that was ordinarily healthy appear comparatively unhealthy. For example, Kirkdale, which ordinarily had between 7 and 8 deaths a year, had 35 in 1832, raising its overall death rate for the 20 years between 1823 and 1842 by more than two deaths per thousand. Salford also suffered in the epidemic of 1832, but Lancaster and Preston escaped. Following Baly, I have calculated separate death rates for all four prisons both including and excluding the deaths in 1832, a year that also provides a convenient midpoint for comparisons of the two halves of the period.

A fifth problem is the demographic bias of the prison population. With the exception of debtors, prisoners tended to be young men in the healthiest part of their life span. There were, however, some important qualifications to this advantage. First, the prisoners tended to be poor and to come from sections of the cities with relatively high death rates. Second, there was that unknown number of pregnant women and newborn infants, who were at very high risk. Third, certain activities that posed a serious risk to health were also grounds for committal to prison, particularly public drunkenness and prostitution. Finally, there were those few prisoners who deliberately sought committal to take advantage of the prison hospitals. In addressing this problem, Baly decided to compare the incidence of death among prisoners with that of the general adult population (aged 15 to 75), but this was at best an extremely rough comparison.

A final problem is the custom of providing free pardons for prisoners who suffered from a chronic illness and seemed likely to die in prison, a practice that lowered the prison mortality rate. Fortunately, Baly went through the lists of pardons for Millbank and estimated how many of them would have resulted in death before the end of the original sentence: 123 out of 355. Baly then used this ratio to estimate how many of the prisoners pardoned at Wakefield, Liverpool, Preston, Lancaster, Chester, and Derby would also have died. He went through the same process for the thirty-six most important English prisons, except that he also had to extrapolate from the six prisons named above to obtain a probable pardon rate. This procedure produced a rather rough estimate, but one that no modern writer is likely to better. According to Baly's estimate, these pardons would add nearly four deaths per thousand a year to the official mortality rates of the larger provincial prisons. Because terms were much longer at Millbank and the pardon rate consequently higher, there was a difference of nearly thirteen per thousand there.

Baly used these calculations to show that the prisoners in Millbank, with an official death rate of 18.147 per thousand (not counting deaths from cholera) and a corrected death rate of 30.976 per thousand, were considerably less healthy than the adult population of London, with a death rate of 15.391. He also proved that death rates increased very rapidly after the first year or two of imprisonment. When these figures are applied to Lancashire, however, the issue is more difficult to resolve, since the death rate in Lancashire towns was considerably higher than that for either England as a whole or for London, while the death rate in Lancashire prisons was relatively low. For the five years between 1838 and 1842, Baly found an average death rate in 36 British prisons of 19.013. In those five years, however, the rates at all the Lancashire prisons, including the Castle, were lower than the English average. Lancaster's rate was 14.43 (my rate, including debtors; Baly's rate for criminals was 15.94); Salford's, 17.68 (Baly, 16.86); Kirkdale's, 17.16 (Baly, 16.96); and Preston's, 6.22 (Baly, 5.34).

These figures represent the actual prison death rates, which were lower than the annual total mortality rate of Preston (31.08) or Liverpool

(33.88 in 1841) and lower than the annual adult mortality rate of Liverpool (18.19). If to these are added a little less than four deaths per thousand per year, Baly's estimate for pardoned prisoners, then Lancaster, Salford, and Kirkdale all have mortality rates similar to that of Liverpool's adult population, although still well below the total mortality (including children) of Lancashire's industrial areas. In 1851, total Lancashire mortality was 31.25.[37]

Preston's consistently and extraordinarily low death rate presents a special problem. It was independent of changes in staff and discipline, although the relatively greater separation between prisoners no doubt helped. Preston was smaller than the other Lancashire prisons, being only a third the size of Salford. Like the Castle, it largely escaped the cholera of the early 1830's, but in the period studied by Baly, cholera was a relatively minor cause of death. There is no evidence that a high pardon rate was responsible; between 1841 and 1843 Preston had two prisoners pardoned on the grounds of health while Lancaster had eight; nor do sentencing policies and average terms of confinement explain Preston's achievement. John Clay often referred to Preston's remarkable healthiness in his reports. In 1844 Clay and the other authors of the *Report on the Sanitary Condition of Preston* pointed out that the adult death rate in the town was five times that of the prison, suggesting that many lives were lost unnecessarily.*

On the whole, the average person's chances of dying probably increased slightly upon commitment and rose with the length of imprisonment, although this was not true for certain groups of prisoners, particularly those in Preston and those already sick or starving. The average person was less likely to die in a Lancashire prison than in many other, though not all, large county prisons. Baly's calculation of death rates in county gaols varied from a deplorable 45.751 at York Castle to 11.981 at the Gloucester county gaol. His rates for the houses of correction tended to be somewhat lower than those in the county gaols, although the next lowest, Devizes, at 10.989, was double that of Preston. Considering the comparatively large size of Lancashire's institutions and their relatively

---

*Harris Library, Preston, John Clay, *Report on the Sanitary Condition of Preston* (1844). For Clay's views on cholera see *Cholera Morbus: A Sermon Preached on the 21st. Day of March, 1832* (Preston, 1832). March 21 was the day appointed by Parliament for national fasting and prayer to avert the cholera. Clay could not quite bring himself to say that God sent cholera as a retribution for sin, so he suggested it was most frequent among the sinfully dirty.

long term of imprisonment, their record was creditable, particularly given the surrounding population's general state of health.[38]

A comparison of the average death rate of the period between 1823 and 1831 with that of the period between 1833 and 1842 shows an increase in the death rate in the three houses of correction. At Preston and Kirkdale it was less than one death per thousand; at Salford it was nearly three deaths per thousand. At Lancaster, however, the death rate fell by about five deaths per thousand, from 20.30 in 1823-31 to 15.24 in 1833-42. It seems likely that the death rate thereafter fell substantially at all four institutions. At Lancaster between 1843 and 1846, only ten prisoners died and the rate fell to 6.7. At Preston only two prisoners died and the death rate fell to a remarkable 3.2. Because of the great variation in mortality rates from year to year, however, the trend one sees depends heavily on the precise terminal years chosen.

Information on Millbank's morbidity is poor and difficult to evaluate, but Baly did examine the incidence of fatal diseases there. He compared Millbank's diseases with those of London and concluded that though slightly more prisoners died of fever in the prison than in the town, by far the greatest cause of death and the most important cause of the difference between Millbank's and London's death rates was tuberculosis. In the county prisons the pattern was different. Baly constructed a table of actual deaths in prison in sixteen large county prisons, including Lancashire's four. The dates covered varied considerably, ranging from nineteen years for Lancaster to only one year for Exeter and Winchester, but Baly added up the annual average of prisoners for each year in every prison where data were available and used this figure to calculate overall deaths per thousand live prisoners. The variation in the numbers of years covered would have distorted the incidence of disease slightly, since it fluctuated from year to year, but except in the case of cholera this factor probably did not make too much difference to the final result. Because of the state of the records, Lancashire's pattern of morbidity received disproportionate weight.[39]

Tuberculosis remained the greatest killer in the county prisons, although its incidence was much lower than at Millbank and did not account for the discrepancy between prison and external death rates. Consumption, or respiratory tuberculosis, accounted for 102 out of 499 deaths, for a death rate of 3.933 per thousand live prisoners. Other tubercular diseases took a further seven lives. The next most important causes of death were the other respiratory diseases, including asthma, bronchitis, pneumonia, and pleurisy. Together they took 101 lives, for a death rate of 3.895.

Typhus was still a very serious problem, despite the complacency with which Victorians referred to Howard's "fever-ridden gaols." In 1817, for example, Preston suffered an epidemic that killed three prisoners and infected at least seventeen more, forcing the establishment of a "lazaretto" on the other side of town. In 1822 67 Crown prisoners at Lancaster caught typhus in one week.[40] At the time of Baly's compilation, typhus alone took 62 prisoners out of the 499 who died, or 2.391 per thousand. It was inevitable that typhus should appear in the prisons, because it had never been eradicated from the poor and filthy Lancashire slums, but the prison surgeons had grown more skilled in treating it and containing outbreaks.

"Bowel complaints" was the next most important category of disease. This included cholera, dysentery, diarrhea, enteritis, ulceration of the bowel, and intestinal disease. Dysentery and diarrhea together took 38 lives, cholera only 5, and the entire group took 54 lives, or 2.031 per thousand. Prison surgeons were mystified about the causes of these ailments, though for the milder cases opiates offered an effective treatment.

Baly argued that these figures seriously underestimated the incidence of tuberculosis in English prisons, for two reasons. First, since tuberculosis was a slow, chronic disease whose course was easy to predict, patients who were likely to die of it in a relatively short time were more likely to obtain pardons than were prisoners killed by other diseases. Typhus and other fevers killed so quickly that if prisoners died of them at all they would die in gaol. Since there were no adequate statistics for the number of tubercular patients pardoned each year in the county prisons, Baly could not adjust his figures for this factor. Second, because tuberculosis was a slow disease and because the average term of imprisonment in the county prisons was relatively short, persons infected with tuberculosis when in prison would not have time to die of it before their release. The only prisoners dying in gaol of consumption were those who already had the disease upon commitment or those sentenced to very long terms. Baly cited indirect evidence suggesting that tuberculosis was often caught in prison, and argued as well that the known conditions of prison life were likely to encourage the disease's spread. He listed these causes as "1st, deficient ventilation; 2nd, cold; 3rd, want of active bodily exercise, and sedentary occupations; 4th, a listless, if not dejected state of mind; and 5th, poorness of the diet." He also argued that many of these conditions, such as "cold, scanty food and bad air," were not necessary to imprisonment and could be corrected.[41]

Baly's recommendations for remedying the situation reveal the shift that had taken place within English medicine from the contagionism of the late eighteenth century to a more miasmatic stance. Baly says little about the need to separate or quarantine prisoners, to screen and disinfect them on admission, or to prevent the transmission of disease through cleanliness. Instead, he concentrates on the need to choose a healthy situation for new prisons so as to avoid the effects of noxious miasma. His suggestions also reflect, however, the nature of the diseases that preoccupied him, particularly tuberculosis, against which "contagionist" measures could do little. The body has natural defenses against tuberculosis and, as long as it is otherwise healthy, can usually resist or contain it. Conditions that lower resistance, such as a poor diet, depression, or other diseases, can lead to infection or reactivate a previously quiescent case. Moreover, though tuberculosis bacilli are not affected by cold and can live for months, they are readily destroyed by sunlight. The adoption of Baly's recommendations that the prisoners get more food, exercise, air, and heat would have helped to mitigate the disease's effect. The complete isolation of all cases would have helped control its transmission, but tuberculosis was difficult to diagnose in its early stages.

The relentless cleanliness of many mid-Victorian prisons, which some modern writers have found so objectionable, probably helped somewhat to contain the incidence of other diseases, particularly typhus. The prison surgeons were hampered not so much by a lack of will as by ignorance. As Baly himself lamented, speaking of bowel diseases, "in one prison the greater prevalence of the disease in the summer season is ascribed to the use of *old* potatoes; in another, to the use of *new* potatoes. In a third, the gruel is thought to be the *cause*; while in a fourth, a bason [*sic*] of gruel at night is given as a *preventative*."[42] Despite these setbacks, it seems likely that the "reformed" prisons lived up to the purpose that had guided their foundation: to reduce the mortality of prisoners below the level that had prevailed in the late eighteenth century and to bring it close to that prevailing in the outside world, so that a sentence of imprisonment need not be tantamount to a sentence of death by fever. The death rates make it clear that the prisons still had a long way to go before they could be considered healthy places, and the variations in death rates between prisons show that to some extent the death rate could be affected by deliberate policy decisions. Nevertheless, epidemic disease could never be eliminated from the prisons until it was controlled in the population outside.

## The Debtors

Debtor self-government at Lancaster Castle persisted into the early nineteenth century largely unchanged. The central association continued to run a mock court, punish offenders, appoint officers, and subscribe to newspapers, but as the century progressed it seems to have gradually lost much of its importance.[43] The central courtroom was lost in 1807 because of overcrowding. Many of the association rules were incorporated into the official rules made for the debtors by the justices, and later by the Home Office, and were thereafter enforced by the gaoler rather than by the debtors themselves. Under the rules of 1841 the governor gained complete control of all charitable contributions and the right to punish debtors for quarreling and disorderliness.[44]

Whatever happened to the central association, the system centering on the different rooms continued to flourish. When new debtors arrived they were shown around the debtors' side of the Castle, known as the "half-crown side." They then chose the room they wished to enter and paid their "room money" to the "room's man." In 1843 the room money varied from 5s. for the Constables, a large room set aside for the poorest debtors, often from the Court of Requests, to 35s. for Number 4 and Number 8, which held only eight prisoners each. There were 32 rooms in all, two being set aside for women. The popularity, cost, and status of a room at any given time depended on its inhabitants and the skill of its room's man.[45]

The room's man filled a role similar to that of the landlady of a boardinghouse. Several made a good profit from their position. One room's man was said to have earned £800 by acting as a moneylender. In the 1860's the Quakers, a large room in the Lungess Tower, became the most popular because its enterprising room's man (who spent 32 years in the Castle) had furnished it in style with "easy chairs, sofas, a piano, and every thing to make the room look comfortable." The rooms' men of the wealthier rooms could count on a good profit from providing full board for their charges, who paid 7s. to 10s. a week for cooked meals and a daily bottle of ale. The wealthier rooms also offered such amenities as books, newspapers, games like dominoes and checkers, and even waiters at meals.[46]

While rooms' men held their posts until released from the Castle, other officers were elected monthly by every room. The Quakers had a chairman, a vice-chairman, a secretary-treasurer, a constable, a postman, and a cock-catcher, whose job was to introduce new members to the room. A popular method of separating incoming debtors from some of their money was to elect them president; a newly elected president was expected to provide dinner beer for three days and a special dinner on Sunday. The more gullible were then accused of misdeeds by the constable, tried, found guilty, and demoted. They were then urged to apply for a fresh trial, vindicated, reinstated, and forced to supply more beer and another Sunday dinner.[47]

Each room had its own rules and regulations, covering such items as cleanliness, clothing, mealtimes, indecent language, quarreling, writing on the walls of the water closet, and damage to communal property. The constable was responsible for keeping a record of all charges made. In the Quakers all accusations were heard at a weekly court, which had the power to punish offenders with fines or by "sending them to Coventry." Members of the room prosecuted the cases; the accused either defended themselves or chose defenders. A mock court also assembled to try the cases of debtors entering at the suit of hostile creditors in order to advise them whether to compound for the debt or go to court. In the Quakers it was an offense to make any complaint to the governor or the turnkeys unless the court had previously heard the case.[48]

Despite the many rules against drunkenness, gambling, profanity, quarreling, and misbehavior, the debtors' side of the prison was always relatively disorderly. Neither the inmates nor the officers objected to a certain rowdy conviviality as long as it was kept within reasonable bounds, but the prison inspectors complained of that atmosphere again and again. "The debtor," William John Williams lamented in 1837, "gradually loses his self-esteem. From want of occupation he descends to the association of those around him, and participates, by degrees, in their low and . . . intemperate enjoyments. He becomes . . . careless in person, dress, language, and habits. . . . Very few, I fear, are discharged, after a long sojourn, without having their sensibility seared, or their principles weakened, by daily contact with misery and vice."[49] Frederic Hill, Williams's successor, expressed a similar disgust: "Instead of being a place of rigid economy and sober reflection, the debtors' side of Lancaster Castle is like a somewhat noisy tavern and tea-garden;

the prisoners idling about, smoking, drinking, talking in a loud voice, and playing at skittles and pitch-farthing."[50]

Though it was almost impossible to control the debtors' consumption of alcohol, the evidence suggests that extreme drunkenness was less common by the 1840's than it had been at the beginning of the century. Hansbrow noted in 1843 that he had locked up a drunken debtor, "a rare occurrence this now-a-days."[51] Few entries in his journal compare with the epic drunken battles to be found in Higgin's. Gambling remained common, and Hansbrow did not make very strenuous exertions to stamp it out, merely confiscating the cards used and on one occasion remonstrating with the players for wasting their time indoors on such a fine day.

Many debtors spent their time in more innocent ways. Music and bowling were popular. A guide of 1843 offers a glimpse of the activities going on in the Constables: "in one of the windows is perched an industrious cobbler, . . . in another an unfortunate tailor. Over a fire of no ordinary dimensions, about half a dozen are leaning; in different parts of the room are groups in earnest conversation; here and there a few lie at full length on their bedsteads; . . . a party in a corner are exceedingly busy at a draught board; and . . . the room is nearly filled with tobacco smoke, emanating from a small knot of furious politicians."[52] One debtor, Edward Slack, occupied himself profitably by drawing the scenes around him and published a book of sketches on his release.

The high point of the debtors' year, although the prison inspectors no doubt disapproved, was a mock election to choose the "representatives of the ancient borough of John of Gaunt." Hustings were erected, deputations waited on potential candidates, election squibs were plastered all over the pump, and hopeful candidates offered bribes and treats on a large scale. The average expense of an election was estimated to be £50. The Conservative candidates invariably won.

On the whole, the condition of debtors changed little in the course of a hundred years. As late as 1835, debtors on the county allowance still received their pound of bread a day and ten pounds of potatoes a week; the only addition had been two pounds of oatmeal a week. They still lived in Norman towers, although a few new rooms and an arcade had been added for their benefit. They could still bring in their own bedding, now subject to inspection for cleanliness, and they still cooked over the open fires in their rooms. They still, if they wished, pursued a multiplicity of trades and shopped for meat, vegetables, and fish at the market held within the Castle. As they were not clothed by the county, many were still to be seen in rags, with "care-worn and haggard visages which express all the horrors of a withering poverty."[53] The gaoler had gained a little more formal control over their behavior, and the institutions of self-government had lost some of their strength, but these developments had not made any major alterations in their daily lives. Prison life had become slightly safer and more peaceful, mirroring changes in the outside world, but on the whole, prison reform had passed the debtors by. As far as they were concerned, the only really significant nineteenth-century reform was the complete abolition of imprisonment for debt in 1869.

## The Criminals

To radical historians, the middle of the nineteenth century represents the apotheosis of the strictly regimented prison. Michael Ignatieff gives a vivid account of the solitary life of a Pentonville convict, implicitly comparing it with the freer existence of the eighteenth-century prisoner.[54] "The opening of Pentonville in 1842," he writes, "represents a point of culmination in the tightening up of social controls underway since 1820."[55] The implied comparison is not entirely justified, since Pentonville was a national prison, built to hold men who in the previous century would have been executed or transported. Nevertheless, many elements of the Pentonville regime were also apparent in the county institutions, which by then were holding increasing numbers of felons.

All the Lancashire prisons claimed to follow a daily schedule that was relatively similar to that at Pentonville. At dawn in winter or at a fixed hour in summer, a bell would ring. After ten minutes the cells were unlocked and the prisoners went down to wash. They then worked until breakfast (8:30 at Lancaster). After breakfast they went to chapel for about thirty minutes and then returned to work until lunch (noon at Lancaster). A period of exercise followed lunch, then labor again, then supper. After supper, some prisoners were locked up, some took exercise, and some had a period of relative liberty.[56]

Such a schedule sounds rather forbidding in the official reports, but the entries in the governors' journals and the perpetual complaints of the prison inspectors show that the prisons often failed to live up to their strict routine. On the whole, prisoners probably suffered more from boredom than from overexertion. Lancaster Castle claimed a winter workday of seven hours, but in midwinter it was probably closer to five. Even after Preston converted to the separate system, many convicts there continued to work in large communal shops and suffered similar restrictions on their hours. William John Williams pointedly quoted the comment made by a hatter as he was being discharged from Lancaster: "I must now work a great deal harder than I have been doing here."[57] Any remaining impression of strict discipline is dispelled by such entries as the following in the Lancaster gaoler's journal: "The female crown prisoners reported for having returned their cotton unpicked. I am quite sure this is the result, not only of idleness, but of misapplication of time, for when I yesterday visited the penitentiary, the women were playing at blindman's buff in one shop, while those in the other were dancing."[58]

Lancaster Castle's old buildings, which were generally comfortable if difficult to supervise, and its humane but not strict government made it by far the most popular of Lancashire's prisons among seasoned criminals. Williams persistently demanded that the Castle impose silence, abolish paid convict labor, and institute compulsory instruction to clear itself "from the moral obloquy of being preferred by the criminal population to the other prisons of the county."[59] When Frederic Hill in 1847 asked inmates at random what they thought of the prison, he received answers such as "We are all very comfortable," "We are well attended to," and, at greater length, "My bedding is very clean. It is cleaner and better than I could get outside the prison. . . . If I was to work hard from Monday morning till Saturday night, I could not keep myself and my boy in the same comfort that I am kept in here. . . . The officers are all nice well-behaved men."[60] "The prisoners," Williams complained, "are frequently heard to declare themselves a great deal worse off out of the prison than within."[61]

Though the other three Lancashire prisons were less comfortable, their discipline also left a good deal to be desired. Despite the praises of visitors to Preston it seems evident that by 1820 its keeper had become corrupt and had taken to playing cards with his charges. Later keepers did little to improve matters until the mid-1840's, when Clay finally succeeded in persuading the justices to adopt some of his radical suggestions. In 1839 Williams wrote that he regretted that "some endeavours have not been made to place this prison in a more creditable state of discipline. The defects and improprieties . . . are still unsupplied or unchecked, and are quite independent of the question whether this or that system of discipline should be introduced, being such as ought not, with propriety, to be tolerated under any. If I am not greatly mistaken, there is a disposition to employ physical rather than moral means in the government of this establishment. . . . I am persuaded that, in many instances, imprisonment here is looked upon as the reverse of a punishment."[62] Lancashire, which had been in the forefront of reforming counties in the late eighteenth century, was growing tired, its prisons were growing shabby, and their management had been overwhelmed by the endless tide of bodies.

The discipline at Salford, in Williams's eyes, was vestigial:

From the variety of employments carried on in various parts of the prison, and their want of concentration, it is quite impossible that any effectual supervision can take place. During the day prisoners of both sexes are continually traversing the yards. . . . The matron states—"I have found a great inconvenience in the number of the male prisoners who come to the female side. . . . They bring . . . shoes to bind, wool to pick, cotton to wind, and every morning coals into the cookhouse, where they see the female cooks. . . ." When I was visiting them a male prisoner was engaged in painting the exterior window sashes, women being at work within, without an overlooker. Tobacco in large quantities is thrown over the walls.[63]

The radical publisher John Doherty, briefly imprisoned in Salford in 1832, claimed that he found lice in his bedding. The beef for the prisoners' dinner "stunk most intolerably; so much so, that after . . . smelling several lots, I was obliged to go into the air to prevent me being sick."[64] As late as 1850, Hepworth Dixon was writing that the Salford New Bailey, once a monument to Howard, was "thoroughly *bad.*" Silence was enforced only partially, prisoners were not classified, the labor was unproductive, little instruction was offered, and the discipline was "loose, irregular, and unsatisfactory."[65] The New Bailey was probably the least popular of Lancashire's institutions among the prisoners themselves; the cells were overcrowded, the food was scanty, and the prisoners were especially likely to prey on one another.

In the eyes of the inspector, however, Kirkdale was the worst of all. On early visits, Williams found treadwheel prisoners talking loudly to each other without proper supervision and "in a most filthy state, their legs and feet encrusted with dirt."[66] Tobacco was everywhere. The workrooms were untidy and neglected. A group of prisoners in one of the dayrooms was brewing coffee that had come over the wall. Thefts were frequent; one of the turnkeys admitted that "there is an idea among the prisoners that they can obtain offices . . . such as that of cook, for money."[67] Breaches of discipline were rarely reported to the governor. At least one of the monitors, a prisoner, carried a leather thong for punishing the boys under his charge. Williams concluded that

the general discipline, and entire system of management in this prison is . . . most faulty, and calculated rather to encourage crime than repress it. Scarcely any of the penalties awarded by the law are inflicted with due severity. . . . Imprisonment here generally, from the prettiness of the garden, the temporal advantages, and the constant communication which takes place between all classes of prisoners, is little more than nominal. The chaplain . . . states "that a female prisoner . . . appeared greatly distressed at coming in, but . . . seeing the garden her grief vanished, and she exclaimed with astonishment, 'Dear me, what a pretty place!' "[68]

The real problem at Kirkdale was the reluctance of the justices to discharge the governor and matron, who had grown too old and frail to carry out their duties. When Williams returned the following year, no improvements had been made. The many improprieties, he wrote, "plainly manifest either gross neglect of duty in the officers or something worse."[69] Williams, however, had little influence with the justices. It was not until his tenth report, written in 1845, that he finally had the satisfaction of noting that a general improvement had taken place in the management of Kirkdale since the replacement of the gaoler and matron.

It is difficult to escape the conclusion that Lancashire prisoners were seldom strictly regimented during the day. The prison buildings were too old or too poorly designed, the prison staff too small, the justices too anxious to save money by assigning prisoners to maintenance work or to trades they already knew, for the constant vigilance that would have been necessary. Only at Preston, for a brief period, was an order imposed that Hepworth Dixon found "admirable; in fact too admirable," because the prisoners' eyes never wandered from their work.[70]

Though the prison days offered many diversions, the prison nights were often intolerably long. In the winter prisoners might be locked in for as many as seventeen hours at a time. Legislation had prohibited the assignment of only two prisoners to any cell; the cells could hold one prisoner or three or more. When prisoners were alone they suffered intense boredom. When several prisoners shared a cell they were uncomfortable: the cells were too small, they got on each other's nerves, and they were often afraid of one another. Serious assaults were comparatively rare in the prisons, although they did take place occasionally; an insane prisoner at Preston kicked a fifteen-year-old boy to death in 1842.[71] Higgin and his staff had once gone in constant fear of the gangs of desperate convicts who perpetually plotted to overpower their guards and escape. Such attempts had become much less common by Hansbrow's day; aside from occasional episodes of pushing, turnkeys were rarely assaulted, although they were often threatened.

Entries in the gaolers' journals and the occasional comments of prisoners themselves show that the communal life they led was not always idyllic or cooperative. Three Lancashire prisoners testified before the Select Committee on Gaols and Houses of Correction in 1835, when it was considering converting prisons to the silent system.[72] One inmate from Lancaster Castle stated that he shared a yard and dayroom with 20 to 30 others. No officer was present. At night they slept either one or three to a cell and there was

noise and singing for Two or Three Hours. . . . Some of all Sorts were there; much Talk about Crime; much swearing and indecent Talk; some had been in Prison before, some had been transported before, and some who seemed to take a Delight in telling what they had done. . . . A wretched bad Place altogether, . . . worse before Trial than after Trial . . . for Contamination; nothing to do, and always contriving Mischief. . . . Had rather be in a Place by himself, or in total Silence, than be amongst such a rough Set; it is the biggest Punishment to be amongst such; always quarrelling and fighting, and no Peace.

An eighteen-year-old thief who had spent ten weeks at Kirkdale before his trial and twenty weeks after said he "spent the day in Idleness. . . . There was very bad Talk; the longer a Man stops in such a Place the worse he is." The third witness stated that at Preston no officer was present in the ward to keep order and to protect prisoners from their companions.

Even for prisoners who were cynical to begin with, or who had become "hardened" by frequent internments, there were many sources of fear and tension. Even after the establishment of county lunatic asylums, prisoners who were insane or "half-crazed" posed a constant hazard to their companions and presented a persistent conundrum to their harassed gaolers. Lunatics remained common in the houses of correction, which continued to serve as convenient dumping grounds for problem cases. Seven of the thirteen visits to Kirkdale made by the visiting justices in 1844-45 were to see insane prisoners.[73]

Lancaster Castle was by this time supposed to be free of lunatics, but they frequently appeared nevertheless. Juries were often reluctant to acquit even distinctly eccentric offenders on the grounds of insanity. Official ineptitude accounted for the presence of others, much to Hansbrow's annoyance. In 1846 he wrote that he had received a "perfectly insane" convict from Preston. "I am at a loss," he added, "to understand why . . . the Preston authorities have not effected his removal to an Asylum . . . and . . . avoided the painful exposure of an unfortunate and irascible being in a Court of Justice."[74]

Once insane prisoners had been sent to gaol, they were unlikely to be removed. Even when the gaoler was convinced that a prisoner was genuinely mad, the transfer process was slow and unreliable. In July 1845 Hansbrow wrote that a female felon had had another access of insanity and had been placed in the hospital with some difficulty. When he visited her he found her "quite frantic—screaming, dancing etc." He noted that he intended to take steps to remove her to the asylum, but she was still in the Castle on October 9.[75] Because malingerers hoping to avoid the full penalties of the law often chose to simulate insanity, prison administrators, unable to distinguish the false from the true, preferred to err on the side of skepticism. In 1843 a Lancaster felon named Ann Ray, whose behavior had already been bad, assaulted one of her companions, beating her severely about the head and trying to kill her. Ray was brought before a visiting justice and "behaved most violently" when he sentenced her to 25 days' solitary confinement. A few days later Hansbrow wrote that she had refused to eat for three or four days and that "whenever I have visited her . . . I have found her singing wildly, and in other respects acting like a maniac." The justices and two doctors came to see her but decided that she was only simulating insanity. "If so," said Hansbrow, unconvinced, "she is acting her part very skilfully."[76] Within four days, Ray was in the hospital, where she and a companion were so violent that the matron was forced to put them in straitjackets. Even then, she managed to break four panes of glass.

Insane prisoners posed the most dramatic threat to the tranquillity of the prison and to the safety of their fellow prisoners, but they were not the only discordant element in prison life. Less visible but more pervasive were the effects of the inmate subculture. This was organized around the bartering or purloining of food and the exchange of contraband such as tobacco, writing paper, extra clothing, and, occasionally, opium. The extent of such trading depended on the conditions in the prison and the vigilance of the staff, but it was present everywhere. At

Lancaster the chief sources of trouble among the criminals were the boys, who traded their bread to some of the older men in exchange for protection from the other prisoners. The head turnkey told Williams in 1843 that "the boys give their food to some of the men, and those men side with them. No man dare complain of the boys, for he is sure to be beaten or annoyed." Two of the monitors confirmed this, and a prisoner asked to be put into solitary because: "I am ruptured, and the boys are always jeering me about it." Another prisoner said, "I have no fault to find with the officers. . . . If the boys were quite away from us there would be no reports. The men induce the boys to commit faults; there would be no more complaints than from the other wards if the boys were away from us."[77] That summer the boys were more fully segregated in a silent shop of their own, which alleviated this source of irritation.

This problem with boys and their older "protectors" may suggest homosexuality. Patricia O'Brien has found considerable evidence of sexual and sentimental attachments among French prisoners in the nineteenth century.[78] Evidence of such activity in Lancashire prisons is very scarce, however, both in the inspectors' reports and in the gaolers' journals, which might be expected to be more frank. The biggest sexual problem was keeping the women separate from both the male prisoners and the male prison staff. The county was very slow to hire female matrons and turnkeys for the women's side of the prison, and a female convict in Lancaster created a scandal in 1820 when she accused a turnkey of making improper advances to her.[79] I have found only one unambiguous reference to homosexual advances. William John Williams included in his 1839 report on Kirkdale an extract from the chaplain's journal about "an abominable crime committed by two young men." Four days later the boys were brought before a magistrate and charged with robbing younger boys of their provisions and beating and kicking them. Further charges stated that they were guilty of a "crime formerly capital" and that one of them had made an attempt on another boy who had reported it to a turnkey and refused to share the same cell any longer. These charges, however, were dismissed because they rested solely on the testimony of "criminals." Shortly thereafter, all prisoners were placed in separate night cells.

Clay's biography contains a more ambiguous reference to "vile practices and disgusting profligacy, to which the turnkeys were suspiciously blind."[80] Although the chaplains were far less tolerant of sexual activity than was the secular administration, sexual advances were a potentially serious source of discord and violence among the prisoners and probably encouraged increased segregation. Certainly, the complaints about the "corrupting influence of prison" and the demands for ever more complete separation carry an undertone of sexual anxiety. It is difficult to see how infractions could be prevented, with a staff distinguished by its absence and a magistracy reluctant to accept the unsubstantiated complaints of "criminals." Nevertheless, it seems likely that there were comparatively few cases of brutal aggression in sexual affairs, as in other aspects of prison life, and that the absence of reported instances of homosexual rape bears some relation to reality. In this, as in other aspects of prison discipline, a comparatively low level of violence was due more to the habitual behavior of the prisoners than to any efforts by the staff.

A significant prop of the prison subculture was the sale of food, which supported the underground economy and provided a frequent occasion for violence. Hansbrow vigorously attacked the practice by having suspected sellers take their meals at a special "traffickers mess," which was closely superintended by a turnkey. All uneaten food was returned to the kitchens. The governor believed that in making these assignments he was protecting prisoners from their own folly or from the intimidation of others, but often the prisoners themselves felt they were being singled out for punishment. Food continued to be bartered sporadically at Lancaster, but neither there nor at Preston, where the supply was relatively generous, did the problem attain the proportions it did at Salford, where the diet was poor and the large size of the prison population completely precluded superintendence by the inadequate staff. Doherty contrasted the "thin, tasteless and almost black" gruel, sour black bread, and stinking meat of the New Bailey with Lancaster's "thick and palatable" gruel, "sweet and wholesome" meat, and bread "of the very best quality."[81] Hansbrow wrote that he had disciplined a man for having 2s. 6d. in cash that he had smuggled in from the New Bailey "under the impression that the diet of this Gaol would be as meagre as that of Salford, and that *here*, as he tells me the prisoners did *there, he might purchase his* comrades' food; but that he found *he had no use for his money*."[82]

Quarrels over food, barter, and loans were a frequent source of tension between prisoners, who often felt they had received the short end of the bargain but did not dare to complain. Another source of tension was the hostility that the prisoners showed as a group to those who did not fit in because they were too religious, feeble-minded, or deformed, or because they came from the countryside or another country. In 1844 a felon approached Hansbrow "under apparently very excited feelings" to complain that the schoolmaster "was in the habit of referring to his being an Irishman, which brought down upon him the ridicule of his comrades."[83] Two years later the gaoler wrote that a Jew named Philip Lipman claimed that the persecution of other prisoners had forced him to quit school. He added, "I fear there is too much truth in his complaints—because he is a foreigner."[84]

The communal feeling that sometimes led prisoners to turn on the misfits in their midst also enabled them to act together to protect their interests. Like the workers in the mills outside the walls, the prisoners cooperated to restrict the amount of work exacted of them. Hansbrow wrote in 1845 that a felon complained that potatoes were thrown at him and that he had been threatened because " 'he does *too much* work!' as a Weaver! I really am at a loss to understand the meaning of this."[85] Four months later a felon refused to continue power-loom weaving because his companions threatened him for working too hard. The army-trained governor was incredulous when he heard such tales, but any factory master could have enlightened him.

The prisoners also banded together to air grievances. The most common cause of complaint, even at Lancaster, was the food. In 1843, for example, the Castle prisoners refused to work because they felt they had been given bad potatoes. A visiting justice promised them he would try to obtain a better supply and the prisoners then returned to work. They were reproved but not punished. The most serious incident of this sort recorded in Hansbrow's diaries came in 1848, when a prisoner was taken sick in the night and died two hours later in the infirmary. The next morning the convicted felons refused to work until they saw the governor, the surgeon, and a magistrate. They complained that the turnkey on duty the night before had been slow to answer their call for help. The turnkey denied the charge and Hansbrow reminded the prisoners that officers on night duty were constantly disturbed by false alarms and that he himself had warned them of the danger of "crying wolf." He promised that any prisoner who had something to say would be allowed to testify at the inquest, and they all returned to work. The next day the prisoners on three wards, led by a man named Buck, complained that the potatoes were bad. Although prisoners were always reprimanded for such concerted protests, there seems to have been a tacit understanding that they would not be punished as long as they behaved peaceably and returned to work once they had made their point.[86]

Prisoners were punished, however, for a wide range of other offenses. Evidence about the frequency of such punishments can be obtained from the schedule B returns in the *Parliamentary Papers*, although the accuracy of this source is open to some question. Nevertheless, when the records of the four county prisons are viewed together, some facts seem evident. One is the relative infrequency with which any prison resorted to the harsh corporal penalties of whipping or ironing. Irons were nearly always reserved for men who attempted escape; their use is probably a better indicator of the security a prison maintained than of the severity of its discipline. Whippings, however, are another story. They were reserved for prisoners who had committed serious offenses and remained unmoved by other penalties. The average number of whippings at the New Bailey, which had been 1.4 per year from 1823 to 1837, suddenly rose between 1838 and 1845 to 14, suggesting that the governor was anxious to reimpose discipline on an essentially disorderly institution. The prison had failed, but the staff was not yet ready to admit defeat. By contrast, both Lancaster and Preston consistently imposed minor punishments with few whippings (about one per year at Lancaster and two every three years at Preston), suggesting the relatively gentle maintenance of order. Kirkdale, after seventeen whippings in 1825, imposed few punishments at all until 1841, suggesting that the staff had simply given up altogether.[87]

Few convicts ever experienced a whipping. Except at the New Bailey, there were rarely as many as six in one prison in a year. The milder punishments, however, were much more common. Governors had the right to sentence offenders on their own authority to up to three days' confinement on bread and water in a dark cell. They also administered a number of other minor penalties, of which the most important was the stoppage of some or all of a prisoner's food. Early reformers, such as Bayley, had encouraged the use of dietary sanctions, but in the early 1850's, as a result of several well-publicized scandals, including one at Manchester borough gaol in 1851, dietary penalties were banned.[88]

At Lancaster Castle, the incidence of most punishments remained relatively stable between 1823 and 1847, despite a change of gaolers in 1832. In each of the houses of correction, however, there was a year in which the number of minor punishments suddenly increased to a much higher level, remaining high or even increasing thereafter. At Salford, the total number of punishments went from 373 in 1835 to 2,369 in 1836 and to 4,181 in 1837. At Preston the total rose from 458 in 1842 to 3,089 in 1843, and at Kirkdale it rose from 521 in 1843 to 2,910 in 1844. This increase seems to have been due as much to accident and new staff as to the consistent application of a new policy. The rise at Preston coincides with the period of Clay's ascendancy and, in particular, with the completion of a wing of separate cells and the enforcement of the silent system in 1843. Preston also had a new governor that year. Similarly, an increase of penalties at Kirkdale in 1844-45 corresponds with the appointment of a new governor there who was attempting to correct the very lax administration of his predecessor. At both of these institutions, the adoption of the silent system brought an immediate increase in the number of penalties, since speaking became a punishable offense. It was this irritating proliferation of minor punishments for natural infractions that was the chief complaint of the silent system's critics.

The New Bailey had four different governors in the 1840's, but the significance of any changes in the number of punishments there is obscured by the returns' patent unreliability in recording minor penalties before 1834. The returns for the 1840's, however, show a relatively high incidence of minor penalties in an institution that was making only a lackluster attempt to enforce silence: prisoners were told not to speak on the treadwheel but were not supervised by an officer, while prisoners in the wool-picking rooms were allowed to speak in low tones. Hepworth Dixon, who visited the New Bailey in the late 1840's (probably in 1848), commented on the large number of punishments there, which had reached 8,407 a year by the date of his visit. He blamed this "monstrously high" figure on the poor design and bad discipline of the gaol.[89]

The general level of punishment was quite low at all three houses of correction until the early 1840's. This fact suggests that the prison staff were not making any effort to "reform" the prisons in the direction of a more stringent discipline until the Pentonville period. The reasons for the rapid escalation thereafter are diverse, but even a relatively large number of punishments was compatible with a very old-fashioned regime. Even if they had wished to, the New Bailey staff could hardly have enforced discipline on a Pentonville scale; in 1843 the total staff numbered 27, including professional men like the surgeon and chaplain, administrators like the governor and steward, industrial staff like the miller and the taskmaster, and gatekeepers and watchmen. There were only ten full-time turnkeys trying to maintain order among about 700 inmates, and not all these men were on duty all the time.[90] By the time of Hepworth Dixon's visit the number of staff members had risen, but only to 42.

The other county prisons were similarly shorthanded. In 1843 Lancaster Castle had a total staff of 28 men and women, including 14 "monitors" and "monitoresses" and only 5 turnkeys.[91] Kirkdale in 1836 had a staff of 23, including 10 turnkeys, and Preston in the same year managed on a staff of only 16, including 5 turnkeys.[92] Even Manchester's eventual complement of 42 seems ridiculously small by modern standards. It is obvious that nineteenth-century turnkeys could hope to keep order only with the cooperation of a large proportion of the prison community.

This impression of comparatively mild discipline and the relative infrequency of life-threatening offenses is confirmed by the surviving volumes of the Lancashire gaolers' journals. Most violence occurred in the course of fights between two or three men, and the most dangerous weapons used were the heavy wooden clogs the men wore at work. Most of the offenders who were reported to the governor received a penalty, but most penalties were small: an hour or a few hours in the lockup, rarely more than a day. In one case, Higgin went so far as to forgive a man who had threatened to kill him with a piece of iron. Frederic Hill commented that though Hansbrow's journal contained "scenes of gross misconduct on the part of some of the prisoners, implying a very imperfect state of discipline, several entries in the journal show a habit of patient investigation by the governor, an anxious desire on his part to avoid inflicting unmerited punishment, and a general willingness to render friendly services to the prisoners."[93]

If prison life in nineteenth-century Lancashire was far from being a communal Eden, it was equally far from serving as the highly regimented "machine for grinding men good" evoked by the radical critics of reform. The main problems were the traditional ones: corruption, peculation, overcrowding, dirt, lax discipline, and violence or intimidation directed against some prisoners by others. Increased discipline, and particularly increased cellular confinement, reduced the contact between prisoners and increased their physical security as it reduced their freedom to do and say what they pleased, but with the partial exception of Preston that discipline never came close to altering, manipulating, or controlling prisoners' minds as the reformers had hoped and as the critics have charged.

# CHAPTER 8

# Toward the Future: John Clay and the Separate System

## Prison Labor and William Liddell

However lax Lancashire's other prisons had become, Preston symbolized for the whole nation the fluctuating currents of reform, from "Benthamite" labor regimes to "Evangelical" isolation. The Rev. John Clay, Preston's chaplain, was the chief local proponent of the separate system, and his writings made him a figure of national importance. His effort to introduce the silent and separate systems constituted a sustained attack on the prison community and on the way early Victorian prisons were run. For historians, Clay's explicit social theory and apparent success in implementing it make his work central to the case for a "social control" model in the Pentonville period. An examination of the way in which prison reform was adopted in Preston, however, reveals that even there it was limited in scope and never fully implemented. Even at Preston, reform was bedeviled by the problems of unintended consequences and limited resources. Nonetheless, the dilemmas raised by Clay's approach to crime are still with us today.

Preston began to have a prominent role in national penal policies even before Clay arrived, when it undertook its first great experiment: the enforcement of a comprehensive labor system. Eighteenth-century reformers had been unanimous in calling for the more thorough imposition of labor in the prisons. They frequently referred to the success of the Dutch *rasphouses* in setting their inmates to work and lamented the relative idleness of the English prisoner even in the bridewells established to teach habits of industry. Howard cited with approval the Dutch maxim "Make them diligent and they will be honest." Bayley quoted it to his colleagues.[1]

Lancashire was relatively successful in finding work for its inmates, because the growing textile industry provided steady employment at least until the hungry forties. On his visits to the north, James Neild commented very favorably on the profitable labor of its prisons. Nevertheless, even in Lancashire there was never a time when profitable labor was successfully imposed in all four prisons at once. At Preston, however, it served as the cornerstone of prison life for some years. Its eventual failure is a story of clashing ideologies and conflicting personalities.

Preston's industrial policy was introduced by its keeper, William Liddell, shortly after his appointment in 1817. He later commented that "my reason for setting them to work was this, when the men have been tried, and the jury have found them guilty, the magistrates would ask them what they had to say for themselves; they would say, 'I could not help it, I was a sailor and could not get a ship; or I could get nothing to do, and I went to the parish officers and they gave me a shilling and turned me away:' and I then determined I would give them a trade."[2]

Three Preston textile firms employed the Preston inmates to weave cotton and cambric. They were encouraged by an allowance of one-fourth the gross value of their work and by the occasional offer of an extra noggin of gruel. Only those with terms of six months or more, or with previous training, became weavers; the others were employed in batting and picking cotton or other simple tasks. The looms of Preston soon became a national symbol of industrious imprisonment. In 1819 Liddell testified before the Select Committee on Gaols as an expert witness. Elizabeth Fry and Joseph Gurney, who visited Preston at about the same date, praised his efforts. "The Governor," Gurney wrote, "has met with great success in two respects. He has, by his kindness, gained the hearts of his prisoners . . . and he has contrived to provide them all with full employment. The consequence is, that he governs with comfort to them, and facility to himself. . . . One thing seems wanting; —namely, more religious care and instruction."[3]

Liddell agreed with Gurney; he acknowledged to the committee that the chaplain came only to hold the Sunday service and that the prisoners received no instruction. Asked whether his system had any effect on their moral character, he replied, "I think a little more religious instruction would be better for them." This suggestion was soon carried out;

under the provisions of Peel's Act, the justices appointed schoolmasters to instruct the illiterate boys. More important, in 1821 they had replaced the aged and ineffective chaplain with a zealous and energetic young man: John Clay. It was this appointment that brought about Liddell's downfall.

By the early 1820's, many Englishmen were beginning to have second thoughts about the desirability of industrial prisons.[4] The Benthamites, who had little faith in spiritual regeneration, stuck firmly to the value of productive labor, on the grounds that it was the most profitable way of keeping prisoners occupied, that it could do no harm, and that it might lead prisoners to develop good habits. The true Benthamites in prison administration continued to emphasize the advantages of productive labor throughout the first half of the century; among them were William John Williams and the Hill brothers.[5] This policy, however, was under attack from two sides. On the one hand, the "Evangelicals" maintained that labor regimes were hardening prisoners and failing to bring about that creative anguish that alone could transform the spirit and reform the mind. On the other hand, the "common-sense school" regarded with dismay the many improvements in the physical comfort of prisoners that the reforms had created. Prisoners, they pointed out, now had better food, clothing, shelter, and medical attention than did many free laborers. They worked shorter hours, and weaving was not an arduous trade. Imprisonment was actually becoming attractive to the poor.[6]

Though useless hard labor schemes were popular with certain segments of the population, however, the loss of income that they entailed was not. Lancashire magistrates, sensitive to increases in the rates and surrounded by manufacturers anxious to find more labor, were never enthusiastic about demands that they convert profitable prison manufactories into places of worthless and unpleasant activity merely to make prisoners more uncomfortable. Indeed, despite objections from all sides, they did their best to extract useful labor from their recalcitrant subjects and even paid them when necessary to encourage effort. After a certain amount of campaigning by zealous reformers, led by Clay, they did introduce treadwheels into all four county prisons in the 1820's, but the power the wheels provided was applied to practical objects, and their use often depended on the power requirements of the prison rather than on the number of inmates deserving hardship. For example, the Kirkdale wheel ground grain into flour. The Lancaster wheel ran the power looms, a system used nowhere else in England. When crank labor was introduced into Kirkdale's separate cells in 1851, it pumped water for the prison.

To the disgust of William John Williams, Lancashire prisons not only continued to employ prisoners as needed in miscellaneous tasks around the buildings and grounds but also paid them a little extra for such work. At Preston, for example, on August 15, 1836, 21 felons and 35 misdemeanants, out of a total population of 161, were grinding flour on the treadwheel. Forty-three prisoners were weaving, winding, or picking cotton, three were cooking, one was acting as a personal servant to the matron, and twelve were serving as "constables." A joiner, a painter, a barber, a flour carrier, a miller's assistant, two whitewashers, and six laborers were pursuing their trades. Four chapel singers and four gardeners received an extra allowance of food. Williams complained that paying the prisoners was bad enough, but giving them extra food when the diet was ample "appears quite preposterous and likely to encourage the very opposite to habits of frugality."[7] He objected even more strongly to the use of prisoners to maintain the large and beautiful ornamental garden just inside the gate. His successor, Frederic Hill, however, a strong proponent of industrial labor, cooperated closely with the justices to introduce a variety of trades.

Prison officials had initially greeted the treadmills with enthusiasm. Convicts, it was said, loathed them and were staying away from prison in droves. John Clay reported that news of the hated machines was being spread through the poorer classes by means of broadside ballads. The authorities' enthusiasm quickly waned, however. Humanitarians began to rally against the common-sense school, claiming that treadmills were cruel and harmful to health. They stunted growth, overheated the body, caused hernias, and brought on miscarriages. In the meantime, ironically, prison officers discovered that treadmills, when used moderately, were not all that unpopular among their charges. While a fat man might endure agonies climbing the "endless staircase," old lags soon mastered the art of sliding their feet from one rung to the next with a minimum of effort and used the opportunity to converse with their friends. As late as 1850, Hepworth Dixon wrote that "a strong proof of the want of more and harder work in the castle [Lancaster] is—that prisoners *desire* to go on the wheel: they say they are starved in the winter months, and want heavier labour to keep them warm!"[8] His comments were confirmed by bemused justices and gaolers all over England. Humanitarians never believed these reports and succeeded in prohibiting treadwheel labor for certain groups, particularly women and boys, but it continued in use in a desultory way, especially in those prisons where the power it provided was useful.

At Preston, John Clay quickly became disillusioned about the deterrent effect of treadmill labor. He began to seek other solutions to the problem of crime and soon began to oppose Preston's emphasis on profitable labor and its disregard of the sinfulness and spiritual needs of its inmates. His son's description conveys Clay's jaundiced view of Liddell: "a rough and ready bully, with a flavour of good nature, and wit enough to manage the prison cheaply. . . . He had been successively sergeant in the army, butler to a county magnate, and a publican. His military experience, his old master's influence, and (it was said) the excellence of his tap, procured him the post. . . . Economically he worked the prison with success, and being a kind-hearted man, though coarse and violent-tempered, he neither practiced nor permitted cruelty."[9]

Liddell's failure to discipline his staff had become evident shortly before Clay's appointment, in the same year Gurney's journal was published. The Preston Michaelmas Quarter Sessions of 1820 dismissed two turnkeys for misconduct. Disgruntled, these men in turn preferred charges against the gaoler, surgeon, and chaplain, claiming that the bodies of prisoners dying in confinement had secretly been given to Lancaster surgeons to dissect. Two justices found that this had indeed happened, although they cleared the surgeon and other officers of participation or knowledge. They also found that "some irregularities have certainly existed . . . from the want of rules and regulations, of which there does not appear ever to have been any at all sufficient for the . . . conduct of the officers."[10] After this wholesale rejection of the work of the late-eighteenth-century reformers, however, the justices blamed the two discharged turnkeys for most of the "irregularities."

Clay cooperated with Liddell for some time, but it became increasingly clear that the two men's ideas about the governance of the prison were incompatible. Clay's son credited Clay with the appointment of a schoolmaster and a matron, although the fact that both were required by the act of 1823 may have been a more important factor. The matron, however, was a friend of his and he supported her against the governor. Walter Lowe Clay wrote that her appointment "considerably embarrassed" Liddell's "household arrangements" and that Clay's reforms "began to trench on his own privileges." For his part, Clay was disgusted by the "open riot and blasphemy" in the yards—where prisoners stole, gambled, boxed, and smoked with impunity—and even more distressed by the "vile practices" that were ignored by the turnkeys.[11]

About five years after his appointment, Clay wrote to the justices, charging Liddell with misconduct. At first they rejected his charges and publicly censured him for making them. The matter rested there for some time, until newspapers published a story that Liddell had "tortured" an inmate by putting her in a scold's bridle. The fact that this action alone was considered scandalous and newsworthy is a sign of the quiet change that had been taking place in public sentiment during the Age of Reform, despite the superficial complaints about "coddling criminals"; at the end of the eighteenth century scold's bridles had been used without arousing any comment.[12] The Home Office inquired into the matter and an embarrassed justice, Thomas Hesketh, wrote that the bridle had been in Preston for many years but that the justices "were not aware that it had been used in modern Times" until they had investigated.[13]

Once again, the justices initiated an inquiry into Liddell's conduct, urged on by the newspapers and, according to Walter Lowe Clay, by a "fatal suspicion that he was too lenient to poachers."[14] On March 28, 1827, they resolved that Liddell's "general habits . . . were those of intoxication."[15] After three days of hearings, they dismissed him for intoxication, neglect of duty, neglect of classification and cleanliness, gambling, improper delegation of authority, failing to discipline staff, peculation, and improper and unkind behavior to the matron. Oddly enough, Walter Lowe Clay found Liddell's dismissal rather harsh because, he said, no better conduct was expected of the gaolers of the time. Perhaps Liddell seemed better in retrospect, for Clay and the new governor, Capt. Anthony, were almost immediately at odds over Anthony's opposition to the "introduction of educational and religious influences," and his imposition of "Quarterdeck discipline, rough, capricious and tyrannical."[16]

This recurrent conflict at Preston can be seen in several perspectives. In one way it was purely a battle for power between the governor, who officially ran the prison, and the chaplain, who thought he knew how it should be run. On another level, the conflict can be seen as a confrontation between reformers and the unreformed prison. Many people were not as convinced as Clay was that swearing and smoking should be stamped out at any cost, including the prohibition of any speech or communication between the prisoners. The Preston justices had never been great reformers; they had trailed the field in the late eighteenth century and had been prepared to overlook many admitted "irregularities" in 1821. Clay complained, with some justification, that Preston was so comfortable that it was attracting prisoners; the resistance of the justices to his costly suggestions for making prison less pleasant was not necessarily a sign of inhumanity. Walter Lowe Clay himself conceded that Liddell was not a cruel man. Like most reformers, Clay was campaigning on two fronts: to increase physical comfort while simultaneously introducing psychological discomfort to maintain lesser eligibility.

On a third level, the conflict was between two competing systems of reform rather than between reform and tradition. Liddell, after all, was considered a reformer by his contemporaries, although apparently the passage of years had relaxed his energy and honesty. He had undoubtedly succeeded in making his charges industrious, but the "Evangelicals" were no longer prepared to agree that that was sufficient to render them honest.

However one looks at the conflict, three things are clear. The first is the importance of an uncensored press in prison affairs. Liddell had already triumphed in two investigations and the justices had actually censured those who had dared to bring charges against him, when newspapers forced a third investigation. By publishing the testimony the local papers made it very difficult for the justices to retain Liddell, whatever their wishes. The press was an unreliable check, ignoring ordinary, everyday peculation and pouncing eagerly on sensational allegations, but nevertheless, it played an important role in prison life.

The second conclusion is that many of the eighteenth-century reforms had been relatively ineffective. There can be no question that the prisons of the 1830's were very different from their predecessors. In the 1770's Preston had contained a huddle of about a dozen prisoners who lived without water and slept in "eleven Closets." By 1830 it was a large and organized institution that provided food, clothing, baths, employment, medical services, education, and religious training to about 200 prisoners living in 138 sleeping cells and working in a large complex of buildings containing workrooms, common rooms, kitchens, a chapel, a reception wing, a boiler house, bathhouses, a treadwheel shed, a governor's house, sickrooms, and separated airing yards. Yet in many ways the prisons had changed little. The most common complaint made by the prison inspectors was that prison discipline was too lax. For one reason or another it had been easier to improve the physical plant in which prisoners lived than to subject them to a more rigorous discipline. The new buildings had become as dirty and crowded as the old ones had been; the carefully written rules were dismissed by the justices as "not at all sufficient" and were in any case largely ignored.

Measures to prevent bribery and peculation were almost totally ineffective. In fact, the opportunities for such activities had increased; once the state undertook to provide for the needs of prisoners, in place of the earlier direct trading for commodities between individual prisoners and suppliers, the prison staff were in the position of middlemen who could alter the quality of the goods provided to almost any extent. It was difficult to compare what the contractor provided with what the prisoner received. Such peculation was also common among the few prisoners in the privileged positions of cook, clothing supplier, warehouseman, or laborer; indeed, the offense was so common that the offenders were rarely punished severely when caught.

The final conclusion is that the prison staff were gaining in importance. Liddell's story is another example of the fact that the eighteenth-century reforms had increased the power of the governor without increasing the justices' control over prison affairs. Of equal significance in this case was the growing importance of the other professional members of the prison staff: the surgeon who stopped the punishment of the bridled woman, the chaplain who brought charges against the governor, and the matron who testified against him. Though historians have paid a great deal of attention to the national inspectorate's place in the growth of reform movements, they have neglected the development of a professional and experienced group of administrators within the local institutions themselves. Of these, the gaoler or warden wielded by far the most power, but other professional staff members were often more vocal. The comparatively high wages paid to prison staff meant that those posts were far more likely to attract able and ambitious men and women than were such institutions as the workhouses. These staff members were, in turn, more likely to gain a hearing for their demands for further reform. Chaplains and surgeons were particularly well placed to collect the evidence to back up their demands. It was Clay's assiduity in collecting such evidence and in publishing his recommendations that was to make him an effective campaigner for the separate system, both in Lancashire and in England as a whole.

## John Clay and the Separate System

Clay arrived at Preston with the very traditional view that the role of prisons was to deter criminals. If anything, his early reports reveal a rather retrograde attitude. While Bentham deplored the use of hard labor, Clay helped introduce the treadmill and praised it highly in his second report in 1825. In the same report, he commended the effects that a sound whipping had on juvenile criminals. Even more extraordinary, at a time when prison administrators were trying to abolish "kangaroo courts" among prisoners, was his complacent remark that the convicted felons' ward had established a set of rules against swearing and irreligious conduct. They enforced these rules by mock trials, punishing those found guilty by whipping them with a leather strap or knotted cord. Further experience and the failure of the treadmill forced Clay to reconsider his theories and to try to discover the causes of crime in the hope of developing more effective remedies.

Almost as soon as he arrived at Preston, Clay had begun to interview convicts on their admission and to collect statistics about them. His first report to the visiting justices, in 1824, included a table of commitments and recommitments and the comment that he hoped crime had not increased with the increase in population of the surrounding area. By 1827 he had carried out a more subtle investigation into the relationship between industrial development and crime, using his carefully compiled statistics.

Lancashire had a long tradition of interest in statistics and their application to social policy, dating back to the work of Percival and his associates a half century earlier. Percival's son-in-law, Benjamin Heywood, and a circle of his friends and relatives would found England's first statistical society in Manchester in 1833. Like them, Clay took a fundamentally optimistic view of Lancashire's industrial society. While modern historians have emphasized the hardship, strain, and class bitterness caused by the Industrial Revolution, these men, most of whom had at least an indirect interest in economic development, saw it as a source of social strength.

To Clay, regular employment was a stabilizing force. He believed that factories were so effective in disciplining their workers that they reduced the need for other institutions of control or authority. The problem came not from factories but from those places where the factory discipline did not reach, especially from the large numbers of men attracted to urban areas by casual employment. These men were particularly likely to have bad habits and to drink whenever they had the opportunity. Since they could afford to drink more when times were good and they had more money, they contributed to a rise in the crime rate in good times. Since many crimes were committed on impulse, by persons who were not well able to weigh the consequences of their actions, deterrent policies were not likely to succeed.[17]

Despite his initial difficulties with the Preston bench, Clay soon managed to convert its chairman, Thomas Batty Addison, recorder of Preston and chairman of the Annual General Session, to his views. In 1827 Addison summarized Clay's ideas in his own general report on the Preston house of correction. Because factory labor provided its own discipline, he wrote, few factory workers committed crimes. It was pieceworkers, "who are under no restraint as to the Regularity of their Employment; or the Hours of their Labour," who filled the prisons. Industrialization itself would reduce the need for other institutions of control.[18]

Clay discovered that about three-fifths of the prisoners in Preston had been fully employed at the time they had committed their crimes. He drew a sharp line between "hardened" professional criminals, who supported themselves by regular and systematic thefts and accounted for a great deal of loss but were skilled at avoiding capture, and casual criminals, those who supported themselves by honest labor but committed crimes on impulse. Only a few were driven to crime by need or hunger. Neither factories in themselves nor the periodic industrial depressions that caused severe suffering among Preston's working classes were sufficient to explain changes in the crime rate. Factory hands themselves usually constituted less than one-fifth of all employed prisoners, a proportion that dropped to 14 percent in 1851.[19]

One piece of evidence supporting this view was the explanation that prisoners themselves usually gave for their crime. A relatively large number attributed their offense to drunkenness, while few pleaded need as an excuse. For example, in four months of 1836, 88 out of a total of 198 prisoners—by far the largest segment—attributed their crime to drink, and only 11 to need. In the whole year, among felons alone, 77 out of a total of 187 alleged "drunkenness" and only 12 "want" as the cause of their offense.[20]

Later in his life, as national crime statistics became more available, Clay tried to show that industrial regions were not more criminal on a per capita basis than agrarian ones. He argued that the effects of urbanization should be separated from those of industrialization. He analyzed per capita committal rates for the counties and regions of England, as well as within Lancashire itself, and pointed out that Liverpool, a non-industrial port, was responsible for far more crime per capita than the industrial centers farther north. The four manufacturing towns—Manchester, Salford, Bolton, and Preston—combined had a population one-fifth larger than Liverpool's, but Liverpool's summary convictions for robbery were seventeen times larger than those of the other four towns. Moreover, such agricultural counties as Rutland and Hereford had higher crime rates than north Lancashire.[21]

Clay's most important contention was that there was a direct correlation between the crime rate and the business cycle. When times improved, the crime rate rose—because, according to Clay, a large proportion of crime was caused not by fundamental dishonesty but by drink. When times got hard, fewer working men could afford alcohol and the resulting drop in drink-related offenses (particularly assault) more than compensated for the slight rise in need-related crimes (particularly larceny). V. A. C. Gatrell and T. B. Hadden's recent study of the differential correlations between property and physical crimes and the business cycle in nineteenth-century Lancashire has confirmed Clay's basic analysis of these trends.[22]

Clay was not merely an apologist for industrialization, nor was he a simple-minded moralist. If the immediate cause of crime was human failing, that failing was brought about by the deprivations of poverty. While he found that most criminals were working when arrested, he also found that the average wage was very low. He was an active campaigner for improved public health measures and better housing for the poor; as a member of the commission established by the mayor in 1842 he wrote the *Report on the Sanitary Condition of Preston* used by Chadwick. His tables demonstrated the abysmal ignorance of convicts: for example, only about half of all prisoners could name the months of the year, and about 40 percent did not know who the sovereign was.[23]

In fact, Clay was probably led by his own experience to overstress the environmental causes of crime; though he denied that the poor were necessarily criminal, he assumed that nearly all criminals were poor. He did not adequately consider the possibility that poor offenders were disproportionately likely to be arrested and gaoled. He saw the poor as criminal and the rich as immoral for demanding "indiscriminate vengeance on all sorts and conditions of criminals, as if the comfort and ease of the vocal, self-asserting respectability . . . was altogether to outweigh the rights, temporal and eternal, of the helpless inarticulate mass . . . below."[24] This nascent environmentalism, buttressed by a statistical method that assumed that aggregations of behavior had meaning, led Clay to espouse an uneasy and often shifting compromise between attributing crime to individual moral failure and blaming it on the larger failures of society. It was this compromise that underlay his penal policy.

Clay rapidly abandoned his original belief in deterrence as the primary goal of imprisonment. He argued that deterrence offended against natural justice on two grounds. First, it was unjust to punish convicts merely in order to terrify someone else, because the convicts then suffered not for their own criminal acts but for the propensities of others whom they could not control. Second, criminals were not wholly responsible for the weakened morals that led to their crime. Deterrence was not only unjust but also ineffective, since criminals never expected to be caught, while those who actually were caught were merely hardened by brutal punishment. At the same time, however, Clay complained that under Liddell, Preston had become so nondeterring that the poor committed crimes in order to be gaoled.

By 1827 Clay had begun to campaign for the "American system," a compromise between the silent system of Albany and the separate system of Philadelphia. Though he could not claim to have developed these systems, he was quick to seize on their possibilities. *Encellulement* offered the hope of ending the corruption of prisoners, which had made the prisons less a remedy for than a cause of crime. At the very least, cellular confinement would not make prisoners worse. More than that, it might even encourage reform. Clay did not, like some of his more enthusiastic contemporaries, believe that solitary confinement and private meditation alone would reform criminals. His experience, however, showed that it "softened" the inmates' minds and made them more receptive to the active program of religious teaching and education he wanted to establish. Since prisoners were weak almost by definition, once separated from their bad companions they could be influenced to do good rather than ill.*

Clay seems to have adopted the American system out of despair. As he campaigned for it, however, he found that it had positive aspects. Imprisonment could now be justified as a means of reforming rather than of deterring or punishing criminals. Clay began to refer to the "self-adjusting" nature of the system; since it punished criminals only by leaving them alone with their conscience, the minute the prisoners reformed and their conscience ceased to bother them, they were no longer undergoing punishment. Until that time, however, no punishment could be more severe than the self-reproaches of a guilty person with few distractions and no hope for a better future. Moreover, however terrible their crime or however pure their innocence, the criminals had a right to be protected from contact with other offenders. Finally, although mild enough to be used even for untried prisoners, the system was yet sufficiently severe to deter offenders. Such arguments reveal Clay's own ambivalence; since he could not really determine who was responsible for crime, he was compelled to argue for a system that provided at one and the same time for punishment and for nonpunitive "treatment."

Like many prison chaplains, Clay preferred the separate to the silent system. The latter, he felt, did not produce "that deep and earnest self-examination which is the necessary prelude to self conviction and conversion."[25] After Rev. William Crawford visited the American prisons in 1833, Clay began an intense and prolonged effort to persuade the Preston justices to adopt the separate system, or else the silent system as second best. In 1834 he persuaded the bench to agree to the adoption of a modified American system, but the agreement was not implemented. In subsequent reports he continued to harp on the subject. By 1840 he could report some progress. A number of solitary cells had been made, though they were only certified for one month's confinement, and the

---

*For the early history of separation see Robin Evans, "A Rational Plan for Softening the Mind: Prison Design, 1750-1842" (Ph.D. dissertation, University of Essex, 1975). See also Philip Collins, *Dickens and Crime* (London, 1965), chap. 5, "The Separate System"; and David J. Rothman, *The Discovery of the Asylum* (Boston, 1971), chap. 4, "The Invention of the Penitentiary." The silent system permitted prisoners to work in groups by day but forbade any communication between them. It was often enforced by prisoners acting as monitors. The separate system, or "Philadelphia system," kept prisoners entirely apart in single cells but, unlike solitary confinement, allowed them books, light, work, a full diet, and frequent visits from prison staff. "Encellulement," the term used by W. L. Clay, is a better description of the Preston system than is "separation."

silent system was in use in much of the rest of the prison. In 1841 he noted that after another year's trial, the system seemed to be working. In 1843, a year after Pentonville opened, a corridor of separate cells appeared at Preston. In his report for that year Clay commented that the discipline of Preston had improved continuously in the years since 1828 (the year of Liddell's departure) and dramatically over the past eighteen months (following Anthony's departure). The silent system was now fully enforced. In 1845 the treadwheel was removed and, for the first time, all prisoners were separated before as well as after trial. By 1848 Clay proudly pointed out that committals and crime had decreased more in north Lancashire than in any other county over the past five years. He attributed the trend to the introduction of the new system at Preston.

Although Clay referred to the discipline he introduced as the "separate system" and argued vigorously for its advantages over the silent system, in fact the separation was so modified that it is difficult to assign it to either category. His son used the word "encellulement." Clay was appalled by the high suicide rate at Pentonville, although Crawford was prepared to write off a few extra deaths as the cost of more effective reformation. Accordingly, Clay altered the system to permit a good deal of silent contact between prisoners. They exercised together, took their lessons together, gathered together in an open chapel, and often worked together in large shops.

Clay had originally opposed the imposition of prison labor on prisoners sentenced to short terms and was later to argue against Maconochie's mark system (differing for once from Matthew Davenport Hill, the recorder of Birmingham) on the grounds that it aimed solely at making men industrious. Preston's convicts were already industrious. By 1851, however, when half the entering prisoners had been unemployed outside, he changed his mind and argued that industrial occupation was essential to preserve mental health and prevent depression.*

*The mark system, or social system, developed by Alexander Maconochie required prisoners to earn their discharge from prison by performing a certain amount of hard labor. Each unit of labor earned them so many marks toward the total set for their release. After a period of separation, prisoners worked in groups of six to eight and marks were awarded to the group as a whole. Matthew Davenport Hill was responsible for introducing the system to Birmingham, but it was discredited in 1853 after a scandal following the suicide of a boy assigned to a defective crank. See Sidney Webb and Beatrice Webb, *English Local Government*, vol. 6: *English Prisons Under Local Government* (London, 1963; orig. ed. 1922), pp. 164-70; and Philip Collins, *Dickens and Crime* (London, 1965), chap. 7.

Like M. D. Hill, Clay began to think of prisons as moral hospitals where prisoners would come to be cured of the moral aberrations engendered by a lack of religious training and education. If prisons were reformative rather than punitive, and if crimes were symptoms of a diseased state, then, clearly, the answer was to send more people to prison earlier in order to nip the evil in the bud and to protect the convalescents while there from further contamination. Clay originally expressed doubt about the value of incarcerating offenders, juveniles in particular, because it just made them worse. As Preston more and more nearly approached his ideal, however, he felt able to recommend incarceration as a universal panacea.

Since imprisonment was no longer imposed as a sort of social vengeance, the idea of simple justice, of fitting the punishment to the crime, became less relevant. Clay believed that only a long spell of reformative imprisonment could truly break criminals of their bad habits, so he advocated ever longer sentences. He was perfectly willing to countenance sentences that, had they been imposed merely for punishment, would have seemed grossly disproportionate to the original offense. The culprits would remain until they had undergone a complete cure. It is possible, though it cannot be proved, that Clay's success in convincing the justices that imprisonment was beneficial increased their readiness to sentence offenders to gaol for such petty offenses as public drunkenness—especially since the number of drunken offenders already in gaol proved the seriousness of the problem. (Lancashire had the highest commitment rate for drunkenness in the country; it accounted for approximately half of all county committals.) This was the danger from reform that Sir George Paul had feared in the previous century.

It was probably owing to Clay's growing influence that the separate system was also partially introduced into Kirkdale and Salford. William John Williams strongly supported the silent system, which had the additional recommendation of cheapness. Frederic Hill, an adamant opponent of silence, also disliked the complete imposition of separation. Several local leaders believed, in the words of the chaplain of Kirkdale, that prison reform was pointless "as long as the state of society remains what it is outside."[26] Nevertheless, old cells were altered and new ones built in order to make at least partial separation possible.

At Lancaster, where architectural barriers made large-scale adoption of the separate system impracticable, Hansbrow was converted by his experiments with his more difficult charges. He began "putting apart" those who broke prison rules on full diet in their cells as a way of evading the regulation that restricted gaolers' punishments to three days of solitary. (Hansbrow frequently found the justices' decisions frustrating; on one occasion a prisoner repeatedly and brutally kicked another, splitting his lip and knocking out a tooth, but the justices refused to punish him on the grounds that he had committed only a single offense, while their jurisdiction was limited to *repeated* infractions of the rules.) Several of these isolated offenders came to thank him for the period of reflection. By 1849 he was noting in his journal that Crown prisoners improved "rapidly and perceptibly" in health and appearance when put apart. He attributed the change to the absence of irritation from other prisoners and to the sequestered prisoners' inability to part with their food.[27] In 1850 he wrote with regret that a felon newly released from solitary had begged to be put apart but that he had no space to do so.

The Home Office was putting more pressure on the local prisons to tighten their discipline and introduce separation. The prison inspectors for the Home District had long since agreed that the separate system should be enforced throughout England, but it is difficult to know what effect they had in Lancashire since they and the surveyor general, Joshua Jebb, were on very bad terms with Williams.[28] Nevertheless, it seems likely that Clay's work was the decisive element in persuading the committee of justices appointed in 1846 to adopt the separate system completely in Kirkdale and Preston and to convert Lancaster into a women's and debtors' prison. (No immediate plans could be made for Salford because the borough of Manchester and the hundred had not yet come to an agreement about city prisoners.) It was the committee's work that inspired the county to embark on the building program that soon aroused loud protests from the ratepayers. By 1851 the county was firmly committed to a policy of separation.[29]

The official adoption of separation by the government, the acquiescence of the magistrates, and the triumph of the reformers should not obscure the limited way in which the separate system was actually implemented. The controversy over the idea has concealed its tenuous existence in fact. The adoption of separation was bedeviled by all the problems that had impeded prison reform since the eighteenth century. The expense of total conversion and the ratepayers' revolt acted as important brakes on its introduction, as did the delay common to all governments and especially to those dependent on unenthusiastic committees of amateurs. By the time Lancashire was actually prepared for conversion, the separate system was again falling out of fashion, in favor of the mark system.

Another difficulty was the unpredictability of prison populations: in 1851 Preston contained 168 cells certified for separation, as well as 108 cells that could not be used for separation and 34 cells too dilapidated for use. Since Preston's average population in that year was 367, it is difficult to see how more than two-thirds, at most, could have been separated even at night. Only 168 prisoners could have been separated by day as well. While the municipalities of Manchester and Liverpool were able to introduce separation (and crank labor) into their newly completed prisons in the 1850's, matters changed little in the county prisons.[30] In 1863 Preston still had only 168 separate cells; Kirkdale, despite much building, had only 162; and Salford, with a population of nearly 500, had 101. The new inspector, Herbert P. Voules, who was now responsible for half of England, supported separation only at night; by day he encouraged industrial labor and open schooling. Lancashire prisoners spent up to five hours a day in associated schooling even when they were nominally separated.[31]

Lancashire was not atypical in this lackluster approach to prison reform. Only one prison in all of Wales had any separate cells at all. The Select Committee on Prison Discipline complained in 1863 that "there are so many interruptions to the regularity of prison discipline, instruction is given at such various times, and the communications which pass between prisoners and other persons are so frequent, that separation, though it exists nominally in many, is really to be found in few gaols."[32]

Nevertheless, the middle of the nineteenth century represents the culmination of a period of continuous change that began in the late 1780's. Several writers have implicitly or explicitly attempted to separate the "good" reforms of the 1780's, which were aimed at improving prison conditions and protecting prisoners, from the more equivocal reforms of the early nineteenth century. There is little justification for this approach. Many nineteenth-century reforms grew out of concerns that the eighteenth-century reformers had expressed as well: a rising crime rate, an apparently disorderly and mobile populace, alcoholism, lack of secular and religious instruction, and a poor environment. Bayley and Clay, though very different in background, religion, and political sympathies, nevertheless worked for many of the same causes: Sunday schools, other education for the poor, prison reform, curbs on drinking, and public health measures. Clay had begun at Preston by campaigning for typical eighteenth-century measures: the abolition of bribery and peculation, the banning of blasphemy and gambling, greater order and discipline, and greater cleanliness. Ever since the introduction of cellular prisons in the late eighteenth century, a trend toward the separation of prisoners had been growing; the separate and silent systems were merely its logical conclusion.

The separate system rested firmly on the "liberal" assumption that prisons should be reformative rather than punitive, and its result was longer sentences. Though Lancashire prison terms remained relatively short, many juveniles were sent to "reformatories" for long periods of time. The probation system was also a direct product of the assumption that the punishment should fit the moral state of the criminal as much as the original crime. Whatever its advantages, the overall effect of probation as it operated in England was to undermine the convict's right to judicial due process, since his sentence was determined not by a judge after trial by jury but by a board of appointed officials whose decision was made in secret and could not be appealed. When this effect was combined with the restrictions on the prisoner's liberty while in prison entailed by *encellulement*, the net effect of this "liberal" theory was increased restriction.

Yet we should not condemn the silent and separate systems and the reforms they brought with them too quickly. There is evidence that some convicts were grateful for changes that not only saved them from being "corrupted" but also protected the weaker prisoners from abuse. It became more difficult for felons to whip each other with knotted cords, or to tease the weak-minded in the hope of provoking an amusing display of fury, or to steal each other's food. Improved prison discipline was protective as well as restrictive.

The adoption of a reform-oriented view of imprisonment also promised an end to the escalation of the harshness that deterrence involved as each new penalty failed and was replaced with something more arresting. If reformation implied the lengthening of sentences, deterrence implied the imposition of unpleasantness, such as the treadmill and crank, merely to "torment" convicts. As fears that prisoners would spread epidemics waned, belief in deterrence also led to a lack of public interest in reducing overcrowding and in maintaining decent prison conditions. This public apathy, which was the prevalent attitude throughout the nineteenth century, also resulted in some cruelty.

Whatever its advantages, however, this "liberal" view of imprisonment as a means of rehabilitation instead of deterrence or vengeance resulted in an advocacy of substantially longer and less certain forms of imprisonment, much greater restrictions on the prisoners' liberty and freedom of speech, the attempted destruction of the last remnants of a prison community, the further isolation of prisoners from the outside world, and an increasing resort to incarceration to solve social problems.

# Conclusion

Though prisoners often did suffer in the "reformed" prisons, they suffered from corruption and peculation, bad food, filth, cold, uncomfortable cells, and intimidation by other prisoners. These were old and unsolved problems, not new instruments of manipulation. Lancashire was both the industrial and the ideological heart of the new order, yet with the single exception of Preston for a brief period, Lancashire's prisons bore no more resemblance to the highly regimented model of Pentonville than Lancashire's Poor Law did to the rigorous visions of the New Poor Law commissioners.

As with the New Poor Law, Lancashire's foot-dragging suggests that the theory that links the development of industrialization with the rise of repressive institutions is in need of some qualification. Lancashire—the home of Preston's Gradgrinds and of Manchester's economists, the industrial center of the nation—was, after all, also a center of resistance to Chadwick's principles. As with the New Poor Law, there are several reasons for the fact that Lancashire, after an initial burst of reform, began to lag.

First, Lancashire's county government was still in the hands of an old aristocracy rather than a new bourgeoisie. The county's great wealth, which benefited the gentry as well as the middle class, probably actually helped delay the movement of "traders" onto the bench. Successful merchants finally achieved admission to the bench by the middle of the century, but the old rulers, through a mixture of compromise and hard work, still retained much of their influence. In any case, since the newcomers had specifically challenged the extravagance of the old guard, it was difficult for them to propose any broad new programs involving considerable expense. They were more interested in reducing chaplains to curates' pay than in hiring the most able and zealous young reformers. Gentlemen like Hesketh, or established professionals like Thomas Batty Addison, were prepared to support a good measure of reform but not a complete revolution in prison management. That had been possible only at the end of the eighteenth century, when an absolute crisis, combined with fear, had been exploited by Bayley—who, as a Nonconformist, a Whig, and a Mancunian, was a Lancashire anomaly.

Second, as with the New Poor Law, Lancashire had begun to reform relatively early. In the late eighteenth century, both the gaoler and the justices seem to have been eager to reform the Castle and were in some cases waiting for legislation that would make it possible. The county was quickly prepared to engage in massive and innovative rebuilding at the gaol and the houses of correction. It thus experienced the fate common to many innovators; early experiments were soon overtaken by versions refined by experience, while the experimenters were left with outdated goods that were too new and expensive to replace. Lancaster Castle's architectural intractability saved it from extreme innovations (though the felons' towers were a costly mistake), but Salford exemplified these problems. Built in the first flush of enthusiasm for a plan that rapidly became outmoded, Salford was too inflexible to adapt to the changes in penal theory and prison population. Once considered one of England's most "humane" prisons, it soon became known as one of the worst. Lancashire's heavy early investment in reform made it much more difficult for the county to begin anew.

Third, Lancashire was simply overwhelmed by the extent of the problems caused by industrialization. It resisted the New Poor Law at least in part because no institution was adequate to contain the multitudes displaced by cyclical employment. Urbanization had grown beyond the power of any institution of social control to contain it. Justices and governors were fully occupied just trying to house, clothe, feed, and clean up after the constantly increasing number of prison inmates. They built their new cells on a new plan, but they could not afford to destroy the old ones. Even the new cells soon became so crowded as to preclude separation; in the old cells separation would have been both cruel and illegal. Nor were there ever enough prison officers to enforce an effective discipline. A shortage of staff often forced prison administrators to leave prisoners to their own devices. It was not until the crime rate at last began to ebb, at midcentury, that the justices were able to win enough distance and flexibility to consider major policy changes on a countywide basis.

This is not to suggest that reform did not take place. It did. The prisons of 1845 were very different places from their predecessors of three or six decades before. They were larger, more highly and formally organized, and more firmly controlled by a professional staff headed by a more powerful governor. These efforts had improved the prisoners' comfort, security, protection from others, and, probably, health. The traditional historians were correct in recounting these improvements, although they failed to weigh the full costs.

This study suggests that the radical historians have seriously oversimplified their case. In particular, they have failed both to delineate the different groups interested in reform and to appreciate the complexities of their interaction. They have assumed that a united elite was acting with a clearly defined motive, the maintenance of domination, and have failed to appreciate both the multiplicity of intentions and the fact that many actual changes had not been intended at all. The cast of actors with a say in the administration of Lancashire prisons included: a Parliament that on occasion heeded Henry Hunt and Francis Burdett as well as Whigs and Tories; a county bench that contained radicals such as George Williams, reformers such as Thomas Butterworth Bayley, professional clergymen and lawyers such as W. R. Hay and Thomas Batty Addison, conservative country gentlemen such as William Hulton, and reluctant reformers such as Thomas Hesketh; prison inspectors who disagreed violently with each other; the Home Office; Assize judges; gaolers; professional staff members; journalists and their readers; ratepayers; and, finally, prisoners themselves.

If the radical version oversimplifies both the groups involved and their motives, however, it correctly reveals the darker side of prison reform. The radical case may assume an overly conspiratorial elite, but the traditional account is naive in assuming a universal benevolence. For many actors in this story, self-interest and altruism were inextricably mixed. The gaoler sought both greater autonomy for himself and better discipline. The professional staff sought both personal advancement through the composition of impressive reports and better conditions for prisoners. The journalist sought both the correction of scandals and new readers, the politician both reform and adulation, the justice both greater personal security from disease and crime and the better protection of those under his charge, and the prisoner both personal revenge for sometimes imagined slights and greater justice.

The radicals have also performed a service by renewing interest in the painful balance between freedom and security. The Age of Reform may have brought prisoners greater protection from disease, hunger, and violence, but they paid heavily in loss of freedom and community life. The choice between freedom and security is not a simple one, since for many, security is a form of freedom. Hunger and fear impose their own restraints on behavior. Any society that does not to some extent restrain its citizens leaves them free to prey on each other, and such a state of affairs may also severely restrict the choices people can make about their own destinies. Nevertheless, there comes a point at which restraints imposed in the name of security smother other needs and values.

Finally, the radicals were correct in claiming that prison reform succeeded in convincing a large segment of the public that prisons ought to be reformative while utterly failing to fulfill that goal. An unjustified faith in reformation may in turn have led judges to sentence to institutions many who should not have gone to them. Whether this means that we should eliminate penal institutions entirely, or merely that we should recognize that they serve other ends, must be a subject of further debate.

Reference Matter

# Notes

Information on the major manuscript collections and parliamentary papers consulted by the author, together with the abbreviations used in citing documents, can be found in Document Sources, pp. 255-59. In citations of LCRO sessional records, "Lanc." refers to Lancaster, "Manc." to Manchester, "E" to Easter, "T" to Trinity (or Visitation or Summer), "M" to Michaelmas, "Ep." to Epiphany, and "AGS" to Annual General Sessions. To avoid confusing the reader wishing to pursue references, all dates given are as found in the documents. That is, all dates are Old Style until 1752, and the Epiphany Sessions meets *after* the Michaelmas Sessions of the same year. This follows the arrangement of the Order Books, which are in volumes covering one year each.

## Introduction

1. Erving Goffman, "On the Characteristics of Total Institutions," in D. R. Cressy, ed., *The Prison: Studies in Institutional Organization and Change* (New York, 1961).

2. E.g., David Roberts, *The Victorian Origins of the British Welfare State* (New Haven, 1960); O. MacDonagh, "The Nineteenth-Century Revolution in Government: A Reappraisal," *Historical Journal* 1 (1958): 52-67; Henry Parris, "The Nineteenth-Century Revolution in Government: A Reappraisal Reappraised," *Historical Journal* 3 (1960): 17-37; Jennifer Hart, "Nineteenth-Century Social Reform: A Tory Interpretation of History," *Past and Present* 31 (1965): 39-61.

3. Sidney Webb and Beatrice Webb, *English Prisons Under Local Government* (London, 1963; orig. ed. 1922), p. 247. This superb study is volume 6 of *English Local Government*.

For other studies of local prisons or county prison systems see: James Horsfall Turner, *The Annals of Wakefield House of Correction* (Bingley, 1904); K. Tweedale Meaby, *Nottinghamshire: Extracts from the County Records of the Eighteenth Cen-*

*tury* (Nottingham, n.d.); P. Styles, "The Development of County Administration in the Late XVIII and Early XIX Centuries, Illustrated by the Records of the Warwickshire Court of Quarter Sessions, 1777-1837," Dugdale Society Occasional Papers 4 (Oxford, 1934); Albert John Rhodes, *Dartmoor Prison* (London, 1933); J. Stevens Cox, *Ilchester Gaol and House of Correction*, Ilchester Historical Monographs 4 (Ilchester, 1949); I. Wyatt and J. W. Wyatt, "Prisoners in the County Gaol, 1789-1814," *Gloucestershire Historical Studies* 2 (1968); M. B. Weinstock, "Dorchester Model Prison, 1791-1816," *Proceedings of the Dorset Natural History and Archeological Society* 78 (1958): 94-109; W. Payne, *Stafford Gaol and Its Associations with a Record of County Crime and Criminals* (Stafford, 1887); Esther Moir, *Local Government in Gloucestershire, 1775-1800*, Bristol and Gloucestershire Archeological Society, Records Section 8 (1969) and Moir, "Local Government in Gloucestershire, 1775-1800" (Ph.D. dissertation, Cambridge University, 1955); Elizabeth Melling, ed., *Kentish Sources*, vol. 6: *Crime and Punishment* (Maidstone, 1969); R. K. Howes, "The Reform of Gloucester Prison," *Gloucestershire Historical Studies* 5 (1972); Royal Commission on Historical Monuments, *York Castle, an Illustrated History* (London, 1973).

See also four recent long studies: Wayne Joseph Sheehan, "The London Prison System, 1666-1795" (Ph.D. dissertation, University of Maryland, 1975); Eric Stockdale, *A Study of Bedford Prison, 1660-1877* (London, 1977); Peter Southerton, *The Story of a Prison* (Reading, 1975); and J. R. S. Whiting, *Prison Reform in Gloucestershire, 1776-1820* (London, 1975).

4. For examples, see Gordon Hawkins, *The Prison, Policy and Practice* (Chicago, 1976), chap. 1, "The Prison and Its Critics," pp. 1-29.

5. Gertrude Himmelfarb, "The Haunted House of Jeremy Bentham," reprinted in *Victorian Minds* (New York, 1968), pp. 32-81.

6. *Ibid.*, p. 77.

7. See L. J. Hume, "Jeremy Bentham and the Nineteenth-Century Revolution in Government," *Historical Journal* 10 (1967): 361-74, and Hume, "Bentham's Panopticon, an Administrative History," part 1, *Historical Studies* 15 (1973): 703-21, and part 2, *Historical Studies* 16 (1974): 36-54; Barbee-Sue Rodman, "Bentham and the Paradox of Penal Reform," *Journal of the History of Ideas* 29 (1968): 197-210; Robin Evans, "Bentham's Panopticon: An Incident in the Social History of Architecture," *Architectural Association Quarterly* 3 (1971): 21-37, and Evans, "Panopticon," *Contraspasio* 10 (1970): 4-18; William C. Bader, "Jeremy Bentham: Businessman or 'Philanthropist'?," *Albion* 7 (1975): 245-54; and Rod Morgan, "Divine Philanthropy: John Howard Reconsidered," *History* 62 (1977): 388-410. Himmelfarb herself explicitly criticized this view during the 1980 meeting of the American Historical Association, at the session on "Social Reform and Social Control in Britain in the Era of the Industrial Revolution."

8. David J. Rothman, *The Discovery of the Asylum* (Boston, 1971), pp. 294-95.

9. Michel Foucault, *Madness and Civilization*, trans. Richard Howard (London, 1967), and *Discipline and Punish*, trans. Alan Sheridan (London, 1977).

10. Foucault, *Discipline and Punish*, p. 268.

11. *Ibid.*, pp. 227-28.

12. Michael Ignatieff, *A Just Measure of Pain* (New York, 1978), pp. 214-15. This book is a revised version of a Ph.D. thesis submitted to Harvard University in 1976. I would like to thank Dr. Ignatieff for permitting me to see early manuscript versions of this thesis.

13. *Ibid.*, p. 209.

14. *Ibid.*, p. 211. For other "radical" accounts, see Morgan, Hume, and Bader. See also Robin Evans, "A Rational Plan for Softening the Mind: Prison Design, 1750-1842" (Ph.D. dissertation, University of Essex, 1975). I would like to thank Dr. Evans for providing me with a copy of this work. For the use of Ignatieff's conclusions by penologists, see Michael Sherman and Gordon Hawkins, *Imprisonment in America: Choosing the Future* (Chicago, 1981).

15. Michael Ignatieff, "State, Civil Society, and Total Institutions: A Critique of Recent Social Histories of Punishment," in Michael Tonry and Norval Morris, eds., *Crime and Justice: An Annual Review of Research*, vol. 3 (Chicago, 1981), pp. 153-92. I am very grateful to Dr. Ignatieff for providing me with an early draft of this article.

16. Peter Linebaugh, "The Tyburn Riot Against the Surgeons," in Douglas Hay et al., eds., *Albion's Fatal Tree* (London, 1975), pp. 65-117: "To the surgeons, their spokesmen, and the lords and squires sitting in Parliament, not only was humiliation at the death of one of the 'Scum of the People' a passing matter, but such further 'Marks of Infamy' as public dissection became a part of the policy of class discipline" (p. 117). Linebaugh offers no evidence in support of this contention, nor does he specify whether "scum" referred to convicted felons or to the poor generally. He also does not explain who was feeling humiliated or why.

17. David Philips, *Crime and Authority in Victorian England* (London, 1977). I would like to thank Mr. Richard Trainor of Glasgow University for bringing this work to my attention. See also John Langbein, "Albion's Fatal Flaws," *Past and Present* 98 (1983): 96-120. For a recent analysis of English legal process in an earlier period that also emphasizes the importance of participation by victims and juries, see Cynthia Brilliant Herrup, "Courts, Crimes and Criminals: Legal Structure and Substance in East Sussex 1594-1640" (Ph.D. dissertation, Northwestern University, 1982). I would like to thank Dr. Herrup for permitting me to see this work.

18. See below, pp. 138-39.

19. Eric Midwinter, *Social Administration in Lancashire, 1830-1860: Poor Laws, Public Health and Police* (Manchester, 1969), p. 61. For classic descriptions of the effects of communal inmate resistance on the implementation of of-

ficial rules, see Erving Goffman, *Asylums* (Garden City, 1961), and Gresham Sykes, *The Society of Captives: A Study of a Maximum Security Prison* (Princeton, 1958). For Lancashire examples, see chap. 7.

## Chapter One

1. Sidney Webb and Beatrice Webb, *English Local Government*, vol. 6: *English Prisons Under Local Government* (London, 1963; orig. ed. 1922), p. 31.

2. W. L. Burn, *The Age of Equipoise* (New York, 1965), pp. 176-77.

3. Ursula Henriques, *Before the Welfare State* (London, 1979), p. 157.

4. Bryan Keith-Lucas, *The Unreformed Local Government System* (London, 1980), p. 57.

5. Robin Evans, "A Rational Plan for Softening the Mind: Prison Design, 1750-1842" (Ph.D. dissertation, University of Essex, 1975); Michael Ignatieff, *A Just Measure of Pain* (New York, 1978), pp. 44-79.

6. Rod Morgan, "Divine Philanthropy: John Howard Reconsidered," *History* 62 (1977): 388-410.

7. See, e.g., Douglas Hay et al., eds., *Albion's Fatal Tree* (London, 1975).

8. Jennifer Hart, "Nineteenth-Century Social Reform: A Tory Interpretation of History," *Past and Present* 31 (1965): 39-61.

9. Henriques, p. 261.

10. *Ibid.*, pp. 265-66. Henriques does, however, emphasize the continuing power of the justices.

11. See my Ph.D. dissertation, "County Prison Administration in Lancashire, 1690-1850" (Princeton University, 1980), p. 134, and Webb and Webb, p. 5. Pugh, however, shows that many gaolers were paid to undertake the position (Ralph B. Pugh, *Imprisonment in Medieval England* [Cambridge, Eng., 1968], pp. 165-66). Bribery of sheriffs was prohibited by 12 Rich. II, c. 2; 4 Hen. IV, c. 5; and 5 and 6 Ed. VI, c. 16. An act of 1718 (4 Geo. I, c. 15) explicitly outlawed the sale of gaolerships.

12. R. Sharpe France, "The Lancashire Sessions Act, 1798," *Transactions of the Lancashire and Cheshire Historical Society* (hereafter *LCHS*) 96 (1944): 1-35, is the chief source on the Sheriff's Board and its replacement. The proceedings of the board from 1661 to 1694 are in LCRO, QSV/11.

13. For more about the role of the Assize judges in county administration, see Pugh, pp. 342-43; J. S. Cockburn, *A History of English Assizes, 1558-1714* (Cambridge, 1972); and Esther Moir, "Local Government in Gloucestershire, 1775-1800," Bristol and Gloucestershire Archeological Society, Records Section 8 (1969). For examples of judicial intervention, see Bryan Keith-Lucas, pp. 58-59, and PRO, HO 42/132, Judge J. Bayley to the Home Office.

14. Pugh, p. 191, and Clifford Dobb, "Life and Conditions in London's Prisons," in A. Nicoll, ed., *Shakespeare in His Own Age* (Cambridge, 1965), p. 98.

15. 23 Hen. VIII, c. 2 (1532), and 14 Eliz., c. 5 (1572). On the houses of

correction see W. E. Passey, "Houses of Correction in England and Wales" (M.A. thesis, University of Liverpool, 1936).

16. Walter Joseph King, "The Prosecution of Illegal Behavior in Seventeenth-Century England" (Ph.D. dissertation, University of Michigan, 1977-78), and John Bellamy, *Crime and Public Order in England in the Later Middle Ages* (London, 1973).

17. 22 and 23 Charles II, c. 20.

18. William Oliver Roper, "Materials for the History of Lancashire, II" (Chetham Society, 1907), pp. 227-29. See also DeLacy, p. 53.

19. See William Farrer and J. Brownbill, eds., *The Victoria History of the County of Lancashire*, vol. 8 (London, 1966), p. 6. A drawing of Lancaster Castle in the PRO (MR 15) is attributed to the Elizabethan period. Speed's map of Lancaster also contains a plan of the Castle. A comparison of these images with eighteenth-century drawings reveals no significant change, suggesting that most of the Castle survived Parliament's attempts at demolition. For descriptions of the Castle, see Roper, p. 247; "A Perambulation of Lancaster Castle" (Lancaster, 1973); Edward Higgin, "Memoranda Relating to Lancaster Castle . . . ," *LCHS* 1 (1948-49): 95-102; LCL, plan of Lancaster Castle prior to 1778; LCL, scrapbook 5; City of London Record Office, "Report from the Committee of Aldermen Appointed to Visit Several Gaols in England" (1815-16); and *Parliamentary Papers* (hereafter *PP*) 1812-13 V, Report of the Commissioners on the State of Lancaster Prison, and the Treatment of Prisoners Therein. I would like to thank Mr. K. J. Neale and Mr. Maurice Butters of the Home Office and the Governor, Assistant Governor, and staff of both HM Prison, Preston, and HM Prison, Lancaster, who made it possible for me to visit these institutions and took the time to answer numerous questions.

20. William Harrison, "The Old House of Correction at Hunt's Bank, Manchester," *Transactions of the Lancashire and Cheshire Antiquarian Society* (hereafter *LCAS*) 3 (1885): 89-110; LCRO, QSO, Manc. M 1700; QSO, Manc. Ep. 1720; QSO, Manc. Ep. 1746; QSP, Manc. Ep. 1757; QSO, Manc. E 1773.

21. John Howard, *The State of the Prisons in England and Wales* (Abingdon, 1977; orig. ed. 1777), pp. 439-40.

22. Sylvia Tollit, "The First House of Correction for the County of Lancaster," *LCHS* 105 (1953): 69-90.

23. Howard, p. 439.

24. See DeLacy, pp. 58-59, for a list of larger repairs.

25. T. C. Porteous, "Roger Haydock of Coppull: A Brief Biography and Ten Original Letters," *LCAS* 52 (1937): 4.

26. Historical Manuscripts Commission, Kenyon MSS., no. 527, pp. 159-60.

27. Tollit, p. 77.

28. LCRO, QSP, Manc. T 1703, no. 46.

29. PRO, PL 27/2/2.

30. PRO, PL 27/2, pt. 2; PRO, PL 26/27; LCRO, QSP, Lanc. Ep. 1695. While chained, Arrowsmith was allowed 10d. a week, an increase of 2d. over his previous allowance.

31. PRO, PL 290, PL 26/45; LCRO, QSP, Lanc. E 1756; LCRO, QSO, Preston E 1756; LCL MS. 3204; PRO, T 90/149 (Sheriff's Cravings) year ending Michaelmas 1755. I would like to thank Miss Joanna Innes of Oxford for referring me to the Sheriff's Cravings, a useful source.

32. PRO, PCOM 2/442: Journal, Feb. 1, 1816.

33. LCRO, QSP, Wigan Ep. 1699, no. 9.

34. LCRO, QSO, Lanc. Ep. 1775.

35. For further discussion see DeLacy, pp. 104-11. I would like to thank the parish of St. Mary's, Lancaster, for permitting me to consult this register in the church. See also the Parish Register Society, *The Registers of the Parish Church of Lancaster*, vols. 2 (Cambridge, 1920) and 3 (Cambridge, 1948).

36. Higgin, pp. 101-2.

37. LCRO, QSP, Lanc. M 1693, no. 20.

38. LCRO, QSP, Lanc. T 1703, no. 9. The gaoler in 1703 was the charitable Henry Bracken.

39. LCL, MS. 6615.

40. LCRO, QSP, Lanc. Ep. 1704, no. 27.

41. LCRO, QSO, Lanc. Ep. 1737, no. 4.

42. LCRO, QSO, Lanc. T 1719, and E 1720; QJB/9.

43. LCRO, Ormskirk E 1715, no. 22: "An Account of the Prisoners that hath the Libtie to worke or Begge in the Towne and what weekly Allowance they have paid them." The eighteen prisoners listed took in a total per week of 16s. See also Howard, p. 438.

44. LCRO, QSP, Lanc. E 1711, no. 2; Lanc. M 1748, no. 3.

45. Webb and Webb, p. 18.

46. Wayne Joseph Sheehan, "The London Prison System, 1666-1795" (Ph.D. dissertation, University of Maryland, 1975), p. 239.

47. LCRO, QSP, Manc. T 1703, no. 46.

48. LCRO, QSO, Manc. T 1720; Tollit, p. 76; LCL, MS. 7321 (folder on J. S. Harrison). This figure probably does not include Higgin's earnings from conveyance fees.

49. Tollit, p. 182.

50. Cf. Eric Stockdale, "John Howard and Bedford Gaol," in John C. Freeman, ed., *Prisons Past and Future* (papers given at the Howard Bicentenary Conference; London, 1978), p. 321; LCL, scrapbook no. 2, f. 1; W. L. Clay, *The Prison Chaplain* (Montclair, 1969), p. 113. Though distinguished, Bracken was also quarrelsome. Two disputes involving his household appear in PRO, PL 27/2/2, and a third is discussed by E. Bosdin Leech, "Fovet Medicinam Concordia," *Manchester University Medical School Gazette* 17 (June 1938): 111-14. I do

not know whether this gaoler was related to the Henry Bracken who served from 1699 to 1707.

51. See DeLacy, p. 156, n. 20; LCL, scrapbook no. 2, f. 1; LCL, *Waddington's Guide to Lancaster*, pp. 30-31; Roper; LCL, MS. 7321; LCL, "Biographies."

52. LCL, MS. 7321.

53. See DeLacy, pp. 131-34. Fell tried to have Ellitson indicted at the Assizes.

54. LCRO, QSP, Lanc. M 1695, no. 7; QSP, Wigan E 1699, no. 9; QSP, Lanc. E 1699, nos. 20, 3, 17; QSP, Lanc. E 1703, no. 6; QSP, Lanc. M 1700, no. 13. Similar comments about kind gaolers can be found in other counties, such as Oxfordshire and Bedfordshire.

55. LCRO, QSP, Lanc. T 1730, no. 3; QSO, Lanc. T 1730; QSP, Lanc. M 1748, no. 3.

56. Tollit, pp. 81-84; LCRO, QSP, Wigan M 1689, no. 24; Manc. E 1690, no. 11; Lanc. M 1690, no. 1; Lanc. E 1691, nos. 10, 14. On the Tomlinson affair, see also the *Calendar of State Papers, Domestic*, June 12, 1690.

57. LCRO, QSP, Manc. T 1703, no. 46; Preston M 1703, no. 81.

58. *The Poor Man's Advocate*, July 14 and July 21, 1832.

59. This description of Lancashire rates is based on the following in the LCRO. Rate books: CAV 3 (1793); DDRo (1665); DDX 123/42 (1718); CPV 3 (ca. 1750); DDP (rate book of John Wilcock, 1767); DDX 951/7. Other rate books consulted include: DDF 5 (1645); DDX 603/1 (1752); DDTa 215 (17ᶜ); DDKe 2/17/9 (17ᶜ); DDPt (1622); DDX 114/1 (1675-78); DDT, 2d batch; ZBR 2/2A (n.d., ca. 1640). Many of these books are almost identical, but some have useful prefaces.

Also used were DDGR o/1, "Case for a New County Rate" (1801), and Robert Hindle, *An Account of the Expenditure of the County Palatine of Lancaster for a Period of Twenty-Three Years . . . with Remarks* (London, 1843). See also G. W. Oxley, "The Administration of the Old Poor Law in the West Derby Hundred of Lancashire, 1601-1837" (Ph.D. dissertation, University of Liverpool, 1966), and Oxley, *Poor Relief in England and Wales* (London, 1974), as well as A. F. Davie, "The Government of Lancashire, 1798-1838" (M.A. thesis, University of Manchester, 1966). See also James Tait, ed., *Taxation in Salford Hundred, 1524-1802*, Chetham Society n.s. 83 (1924), and Edwin Cannan, *The History of Local Rates in England* (London, 1896).

60. 43 Eliz., c. 2, 3. The ox ley is Lancashire's equivalent of the purveyance tax, or "purvey," that formed the basis of Cumberland's rating system. See J. V. Beckett, "Local Custom and the 'New Taxation' in the Seventeenth and Eighteenth Centuries: The Example of Cumberland," *Journal of Northern History* 12 (1976): 105-26.

61. LCRO, DDRo.

62. LCRO, DDGr o/1.

63. Webb and Webb, p. 9, n. 1.
64. LCRO, QSO, Lanc. M 1695; QSP, Lanc. T 1696; and, e.g., QSO Lanc. E 1699.
65. Keith-Lucas, p. 55; my calculations from his table. Since other counties may have had peculiarities of accounting similar to Lancashire's, this table should be used with caution.
66. For the restraint this placed on prosecution, see King.
67. This paragraph follows David Philips, *Crime and Authority in Victorian England* (London, 1977), pp. 112-13.
68. LCRO, QSP, Lanc. E 1699, no. 23.
69. LCRO, QSP, Lanc. E 1707, no. 13.
70. LCRO, QSP, Lanc. E 1722; Lanc. Ep. 1767.
71. LCRO, QSP, Lanc. E 1711, no. 1.
72. PRO, T 90/159.
73. LCRO, QSP, Lanc. E 1695.
74. LCRO, QSO, Lanc. M 1695.
75. LCRO, QSP, Lanc. Ep. 1699, no. 17.
76. LCRO, QSP, Lanc. Ep. 1721, no. 2; Lanc. E 1722; QSO, Manc. M 1724; Lanc. T 1725.
77. LCRO, QSO, Lanc. M 1737; QSP, Lanc. Ep. 1737, no. 4; QSO, Lanc. Ep. 1737; AGS, 1822.
78. LCRO, QSO, Lanc. E 1742; Manc. E 1748; Lanc. T 1748.
79. LCRO, QSP, Lanc. E 1695; Lanc. M 1683, no. 6; Wigan Ep. 1699, no. 9.
80. Howard, p. 12.
81. Jeremy Bentham, *Panopticon; or, the Inspection-House, with Two Postscripts* (London, 1791), pp. 149-50.

*Chapter Two*

1. See also Wayne Joseph Sheehan, "The London Prison System, 1666-1795" (Ph.D. dissertation, University of Maryland, 1975), p. 132; and Michael Ignatieff, *A Just Measure of Pain* (New York, 1978), pp. 11-15. Ignatieff sees four early periods of reform: the Elizabethan period, the 1690's, the 1720's, and the 1780's. He bases his conclusion on his national data. My work in Lancashire, carried out before his book appeared, confirms his. On the fluctuations of the "crime rate" see J. M. Beattie, "The Pattern of Crime in England, 1660-1800," *Past and Present* 62 (Feb. 1974).
2. John Howard, *The State of the Prisons in England and Wales* (Abingdon, 1977; orig. ed. 1777), p. 437.
3. Ignatieff, p. 82.
4. Sir Leon Radzinowicz, *A History of English Criminal Law*, vol. 1 (London, 1948), pp. 138-64.

5. PRO, HO 42/4 and HO 42/8. See also Ignatieff, pp. 82 and 85-87.

6. LCRO, QJC. For further discussion see Margaret DeLacy, "County Prison Administration in Lancashire, 1690-1850" (Ph.D. dissertation, Princeton University, 1980), pp. 218-25.

7. For a table of the numbers of debtors filing insolvency papers, see De-Lacy, p. 79, which is a count of debtors calendared in LCRO, QJB. Joanna Innes has informed me that she has compared these numbers with the numbers of debtors listed in the London *Gazette* as filing for insolvency in Lancaster and has found that the numbers seem to bear no relationship to each other. I know of no explanation for this puzzling discrepancy.

8. Numbers for committals of debtors are compiled from the following sources: *PP* 1819 XVII; PRO, PCOM 2/442 (Thomas Houseman Higgin); *PP*, Annual returns of prisons under 4 Geo. IV, c. 64, schedule B. These numbers do not always coincide.

9. Manchester Central Library, Henry Fielding, "Tables Showing the Total Number of Prisoners Committed to the New Bailey, Salford, under the Several Charges Specified . . ." (paper read to the Manchester Statistical Society, 1834-35). I am grateful to the City of Manchester, Cultural Services, Archives Department, for providing me with a copy of this paper.

10. Total committals, Michaelmas to Michaelmas, are in the schedule B returns.

11. The best source for daily average populations is Robert Hindle, *An Account of the Expenditure of the Country Palatine of Lancaster for a Period of Twenty-Three Years . . . with Remarks* (London, 1843). S. Peter Bell calculated his own daily averages in his M.Sc. thesis, "A Social History of Salford New Bailey Prison, 1823-1865" (University of Salford, 1972). Another set of figures is available from the reports in the Annual General Session (LCRO, QSG and QSZ), and miscellaneous figures are available in other LCRO documents (e.g., QAV/3). Unfortunately, due to different calendar years and other variables, there is some discrepancy between the sets of figures. Since Hindle provides the only consistent long series for all four prisons, it has been used whenever possible. See DeLacy, pp. 485-88, for further discussion. Daily average populations are difficult to obtain for most English prisons, and because sentence length varied, total committals are only a rough guide to population levels.

12. I am grateful to Mr. Malcolm Ramsey for enabling me to see a draft of his paper on Paul, read at the 1977 Howard Society Conference in honor of the bicentenary of the publication of *State of the Prisons*. See also Ignatieff, pp. 108-9.

13. Andrew Tennant Scull, *Museums of Madness: The Social Organization of Insanity in Nineteenth Century England* (New York, 1979), pp. 34-36.

14. David Philips, *Crime and Authority in Victorian England* (London, 1977), pp. 112-13.

## Chapter Three

1. The chief sources on Bayley are [Thomas Percival], *Biographical Memoirs of the Late Thomas Butterworth Bayley, Esq.* . . . . (Manchester, 1802), and Sir Thomas Baker, *Memorials of a Dissenting Chapel* (Manchester, 1884). See also Valentine Arthur Charles Gatrell, "The Commercial Middle Class in Manchester from c. 1820 to 1857" (Ph.D. dissertation, Cambridge University, 1971); Michael Ignatieff, *A Just Measure of Pain* (New York, 1978), pp. 62-64; Sidney Webb and Beatrice Webb, *English Local Government*, vol. 1: *The Parish and the County* (London, 1963; orig. ed. 1906); William Wardell Bean, *The Parliamentary Representation of the Six Northern Counties of England, 1603-1886* (Hull, 1890). Letters from Bayley can be found in the Liverpool papers at the British Library, the Public Record Office Home Office letters, the Wilkes papers, and the Dundas papers in the Scottish Record Office.

2. I would like to thank Joanna Innes for informing me of Bayley's proposal to Miss Wilkes.

3. John Brewer, "The Wilkites and the Law, 1763-74," in John Brewer and John Styles, eds., *An Ungovernable People: The English and Their Law in the Seventeenth and Eighteenth Centuries* (London, 1980), pp. 128-71.

4. *Ibid.*, pp. 166 and 170.

5. BL, add. MSS. 38225, f. 114.

6. BL, add. MSS. 38450.

7. J. L. Hammond and Barbara Hammond, *The Skilled Labourer, 1760-1832* (New York, 1967; orig. ed. 1919), p. 62.

8. Percival, *Biographical Memoirs.*

9. BL, add. MSS. 38447, f. 144.

10. Percival, *Biographical Memoirs*, p. 6.

11. *Ibid.*

12. LCRO, QSO, all sess. T 1781, and Manc. T 1787.

13. LCRO, QSO, Lanc. M 1770; Lanc. Ep. 1772; and Lanc. T 1774.

14. 32 Geo. II, c. 28; 13 Geo. III, c. 58; and 14 Geo. III, c. 20, 59.

15. 16 Geo. III, c. 43, and 19 Geo. III, c. 74. Bayley to Lord Sydney, Jan. 26, 1785, PRO, HO 42/6.

16. 22 Geo. III, c. 64.

17. 24 Geo. III, c. 54, 55.

18. LCRO, QSO, Manc. T 1777.

19. Manchester Central Library, 365 C20; *The Report of Samuel Clowes the Younger, and Thomas Butterworth Bayley, Esquires, of the State of the House of Correction at Manchester* (Manchester, 1783).

20. LCRO, QSB/1.

21. *Ibid.*, deposition of Edward Cowburne.

22. LCRO, QSO, Lanc. Ep. 1784. Manc. Ep. 1784; E 1784 adjourned to

Preston, May 13; Lanc. M 1784; Ep. Manc., adj. to Preston, 1785; and all sess. M 1786. On Harrison see J. Mordaunt Crook, "A Reluctant Goth: The Architecture of Thomas Harrison," *Country Life* 149 (1971): 876-79, 944-47, 1088-91, 1539.

On typhus in Lancashire see [?A. Meiklejohn], "The Putrid Fever at Robert Peel's Radcliffe Mill," *Notes and Queries* 203 (1958): 26-35. Typhus was present in Lancaster town from 1782 to 1784, in Preston from 1781 to 1783, at the Radcliffe Mills from Nov. 1782 to 1784, and at Carlisle in 1781. See also John Heysham, *An Account of the Gaol Fever or Typhus Carcerum* (London, 1782), and D. Campbell, *Observations on the Typhus* (Lancaster, 1785). Campbell was a superintendent of the Lancaster Dispensary. Percival was one of the doctors who were called in to control the Radcliffe epidemic.

On public health in the north, see B. Keith-Lucas, "Some Influences Affecting the Development of Sanitary Legislation in England," *Economic History Review* 2d ser. 6 (1953-54): 290-96, and E. P. Hennock, "Urban Sanitary Reform a Generation Before Chadwick," *Economic History Review* 2d ser. 10 (1957): 113-20.

For further citations see John Pickstone, ed., "Health, Disease and Medicine in Lancashire, 1750-1950, Four Papers on Sources, Problems and Methods" (University of Manchester Institute of Science and Technology, Department of History of Science and Technology), and Pickstone, "Ferriar's Fever and Kay's Cholera: Disease and Social Structure in Cottonopolis," paper read to the Society for the Social History of Medicine (Liverpool, July 1980). I would like to thank Dr. Pickstone for sending me copies of these and other papers and for additional assistance. See also my paper, "Social Medicine and Social Institutions in Eighteenth Century Lancashire" (Social Science History Association, Bloomington, 1982).

23. PRO, HO 42/6, Jan. 1, 1785.

24. [?Harriet Martineau], "Convict Systems in England and Ireland," *Edinburgh Review* 117 (1863): 241-68. I am grateful to Mr. Simon Stevenson of Oxford for this reference.

25. On the Life Table see John M. Eyler, *Victorian Social Medicine: The Ideas and Methods of William Farr* (Baltimore, 1979), pp. 73-74. John Heygarth, *A Letter to Dr. Percival on the Prevention of Infectious Fever* (Bath, 1801), and "Observations on the Population and Diseases of Chester in the Year 1774," *Philosophical Transactions* 68, pt. 1 (1778): 131-54. Heygarth, who was physician to the Chester Infirmary between 1767 and 1798, introduced fever wards to the infirmary in 1783, following the typhus epidemic of 1782. On the Aikins see John Fulton, "The Warrington Academy (1757-1786) and Its Influence upon Medicine and Science," *Bulletin of the History of Medicine* 1 (1933): 50-80. On Currie, see William Wallace Currie, ed., *Memoir of the Life, Writings and Correspondence of James Currie, M.D., F.R.S. of Liverpool* (London, 1831), and Rob-

ert Donald Thornton, *James Currie the Entire Stranger and Robert Burns* (Edinburgh and London, 1963).

26. On this group, see DeLacy, "Social Medicine"; notes 3, 9, and 10 contain further citations.

27. The classic source on contagionism and the logic that led medical theorists to modify or reject it is Charles-Edward Amory Winslow, *The Conquest of Epidemic Disease: A Chapter in the History of Ideas* (Madison, 1980; orig. ed. 1943), esp. chaps. 10 and 11. See also Erwin H. Ackerknecht, "Anticontagionism Between 1821 and 1867," *Bulletin of the History of Medicine* 22 (1948): 562-93; Eyler; and Margaret Pelling, *Cholera, Fever and English Medicine, 1825-1865* (Oxford, 1978).

28. Ackerknecht, "Anticontagionism."

29. Peter H. Niebyl, "The English Bloodletting Revolution, or Modern Medicine Before 1850," *Bulletin of the History of Medicine* 51 (1977): 464-83.

30. Richard Mead, *A Short Discourse Concerning Pestilential Contagion and the Methods to Be Used to Prevent It* (London, 1720), pp. 47-48.

31. *Ibid.*, p. 42.

32. *Ibid.*, quoted in Winslow, p. 187.

33. Sir John Pringle, *Observations on the Diseases of the Army*, 5th ed. (London, 1765).

34. Sir John Pringle, *Observations on the Nature and Cure of Hospital and Jayl-Fevers* (London, 1750); and Stephen Hales, *A Description of Ventilation* (London, 1743), and *A Treatise on Ventilation, Part Second* (London, 1758). On the Newgate incident see Ignatieff, pp. 44-45; Wayne Joseph Sheehan, "The London Prison System, 1666-1795" (Ph.D. dissertation, University of Maryland, 1975); Robin Evans, "A Rational Plan for Softening the Mind: Prison Design, 1750-1842" (Ph.D. dissertation, University of Essex, 1975).

35. John Howard, *The State of the Prisons in England and Wales* (Abingdon, 1977; orig. ed. 1777), p. 243.

36. Erwin Ackerknecht, *Medicine at the Paris Hospital, 1794-1848* (Baltimore, 1967), chap. 1, esp. pp. 4-5. See also Richard Harrison Shryock, "The Medical Reputation of Benjamin Rush: Contrasts over Two Centuries," *Bulletin of the History of Medicine* 45 (1971): 507-53; and Niebyl.

37. Ackerknecht, *Paris Hospital*, p. 5.

38. Ignatieff, p. 60.

39. *Ibid.*, p. 61.

40. John Ferriar, "Some Remarks on Dr. Tattersall's 'Brief View of the Anatomical Arguments for the Doctrine of Materialism,'" in *Medical Histories and Reflections* (Warrington, 1792); Thomas Percival, *Essays, Medical and Experimental* (London, 1770). I would like to thank Mrs. Hanks of the National Library of Medicine for providing me with copies of these works.

41. John E. Ransom, "John Howard on Communicable Diseases," *Bulletin of the History of Medicine* 5 (1937): 131-47; and see Niebyl.

42. Percival, who was a close friend of Priestley and corresponded regularly with Benjamin Franklin and the French *philosophes*, was especially suspect.

43. Thomas Percival, *Medical Ethics*, ed. Chauncey Leake (Baltimore, 1957), pp. 77-78.

44. *Ibid.*

45. John Thompson and Grace Goldin, *The Hospital: A Social and Architectural History* (New Haven, 1975). See also Anthony King, "Hospital Planning: Revised Thoughts on the Origins of the Pavilion Principle in England," *Medical History* (1966): 360-73.

46. *Proceedings of the Board of Health in Manchester* (London, [1805]). I would like to thank Miss Margaret De Motte of the Manchester Central Library, City of Manchester Cultural Services, for providing me with a copy of this work.

47. Percival, *Medical Ethics*, p. 173.

48. On the history of typhus see Charles Creighton, *A History of Epidemics in Great Britain* (2d ed. Totowa, N.J., 1965; orig. ed. 1894); Major Greenwood, *Epidemics and Crowd Diseases* (London, 1935); Ronald Hare, *Pomp and Pestilence: Infectious Disease, Its Origins and Conquest* (London, 1954); and Hans Zinsser, *Rats, Lice and History* (London, 1935).

49. E.g., Gloucester, Worcester, Maidstone (PRO, HO 42/4). Fear of fever is mentioned in petitions from Reading, Portsmouth, Stafford, and Dorset. See also Webb and Webb, *English Local Government*, vol. 6: *English Prisons Under Local Government*, p. 57. William Augustus Guy wrote that Howard saw gaol fever in six prisons and heard of it in twenty-one, "so . . . fever haunted at least one-fourth of our prisons" ("John Howard as Statist," *Journal of the [London] Statistical Society* 36 [1873]: 1-18, p. 3). Some of these episodes, however, were well in the past.

50. Heysham, *Account*, and Heygarth, "Observations." See also M. W. Flinn, "Introduction" in Edwin Chadwick, *Report on the Sanitary Condition of the Labouring Population, 1842* (Edinburgh, 1965), p. 9.

51. Friedrich Engels, *The Condition of the Working Class in England*, trans. W. O. Henderson and W. H. Chaloner (Stanford, 1970), p. 113; and Winslow, p. 359.

52. PRO, HO 42/3 and 42/4. See also HO 42/8 (from Kent) and 42/6, Higgin to T. Stanley, MP.

*Chapter Four*

1. Copies of the rules for Lancaster, Preston, and Salford can be found in Margaret DeLacy, "County Prison Administration in Lancashire, 1690-1850" (Ph.D. dissertation, Princeton University, 1980), pp. 311-27.

2. See Michael Ignatieff, *A Just Measure of Pain* (New York, 1978), p. 77. I am grateful to Dr. Ignatieff for providing me with a copy of a paper read at the December 1976 meeting of the American Historical Association that also discusses these points.

3. 2 Geo. II, c. 22, and 55 Geo. III, c. 48.

4. *PP* 1812-13 V, Report of the Commissioners on the State of Lancaster Prison, and the Treatment of Prisoners Therein (hereafter "1812 Comm."), p. 34.

5. *Ibid.*, pp. 11, 85.          6. *Ibid.*, pp. 27-28, 34.

7. LCRO, QSO, Lanc. T 1777.     8. LCRO, QSO, Preston T 1785.

9. LCRO, QSO, Manc. T 1786.

10. PRO, PCOM 2/442, April 18, 1817, entry in handwriting of John Higgin.

11. 1812 Comm., p. 68.

12. *Ibid.*, p. 23.

13. PRO, PCOM 2/442, Oct. 22, entry in handwriting of Thomas Houseman Higgin; Joseph John Gurney, *Notes on a Visit Made to Some of the Prisons in Scotland and the North of England in Company with Elizabeth Fry*, 2d ed. (London, 1820), p. 418; LCRO, Testimony of William Liddell Before the Select Committee on Gaols (extract from the *Parliamentary Papers*).

14. LCL, folder on J. S. Harrison.

15. John Howard, *The State of the Prisons in England and Wales* (Abingdon, 1977; orig. ed. 1777), p. 51.

16. LCRO, QSO, Manc. July 1786; Preston M (2d sess.) 1792. See also 1812 Comm.

17. LCRO, QSO, Manc. T 1777.

18. These diets are taken from the rules. See above, notes 1 and 16.

19. J. C. Drummond and Anne Wilbraham, *The Englishman's Food: Five Centuries of English Diet* (London, 1958), pp. 206-8.

20. 1812 Comm., p. 40.

21. PRO, PCOM 2/442, entry in handwriting of Thomas Houseman Higgin.

*Chapter Five*

1. James Neild, *State of the Prisons in England, Scotland and Wales* (London, 1812), p. 326.

2. *Ibid.*

3. PRO, HO 42/125.

4. The following narrative of the events leading up to Rawlinson's suicide and the commission's investigation closely follows the commission's report.

5. *PP* 1812-13 V, Report of the Commissioners on the State of Lancaster Prison, and the Treatment of Prisoners Therein (hereafter "1812 Comm."), p. 51.

6. *Ibid.*, p. 49.
7. *Ibid.*, p. 65.
8. *Ibid.*, p. 62.
9. *Ibid.*
10. *Ibid.* p. 94.
11. PRO, HO 42/125.
12. *Ibid.*

13. John Howard, *The State of the Prisons in England and Wales* (Abingdon, 1977; orig. ed. 1777), p. 438.

14. *Hansard*, 24: 895-904.
15. PRO, HO 42/125.
16. 1812 Comm., pp. 14-15.
17. *Ibid.*, pp. 15-16, 88.
18. *Ibid.*, p. 17.
19. *Ibid.*, pp. 43-44.
20. *Ibid.*, pp. 64-65.
21. *Ibid.*, p. 69.
22. *Ibid.*, p. 97.

23. PRO, HO 42/126, July 18, 1812.

24. 1812 Comm., p. 21.

25. *Ibid.*, pp. 27-28.

26. *Ibid.*, petition of John Hankin, p. 97.

27. PRO, HO 42/165.

28. J. R. S. Whiting, *Prison Reform in Gloucestershire, 1776-1820* (London, 1975), p. 67.

29. Samuel Bamford, *Passages in the Life of a Radical*, ed. W. H. Chaloner, vol. 2 (London, 1967; orig. ed. 1844), pp. 181-82. See also Henry Hunt, *Memoirs*, vols. 2-5 (n.p., n.d.); Hunt, *Investigation at Ilchester Gaol* . . . (London, 1821); Hunt, *Peep into a Prison or Inside of Ilchester Bastille* (London, 1821); William Bridle, *A Narrative of the . . . Improvements Effected in . . . Ilchester . . .* (Bath, 1822); J. Stevens Cox, *Ilchester Gaol and House of Correction* (Ilchester Historical Monographs no. 4; Ilchester, 1949); and *PP* 1822 IV, Report of the Commission on Ilchester. I would like to thank Miss Joanna Innes for referring me to the Cox pamphlet.

30. On Carlile see Edward Royle, *Radical Politics, 1790-1900: Religion and Unbelief* (New York, 1971).

31. Winifred Proctor, "Orator Hunt, M.P. for Preston, 1830-32," *Transactions of the Lancashire and Cheshire Historical Society* 114 (1963): 129-54. For Doherty see R. G. Kirby and A. E. Musson, *The Voice of the People: John Doherty 1798-1854, Trade Unionist, Radical and Factory Reformer* (Manchester, 1975).

32. *PP* 1840 XXXVIII.

33. *PP* 1825 VI.

34. *Poor Man's Advocate*, July 14, 1832.

35. PRO, HO 42/125, Hay to HO, Manchester, July 26, 1812.

36. PRO, HO 42/129, Higgin to John Beckett (undersecretary of state), Nov. 12, 1812.

37. *Ibid.*
38. PRO, HO 20/1.
39. *Ibid.*
40. LCRO, DDHu 53/59.
41. *Ibid.*

42. *Ibid.* See also Sir Leon Radzinowicz, *A History of English Criminal Law*, vol. 1 (London, 1948), pp. 314 n. 72, 498.

43. LCRO, DDHu 53/59.          44. *Ibid.*

45. PRO, HO 20/1 fol. 124a.    46. *Ibid.*, fol. 102b.

47. These accounts are taken from *Hansard* for the dates mentioned in the text. In many cases they were also recorded in the local press.

48. PRO, PL 28/16; LCL, cause list no. 2, Lanc. Lent Assizes, March 23, 1822 (notes by T. B. Addison).

49. *Preston Chronicle*, March 31, 1832; and *Hansard*.

50. *Preston Chronicle*, Sept. 8, 1832.

51. *Ibid.*

52. *Poor Man's Advocate*, July 21, 1832.

53. *Ibid.*

## Chapter Six

1. Peter Mathias, *The Transformation of England* (London, 1979), p. 122.

2. E. P. Thompson, *The Making of the English Working Class* (New York, 1963), pp. 600, 603-4; Samuel Bamford, *Passages in the Life of a Radical*, ed. W. H. Chaloner, vol. 1 (London, 1967; orig. ed. 1844), p. 125.

3. S. E. Finer, *The Life and Times of Sir Edwin Chadwick* (London, 1952), p. 42. *PP* 1836 XXVII (County Rates Committee). The Rate Consolidation Act was 12 Geo. II, c. 29. See also A. F. Davie, "The Government of Lancashire 1798-1838" (M.A. thesis, University of Manchester, 1966), p. 72. I am grateful to Michael Collinge of the Institute for Historical Research for pointing out to me that joint collections probably camouflaged the rises in the county rate.

4. *PP* 1825 VI.

5. R. Sharpe France, "The Lancashire Sessions Act, 1798," *Transactions of the Lancashire and Cheshire Historical Society* (hereafter *LCHS*) 90 (1944): 33.

6. See Margaret DeLacy, "County Prison Administration in Lancashire, 1690-1850" (Ph.D. dissertation, Princeton University, 1980), p. 436.

7. BL add. MSS. 38447, f. 3 (Liverpool Papers), Bayley to Liverpool, March 4, 1790.

8. Sharpe France. This is the main source for the events leading up to the act and I have followed it closely. It is also discussed in Sidney Webb and Beatrice Webb, *English Local Government*, vol. 1: *The Parish and the County* (London, 1963; orig. ed. 1906).

9. Sharpe France, pp. 10-34. LCRO, QSO, Preston T 1794.

10. LCRO, DDGr Box 0/1 (Case for a New County Rate). See also Davie, "Lancashire 1798-1838," p. 54.

11. LCRO, DDGr Box 0/1, and *Fourth Annual Report of the Poor Law Commissioners for England and Wales*, appendix D: Poor Rate Returns, 1838 (London, 1839). According to these returns, 9 of the 22 parishes in West Derby

Union and 5 of the 20 parishes in Prescot Union paid more to the county than to the poor rate. There were only 9 other such parishes in the whole county, however. In 1804 money spent on "Church rate, County rate, highways militia etc" had exceeded total poor-law expenditures for paupers both in and out of poorhouses (not including law expenses) in 12 parishes in Lonsdale, 11 in Amonderness, 12 in Blackburn, 19 in Leyland, 19 in Salford, and 42 in West Derby (LCRO, poor rate abstract, 1804).

12. David Foster, "Class and County Government in Early Nineteenth-Century Lancashire," *Northern History* 9 (1974): 48-61. See also Foster's Ph.D. thesis, "The Changing Social and Political Composition of the Lancashire County Magistracy, 1821-51" (University of Lancaster, 1971).

13. E. W. Gilboy, "The Cost of Living and Real Wages in Eighteenth-Century England," in A. J. Taylor, ed., *The Standard of Living in Britain in the Industrial Revolution* (London, 1975), pp. 1-20. Lancashire's agricultural problems are analyzed in J. Phillip Dodd, "South Lancashire in Transition: A Study of the Crop Returns for 1795-1801," *LCHS* 117 (1966): 89-107.

14. Davie, "Lancashire 1798-1838," p. 54, and see LCRO, QSG (1809).

15. 55 Geo. III, c. 51. See also *PP* 1836 XXVII, and Davie, "Lancashire 1798-1838," p. 54.

16. *The Preston Pilot*, Sept. 15, 1827; A. F. Davie, "The Administration of Lancashire, 1838-1888" (Ph.D. dissertation, University of Manchester, 1968), p. 4; Foster, "Lancashire County Magistracy," pp. 4-5; Robert Hindle, *An Account of the Expenditure of the County Palatine of Lancaster for a Period of Twenty-Three Years . . . with Remarks* (London, 1843), p. 15. This is the source for Table 10. LCRO, AGS, Sept. 1840.

17. Foster, "Lancashire County Magistracy," pp. 4-5, and "Class and County Government." Hindle, pp. 37-45.

18. Hindle, pp. 37-45.

19. *Ibid.*; AGS, June 1842.

20. *PP* 1836 XXVII; Hindle, pp. 222-23.

21. *PP* 1836 XXVII.

22. D. Gregory, "Rates and Representation: Lancashire County in the Nineteenth Century," *Northern History* 12 (1976): 158-71.

23. *Preston Chronicle*, Sept. 10, 1831. LCRO, AGS, Report of the Committee to Examine Expenditure, Dec. 1849, pp. 16-17.

24. *Preston Chronicle*, March 20, 1831.

25. *Ibid.*, April 9, 1831.

26. Hindle, p. 171.

27. *PP* 1850 XIII, Evidence of Edward Gorst and William Roberts.

28. *Ibid.*, appendix. This includes county, hundred, and constabulary rates. For West Derby, see the evidence of John Livesay. LCRO, AGS, 1848.

29. Gregory, pp. 161-62; *PP* 1850 XIII, Evidence of William Roberts.

30. Gregory, pp. 164-71. I agree with both Gregory's analysis of this attempt and his explanation of its failure; the account below follows his.

31. *PP* 1850 XIII.

32. For Hulton's failings, see Davie, "Lancashire 1838-1888," pp. 70 and 281-82.

33. *PP* 1850 XIII, Report of the Committee.

34. Hindle, pp. 302-3.

35. M. Heather Tomlinson, "Victorian Prisons: Administration and Architecture, 1835-77," vol. 2 (Ph.D. dissertation, University of London, 1975), appendix D. I would like to thank Dr. Tomlinson for permission to consult this work and for other assistance. Richard Wildman, "Workhouse Architecture," in Norman Longmate, *The Workhouse* (London, 1974), appendix. The average cost of a new workhouse was about £5,000.

36. *PP* 1850 XIII, Evidence of J. S. Birley.

37. Longmate, pp. 105-6.

38. Eric Midwinter, *Social Administration in Lancashire, 1830-1860: Poor Laws, Public Health and Police* (Manchester, 1969), p. 62.

39. Longmate, p. 105.

40. Tomlinson, 1: 174-75.

41. E. P. Hennock, "Finance and Politics in Urban Local Government in England, 1835-1900," *Historical Journal* 6 (1963): 212-26.

42. *PP* 1850 XIII, appendix B.

43. *PP* 1850 XIII.

*Chapter Seven*

1. Michel Foucault, *Discipline and Punish*, trans. Alan Sheridan (London, 1977), p. 228.

2. Gertrude Himmelfarb, "The Haunted House of Jeremy Bentham," *Victorian Minds* (New York, 1968).

3. Ursula Henriques, "The Rise and Decline of the Separate System of Prison Discipline," *Past and Present* 54 (Feb. 1972): 61-93, quote from p. 90.

4. See M. Heather Tomlinson, "Victorian Prisons: Administration and Architecture, 1835-77" (Ph.D. dissertation, University of London, 1975); Robin Evans, "A Rational Plan for Softening the Mind: Prison Design, 1750-1842" (Ph.D. dissertation, University of Essex, 1975); and J. Mordaunt Crook, "A Reluctant Goth: The Architecture of Thomas Harrison," *Country Life* 149 (1971): 876-79, 944-47, 1088-91, 1539, for more information on building at these prisons. I am grateful to Dr. Tomlinson for referring me to the Crook article.

5. This tower still stands, although it is no longer used for prisoners' cells. I am grateful to the Home Office, the Governor and Assistant Governor of Lancaster Castle, and the prison staff for enabling me to view these cells.

6. Samuel Bamford, *Passages in the Life of a Radical*, ed. W. H. Chaloner, vol. 2 (London, 1967; orig. ed. 1844), p. 7.

7. Henry Hunt, *Memoirs* (n.p., n.d. but ca. 1820), 3: 628-29.

8. Robin Evans discusses these innovations in "Bentham's Panopticon: An Incident in the Social History of Architecture," *Architectural Association Quarterly* 3 (1971): 21-37.

9. See, e.g., Jeremy Bentham, *Panopticon; or, the Inspection-House, with Two Postscripts* (London, 1791), pp. 148-50: postscript I, pp. 132-33, postscript II, pp. 104-5.

10. Tony Frankland, ed., *Salford's Prison* (Salford, 1978); Society for the Improvement of Prison Discipline, *Fourth Report* (1822), pp. 31-33, and *Fifth Report* (1823). Tomlinson, vol. 2, appendix D, p. 519. I would like to thank the Salford Central Library, Peel Park, for sending me the plans for Salford.

11. Society for the Improvement of Prison Discipline, *Remarks on the Form and Construction of Prisons* (London, 1826), p. 27.

12. John Thompson and Grace Goldin, *The Hospital: A Social and Architectural History* (New Haven, 1975).

13. Evans, "A Rational Plan," pp. 164-66.

14. Tomlinson discusses these problems at length; I am merely summarizing her conclusions. See her "Victorian Prisons," vol. 1, pp. 110-17.

15. LCRO, QJB 58/5.

16. *PP*, Returns under 4 Geo. IV, schedule B.

17. *PP* 1837 XXXII, Second Report of the Inspectors of Prisons for the Northern and Eastern District.

18. *PP* 1837-38 XXXI, Third Report of the Inspectors of Prisons for the Northern and Eastern District. See also Sidney Webb and Beatrice Webb, *English Local Government*, vol. 6: *English Prisons Under Local Government* (London, 1963; orig. ed. 1922), p. 106.

19. Thomas Rogers Forbes, "The Crowner's Quest," *Transactions of the American Philosophical Society* 68 (1978): 33. See also William Baly, "On the Mortality in Prisons and the Diseases Most Frequently Fatal to Prisoners," *Medico-Chirurgical Transactions* (Royal Medical and Chirurgical Society of London), 2d ser. 10 (1845): 113-272, esp. 250.

20. George Holford, *A Short Vindication of the General Penitentiary of Milbank*, 2d ed.; *A Second Vindication . . .* and *Third Vindication . . .* (London, 1825). See also J. C. Drummond and Anne Wilbraham, *The Englishman's Food: Five Centuries of English Diet* (London, 1958), pp. 436-37.

21. *PP* 1847-48 XXXVI, Thirteenth Report of the Inspectors for the Northern and Eastern District.

22. LCRO, QGR 2/41 (chaplain's report, 1847), and QGV 2/8.

23. Second Report. See also S. Peter Bell, "A Social History of Salford New Bayley Prison, 1823-1865" (M.Sc. thesis, University of Salford, 1972).

24. Chaplain's report for 1844.
25. PRO, PCOM 2/445, Aug. 13, 1849.
26. PRO, PCOM 2/443, July 13, 1843.
27. PRO, PCOM 2/445, Sept. 7, 1849.
28. Second Report.
29. LCRO, QGR 1/25.
30. LCRO, QSZ: AGS 1826, 1828.
31. Webb and Webb, p. 135; Drummond and Wilbraham, pp. 437-39. The dietaries printed in Table 12 are taken from the schedule B returns in *PP* 1835 XLIV. These dietaries vary considerably from those reported in the "Digest of Returns" in the "Second Report of the Inspectors," *PP* 1837 XXXII.
32. Returns under 4 Geo. IV, c. 64, schedule B, and *PP* 1843 XXV and XXVI, Eighth Report of the Inspectors for the Northern and Eastern District.
33. LCRO, QGR 3/22.
34. Baly, pp. 113-272. I am most grateful to Miss Valerie Johnston of Oxford for this reference. I would also like to thank Dr. Margaret Pelling of the Wellcome Unit for the History of Medicine at Oxford for her advice on this section.
35. Robert Hindle, *An Account of the Expenditure of the County Palatine of Lancaster for a Period of Twenty-Three Years . . . with Remarks* (London, 1843).
36. Returns under 4 Geo. IV, c. 64. See Document Sources for a list of these returns for this period.
37. Eric Midwinter, *Social Administration in Lancashire, 1830-1860: Poor Laws, Public Health and Police* (Manchester, 1969), p. 74.
38. Baly, appendix.
39. *Ibid.*, Table XX.
40. *Preston Chronicle*, July 10, 1817. PRO, HO 20/1, no. 53, Joseph Baxendale to HO, Jan. 30, 1822. Typhus killed another prison officer at Kirkdale in 1835 (LCRO, QGR 3/38, surgeon's report).
41. Baly, pp. 234-35.
42. *Ibid.*, p. 173.
43. Manchester Central Library, *Laws of Debtors in Lancaster Castle* (Lancaster, 1804).
44. J. Hall, *Lancaster Castle: Its History and Associations* (Lancaster, 1843), pp. 15-20. This book was written for the use of Castle debtors; Hansbrow corrected the proofs.
45. *Ibid.*, p. 14.
46. Isaac Smith, *A Warder's Experiences in Lancaster Castle* (Blackburn, n.d.), p. 10.
47. *Ibid.*, p. 13.
48. LCL, scrapbook 5, *Rules and Regulations for the Guidance of Members of the Quakers Room* (printed broadside, Lancaster, n.d.).

49. Second Report.  50. Thirteenth Report.
51. PRO, PCOM 2/444.  52. Hall, p. 26.
53. *Ibid.*, p. 38.
54. Michael Ignatieff, *A Just Measure of Pain* (New York, 1978), chap. 1, "Pentonville," pp. 3-14.
55. *Ibid.*, p. 193.
56. *PP* 1845 XXIV, Tenth Report of the Inspectors for the Northern and Eastern District.
57. Second Report.
58. *PP* 1839 XXII, Fourth Report of the Inspectors for the Northern and Eastern District.
59. *Ibid.*; see also the second report.
60. Thirteenth Report. This was Frederic Hill's first report on Lancashire prisons. He had previously served as the inspector of the Scottish prisons.
61. Second Report.
62. Fourth Report.
63. Second Report.
64. *The Poor Man's Advocate*, July 21, 1832.
65. W. Hepworth Dixon, *The London Prisons* (London, 1850), p. 310.
66. Third Report.  67. *Ibid.*
68. Second Report.  69. Third Report.
70. Dixon, p. 338.  71. Eighth Report.
72. *PP* 1835 XI, Evidence Taken Before the Select Committee on Gaols and Houses of Correction, appendix.
73. Tenth Report.
74. PRO, PCOM 2/444, March 2, 1846. See Margaret DeLacy, "County Prison Administration in Lancashire, 1690-1850" (Ph.D. dissertation, Princeton University, 1980), p. 609, n. 110, for additional references to insane prisoners.
75. PRO, PCOM 2/443, July 26, 1845.
76. *Ibid.*, March-April 1843.
77. Eighth Report.
78. Patricia O'Brien, *The Promise of Punishment: Prisons in Nineteenth-Century France* (Princeton, 1982), chap. 3, pp. 75-108.
79. LCRO, QAL 1/1: proceedings of the Lancaster Castle Committee.
80. Walter Lowe Clay, *The Prison Chaplain* (Montclair, 1969), pp. 110-11.
81. *Poor Man's Advocate*, July 21, 1832.
82. PRO, PCOM 2/443, Aug. 7, 1843.
83. *Ibid.*, Sept. 14, 1844.
84. PRO, PCOM 2/444, March 11, 1846.
85. PRO, PCOM 2/443, Aug. 19, 1845.
86. *Ibid.*, Aug. 19-20, 1845.

87. For further discussion, see my article, "Grinding Men Good? Lancashire's Prisons at Mid-Century," in Victor Bailey, ed., *Policing and Punishment in Nineteenth-Century Britain* (London, 1981), pp. 182-216.

88. See Tomlinson, vol. 1, pp. 168-70.

89. Dixon, p. 312.

90. Eighth Report. Cf. Ursula Henriques, *Before the Welfare State* (London, 1979), p. 192.

91. Eighth Report.

92. Second Report.

93. Thirteenth Report.

### Chapter Eight

1. John Howard, *The State of the Prisons in England and Wales* (Abingdon, 1977; orig. ed. 1777), p. 121.

2. *PP* 1819 VII, Evidence Taken Before the Select Committee on Gaols.

3. Joseph John Gurney, *Notes on a Visit Made to Some of the Prisons in Scotland and the North of England in Company with Elizabeth Fry*, 2d ed. (London, 1820), p. 419.

4. Ursula Henriques, "The Rise and Decline of the Separate System of Prison Discipline," *Past and Present* 54 (Feb. 1972): 61-93.

5. Matthew Davenport Hill became a close friend of Bentham's toward the end of the latter's life. See Peter W. J. Bartrip, "The Career of Matthew Davenport Hill with Special Reference to His Place in Penal and Educational Reform Movements in Mid-Nineteenth-Century England" (Ph.D. dissertation, University of Wales, 1975). See also David Roberts, *Victorian Origins of the British Welfare State* (New Haven, 1960).

6. "Creative anguish" is a modern phrase, used by King and Elliott to describe the regime at Albany when it opened, but it is an extremely apt description of what the prison chaplains wished to foster in Victorian gaols. For the "common-sense school" see W. L. Clay, *The Prison Chaplain* (Montclair, 1969), pp. 212-19; Philip Collins, *Dickens and Crime* (London, 1965), pp. 70-81; and Sidney Webb and Beatrice Webb, *English Local Government*, vol. 6: *English Prisons Under Local Government* (London, 1963; orig. ed. 1922), pp. 87-89.

7. *PP* 1837 XXXII, Second Report of the Inspectors of Prisons for the Northern and Eastern District.

8. Hepworth Dixon, *The London Prisons* (London, 1850), p. 253.

9. John Clay, chaplain's third report to the Preston Quarter Sessions, 1826; W. L. Clay, p. 113.

10. LCRO, QSZ/1, AGS 1821.

11. W. L. Clay, pp. 110-11.

12. HO, Prison Department, Manchester MSS., register of felons, January 1796. I am grateful to the Home Office for enabling me to see this register.

13. PRO, HO 20/2, March 3, 1827.

14. W. L. Clay, p. 114.

15. *The Preston Pilot*, Sept. 15, 1827.

16. W. L. Clay, p. 115. The dispute grew so bitter that William John Williams hinted that one of the parties should resign.

17. John Clay, chaplain's reports to the Preston Quarter Sessions. Though Clay's reports were published and widely distributed, some have vanished. The reports for 1824-26, 1828-29, 1839-42, and 1844-58 are available in the LCRO (QGR 2). W. L. Clay's *The Prison Chaplain* contains copious extracts from many reports. After 1837 they were printed in full in the schedule B returns in the *Parliamentary Papers*. The reports of the prison inspectors contain some extracts from Clay's journal. J. J. Tobias included excerpts from some reports in *Nineteenth-Century Crime: Prevention and Punishment* (Newton Abbot, 1972).

18. Thomas Batty Addison, general report on the Preston house of correction (Preston M 1827), LCRO, QGR 2/14. Clay's report for 1827 has disappeared, but it seems clear that Addison was summarizing it accurately. Clay returned to the subject in 1850, quoting the 1827 report to show that his views had not changed.

19. Chaplain's report for 1851.

20. Second Report.

21. Chaplain's reports for 1848 and 1849.

22. V. A. C. Gatrell and T. B. Hadden, "Criminal Statistics and Their Interpretation," in E. A. Wrigley, ed., *Nineteenth Century Society* (Cambridge, Eng., 1972), pp. 388-91. I would like to thank Dr. Gatrell for assistance with an early draft of this section.

23. Chaplain's report for 1851. This example has been taken at random; similar tables appear in nearly every report. Cf. Norris Pope, *Dickens and Charity* (New York, 1978).

24. W. L. Clay, p. 212.

25. Chaplain's report for 1842.

26. LCRO, QGR 3/45, Richard Appleton, chaplain's report for Kirkdale, 1850. See also S. Greg, "Notes on Criminal Statistics," MS. copy of a paper read before the Manchester Statistical Society, sess. 1837-38, Manchester Central Library, MS. F. 310. 6. m5. I am grateful to the City of Manchester Cultural Services, Archives Department, for providing me with a copy of this and other Statistical Society papers. James Phillips Kay-Shuttleworth also believed that environmental improvements and education were the only solution to the problem of crime. See *The Moral and Physical Condition of the Working Classes Employed in the Cotton Manufacture in Manchester* (2d ed. Manchester, 1969; orig. ed. 1832). On the views of the Society as a whole, see Michael J. Cullen, *The Statistical Movement in Early Victorian Britain* (New York, 1975), chap. 8, and T. S. Ashton, *Economic and Social Investigations in Manchester, 1833-1933* (London, 1934).

27. PRO, PCOM 2/445, Aug. 27, 1849.

28. PRO, HO 20/4, Williams to Lord John Russell, Wakefield, Nov. 18, 1837, and Dec. 14, 1837. Jebb was even less tactful and more disliked than Chadwick, and it is difficult to believe that his efforts alone could have had much effect on a county already resisting the New Poor Law. See Eric Stockdale, "The Rise of Joshua Jebb, 1837-1850," *British Journal of Criminology* 14 (April 1976): 164-70. I am grateful to Judge Stockdale for providing me with a copy of this article.

29. LCRO, QGR 5/1, Report of the Committee on Prison Accommodation and Discipline (1853).

30. *Ibid.*

31. *PP* 1863 IX, Report from the Select Committee on Prison Discipline.

32. *Ibid.*

# Document Sources

*Major Manuscript Collections*

Bodleian Library
 Burdett MSS.
 Gough collection
 Howard MSS.
 MSS. Top. Oxon
British Library (BL)
 The Liverpool papers
Corporation of London Records Office
 Report from the Committee of Aldermen appointed to visit several gaols in
  England, 1815-16
HM Prison Lancaster and HM Prison Preston
 Miscellaneous newspaper clippings and similar materials
Home Office
 Manchester prison registers. (See also HO entries under Public Record Office
  below.)
Lancashire County Record Office (LCRO)
 CT. Financial papers
 DDB/74/15, 16. Parker collection, calendars of Crown prisoners, 1782-83
 DDGr. Dawson-Greene papers
 DDHe. Hesketh papers
 DDHu. Hulton papers
 DDKe. Kenyon papers
 PP. Prison plans

*The Preston Chronicle*
Probate records, Original wills for the diocese of Chester and the archdeaconry of Richmond
QAF. Financial papers
QAL. Lancaster Castle Committee minutes, 1783-1848
QAV/3. Report on Manchester house of correction, 1783
QGR. Reports by governors, chaplains, and surgeons, 1823-67
QGR/S/1. Report of the Committee on Prison Accommodation and Discipline, 1853
QGV. Prison rules
QJB. Insolvent debtors' papers
QJC. Calendars of Crown prisoners
QSB/1. Recognizance rolls
QSG. MS. Annual General Session minutes
QSO. Quarter Sessions order books
QSP. Quarter Sessions petitions
QSV/11. Proceedings of the Sheriff's Board, 1661-94
QSZ. Annual General Session minutes (printed)
Rate books: CAV/3, CPV/3 (ca. 1750), DDB 64/7 (1710), DDF 5 (1645), DDKe 2/17/9 (17ᶜ), DDN 1/64 (1624), DDP, DDPt (1622), DDRo (1665), DDT (2d batch), DDTa 215 (17ᶜ), DDX 114/1 (1675-78), DDX 123/42 (1718), DDX 603/1 (1752), DDX 678/2, DDX 951/7, ZBR 2/2A (ca. 1640)
Lancaster City Library (LCL)
Biographies file
D6351, no. 20, Letters on the treatment of John Bagguley (1817)
D6351, no. 24, John Higgin on his salary
D6351, no. 30a, Returns and correspondence, Lancaster Castle
Docton, Kenneth H., *Index to the Records of the Jail at Lancaster Castle*
Miscellaneous Assize calendars
Miscellaneous printed guides
MS. 6615, Debtor's rules, ca. 1772
MS. 7321, Folder on J. S. Harrison
PT 8167, "The Insolvent Debtor"
Rules of Debtors, 1804
Scrapbook no. 2
Scrapbook no. 5
Sketches of Edward Slack
Lancaster City Museum
Sketch of "The Quakers" by Edward [S]lack

Manchester Central Library
Papers read before the Manchester Statistical Society
Report of T. B. Bayley and S. Clowes on the Manchester house of correction
Rules and regulations for the Salford house of correction

Public Record Office (PRO)
DL 21/2. Duchy of Lancaster, sheriff's papers
DL 44/271, 423, 812. Miscellaneous papers, Lancaster Castle
HO 12. Home Office, criminal papers
HO 17. Petitions, 1819-39
HO 18. Petitions, 1839-54
HO 20. Home Office correspondence
HO 40. Correspondence on disturbances, 1812-55
HO 42. Correspondence
HO 43. Correspondence
HO 52. Letters from magistrates, 1835-40
HO 74/1-3. Letters to commissioners of inquiry
MPC 179. Maps and drawings
MPH 351. Maps and drawings
MR 15. Maps and drawings
PCOM 2/442-48. Journals and letter book, Lancaster gaolers
PL 25. Assize rolls, Lancashire
PL 26/27-30. Assize indictments, Lancashire
PL 26/285-95. Coroner's inquisitions, Lancashire
PL 27. Lancashire depositions
PL 28/16. Crown office order book
PL 28/22. Crown office order book
PL 28/40/2. Sheriff's papers
PL 28/41. Assignments of Lancaster Castle
SPD Geo. I, II. State papers, domestic
T 90/148, 149. Sheriff's cravings
TS 11/1025. Treasury solicitor's papers, R. v. George Dewhurst
TS 11/6056. Treasury solicitor's papers, R. v. Bagguley, Drummond, and Johnstone

St Mary Priory and Parish Church, Lancaster
Parish registers

Salford Public Library
Journal of Henry Fielding
Plans and pictures of the Manchester and Salford houses of correction

University College London
The Chadwick papers

*Parliamentary Papers*

Returns under 4 Geo. IV, c. 64

| | |
|---|---|
| 1828 XX | 1837-38 XLIII |
| 1829 XIX | 1839 XXXVIII |
| 1830 XXIV | 1840 XXXVIII |
| 1830-31 XII | 1841 XVIII |
| 1831-32 XXXIII | 1842 XXXII |
| 1833 XXVIII | 1843 XLIII |
| 1834 XLVI | 1844 XXXIX |
| 1835 XLIV | 1845 XXXVII |
| 1836 XLII | 1846 XXXIV |
| 1837 XLV | |

Reports of the Inspectors for the Northern and Eastern District

| | |
|---|---|
| First: 1836 XXXV | Seventh: 1842 XXI |
| Second: 1837 XXXII | Eighth: 1843 XXV and XXVI |
| Third: 1837-38 XXXI | Ninth: 1844 XXIX |
| Fourth: 1839 XXII | Tenth: 1845 XXIV |
| Fifth: 1840 XXV | Eleventh: 1846 XXI |
| Sixth: 1841, sess. 2, I | Thirteenth: 1847-48 XXXVI |

Investigations into Individual Prisons

1812-13 V (Lancaster Castle and Lincoln)
1822 IV (Ilchester)

Other Prison Papers

1819 XVII (Number of prisoners and management)
1819 VII (Prisons in England and Wales)
1821 XXI (Returns from gaols)
1822 IV (Prison discipline)
1826-27 VI (Increase in criminal commitments)
1828 VI (Secondary punishments)
1831 XV (Prison expenses)
1831-32 VII (Treadwheel labor)
1833 XXVIII (Number of prisons, prisoners, and cells)
1833 XXVIII (Expense of prisons)
1833 XXVIII (Officers and servants)
1835 XI (Answers of governors, prison discipline, the silent system)
1839 XXXVIII (Amount spent from rates for prisons)
1840 XXXVIII (Prisoners for political offenses)
1840 XXXVIII (Abstract returns)
1843 XLIV (Prisoners for nonpayment of fines)
1843 XLIII (Salaries and size of gaols)

1843 XXV and XXVI (Prison discipline)
1850 IX (Discipline in gaols)
1851 XXII (Digest of returns)
1863 IX (Prison discipline)
General Financial and Other Papers
  1813-14 XII (Lancashire rates)
  1814-15 X (Lancashire treasurer's accounts, 1786-1814)
  1825 VI (County rates committee)
  1826 XXI (Poor Law returns)
  1831-32 XXXV (Population of Lancashire)
  1835 XIV (County rates)
  1836 XXVII (County rates)
  1839 XLIV (Expenditure on poor)
  1850 XIII (County rates bill)

# Index

# Married With Baggage

*Also by Elise Chidley*

The Wrong Sort of Wife

# Married with Baggage

## Elise Chidley

First published in Great Britain in 2009 by Orion Books,
an imprint of The Orion Publishing Group Ltd
Orion House, 5 Upper Saint Martin's Lane
London WC2H 9EA

An Hachette UK Company

1 3 5 7 9 10 8 6 4 2

A CIP catalogue record for this book is
available from the British Library.

ISBN (Hardback) 978 0 7528 8901 6
ISBN (Trade Paperback) 978 0 7528 8902 3

Typeset by Deltatype Ltd, Birkenhead, Merseyside

Printed in Great Britain by Clays Ltd, St Ives plc

The Orion Publishing Group's policy is to use papers that are natural,
renewable and recyclable products and made from wood grown in sustainable
forests. The logging and manufacturing processes are expected to
conform to the environmental regulations of the country of origin.

www.orionbooks.co.uk

For my mother

Huge thanks to Peter Robinson, and to everybody at Orion, especially Kate Mills and Jade Chandler. Gratitude also to Debbie Lynn, Odette Watson, Nicola Featonby-Smith and Julie Camarillo. And thanks, of course, to Patrick and the crew.

# Chapter One

'Let's see, lunch box, water bottle, backpack, pencil box,' Annie muttered as she sailed regally along Shady Oak Road in her brand new silver minivan. 'Bread for sandwiches. What else? Cheese. Peanut butter? Hang on, isn't there some ban on peanut products? Marmite, then. And jam.' Preoccupied with her mental shopping list, she made it all the way to the four-way stop before she glanced in the rear-view mirror and realised with a jolt that something was wrong. Horribly wrong.

The booster seat was empty.

'Oh *God*!'

The minivan leapt forward as she gunned it around the corner, feverishly searching for a place to turn. She shot into a driveway, executed a seven-point manoeuvre in front of some stranger's garage, and then nosed out into the street again. It was only when the driver of an oncoming vehicle hooted and made rude signs at her that she realised she'd forgotten to pull over to the right-hand side of the road. 'Sorry!' she mouthed at the indignant face behind the windscreen as she veered out of the way.

OK, calm down, she told herself. Getting killed at this point would *really* screw things up.

She pictured seven-year-old Lydia trailing around the empty house, calling, 'Annie! Annie?' while, just a block or two away, ambulances used the Jaws of Life to extricate her charred body from the wreckage. Simon would be on the news afterwards, walking around in a blanket, saying, 'I never dreamed she was the type to go off shopping and leave a kiddy alone at home. You think you know a person ...'

He'd never say 'kiddy', of course. But words to that effect.

By the time she pulled up in her own driveway at number five Maple Tree Ridge, she was sweating and shaky.

The place was still standing, at least.

And what an impressive place it was, too. Set in a small, highly exclusive Connecticut town called Norbury, her new home was a two-storey, five-bedroom, five-thousand-square-foot example of New England colonial architecture, complete with glossy black shutters and freshly painted cedar shingles that gleamed brilliant white in the sunshine.

At the tail end of summer, the front borders were still bright with massive late-blooming hydrangeas and mounds of impatiens tucked under neat box hedges trimmed in alternating ball and cone shapes. The relocation agent had pointed out a clump of tall rhododendrons near the triple garage. 'Those will be fabulous in July,' she'd said. 'And look at those lilacs and dogwoods – you'll have a mass of blossom in the spring.' Annie, whose only experience of plants revolved around care of a temperamental African violet on the kitchen window sill of her tiny flat in Islington, had filed away the horticultural names with relish so that she could recount them to her mother.

The enormous front door of her new house was flanked

2

by two impressive round pillars that oozed substance and prosperity. Even the knocker – a large copper lion's head – was a statement of power and wealth. If someone had told her, just a few short months before when she was still ensconced in her one-bedroom flat in London, that she'd soon be living in America, in a house that was bigger than her whole block of flats back home, she would have dismissed the whole idea with a laugh.

Yet here she was.

She'd been in the house exactly a week now, and the novelty had far from worn off – but as she pulled up in the minivan she didn't pause for even a moment to admire the architecture.

Instead, she ducked under the garage door while it was still rolling up, and burst into the quiet kitchen. Casting a quick eye around, she shot past the gleaming granite countertops, on through the family room with its cathedral ceiling and massive plasma TV screen, across the gleaming floorboards of the centre hall (skidding a bit on the Persian rug) and up the main staircase. In the carpeted corridor she hurried past several closed doors, then stopped, breathless, in front of a door with a handmade sign taped to it.

The sign read, 'No groan-ups ecsep Daddy'.

Annie threw the door open without knocking.

Thank God! There she was. Safe and sound.

Lydia Keeler, Annie's stepdaughter, was kneeling on the rug, her fair hair falling over her face, the picture of concentration. She seemed to be wrapping a doll in strips of tissue paper. She didn't so much as glance up as Annie burst in. She obviously hadn't even noticed that she'd been gone for a good twenty minutes or more. Excellent, Annie thought. No need to erode whatever modicum of trust the child was beginning to have in her by blurting out the story of her slip-up.

'Lydia? Um – are you ready to go? Remember, I said we have to buy stuff for your first day of school tomorrow?'

Lydia turned the doll over and began tucking away loose ends of paper with the businesslike air of a nurse.

'Lyddie? You can bring the doll, but we have to go.'

The child looked up with a frown. 'I don''t want to go.'

'I know. It's a pain. But we have to do it or you won't have any lunch tomorrow, or any backpack to put it in. Do you think you want a pink backpack?'

Lydia gave her a withering look, but began to stand up.

'Here, let me brush your hair.' Annie went over to the dressing table, picked up the hairbrush and brandished it briskly. ('Look as if you mean business,' her friend Henny had told her when she'd asked for advice about getting Lydia to do as she was told.)

Lydia heaved a deep sigh and shuffled towards the dressing table. Folding her arms over her narrow chest, she allowed her stepmother to run the brush through her tangles. Every time it caught in a knot, she winced dramatically and shrank a little further away from Annie.

'How's that?' Annie asked after a moment, meeting Lydia's eye in the mirror. 'Your hair is so pretty.'

Lydia stared at herself with an unreadable expression. Then she looked at Annie's face in the mirror. 'You have weird-coloured eyes,' she noted.

Annie glanced at her own reflection. It was true; her eye

4

colour was unusual. Most people called it hazel, but it was lighter than true hazel. She'd once seen a goat with eyes exactly that colour; a sort of greenish gold.

Her hair, at least, was an ordinary colour. Brown.

Annie shrugged. 'I know. There's no exact name for the colour of my eyes. But yours are definitely blue, like your dad's.'

'And my mum's.'

Annie paused a moment. 'That's right. Come on, are you ready?'

'I suppose. Why do I have to go to stupid school, anyway? I hate school.'

'You never know. You might like this one.'

'I won't.'

Dragging her feet and complaining steadily, Lydia followed Annie down the stairs, through the kitchen, through the garage, and into the car. 'Right,' Annie murmured to herself, glancing back at the booster seat full of peevish little girl, 'let's try this one more time.'

They returned two hours later loaded down with, among other things, a Hannah Montana backpack and a Barbie lunch box. Lydia sat at the kitchen counter examining her new possessions one by one, while Annie poured tea for the two of them. Lydia's was mainly milk.

'I can't wait to meet your teacher,' Annie said, stirring Lydia's mug and setting it down in front of her.

'Why?' asked Lydia. 'What's so great about her?'

'Well, I don't know. But I bet she's really nice. I wonder how many kids you'll have in your class.'

Lydia shrugged. 'Who cares?'

'Lyddie, I know you're a little nervous about tomorrow ...'

'I'm not nervous.'

'Really? Great. I'm happy to hear it. It's hard to be the new girl, but you'll soon settle in.'

Lyddie didn't even grace this comment with a reply. Instead, she finished her tea, banged the cup on the counter, slid off the bar stool, and left the room.

'Nice chatting to you, too,' Annie said to the empty air.


As Simon opened the front door that evening, Annie came quietly out of the kitchen and stood in the shadows, watching him shrug off his dark trench coat and hang it up.

Even now, she could hardly believe that this tall, rugged man with sun-bleached hair and piercing blue eyes was actually her husband.

For a while before she met him, Annie had almost given up on the notion of a husband. Oh, she'd had boyfriends, all right. There'd been Nick, the computer whiz; attractive enough in a slightly geeky way, pleasant enough when you could attract his attention, but so wedded to the virtual world that he could be physically in your living room without having a single particle of mental presence there. His passport should have been issued not by the United Kingdom, but the World Wide Web. Their relationship had ended abruptly one night when Annie ripped a handful of electrical plugs out of the wall in an effort to unglue his eyes from the computer screen.

Then there'd been Matty. Matty was too gorgeous-looking for his own good, her friend Henny said from the outset.

A smoking-hot man like that was bound to have a warped view of reality, she reckoned. Annie, of course, didn't pay any attention to Henny's warnings. After all, Matty wasn't a self-obsessed narcissist. Far from it. He was a man with a social conscience. Saving the environment was his explicit personal mission. (He believed everybody ought to have an explicit personal mission.) He'd managed to carve out a career for himself as middleman between people trying to sell green products and trendy young things with enough cash to buy them. He had a huge advantage in doing this. Just by association with his smoking-hotness, he could make any product under the sun seem chic and desirable – even automatic indoor composters.

In the end, what ruined things with Matty was his insistence on recycling ziplock lunch bags. Annie wasn't against recycling, per se. In fact, she was all for it. She just couldn't stomach his particular *method* of recycling, which involved throwing his old, mayonnaise-smeared lunch bags in with the laundry. The daily sight of these bags spinning around with his underwear gave her such an ominous feeling about life with Matty that, after a month-long experiment with 'living together', she asked him (apologetically but firmly) to shift himself and his stuff out of her flat. He didn't try to change her mind. It turned out that, for his part, he was thoroughly disillusioned by her lack of commitment to the worm farm he was cultivating in the corner of her kitchen.

Annie first laid eyes on Simon about a year after she'd broken up with Matty. She met him in Greece, on the final day of a holiday with her red-headed cousin Sarah – a massively self-indulgent few days spent reading paperbacks on the beach and perfecting her tan while Sarah went sailing.

As Annie and Sarah sat under an umbrella outside a restaurant in Lakka on the island of Paxos, waiting for their order of moussaka and spanakopita, a tall, blond man walked by, in earnest discussion with a shorter, broader man whose face Annie didn't even notice. When Annie caught sight of the tall man, her stomach swooped as if she'd hit an air pocket in a light aircraft.

'God! Look at that, Sarah!' she hissed, gesturing discreetly at the man. 'You're always asking me what my type is. Well, that's it. Right there. The tall bloke.'

Sarah obediently looked. Then, to Annie's consternation, she suddenly hailed the men in a loud baritone. 'Simon! Billy! Over here!'

The men turned and squinted their eyes at the pair sitting in the deep shade of the umbrella.

'Hey,' said the stocky man after a second. 'It's Sarah! Sarah Harleigh!'

The two of them made their way over to Annie and Sarah's table. 'Pull up a pew,' Sarah invited.

Annie felt a pleasant shiver go through her as she met the eyes of the tall stranger Sarah introduced as Simon Keeler. He had a stern, weather-beaten face, but his eyes were bright blue, and when he smiled – which he did just once during the whole encounter – they crinkled attractively.

Annie found herself completely tongue-tied, and Simon didn't seem to have much to say either, but Sarah and the other man talked nineteen to the dozen, in incomprehensible nautical language. Distracted as she was, Annie only caught snatches. '. . . Last saw Sarah when she was rail meat on a mono-hull off the Aegean islands ...' she heard Billy tell Simon.

'Yeah, the Meltemi was blowing that day, remember? We had one broach after another,' Sarah replied with gusto.

'But good sailing,' Billy insisted. 'Half the time we had to come in flying a chicken chute ...'

Annie didn't even try to understand what they were saying. She kept stealing glances at Simon, hoping that her blushes didn't show through her sunburn. When Billy at last stood up to go, Simon hastily pushed something across the table to Annie. It was a phone number written in pencil on a linen napkin. Annie still had the napkin to this day.

When Annie finally brought herself to dial the number on the napkin – three weeks passed before she could screw up the courage – she had no clue that Simon was a widower with a seven-year-old daughter. Of course, her cousin Sarah could have told her all this, and more, if Annie had only asked, but from the moment Simon walked away from the table, Annie had felt that gossiping about him with Sarah would be sacrilege.

In fact, she never mentioned him to Sarah at all. She even managed a casual, 'Nah' and a dismissive shrug when Sarah said, 'So Simon Keeler is your type, is he?'

By the time Annie was brave enough to call him, she wondered if he'd even remember meeting her.

But the question didn't come up. The minute she heard his deep, masculine voice on the phone, she dropped the receiver in abject fright, hanging up on him. It was a bit of a relief, really. What on earth could she possibly say to such a man, the solitary example she'd ever actually seen of the exact 'type' that turned her legs to jelly and made her heart pound like all those drums at the Beijing Olympics?

She'd be much better off going out for a drink with Sid Vole, the art director at *Rumour Has It*, the women's weekly magazine she worked for. The state of his hands was a bit off-putting, but she was almost sure the black under his nails was ink of some sort.

But within half an hour the phone rang, and it was him. Simon Keeler. He'd tracked Sarah down through his friend Billy, apparently, and asked for Annie's number. 'What made you do that, after all this time?' she asked when she found the breath to speak.

'Well, I had a crank call a few minutes ago,' he admitted. 'For some reason, before I picked up the phone I had this weird feeling that it was you. But it wasn't, of course. Just some heavy-breathing nutter who hung up on me. So much for sixth sense. But it made me want to talk to you.'

'Oh,' Annie said faintly. 'Um, can you excuse me a moment? I'll be right back.' She ran to her medicine cabinet and threw back an unmeasured dose of Rescue Remedy, her fingers shaking so much that she could barely get the bottle open. The trouble was, the bottle had expired years ago. She'd last used it when her dad died.

No man had ever upset her entire nervous system before, just by talking to her on the phone.

At first, Simon was a bit of an enigma. Something about his face – the stern, shut-off look she would surprise on it when she watched him from across a room – made her think she was mad to believe he fancied her at all. But then he'd catch her watching him, and his expression would dissolve into a lopsided, utterly irresistible grin, and she'd tell herself that he found her irresistible, too.

It was only on their third date that Annie found out about Lydia. It wasn't that Simon deliberately kept his daughter secret. He just didn't talk about her in casual conversation. Holding Annie's hand across the table of a dimly lit restaurant in Islington (close to her flat so that she could invite him back for their first after-date 'coffee' if she happened to feel like it), he confessed that he never quite knew how to explain his situation to new people. If he mentioned Lydia, then he had to mention his wife; and then, obviously, he had to explain that she'd drowned in a boating accident.

It was always a bit of a conversation stopper, he said.

'I'm so sorry,' she gasped, determined to keep the conversation flowing freely. 'What a terrible, terrible thing. When – when did it happen?'

'A little over a year ago. She went out alone on a boat in Cornwall. A storm blew up. She never came back.'

In the candlelight, she realised that his face wasn't stern at all. It was lined with grief.

'Can I meet your little girl?' she asked suddenly.

He raised his eyebrows. 'You really want to?'

'Yes, of course!'

He shrugged ruefully. 'I was thinking this would probably be the moment when you'd tell me goodbye, and thank you, and have a nice life.'

'I think it's too late for that,' she said, only half joking.

He stared at her very hard. 'Annie, I'm leaving for America in four months.'

11

Her heart gave a painful squeeze.

'On ... on holiday?'

'No. To live there. My company's sending me to New York.'

She coloured. 'Oh. Well, then. Of course you don't want me to meet her. Obviously. I mean, what would be the point?'

'I do want you to meet her.'

She looked into his eyes. He held her gaze steadily. 'All right,' she said. 'I'd love to. If ... if you think it's wise.'

'Wise?' he repeated blankly. 'What's wisdom got to do with it?'

Since wisdom wasn't a consideration, she took him back to her flat after dinner in the full knowledge that losing him to America would be altogether more wretched once she'd seen him naked between her sheets.

'Who's looking after Lydia?' she asked suddenly, at a point when she hadn't yet seen him completely naked but had checked out a fair amount of his bare skin at close quarters.

'Polish au pair,' he murmured between kisses. 'Very reliable. Can we just not talk about her now, though? She has a moustache.'

That very Saturday, Annie went round to Simon's big house in Kensington for the first time ever, clutching a gift for his daughter – a handheld puppet. 'I need something I can sort of *entertain* a seven-year-old with,' she'd told the spotty youth in the toy shop. 'Something interactive.'

He'd suggested an MP3 player or a Nintendo DS. 'Do

you have anything more ... I don't know, low tech?' she'd asked, staring doubtfully at the electronic offerings. He sighed, spat out his gum, and suggested a junior magician set – but she didn't fancy the idea of taking pound coins out of people's ears.

Then she spotted the monkey puppet. It was a luxuriant creature with soft faux fur and remarkably lifelike eyes – exactly the sort of toy she'd always hankered after, in vain, as a kid. In her day, she'd had to make do with paper dolls and the occasional home-made rag doll – her mother was a firm believer in creativity, thriftiness, and self-sufficiency.

Taking a quick look around the shop to make sure that nobody from the office happened to have wandered in off the street, she stuck her hand inside the puppet's body and made it perform a few experimental hand claps, bows and head nods. In a low voice, the monkey said, 'Hello there, folks, Peanut at your service.'

'I'll take it,' she told the spotty youth.

'Well, it's your decision,' the youth replied, eyeing the monkey with distaste.

Simon's daughter, as it turned out, was even less enthusiastic about the monkey than the shop assistant.

Lydia, small and blonde, ethereal as a dandelion, was huddled in a corner of a handsome leather sofa when Annie first laid eyes on her, wearing pyjamas and an expression of deep distrust.

'Lydia, this is my friend Annie,' Simon said a shade too heartily, drawing Annie into the room by the hand. The room itself was a little intimidating, Annie thought. It was what you'd call well appointed. The ceiling was high with lavishly adorned cornicing. The furniture — plentiful, dark and gleaming — bore absolutely no resemblance to her own eclectic collection of catalogue-bought, some-assembly-required pieces. It was all terribly solid and — well, *married* looking, whereas her own style was more student-meets-underpaid-magazine-writer.

'Look, I've bought you a present!' Annie found herself saying in a bright, sing-song voice. 'See? It's a monkey.'

The child stared at the proffered toy in absolute silence, making no move to accept it.

Bit of an awkward moment, really.

Simon, of course, tried to smooth things over. 'Come on, Lydia, take the monkey. He's really cute! You'll hurt his monkey feelings if you don't.' Then, as if on cue, his BlackBerry rang. 'I'm sorry, but I really must get this call,' he murmured, walking out and leaving Annie alone with Lydia and the monkey.

Quick as a flash, Lydia took a cushion and placed it in front of her, between herself and the newcomer.

'Hey folks, Peanut at your service,' Annie offered gamely, waggling the bright-eyed monkey. 'What's your name?'

Lydia said nothing.

Annie stepped over to an armchair and crouched down behind it so that Peanut was poking up over the back. Maybe Lydia would feel less threatened if she were out of sight. 'Can you guess what my favourite food is?' Peanut asked.

Apparently, Lydia couldn't.

'I bet your favourite food is, let's see now, Brussels sprouts?'

Lydia chose not to comment.

'How about I sing a little song for you?' Peanut was really struggling now. Annie wracked her brains, trying to think of a suitable ditty for him, but all that came to mind was Humpty Dumpty. Well, it would have to do. 'Humpty Dumpty sat on a wall,' she began. Only it wasn't a song, was it? More of a dirge, really. 'Humpty Dumpty had a great fall.' She snatched Peanut out of sight. 'All the king's horses and all the king's men couldn't put Humpty together again.' She eased her hand into view again and had the monkey drag himself along the back of the chair, groaning and moaning, as if gravely injured.

Loud clapping broke out!

Relieved, Annie stood up with a smile. 'I knew you'd . . .' She trailed off. The applause was coming from Simon. Lydia was still sitting in her corner, knees pulled up to her chin, arms folded around her legs.

'Daddy,' the child said clearly – and these were the first words Annie ever heard her say, 'can you please make the mad lady go away?'

Things had improved a lot since that first encounter, of course. Nowadays, Lydia spoke directly to Annie on a daily basis. She was never chatty, but at least they'd progressed beyond those early days when she spoke to Annie only through Simon.

Simon was kicking off his shoes when Annie came up behind him and put her arms around his chest, feeling the warmth of his skin through his fine-gauge woollen jumper. As he turned towards her she stood on tiptoe to kiss him on the lips – not a wifely peck, but a passionate, newly-wed, rip-my-clothes-off-now kind of kiss.

'Mmm,' he said, taking a step back and looking at her with his raffish grin. 'That was quite a welcome. What's with the apron?'

She looked down at the candy stripes (she was using a smock she'd bought that very day for Lydia's school art classes) and wrinkled her nose. 'I know, I'm not sure pink is my colour. It suits Lyddie much better. The thing is, I've been making spaghetti bolognaise, and I didn't want it spattered all over my clothes again.'

'Spaghetti bolognaise. Hmm.' His face went thoughtful.

'Don't worry, the mince isn't like bullets this time,' she assured him. 'I defrosted it first.' Cooking was not one of her strong points.

'Right. Sounds good. Hang on, I'll just run up and check on Lydia.'

While he was upstairs, she poured them each a glass of wine and turned on the gas fire, feeling very domesticated. It wasn't really cool enough yet to warrant the fire, but flames set a nice romantic tone.

'How is she?' she asked when he came back downstairs in old corduroy trousers and a T-shirt. He took his wine and sank down beside her on the sofa.

'Asleep. Looks like I'll have to take an earlier train if I ever want to see her conscious.'

'How was work?'

Simon was a rising young executive with ChefPro, one of Britain's top five food production companies. He and his team had been sent over to New York to investigate the viability of setting up a new chain of fast-food outlets, starting out on the East Coast and gradually expanding across America.

Simon shrugged. 'It was ... interesting. We're processing results from the first focus group. They're not as decisive as we'd like.'

'So, which pie do they like best?' Annie asked, sipping her wine. 'I bet it's the chicken and mushroom.'

He put his glass down and stretched, yawning. 'That's the funny thing. If you don't tell them what they're eating, a surprising percentage like the steak and kidney.'

'New style or old style?'

In an initiative spearheaded by Simon, ChefPro was working on an updated version of its trusty staple, the meat pie. At Simon's urging, the test kitchens were developing lower-fat pies made with gourmet ingredients and fresh herbs. Disappointingly, the new pies were not finding much favour with the British market. Simon was counting on them going down a storm in America. 'Olde World made new' was the working catchphrase for the chain.

'Well, that's the problem. I don't think we've nailed it yet with the new-style pastry. The old recipe is winning hands down.'

'Oh dear. If only saturated fats weren't so bad for you.'

'Exactly. And if only wholewheat wasn't so chewy.' Simon shrugged and took a sip of his wine. 'Don't worry, we'll get it right. It just takes time.'

Later that night, as Simon lay sleeping, Annie slipped out from under his heavy arm and crept across the landing to the room known as the den. Closing the door softly, she turned on the light and looked around the snug room. She liked it in here, mainly because it was small and informal enough to feel comfortable. They had rented the house fully furnished, and the reception rooms downstairs were decorated with such rigorous professionalism that Annie always felt that she herself was a bit of a blot on an otherwise blameless landscape in her everyday jeans, T-shirt, and ponytail. Pyjamas and a ratty old gown, she felt, would be an absolute affront to the sensibilities of these rooms.

Annie's small flat in Islington had been bursting at the seams with clutter, but when her pictures and knick-knacks were spread across this large house in Connecticut, they virtually disappeared into the woodwork.

Unlike Annie, Simon had brought almost nothing from London; just clothes and a couple of photo albums that he buried under socks in his chest of drawers. Simon had encouraged Annie to go out and buy whatever she fancied to make the Connecticut house feel like home, but just at the moment she couldn't imagine what that would *be*. Books and a teapot, maybe? After all, she couldn't exactly change all the formal furniture for something a little more relaxed, could she?

Annie picked up the cordless phone, sank down onto the sofa and glanced at her watch. It was two in the morning. Safe, then, to call England.

But who to call? Her mum? She pictured her sixty-four-year-old mother jumping with fright over toast and tea in her Surrey kitchen as the phone shrilled out so early in the morning. No, she didn't want to worry Mum.

It had better be Henny again.

Henny Foster was married. She'd been married for ages. She even had children – one of whom was a little girl just a year older than Lydia. This, and the fact that Annie Harleigh and Henny Foster had known each other since they were ten years old, made Henny the perfect person to unburden herself to – not that she really had *burdens*, of course; just a touch of, hmm, would you call it homesickness, or was that too childish?

Henny picked up the phone after only a couple of rings. From across the Atlantic, her voice sounded surprisingly loud and robust. 'Hello?' she bellowed. '*Annie?* Do you know it's seven in the morning? I'm just trying to get Lulu through her flashcards for her spelling test. It's "i" before "e" except after "c". Go away and write it down a couple of times – receive, receive, receive. Right, I only have a few secs, Annie. What's going on?'

'I can't sleep again,' Annie said sheepishly. 'I just needed to talk to someone.'

'Why don't you wake up Simon?'

Annie played with the loose threads of her gown. 'I don't want to worry him,' she admitted.

'Is it about Lydia again?'

'Sort of. Have you – um, have you ever gone shopping and forgotten the kids at home?'

'Annie! You didn't!'

'Well, only for a few minutes. It really didn't take me long to realise I'd left her behind. But that was a hairy moment – you know, when I looked back and saw the empty seat.'

'Good grief. I bet it was. What did Simon say?'

'Do you know, I didn't actually tell him. I mean, it wasn't

a big deal. And I'd hate him to go off to work thinking maybe it wasn't safe to leave Lyddie with me all day.'

'Yes, I see what you mean.'

'It's Lyddie's first day of school tomorrow. Well, *today*, I suppose. I'm a bit stumped about what to make her for lunch. She doesn't like ham or cheese, and she's not allowed to have peanut butter because of allergies. I thought I'd give her Marmite but they've never even heard of it at the supermarket.'

'Annie, you've called me at seven in the morning to ask what sandwiches to make?'

'No, of course not. It's just ... I felt like talking to someone, that's all. Plus I wanted to ask you, what do you normally do when the children are at school? I'm ... you know, just trying to plan my day tomorrow. I mean, what is it most mums *do* all day?'

There was silence on the other end of the line for a moment. Then Henny burst out, 'Oh, for God's sake, Annie! Don't you know that's just about the most insulting thing you could ask me?'

'Look, you know I'm not trying to insult anybody! It's a perfectly valid question. I'm used to getting up, putting on my clothes and going out to work!'

Annie had been features writer for *Rumour Has It*, the women's weekly best known for never allowing the truth to get in the way of a good story.

'Well, it's the same thing now, for heaven's sake! Except your work is at home.'

'You mean – housekeeping?'

Henny sighed. 'Well, houses do need a certain amount of

20

keeping, that's for bloody sure. The dishes and the laundry and the vacuuming. Changing sheets, making beds, cleaning loos, scrubbing bath rings, sweeping bloody floors.'

'The thing is,' Annie said a little self-consciously, 'I don't have to do as much of that as you'd think. Simon thought we should have a cleaning service, since the house is so big. They did a massive clean-up after we moved in, and they're going to come in twice a week. And all his shirts go out to the dry-cleaner.'

'Well, even so, you're cleaning up after Lydia all the time, I'm sure.'

'Um, not really. She's a very tidy child. Doesn't really have many toys. Makes her own bed.'

'OK,' said Henny evenly. 'I'm trying to sympathise, I really am, but right now I'm a bit short of time because I've got to go and strip a wee-soaked bed, make three lunches, write a note to the teacher, make sure everyone has their trainers, and ice a batch of fairy cakes for the school fete.'

Annie sniffed. 'Oh God, I sound spoilt rotten, don't I?'

'No,' said Henny. 'You sound bored and lonely. I suppose it's not nearly as hectic, dealing with just the one child. Have you thought about getting a part-time job?'

Annie sighed. She'd thought about getting a part-time job, all right. She'd had lurid, feverish, just-short-of-erotic dreams about getting a part-time job. New York, the Big Apple, was just a tantalising hour away by train. She could only imagine what fabulous opportunities awaited an ambitious journalist in the *actual* city of *Sex and the City* fame.

'Can't do it,' she said, trying to keep the hollow regret out of her voice. 'Don't have the right paperwork. I'm here as a spouse, that's all. I tried to set up some freelance work before I left the UK, but it didn't pan out.'

If Annie had never in her wildest dreams imagined she'd marry a man who would whisk her away to a fully furnished mansion in a foreign country, she had also never imagined she'd marry a man with a fully furnished family. She'd never imagined she would wind up sacrificing her career to be a mum before she'd even had a baby.

Given the choice, she would have liked to get a bit of practice on a dog or a cat first. She'd had a goldfish once, a few years back. Goldfish were pretty fragile, it turned out. Little girls were much more robust; or so she hoped.

So here she was, thrust all unprepared into a stage of life she had always thought of as very distant, possibly even unattainable.

She'd been handed married life on a platter: husband, daughter, house, garden, cleaning lady, landscaping service, credit card. And it was great. Of course it was. Only sometimes she walked into the beautiful house, sat down in the fabulous stainless steel and granite kitchen, and wondered exactly what she was supposed to do next.

'Well – well, you'll just have to get involved with the school then,' Henny said decisively. 'Offer to shelve books at the library, that sort of thing. Look, I really must go. Shoe crisis. Talk to you soon.'

What sort of a shoe crisis? Annie wondered. Knowing Henny, it wouldn't be something simple, like a lost shoe. No, it would be a shoe stuck halfway down the Labrador's throat, or the three-year-old using his boots as boats in the garden pond.

Annie reached for the chenille throw draped fetchingly over the sofa, and wrapped it around her body. She was getting a little cold. So. Volunteering at the school. She pictured herself arranging flowers for the school secretary's desk. Or – or helping the lunch lady dole out chicken nuggets. Or sharpening all the pencils in the second-grade classroom. Or holding a lollipop sign and helping kids cross the road. Or something ...

'Would my lady care for a cup of tea?'

Annie opened her eyes reluctantly and sat up. Looking around, she realised she was in the den, and fingers of light were filtering in through the window.

'Was I snoring then?' Simon asked mildly. He towered over her in his dark suit, freshly showered and shaved and really quite fragrant, briefcase in one hand, a steaming mug in the other.

Annie accepted the tea and took a tiny sip. 'No, of course not. You only do that if you've had too much whisky. I just couldn't sleep, that's all.'

Simon raised his eyebrows. 'Something on your mind?'

'Not really. It was just – you know, jet lag.'

'Jet lag? After a whole week?'

Annie laughed a little uneasily. She didn't want Simon catching wind of her homesickness, or boredom, or what-ever it was. He had enough on his plate, worrying about his New Age pies, and about Lydia's adjustment to their new life. 'I have a very sensitive internal clock, as it happens,' she told him. 'It has to do with the fluid in your inner ear, apparently.'

'Really? Hmm. Well, feel free to wake me next time your inner ear starts playing up. I'm sure we'll think of something to do.' He leaned in to kiss her, and she felt the familiar rush of blood to various parts of her anatomy, including her face. He tasted quite deliciously of tea.

She pulled away reluctantly. 'Hey, you'd better get a move on or you'll miss your train.'

'I could miss it just once,' he said, putting his briefcase down with a clatter and lowering himself onto the sofa. Just as he was sliding his hand into the warmth of her dressing gown, raising a trail of goose-pimples, his BlackBerry gave its strident ring.

'Bugger,' he said, fishing it out of his pocket and glancing at the screen. 'I forgot the teleconference on the bloody train. Sorry, love, got to go after all.' He turned to look her smack in the eyes. 'You're not worrying about anything, are you? I don't like waking up to find you gone. Much prefer to see you drooling on the pillow.'

'Bloody cheek!' She grabbed a cushion and he stood up quickly, grinning as he backed away from her. 'I don't *drool*!' she cried. The cushion caught him smartly in the small of the back just as he exited the room.

# Chapter Two

Bradley Elementary School was a five-minute walk along wooded streets from the Keelers' house on Maple Tree Ridge. Annie had taken Lydia over to explore the playground several times already, to familiarise her with her new stomping ground. Normally the walk was punctuated with groans and moans from Lydia: 'Why do we have to go? I was playing a game. I don't *want* to go on the swings.' But today they walked in silence, the shiny pink Hannah Montana backpack rattling slightly with every step Lydia took.

As they stepped through the double doors into the school's front lobby, Annie glanced at the little girl, trying to gauge how she was feeling. Her head was down and her fair hair fell over her face, making it impossible to see her expression. 'Lyddie? You OK?'

Lydia nodded without looking up.

'So like I said, I put in a plain butter sandwich, but there's also one of those mild mini cheeses that you like. If you eat them both, then bingo! You've eaten a cheese sandwich.'

'OK.'

'Let's see ... I think the second-grade wing is this way. Funny how empty the place is. We're early, I suppose.'

After a few false turns, they found Miss Scofield's room and verified that Lydia's name was on the list of students pinned to the door.

'You can go now,' Lydia said, her face very white and set.

'What, and leave you standing out here in the corridor? You've got to be joking. Come on, let's see if Miss Scofield's in there yet.'

She knocked on the door, and a voice asked them to come in.

'Right,' said Annie, tucking Lydia's wayward hair behind her ears, 'let's go and introduce ourselves.'

Lydia pulled her hand out of Annie's grasp. 'I don't think you're supposed to come in with me.'

'Rubbish,' said Annie. 'Miss Scofield will be happy to meet me. Come on!'

She pushed the door open and walked in, smiling at the woman behind the desk, who blinked up at her in surprise. 'Hi, I'm Annie Har— Keeler and this is Lydia. We've just moved here from England.'

'Right. Good to meet you, Mrs Har-Keeler. I'm Melissa Scofield. Hi, Lydia, great to meet you.'

Lydia looked very hard at the floor.

'So, we're early.'

'Yes, you are. That's OK. Lydia can find her desk and do a little colouring while she waits. Look, Lydia, this is where you hang your backpack.' Miss Scofield showed her a hook with her name underneath it, and Lydia duly hung up her bag.

While the teacher settled Lydia at a desk, Annie looked

at the displays on the bulletin boards. 'This is all very bright and cheerful,' she remarked.

'We try to make it a happy room,' said Miss Scofield. 'Now, Mrs Har-Keeler, I assume you've had your package from the school secretary? We do have a parents' evening in a couple of weeks when you get to come in and hear about the curriculum.'

'Yes, thanks, I got the letter.'

'Good.' Miss Scofield stood and smiled at her.

Annie smiled back.

'So ... walkers normally stay out in the playground until the whistle blows,' the teacher said. 'They all line up by grade outside once the buses have arrived.'

'OK,' said Annie.

'No real need for moms to come inside at drop-off,' Miss Scofield added.

Just then a scuffle of feet and a hum of voices broke out in the corridor.

'Here they come.' Miss Scofield walked over to the door and threw it open.

Children began to pour into the room, chatting excitedly as they searched for their designated coat hooks. Lydia, seated at her table, stared fixedly at the piece of paper in front of her, but didn't make any pretence of actually colouring in.

When the children had all hung up their backpacks and found their seats, Miss Scofield clapped her hands briskly.

'Girls and boys,' she said in a carrying voice, 'good morning and welcome to second grade. I'm Miss Scofield and I'll be your teacher this year.'

A boy raised his hand. 'Who's that?' he asked, pointing at Annie.

'Um ... that's Mrs Har-Keeler, Lydia's mom. Lydia is new to Bradley this year. Boys and girls, say hello to Lydia, please.'

'Hello, Lydia,' the class droned.

Lydia didn't look up from her piece of paper but the tips of her ears, visible because Annie had tucked her hair behind them, were seen to go very pink.

'Oh, and we have another new pupil in the classroom this morning,' the teacher went on. 'Let's all say hello to Hailey.'

'Hello, Hailey,' the boys and girls chorused. A plump girl with a mop of dark hair gave a jaunty wave.

Miss Scofield crossed the room to where Annie was standing. 'Thanks for coming in,' she said pointedly.

'Right. No problem. I'll ... I'll be on my way, then.'

'Probably a good idea. We do encourage moms to come into the classroom, by the way, for specific volunteer opportunities. I guess you'll be heading over to the second-grade coffee at the cafeteria to put your name down for some of those.'

Annie smiled. 'Oh yes. That's at nine, I think. I'll get out of your way, then. Bye, Lyddie. Have a good day.'

Lydia glanced up at her briefly but didn't return the kiss she blew.

It wasn't worth going home, Annie decided, before this 'coffee' thing, so she gave herself a little tour of the school, glancing in at the library, the gymnasium, and the art room.

A few minutes before nine, she found her way to the cafeteria, a big, clattery room with a linoleum floor and rows of long metal tables with attached benches. Women were buzzing around a table laden with boxes of doughnuts and cartons of coffee, greeting each other with air kisses and shrieks of joy.

Annie looked at them with interest. Almost to a woman, they had long blonde hair, deep tans, sunglasses perched on their heads, and good pedicures displayed by colourful flip-flops beneath bright Capri pants. The only make-up they seemed to be wearing was a hint of lipgloss. They looked as if they were all on holiday at some island resort. In her 'meet-the-teacher' outfit – a favourite black skirt, closed-toe heels, and a fitted white blouse – Annie felt like a penguin among birds of paradise. Her own Greek tan was long gone, by now.

'Hi, I'm Susie Stein, room mom for Miss Scofield's class.' A tall woman with a blonde ponytail was standing before her holding out her hand. Annie took it and was engulfed in a firm handshake. 'I don't recognise your face. Are you one of the new moms?'

Annie laughed. 'Is it that obvious? Yes, I'm a new mum.' In more ways than you can imagine, she might have added.

The woman looked at a list in her hand. 'So, let's see, I bet you're Annie Keeler?'

'That's right.'

'Great! Love the accent, by the way. Here, there's someone you should meet.' Susie's eyes raked the room with a predatory look. 'Ah, there she is. Come on!'

Feeling faintly apprehensive, Annie followed Susie as she

snaked through the crowd. Reaching a small knot of women, Susie stopped and tapped someone on the shoulder. A woman with a cloud of dark hair spun around, eyebrows raised.

'Hey, Heather. I want you to meet Annie Keeler. She's new to the school, just like you, and guess what? She has a daughter in Miss Scofield's room, too.' With an encouraging smile to both of them, Susie Stein sailed away on other important business.

Annie and Heather eyed each other silently for a moment.

'So,' said Heather, 'that's sorted us out, hasn't it?'

Annie gave a snort of surprised laughter. 'Right, except we probably have nothing in common and won't have a word to say to each other.'

'Yeah, and then Susie will have to come back and tell us to play nice.'

'Oh God, you're right. We'd better look like we're chatting. So. Heather. Pleased to meet you. You really have a daughter in Miss Scofield's class?'

Heather grinned. 'That's right. Hailey. And you have Lydia.'

'How do you know?'

Heather glanced down at the booklet in her hands. 'It's in the directory. You'd better get one – over on that table. By the way, have you heard the scoop on Scofield yet?'

'No. I hope they didn't stick all the new kids in with the dud teacher.'

'Oh, she's not a bad teacher. Word is, the kids love her but she doesn't go down that well with parents. She doesn't tolerate helicopters, you see.'

'*Helicopters?*'

'Moms who hover. You know, the overprotective types. If she had her druthers, she'd have no mom volunteers at all in her room.'

'Oh God! I think I was hovering this morning! We came in early and I hung around, you know, just to make sure Lyddie was going to be OK ...'

Heather pulled a sympathetic face. 'She has separation anxiety?'

Annie had a brief flash of Lydia's disgusted face as she blew her a goodbye kiss. 'Not exactly,' she said. 'But it's a whole new country for her, never mind a whole new school. I felt I should stick around as long as I could.'

'Hey, did you sign up for mystery reader yet?' Susie Stein was back, waving a piece of paper at them. 'We also need more volunteers for math games.'

Heather drifted away as Annie took a look at the sign-up sheets, and she didn't see her again until she was walking home. As she was approaching the pedestrian crossing at Shady Oak, she noticed a familiar-looking figure standing with folded arms, waiting for the light to change. It was hard to mistake Heather's cloud of dark hair, even after such a brief meeting.

Annie felt a grin breaking out as she caught up with her. 'Hello again,' she said. 'You're a walker too?'

'Yes, we're on Tulip Street, right across from the school,' Heather said, pointing with her chin at the street sign on the other side of the road. 'So no bus for us.'

'And you're new in town?'

'Yeah. We moved in over the summer. Just from Westport, though, so no culture shock.'

'Westport. That's a few miles north of here, right?'

'Yeah. We've shaved five minutes off my husband's commute. He crunched the numbers to see how much time that would buy him over the course of a year, and figured the move was worth the hassle. You guys moved from England?'

'That's right. About a week ago, so we're still settling in.'

The traffic light changed and they began to cross the street together.

'So what do you think of all this?' Heather waved her hand to encompass the wide street with its pretty, wooden-framed houses set well back from the road, each with a rolling green lawn that ran down to the pavement, one or two bordered by a low stone wall or white picket fence, but most simply open to the world. Trees towered over the houses, casting a luxurious shade.

Annie shrugged. 'It's gorgeous, of course. But I'm still getting used to it. I mean, I grew up in a village, but for the last ten years or so I've been in the thick of things in London.'

'Yeah, it was tough for my husband too, when we first moved in from the city,' Heather said. 'I grew up around here, so it seems pretty normal. As a matter of fact, I don't miss the city at all.'

'Which city?'

Heather gave her a strange look. '*The* city. You know. New York.'

'Oh, right.'

'Yeah, we made the trek to suburbia a couple of years

ago, when Hailey was ready to go to school. I was happy because it meant I could keep a horse again. I was crazy about horses, growing up. Still am. Do you horseback ride at all?'

'*Horseback* ride?' Annie felt her stomach plummet.

'There's this really good barn just up the road – another reason why we moved to Norbury. I've had my horse there for some time, and it was a real pain driving over from Westport every day. Anyway, if you're interested in riding, you should get your name in front of them as soon as possible. They don't have a lot of openings for new riders.'

'Actually, horses aren't my thing. I've never been on one in my life, and I'm not sure I want to.'

'Pity,' said Heather with a shrug. 'I guess Lydia doesn't ride either?'

'I don't know. I don't think so.'

Heather raised her eyebrows in confusion. 'You don't *think* so?'

Annie shrugged. 'I'm pretty sure she doesn't – but then, I'm not her mum.'

'You're the nanny?' Heather asked, looking thoroughly confused.

'No, no, the stepmum. Um … look, my house is just around the corner. Do you … do you want to come in for some tea?' She felt suddenly as nervous as if she were asking some man out on a first date.

To her relief, Heather grinned with real pleasure. 'Sure, but I'll have coffee, if that's OK,' she said. 'The coffee at the meeting was lukewarm by the time I got to it. I could use another cup.'

'Great!' Annie resigned herself to drinking coffee too, although she'd never liked it much.

Annie took her guest through the garage into the kitchen. The front door seemed too imposing for casual use. As Annie fussed with the coffee maker, Heather settled herself on a bar stool and looked around the room with interest. Annie remembered how she herself had first reacted, standing in this huge, sunny room beneath the cathedral ceiling, gazing with open mouth at the curvaceous custom cabinetry, the Viking gas stove built in to look like an imposing country fireplace, the generous granite island in the middle of the room. She was pretty sure Heather wouldn't be half as impressed. She probably lived in an even grander house.

But, shaking her head, Heather gave a small whistle of appreciation. 'I'm having a major attack of kitchen envy,' she said. 'This is a great space.'

Annie grinned. 'Isn't it? I can't take credit for the decorating. It came this way – French chateau style, apparently.'

'Well, that explains all the toile, anyway. Did you look at many other houses before you bought this one?'

Annie bit her lip. 'Well, no,' she said. 'And we didn't buy it, actually. It's a rental – part of our ex-pat deal. It was the first place the relocation lady took us, and we didn't think we could do better. My husband really loved the idea of Lyddie walking to school.'

'God, I wish our house-hunting had been half as quick,' Heather said. 'We must have looked at forty, fifty houses before we found something in our budget that we could work with. That was before the bottom fell out of the property market, of course. But then, we were only moving locally; we had all the time in the world. You probably had just a week or two to find a place.'

'Three days, as a matter of fact,' said Annie, remembering their flying visit at the beginning of the month. 'But we were sort of on honeymoon so we didn't want to waste it house-hunting.'

'On *honeymoon*?'

'We got married just weeks before we moved,' Annie explained.

'Sounds very whirlwind.'

'Oh, more like a rollercoaster,' Annie admitted. 'It was only four and a half months from the time we met to the time we married.'

'Four and a half months!' Heather sounded incredulous. Annie was used to incredulity. Almost everybody she knew had been incredulous when she and Simon announced their plans. Nobody got married after four and a half months, people told her. It simply wasn't done.

'There's no law against it,' she'd told a number of people, including Simon's risk-averse brother, John, and Annie's reckless cousin, Sarah.

'If there isn't, there should be,' Sarah responded in no uncertain terms. 'After four and a half months, everybody's still on their best behaviour. You've only seen the tip of the *tip* of the iceberg, after four and a half months. You want to see what he's like after a year. That's when he'll let his guard down and stop waxing his back.'

'He doesn't wax his back!'

'Well, how the hell would you know?' Sarah demanded. 'Which proves my point.'

The trouble was, Annie knew that people weren't just incredulous. They were also cynical.

Annie had overheard her friend Henny making a little crack to Sarah on the very day she and Simon tied the knot at a register office in Islington. Henny and Sarah had walked into the cloakroom at the pub where they were all having a celebratory lunch, both a bit tipsy, neither of them realising that Annie was in one of the cubicles. 'You have to hand it to Simon; he doesn't mess about,' Henny was saying loudly as they came in. 'Sacked the nanny already, has he?'

Annie heard Sarah's hoot of laughter. 'Yeah, I bet. But it's a win–win situation, don't forget. I mean, our Annie was probably starting to fret about her shelf life. She's not like me – God knows, I don't care if I never get shackled. Still, Simon's a good bloke. Nanny be damned, he wouldn't be doing this if he didn't fancy her rotten.'

Then Henny said, 'Yeah, they can't keep their eyes off each other. Or their hands, for that matter. But I just hope he's not kidding himself, that's all. If he lets her down—'

'We'll chop his balls off,' said Sarah. And they'd both roared at their own wit.

Annie's mother wasn't incredulous or cynical, though. Far from it. In fact, she thoroughly approved of the speedy courtship. 'Sensible to get married as quickly as you can, if both parties are willing,' she said. 'Think of the money you'll save on heating and rent. Why keep two homes going when you can make do with one?'

\*

Annie nodded at Heather. 'That's right, four and a half months. We probably wouldn't have moved so quickly, only Simon had this job lined up in New York. And I had to get my visa sorted out.'

'Hmm.' Heather was staring at her with curiosity. 'But when you know, you *know*, right?'

'Exactly,' agreed Annie. 'People dilly-dally so much about tying the knot these days, it's ridiculous.'

'Oh, absolutely,' Heather agreed. 'Rob and I were like that. Four years in, we still hadn't set a date. All that time wasted when we could've been making babies. Who knew we'd have fertility issues? But God, I wish I'd gotten him to freeze his sperm back when it was healthy.'

Annie was speechless for a fraction of a second. 'Well, there you go,' she said faintly. As she busied herself pouring milk into a jug, she was thankful that her hair had a habit of flopping forward and hiding her face. She didn't want Heather to catch her pressing her lips together to suppress laughter. Surprise sometimes took her that way.

'So what does your husband do?' Heather asked after a moment.

Annie felt her eyebrows shoot up. She was used to a bit more beating about the bush. 'Um ... he works for a big food company. Do you take milk and sugar?' She didn't want to sound evasive, but neither did she want to come right out and say that he was VP: Development for ChefPro. Her mother (not to mention her father, her teachers, and every other adult who'd ever had any authority over her) had drilled into her a dread of seeming boastful.

'Really? Mine's an executive with one of New York's

top ad agencies specialising in digital media. They're pretty much on the bleeding edge.' No false modesty here, apparently. Heather waved aside the milk. 'You don't have any fat-free half-and-half?'

'Sorry, I don't even know what that is.'

'I'll take it black then, and no sugar. Thanks. So, you were saying about Lydia?'

Annie pressed her lips together as she handed Heather her mug. 'Yes. Lydia. Um. Where to start ... Her mother – her mother, well, she drowned in a boating accident.' Annie blinked quickly. She could never tell this story casually.

Heather's eyes widened and her hand flew to her mouth. '*Drowned?* Oh my God.'

'I know. Lydia was five.'

The two of them stared at each other, instinctively observing a moment of silence.

'How did it happen?' Heather asked at last, with a sort of fascinated horror.

Annie told her what she knew – the bare bones of the story. She herself had filled in so much – the worry that must have grown into fear when Beth Keeler didn't come home; the barely contained panic as the coastguard made its search; the stunned disbelief when the boat could not be found; the flat-out agony when nightfall forced the search party to postpone its activities until dawn.

'They were on holiday in Cornwall,' she said. 'They always went there in the summer time – they were both mad about sailing, you see. Beth went out on the water alone one day and got caught in a storm. The boat went under.'

Heather's hand was at her mouth. 'No! Did they find her body?'

Annie nodded. 'It washed up eventually.'

'Jesus. The poor kid. I mean, it had to be pretty bad for your husband, but that's a kid's worst nightmare: Mom just goes off one day and never comes home. How's she dealing with it?'

Annie shrugged. 'So-so,' she said non-committally.

'Does she accept you as a mom?'

'Well, sort of. She doesn't call me mum or anything. And she won't let me hug her.' Annie thought ruefully of the many fruitless attempts she'd made to fold Lydia's stiff little body in a warm embrace. The last time, the child had all but headbutted her. 'The most I can do is pat her head. But, you know, things are getting better. At least she speaks to me now.' She was determined to sound bright and breezy, but somehow a catch had crept into her voice.

Heather patted her hand. 'Don't worry, Hailey doesn't do hugs any more, either. It's the age, I think.'

'Yeah, probably.' Annie fell silent, thinking.

Motherhood was supposed to come naturally to women, and yet she found herself second-guessing almost every 'motherly' thing she did. Perhaps she was missing some vital maternal gene? Or maybe you had to go through the whole pregnancy thing first, before the nurturing instincts kicked in properly?

Right now, she felt like an impostor among the Bradley Elementary mothers: an undercover journalist posing as a mum. But she wasn't undercover. This was all real. Nobody was going to send her home to write a punchy story about

39

stay-at-home-motherhood among the prosperous commuter towns of south-western Connecticut. No. She wasn't here to find out how the other half lived.

She was here to live with the other half.

It was all a bit disconcerting.

'So how's Lydia with her dad?' Heather asked, bringing her back to the moment.

Annie thought about that. 'They're very close,' she said after a while. In her mind's eye she saw the two of them on the plane trip from Heathrow, their heads bent over the colouring-in book the air hostess had supplied, the crayon very small and out of place in Simon's big, tanned hand. 'They seem to have a special kind of bond. They've been through some tough times together. Sometimes ...'

'Sometimes what?'

'Oh, nothing.' She wasn't going to say out loud that sometimes she felt a bit left out, a bit excluded. She was ashamed of that thought, quite honestly. But as vigorously as she squelched it, it always seemed to pop back up.

Instead, she blurted out, 'Do you mind if I ask you something, Heather? I mean, it's a weird question, really. I just want to know: as a real mum, do you – well, do you *like* the job?'

Heather did a bit of a double-take.

'Oh, I don't mean do you love your *daughter*. Of course, you do. God, you'd probably jump in front of a bus for her. I mean, do you like the actual, you know, *work* you have to do as a mum? Cooking and cleaning the kitchen and making packed lunches and helping with homework and all that? You're not supposed to say, are you, but looking after kids

. . . it's sort of – boring. You're *busy* all right, you're just not – not mentally occupied.'

'Actually, I love it,' said Heather. 'I like being my own boss, coming and going as I please, planning my day to suit me, getting things done on my own schedule. Hey, it's hard work – *manual* work, a lot of the time. Carrying groceries, cleaning windows, folding laundry, weeding borders. But it's varied, that's what's so great. Except in the afternoons, when it's mostly driving. But I don't envy the poor bastards stuck in their cubicles all day, I can tell you.'

'So you don't sort of wonder why you bothered to go to uni? I mean, when you're scrubbing soap scum rings off the bath tub?'

'Uni? You mean college? Well, it's good to be able to explain quantum physics, when they ask.' She laughed and shook her head. 'Look, staying home with the kids isn't a life sentence. I was out in the workplace before I had Hailey, and I'll be heading back when she's older. These kids, they'll be all grown up in a New York minute, that's the scary thing. But right now I'm living in the moment.'

Annie looked at her with respect. A spark of hope flared inside her.

'It helps to get a hobby,' Heather added. 'I'm into the horseback riding to keep me sane. Other people play bridge. Tennis is a good one too, so I hear.'

Annie pressed her lips together. 'A hobby, huh? Well, I couldn't do riding. I'm terrified of horses. And I was never much good at tennis. I *suppose* I could try bridge. It just sounds so old-ladyish.'

'You could always be one of the ladies that lunch,'

Heather suggested. 'You know, get into the social network by joining a couple of charities. Calamities International was huge back when the tsunami hit, of course, but right now Hand-Me-Down is the hot one in town. People like it because of the ball. Big black-tie event at one of the country clubs.'

'I was thinking of doing something at the school, just to start with,' Annie said.

'Good idea; they're always looking for help. Oh, look at the time, I have to go.' Heather set her mug down. 'Got to run over to the barn real quick. Thanks for the coffee.'

Annie stood at the kitchen window, watching her new friend hurry home along the street. There she went, the woman who was her own boss and could arrange her own schedule. Annie felt a smile breaking out. It was amazing what a change of perspective could do for your state of mind! She now felt quite cheerful and upbeat about scheduling herself to go to the supermarket to restock the fridge.

The next morning, after she had walked Lydia over to school, Annie had a brilliant idea. She would take the train in to New York and surprise Simon with a visit! Why on earth not? There was nothing to stop her.

She hadn't set foot in his offices yet, and she was dying to see the view of Central Park from his twenty-fourth-floor window. She was also eager to say hi to his team of five. She'd met a couple of them in London and they seemed like a nice bunch. They were young and single, and living in apartments in Manhattan. Lucky things, a disloyal part of her brain murmured; *they* hadn't been exiled to the suburbs.

In anticipation of wandering along Madison Avenue and peering into designer shop windows, she hurried home and threw aside the Capri pants, flip-flops and T-shirt she'd put on that morning in a bid to fit in with the Bradley Elementary mums. Instead, she pulled on her favourite knee-high leather boots and a long-sleeved jersey-knit dress. She piled her hair up in the chignon she'd worn almost daily to work, back in London, and added dangling earrings. Ah. Now she felt better.

She took an eye pencil and drew in the dramatic line she liked to wear on her upper eyelid. Round here, she felt like Amy Winehouse if she applied her usual London make-up; but in New York, she reckoned, she could get away with it.

Feeling all charged up, she drove the minivan to the train station and managed to park it without scraping anything. (Simon hadn't noticed the marks on the back bumper, and she hadn't felt the need to tell him about her close encounter with a pole at the supermarket. After all, a person who hadn't driven anything larger than a Renault 5 in her life needed time to get to grips with the outsize dimensions of a monster like the minivan.)

She felt an intoxicating sense of freedom as she jumped onto the train, holding her polystyrene cup of tea and a newspaper. God, this was like the old days, she thought, settling down in an empty seat and turning to the entertainment section of the paper where she ran a knowing eye over the gossip pieces. She could pretend she was on the Victoria line, going in to work. She'd be going to the weekly brainstorming meeting, and she'd suggest a story

43

on ... let's see, on this woman who'd had eight babies with fertility treatment, despite having no husband, because she felt so alone in the world. Or on the divorcing couple who were suing each other over a kidney he had donated to her way back when they were happy. God, both those stories seemed so sad and so, well, *personal*. Maybe she could find something a bit more upbeat, like a celebrity cat fight.

Hang on. She didn't actually have to find a story! She wasn't actually going in to work. She could sit back, relax, and enjoy the ride.

When the train pulled in to Grand Central Terminal, Annie stepped off onto the crowded platform with a sense of exhilaration. After the humming silence of her big, empty kitchen, it felt good to be jostled by a stream of people all striding purposefully towards unknown destinations in this great city. She felt as if she was back in the engine room of life again, back where things happened and news was made; yip, she was pumped full of adrenalin and ready to take on the world.

Finding her way onto Madison Avenue, she decided to walk a few blocks north, and then catch a taxi to Simon's building on the Upper East Side. Standing at the traffic light with several hundred other people beneath towering steel and glass buildings that blocked out the sun, breathing in the gasoline fumes and listening to the honking of horns, Annie had a sudden image of the quiet traffic light outside Bradley Elementary, where the only things towering over you were trees.

Gosh, she was glad to be here, absorbing the energy and general oomph flowing all around her.

A car swept past, cutting the corner so tightly that she and several other pedestrians had to jump backwards to save their toes from being run over.

So invigorating!

She was enjoying the hustle and bustle so much that by the time she decided to flag down a taxi, her feet were aching in her high boots, and she was sure she had developed a blister on her left heel. Just a few days of wearing flats, she reflected bitterly, and her feet had gone soft.

ChefPro's corporate headquarters in New York were housed in an impressive building within spitting distance of Central Park. As Annie stepped into the lift, she found herself grinning happily at the worker bees sharing the tiny space with her. Nobody grinned back, but that didn't dampen her spirits. She couldn't wait to see Simon's face when she walked into his office!

As it turned out, she was going to have to wait.

The woman behind the desk in ChefPro's lobby told her in a low voice that Mr Keeler was in a meeting, and wouldn't be available for at least half an hour.

'Oh? That's too bad. Never mind, I can wait.'

The woman raised her eyebrows. 'Is he expecting you?' She was paging through a book, apparently looking for any sign of an appointment.

'No, but—'

'He really is very busy. I'm not sure he'll be able to see you without a—'

'I'm Annie,' she burst out. 'You know – his *wife*. Annie.'

The woman, about fifty years old but trying to conceal

the fact beneath a layer of white foundation, allowed herself a small smile. 'Oh, that's different then. I'll show you to his office. You can wait there.'

He had a corner office, Annie was pleased and proud to see, complete with a big desk, and a new-looking leather couch in front of a glass coffee table. 'Can I get you a coffee?' the woman asked.

'Oh, no, that's OK. I'm just going to sit here and enjoy the view. Gosh, look at those treetops down there.'

The woman walked out quietly and closed the door.

The couch was very comfortable. After a few moments, Annie decided that it wouldn't hurt to lie down. She was rather tired, actually. Insomnia was becoming a bit of a nightly menace. Maybe she really did have a malingering case of jet lag.

She sank back into the soft leather, but couldn't get comfortable, mainly because her feet hurt. She wondered if she had a blister or just a tender spot. Might as well check, while she had some privacy. Glancing at the closed door, she slipped her boots off and had a look at her heel. She couldn't really see it properly through her tights, so, after a tiny hesitation, she pulled them off. There. Now she could see what was going on. Her heel was bright red, but as yet there was no sign of an actual blister. She stretched her feet and twirled her toes. Ah. Bliss!

No harm in leaving the boots off, just for a bit. After all, she had about half an hour to kill. Maybe she'd close her eyes and do a bit of meditation.

Seconds later, or so it seemed, she felt somebody shaking her by the shoulder and calling her name.

She opened her eyes and found herself looking up into Simon's face. He looked a little wild around the eyes.

'Annie? Annie? Are you OK?'

'Is she OK?' another voice asked.

Annie sat up, rubbing her eyes. 'Of course I'm OK.'

There seemed to be several people in the room, all of them staring at her.

'Pull your skirt down,' Simon whispered urgently.

Annie looked at her lap. Her dress seemed to have ridden up quite a lot higher than was decent. She adjusted it hastily, smiling at the small crowd. She recognised a couple of faces but couldn't think of names. 'Oh, um, hi,' she said brightly to a blonde woman who looked especially familiar. 'How are you liking New York? Settling in nicely? We must really have you all up to Norbury for lunch or something.'

The woman smiled a cool, amused smile. 'The name's Cindy,' she said.

Simon straightened up and ran his fingers through his hair. 'OK, everybody,' he said. 'How about you all go back to your desks, for now, and start putting your thoughts on paper. We don't want to lose the momentum, but obviously we can't get down to brass tacks right this minute. Why don't we reconvene in an hour?'

'Right,' people mumbled and began to shuffle out, some of them taking a last glance over their shoulders at the fascinating sight of their boss's wife, standing there all groggy and rumpled in her bare feet.

The minute the door closed, Simon pointed at something on the floor. Annie followed the line of his finger to the small puddle that was her tights.

'Oh shit,' she said, scooping them up and tucking them under her arm. 'I'm sorry. God, I wonder what your minions are thinking?'

'Annie, what's going on? Why are you here?'

Annie was feeling her chignon, which seemed to be falling out and flopping down her back. 'Surprise! I came to take you to lunch.'

'Lunch? But it's past two.'

'It's – what? But I got here at eleven!'

'Crikey. You must have been sleeping for hours.'

'I didn't mean to go to sleep. I . . . I was meditating.'

To her great relief, he burst out laughing. 'Meditating? You were in a REM cycle, my love, eyelids twitching like crazy. So where's Lydia?'

'Well, she's at school, of course.' Some vague uneasiness was beginning to stir in Annie's still fuzzy brain.

'At school? But doesn't she get out at three?'

Annie felt the blood drain out of her face. Her mouth was suddenly so dry she could hardly talk. 'Um, what did you say the time was?'

He looked at his watch. 'It's after two. You don't have a hope in hell of making it back in time.'

'Oh God. Oh Jesus. What do we do now?' She was picturing Lydia standing outside the school, waiting for her stepmother to show up. All the other walkers would leave. All the buses would leave. The car park would be deserted. The teachers would lock up and go home. And Lydia would just keep standing there, lost and alone, an obvious target for kidnappers and child molesters.

Or, no, she might decide to walk home by herself. Yes,

that was what she'd do. She'd wait for a while, and then when Annie didn't show up, she would try to go home alone. She'd walk over to the traffic lights, and of course the crossing guard would be long gone, and, being just seven years old, she might or might not have sense enough to wait for the light to change.

Annie shook her head against an image of a car flying down Shady Oak towards the intersection just as Lydia lifted her foot to begin crossing.

'Is there somebody you can phone?' Simon's voice was hard and cold.

'Um – somebody? Well, the thing is, I don't actually— Hang on.' With a sudden surge of hope, she remembered the school directory. At the urging of the PTO woman who was selling them at the second-grade coffee yesterday, she'd bought two copies: a big one to keep at home, and a small one to keep in her bag. 'I have a directory! A school directory! I'll phone and ask somebody to pick her up.'

'Who?'

'Um – this woman! This woman I met yesterday. Her name is Heather. She has a girl in Miss Scofield's class and they live on Tulip Street. She's nice. Remember, I told you she came in and had coffee with me? I bet she'd take Lyddie!'

'OK,' he said briskly. 'Do it.'

She went over to his desk, sat down on his throne-like swivel chair and began paging through the directory. 'The thing is,' she said in a quivery voice, 'I don't actually know this woman's surname. I mean, I know she's called Heather and her daughter is Hailey, and she's in Miss Scofield's class, but the names for the whole school are listed alphabetically by bloody surname.'

'Oh, for God's sake. Here, give it to me.' He took the directory from her shaking fingers and paged through it himself, running his eyes down the columns of names.

'Here,' he said. 'Heather Gibson, 7 Tulip Street.'

'Thanks,' she whispered, and dialled the number.

After five interminable rings the phone connected to Heather's voicemail. 'You know who we are and you know what to do,' a child's voice told her precociously.

'She's not home,' she told Simon, putting the receiver down. 'Oh God, let me see if I can call someone else ... Maybe that Susie woman ...'

'You'd better call the school,' Simon said. 'Ask them to keep her there until you get back.'

Annie paled at the thought of phoning up the superior-looking school secretary and revealing the shameful news that, just minutes before pick-up time, she was miles away in New York City with absolutely no plan in place.

She glanced desperately at the directory again. 'Hang on! Heather's mobile number is listed, too. I'll try that!'

Simon was pacing the room now, his face grim.

'Please pick up, oh please pick up,' Annie was whispering to herself when Heather's voice suddenly spoke into her ear.

'Hello? Who is this?'

'Um ... Heather? Heather, it's me, Annie Keeler.'

'Annie who?'

'Annie Keeler. From the second-grade coffee morning yesterday.'

'Oh. Right. Annie. Of course. How's it going?'

'Fine, fine. Well, not that great actually. The thing is, I'm ... well, I'm in New York right now and I'm not going to be able to get home in time to pick Lydia up from school. So I wonder if you could do me a huge favour and take her for me?'

'You mean, like, today?'

'Yes, today. If you could. If at all possible.'

'Oh geez, today isn't that great for me. I'm sorry but—'

Annie's eyes flew to Simon. He was frowning at her and mouthing something. The sternness of his bright blue eyes unnerved her. She turned away from him and said, very low: 'Please! It's an emergency. I don't know anyone else to ask.'

There was a moment of silence. Then Heather said, 'OK, I'll do it. Just call the school and let them know, OK? I'll be in my car today, not walking. Have the teacher tell her what's going on so she won't think some strange lady is kidnapping her.'

'Of course. Thanks! Thanks so much. I'll see you around four.'

'Seven Tulip Street,' Heather told her. 'Don't worry, she'll have a blast with Hailey.'

Annie hung up and turned to Simon with shining eyes. 'It's OK,' she said. 'It's all organised. Heather will take her home. I just have to call the school and fill them in.'

He nodded curtly, his mouth still tight. 'Good. Better get your boots on, too.'

Minutes later, as Simon rode down in the lift with her, she quipped, 'Well, at least Lydia gets her first play date out of the whole thing.'

Simon, head down, hands in his pockets, glanced up. 'This is no joking matter,' he said in a tone she'd never heard before. 'I know you're new to the whole parent thing, but you can't slip up like this, Annie. It's just not on. The stakes are too damn high.'

She gulped. 'I know. I'm sorry. But to be fair, it's not as if I just forgot about Lyddie. If I hadn't fallen asleep I would've had more than enough time to go to lunch and get the train back in time for pick-up.'

He clenched his jaw, making the muscles pop out. Clearly, he was livid, biting back words. He didn't say another thing until he'd flagged down a taxi and was holding the door open for her. By then, he seemed to have regained some control.

'We'll talk about doing lunch another day,' he said, his voice strained. 'But for God's sake, no more surprise visits. I don't have a lot of wriggle room just at the moment. The schedule's very tight if we're going to launch on target.'

'Sorry. I should have known you probably couldn't just drop everything and go out. And I'm so sorry about Lydia.'

He shrugged. 'No harm done. See you later.' He slammed the door, tapped the roof of the car, and stepped back onto the pavement.

She looked back as the taxi nosed its way into the traffic, half expecting to see him still standing there, waving. But he was hurrying back towards his building, and he had disappeared through the glass doors even before the taxi pulled away from the first set of traffic lights.

# Chapter Three

By the time Annie arrived at Heather's house, she had managed to convince herself that the day hadn't really been a total disaster, despite the unfortunate turn of events at Simon's office. After all, she had accomplished quite a lot – received a much-needed shot of urban energy, seen the truly spectacular view from Simon's window, shown him that she took an interest in his career, and demonstrated crisis-solving skills in her capacity as stay-at-home mother. She had also, as a spin-off benefit, organised a play date for Lydia.

The fact that she'd been caught snoozing on the office couch with her dress hiked up and her tights in a heap on the floor – well, you couldn't really put a positive spin on that, but in the big scheme of things a little mistake like that didn't do anybody any harm, and it had probably given Simon's team a bit of a chuckle and, who knew, maybe even drawn them together in a morale-building sort of way.

Anyway. The long and the short of it was, one of these days she and Simon would go out to lunch in Manhattan in a calm, civilised, pre-organised fashion, and they would laugh their heads off at the way her surprise visit had misfired; because one of her strong points, and probably one of the reasons Simon loved her, was that she *could* laugh at herself.

She took a tissue out of her bag, dabbed her eyes, blew her nose hard, and rang the doorbell of 7 Tulip Street. Moments later, the door inched open a crack and Annie could make out Heather on the other side, peering at her through her cloud of hair, which seemed to be hanging over her face in its entirety today.

'Oh, it *is* you.'

'Yes, it's me. Thank you, thank you, thank you for taking Lyddie. You absolutely saved my bacon. Did everything go OK? Lyddie didn't freak out or anything?'

'Oh no, everything was absolutely fine. They're down in the basement right now, watching a movie. Look, Annie, are you in a rush? Do you have a minute to come in?'

'Sure.' Annie began to look at her watch, but Heather reached out and almost yanked her over the doorstep.

'This way,' she said, striding off into the house. Slightly confused, Annie hurried after her.

When they reached the kitchen, Heather lifted the hair away from her face in a big, handheld ponytail, and turned to look at Annie.

'Now you know why I didn't really want to take Lydia today,' she said.

Heather looked as if she'd gone a few rounds with a prize fighter. The right side of her face was bruised along the cheekbone, and she was all swollen and slightly bloody around the mouth.

Annie felt her eyebrows shoot up. She opened her mouth to say something and then snapped it tightly shut.

Somebody had beaten Heather up. That was the only possible explanation for her battered appearance. You didn't get injuries like that from walking into a lamp-post. And, of course, it could only be her husband, because if there'd been a mugging or a burglary, surely somebody would have mentioned it to her already.

So Annie shut her mouth and shook her head mutely.

With a short sharp laugh, Heather pulled out a kitchen chair and dropped into it. 'Hey, don't look at me like that,' she said. 'It's not what you think. Sit down a moment and I'll explain. I haven't been smacked around by Rob, I promise you. I've just been to the doctor, that's all.'

Annie pulled a face of disbelief. 'The *doctor*?'

Heather giggled like a schoolgirl. 'Dermatologist. See, Rob's away for a couple of weeks, and I — well, I decided to try some surgical beauty treatments. This is the Botox.' She pointed to the bruise on her cheekbone. 'And this is the filler.' She indicated her swollen and bloody mouth.

Annie's mouth fell open. 'What?'

'Come on, you know what I'm talking about. You must have wondered about this kind of stuff yourself.'

Annie ran her finger nervously over the faint frown line between her brows. 'Yes, maybe, but—'

'Anyway, I decided now's the time to do it. Just to see if it freaking works. Please don't tell Rob, though. Or anybody else.'

'Of course I won't tell Rob. I've never met him.'

'Oh yeah, that's right. See, this is a birthday present for Rob, but he's never going to know about it. Not the details, anyway. He's a real visual kind of guy. He likes me to look my best. It makes him happy, so I'm doing what I can. OK, that's my confession and you'd better freaking keep quiet about it. Not a word to anyone, do you promise? I know these stay-at-home moms. They live for gossip.'

Annie felt a sudden rush of affection towards this woman. 'Who would I tell?' she asked with a little laugh. 'I hardly know a soul.'

'That's why you're the perfect person to help me out.' Heather nodded her head briskly.

'But why does it have to be a secret? Shouldn't you just be brazen about it? I mean, doesn't everybody do Botox?'

Heather shrugged. 'Maybe. But nobody advertises it, do they?'

'I suppose not. Come to think of it, I don't see people walking around looking as if they've had a punch-up all that often. Is it usual to bruise and swell like that?'

Heather jumped off her bar stool and began to rinse dishes at the sink. 'Apparently not,' she said. 'Apparently I have aberrant blood vessels around my eyes.'

'What?'

Heather tilted her face to one side. 'See? Here? Aberrant blood vessels. Apparently I have such expressive eyes that I've developed this huge muscle just to create extra crow's feet, and the huge muscle needs to be fed by extra veins that normal people don't have in their faces.'

Annie could feel her mouth twitching.

'Go on, laugh. I'd laugh too but it hurts too much. It's the gunk he shot into my naso-labial grooves. He told me it was going to be a quick fix, instant gratification, but then he didn't know I was a sweller.'

Annie found herself snorting into her hand. 'I'm sorry,' she gasped. 'I'm really very sorry. It can't be that funny from where you're standing. Look, is there anything I can do to help out?' She was thinking along the lines of doing a small grocery run for Heather, or maybe walking Hailey to and from school for the next few days.

Heather stopped her frantic dish-rinsing. 'As a matter of fact, I was hoping you could do a couple of things for me,' she said. 'It's ... it's a lot to ask, I know, but you're the only one who's seen me like this and I'd kind of like to keep it that way. The fewer people who know about the surgery, the better. Could Hailey walk to school with you guys for a couple of days?'

'Good grief, of course!' said Annie. 'I mean, after what you did for me today ...'

'Great! I drove in to pick the girls up today, and it was OK because my windows are tinted, but I was real nervous in case somebody came up and tapped on the glass. Oh – and there's another thing. Any way you could go to the, um, barn and, um, sort out my horse for me?'

Annie took an involuntary step backwards. 'Go ... *where*? Hang on. Didn't I tell you I'm not a horse person?' Shocked as she was, Annie still had her wits about her enough to notice a flash of navy blue in the far corner of the kitchen. Lydia had sneaked into the room and was trying to hide under the table.

'I'm not asking you to actually handle the horse,' Heather said quickly. 'I'll send Hailey with you. She can put the halter on and walk Pompom to and from the paddock. She'll help with the mucking out too. She knows all about it.'

'Mucking out?' Annie's head was reeling. She needed a friend in this new life of hers, but did she need one this badly?

At that moment, Lydia crawled out from under the table.

'Oh, hi, sweetie,' said Heather. 'Is the movie over?'

Lydia didn't answer. Instead, looking at Heather with a directness and intensity Annie had never seen in her before, she asked, 'Is Pompom a horse?'

'Yes, Pompom is a horse,' Heather said quickly. 'A big chestnut mare with beauty-queen legs and one white hock. She's a sweetheart, old Pompom. Your mom doesn't need to be scared of her.'

Lydia looked curiously at Annie. 'You're scared of horses?'

Annie shrugged. 'They're not my favourite animal.'

'I'm not afraid of horses,' declared Lydia.

Lydia hadn't volunteered this much information about herself, ever. Annie's pulse picked up a bit of speed.

'You've been around horses?' asked Heather.

Lydia frowned. 'I think so. Long ago. In the old days. Can we see Mrs Gibson's horse, Annie?'

Oh no. What was she going to do now? She couldn't agree to look after some whopping great brute with sharp hooves and yellow teeth. She couldn't muck out a stable! She imagined a small room full of enormous piles of dung, guarded by a vicious quadruped.

'There's really nothing to it,' insisted Heather. 'Just take Pompom to the paddock, shovel out the wettest sawdust, change the water, fill the feed basin and stuff some hay into the hay net. Don't even bother to groom her. Hailey could practically do it all herself, except she can't drive over there.'

Annie drew breath to say no, she couldn't possibly take it on, Heather would have to phone up someone else, or – if she didn't know anybody else well enough to ask such a preposterous favour, which was quite possible since she was new in town – then she'd have to find some service that could do it for her. There must be such a service here in New England; flyers had been piling up in her mailbox for everything from picking up the doggy-do in your backyard to helping you organise your closets.

Then she felt a small hand sneak into her own and give it an urgent squeeze.

Lydia had never initiated physical contact with Annie in her life.

'OK,' Annie rasped. 'I'll do it. Just this once, mind. You'll have to find somebody else to take care of it tomorrow.'

Heather beamed at her, her swollen face contorting strangely. 'I knew you'd come through for me,' she said. 'There's a guy over at the barn who would probably do it for me, but I'd feel kind of weird asking him to help out. I mean, I'd have to lie about why and everything. Listen, you'd better hurry. I'm normally over there by now.'

'Right,' said Annie, 'it's facing the wrong way. How do I get it to turn?' She was staring at the big gleaming rump of Heather's socking great horse. Lydia and Heather's daughter, Hailey, were too short to see over the stable door.

Hailey, a stocky, forthright child with short, dark hair and no discernible gap between her eyebrows, suddenly reached up and undid the bolt on the door.

'Hang on!' cried Annie, quickly slamming the door shut. 'What if it runs out?'

'Don't worry, Mrs Keeler,' said Hailey. 'Pompom doesn't do that.'

'Be careful of its rear end!' Annie cried as the child opened the door a crack and slipped into the stable. 'They kick if you go up behind them!'

But Pompom didn't kick. Hailey touched the horse gently on its rump, then slid her hand along its side as she approached the business end, all the while crooning some sort of horse baby-talk. Suddenly the creature lifted its head and lurched around in the narrow box, clacking its hooves together as it went. Annie shrieked, convinced Hailey was about to be trampled underfoot, but the child stepped nimbly out of the way and then actually manoeuvred herself in front of the horse's broad chest and reached an arm up around its neck.

'Pompom, good *girl*, Pompom,' she sang, holding her hand out flat. When the horse dipped its head to nuzzle her palm, Hailey expertly slid a halter over its long nose and buckled the strap that went behind its ears.

'There,' said Hailey. 'Good, good girl. Can you open the door again, Mrs Keeler?'

Annie unbolted the door, which she'd fastened in panic the minute Hailey entered the stable.

'Stand back,' said Hailey, and without further ado led the horse out into the brick courtyard.

Yes, Annie remembered horses all right, and she hadn't got it wrong. They were just as big and lethal-looking as they'd been when she was ten, and her friend Henny had dragged her along to the stables near Guildford to observe one of her riding lessons. Annie's introduction to horses hadn't gone well. She'd been standing at Henny's elbow, watching her adjust the belt-like thing that kept the saddle on, when the peevish school pony whipped its head around and savaged her in the arm. Horses didn't have sharp teeth, but what they lacked in edge they made up for in brute force. Annie's arm had been bruised for weeks.

Her heart was in her mouth now as she calculated what damage the creature could do to chubby little Hailey if it suddenly got a bee in its bonnet and decided to skitter off, kicking aside obstacles to its escape. What nonsense to think that this child, who (though robust) couldn't weigh more than five stone, would be able to restrain the pea-brained thousand-pounder if it suddenly stopped cooperating.

'Lydia! Keep back! Don't touch!' Annie said. Lydia had stepped up beside Hailey and was now standing directly in the monster's bolt path.

'It's OK,' said Hailey. 'Pompom is a big softy. She won't hurt anybody. Do you want to hold the rope, Lydia?'

'NOOO!' yelled Annie. Everybody jumped in fright, including the horse.

'Um, Mrs Keeler, horses don't really like shouting,' Hailey said soothingly. 'Don't worry, everything will be OK.' Annie didn't know if this horse-whispery tone was meant for herself or Pompom. 'Come on, Lydia, let's just walk her to the paddock, shall we?'

The girls walked off, Pompom nodding her enormous head as she tapped along delicately behind them. Annie brought up the rear, rather distantly so as to be out of range of the deadly back hooves. As their small procession made its way to a pathway outside the stable yard, a woman with a hose trained on a muddy horse box gave them a perky wave. 'Hi, Hailey, where's Mom today?' she called.

'She's home,' Hailey called back, making the horse jump again. 'She doesn't feel good so Mrs Keeler is helping.'

The stranger, elegant in navy jodhpurs, riding boots and chaps, raised her eyebrows at Annie in her yoga pants and white sneakers threading her way gingerly along the muddy path. Annie found herself thanking her lucky stars she'd changed out of the jersey knit dress and high-heeled boots. She gave the woman a brisk wave back. No wonder Heather hadn't wanted to show her face around this place. Annie hadn't given much thought to horsy people, but at the back of her mind she'd supposed they were non-threatening types, tending towards buck teeth and big behinds. But if this stylish blonde woman was anything to go by, she'd been dead wrong.

At that moment Pompom lifted her tail, gave a few perfunctory blasts, and dropped a big pile of steaming dung in Annie's pathway.

'Wasn't it lovely?'

They had already dropped Hailey home and were heading back to their own house. Annie, exhausted and muddy, nursing a sore shoulder that she seemed to have put out while shovelling muck, felt a rueful smile break out.

'It was smelly,' she said. 'And cold. And I can't *believe* I said I'd do it again.'

That evening Simon came home well after eight, but when he went up to Lydia's room to kiss the top of her head he found her wide awake, waiting in the dark for him. 'She scared the living daylights out of me,' he reported, crashing down on the sofa next to Annie, 'suddenly rearing up under the duvet when I crept in. Looks like she's had quite a day. First the play date, then the horse jaunt.'

'I'm guessing she's been around horses before,' Annie said, giddy with relief because the grim mood he'd been in at the office seemed to have lifted.

'God, yes, the holiday place we used to rent in Cornwall was on a farm. There was this field full of muddy little ponies. Shetlands, I think they were. Lyddie loved them. Beth used to ...' He paused and cleared his throat. 'Lydia used to ride one of them round the field.'

Annie was silent a moment, picturing a mother and child in a green field, the mother with her hands wrapped in the rough mane of a shaggy pony, her other hand holding the little girl steady on the animal's back. Perhaps Simon would have been leaning up against a gate, shouting encourage-ment as Lydia bounced along.

Annie burrowed closer to Simon's warm body, listen-ing to the rhythmic thump of his heart, wanting to make him smile again. 'You should have seen her this afternoon, filling the hay net and spreading sawdust. She was in her element! Almost makes me glad I messed up and couldn't get to school in time for pick-up. Hey! Maybe I should look into riding lessons for her!'

Simon froze a moment. Then he drew slightly away from her.

'Steady on,' he said. 'I mean, I'm happy with her going over there to see the horses – but *lessons*? I don't know.'

'I thought you wanted her to be busy and get lots of exercise?'

Simon took her hand. 'I do,' he said. 'But she isn't even *asking* for riding lessons. I'd rather she did something more active – some sort of ball sport. Riding is just sitting on your bum, when you get right down to it. What do the girls play around here. Hockey?'

'Soccer, apparently,' Annie said. 'But do you really think—'

Simon interrupted by leaning in for a kiss. Just before their lips met, she saw the corners of his mouth tug up into a smile.

'What are you grinning at?' she mumbled against his lips.

'You,' he murmured back. 'You're wearing this fabulous perfume. Eau de dung, perhaps?'

She pulled away quickly, dismayed. 'Oh no! I meant to have a shower but I didn't get the chance.'

'Never mind.' He drew her back towards him. 'I need one too. We can scrub each other's backs.'

'Couldn't you give her some aspirin?' Annie asked Heather over the phone three days later.

Heather had phoned to break the news that Hailey had

64

a fever and wouldn't be able to help Annie muck out the stable that afternoon.

'Annie, it's strep throat, it's infectious,' Heather said. 'You won't want Lydia to be around her. Oh, and you should *never* give a kid aspirin, by the way. Look, I know you're a bit nervous to do it on your own, but surely you can see that Pompom is a doll?'

A *doll*?

'But ... but your face is nearly normal now,' Annie protested.

'The bruise on my cheek is a freaking rainbow. You saw it yesterday! It didn't just disappear overnight. Look, I promise to send Hailey out with you tomorrow. Overnight on the antibiotics and I know she'll be up to it. I hate to ask you, but no *way* am I going to the barn like this. I mean, I can get away with doing the school run in the car now, but the barn is different. You've seen the women over there. Freaking queen bees. And it's not as if I can explain myself to them. How could I? Just walk up and say, Oh, by the way, this is Botox, not a black eye?'

Annie could see her point. All this week she'd been noticing the sort of people who frequented the barn. Something about these elegant and moneyed women with their sharp eyes and careful hair was just plain scary.

'OK,' she groaned into the phone. 'I'll do it.'

'Just think how thrilled Lydia will be!'

'Oh yes. She'll be doing backflips, I'm sure.'

Taking a deep breath, Annie opened the stable door a crack and eased herself into the dragon's lair.

'Whoa, girl, whoa,' she called. She must have spoken too loudly or in the wrong tone of voice, because Pompom immediately stopped ripping at the hay net, threw her head up, then flung her whole body round in a tight circle, narrowly missing standing on Annie's foot.

Annie pressed herself against the stable wall, cursing beneath her breath. Really, this went way beyond the call of duty. Heather was going to be paying Annie back for the rest of her life, and possibly well into her afterlife.

'Whoa, girl,' she called again, trying for a low, crooning note.

'Are you OK?' Lydia asked from the other side of the door.

'Fine,' Annie called back.

The horse flattened its ears but otherwise didn't react. Annie stretched out one hand and connected gingerly with Pompom's shiny rump, just as she'd seen Hailey do. The animal threw its head up and did that abrupt circle again before returning to the methodical savaging of the hay net.

Annie decided she'd dispense with the foreplay. Gritting her teeth, she crept towards Pompom's head, body pressed against the wall, heart pounding so loudly she was pretty sure the horse could hear it. When she finally got within striking distance of her target, she cleared her throat and held out her hand, the way she'd seen Hailey do. 'Come on, Pompom, come on, come on, girl.'

Pompom nodded her head rapidly and rolled her eyes at her.

'Come on, you bloody great monster, come and eat out of my hand like you're damned well supposed to.' This she

66

murmured between her teeth, aware of Lydia on the other side of the door.

The horse stamped her hoof and sidled towards her. Then she extended her neck and bumped her nose against the outstretched palm. 'Ha!' Annie yelled, and lunged at the horse with both arms, trying to catch her around the neck.

Pompom snorted and jerked away, slamming her considerable backside into the wall. 'What's happening?' Lydia's voice cried out.

'Nothing, nothing, everything's fine,' Annie called back with false calm. Her blood was up now. There was no way this animal was going to make a fool out of her in front of her stepdaughter.

After giving them both a moment to get over the excitement, she began sidling up towards Pompom's head again. 'Come on, girl, come on, look what I've got for you.' Why hadn't she brought a carrot or something? Why had Hailey gone and made it look so easy?

In desperation, she snatched some hay from the net. 'Come on, girl, look here, nice hay.'

It turned out that Pompom wasn't that bright a spark, after all. She didn't seem to realise she was being tricked as she curled her lip out towards the stolen handful of hay. While the horse's head was down, Annie managed to throw the rope around her neck, and once she'd done that, Pompom seemed to know she was beaten. With wisps of hay hanging out of her mouth, she allowed Annie to slide the halter over her nose and fasten it. Annie was amazed. Didn't the brute know her own strength, then? She could have thrown Annie aside with a quick jerk of the massively muscled neck, but apparently now that she was tethered, she was quite prepared to behave herself.

Flushed with pride, Annie called to Lydia to open the stable door. She had a momentary feeling of panic, as she pulled the horse into motion, that Pompom might take the opportunity to knock her down and make a run for it, but the horse had apparently resigned herself to business as usual.

'Here, you can hold her too,' Annie told Lydia as she led Pompom out of the stable yard. Smiling, Lydia took the end of the rope.

'She's a nice horse, isn't she?'

Although Annie was still shaking with stress after her ordeal in the stable, she responded with an enthusiastic yes. When you got right down to it, this horse was worth its weight in gold; because Lydia only smiled for her dad.

They set off towards the paddock, Annie beginning to feel almost confident. The worst was surely over. Catching Pompom to bring her back to the stable might present a problem, but Hailey had never had any difficulty. In fact, Pompom, knowing that her evening feed awaited, had always come trotting over to be caught.

As they rounded a bend, they approached what Hailey had described as the lungeing arena. It was a circular area neatly fenced to shoulder height with wooden palings. Just the day before, Hailey had taken Pompom in there and made her trot around in circles at the end of a long rein for about twenty minutes, for exercise.

Today there was a horse in the lungeing arena, but it wasn't being exercised. It seemed to be exercising itself, though, running up and down the fence with an arched neck and flared nostrils. The moment Pompom caught sight of this horse, she stopped in her tracks, raised her head, and gave an almighty bellow that nearly deafened Annie. It didn't sound like a whinny or a neigh, or any noise that a horse was supposed to make. It was a loud, quivering blast of anguish, and Annie nearly fell over with fright. Out of the corner of her eye, Annie saw Lydia freeze in confusion.

'It's OK,' Annie said bracingly into the pulsating aftermath of Pompom's cry. 'It's OK. Everybody calm down. It's just another horse. Don't worry, Pompom, the bad horsy can't get out. We just have to walk by. Everybody will be OK. Come on, let's just walk on by.'

She was trying to sound both calm and authoritative, and Lydia certainly looked a little reassured, but Pompom didn't seem to have caught her tone. In fact, Pompom's eyes seemed in danger of popping out of her head. Her nostrils now appeared as wide as Martini glasses, and her head was up in the air at an unnatural angle that pulled the rope taut in Annie's hand.

Annie gave the rope a little tug. 'Come on, Pompom, let's go,' she begged.

Pompom took a deep breath and bellowed again. This time, the horse in the lungeing arena bellowed back and began to gallop in earnest around the circumference of the fence.

Annie's heart banged hard against her ribs. She yanked at the rope again. 'Come on, you stupid, *stupid* beast.'

'Don't talk to her like that,' cried Lydia.

And then Pompom reared up and tore the rope out of Annie's and Lydia's hands. Snorting and kicking up her heels, Heather's precious mare clattered off towards the distant car park, trailing the rope behind her. Annie gave a scream of pure panic. She had a sudden mental image of the beast with its iron hooves kicking out at all the parked Hummers and SUVs. An even worse scenario popped into her head. What if a car suddenly pulled in at speed, and there was a collision, and the horse's long legs were snapped at the knee, and the car was a write-off, and a child inside broke its neck ...

Just as Pompom seemed about to do her best to turn these horrors into reality, the horse had a sudden change of heart. Annie and Lydia were halfway across the grassy field by now, in hot pursuit, when Pompom gave a joyful buck, turned around, and began galloping at breakneck speed back towards the lungeing arena.

Annie switched directions to run after her, lungs screaming for air.

Pompom raced up to the other horse, screeched to a halt, and stood nostril to nostril with it for a moment. Then both horses squealed and did some jumping about. Then the big sand-coloured horse in the arena stretched its head out, flattened its ears, and appeared to bite a chunk out of Pompom's neck. Pompom did the screaming whinny, reared in the air, and clunked one hoof against the fence.

Oh dear God, something bad was bound to happen soon. Annie hadn't realised horses were so aggressive. Would it be like a dog fight, with one of them lying dead on the ground at the end? Could they rip each other's throats out with their grass-eating teeth?

Annie felt in her pocket for her phone – but who to call? Surely in a situation like this, Heather would throw caution to the winds and come flying over to help, despite her rainbow-coloured face and strep-infected child? Or maybe she should dial 911? She pictured the commotion of sirens blaring and lights flashing as the entire Norbury police force pulled into the barn's car park, closely followed by the fire engine. The police never seemed to go anywhere without the fire engine, she'd noticed. If the huge shiny truck didn't drive Pompom over the edge, nothing would.

'Having trouble, ma'am?' a voice drawled.

Phone in hand, Annie glanced over her shoulder. A man who looked remarkably like a cowboy out of a spaghetti western stood behind her, complete with hat, narrowed eyes and tasselled leather chaps worn over jeans. He lacked only a bandanna and a cheroot to be picture-perfect for a role in a John Wayne classic.

'The brown one's mine,' Annie replied. 'Well, not mine. My friend's, but I'm supposed to be looking after it. I don't know whose bloody horse that is in the arena but it's taunting Pompom like anything. Took a bite out of her neck just a moment ago.'

'The palomino?' said the cowboy. 'He's mine.'

'Well, get over there and bloody stop him, can't you? I don't know what he's been saying to Pompom, but he's really giving her the heebie-jeebies. She's ready to go for the jugular. Quick, do something before they hurt each other!'

The horses were squealing back and forth in a loud, threatening fashion, the sand-coloured one rearing up and slamming his chest into the fence.

To Annie's outrage, the cowboy laughed.

'They're not trying to hurt each other. Pompom's in heat,

is all. My boy's just been gelded but she ain't picky, I guess. Reckon his brain hasn't figured out his balls are gone.'

Annie felt her face flush, and she glanced at Lydia. The child was staring at the stranger with wide eyes. 'Can you keep it clean,' Annie hissed at him.

His face broke into a lazy smile. 'Sure I can,' he drawled. 'Here, you need help getting that mare away from Stanley?'

Relief made Annie weak at the knees. 'Oh yes, yes,' she said. 'Please! I know almost nothing about horses, you see, and to be honest I find them a bit ... intimidating.'

'You don't say.' The man sauntered off towards Pompom, making some kind of clicking noise with his mouth as he went. Pompom could barely take her eyes off the palomino, but she had the humans covered with her peripheral vision. As the man moved closer, she gave a contemptuous snort and danced off sideways, still keeping her eyes on the prize. The man began to move very slowly, perhaps an inch at a time, his hands at his side. Pompom watched and snorted and danced. It was clear that she wasn't planning to let him get within spitting distance of her.

But she'd forgotten the lead rope hanging from her halter.

Before she'd figured out what he was up to, the cowboy was standing on that rope with both of his boots. Feeling the resistance, Pompom tried to lunge away, but the cowboy bent down quick as a striking snake and took the rope in his hands. Then, still clicking his tongue and talking softly, he began to reel her in.

He made it look so easy.

Within seconds he was holding the halter at the metal

ring and marching an unrepentant Pompom away from her wildly protesting would-be lover. Annie ran to catch up with them, and Lydia followed.

'Oh, thank you so, so much,' Annie panted. 'Can you put her in the first paddock? We just have to muck out her stable. We'll do it really, really fast. And then – I wonder if I can ask you – I mean, I'm not sure if you were planning to leave right away, but—'

'I'll bring her back past Stanley for you, no problem,' he said. 'No sense getting everybody all worked up again.'

Back in Pompom's stall, Annie rolled up her sleeves and got busy shovelling and raking as fast as she could. She just wanted to get the job over and done with so they could go home. Lydia didn't seem to sense the hurry. She moved about in a leisurely fashion, unhooking the hay net, tipping out the last of the water in the bucket.

'What does "in heat" mean?' she asked just as Annie was about to set off for the compost heap with her wheelbarrow.

Damn.

Annie clung to the handles of the wheelbarrow with white knuckles. 'Um ... it sort of means Pompom wants to ... to find herself a boyfriend. A horse boyfriend, of course.'

'Oh,' said Lydia, and went back to spreading clean sawdust with no further sign of interest. Annie lingered, feeling she should explain things better. Wasn't this, after all, what those parenting books called a 'teachable moment'? Lydia hardly ever offered such moments, because she hardly ever said anything at all.

But Annie flinched as she thought of ways to develop the theme. She could explain that Pompom wasn't angry with the other horse, just excited to see him, and that was why she'd acted like such a lunatic. She could explain that Pompom really wanted to be in the lungeing arena with the other horse so they could make babies. She could explain further that this would be a futile exercise because the boy horse lacked the necessary equipment.

Or she could just move on by with her wheelbarrow.

After a moment of reflection, she just moved on by with her wheelbarrow.


On their way home, Annie stopped off at the drugstore on the town's oak-lined main street. 'Do you have anything for somebody who has a bad, um, you know, mark on their face?' she asked the woman behind the counter. Lydia, toying with a small stand of key rings, seemed entirely uninterested in the conversation.

'A mark? You mean, like a birthmark?'

'Yes. Like a birthmark.' Annie fluttered her hand around her cheekbone. 'Sort of a multicoloured birthmark.'

'I'll show you what I have.'

Twenty minutes later, Annie was ringing Heather's doorbell. When Heather cautiously opened the door, lurking well back in the shadows of an unlit hallway until she saw who it was, Annie thrust a brown bag into her hands. 'This is for you,' she said. 'It's make-up. You put the green stuff on first, then the thick paste. It's supposed to be really good. Slap it on with a spatula if you have to. But I can't go back to the stables tomorrow. I'm sorry. I just can't.'

'Jesus, Annie, what happened?'

'Your horse,' Annie hissed. Then she looked down at

Lydia and swallowed back a few choice expletives. 'Your horse is in *heat*.'

According to Heather, the cowboy at the barn was Dan Morgan, a well-known personality in these parts, well nigh a celebrity. Although he looked and acted as if he'd been out riding fences all his life, he was in fact some sort of oil tycoon who'd moved east for mysterious reasons, and spent much of his free time (of which, like Annie, he seemed to have an abundance) dispensing horse wisdom at the barn. People came to ask his advice about horses that wouldn't box, horses that refused to jump, horses that reared, crib-biters, wind-suckers, bolters, buckers, even horses with bizarre diagnoses such as emotional dissociation and sensory overload.

Beneath his rustic speech patterns and aura of countrified simplicity lurked a deep and complex personality, Heather reckoned.

'I don't know about that,' said Annie, 'but it's funny how you notice a man's bum when he's wearing those leather legging thingies.'

'I think you mean butt,' said Heather. 'A bum is a home-less person sleeping in a cardboard box in a doorway.'

Annie shook her head. 'You're wrong! A butt is the tail end of a cigarette.'

'It's a tail end, whichever way you look at it,' Heather laughed.

Annie wondered briefly if she could persuade Simon to wear a cowboy hat, jeans and leather legging thingies. She rather thought not. Shabby old corduroys were more his style.

# Chapter Four

'She had this trip to the south of France lined up, but then she broke up with the chap who was organising it, and he's taking someone else instead,' Annie told Simon that Saturday afternoon as they walked around the nature trail at Fairacres Park with Lydia.

Simon raised his eyebrows, looking faintly amused. 'Which chap was this? I can't keep up with Sarah's boyfriends. I wonder why she'd want to come here? It's not really her kind of place. I don't think there's a singles scene in Norbury at all. It's just families, as far as I can tell. Of course, she could take the train in to Manhattan and go clubbing.'

'She's coming to see *me*, of course,' said Annie.

Annie and Sarah were very close, for cousins. They were like sisters, without the rivalry. Because her parents travelled abroad a lot, Sarah – the youngest in her family by far – had spent countless weekends and school holidays with Annie's family in Surrey. Conveniently, the weekly boarding school she attended was only about an hour's drive from their home. Annie, an only child, had practically worshipped the ground her older cousin walked on.

'Anyway, she enjoys meeting all kinds of new people,'

Annie said. 'Not just men. We should have a dinner party or something for her.' They could see Lydia ahead of them, poking at things with a long stick, and then running on a few strides to make sure the grown-ups didn't catch up with her.

Simon smiled down at Annie. 'A dinner party. Wow. Do we know anybody to invite yet?'

Annie gave him a playful kick. 'Idiot. Of course we know people. There's Heather, and I wouldn't mind asking this other mum who lives on our street, Jennifer Miller. She's a bit prim, but I've got a feeling she could be a different person altogether after a glass of Pinot Grigio. And maybe we could invite a chap for Sarah.'

'A chap? What chap?'

Lydia waved a hand. 'I don't know. Don't you have any single blokes on your team?'

Simon gave a sudden snort of laughter. 'Well, yes, there are a couple – but I wouldn't want to introduce any of them to Sarah Harleigh! I'd never live it down.'

'Sarah's not so bad!'

'Sarah's great. She's a hoot. But even you have to admit, she's a bit of a rough diamond.'

'You'd be embarrassed to introduce your colleagues to her?'

'Bloody right I would. If she takes a fancy to somebody, next thing you know she's clubbing him over the head and dragging him off to her room by the ankle.'

'Rubbish!' She kicked him a bit harder, but still playfully. With lightning reflexes, he grabbed her foot and held her hopping and helpless.

'Look, we don't have to be pimps for Sarah,' he said. 'She's tough. She can take an evening of being the only single woman in the room. Or we could just scrap the whole dinner party idea.'

'No, no, I want the dinner party. Whoooa,' she yelled as she began to topple over backwards. Simon released her foot and leapt into action, managing to catch her before she fell. For a moment she lay in the tight band of his arms, looking up into bright blue eyes that seemed to be chinks of the crisp autumn sky itself. Then he dipped his head to kiss her.

Annie felt somebody tugging urgently at the back pocket of her jeans. Delicious though it was to be tasting Simon's cool lips, she drew away from him. Lydia was standing nearby with an unreadable look on her face, arms crossed over her narrow chest.

'Daddy,' she said in a louder voice than usual. 'Why are you doing that? Why was Annie kicking you? Is she in heat?'

There was a stunned silence. Simon turned speechless eyes on Annie. Annie shrugged helplessly. Simon cleared his throat. 'Darling, Annie's not a horse,' he said. 'We were just ... just having a little fun.'

'I don't like you doing that,' Lydia said, glaring up at him. 'It's stupid.'

He squatted down next to her. 'Come here, sweetie.' He held out his arms and after a small hesitation she slumped into them. Annie could see her petulant face resting on his shoulder. He looked up at Annie. 'Will you give me a minute to talk to her?' he asked.

She nodded and walked away from them quickly down the trail. They didn't catch up with her again – she made sure of that by breaking into a run as soon as she was out of sight around a corner.

She'd never been on a nature walk in a park with her own dad. He wouldn't have been caught dead in a park – he reckoned they were riddled with druggies and dog poo. But he used to play cards with her, when she was growing up. Gin rummy, cribbage, even poker. He made her win her pocket money off him, and the truth was she often found winning the money more fun than spending it.

As she waited at the car, watching Simon and Lydia draw closer, a strange melancholy came over her. They were chatting away, engrossed in each other's company: the tall blonde man and his skinny blonde daughter. They didn't look anything like her dad and herself at seven years old. Her dad had been of average height and slight, and he had always worn a tie, even when he was on holiday. His hair had been the same colour as Annie's own – plain brown. Yet, in some inexplicable way, the sight of these two reminded her almost unbearably of herself and her dad, whose face she hadn't seen since he died of a heart attack when she was in her early twenties.

'Ah, *there* you are,' Simon said, lifting his head and looking straight at her.

She unpeeled herself from the car and waved at them.

Their approach was slow and awkward now, because Lyddie was holding Simon's right hand in both of hers and jumping forward every few steps with curled-up legs, so that she could swing from his arm.

'Come over and give me a hand with this monkey, will you?' Simon called.

Annie felt the smile breaking out on her face as she ran over to join them.

'Lyddie, take Annie's hand and we'll both swing you,' Simon suggested.

Lydia tightened her two-handed grip on Simon's hand.

'Go on,' said Simon. 'Trust me, this is one of those things a dad can't do alone.'

'Yes, you can!' Lydia threw her weight onto his hand to prove her point. He let her dangle a moment, then lowered her to the ground.

'But not very well,' he said.

Annie held out her hand. Lydia detached one of hers and slid it reluctantly into her stepmother's grasp.

'OK, here we go,' said Simon. 'One, two, three ... *up!*'

Lydia flew so high into the air that for a moment Annie had a glimpse of her pink trainers against the blue sky. As she swung up, she shrieked with glee.

Inspired by the idea of throwing a dinner party, Annie thought she'd better try to kick-start Lydia's social life a bit, too. 'Is there anybody you'd like to have round to play, other than Hailey?' she asked one evening while Lydia was brushing her teeth. They had already returned Heather's favour and had Hailey round. It hadn't been a particularly successful play date. Hailey had spent the entire time kicking a ball about outside with Annie, while Lydia played with her bald doll up in her room.

'No,' said Lydia. 'I like playing by myself.'

'Yes, I know, but ... Look, who do you sit next to in class?'

'This girl called Courtney.'

So Annie looked up the name in the school directory and cold-called Courtney's mother. Mrs Phelps sounded a bit surprised to hear from her, but duly agreed to send her daughter over.

To prevent Lydia from hiding away in her room again, Annie decided to take the girls to Dogwood Park, where there was apparently a very nice playground.

And it *was* a very nice playground, as it turned out. The only trouble was, it seemed to be entirely made up of activities that were best tackled alone. You didn't need a companion when you were rock climbing or balancing your way over a wobbly rope bridge or hurtling down a tubular slide. In fact, a companion during these feats of derring-do was a bit of a liability, or so she gathered from the way Lydia and Courtney shot off in different directions the moment they set foot in the place. But that was OK. They were probably bonding, nonetheless. Common experiences brought people together, everybody knew that; even if they ignored each other while experiencing them.

Annie settled down on a bench and looked around with interest at the other adults in the park. She noticed a tired-looking woman with dark hair tucked behind her ears walking around behind a bandy-legged toddler. Standing up slowly, Annie stretched in a nonchalant way and ambled over towards the woman. She didn't want to look like a stalker, but she was in desperate need of adult conversation. She hadn't spoken to a soul all day. She'd never really thought, before, of the solitary nature of the life of a stay-at-home mum. The truth was, she'd never thought *at all* about the life of a stay-at-home mum.

She waited till the dark-haired woman glanced her way, then smiled and said, 'You'd think they'd have a see-saw at a big playground like this, wouldn't you?'

The woman looked a little startled. 'See-saw?'

'Yes. Didn't you just love see-saws when you were little?' She demonstrated an up and down motion with her hands.

The woman frowned. 'Oh, you mean a teeter-totter? They don't put those in parks any more. Too much liability.'

'Liability?' Annie echoed, but the woman was waving to somebody across the playground.

'Gotta go,' she said, giving Annie a polite smile as she hauled her toddler up onto her hip and crossed the wood chips towards her friend.

Annie watched her walk away, feeling wistful.

This was one of those moments when she felt as if she'd give anything to be back inside the fuggy offices of *Rumour Has It*, at her familiar desk in her familiar cubicle, surrounded by the motley crew she'd worked with for four years. Oh, she'd spoken to them by phone a few times since she left, and her friend Amanda, the copy editor, kept sending her silly email jokes, but it wasn't the same thing as being in the office with everybody.

With a brisk shake of her head, Annie put her old life out of her mind. She'd given up her job at the women's weekly without a moment's hesitation, despite predictions that she was shortlisted to fill the shoes of the retiring assistant editor. She hadn't felt a single pang as she cleared her desk and emptied her half-shelf in the office fridge. Indeed, she'd even handed over her top secret Ideas file to the incoming staff writer.

Yes, she'd been on the up and up at the magazine, but no, she didn't regret leaving, not for a moment – even though she'd been planning to springboard off her position as assistant editor into a magazine with slightly more credibility than *Rumour Has It,* which was a bit of a bottom-feeder in the industry, if she were honest. Something like *Marie Claire* would have done nicely.

The truth was, she'd always been ambitious – a fact that her career path didn't really reflect, at first glance. Early on, she'd found that there were far too many girls fresh out of university willing to work for *Tatler* for almost nothing. But Annie was cunning. When the direct route to women's magazine stardom seemed to be blocked off by congestion, she'd decided on the road less travelled.

So she'd taken a job first with a magazine for doll's house and miniature collectible enthusiasts, then with an online aquarium hobbyists' journal. Her lucky break had come when she'd heard through the friend of a friend that *Rumour Has It* was looking for a general dogsbody. She did that for about a year, until one of the copy editors suddenly threw in her job in order to follow her boyfriend to a Buddhist retreat in India.

Without fanfare or fuss – without even a pay rise – Annie took over the vacant desk and the unfinished proofreading. Her considerable talent for idea generation (i.e. for reading competing magazines and mining their stories) soon emerged. And the rest was history.

But she would have given up a lot more than her career to marry Simon Keeler.

As a matter of fact, she *had* given up a lot more than her career to marry Simon Keeler. She'd given up her flat, her ancient Mini, her handmade curtains, her hand-picked furniture, the land of her birth. Not to mention her friends, her family, and her gym membership.

But it wasn't the adrenalin-rush of working in media that she missed. It wasn't even the perks (although it *was* hard to live without the cosmetics samples, free books and other small bribes that streamed in almost daily). It was being in a place where people knew (and cared) that she took her tea weak with one spoon of sugar and a dash of milk.

Annie gave herself a mental shake and surveyed the playground, looking for Lydia's white shirt and Courtney's purple one. Lydia was on the swings and Courtney was ... oh no, Courtney was running up to another little girl who'd just arrived. They were squealing with excitement, hugging, and generally acting like long-lost lovers. And now they were glancing over at Lydia and talking in low voices. Annie felt her heart begin to thump. Lydia looked back at the girls, then dropped her eyes and slumped down in the swing. The girls giggled and ran off together, hand in hand.

For a few minutes, Annie watched Lydia dangle on the swing, shoes stirring up wood chips, while Courtney ran around noisily with the newcomer. Then she stood up and walked casually over to her stepdaughter.

'Can I give you a push?' she asked.

'No thanks.'

'Are you sure? It's more fun if you go a bit higher.'

'I don't want to go higher.'

A shrill cry caught their attention. Courtney was scream-ing with laughter as her friend tried to catch her.

'Is that other girl in your class?' Annie asked.

Lydia shrugged.

Annie looked at her watch. It was only four o' clock. Courtney's mother was coming for her at five thirty. An hour and a half. Eternity. 'You know what?' she said sud-denly. 'I think we should head on home now. I've had about enough of this park for one day.'

'All right,' said Lydia. Annie couldn't even tell whether she was relieved or disappointed.

Thankfully, Courtney came away from her friend obedi-ently when called. 'See you tomorrow, Samantha,' she yelled to the girl through the open window as they pulled away.

'Does Samantha go to Bradley?' Annie asked in a bright voice.

'Yes, and she lives on my street, and she's my BFF,' said Courtney.

Bully for you, Annie thought. 'That's nice,' she said. Lydia said nothing at all. You couldn't blame her, really.

'So – what games do you play at recess?' Courtney asked Lydia after a moment. She was obviously a girl who couldn't abide dead air.

Lydia didn't reply.

Annie glanced in the rear-view mirror at Courtney's confi-dent, slightly sneering face, her heart sinking. She stole a look at the small, clenched face of her stepdaughter. Lydia was staring out of the window, one shoulder raised protectively.

'I never see you on the blacktop,' Courtney continued.

'Do you go over to the monkey bars? *We* always play on the blacktop in the corner near the portables. We play ponies. Sometimes we play tag, but mostly it's ponies. I play with Samantha and McKenna and Brittany. Who do *you* play with?'

Annie looked at Lydia's face again in the rear-view mirror. She was still staring stonily into the distance.

'Can you do the monkey bars, Courtney?' Annie asked hastily. 'Lydia can. She's really good. She can go from one end right over to the other side. I've tried it myself, but I can't do more than a couple of bars.'

'Sure, I can do the monkey bars,' said Courtney. 'Everybody in second grade can. But we pretty much don't bother with the monkey bars any more.'

'Really?' Annie cursed silently. She'd thought Lydia's unexpected prowess on the bars would give her a bit of an edge. But no. The bars were passé, apparently. Good grief, they were a tough bunch these Norbury second-graders, agile as monkeys and nonchalant with it.

'Can we take the bikes out?' Courtney asked when Annie pulled up outside the house.

'Bikes? Um ... we don't have bikes,' Annie said.

Crikey. She didn't even know whether Lydia could ride a bike. That was something she needed to fix.

'How about scooters, then?'

'Sorry, no scooters.'

'Trampoline?'

'No trampoline.'

'So what do you guys have?' Courtney asked, looking genuinely curious.

'Um ...' Annie was stumped.

'We have TV,' said Lydia.

The girls spent the rest of the afternoon slumped in front of *Sponge Bob*.

'It went very well, I thought,' Annie said staunchly as they waved goodbye to Courtney from the driveway.

'It totally sucked,' said Lydia, uttering her first Americanism.

'This is effing unbelievable,' said Sarah, staring out of the car window at the pastel-painted wooden-framed houses on their artfully landscaped grounds. They were driving through Norbury, on their way back from the airport. 'Look at the picket fences! The rolling lawns! The stars and stripes all over the place! I thought this kind of thing was a figment of Hollywood's imagination.'

'No, it's real,' said Annie proudly. 'You won't see any pebble-dash here, let me tell you. And no terraces. People aren't into sharing walls.'

'And the gardens are huge!'

'Not gardens, backyards. Yes, around here they're all one or two acres.'

'And look – hay bales and pumpkins all over the place! It's a seasonal extravaganza. Slow down, I want to look at that scarecrow. Crikey. Is that a cashmere scarf he's wearing? God, maybe I could nip out and nab it. Just kidding,' she added as the minivan leapt forward in sudden haste. 'Can you imagine people at home bothering with all this? It's a paradise for kids, isn't it? I can see what Simon was thinking when he moved, now.'

'Yeah, well. It's a bit of a paradise for mums, too. It's all about convenience, you see. Every kind of appliance you can imagine. And so much space everywhere! You never have to battle for parking. Nail salons on every corner. Big supermarkets with plenty of room to turn your trolley in the aisle. Trolleys with wheels that work. And if you don't have time to take care of something, like – I don't know – walking your dog or ironing your shirts, you just call up a service.'

Sarah settled back in her seat and gave a low laugh. 'Yeah, nice for some. Where do the real people live, the ones who are going to be repossessed?'

Annie pulled a face. 'Don't know, really. Want to see the beach?'

The town's private beach was deserted this school morning. Annie and Sarah put on their jackets and took a seat on a bench, looking out at the calm water of Long Island Sound and listening to the gulls.

Sarah examined the distant boats, bobbing at anchor, with beady-eyed interest. 'Wow, Annie,' she said musingly after a while, 'you've gone and landed with your bum in the butter, haven't you?'

Annie felt a slight prickle of resentment. 'Things aren't always as cushy as they look,' she said with a shrug. 'And that's butt, not bum.'

'It's bum to you and me, my girl. How hard can it be, looking after one kid in a big mansion, with all kinds of help laid on? Look, I'm not taking a dig at you. I'm happy for you, that's all.'

Annie was silent.

Sarah gave her a shrewd look. 'What's going on?' she asked after a moment. 'Is there a serpent in paradise?'

Annie stood up briskly and walked off towards the water's edge. Staring out at the distant shape of Long Island, she was appalled to feel tears forming in her eyes. After a while, Sarah came and joined her.

'You're homesick,' Sarah said. 'Settling into a new place must be hard. No friends, no family.'

'No job,' added Annie. She dashed her hand across her eyes. 'God, listen to me. I'm not normally so pathetic. It's just ... seeing a familiar face, you know. I'm actually very happy here. Very.'

Sarah grinned and ran her hand through her springy red hair. 'Look, love, you don't have to convince *me*. I'm bloody green with envy. Of course you're happy. I mean, you've got all this,' she gestured at the beach, the bobbing boats, the distant houses with their lawns running down to the water, 'and the lovely Simon Keeler to boot.'

Annie smiled and blushed with pleasure. 'He is lovely, isn't he?'

'Yeah, and he's not just a pretty face. I've sailed with him. He's a good man in a squall.'

Annie nodded. 'I bet he is.'

'Why isn't he sailing any more?' Sarah asked abruptly. 'It's a crying shame. He ought to be out on that water! He tells me he hasn't even joined a club.'

Annie clicked her tongue and stared out over the water. 'I don't know,' she said after a moment. 'I certainly haven't pressurised him to stop, if that's what you're thinking. Maybe he just doesn't want to take away from family time.

There's little enough of it, as it is.' She leaned over, picked up a smooth pebble and turned it around in her hand. It was a beautiful stone, flecked with orange and green. Studying it as if she was going to have to draw it from memory, she asked suddenly, 'Did you know Lydia's mother?'

Sarah picked up a couple of pebbles too. She didn't look at them, just weighed them in her hand then threw them far out across the water, making them skip over the surface with the practised ease of a teenage boy. 'Beth? Yeah, I met her a few times. Never got to know her very well.'

'So? What was she like?'

Sarah began to walk towards the rocky outcrop that marked the end of the beach. Annie followed, still holding her pebble.

'Oh. You know. She was thin and blonde. White eye-lashes. Looked frail, you wouldn't have thought she weighed enough to be rail meat.'

'For God's sake, what *is* rail meat?'

Sarah glanced at her in mild surprise. 'Well, it's the people who sit on the rail to balance the boat when it heels, of course. But Beth was stronger than she looked. One of those wiry women with muscles like steel cables.'

'Different from me, then.' Annie glanced at her own arm. Muscles like steel cables did not lurk beneath her jumper, she knew for a fact.

'Of course. And you should be glad of that. Wouldn't like to think he was looking for a clone, would you?'

'Good God, no, now you put it that way. But ... it's just hard. Dead people are a bit intimidating, aren't they? They can never put a foot wrong.'

90

Sarah gave a snort of surprised laughter, then shook her head in disbelief. 'Oh Annie ... Does he go on about Beth, then?'

'No, the opposite. He hardly mentions her. Do you think he loved her very much?' Annie asked wistfully.

'I would hope so. He loves *you* very much, that's pretty obvious.'

'I know he does,' Annie said, fiddling with her pebble. 'But – sometimes in the middle of the night, when I can't sleep, I go into a bit of a cold sweat. You see, I can't help thinking I'm in over my head with all the mum stuff. I mean, I don't mind teaching myself to cook and all that. It doesn't matter if a casserole gets overdone or a cake flops. But you don't want to be overdoing or flopping a *kid*.'

Sarah shook her head. 'Come on, Annie. Don't be so hard on yourself. Lyddie has to be better off with you than she was with the nanny. Just keep doing what you're doing and everything will sort itself out in the long run. I mean, of course you'll make mistakes, but you'll never go too far wrong.'

'How can you possibly know that?'

'Well, because you care enough about all this to worry, in the first place. Your heart's in the right place. And that makes up for almost everything else.'

Annie gave a sniff. 'It had better,' she murmured. Then, brushing the sand off her hands briskly, she added, 'Anyway, let's move this tour along. I want to show you the real centre of Norbury life.'

Fifteen minutes later, they stood on the shiny marble floor of the Fairfield County Leisure Store, looking at the displays of hundred-dollar ribbon belts, indecently expensive flip-flops, and 'resort wear' embroidered all over with tiny dolphins or elephants, like a bumpy fabric rash. Everything seemed to be either hot pink or lime green, or both.

'Bit chilly for this sort of gear,' remarked Sarah.

'Not if you're flitting off to St Kitts,' Annie explained. 'Oooh, look at the lovely tennis outfits. I have to confess, I've bought one of these already.'

Sarah squinted at the lycra skorts and sports bra tops. 'Why would you buy a tennis outfit? You don't play, do you?'

'No, of course not, but *everybody* in town wears them. I'm sure they can't all be playing, either. They're cute, aren't they?'

Sarah shook her head austerely, and they moved on.

'Look at this lot,' said Annie when they reached the children's section. 'The unofficial school uniform of the town. The right footwear is the foundation stone of any respectable winter wardrobe, of course.' She pointed at a rack of slipper-like sheepskin boots.

'Those things? Oh my God! Look at the price of them! I'd never spend that on a pair of boots for myself, let alone a kid. You didn't buy these for Lyddie, did you?'

Annie wrinkled her nose. 'Not yet. Oh, these are the backpacks. You get them monogrammed and they have matching lunch boxes. I didn't know about them when I got Lydia's, so she's walking around with a Hannah Montana backpack, poor girl. Of course, I can't bring myself to replace it – what a crying waste of money, and what on earth would Mum say?'

Sarah chuckled. Annie's mother was known to be such a scrimper and saver that she'd keep the wax from cheese to make home-made candles.

'Oooh, look, these are the must-have North Face jackets.' Annie pointed excitedly at a colourful rack. 'Lydia *does* have one of those, I'm proud to say. I got the last one in her size. I'm not sure teal is her colour, but still.'

Sarah picked up a jacket and squinted at the tag. 'Annie, this thing costs more than a hundred dollars. And she'll be out of it by next year, right?'

Annie shrugged. 'I know. Mum would just faint with horror. But Sarah, I want Lydia to have a fighting chance out there. She wouldn't have a hope in hell if I sent her out in some geeky anorak. I mean, these kids have their own embossed stationery, their own monogrammed bath robes ... They go into Manhattan to get their dolls' hair done, for God's sake.'

'I don't know,' said Sarah, shaking her head. 'Kids seem to get too much, these days. Put them all out on the water on a Sun Fizz, that's what I say. That'll soon teach them a bit about real life – sail too close into the wind and over you go.'

'Sarah, you're sounding like somebody's grandfather. Come on, let's get out of here. I shouldn't have brought you in, really. I'll take you down the road to Target. You'll like it much better.'

Three days later, Annie pushed the last napkin through its beaded napkin ring and stood back to admire the table. She'd decided on a sleek, simple look, with pillar candles down the centre of a table-runner in jewel tones.

As she tweaked a place mat, she heard a muffled cry from the kitchen. 'Hang on, I'm coming!' she called back.

For once, she wasn't too worried about the actual food component of the dinner party. Sarah had offered to make the shrimp cheese balls that she was so justly famous for in Kilburn, plus they had some mini pies from ChefPro, and Simon was roasting a leg of lamb with rosemary potatoes and a colourful tray of autumn vegetables. Between them, they'd agreed to let Annie boil up some peas and make a green salad. Dessert was ready-bought cheesecake jollied up with a scattering of fresh blueberries; not exactly gourmet fare, but a good, hearty meal of the English Sunday lunch variety.

In the kitchen, Simon stood at the open door of the fridge, running his eye over its contents. 'Do we have any mint?' he asked urgently.

Mint! She knew she'd forgotten something. 'I don't think so,' she said with a rueful grimace. 'Do we really need it?'

Simon's eyebrows went up. 'Well, yes, given that we're making leg of lamb with mint sauce. Look, I'll dash out and get some.'

'But ... but people will be here in twenty minutes,' Annie protested. 'Sarah's already gone up to change!'

'I'll be quick,' he said firmly. 'Lamb without mint is like ... I don't know, coffee without milk.'

'Some people like it black!'

'Not me.' His tone was decisive. 'Don't worry, I'll be right back. You won't even miss me.'

'Can I come, Daddy?' Lydia's voice surprised them. They

hadn't noticed her, sitting quietly in the bow window. Simon cocked an eyebrow at Annie.

'I wanted to get her ready for bed,' Annie said. 'But OK, if you're quick.'

'Don't forget to turn off the oven if I'm not back by seven,' Simon called over his shoulder before slamming the kitchen door.

Annie stood alone for a moment, listening to the car start up and drive away. She pulled a little face at herself. She couldn't remember ever feeling this panicky about a dinner party – and normally she had a lot more *reason* to panic, because normally she was the cook, and normally she was cooking something complex and way beyond her limited abilities, like Fricassee de Mer.

But tonight her nerves had nothing to do with the food. The truth was, she felt a bit like an old-fashioned debutante, launching herself on society in the hope that she would 'take' and find herself accepted into fashionable circles.

Although Heather was a newcomer to the town, she'd lived in the Connecticut suburbs long enough to understand how things worked, and she'd already warned Annie that if she wanted Lydia to be on the birthday party circuit, she'd better get out and do some networking. Happily, it turned out that her neighbour, Jennifer Miller, was one of the queen bees in town. If Annie impressed Jennifer, then she might be admitted into the inner circle of school mums, and Lydia's social life would prosper accordingly.

Annie glanced at her watch. Time was ticking on and she'd better get herself showered and ready to 'receive'.

But she was still in front of the mirror, hair damp, trying

to choose between a ribbon of beads (creative, playful) and a solid gold rope of a necklace (sophisticated, bold), when the doorbell rang. 'I'll get it,' Sarah foghorned as she thundered down the stairs.

Oh no. This wasn't how she'd pictured her first dinner party in Connecticut; her first dinner party as a married woman, really. She hadn't for a moment imagined that her husband would be out, nor that her cousin Sarah – all very well in the right context, but rather rough and ready for a formal sort of evening – would be welcoming people at the door.

She took a steadying breath. If her fledgling friends were put off by Sarah's frank, no-nonsense style, then they could jolly well bugger off home again.

Still, she hoped it was Heather at the door, not Jennifer Miller. She couldn't imagine Heather being fazed by anything or anybody – or being judgemental, for that matter.

As Annie descended the stairs, careful not to trip in her heels, she heard Sarah's voice: 'Let's see, are you the horsy one or the posh neighbour? I'm the London cousin, of course. Lord and lady of the manor are still hosing down. Here, hand that wine over, I'll take it to the wet bar and let it breathe. As for the flowers, you'd better hold onto them till Annie comes down. I wouldn't know where to find a vase in this place.'

When Annie got there, Jennifer and a nondescript man with blondish hair, presumably her husband, were still standing in the hallway, but Sarah was nowhere to be seen. The Millers were dressed impeccably, like mannequins from the Fairfield County Leisure Store. Annie tweaked at her pencil skirt, suddenly aware that its cut was probably more suitable for the office than for dinner at home. She should have bought herself something with box pleats, like Jennifer's.

Jennifer's face formed a small, polite smile as Annie came into view.

'Annie, how nice to see you. Your cousin let us in. She's gone off to decant the wine, I believe. This is my husband, Drew.'

Drew held out his hand, and Annie took it automatically. He had a light, very dry grip. 'So pleased to meet you,' she murmured. 'Come on in and sit down. Oh, these are for me?' She took the bouquet of flowers and buried her nose in them. They had absolutely no scent. 'I'll just find a vase.'

As she spoke, the doorbell rang again. 'Why don't you go through,' Annie told the Millers, gesturing at the formal living room, 'and I'll be right back.'

Still clutching the flowers, she opened the door on a small crowd. Heather was in the forefront, with two men hanging slightly behind her. One of them was Dan Morgan, the cowboy, and the other – dark-haired and handsome in a TV-anchorman way – was presumably Heather's husband.

'Heather! How lovely to see you! Dan! So glad you could make it!' It had been Heather's idea to invite Dan, to even up the numbers. Apparently, she knew him well enough to approach him with an invitation on a friend's behalf.

'And you must be ...' Annie looked at Heather's husband in a hostessy way. To her great surprise, he returned her polite glance with a scorcher of a look that drew an involuntary blush up from the soles of her feet to the tips of her ears.

'Rob,' he replied, holding out his hand for her to shake. Even his voice was ridiculously attractive. 'I'm delighted to meet you. I've been hearing "Annie this" and "Annie that" for the last couple of weeks.'

Annie nodded awkwardly, aware of her cheeks still burning away. She hoped Heather hadn't noticed her sudden rosiness. 'Yes. Well. I've heard a lot about you, too. Anyway, come on in. I'll introduce you to the others.'

As she walked into the living room, holding the flowers like a bouquet, she was stopped in her tracks by the sight of Sarah handing around nuts.

Now, Annie had always adored her cousin Sarah. She'd looked up to her when she was just a little girl, and Sarah an adolescent, with something like hero worship, because Sarah had always seemed so confident, so outspoken, so chummy with boys and men, so comfortable in her own skin. But Sarah had never known how to dress, and it looked as if her sartorial skills had now slipped askew entirely.

She was wearing a tiny, body-hugging tie-dyed T-shirt over a pair of loosely fitting combat pants. The T-shirt looked vaguely familiar. With a jolt, Annie realised it was the shirt Lydia had dyed at school for second-grade field trips. For God's sake! It was a shirt for a seven-year-old! If that weren't enough, when Sarah turned to put a bowl of olives on the table, Annie was mortified to see her cousin's lime-green G-string rising up over her hips out of the baggy pants.

As Sarah straightened up, her earrings caught Annie's eye.

They seemed to be mini Navajo dreamcatchers, complete with beads, shells and feathers in unlikely colours.

Annie's eyes flickered in growing disbelief to Sarah's feet. Oh no! Clunky brown Doc Martens. Annie hadn't seen a single soul, not even a teenage boy, wearing boots like that in these parts.

'Sarah!' Annie cried in an artificially bright voice, 'I want you to meet Heather and her husband, Bob.'

'Rob,' said Heather's husband in his throbbing voice. Annie was surprised to see that his eyes were fixed on Sarah with the intensity of a lion spotting a really juicy-looking wildebeest. She prayed Heather wouldn't turn around and catch that look.

'Right. Rob.' Annie cleared her throat. 'And everybody, this is Dan Morgan, a friend of Heather's.'

'A family friend,' Heather said quickly.

Dan Morgan smiled lazily around the room. He was hat-less, but clad in jeans and boots as if he might be called on to mount a mustang at any given moment. Even indoors at night, he had the squinty-eyed, weather-beaten look of a man used to spending most of his time out on the range. Jennifer Miller gave everybody a small wave with her fingertips, and Drew stood up to offer the newcomers his dry handshake.

Gosh. They were a bit of an ill-assorted group, now Annie came to think of it. What on earth would they talk about?

'Where's Simon to do the drinks?' Sarah demanded. 'Give him a kick up the backside if he's still in the shower. Tell you what, I'll start mixing the Bloody Marys. Everybody has to get one down the hatch in the first five minutes. House rule.'

'Steady on, Sarah!' Annie protested, tossing the flowers down on a table. 'There's no house rule, of course,' she added brightly to the company at large. She'd read that Americans didn't drink nearly as much as English people, and she didn't want her household to be known for forcing the demon alcohol upon the fine, upstanding citizens of Norbury.

Moving closer to her cousin, she hissed, 'Simon's buggered off to buy some mint, so let's just keep them occupied till he gets back. Maybe give them your shrimp cheese balls. Oh, and the mini pies.' Aloud, she said, 'Anybody care for an Evian? I also have iced tea, orange juice ...'

'I think I'll have that Bloody Mary you mentioned,' said Jennifer Miller, dipping a carrot in guacamole.

'Sounds good to me,' Drew chimed in. 'And make it bite.'

Annie's eyebrows rose. Clearly, whoever had written the culture-shock book on America hadn't spent much time in this particular part of Connecticut.

Before long, everybody had a lethal red cocktail in hand, and conversation was becoming quite general and relaxed. Annie was just beginning to enjoy a chat with Drew (who turned out to have a dry sense of humour) about his many peculiar experiences on the 5:37 back from the city, when − with a stab of alarm − she realised it was nearly eight o'clock and there was still no sign of Simon. 'Excuse me a moment,' she told his surprised face, and darted upstairs to call Simon on his mobile.

When the mobile began to ring loudly from his bedside table, she threw her own phone onto the dressing table in disgust and forced herself to go back downstairs into the fray.

By eight twenty, she was pretending to listen to people with a fixed smile on her face, barely able to concentrate on a word they were saying. At least the party was going with a definite swing. Nobody had asked her where on earth her husband was, or why dinner was still not served, and she couldn't help feeling desperately grateful to Sarah for her steady flow of cocktails from the wet bar, not to mention her prawn cheese balls, which people were wolfing down with alacrity. But still; it was only a matter of time before it became clear that mine host was definitely not among them.

At 8.27, Annie abruptly slammed down her glass and hurried off to the kitchen, in the middle of a story Dan Morgan was telling about a neurotic horse with a passion for a billy goat. She'd suddenly remembered the lamb roast, all unattended for the last hour or more.

The smell of burning reached her in the dining room. Luckily, it hadn't yet snaked its way into the formal living room. That was one of the advantages of a big house. Chaos and disaster could be contained.

The kitchen itself was full of an oily black cloud that had Annie coughing and grasping her chest. Clearly, the smoke alarm had a flat battery.

In a panic, she switched on the extractor fan and flung windows open. Wrapping a dishcloth around her lower face, she eased open the oven door.

The bright red and green peppers had turned into pepper-shaped ashes. The potatoes looked uncannily like charcoal.

The leg of lamb itself had shrunk down to the size of a tennis ball and was profoundly black.

Oh! She was going to murder Simon with her bare hands. Why hadn't he put the oven timer on?

And what in God's name was she supposed to do now, with six people expecting to sit down to some sort of cordon bleu meal within minutes, and the host still AWOL?

The cloud of smoke had dispersed and Annie was on the phone when the back door opened and Simon erupted into the room on a cool breeze, carrying a bunch of mint and looking full of suppressed energy.

He opened his mouth to speak, but Annie hushed him fiercely and continued to read out her credit card number to the person on the other end of the line.

When she'd given the last details, she put the phone down and looked at Simon.

'How's it all going?' he asked. 'Everybody here yet? How's the roast?'

She gestured wordlessly at the oven. He went over and peeked inside. There was a pregnant pause as he took in the sight of the cremated remains of his hearty feast.

He straightened up and closed the oven door gently. He turned to face her, still holding the bunch of mint. He opened his mouth, but no words came out.

'I've ordered pizza,' she said into the silence. 'I tried to get Chinese, but the kitchen was closed.'

He was shaking his head now, and pressing his lips together. 'I take it you forgot about turning off the oven?' he managed to utter after a moment.

For God's sake. He was trying not to laugh. The bastard was trying not to *laugh*.

And then, without warning, she felt the laughter welling up inside her too, like a violent need to sneeze. She choked it down relentlessly. If she started laughing now, she wouldn't be able to stop. 'Of course I forgot to turn the bloody oven off,' she said. 'But I don't suppose it matters. Everybody's getting sozzled on Sarah's concoctions so they probably don't care about dinner any more. Hang on – where's Lydia?'

Simon hesitated a moment. This seemed ominous to Annie. He wasn't a hesitant sort of man. Then suddenly he walked over to the kitchen door and called out, 'You'd better come in now, Lyddie.'

The child staggered up the stairs into the kitchen, carrying some sort of heavy, awkward bundle wrapped in a towel.

For heaven's sake. It looked like – but it couldn't be – it *looked* like the body of a dog.

Oh no. It *was* the body of a dog. The thing's head hung down at an impossible angle, and its blackish tongue lolled out of its slack, open mouth.

Lydia lowered the dog's floppy body to the floor and squatted down beside it. No rigor mortis as yet, Annie noticed with some part of her brain that was still capable of thought; that would make it easier to shove it into a cupboard, at least. Oh, she was forgetting the basement. They could stash the body down there.

'I'm sorry, Annie,' Simon said ruefully. 'I know this is the last thing you want on your doorstep tonight.'

'Understatement of the bloody year! Who goes out for

a bunch of mint and comes back with a dead dog?' The laughter was boiling up in her again, but she was tamping it down.

'He's not dead,' said Lydia fiercely.

'Of course, he's not dead,' said Simon. 'Why would I bring a dead dog home?'

'I don't know — to give it a decent burial? Are you sure it's not dead? I don't see it breathing. And the way its head was hanging down ...'

'Look, he's very much alive, take my word for it. We found him in the car park at the supermarket, cowering near the trolleys.'

'Was this before or after you bought the mint?'

'Well, *after*, of course. His leg was all matted with blood and he was out of his mind with fear. We thought he might've been run over, but the vet—'

'The vet?'

'We rushed him to an emergency vet. That's what took the time. The vet says it's probably an injury from a dog fight. He had to have stitches. Poor chap doesn't have a collar or a chip under his skin, so we couldn't contact anybody. He's out for the count because the vet gave him something to calm him down. A tranquilliser.'

'Good grief, poor thing. Can we tuck him away somewhere quiet? I mean, just while we're trying to throw this dinner party? He does look exactly like a dead dog—'

At that moment, a posse led by Dan Morgan burst into the room. 'Everything OK in here? We heard voices ...'

Simon caught Annie's eye and she bit her lip hard to keep from folding up with hysterical laughter. 'Don't worry, everything's fine. Everybody' — because everybody did indeed seem to be in the kitchen — 'this is Simon. Oh, and Lydia. Lydia, say hello to everybody.'

Lydia didn't even look up. She was still bent over the dog, stroking him gently, whispering in his ear.

'What's up with your dog?' asked Jennifer. 'Is he OK?'

'They don't have a dog,' said Heather and Sarah together.

'It's a stray,' Annie told them with a helpless shrug. 'They found him at the supermarket. He's not dead, by the way, just looks it. Anyway, sorry about the hold-up, everyone. Dinner will be ready any moment. Did I mention, we're doing this sort of ironic new thing where you order pizza and serve it on your best china with a green salad?'

Sarah looked at her sharply, but no one else showed the slightest flicker of interest in the status of their dinner. They were too busy talking dogs.

'We have a Golden,' Jennifer was saying. 'Great breed, but our Sunny is a little hyper. We could never get her crate-trained so now she just has her own room. I mean, the guest bedrooms just stand around empty all the time; we figured, why not use one of them? It's the one place in the house she never poops.'

'Goldens are OK, but you can't beat an American Indian dog,' declared Dan. 'Now, there's a thinking breed. Gutsy, too.'

'I've been told there *is* no such breed,' Drew interrupted. 'We looked into them, ourselves. They're supposed to be hypoallergenic, right? But most reputable dog breeders will tell you they're extinct.'

'Bullshit,' said Dan. 'You come over some time and see my dog, Blue. Then you try telling me the American Indian dog is extinct!'

'You're extinct, too, cowboy, but you don't know that either,' Heather's husband muttered under his breath. Annie, who was standing close enough to hear, gave him a startled look. He grinned back at her and closed one eye in a slow wink. She looked hastily away.

'Hush, everybody – he's coming round,' said Simon.

The dog huffed loudly a few times, then unpeeled his tongue from the hardwood floor and retracted it into his mouth. Annie pushed her way through the crowd and squatted down beside Lydia. 'Careful, now,' she told the child. 'He'll be confused and scared. He might try to bite.'

Lydia gave her a contemptuous look.

The dog, still woozy, began to scrabble at the floor with its front paws, presumably trying to stand up. Just then the doorbell rang, and to everyone's surprise and consternation, the dog began to howl. The hound of the Baskervilles probably never made half as much of a racket.

Showing remarkable aplomb, Simon hastened to the door to forestall any further ringing. Moments later, he came back into the kitchen, followed by a man in a red uniform bearing four large boxes of pizza.

'Looks like dinner is served,' Simon announced. 'And, um, does anybody have cash for a tip? He's telling me I can't put a gratuity on a credit card.'

The men reached into their pockets, pulled out their wallets, and began rummaging for dollar bills.

*

'You have to give me the recipe for those cheese balls,' Jennifer Miller trilled to Sarah as she and her husband left the house some time after midnight.

'You guys sure know how to throw a party,' Dan Morgan added, pumping Simon's hand and then surprising Annie by leaning in to kiss her cheek.

'We had a blast,' Heather chimed in, holding onto Rob's arm a little unsteadily. Rob merely grinned and winked his agreement.

Annie felt as if she were floating on a cloud as she, Simon and Sarah moved between the rooms, clearing up. Who cared if the evening had been a bit unconventional? Anybody could throw a perfect party, but it took an inspired few to throw an unforgettable one.

And then Simon walked into the kitchen with a silver tray. One look at his face and Annie knew that something was horribly wrong.

'The mini pies,' he announced, proffering the tray for inspection. 'They barely touched them.'

Annie glanced at the plate. 'That's not true,' she said staunchly. 'There were more than a dozen on the tray to begin with—'

'There was a baker's dozen,' Simon said. 'Four steak and kidney, four chicken and mushroom, five steak and pepper. That's how they come in the wholesale box.'

'OK, so thirteen ... That means, let's see,' she counted pies quickly, 'five people tried them.'

'Tried and *rejected* them.' He was pointing to a small stack of plates on the counter, unmistakably mounded with the remains of several pastries.

'Well, you have to realise that women often don't finish things they put on their plate because they're always dieting,' Annie said.

'They didn't leave a crumb of my cheese balls,' Sarah put in. Annie gave her a black look. 'I'm just *saying*.' Sarah shrugged and sauntered out of the room.

Annie went over to Simon where he stood staring at the nibbled-at leftover pies, his arms crossed over his chest.

'One pie,' he said hollowly. 'That's all they ate, between the lot of them.'

She slipped her hand into the crook of his arm. 'They're just not *used* to pies, that's all,' she said. 'It's ... it's a case of education.' She gave a little laugh, hoping to lighten the atmosphere. 'Maybe we should've started them off on pies stuffed with shrimp cheese balls.'

At that moment the dog, who'd been lying quietly in the corner of the kitchen looking dead again, scrambled to its feet and vomited violently. Annie grabbed a paper towel and set to work hastily to clean up the mess. The dog had obviously bolted down its food without bothering to chew it. She fervently hoped Simon hadn't noticed the distinctive fluted edges of pastry crust.

# Chapter Five

Annie woke the next morning with a horrible jolt, head throbbing, vision strangely sharp, filled with a vague sense of unease. Instinctively, she reached a hand out for Simon, for the sheer physical comfort of his warm body beside her, but he wasn't there.

Pulling on her dressing gown, she wandered downstairs, hoping Simon had put the kettle on. She was suffering the after-effects of too many of Sarah's Bloody Marys, and was sorely in need of a cup of tea. As she opened the kitchen door, the dog looked up from a mess of half-chewed pizza boxes, wagged its tail with joy, and came skittering over to her, leaving a trail of wee droplets on the stone tiles.

Of Simon there was no sign.

She was about to move on to the family room when she spotted a note on the counter. She grabbed it and read it at a glance. It was pithy, to say the least: 'Emergency call from the big boss in London. Had to go into work. Please feed and walk dog. Sorry about pizza boxes. Simon.'

'He works on Sundays?' Sarah sounded incredulous a little later as she sat at the counter eating a piece of dry toast.

'Not usually,' Annie said, wishing Sarah wouldn't talk quite so loudly.

'You know, sometimes you wonder if it's all worth it.' Sarah stood up, yanked her G-string (purple, this morning) into a more prominent position above her low-slung tartan pyjama bottoms, and made a sweeping gesture that took in the kitchen, the house, the yard, the whole of Annie's new world. 'The eighty-hour weeks, the long commute, the weekend hours. I mean, I know Simon's pretty high-powered, but wouldn't it be better to have a less demanding job and spend more time with his family?'

'He's really committed to his career,' Annie said defensively. 'ChefPro has given him a huge responsibility, and he takes it very seriously. You have to, if you have a top job.'

At that moment Lydia walked in, trailing the dog, which she'd christened Patches despite the fact that it was a solid yellowish colour without a single patch to speak of unless you counted the pink battle scar on its nose.

'Where's Daddy?' she asked. 'I've looked all over. He said we'd take Patches to the park.'

Annie paused in the act of refilling a bowl with water for the dog. 'Sorry, love, but Daddy had to go in to work. We can still go to the park, though.'

Lydia scowled and folded her arms over her chest. 'He always has to go to work,' she said, her voice wobbling. 'I never see him any more. All I ever see is stupid old *you!*' She ran from the room and back upstairs. In the distance, they heard a door slam.

Sarah raised her eyebrows at Annie. 'God,' she said, 'somebody's got an attitude.'

'You'd have an attitude too if your mum had died when you were five,' Annie retorted. 'And it's true. She doesn't get to see him very much.'

'Maybe so, but you shouldn't let her speak to you that way, Annie. It makes me want to give her a good ticking off. She has no *idea* how lucky she is to have you as a step-mum.'

'You're dead wrong. Turns out I'm not that great as a stepmum.'

'Rubbish, you're brilliant.'

'Ha, that's what you think. But then you weren't here the day I went shopping and left her at home. Or when I took the train to New York and couldn't get back in time to pick her up from school. Or when I forgot to go into the classroom for maths games. Or when I slept late and sent her to school without lunch. Or when I—'

'Annie. Stop. Those things don't *matter*. What matters is that you're trying your best, really throwing your back into it.'

At that moment the dog spat out a masticated mess that Annie recognised as the remains of her contact lens case. With a jolt it dawned on her that she'd slept in her lenses, which explained the uncannily clear vision and horribly dry eyes. Perhaps she'd go up to her room and have a little cry, in the interests of rehydrating the things. She would never peel them off her eyeballs, otherwise.

It was Monday morning, elevenish, and traffic was relatively light on the I-95. Sarah sat in silence beside Annie, watching her drive. As they approached the exit for the

Whitestone Bridge, Sarah said, 'I heard Simon come in last night. Must've been close to midnight. What time did he leave this morning?'

'Around six thirty.'

'God. No wonder I missed him. Will you tell him good-bye for me?'

'Of course. But you might just see him in the next couple of days, you know. I told him to look you up if he had time.'

'What – are you saying he's going to be in London?'

'Yip, that's right. He flew out earlier this morning.'

'Talk about sudden!'

'Yeah, well. He was in talks with the big boss all of yesterday. He's going to consult with the research people in the test kitchen. He has some serious concerns about the texture of the lower fat pastry.'

'Crikey. I never knew the pie business was this intense. So why don't you and Lydia come out too? Hop on a plane? Auntie Gladys would love to see you.'

Annie shook her head regretfully. 'God, I wish I could. But Simon and I agreed we can't take Lyddie out of school. She's just settling in and we don't want to risk whisking her off home on a flying visit and getting her all homesick. Besides, she has her first soccer practice this week, and Simon doesn't want her to miss it.'

'That's too bad,' said Sarah. After several minutes of silence, she stole a glance at Annie. 'Good party on Saturday night, wasn't it? Did that bloke try to feel you up? Your friend's husband?'

A car pulled sharply in front of Annie, narrowly missing

the nose of her minivan, and she jammed both hands down on the horn. The driver stuck his hand out of his window and gave her the finger. She hooted again. At this rate, she'd provoke a drive-by shooting.

'No, of course he didn't try to feel me up!' she said when the other car had darted off out of sight at high speed.

'Really? Well, he tried it on me.'

Annie glanced at Sarah, her mouth hanging open. 'Are you *sure*? Rob Gibson tried to feel you *up*?'

Sarah laughed. 'Sneaky bugger twanged my G-string when I squeezed by his chair to go to the loo.'

Annie shook her head. 'Oh God, poor Heather.'

'Oh, I don't think he means anything by it,' Sarah said. 'It's just *noblesse oblige* or something.'

Annie snorted. 'What kind of *noblesse* would that be?'

Sarah shrugged. 'You know. Chivalry. Gallantry. His way of acknowledging a single woman.'

Annie shook her head some more and lapsed back into silence. She didn't want to cast aspersions on Sarah's credibility, but she was having a difficult time believing Rob Gibson would twang a G-string right in front of his wife.

As they approached the airport, Sarah said, 'Look, don't park the car and come in. Just drop me at the door and bugger off home. I'll go and find a coffee.'

'No, I'll come in and see you off.'

'Please don't. Honestly. I sort of fancy being alone. I hate goodbyes, anyway, especially long-drawn-out ones. And you've got to get back anyway; that dog's probably tearing down the curtains by now.'

Annie nodded. 'Well, OK — if you're sure. I hate goodbyes

too. Did you have an OK time? I mean, it wasn't the south of France, but ...'

'Oh, it was great. That bloke at the dinner party did my ego no end of good.'

'I hope you didn't encourage him, Sarah. I think Heather has a bit of a hard time keeping him in line.'

'No, I don't mean him. The cowboy bloke.'

'Oh?'

'Yeah. We ended up having a bit of a snog in the loo.'

'Sarah! You're *impossible!*' Annie was surprised at how irritated and out of sorts she felt to hear this news. After all, what right did she have to feel proprietorial about a man just because he happened to have rescued her from a couple of amorous horses?

Sarah chuckled. 'You need to loosen up a bit, Annie. You're getting quite prim and proper. Soaking up the puritanical New England spirit like a bloody sponge.'

Annie grinned back at her. 'You're right, I should get a grip. Nothing wrong with a bit of snogging in the loo at a dinner party.'

Still, a certain sense of relief was mingled with the regret Annie felt as she watched her cousin drag her battered rucksack out of the boot of the car and stomp away in her Doc Martens.


'Let me see if I can make him smile,' Lydia said later that day, after school. She was sitting behind Patches, holding him still so that Annie could take a photo with the digital camera. She leaned in now and pulled the sides of his mouth up, exposing black lips and yellowing teeth.

'Maybe not,' said Annie. 'His owners might not recognise him if you mess with his face.'

'No, no, please! Take it like this!' Lydia insisted, pulling the dog's lips up even higher.

'Oh, all right, then. But he looks really weird.' Annie took a couple of shots and looked at them doubtfully in the viewfinder. 'Come on, let's see what we've got.'

She and Lydia spent a happy afternoon printing out posters advertising the fact that they'd found Patches, and then attaching them to lamp-posts around town.

'Is it usual to offer a reward to the owner for *claiming* a lost dog?' Jennifer Miller asked, stopping her Hummer to read the poster that Annie was stapling to the tree trunk at the end of their street.

'Maybe not,' said Annie, 'but these are special circumstances.' And she rolled her eyes towards the dog, who was lying on the pavement at the end of his leash, savaging a stick.

Jennifer smiled. 'Gotcha,' she said.

'We put an ad in the paper too,' Annie told her.

'Well, good luck to you!' Jennifer trilled as she pulled away.

Whenever the phone rang over the next few days, Annie ran to pick it up, half expecting it to be the dog's grateful owner. But mostly the calls were from Simon, sounding tense and stressed, telling her that he needed to stay in London for just a few more days.

Then one morning the phone rang and her caller ID told her that the Board of Education wanted to talk to her.

She picked up the receiver with sweaty palms. She'd

never been called up by a Board before, and frankly she felt a bit apprehensive.

But it was only Lydia's teacher, Miss Scofield. 'Mrs Har-Keeler? Melissa Scofield here.'

'I've been meaning to say, it's actually just "Keeler".'

'You dropped the double-barrel, huh? Look, there's no problem in the classroom. I'm just calling to ask if you could come in at ten o'clock on Friday for Lydia's show-and-tell slot? I don't usually ask the mom to come in, but in this case ...'

'Um – in which case?' asked Annie. 'I mean, of course I'll come in – but why, exactly?'

'Well, because Lydia doesn't speak.'

'Doesn't – speak? Well, I know she's a bit quiet, but—'

'Oh dear. I thought you were aware ... Are you saying Lydia used to speak at her old school?'

'Well, I don't really know, to be honest. I met her during the summer when she wasn't *at* school.'

There was a brief silence.

'You *met* her?' Miss Scofield's voice was faint.

'That's right. I'm her stepmum,' Annie explained. She had wanted to send the teacher a letter, outlining Lydia's home life, but Simon had thought it might be good if Lydia just went to school like any other child from a normal nuclear family. He'd thought that she might cope better if people treated her the same as all the other kids in the room. At her school in London, apparently, the whole staff had been very aware of her 'situation' – and Simon reckoned all the walking around on eggshells (they'd banned any talk of Mothering Sunday in her classroom, for example) hadn't actually been that helpful.

'Oh, I see,' said Miss Scofield in a speculative sort of way. 'Was it by any chance an acrimonious divorce? I only ask because I want to understand how Lydia's mind is working.'

'It wasn't a divorce,' Annie said. 'Her mum died in a boating accident.'

'Ah,' breathed Miss Scofield. 'That explains a lot.'

'So you want me to come in on Friday?'

'Yes, and could you please help her choose something to show the class, something special to her in some way.'

'No problem,' said Annie. 'I'll be there.'


'I don't *have* anything special,' Lydia said that afternoon, folding her arms over her chest and glowering at Annie. Suddenly she narrowed her eyes. 'Why is your hair *grey* today?'

Annie shook back her hair self-consciously. She'd just come from the salon where, in the 'when-in-Rome' spirit, she'd taken a deep breath and asked for highlights.

'It's not grey. It's ash blonde.' She felt a bit dubious about the colour herself, but the colourist had assured her it was a very popular shade. 'But never mind my hair. You *must* have something special. Everybody does. How about ... Oh, I don't know, a photo of Daddy?'

'I don't want to take a photo in. You have to pass it round the room, and people *breathe* on it.'

'Well, how about a toy, then? Your doll?'

'I'm not taking my doll.' Her lower lip was beginning to stick out mulishly.

'Why not?'

'They'd laugh at it.'

'Would they? I'm sure all the girls in your class have dolls.'

Lydia pulled a strand of hair into her mouth and began to chew ferociously. 'My doll is *bald*, and she has those holes in her head where the hair goes in.'

Annie shrugged. 'Fair enough. So – what about, I don't know, a book? Maybe we could read them a little story or something?'

Lydia got up and left the room without a word.


Annie phoned Henny on Thursday morning to see if she had any suggestions about what Lydia should take in. 'It has to be something that means a lot to her,' she said. 'But she won't take her doll, or even a book. Do your kids ever have show and tell?'

Henny's laugh reverberated down the phone. 'We took a kitten in when Lulu was in Reception. What a bloody disaster! The bloody thing got scared, scratched up a boy's arm, and hid behind the radiator. We couldn't get it out until the end of the day, when all the kids had gone home. It mewed piteously all morning. The teacher was ready to kill me.'

Annie paled at the thought. It had crossed her mind to ask if they could take in Patches. 'Right, so no live animals. Any other ideas?'

'Oh, the boys like to take in trading cards. Lulu once showed her grandad's stamp collection.'

'OK. So some kind of collection. That's a good idea. Except, dammit, we don't collect things. I mean, other than Simon's ties, or my shoes.'

'Take it easy, Annie. This isn't a boardroom presentation. It's show and tell. It really doesn't matter what she takes in. As long as she can say a couple of words about it ...'

'Well, no hope of that either,' Annie said. 'She's gone schtum at school. Won't talk at all. I have to go in and say her piece.'

'Oh. That's not so good.'

'I know. God, I wish I could wave a magic wand and make everything OK for her. If only she had a sidekick at school ... I mean, there's this girl, daughter of a woman I know, and they've had a play date, but when I asked Lyddie if she wanted to invite her back, she said she would rather not.'

They were both silent for a moment, thinking of the horrors of school without a sidekick.

'Is she homesick?'

'She doesn't say. She's not a big talker even at home.'

'Did she have a best friend in London?'

'I've heard some talk of a girl called Emily.'

'Maybe she could write her a letter or something?'

Annie perked up. 'Yes, that's an idea. But in the meantime, what about the bloody show and tell?'

'Leave the ball in her court,' Henny advised. 'She'll come up with something.'


In the end, Lydia said she'd take in a plastic teaspoon.

'A plastic *teaspoon*?' Annie asked, incredulous. It was Friday morning and they were running late.

'Yes, I keep this spoon in my backpack,' she said. 'I got it in the cafeteria.'

'And it's *special* to you?'

But Lydia only shrugged.

Annie turned up at the school at ten o'clock in some trepidation. The children were already sitting cross-legged on a brightly patterned mat in readiness for show and tell, and they all turned to stare as Miss Scofield greeted her. Lydia was seated in front of the class on a small chair. Her face was as white as chalk.

Right. Annie certainly wasn't going to let the little monsters scare Lydia. Or her, for that matter. She strode confidently into the room and sat down on the empty chair next to Lydia.

She looked over at Miss Scofield, a small, plump woman with shoulder-length brown hair. Miss Scofield gave her a firm nod.

Annie glanced back at the children. Their faces were up-turned in expectation. She cleared her throat. Gosh, there were a lot of them. 'Good morning, girls and boys. My name's Annie Keeler and I'm Lydia's stepmum. I've come to help her do show and tell.'

Several hands shot into the air. Annie smiled at a boy with ears like open car doors. 'Yes?'

'Why are you talking like Harry Potter?' the boy asked.

Annie went on smiling. 'Because I come from the same place Harry Potter does.'

'Hogwarts?' he asked excitedly.

'No, I meant England.' She nodded her head at a girl with pigtails.

'What's a stepmom?' the girl asked.

'Um.' Annie looked desperately over at Miss Scofield who raised her palms and gave a discreet shrug.

'A stepmum. Well, a stepmum didn't give birth to you, but she's married to your dad.'

'What's give birth?' another voice demanded.

'Where's her *real* mom?' somebody else chimed in.

Miss Scofield stood up and clapped her hands. 'Boys and girls,' she said ominously. 'We need to remember our manners. Do we shout out in class? No, we don't. We raise our hand. We wait to be called on. Think about the choices you're making, boys and girls. OK?' Then she sketched a bow in Annie's direction. 'Please go on, Mrs Keeler.'

Annie thought she wouldn't take any more questions just for the moment. 'Right, let's get on with the programme, shall we? So. Lydia has chosen to bring in a ... um ... well, a plastic spoon, as a matter of fact. Could you show them, Lydia?'

She held her breath, waiting for a huge eruption of laughter. Strangely, it didn't come. Lydia pulled the spoon down out of her sleeve and held it up with a hand that trembled slightly. Annie gave a sigh of relief. It wasn't just an ordinary plastic spoon, after all. Lydia had drawn a face on the round surface, and the handle had been transformed into a narrow dress, skinny legs, and shoes.

Hands shot up again. With her spoon, Lydia pointed at Hailey Gibson. 'Where did you get the spoon?' Hailey asked.

Lydia leaned over and whispered in Annie's ear, 'Cafeteria.'

'She got it at the cafeteria,' Annie reported.

Lydia selected Courtney Phelps next. 'What's its name?' Courtney asked.

'Doesn't have one,' Lydia hissed, her hand shielding her mouth, perhaps in case anybody in the audience could lip-read.

Annie nodded. 'She hasn't named the spoon just yet. She's still thinking about it.'

'Why is it sad?' somebody else called out.

The spoon's expression was miserable, it had to be said. Its mouth was an upside-down U, and there was even a tear trickling down next to its nose.

Lydia shrugged and stuffed the spoon up her sleeve again.

'Let's take one last question,' said Miss Scofield.

Annie glanced at Lydia, but her head was down, her hair falling like a curtain across her face. Hastily, Annie pointed at a boy who was stretching his hand as far into the air as it would go.

'Isn't it stealing to take a spoon from the cafeteria?' he asked triumphantly.

'Of course it's not,' snapped Annie. 'It's a plastic spoon. Disposable. I bet you throw away two or three of them every day.'

'No, I don't,' said the boy. 'I eat a packed lunch from home and I bring my own *fork*.'

Suddenly Lydia tapped Annie on the shoulder, then whispered in her ear, 'Tell him I got it out of the bin.'

'For your information, she says she got it out of the rubbish bin,' Annie reported.

'She means the garbage,' somebody cried.

'Eeeewwww!!'

'Gross!'

'Yech.'

Miss Scofield was on her feet, clapping as hard as she could. It wasn't applause. 'That's enough, boys and girls. Let's say thank you to Mrs Keeler for coming in.'

As they chorused a thank you, Annie ruffled Lydia's hair, but the child wouldn't look up and meet her eye.

# Chapter Six

'Your hair – it's different,' Simon remarked on Friday night as he rifled through Annie's purse looking for cash so he could tip the taxi driver, all the while fending off Patches, who was overjoyed to see him.

'Yes, I had highlights. You know, it's virtually the law around here; you have to be blonde.'

'Ah, I see. It's – yes, very nice. But I think I prefer your natural colour.'

'You like brown? Plain brown?'

He took a strand of her hair in his hand and considered it. 'It wasn't plain,' he said. Then he pulled her into his arms. 'I missed you,' he murmured against her lips. 'It's been a *long* five days.'

'I missed you too. It's weird in this place without you.'

But the romantic mood didn't last long. By the time Simon had dragged his suitcase upstairs, it had burned off like morning fog.

'I thought that damn dog was sleeping in the kitchen.' Simon jerked his chin at the laundry basket in the corner, now doing duty as a dog's basket.

'Oh, he howls and scratches the door if you leave him in

the kitchen,' Annie explained. 'As soon as that tranquilliser wore off, he started getting very exacting about house rules. He reckons the kitchen is no place for a dog to sleep.'

'In that case, the sooner we find his owner, the better.' At the tone of Simon's voice, Patches – still capering about with excitement – slunk back to his corner and settled down.

'Well, we're trying. But I thought you liked dogs. I mean, you went to all that trouble to rescue him.'

'Yes, I like dogs, but I wouldn't have gone out and chosen a . . . a cringing yellow cur. I brought him home for Lyddie's sake.'

'Gosh, you sound – tired,' Annie said, flinching at his tone of voice. 'Was the flight OK?'

Simon shrugged as he twiddled with the combination lock on his suitcase. 'Oh, it was fine – but I'm pretty knackered. It's been one bloody meeting after another for days.' He shook his head and with a visible effort tried to switch gears. 'But how are you? And how's Lyddie been?'

He had been into Lydia's room already. Annie had glanced in on him standing there, lit up by the night light, gazing down at the top of his daughter's head with a rather vulnerable expression on his face. She had walked away quickly, not wanting to intrude on the moment.

'Oh, she's been fine! Very helpful with Patches. You know it's her first football – I mean, soccer game tomorrow, right?'

She said this a little anxiously. It wasn't an exaggeration to say that Lydia was actively dreading this first game. The child had attended one practice under protest, and Annie had let her skip the second one when she said her tummy hurt. The stomach ache had disappeared miraculously once the threat of soccer practice went away, but that was going to be their little secret. In any event, Annie thought that two practices a week was a little intense for seven-year-olds.

Simon's strained-looking face lit up. 'Her first game? Great! I'm really looking forward to it!'

'I wouldn't get too excited,' Annie said. 'She doesn't seem all that keen on playing, as a matter of fact.'

'She's probably a bit nervous. Perfectly normal to be nervous your first time out.'

'Maybe, but I'm just not sure soccer is going to be her thing.'

His face stiffened. 'Let's just wait and see, shall we? I reckon being part of a team will be really good for her. Help her make friends and build up her confidence.'

'I think you only make friends and build up your confidence if you're actually any *good* at the sport involved,' Annie muttered. She spoke from personal experience, but she wasn't about to treat him to anecdotes about her brief career in hockey, that was for sure.

'What did you say?'

'Oh, nothing.'

He looked at her with narrowed eyes for a moment. 'All right. I'm going to hop in the shower now.'

He disappeared into the en suite bathroom, then stuck his head back around the corner. 'Don't feel you have to wait up any more. It's late.'

Annie looked across the room and met the dog's eye. Curled up in the basket again, he looked strangely downcast.

Brooding on the idea that he was a cringing yellow cur, no doubt.

With a sigh, Annie climbed between the sheets, but when she heard the shower running, she got out of bed, shrugged off her nightie, and tiptoed towards the bathroom. She would take him by surprise in the shower; see if he could keep up his bad mood while she lathered his back!

He didn't notice when she slid the frosted glass door open. He was standing beneath the powerful jet with his eyes closed, hands hanging at his sides, his head raised to receive the needles of water directly on his face. The sound must be drumming in his ears like the Niagara Falls, drowning out everything but his thoughts.

She stood and stared. Something about his attitude was deeply disturbing. He looked like a man trying to wash away some terrible misfortune. He looked like a man who needed to be alone.

She took a deep breath and stepped back quietly, on her way out. He need never know she'd seen him like that, in such an attitude of despair.

But at that moment he turned his head and opened his eyes. 'Annie?'

'I — I was just using the loo,' she said quickly, covering her bare breasts with her arms. 'Thought I'd ... you know, take a peek at you before heading back to bed.' Oh, very good, Annie. Now he had this attractive image of her perched naked on the throne, perhaps ogling him through the frosted door before giving in to her peeping Tom impulses.

He frowned for a moment, his expression bleak. Then, in an instant, his face cleared, his eyes lit up, his mouth twitched, and she could almost believe she'd imagined the grim look in his eyes. 'Heading back to bed?' He held out a dripping arm to her, the hairs all flattened against his skin. 'Not bloody likely. Come on in, the water's lovely.'

With a fair imitation of a surprised laugh, she allowed him to pull her into the spray. It *was* lovely in the shower, all steamy and warm. Quite interesting, too. Kissing, for example, presented a bit of a challenge because the shower-head was set to such a high pressure that if you turned your head the wrong way, the water could catch a lip and peel it right away from your teeth. Or—

'Ouch!' Simon yelped as Annie snapped shut her mouth and leapt away from him, coughing and spluttering. 'God, I think you bit my tongue!'

'Did I? Oh no! Sorry,' she coughed. 'Water ... went straight up my nose. Down my throat, too. Felt like I was drowning. Can you turn the shower to a softer setting?'

Simon was trying to look at his tongue in the shaving mirror. 'It's only a nick,' he said with evident relief. 'Tongues are oversensitive, apparently. I thought you'd bitten a chunk out of me. A softer setting. Let's see, now.' He fiddled around a bit and managed to control the flow. Gratefully, she moved back into his wet embrace, telling herself that she didn't feel squeamish about kissing someone with a bleeding tongue. Just as they had worked up a bit of a lather between them, Annie felt a soft, brushing sensation against the backs of her knees. She had no idea how Simon was managing to reach down there, not with his hands where they were right now. Suddenly, something sharp and distinctly outside her idea of foreplay dug into her back at waist height.

She swirled round with a horrified yell.

'Oh! For God's sake! It's the bloody dog.' Patches, hair plastered down on his muzzle so that his head looked too small for his body, took this is a shout of encouragement. He jumped up a second time, this time catching her on the bare stomach with his claws. He must have nosed open the sliding glass door. 'Aaargh! Get him *out* of here.'

With admirable speed, Simon nipped out of the shower, slung a towel around his waist, grabbed the dog by his collar, and dragged him away from the scene. Annie heard the thump of the bathroom door closing, and he was back.

Right. Somehow they seemed to have taken two steps back and were obliged to start all over again. At this rate, they'd drain all the hot water before they got to the crux of the matter.

But hello, things were actually progressing with a bit of speed now. Gosh, that was rather nice. Mmm. Yes, the water was definitely at just the right pressure now.

Abruptly, they sprang apart as a cacophony erupted in the bedroom: muffled crashing and clanging sounds mingled with the high-decibel frenzy of a dog barking at the top of his vocal range.

'*Bloody* animal!' Simon dashed out of the shower again, this time not pausing for a towel. Annie followed hot on his heels, wondering how on earth a dog could actually *make* so much noise.

The state of the bedroom indicated exactly how. Patches, obviously distressed at being shut out of the fun, had upturned the round table in the corner (the crashing), which held a decorative pewter wash basin and pitcher (the clanging), barking like mad all the while. The moment his new owners burst out of the bathroom, he fell silent, flattened his ears in an ingratiating way, and wagged his tail.

'Oh, for God's *sake*,' said Simon, setting the table back on its legs. 'If we throw him out of the room altogether he'll probably go ballistic and wake up Lyddie.'

Annie was shivering now. Wet and bedraggled, she stepped into the walk-in closet and retrieved her dressing gown.

'Maybe we should just go to bed,' she said, throwing a towel in Simon's direction. 'My skin's getting all wrinkly.'

'Yeah, mine too.' Simon began drying himself vigorously. 'My parents' dogs don't behave this way,' he said after a moment. 'They just fetch sticks and chase rabbits and lie about the place asleep, like animal skins. They don't *bother* anybody.'

Simon's parents lived on the outskirts of Carlisle in Cumbria, in a substantial country house set among fields. His dad was a doctor, and his mother made a career of being flamboyant and arty. When Simon drove Annie up to meet them, she was charmed by the easy, bucolic rhythm of their life – a fire in the grate every night, wine glasses on the table, dogs all over the place, Simon's mum's glazed pots adorning every surface, a succession of casual dinner parties with red-faced neighbours. In retrospect, the dogs had been very self-effacing. She'd only noticed them as a sort of background motif. Not once had any one of them forced its way into a shower cubicle and jumped all over her.

'I suppose he feels all unsettled, poor thing,' Annie said, glancing at Patches. He looked up at her with mournful eyes and wriggled his behind in an ingratiating way. 'You're a bad boy,' she told him severely. He wagged his entire body at her. 'Oh, Lord,' she said, turning to Simon. 'I think we left the shower on.'

When she came out of the bathroom after turning off the tepid water, Simon was already under the covers. She slipped off her dressing gown and climbed in beside him, nuzzling up against him.

'Annie,' he said, inching away from her, 'it's nearly one in the morning and I'm knackered. Let's just give it up as a bad job, shall we?'

Annie got out of bed the next morning with a feeling of foreboding. Simon was up already, in the kitchen making tea and reading the *New York Times*, now delivered daily. He was humming as Annie drifted downstairs in her dressing gown. *Humming!* After all his doom and gloom last night!

'You sound happy,' Annie said.

'Here, have some tea.' Simon pushed a mug towards her. 'I'm planning to go outside and kick the ball around with Lydia when she comes down. Get her warmed up for the game a bit.'

'Hmmph. You'll be lucky,' Annie said, but so low that he didn't hear.

Even when Simon saw Lydia's fed-up face as she trailed downstairs in an enormous white T-shirt that came down to her knees, almost entirely hiding her red shorts, he wasn't downcast.

'How about some porridge to line your tummy?' he suggested. 'You need some decent fuel if you're going to crush your opponents to smithereens.'

'It's not really about crushing your opponents,' Annie said quickly, seeing sheer fright take over from long-suffering misery on Lydia's face. 'You know, at this level they don't even keep score. No goalies. No positions. No offside rules. It's just about getting out there and having fun.'

'Ah, that's what they tell you,' Simon said, sprinkling sugar on Lydia's porridge. 'But it's *always* about crushing your opponents. Here, get this down you and we'll go outside and practise passing.'

Lydia slumped down over her bowl, hair trailing in the cereal. She ate so slowly that Simon was pacing the kitchen floor by the time she was ready to go out with him.

Ten minutes later, they came trooping back inside.

'That was quick,' observed Annie.

'No point tiring her out before the game,' Simon replied, listening to the distant thump of Lydia stomping her way back upstairs. He looked a lot less enthusiastic and a lot more thoughtful than he had earlier.

'Simon, do you really think we should insist on the soccer?' she asked, sensing that this might be a good time to press her point home. 'I mean, given how much she seems to hate it?'

Simon folded his arms across his chest and propped himself on a bar stool. His face was serious. 'Annie, she needs to get out of the house. She needs to be busy and do something outdoorsy. Every week there's some new article in the paper saying that kids today aren't getting enough exercise. Lyddie spends far too much time holed up in her room; it can't be good for her health. Besides, how do we know she hates it? She's never even played a game.'

'Would – would Beth have wanted her to play soccer?'

Simon froze for a fraction of a second. Then he shrugged. 'I'm not sure, to be honest,' he said slowly. 'Lyddie was only five when ... The whole sport thing hadn't come up, at that stage. But, you know what, that was *then* and this is now. Lydia needs something to get her blood pumping. Don't you think?'

An image of Lydia's pale, drooping face popped into Annie's mind. She found herself nodding. 'OK,' she said. 'You have a point. The soccer might sort of energise her, I suppose. Hey, guess what? I think this is what they call "tough love" in the parenting books.'

Over at the middle school field, they found Heather already set up on a folding chair, holding a giant Styrofoam mug of coffee and reading *People* magazine.

'Too bad Rob isn't here,' Heather said. 'He's on one of his eternal business trips.'

Annie hadn't thought to bring chairs, so she and Simon were obliged to stand on the sidelines, looking unduly prominent.

After the first few minutes, though, Heather was on her feet too. It turned out that Hailey had the killer instinct on the soccer field. Annie found herself screaming wild encouragement alongside Heather as the little girl tackled child after child on the blue team, stealing the ball from between their feet with consummate ease, and running it down the length of the field with a turn of speed that left everyone else eating dust, one elbow at the ready in case anyone dared challenge her. Nobody did. In the first ten minutes she scored three goals.

Lydia had something of a different game plan, naturally.

'She's obviously playing defence,' Simon said staunchly. She could be seen at the inactive end of the field, wandering about near the goal posts, kicking at clumps of grass, squatting down to pick dandelions, sucking her hair (possibly there was still some cereal in it), and at one stage lying on her back, apparently gazing at the sky.

It was while she was sky-gazing that a member of the blue team managed to wrestle the ball off Hailey and give it a huge kick that sent it flying unimpeded towards Lydia's end of the field.

'Lydia, get up!' yelled Simon. 'Get up and get ready! Clear the goal! Come on, come on, get *up*!'

Lydia must have heard her father's desperate cry. She got to her feet in a leisurely fashion, brushing blades of grass from her T-shirt. A bit of a titter broke out among the spectators. As she adjusted her clothing, she happened to glance at the ball, still rolling towards the goal, but beginning to lose steam. Then she looked at the pack of girls stampeding towards her, all intent on the ball.

Unhurriedly, she walked up to the ball, got behind it, and gave it a tentative kick. Her cleats seemed to catch on the top of the ball, and her legs shot out from under her. Down she went onto the turf again, but all of a sudden she seemed consumed with a sense of urgency. She sprang back to her feet, glanced in a panicky way over her shoulder, and kicked inexpertly at the ball a second time. Her toe caught it with just enough impetus to send it rolling slowly towards the goal post. It trickled into the net just as the pack caught up to her.

It was a goal. Definitely a goal.

Annie punched the air in triumph, and turned to hug Heather, who didn't look as excited as Annie would have expected.

Simon was doubled over, hands in his hair.

'Own goal!' shouted the umpire, and the titter erupted into a generalised guffaw.

'Oh,' said Annie. '*Own* goal. I suppose that's not good.'

'Not so much,' said Heather, pressing her lips together.

'Well, she had the right instincts, wanting to score,' Simon said, recovering his composure with visible effort. 'I just need to spend some time explaining the rules to her. Maybe we can watch a couple of Premier League games together. She's bound to get the hang of it.'

'You're right,' said Heather, a shade too heartily. 'This is her first game. So she made a mistake? We all make mistakes. She'll be unrecognisable by the end of the season, you'll see.'

'You don't think we should just let her give it up?' Annie asked.

'What, tell her that now we've seen her play we agree she's a no-hoper?' Simon asked, incredulous.

'He's right,' Heather said. 'If you take a fall, the worst thing you can do is walk away. Got to get back up on that horse again.'

Gosh, Annie thought, being a parent was a pretty brutal business. All her instincts were telling her to grab Lydia off the field, whisk her away home, throw the ugly soccer clothes into the rubbish bin, and tell the child that she never had to go back. Obviously, she had a lot to learn.

135

# Chapter Seven

If Saturday's soccer game was a bit of a downer, Sunday was going to be great — because Annie had decided to surprise Simon with a family day on a rented sailing boat.

Sarah had planted the seed of the idea in her mind, when she'd asked whether Simon was doing any sailing.

Sailing had been a huge part of Simon's life when he was married to Beth. Annie knew this because she'd seen the photos in the albums he kept in his underwear drawer.

Boats were the backdrop of every second photo she looked at. Simon and a smiling, freckled Beth seemed to have spent their honeymoon sailing. They seemed to have entered sailing races together. They seemed to have drunk a lot of champagne while sitting on top of white hulls. If there was a picture of them standing next to a car, then the car was hooked up by a tow bar to some kind of boat on a trailer. And all the while, they seemed to have been deliriously happy. Simon didn't look bleak and brooding in a single one of the pictures.

The only pictures without a nautical theme were those of Lydia; Lydia in nappies, lying asleep in a white crib, plump and bald; or toddling around the London house half-dressed, grinning over her dimpled shoulder in delight at whoever was taking the snapshots.

The photos screamed the truth. Sailing hadn't just been a huge part of Simon's life. Sailing had *been* his life. She suspected he'd given it up on her account. It was true she'd never expressed much interest in being out on the water, but she was game for anything. He should have known that!

Why exactly Annie wanted the sailing expedition to be a surprise, she wasn't sure, but she kept picturing Simon's face as he stepped out of the car and first caught sight of the boat. He'd be bowled over, delighted, touched, enthusiastic as a little boy. He'd turn to her and kiss her hard – a big, sloppy smooch that would make Lydia groan and roll her eyes. Then he'd help her and Lydia on board, and they'd sail off into the sunshine with Simon at the steering wheel – or whatever it was called. She could hardly wait.

Not having the slightest idea of how to go about renting a boat, she had enlisted the help of Heather and her neighbour, Jennifer Miller, both of whom, as it turned out, knew people with boats. After a few false starts, Jennifer came up with the name of an acquaintance who, for a staggering fee, was willing to let the Keelers use his boat, which he kept at the Norbury Yacht Club.

'It looks awfully big,' said Annie in sudden fear as she, Jennifer, and the boat-owner's wife stood on a wooden pier looking at the tethered craft. 'I hope Simon knows how to handle it.'

'If he can't handle this boat then he's no sailor,' declared the owner's wife. 'In the right conditions, my thirteen-year-old daughter can take her out single-handed.'

Annie felt a bit miffed. 'He's an excellent sailor,' she countered. 'I just don't know a lot about boats, that's all. This one seems more like a ship. But OK, we'll take it.'

Sunday morning dawned cloudy and humid; not the kind of weather she'd been hoping for, but at least it wasn't raining.

Over breakfast, Annie said casually, 'I promised Lydia we'd drive around and take a look at the autumn colours today.'

With a piece of toast halfway to her mouth, Lydia said, 'No, you didn't! I said could we go to the park with Patches, and you said—'

Annie gave Lydia a big, fake smile. '*Remember* what I said?' She winked meaningfully and jerked her head at Simon, who was lost behind newspaper and showed no signs of listening.

She and Lydia had discussed going out on the boat. Originally, she'd wanted the trip to be a surprise for Lydia too, but in the end she'd decided not to risk finding out, at the last moment, that Lydia had some sort of phobia about going on the water.

'Oh, I'm not scared of sailing,' Lydia had told her. 'It's just sort of boring. But I'll go.'

'Oh yes. Right,' Lydia said now, visibly remembering about the surprise.

'So, I thought we'd leave at about ten and maybe pick up some lunch along the way? It could be chilly so we'd better bring sweatshirts.'

'Hmmm?' Simon glanced around the paper at her, giving

a glimpse of weekend stubble and bed-head. She wanted to go over, sit on his lap, and run her fingers through his tousled hair – but Lydia wouldn't like it.

'We're going out,' she said loudly. 'A drive into the country.'

'OK,' he shrugged, looking faintly mystified. 'Fine by me.'

'I might as well drive,' she added. 'It's a bit of a tricky route.'

'A tricky route?' he asked. 'Where exactly are we going?'

'To look at the leaves. The famous New England autumn foliage. People drive all the way from New York city to see it – and I happen to know where the best trees are.'

'Good grief, do you always take your foliage so seriously?' he teased.

'Always,' she said, grinning back. Already, he was beginning to look less distracted – and more like the Simon of old.

'Hurry up and eat, Lydia!' Annie chivvied. 'We need to get going. Oh, and grab your trainers. Maybe a jacket too, in case it cools down. I've got the camera.'

About half an hour later, as they pulled into the unobtrusive driveway of the tucked-away club, Simon looked around in mild confusion. 'Aren't we going up north to see the leaves?' he asked. 'What's this place?' He obviously hadn't noticed the tiny Norbury Yacht Club sign, discreetly engraved in stone.

'Just wait, you'll see,' Annie told him, slowing down as

she approached a gate. 'Annie Keeler,' she told the man in the glass booth. He consulted a clipboard, made a laborious notation, and lifted the boom.

As they pulled into the car park, Lydia cried, 'Look at all the masts!'

Simon grabbed Annie's arm. 'What's going on?' he asked urgently.

She smiled a Mona Lisa smile. 'Come with me,' she said.

She walked confidently along the marina to the place where their vessel was berthed. The boat wallowed in the water, waiting for them, already stocked with borrowed life jackets and a cool box of picnic fare that she'd stowed on board on Friday: juice, champagne, cheese, smoked salmon, thin-sliced roast chicken, even a jar of peanut butter for Lydia. She'd made a loaf of bread overnight in the bread machine, and it was wrapped in a dish towel in the boot of the car, along with a bag full of towels, swimsuits, sunscreen and flip-flops – just in case the mercury rose. She'd packed the car that morning while Simon and Lydia were still asleep.

'This is our boat for the day,' Annie announced, waving her arms in a grand gesture.

For a moment, Simon said nothing at all.

Well, clearly he was speechless. That was all right – just as long as he was speechless with joy.

But when he turned to look at her, she knew right away that joy had nothing to do with whatever he was feeling.

'I can't believe you did this,' he said at last. She sensed by the tone of his voice that he was working hard to control some quite violent emotion. 'I'm sorry, Annie. I'm not going sailing on some rented boat on a morning so still you couldn't launch a bloody kite. You really know nothing at *all* about sailing, do you?'

Annie blinked hard. 'But the wind might pick up,' she said. 'And isn't there a motor on this thing?'

'You think I want to motor around on a glassy pond like some sort of ... Come on, Annie, let's just go home.'

Suddenly, Lydia raised her voice. 'Daddy, you're *mean*,' she said, her face clenched in reproach. 'You're hurting Annie's *feelings*. She was just trying to give you a nice surprise.'

Annie gulped and looked at Simon. His face had gone pale and still. For a couple of heartbeats, nobody moved. It seemed to Annie that none of them even breathed.

Then Simon put his hand on Lydia's shoulder. 'You're right,' he said. 'That was pretty uncivilised. I'm sorry.'

'Annie's the one you need to say sorry to,' Lydia told him, shrugging off his hand.

He pressed his lips together and turned to Annie. 'Sorry.' He sounded sheepish and sincere. 'I don't know what came over me. I can see you've gone to a lot of trouble. But if it's all the same to you, I'd really rather not go out on this thing. Can we just look at autumn leaves instead?'

Annie shrugged and managed a smile. 'OK,' she said. 'Mrs Van Hausen who owns the boat would be pretty miffed to hear you write it off that way.'

Simon cast a critical glance at the rejected vessel. 'It's built for stability, not for speed. I suppose they take the family out for little jaunts.' He spoke with such disdain for that sort of sailing that she cringed inwardly. She'd really misjudged his whole attitude to the sport; hadn't realised for a moment that pottering around with his family on board a nice safe boat would be absolutely abhorrent to him.

As Simon lugged the cool box off the boat, he suddenly said, 'I don't miss sailing, you know. It's all over and done with, for me. I'm quite happy to be a landlubber these days.'

Annie shrugged her scepticism. He took her by the shoulder and looked deep into her eyes. 'Annie, you need to believe this. I'm not hankering to go back out there.' He gestured at the smooth grey waters of the Sound. 'I'm happy the way we are. That was then, and this is now. I want to live in the now.'

And, suddenly, she believed him.

Against all odds, they ended up having a rather wonderful day; the sort of day that becomes a landmark in family history. They drove up north, where the leaves were indeed turning crimson, orange and yellow in a spectacular way. By accident, they stumbled on a pick-your-own apple farm and spent a happy half-hour watching Lydia fill bags with fruit.

'What on earth will we do with all these apples?' Annie asked, as Lydia put a fourth laden bag into the handcart Simon was pushing.

'God knows,' said Simon. 'But look at her face.'

And they stood together with their arms entwined, just watching Lydia's pleasure as if it were a spectator sport.

Hungry for something more substantial than apples, they drove on to a charming little waterfront town. They ate their picnic lunch barefoot on a rocky outcrop at the beach, gazing over the tranquil waters of Long Island Sound.

Stealing glances at Simon's thoughtful profile, Annie realised that he might never again look like the happy-go-lucky young man in the photos with Beth. And yet his face had more depth to it now.

He must have felt her eyes on him. He turned his head and looked directly at her, his pupils dilating slightly as if to take her in all the better.

'Happy?' he asked.

She nodded, speechless.


'Annie? Annie, guess what?' Heather's voice sang out over the phone one morning in triumph. 'I've just been over at the barn and — you won't believe it — but a space has opened up in Hailey's Wednesday class! The Moretons are leaving town, relocating to Dubai for a couple of years, all kind of sudden. So there's a slot for Lydia!'

Annie scratched her head, straining to bring her mind to bear on whatever it was Heather was babbling about so excitedly. 'I'm sorry, a what?'

'A slot! In the Wednesday class!'

'You mean a riding class?'

Heather groaned audibly. 'Yeah, that's it! A freaking riding class! But you have to move quickly, like *now*, because it's not going to last long. I told them you'd be calling, but they won't hold the space for more than a couple of hours. There must be ten families lined up to snatch it out from under you.'

'I— *what?*'

'Yeah, it could get ugly. There's a waiting list. I put Hailey on it right before kindergarten and she only got in halfway through first grade. These slots only come up once in a while. It's more competitive than country club membership, or getting a mooring for your boat at Norbury Harbor. You have to jump on it! Play your cards right and she could be riding this afternoon!'

Annie's heart began to pound with excitement. 'Oh God, Lydia would be thrilled, wouldn't she? Have you got the phone number?'

Heather rattled off a number, and then repeated it more slowly at Annie's request. 'Ask for Mrs Winter,' Heather instructed. 'She's a piece of work, but she owes me.' Annie wrote down the details and thanked Heather profusely. By now, it was beginning to seem to her that getting Lydia into the riding class had been her most fervent ambition ever since they'd arrived in Norbury.

As she hung up, she remembered that Simon wasn't actually that keen on Lydia riding at all.

But surely he'd think differently if she told him the circumstances? How the Moretons had left unexpectedly for Dubai, how ten other families were circling, how this was possibly their last chance to get Lyddie on a horse until she was a teenager? She was sure he'd be excited about the opportunity, but she'd better check in with him before signing Lydia up, just to be on the safe side.

Taking a deep breath, she punched out the number of his mobile phone.

The phone rang only once before Simon picked up.

'Simon? Oh, hi. I was just calling to—'

'Annie, is it an emergency?' Simon's voice was strangely hushed.

'No, but—'

'OK, because I'm in a meeting. Quite an important one. Can we talk later?'

'But it's about Lyddie—'

'I trust you absolutely to handle anything in that department.' He really didn't sound himself at all; very muted and brisk. Not particularly loving.

'Really? You trust me *absolutely*?'

'Of course! Look, I'm sorry but I really have to go now.' And he hung up on her.

Annie stared at the phone for a moment. She thought about calling him again and insisting on getting his opinion, but something in his tone gave her pause.

He was busy, clearly. Strategising about selling pies to the American market was a highly stressful job. Pies-as-fast-food was a foreign concept to American culture, and ChefPro was taking a huge leap of faith with this whole project. She knew that. She and Simon had talked about it often. Obviously, he was tense. Obviously, he hadn't cut her off on the phone just because he didn't feel like speaking to her. Of course he wanted to speak to her. He loved her, after all. He'd married her, hadn't he? He'd stood up in a register office and proclaimed his desire to be shackled in a monogamous bond to Annie Harleigh for the rest of his life. He'd done it of his own free will. The whole thing had been his idea in the first place! She couldn't have *been* more surprised when he'd popped the question. In fact, she'd been just about incredulous.

He'd proposed to her on a Wednesday afternoon during the lunch break. He'd taken her to a small restaurant on Islington Green, sat her down at a table, waved a waiter away, extracted an envelope from his briefcase and burst out, 'Have you ever given any thought to living in America?'

When she gaped wordlessly back at him, displaying a half-chewed mouthful of bread, he put the envelope down, raked his fingers through his hair, and muttered, 'God, Simon Keeler, try that again.'

Then he leaned across the table, disengaged her hand from her bread roll, took it in his own, and said urgently, 'I can't change my plans, Annie. Everything's in motion. The whole American pie push is my idea. It can't go forward without me. I've found renters for my house, told Maria to look for something else. But, the thing is, I can't let you go. I just can't. It's mad, I know, but would you consider, sort of, marrying me?'

Annie chewed and swallowed. A pulse was beating in her throat, and she put her hand over the place in case it was throbbing visibly. But she couldn't speak.

'Connecticut's a fantastic place,' he went on, impatiently declining a menu. 'They say the sky is blue most days, even in winter. And the town I'm thinking of is close to New York, so we'd be able to go in to the city for theatre and museums and shopping. The summers are really hot, and Norbury has its own beach. Plus the schools are brilliant, a really great environment for Lydia. I don't know how they do it, but they churn out kids with enough self-confidence to run for president by the time they're twelve. Look, I know it would be a sacrifice,' he added hastily. 'You'd have to give up your job, and I'm not sure we'd be able to wangle papers for you to work over there. So – well, I know I haven't got a hope in hell, but I'm asking you anyway.'

'What's in the envelope?' she rasped, ignoring the waiter at her elbow.

'Forms for my US work visa. Here, have a look.' He took some papers out and spread them on the table. 'I . . . I could put you down as my fiancée. That way they could get going on the paperwork. And we could get married before we go. Maybe in August? I mean, that's if you want to. I don't even know if you want to, but I feel as if maybe you do. Because I do. Very much. I can't imagine going off right now and never seeing you again. Or . . . or trying to have a long-distance relationship. Weekends here and there. Phone sex. I don't know if I could bear it.'

Phone sex? Golly, she didn't even know how to do that. Tears sprang to her eyes. 'Are you serious?'

'Deadly serious. Annie, I think I knew I loved you when I saw you that first time in Greece. I just sort of *recognised* you, in some weird way. I feel as if I've known you for ever.'

'I feel the same,' she whispered back, but he didn't hear her. He was delving in the envelope again, almost feverishly.

'Here, I have some photos of Norbury – you know, the town I'm going to live in. Look, this is the beach – it's right on Long Island Sound. And this is one of the elementary schools. And this is, let's see, I think it's a pond in the park. They skate on it in winter, apparently, and play ice hockey. Oh, and this is a typical house. They're all made of wood, with massive gardens—'

147

'Are these people taking the piss?' a low but carrying voice suddenly asked. Both of them became aware for the first time of a man in a white hat looming over their table. 'When are they going to order their effing food? We're trying to turn tables over here.'

Annie froze in horror.

'It's not *my* fault, mate,' another voice hissed back. 'I keep showing them the bloody menu but they won't look at it.'

'Oh God, I think we'd better order,' said Annie. 'I'll have the chicken. Any chicken. And yes, I'll marry you, Simon. Of course I will.'

Oblivious of the disgruntled chef and waiter, Simon stood up, pulled Annie to her feet, and kissed her across the table in a clatter of knives and forks.

Back then, Simon always had time for her if she called him at work. He never cut her off, never spoke to her curtly.

Annie found a tissue and blew her nose. Married life was different, obviously. Certain things were taken for granted, certain niceties could be dispensed with. It didn't mean that the way he felt about her had changed in any way.

Since it was up to her, she decided she would phone Mrs Winter at the barn. Lydia was bound to like riding lessons a lot more than she liked soccer. (So *there*, Simon.)

In about five minutes, she had secured the coveted spot.

Later that day, Annie stood on the pavement outside Bradley Elementary, holding a bag from Fairfield County Leisure, and grinning idiotically.

Waving at Lydia as she emerged from the building, she

pumped her arms up and down in a pantomime of running, but Lydia frowned, dropped her eyes, and came forward at her usual snail's pace.

'Lyddie! Hurry, hurry! Come and see what I have in this bag for you!'

Lydia's head shot up in surprise, and she did speed up ever so slightly.

'Here,' said Annie, thrusting the bag at her, 'take a peek.'

Lydia glanced around at the other children; some were watching curiously. She hesitated a moment, then reached into the bag and pulled out the contents.

'Oh, thanks,' she mumbled. 'A pair of trousers.'

'They're not trousers! They're jodhpurs.'

'Jodhpurs? What's a jodhpur?'

'Horse-riding trousers.'

Lydia stared at her in silence.

'That's right! You're starting riding lessons! Right now! Today! This very afternoon!'

Lydia's face went pale, then flushed painfully. 'Me? Riding lessons? Today?'

'Yes, now! Come on, we'll rush home and have a quick snack first. I hope the jodhpurs fit. I took a pair of your jeans into the shop and they said these should be the right size. We'll get riding boots as soon as we can, but for now you can wear your brown cowgirl boots.'

Lydia stood very still, not moving or speaking.

'Come on, come on, let's get going. It's going to be a bit of a mad dash to get there on time.'

Lydia remained frozen.

'Oh God!' Annie clapped her hand over her mouth. 'I'm such an idiot! You don't even *want* horse-riding lessons, do you? And I've gone and paid for four months upfront. Never mind. I totally understand. I wouldn't want to go either, to be honest. I can probably still cancel.'

Lydia tightened her hand around the jodhpurs. 'No,' she said, shaking her head. 'Don't cancel! I want to go.'

Annie stared at the child. Lydia wasn't smiling but when she glanced up at Annie her eyes burnt with secret elation.

'Oh, *you* . . . You really had me going there.' Annie dived at Lydia, tickling her vigorously on the ribs and under her arms, overcome by the urge to blow the lid off her give-nothing-away composure. Startled, Lydia gave a hoot of laughter, then took off at a run, her backpack thumping up and down, the bag containing the jodhpurs ballooning up with air as she went. Annie followed, delighted. A small group of kids still waiting to be picked up stared after them in wonder.

What demon prompted Annie to take Patches to the barn that afternoon to watch the riding lesson, she couldn't really have said. Of course, she was a bit nervous about leaving him alone in the kitchen now that he'd chewed up several chair legs. She could only hazard the vaguest guess at the kind of damages they'd have to pay when they vacated the premises if Patches were left unattended too often. Because of his destructive streak, she'd taken to leaving him in the garage, where there wasn't much he could sink his teeth into. Lydia had even set up a little home for him out there – a folded blanket in a large cardboard box, a selection of chew toys, a bowl of water.

Annie was fully intending to leave him in this cosy holding pen, but when the minivan door slid open, Patches jumped into the back before she could grab his collar.

'Oh, can't he come?' Lydia begged. 'I've seen loads of people with dogs at the barn.'

Annie had seen them, too, these glamorous women and their dogs. They would pull up in their tank-sized SUVs, flicking the obligatory long, straight hair over their shoulders, and Annie would wonder how they got their highlights to match the exact shade of the golden retriever or yellow Labrador poking its head out of the passenger window.

The retrievers and labs wore bandannas, and sometimes plaid waistcoats. Their collars were in the style of the Fairfield County Leisure Store's famous hundred-dollar ribbon belts. Many were green, embroidered with pink flamingos.

Patches, of course, couldn't hope to hold a candle to these high-bred beauties. He was a mongrel through and through, with absolutely no pretensions to expensive pedigree, or any pedigree at all. But he was all dog, and she wasn't ashamed of him.

'OK, he can come,' Annie said, peering into the minivan at Patches cringing on the back seat with flattened ears, waiting to be evicted.

'Yippee!' Lydia yelled, jumping into the car and throwing both arms around the dog's neck. 'I can't wait to introduce him to Pompom.'

Annie's heart lifted at the exuberance in her voice.

As they nosed out of the driveway, Lydia suddenly asked, 'Annie, are you going to have a lesson too?'

'*Me*? Good grief, no.'

'But you're wearing jodhpurs.'

'Um ... yes. Well, you know. Just thought I'd show the right spirit.' She was beginning to wonder, now, if her outfit was a bit much. She'd noticed that jodhpurs were de rigueur among the women at the barn – but maybe that was only if you actually rode the horses. Maybe there was another dress code for non-riding mothers. She might just leave her new whip – no, 'crop' – in the car.

The riding instructor was holding the reins of a small, nondescript pony as they half-ran up to the arena, about five minutes late for the lesson. Heather had offered to drive Lydia to the barn, but Annie had declined the offer, thinking she'd better stay and watch, since it was Lydia's first time.

Hailey and another girl were already up on ponies, walking around the perimeter of the arena, looking very calm and collected. Several heads turned as Annie and Lydia approached, perhaps because of the strangled noise Patches was making as he strained against his collar. Every now and then he'd stand up on his hind legs and hop forward like a circus dog in his desperation to arrive more quickly at the scene of the action. Then again, the onlookers might have been admiring Annie's jodhpurs coupled with her knee-high patent leather platform boots. (Like Lydia, she didn't yet own actual riding boots.) The effect, if Annie said so herself, was pretty spectacular.

Lydia's new riding instructor, dressed in jeans, trainers and a fleece jacket, surged forward to greet them. 'You must be my new girl. Linda, right? Oh, *Lydia*? OK. I'm Christine, and your pony is Milkdud. Now, before we start this lesson we need to get one thing straight.' She lowered her eyebrows at Lydia. 'While you're up on the pony, what I say goes. If I ask you to sing the stars and stripes, you sing it. If I ask you to wriggle your fingers, you wriggle them. If I ask you to pat your belly and rub your head, you do that too.'

Lydia, who was usually mute when she met new people, looked up and whispered, 'I don't know the stars and stripes.'

'That's OK, I'm not actually going to ask you to sing.' Christine pushed her sleeves up to her elbows. 'But you get it, right? You do as you're told when you're up on the pony. Come on then, let's get this safety helmet on you. Oh, and Mom, could you take the dog behind the palings, if you're staying to watch?'

Mom? Wow, she *did* look the part, after all. Feeling highly satisfied with the whole turn of events, Annie gave Patches' leash a tug and retreated behind the fence Christine had indicated. The dog resisted with all his might, digging his paws into the ground, but she was able to drag him over by brute force. He was still making the strangled noises but at least he wasn't barking.

Beetle-browed Christine boosted Lydia up onto Milkdud's back, then spent some time showing Lydia how to hold the reins and where to put her feet. Annie was relieved to see that the pony stood stock still, looking bored out of its mind. At a click and a tug on the reins from Christine, Milkdud moved off at a lumbering walk, Lydia concentrating hard under her black hat. Christine shouted inscrutable orders to the other two – 'Change the rein across the diagonal, rising trot at K, sit deep and shorten the reins, get those ponies

on the bit!' – turning aside every now and then to murmur
something to Lydia. After a few minutes, she moved away
from Lydia and into the centre of the arena. 'Prepare to
walk ... and *walk*,' she called to Hailey and the other girl,
who slowed their horses down. 'Now, overtake Milkdud
on the inside and let him follow you. I want all the ponies
on a long rein, lengthening their stride please, girls. I want
feet out of stirrups. You too, Lydia. Now, stretch your legs
and point your toes down, down, down. Right. Feel that?
That's absolutely the wrong way for your leg and foot to
be. Now, toes up and push your *heels* down. Bend slightly
at the knee, wrapping your legs around the pony but not
squeezing. OK. Good. Now, let's move into a circle, bending the pony round your inside leg ...'

As Annie watched, Patches began to act strangely. He
started whimpering low in his throat then gave a high-
pitched bark.

'Hush,' Annie scolded. 'You'll scare the horses.'

'That your girl on Milkdud?' drawled a vaguely familiar
voice behind her. Annie turned to see Dan Morgan strolling
up.

For some reason, an image of Dan and Sarah in a lip-lock
in her loo popped immediately into Annie's mind, and she
felt herself blush. At that same moment, Patches lost all
self-control and gave a giant tug on his leash. Caught by
surprise, Annie felt the leash slip through her slack fingers.

'Patches!' she yelled as the dog dived under the fence and
began to charge the horses. 'Come back here! Come *back*!
Come back at *once*!'

But it was no use. With helpless disbelief, Annie watched

as the dog streaked across the arena, barking fiercely, making straight for the pony Lydia was riding. Christine put her hands on her hips and bellowed, 'Get that freaking dog out of here!'

In slow motion, or so it seemed to Annie, Patches launched himself into the air and sprang at the mousy brown quarters of Lydia's pony. In mid-leap, he managed to grab a mouthful of the pony's shaggy tail. He locked his jaw, eyes bulging, and held onto the tuft for dear life. With a snort, the spooked pony began dancing and kicking. Lydia, her face rigid with shock, dropped the reins entirely and clung to the saddle. Patches, caught on the pony's tail like a burr, was shaken and tossed about – but not dislodged.

'Oh, stop that horse, stop it now,' Annie cried, her heart in her mouth, ducking under the fence and running at the animals with no idea of how to break up the fracas, but a vague notion of plucking Lydia off the pony's back.

'Get that dumb mutt outta here!' cried Christine. 'Get him outta here NOW!'

Suddenly Lydia's pony let loose with a giant two-legged kick that found its mark. Patches went sailing through the air, legs flailing. The pony skittered away, snorting with satisfaction, with Lydia still on board, though barely. Patches hit the ground running. He spotted Annie and went bolting back to her for protection, tail well between his legs.

The riding instructor stood and shouted at Lydia as she was jostled about like a bag of potatoes, 'Take up the reins and pull her in! Sit down, sit down, sit *down*, for God's sake. Whoa, whoa, *whoa*.'

It wasn't until Dan Morgan stepped casually into the

arena, strode into the path of the bolting pony and – somehow, miraculously – caught it by the reins, that Lydia lost her seat altogether, and slithered slowly off the pony's back to fall in a heap at Dan's feet.

'It's a miracle she didn't break every bone in her body,' Annie told Heather shakily as she dropped Hailey off home. 'Totally my fault. I've been banned from bringing Patches to the premises ever again. I think the woman was toying with banning me too, only I've already paid for the four months.'

'Are you all right, honey?' Heather asked, bending down to peer into Lydia's face. 'Any bruises?'

'I'm fine,' said Lydia with a shrug.

'You should've seen her!' Hailey piped up. 'Milkdud was going nuts, and she stayed up on him. It was so cool. She was like – like a circus rider. Was it scary, Lydia?'

'Really scary,' said Lydia, looking up with bright eyes, 'especially that big buck just before the pony kicked Patches. Poor Patches. I'm glad he's OK.'

'I saw your fanny come right up off the saddle then,' enthused Hailey. 'I don't know how you stayed on!'

Fanny? Good grief. Annie glanced at Heather but she seemed unperturbed by this sudden use of obscene language.

'Hey, I *wish* I could've seen that,' Lydia said wistfully. 'Do you think you could draw a picture of how it looked?'

Hailey raised her unibrow. 'Sure,' she said. 'Mom, can she stay and draw with me?'

Heather began to shake her head slightly, but before she

could say a thing, Annie cut in. 'Yes, yes, of course she can stay. Right, Mrs Gibson? It's late for a play date, but since it's been such a big day, we'll make an exception. Won't we?' She caught Heather's eye with a pleading look. Surely she wouldn't pull the plug on the first real overtures of friendship Annie had ever seen Lydia make?

'All right,' said Heather with a sigh. 'She might as well stay for dinner, too. It's only going to be scrambled eggs. Do you like scrambled eggs, Lydia?'

Lydia smiled, not the small, polite smile she sometimes forced onto her face when pressed by Annie, but a normal, genuine, child's smile. 'Yes, I like eggs,' she said. 'If they're not too dry.'

As the girls scampered into the house together, Annie found herself beaming too. 'I've never seen Lydia so happy. Thank God for those bloody horses.'

Heather nodded her head. 'Didn't I tell you to get involved with the riding?' she said. 'Horses are like dolphins, you know. They have a therapeutic effect on people.'

Annie laughed ruefully. 'Well, not on me and Patches,' she said. 'D'you know who came to the rescue, by the way? Your friend, Dan Morgan. He jumped in there like the Lone Ranger and caught the pony's reins. The stupid thing was still running around like a headless chicken even after it booted Patches. Poor dog, he was kicked a good twenty feet or more into the air. Flew off like a cannonball.'

Heather's grinned. 'Really? Must have been kind of funny. And Dan helped out? Wish I could've seen it.'

The story of the afternoon's adventures didn't go over half as well with Simon.

'I'm sorry, *what*? It sounded like you said Lydia fell off a horse.' He stood in the front hallway that evening, frozen in the act of taking off his coat. Perhaps she shouldn't have begun the tale the minute he set foot in the door. Maybe she should have primed him with a glass of wine first.

'Well – yes, that's what I said.' Annie could hear the tremble in her own voice. 'But don't worry, she's not hurt. Not even bruised.'

'Hang on, hang on. Backtrack a moment, here. How did she come to be riding a horse? Did she go over to the stables with the Gibsons?'

'No, Heather had nothing to do with it. Well, very little to do with it. The thing is, Lyddie was having her first riding lesson – mostly walking, you know, so very, very safe – when Patches—'

'*Riding* lesson?' Simon paused in the act of kicking his shoes off, his face incredulous.

Annie bit her lip. 'Um, yes. You see, Heather rang up this morning to say a slot had opened up in the group lesson Hailey goes to—'

But he was gone, thudding up the stairs in his socks, to see for himself that Lydia was really in one piece.

When he came back down again Annie was in the kitchen, stir-frying chicken and vegetables in a wok.

'You see?' She looked at him through the sizzle and steam. 'She's just fine. Not a mark on her.'

But Simon ran both hands through his hair and took a few quick, agitated steps around the kitchen. 'Annie,' he said with an audible effort to be calm, 'how do we know she doesn't have concussion? I thought I made it clear that I don't want her going up on a horse.'

Annie's stirring hand slowed right down. 'Well, um, the way I remember it, you said since she wasn't *asking* to ride, we should leave it at that ...'

'OK, so maybe that's what I said. But I thought you understood. I thought you knew I didn't want her riding.'

'Well, yes, but—'

'Annie, my brother says that accident stats for horse riding are right up there with fractured skulls from trampolines and bunk beds.' Simon's brother was a senior executive in a major insurance company. 'He says he'd rather let his daughter ride a *motorbike* than get up on a bloody horse.'

'Come off it, Simon. I'm sure there are far more fatalities from road accidents than from falling off horses and bunk beds *combined*.' Annie was starting to feel indignant.

'Look,' Simon said firmly, 'I'm just not comfortable with this whole thing. She's already fallen off once. It's an unnecessary risk. A gratuitous bloody worry that we just don't *need* in our lives! You're going to have to cancel the lessons.'

'But ... but I phoned to ask you. You left it all up to me. I mean, you *specifically* gave me the go-ahead to do whatever I thought was right.'

'Well, I made a mistake, in that case! I didn't know what the hell it was all about!'

'You mean you *don't* trust me absolutely to make any and all decisions for Lydia?'

'Annie, it's not a case of trust. I'm her *father*.'

'And I'm not her mother?'

'No,' he said. 'You're not.'

They stared at each other in silence for a moment.

Then Simon sank onto a bar stool. 'Bugger it,' he said. 'That didn't come out right.'

'No, I think it came out exactly right,' Annie said. 'Who am I to make decisions for Lydia? I mean, really? I've only known her a few months. I have no experience dealing with kids. She doesn't think of me as her mum. I have no more rights than ... than a nanny. Probably fewer. I mean, an experienced nanny would be a lot better at all this than I am.'

'Rubbish,' said Simon. 'You're doing a fantastic job with Lydia. I'm well aware of that. You *are* her mother, to all intents and purposes, and I love you for all that you do for her. It's just that a – a *biological* parent is a lot more likely to have irrational fears. That's all.'

Annie reached for the plates and began serving up their food with jerky little movements and lots of clattering.

'Annie,' he said, 'I'm sorry. I *do* trust you with Lydia. I trust you absolutely. But I just can't stop thinking about how big and solid horses are, and how small and breakable children are. So can you please just humour me on this?'

She turned towards him quickly, ready to forgive ... and knocked a glass of water off the counter with her elbow. It shattered on the tiles with an unnerving crash.

'Oh *bloody* hell,' Simon muttered, striding across the room and throwing open the pantry door. 'Is there such a thing as a dustpan and brush in this stonking great house, or are we too posh for that?'

She put her spoon down carefully on the glass stove top. 'So now you don't like the house?'

He was still throwing cupboard doors open. 'Of course I like it,' he growled, staring in frustration at a pyramid of plastic containers. 'We chose it together. How could I not like it? It's a bloody mansion! It just doesn't feel much like *home*, that's all.'

'The brush and pan are round the corner, in the cupboard next to the washer and dryer.' Annie worked hard to keep her voice even.

Shaking salad greens out of a bag onto their plates, she glanced at him, squatting on the floor brushing fragments of broken glass into the dustpan. He was still in his suit, his tie loose and crooked, his blond hair in disarray. She watched his broad, muscular hands wielding the brush, distracted by their brisk competence.

As she stared at him, his eyelids lifted and he looked straight up at her with his direct blue gaze. She was taken aback by the bleakness of his expression.

'Food's ready,' she said hastily. 'Let's just eat and deal with the mess later. I'll have to vacuum.'

He dumped the glass fragments in the bin, then sat down on a bar stool and accepted the plate she handed him. For a moment he sat staring at his food. Then he flicked his eyes at her from beneath raised brows. 'I just don't have the stomach for chances any more,' he said.

Suddenly, Annie's throat ached for him. She swallowed hard. 'No worries, the riding lessons are history,' she said. 'Um – and I know what you mean about the house. It's not that homely. I can't work out why, exactly. I suppose it's because we didn't pick the furniture.'

Simon held his loaded fork and looked around the kitchen,

his eyes resting on the toile 'window treatments'. 'I suppose so. But it's also, I don't know, so *tidy*. Beth always—' He caught himself immediately.

Annie took a quick gulp of water. 'Beth always what?'

He shrugged. 'I don't know. She had a lot of clutter, I suppose. And she always stuck bits of Lyddie's art up on the fridge.'

Lyddie's art? Lyddie didn't produce art. Annie hadn't seen a single stick figure to date. Oh God. That was probably a bad sign. She, Annie, must be crushing the child's creativity. Hang on! Hadn't Lyddie talked about drawing pictures with Hailey that very afternoon? She must ask Heather to check and see if she had actually put crayon to paper.

She cleared her throat and initiated a hasty change of subject. 'So what do you think of my Japanese stir-fry?'

Simon came back from some faraway place and glanced at his fork as if seeing it for the first time. 'Right. Looks great.' He took a mouthful and chewed with a thoughtful expression.

'So?'

His brow wrinkled. 'It's – quite nice. But it doesn't really taste Japanese, to be honest. What sort of seasoning did you use?'

Annie looked down at her own plate. The food looked good, if she said so herself: nicely browned chunks of chicken vied for attention with a colourful palette of vegetables: red peppers, tiny sprigs of broccoli, and adorable, bright yellow mini cobs of corn. 'You know, just the usual simple elements of Japanese cuisine: garlic, ginger, a base of soya sauce.' She glanced over at the stove top as she spoke, her eye falling on the bottle of soya sauce.

Only it wasn't soya. It was the Worcestershire sauce she'd been so happy to find the other day in the supermarket's mainly Mexican 'international' aisle.

Simon spotted the Worcestershire sauce at the same moment she did.

His mouth quivered and his eyes glinted with appreciation. 'Tuck in yourself,' he urged. 'It's a bit of a carnival on the tongue.'

'Oh God, I'm sorry. But in fairness, both bottles are black with yellow labels!'

He burst out laughing, and she couldn't help but laugh with him. All the tension and strain that was thickening the atmosphere in the room suddenly went swirling round at high speed and drained away abruptly, like murky water disappearing down the pipes when you pulled the plug on the kitchen sink.

Promising Simon that she'd cancel the riding lessons was one thing. Breaking the news to Lydia was something else entirely.

Simon offered to do it himself, since he'd been the one to throw the spanner in the works.

'No, Simon, don't do it,' Annie said. 'Don't go telling her you asked me to cancel the lessons.'

'Really? Why not? It won't be fair if she blames you.'

'No, don't you see? If you explain everything to her, it's going to look ...'

He stared at her a moment. 'It's going to look as if you're not allowed to make decisions about what she does and doesn't do,' he said slowly. 'Oh God. I hadn't thought of that.'

She nodded briskly. 'She'll be angry with me,' she said, 'but I think that's OK. She'll get over it. I just – I want her to think that I know what I'm doing, that's all.'

At six thirty the next morning Annie lay awake in bed, watching Simon get ready for work. Normally she slept through his daybreak rituals, but today the alarm clock had found her wide awake, staring into the darkness. 'I'm sure she'll take it OK,' she suddenly murmured. 'I mean, she does like riding, but it doesn't seem to be an all-consuming passion or anything. She'll be fine.'

'God, I hope so.' Simon ran a comb through his damp hair and snapped his fingers at Patches, who rose from the laundry basket with a resigned groan and tottered over towards the door. Patches was a bit of a night owl and didn't relish being turned out of doors so early in the morning.

Simon leaned down to kiss Annie goodbye. Drowsy and affectionate, Annie surged up out of the sheets to put her arms around his neck. He smelled of soap and toothpaste. She smelled a little earthier, apparently. 'Phew,' he murmured, setting her gently aside. 'Quite a lot of garlic in the food last night.'

She felt herself deflating on the pillow like a balloon with a slow leak.

Then, one hand on the door, he turned to give her an indescribably raunchy wink, perking her back up instantly. With his muscular build and dark tan, he looked indecently raffish in his white shirt. 'See you later,' he murmured, and was gone.

Annie stared at the closed door.

How was it possible to be married to a man and still yearn for him as if you'd just had a one-night stand after meeting him in a pub and weren't quite sure whether you were ever going to lay eyes on him again?

'Do you have any aches and pains from your fall?' Annie asked Lydia as she put her porridge in the microwave to warm up. Lydia, trailing around the kitchen in pyjamas and bare feet, swept the long hair out of her eyes and gave a confused shrug. 'No, I told you, I didn't hurt myself.'

'I know, but sometimes muscles sort of stiffen up over-night.'

'Is my porridge ready?'

'Yes, here you go.' Annie watched as the little girl settled herself on a stool and began sprinkling sugar. 'So – you and Hailey had fun yesterday afternoon?'

Lydia shrugged again.

'Did you draw any pictures?'

'Loads.'

'You didn't bring any back to show me.'

'No, we threw them away.'

'Oh. Why?'

''Cos Mrs Gibson says it's about process not product.'

'I see. Next time you draw something, could you give it to me?'

'Why?'

'So I can stick it on the fridge to brighten up the kitchen.'

'OK.' Lydia stirred her porridge and sampled it experi-mentally. Apparently, it needed just a soupçon more sugar.

Watching her sprinkle, Annie took a deep breath, closed her eyes a second, then suddenly blurted, 'I'm sorry, sweetie, but I'm going to have to cancel the riding lessons.'

Lydia froze mid-sprinkle.

'What did you say?'

'Um ... the riding lessons. I'm going to have to cancel them. You see, your dad and I were talking and we realised that we don't want you riding, after all. We would rather have you do something less dangerous like – I don't know – chess.'

'But – but you *said*! You said I could do it. You said you'd already paid for it! I didn't even ask to do it! You bought me jodhpurs and *everything*! You said we'd buy riding boots today after soccer!' Her voice was rising ominously.

Annie pressed her fingers into her eyeballs and breathed in through her nose. 'I'm sorry, love. We've ... we've reconsidered and we don't want you riding.'

'Is this because I fell off?' Lydia cried. 'I didn't even hurt a hair on my head! Not even my little finger! Christine said I did a great job staying on. She said I was a natural!'

'My darling, I'm sorry. I'm so, so sorry. But we've decided. No more lessons.'

Lydia jumped up, dropping her spoon on the counter and scattering sugar all over the place. 'You know what you are?' she screamed. 'You're a big, fat *meanie*!' And she ran for the stairs, heaving with sobs.

Annie stood in the middle of the kitchen, arms folded to stop her hands from shaking visibly. 'So,' she said out loud to Patches, who was licking sugar off the tiles, 'that went surprisingly well, don't you think?'

# Chapter Eight

'She's moping,' Annie told Simon a few days later, 'definitely moping.'

'I've noticed it too.' They were sitting on a bench at the beach on a Saturday morning, watching Lydia wander aimlessly over the sand. It wasn't really a beach day. The wind was blowing, whipping the normally flat water into little troughs.

'So I have a plan.'

He looked at her with interest. 'Yes?'

'Let's tell her we're keeping Patches.'

His brows snapped together.

'Don't you see?' she said quickly. 'It's a great plan. I mean, what are we going to do with him, anyway? Take him to the pound to be put to sleep? Nobody's going to claim him, that's pretty clear. We've advertised him up and down Fairfield county.'

'Annie, it wouldn't be responsible to keep him. You seem to forget, we're only here for a couple of years. We're not permanent enough to be dog owners!'

Annie jumped up and stood in front of him, radiating energy and determination. 'That shouldn't stop us. It's much easier to take dogs around the world nowadays. You just have this chip thingy inserted under their skin, and they don't even have to go into quarantine. Come on, Simon! He's a good dog.'

'He's a nightmare bloody dog.'

'But you like him. I know you do. And think how happy Lyddie would be!'

'Oh, for God's sake, Annie. Haven't we got enough on our plates?'

'I've got hardly anything on my plate, to be honest. Taking Patches for a walk every day has been a godsend! It gives me something to do, gets me out of the house, even helps me meet people.'

Simon looked at her with narrowed eyes. 'You're serious, aren't you?'

'Of course I'm serious.'

He sighed. 'Well, OK then. I guess we're stuck with the cringing cur.'

Annie was already running across the sand towards Lydia. 'Quick, quick!' she called. 'We have good news.'

Lydia glanced up from the shells she was poking at with a stick. Seeing Lydia racing towards her, she frowned in a resigned sort of way, threw her stick down, and began trudging to meet her.

'Is it time to go?' she asked.

'Probably,' said Annie. 'I don't know about you, but my hands are freezing. But come back to Daddy. We have something to tell you.'

'You tell her,' Simon said when they reached him. 'It's your idea, after all.'

'OK. Lyddie, your dad and I have been talking and ... well, since nobody has claimed Patches, we've decided to keep him.'

Lydia held very still.

'Do you understand? We're keeping Patches. You'll have a dog!' Annie was disappointed. The child didn't look in the least bit overjoyed. She hadn't even cracked a smile.

Lydia rubbed her sandy hands against her fleece jacket. 'You're just saying that,' she said. 'Tomorrow you'll tell me you made a mistake. Just like with the riding lessons.'

Annie threw Simon a horrified look. 'No, honestly. I promise you! I'm not just saying it! You can keep Patches.'

Lydia looked at her father. 'Is it true?'

He stood up and put his hands on her shoulders. 'Yes, it's true. We're not going to change our minds.'

Lydia jumped up into his arms, pressed her face into his coat and began to sob. 'It's OK,' he said, patting her back and raising his eyebrows at Annie. After a moment the sobs dried up, and she rubbed her face on his sleeve.

'Let's go back and tell him,' Lydia said. 'Let's go and tell him he gets to stay.'

This was more like it, Annie thought. Far more like it! 'Yes, and let's go to the pet shop and get him his own basket,' she suggested. 'And his own feeding bowl.'

'And maybe another toy to chew on,' Lyddie said.

'Or several dozen toys to chew on,' said Simon, who had lost a slipper and sundry belts to Patches' incorrigible oral fixation.

\*

On Monday, Annie took Patches along to the vet to have his jabs done. After he knocked the vet's glasses off his face, then urinated on the stainless steel examining table with excitement, the man in the white coat recommended manners lessons. He also recommended crate training, which apparently meant putting the dog in a cage every time you left the house. This was after Patches vomited on the table, giving him an opportunity to see the contents of his stomach, which included fragments of wax crayon, sticks, pieces of brightly coloured plastic, a small spring, and a length of string. He told her Patches was about one year old, and strongly advised her to get him 'fixed' as soon as possible.

'I'm not sure the world is ready for this dog to start re-producing,' he noted in a far from jocular tone.

But what did Annie care if the vet didn't approve of their dog? Lydia was happy!

She was happier still when a little note arrived in the post from a girl called Emily Cooper, who used to be her best friend at St Thomas Church of England Primary School in Kensington.

Annie had passed on Lydia's address to the headmistress of St Thomas. She had almost given up hope of anything coming of it when the letter, in its blue airmail envelope, appeared in their mail box.

'Der Lidia, how are you? I am fine. It is raning here. LOL Emily.' This riveting piece of correspondence was illustrated with a stick-figure scene of people holding up umbrellas. It made Annie feel quite homesick.

Lydia wrote back: 'Dir Emly, how are you? I am fine. I

have a dog. Love Lydia.' Annie photocopied the letter and stuck it on the fridge. The drawing of Patches was quite masterful, in her humble opinion.

The next day, as Annie sat in her idling car, waiting to take Lydia and Hailey to soccer practice, she found herself hailed through the car window by Donna Knopf, one of her Maple Tree Ridge neighbours.

'Annie? Hey, how's it going?'

'Very well, thanks, how about you?'

'I'm good. Everything's good. Hey, I'm wondering if you could do me a favour?'

Annie felt quite flattered. She would never have thought she could do anything to help out Donna Knopf, who was one of those highly organised women whose main job in life seemed to be to make other women feel inadequate. Recently, when the mothers had been asked to bring in treats for the staff at Bradley Elementary for teacher appreciation day, Donna had brought in a cheese moulded into the shape of an owl, layered with sun-dried tomatoes, and artistically decorated with pine nuts for feathers. Annie had brought in a plastic box of violently coloured cookies.

Annie smiled through the car window. 'Of course, happy to help. What do you need?'

'We're looking for a fourth for our tennis clinic tomorrow. One of the gals has something else on. So — are you up for it?'

'Aaah,' Annie's voice was a squeak.

'I know you play,' Donna added. 'I've seen you walking around in tennis outfits.'

'Well, um——'

'Of course, if you're a tennis snob ...? I mean, we're just giggle and hit.'

Giggle and hit? Annie wanted to lean out of the window and kiss Donna with relief. She could do giggle and hit any day of the week. After all it wasn't as if she'd never held a tennis racquet in her life. She'd had several lessons at school! 'A tennis snob? Me? Gosh no, I'm just trying to keep my eye on the ball, myself. I'd love to play! I'm really bad, though, I'm warning you.'

Donna smiled. 'Oh, you English. Always so modest! I'll email you the details. See you later.'

Gosh. Tennis. Simon was bound to be impressed if she started playing tennis. He was definitely in favour of competitive sports, as testified by his initial excitement about the soccer. Come to think of it, he didn't really know much about Annie's athletic abilities. He wouldn't know how downright astonishing it was that she was going to make up a foursome at Winterton Indoor Courts. For all he knew, she could have been a schoolgirl tennis star.

'Annie, open up!'

Lydia stood on the kerb, banging on the car door. Coming out of her reverie, Annie pressed the button to open the remote-controlled sliding door for the girls. They piled in, throwing backpacks onto the floor and then walking over them with a fine disregard for their contents. Annie thought she could hear pencils snapping and leftover sandwiches squishing.

'Come on, girls, get out the soccer gear and start changing,' Annie called over her shoulder, easing out into the minivan traffic.

'Sock puppet!' yelled Hailey, holding up a hand encased in a navy-blue soccer sock. 'I'm Wally Worm and I eat nothing but blueberries,' she announced in a high, distorted voice.

Annie glanced at Lydia in the rear-view mirror – then did a double-take, her mouth falling open. Her stepdaughter's eyes were glittering with excitement! *Glittering!* 'I'm Molly Worm,' Lydia cried, shoving her hand into her own sock. 'And I eat nothing but ... chewing gum.'

Annie squeezed her eyes shut and opened them again, then glanced quickly over her shoulder. Sure enough, Lydia still had her hand in a sock, and was still talking in the squeaky tones of Molly Worm. This was a side of Lydia she'd never seen!

Alas, by the time Heather delivered Lydia back to the Keeler house later that afternoon, her playful side had disappeared. As Lydia yanked off her shin guards, Annie asked brightly, 'So, how was soccer?'

Lydia shrugged and threw her boots into the cubbyhole where her shoes were stored. 'Bad,' she said. 'Like always.'

'Would you like a snack? Some juice?'

'No.'

'We'd better take a look at your homework, then.'

'I can do it by myself.'

'Well, OK. But I'm right here if you need me.'

'I won't need you.'

In a flash of sheer genius, Annie grabbed one of Lydia's socks. She hesitated a moment then stuffed her hand into its slightly damp depths. 'I'm Molly Worm,' the sock said, 'and I just love helping out with homework!'

Lydia pulled a disgusted face. 'You're putting your hand in a sock,' she said. 'That's really gross!'

'I thought we'd have steak tonight,' Annie told Simon later as he poured himself a large tumbler of iced water. 'Something quick and simple.'

The fine lines around his blue eyes seemed more deeply etched than usual as he glanced at her over the rim of the glass. Closing his eyes, he drank deeply, without stopping to breathe, as if he hadn't had the chance to quench his thirst all day. Then he put the glass down, wiped his mouth with the back of his hand, and took a gulp of air. Not looking at her he said, 'I think I'll pass on dinner tonight. We were sampling pies at the office, and I'm stuffed.'

'Oh. Fair enough. I'll probably...I'll just make myself an omelette or something. We can have the steak tomorrow.'

'I should've called and let you know.' He looked genuinely contrite. 'You could have eaten with Lydia.'

'Nah. Plain pasta with grated cheese on the side isn't my favourite splurge. Never mind, I feel like something light anyway.'

He wandered off to watch TV while she made her solitary dinner. By the time a leathery omelette was on her plate, she seemed to have lost her appetite, but she took it through to the family room on a tray and sat down beside him.

He was watching a programme about a man who travelled the world eating unusual foods. 'Ah, goat's scrotum,' the man was saying, holding up a bowl of some indescribably foul-looking stew to the camera, 'a specialty here in

Uzbekistan. Mmm! Slightly ripe, and rubbery on the tongue, but meaty and delicious.'

She took a bite of her omelette, chewed, and swallowed with difficulty.

Instead of watching TV, she was watching Simon's profile in the light from the giant screen. She liked to look at him. He felt her gaze and turned to look at her with a quizzical expression. A faint stubble shadowed his strong jaw, and a tiny smile played on his lips. 'Is the omelette good?' he asked, tilting his head at the forkful of food that lay untouched on her plate.

'What do you think?' she asked. 'It's slightly ripe and rubbery on the tongue, to be honest.'

She met his eye and they both burst out laughing.

'By the way,' she told him when they'd stopped laughing, 'I forgot to mention to you – I've been invited to play tennis tomorrow.'

He raised his eyebrows. 'Really? That's great! I didn't even realise you played.'

'Oh, I haven't played in ages, but I used to pick up the racquet now and then at school,' she said nonchalantly.

He stared at her in silence for a moment. 'Well, have a good game,' he said at last. She was half convinced she saw his mouth twitching, as if he were suppressing a grin. 'I'm glad you're getting out and meeting people.'

It was only at the last minute the next morning that Annie realised she'd made a horrible mistake. She'd promised to play tennis, but she didn't have a tennis racquet. She had the outfit, all right – in fact, she had several. Tennis gear was simply so common around Norbury that no one ever batted an eyelid to see someone pushing a trolley around the supermarket in a cute little skort and top. It seemed to be the only form of skirt you could wear in town without raising eyebrows. Plus, if she decided to go jogging – which she was often on the brink of doing – then she'd have something to jog in. To complete the image, she'd even bought some blinding white tennis shoes. But no racquet.

It was as she was closing all the kitchen doors and settling Patches down in the garage with a bone in preparation for her departure for the courts that she realised she was missing this vital piece of equipment. Clearly, there was no time to run out and *buy* a racquet. In desperation, she phoned Heather.

'Yes, I think I have a racquet,' Heather said, sounding a bit surprised. 'I can probably dig one up.'

'Oh, thank God! I'll be round in five minutes to pick it up. You're a lifesaver.'

Heather had the racquet ready as Annie pulled into her driveway. 'It's quite a good one, I think,' she said as she handed it to Annie through the car window. 'An Agassi.'

'Oh, great,' said Annie, suddenly feeling horribly nervous. 'I'll look after it.'

'Have fun,' Heather called as Annie inched out onto the street, keeping her eyes open for toddlers on bikes. 'Break a leg!'

By the time she pulled into the car park of the Winterton Indoor Courts Annie was in a bit of a nervous froth. 'Calm down,' she told herself as she got out of the car. 'It's only tennis, for God's sake.'

Once inside, she went straight to the changing room and locked herself in a cubicle, rather wishing she could stay there until the hour was safely over. Coming out at last, she bumped into Nancy McKenzie, a Maple Tree Ridge resident, tying her hair back in a ponytail in front of the mirror.

'Great to have you playing with us today, Annie,' said Nancy with unnerving intensity. 'Listen, if we're partners, which is your stronger side, forehand or backhand?'

'Um ... forehand, I suppose. But I'm about the same with the backhand. Sort of ambidextrous.'

Nancy frowned at her. 'You're a leftie?' she asked.

'Oh, no. Definitely a rightie.' Annie made a few swishing motions with her right hand. 'But sometimes my ... my shoulder sort of ... seizes up on me. If it does that then my shots are all over the place. I'll even miss a few. With any luck it won't happen today.'

Nancy's eyebrows rose. 'Yeah, let's hope.'

As Annie followed Nancy through a sumptuous waiting area equipped with coffee makers and easy chairs, she worked hard on breathing normally. Just keeping your breath slow and even could go a long way towards curtailing panic, she'd recently read in a magazine. Nancy opened a door and led Annie into a narrow passageway cloaked on one side by a huge, heavy curtain made of something like rubber. As they walked through this dim corridor, Annie heard the repeated slams of racquets hitting balls with unnerving ferocity. People were making load moans and groans as they smashed the ball around. Annie's mouth was as dry as dust now.

Giggle and hit, she told herself. It's nothing but giggle and hit. You'll be fine.

At last they emerged onto a blue court, beneath bright lights. Other courts were visible through immense curtains made of something like fishnet. Two women and – oddly enough – a young man in shorts were standing beside a bench on the side, fiddling with water bottles and shoe laces. 'Come on, I'll introduce you to the pro,' said Nancy.

The *pro*?

'Hey, Jacques, this is Annie. She's taking Kelly's spot for the day. Annie, this is Michelle. You know Donna, of course.'

The boy in shorts – presumably Jacques – held out his hand. Annie took it rather gingerly, aware that her palms were so wet they ought to be wrung out and hung up to dry.

'Right, ladies, let's get going,' said Jacques in an exaggerated French accent that made Annie giggle – until she realised it was real.

Everybody began to unzip their racquets. Annie did likewise. The boy wheeled a huge trolley-load of balls to the side of the court and positioned himself next to it. 'Donna and Michelle, come to the net on my side,' he called. 'Nancy and, um, Annie? Go back to the baseline. We'll warm up down the line. Nice and easy, just keep it in play.'

Baseline? Down the line? What on earth did he mean? Annie looked at Nancy who was walking towards the far end of the court. She followed.

'Why don't you take the forehand? I'm working on my backhand right now,' Nancy suggested.

'Sure,' said Annie, shuffling over to a spot Nancy seemed to be indicating with her racquet.

'Remember, down the line, two balls in play at the same time,' said Jacques, and suddenly a ball came shooting at Annie. She lunged forward and managed to get it with the handle of her racquet. It flew out of the court at a strange angle, not even making it to the net.

'OK, Annie, nice and easy,' said Jacques, shooting a ball at Nancy. Nancy hit it convincingly with the string part of the racquet, and it sailed calmly over to Kelly, who blocked it mid-air and sent it sailing back to her. They began to bat the ball between them. Darn, they made it look so easy. Annie didn't notice any giggling at all.

Donna stood at the net, obviously waiting for a shot from Annie.

'Are you ready, Annie?' called Jacques. This time the ball came more slowly, and seemed to jump up straight onto her racquet. To her delighted surprise, she managed to send it back to Donna. Donna smacked it hard, it flew back at Annie, she put out her racquet, the ball caught the wood and shot straight up into the air.

Jacques stepped up to the net, holding out a hand to stop play, and beckoned Annie.

'Do you always play with a child's racquet?' he asked in a low voice, jerking his head in the direction of Heather's Agassi.

Annie stiffened. 'No, of course not,' she said, glancing at it. 'Now you mention it, it does look a bit ... you know, small. Good grief, I – I must have picked up my daughter's racquet in my rush.'

She shot a look at the other women. They seemed to be biting their cheeks and exchanging sly glances.

'OK,' said Jacques. 'Take mine, I'll go get another one. Meantime, just keep warming up with some mini tennis.'

Mini tennis?

The others had stepped up towards the line in the middle of the court. Annie followed suit. They began hitting a ball between the four of them. Mostly, Michelle and Donna hit it to Nancy, whose backhand didn't seem to need any improving at all. When they occasionally hit a shot in Annie's direction, she was surprised to find that she could almost always get Jacques' racquet on the ball. The results were a bit mixed, though. Sometimes the ball crashed into the rubber curtain at the back of the court. Sometimes it flew towards the ceiling. Every now and then it behaved in a more respectable way and hopped over the net towards Donna or Michelle.

Annie began to relax a little. She was clearly a lot more coordinated now than she'd been as a schoolgirl. She wasn't exactly shining, but at least she wasn't swishing at air.

Jacques arrived back with a substitute racquet, and soon had them in a new formation, Annie and Nancy up at the net, Donna and Michelle behind the baseline.

'Just block the ball, don't hit it,' he recited as he directed a shot at Annie's strings. She managed to get it back over the net quite handily without even moving a muscle. Honestly, she was beginning to enjoy herself. OK, so she'd noticed Nancy doing miniature shrugs at Michelle after some of her more deviant shots, but she was improving in such leaps and bounds that even Nancy was bound to be impressed.

And she could always put down her duff shots to the dicky shoulder she had quickly invented in the changing room.

Maybe tennis was her thing, after all. Maybe she'd get really good at it, and start playing in tournaments, and Simon would bring Lydia along to watch and learn.

'Ready, Annie?' called Jacques – and popped a ball at her.

Ready? Boy, was she ready. She swung at the ball with all her might, every muscle in her body bent on hitting it hard enough to make the thwacking sound that had eluded her so far. And to everyone's amazement her racquet caught the ball exactly right, her arm drove through the stroke exactly right, and the resulting thwack was enough to turn heads on other courts.

Delighted, she watched the ball fly low and bullet-like back over the net.

'Oooof!'

Jacques was suddenly bent double beside his trolley, clutching himself. A moment later, he dropped to his knees, and by the time Annie got over to him he was curled up in the foetal position, groaning in agony.

'Oh my God,' said Michelle. 'Bullseye.'


'So, how was the tennis?' Heather asked, catching up with her as she walked to school to pick up the girls.

Annie winced slightly. 'Um ... you know, all right. By the way, did you realise your racquet is kid-sized?'

'No way! I'm sorry – I guess I bought it for Hailey at some point. Did they crack up when they saw it?'

'A bit. But it was OK. The pro got me another racquet.'

'The pro, huh? Was he hot?'

Annie pulled a face. 'Actually, he looked like a schoolboy. But he was nice. I just hope he's not a bruiser and sweller, like you.'

'Oh, why?'

'Well, I sort of — hit him in the privates with a ball. Quite hard. They were still applying ice packs when I left.'

Heather's eyes bulged. 'You're kidding! *Ice* packs?'

'That's right. They keep them at the front desk.'

'Is this guy married?'

Annie shrugged. 'I don't know. Do you mind awfully if we don't talk about it any more?'

Heather pressed her lips together, suppressing laughter. 'Fine, no problem. So tell me, are you ready for Halloween?'

'Ready as I'll ever be.' Annie shot her a slightly puzzled look.

'God, you're ahead of me then. I still have to go buy candy.'

'Oh, right. Of course.'

'I only have about four fifty-count bags right now. You always need way more than that, don't you?'

'You do?' Fifty-count bags?

'In this town, you do. Especially on a cul-de-sac like ours. It's a perfect street for trick or treating.'

'Do you know, nobody did trick or treating much when I was growing up. It's going to be a first for me.' Annie's dad used to say that if any of the little bleeders had the cheek to ring the doorbell begging for sweets, he'd show them what for with his cricket bat. He was a mild man, her dad, but he didn't hold with yobbos going around threatening home-owners with vandalism if they didn't cough up. And that had pretty much been the attitude of all the parents in the village, as far as she could remember.

For all she knew, trick or treating might be the norm in London for little kids; she just didn't move in those circles. Henny, who lived out in the country, was her only friend with small children. Certainly, no child had ever rung the doorbell of her Islington flat on Halloween. She herself had been to the occasional nuns-and-prostitutes party in honour of the holiday, but that was about the sum of it.

'You do have a costume for Lydia, right?' Heather asked.

'Um ... not just yet. Maybe I could make her something? Cut out some holes in a sheet?'

'You don't see a whole lot of home-made costumes around here,' Heather cautioned. 'Tell you what, why don't you come round and look at Hailey's costumes? She was a purple witch last year. Lydia could be that.'

'Thanks,' said Annie humbly. 'I'd really be stuck without you.'

When Simon came home at ten o'clock that evening, he didn't even ask her about the tennis. She didn't know whether to be relieved or annoyed. Obviously, he'd totally forgotten she was scheduled to play. With little more than a distracted hello, he declined dinner (again) and closed himself up in the den, claiming he had to talk to a pie company in Australia.

Perhaps it was time she enrolled herself in some cooking lessons.

She wasn't going to make a habit of watching daytime TV, Annie promised herself the next day. She was just doing it this time because there was a bit of a lull in her morning, and she owed it to herself to get a broader sense of American culture.

Daytime TV was a bit of a window into the soul of a nation, she reckoned. For one thing, she'd had no idea that so much American justice was meted out over the air. Once you stumbled on Judge Judy or Judge Alex on the job (judges were obviously a casual lot over here: first names all round and not a white wig in sight) there was very little hope of being able to tear yourself away for at least half an hour. You found that you absolutely had to know whether Luella had completely vandalised Billy-Bob's Ford Escort including the custom seat covers in yellow leather – 'Ain't *nobody* got that, man,' as Billy-Bob attested – or whether, as Luella insisted, she'd confined herself to breaking the windshield. And then, of course, you had to weather out the advertising to hear what lessons Luella felt she'd learned from the exasperated knuckle-rapping that Judge Alex had given her.

Better even than the courtroom dramas were the cooking and decorating shows. She almost wished she had a tailgate party to cater for, or a clapped-out old house to refurbish, just so that she could use the foolproof recipe for five pounds of Buffalo-style chicken wings, or create a faux marble headboard using only poster-board and paint. She had no idea what happened at a tailgate party, or what poster-board was, but it all sounded like a lot more fun than sitting in an empty house.

Best of all, though, were the ads for prescription medicines; they were absolutely riveting. It almost brought tears to Annie's eyes to see the difference that medicine was making in the lives of people suffering from all kinds of diseases, from insomnia, indigestion and genital warts, to migraines, attention-deficit disorder and incontinence. One minute these people were down and out, sitting around alone in darkened rooms. Next minute they were running along beaches with their hair streaming out behind them, or drinking coffee with good-looking friends, or even fly-fishing in the sunset.

She just wished the narrator wouldn't always rattle off a list of side effects just when your eyes were misting up. Every drug under the sun, it seemed, carried a small risk of dizziness, headaches, nosebleeds, diarrhoea, blood clots, stroke, and cardiac arrest.

The most common illness in America was erectile dysfunction, judging by the volume of advertising. A bit unsettling, that. Presumably it wasn't infectious. Annie's personal favourite among the ED ads showed a very affectionate couple – identified as 'older' by a few grey strands in their hair, but otherwise well equipped with teeth, hair and the glow of youth – sitting in a romantic restaurant, holding hands over a linen tablecloth and staring into each other's eyes in the candlelight. Suddenly, rudely, a hand knocks at the plate glass window. The lovers glance out to see another youthful elderly couple peering in at them, waving madly. Chums of theirs, obviously. The romantic music fades abruptly, the friends barge into the restaurant, the lovey-dovey couple draw apart. But all is not lost, the voice-over assures viewers. Although the romantic lead has already popped a pill in expectation, apparently, of a quick consummation on the tabletop between courses, he finds himself well able to put off the action until a more convenient time. This was the special magic of the pill in question. Competing pills, Annie gathered, required the pill-taker to get on the job immediately or suffer who knew what debilitating consequences.

As the morning wore on, Annie began to feel very ignorant. She hadn't realised social anxiety was even an illness. The danger of living in a country where it was illegal to advertise prescription drugs, she could see, was that you simply had no idea of the range of new diseases out there.

Around noon Annie jumped up, turned off the TV and decided to take Patches for a walk. A vague headache and a vaguer sense of guilt told her that she'd probably had enough cultural immersion for one day.

She was clipping Patches' leash onto his collar when the phone rang.

'Annie? Annie, is that you?' Henny's voice sounded strangely shrill.

Before Annie could reply, Patches jumped up at her in his pre-walk frenzy and knocked the phone out of her hand. It crashed to the floor, the dog grabbed it gleefully, and Annie went down on hands and knees to wrestle it out of his mouth. It was a little wet when she put it back to her ear, but still in working order. Patches ran off, trailing the leash.

'Yes, it's me. Sorry about that. Bloody dog got the phone. Are you OK?'

'Yes, yes, I'm fine. But Annie . . . your mum . . . she's had a bit of a turn. She's in hospital.'

Time slowed down. Annie watched a speck of dust swirl about in a finger of sunlight, twinkling like a tiny star before it disappeared.

She told herself to breathe. 'A turn?' she managed to ask. 'What's a turn, for God's sake?'

'She fell down. In the kitchen, making dinner. Managed to crawl over to the phone when she came round. The ambulance people called me. Apparently my number's on her fridge door.'

'Yes, I stuck it there when I left,' said Annie. 'For emergencies. Oh God, is this an emergency?'

'To be honest, I don't really know. They're not giving me a lot of information. But I think you'd better come.'

'Of course I'll come. I'll get on a plane this afternoon if I can find a seat. Have you got a number for the hospital? Maybe they can tell me more.'

She wasn't able to get much out of the woman who picked up the phone at Guildford Hospital. 'Gladys Harleigh,' the disembodied voice said. 'Let's see now. Maternity ward, is it?'

'No, no! She's in her sixties. She fell down at home and they brought her in by ambulance. For God's sake, nobody of childbearing age is called *Gladys*!' She clapped her hand over her mouth, shocked by her own rudeness. 'Look, I'm terribly sorry! You see, Gladys Harleigh is my mum, and I'm stuck over here in America, and I don't know what on earth is going on.'

'All right, dear. You just take a deep breath. I'm looking

it up. Yes, she came in earlier today and they have her in Ward D, room 23. It says here she's stable. She had a fall, apparently.'

'Yes, yes, that's her. Does it say anything else? Like, why she fell?'

'Oh, these old folk, it could be anything, my dear. Stroke, heart attack, or maybe she slipped on a wet spot. You'd better come in and see for yourself.'

'Well *obviously* I'm going to, but did I happen to mention that I'm calling from America?'

'If I were you, I'd get on a plane, my dear.'

Annie couldn't get hold of Simon. He was either in a dead spot, or he'd turned off his phone. After the fifth attempt to get him in person, she caved in and left a message. 'Simon, bad news. My mum's in hospital. She had a fall and they don't know what the problem is. I'm trying to get on a flight to Heathrow this afternoon. I'm going to ask Heather to take Lydia. Maybe she can take Patches too, if I beg her. Anyway, please call me back as soon as you can.'

Annie managed to find a seat on an evening flight, and Heather offered to drive her to Kennedy airport. To make it to the flight in time they pulled the girls out of Miss Scofield's classroom early.

'You're going to England? Without me?' Lydia asked as they sped along Main Street towards the I-95; Annie watched as the joy of being busted out of school abruptly faded from her stepdaughter's face. 'Why can't I come too?'

'I've told you. My mum isn't well and I need to go over and look after her. It won't be for long, I'm sure.'

'Yes, but what if it is? I saw your suitcase. It's big.'

'Mrs Gibson will look after you. And so will Daddy, of course. You'll be fine, I promise.'

'But I want to go to England. Why can't I come too?'

'You can't miss school. Besides, hospitals are boring places for kids.'

'No, *school* is a boring place for kids,' Lydia countered. 'I want to come *with* you.'

'Let's not talk about this now,' Annie said, rolling her eyes at Heather. 'I've said you can't come, and I'm sorry but you'll just have to accept that.'


'I'm not dying,' her mother told her the next day from her hospital bed. 'What a terrible waste of money, rushing over here like that. On business class too, you say.'

Annie blinked hard. Her mother's face was papery white and she was festooned with drips. 'Business was all I could get at the last minute. You're not allowed to get excited, Mum. How was I supposed to know you weren't dying, anyway? Am I supposed to wait until you're safely in your coffin before I book my flight?'

Her mother chuckled. 'That would be a waste of money, too,' she said. 'Anyway, it's good to see you. What did they tell you?'

'The same as they told you, probably. They've ruled out heart attack and stroke. They can't find anything major, but they're worried about you blacking out again.'

'How long are they going to keep me flat on my back? It's enough to make anybody weak as a kitten, lying about all day.'

'Not as long as you'd think. They're going to monitor you for maybe another day, then send you home.'

'Good. I can't stand the food in these places.'

Annie slid the box of chocolates she'd bought at the airport towards her. 'Have one,' she said. 'Chocolate always cheers me up.'

'If you were going to spend the money anyway, I wish you'd bought me a book.' Her mum gave a disapproving sniff. 'The government ought to ban chocolate – it serves absolutely no practical purpose, and it costs a fortune.'

'Well, how about giving it to the nurses? It might sweeten them up.'

Her mum shrugged. 'I suppose so. Goodness, don't I sound like an old battleaxe? I'm sorry, Annie-bean. I've had a bit of a scare, to be honest. Now listen, you'll find the house keys in my bag. I want you to get back there as quick as you can to check up on things. For all I know, I've left the thermostat on full blast. Lord knows, I don't want to get back to a runaway fuel bill.'

Annie laughed out loud, giddy with relief. 'A runaway fuel bill! Right, that would be a real emergency, wouldn't it?'

But her relief was short-lived. As she was leaving the ward, a doctor pulled her aside and said, 'About your mother. She's OK for now, but her blood pressure is almost too low, and she's having problems with balance. She's going to need to be very careful in future. Another fall and she could easily break a hip. To be brutally honest, with her profile she could faint again at any time. Ideally, she should have someone around to keep an eye on her until we work out whether this was a one-off. If you can, please persuade her to stay with you for a while, just to keep tabs on her. In the long run, if the syncope recurs, it might even be time to think about some sort of assisted living.'

He hurried away before she had time to say hang on, I can't cope with any of this, I live in America.

When Annie pushed open her mother's kitchen door later that afternoon, she gasped in horror. The white floor and cabinets were dramatically daubed in blood. People in big boots had walked around in the blood and tracked it all over the linoleum. The room looked like the scene of some ghastly massacre.

She stood stock-still for a moment, stunned that nobody had seen fit to mention that her mother had experienced some kind of major haemorrhage during her so-called turn.

Shaking all over and fighting a queasy stomach, she closed the door behind her, slipped her shoes off by force of habit, and inched her way around the blood to the sink, where she found some yellow washing-up gloves and a dishcloth. No paper towels, of course, because her mother 'didn't believe in' disposable goods. Creeping towards the splatters, she took a deep breath, turned her head away, and began to mop up at arm's length.

The consistency was all wrong for blood. So was the smell.

Annie risked turning her head to look at the gruesome mess again.

She gave a sudden peal of laughter, shockingly loud in the still and deserted house.

Tomato soup! Her mother seemed to have thrown a bowl of tomato soup at the cabinet before she fainted. How on earth could she have thought it was blood, for even a moment? Good grief, she must be going mental.

Weak with relief, Annie threw down the dishcloth and went straight through the kitchen, skirting around the soup, to the phone. She hesitated a moment before picking it up.

Annie's mother saw the phone as a dangerous instrument that could lead to unnecessary and uncontrolled spending if not kept under strict quarantine. To that end, she kept it tethered to a small walnut table in the hallway in the direct path of an icy draught that blew up the back of your legs from under the front door while you talked. Furthermore, the phone was so centrally placed that anyone in the kitchen or living room could hear your every word with ease, unless you kept your voice down to a virtual whisper. When Annie was a teenager, her mother's attitude to the phone had been a terrible blight on her social life.

Calculating the time difference in her head, Annie realised that Simon might already be in bed, but she hadn't said a word to him since she got the news about her mum, and she didn't care if she woke him from the sleep of the dead. She needed to talk to him.

Minutes later, she sat on the floor, arms wrapped around her knees, staring sightlessly at her reflection in her mother's glass-fronted bookcase.

She'd let the phone ring through to her embarrassingly sing-song recorded greeting at least six times. That was enough to rouse an entire household six times over, surely. But nobody had answered the call.

Where on earth could the man *be*, this late at night?

Really, there was only one thing for it. With shaky fingers, she dialled Heather's home number.

Somebody at the Gibson house was obviously up and about, even though it must be close to midnight. After a single ring, Annie heard a click and a voice said, 'Yes?'

'Um ... Heather?'

'No, it's Rob.'

Oh dear. Bit of a clanger. What man wanted to hear that he could be mistaken for his wife on the phone? 'Sorry,' she muttered, 'bad line. It's Annie calling from England. Um ... is Heather asleep?'

'Not that I know of. I think she's making lunch.'

'Oh, it's *lunch* time? Thank God, thank God! I thought it was the middle of the night. I was wondering where on earth Simon could possibly be at this hour. I've got it all backwards! What an idiot. Look, can I speak to Heather?'

'Hang on, I'll give her the phone.'

Annie heard a shuffling sound as Rob walked to the kitchen with the cordless phone to find his wife. Then his muffled voice said, 'It's Annie Keeler. She sounds a little spacey.' Moments later, Heather was on the line. 'Annie! How is everything? Is your mom OK?'

'Yes, thank God. She seems fine. How's Lydia?'

'She and Hailey passed out at around ten last night. It was cute – their first sleepover.'

'Around *ten*? Um, where was Simon?'

'He called in from the office. He had some huge meeting or other. It went on late. We decided he'd just leave Lydia here rather than come in and drag her home at midnight.'

'So ... how did he sound?'

'Tired. Worried about you. I can't believe he didn't call you today.'

Heather didn't sound too bright and bushy-tailed herself, Annie thought but didn't say.

'Well, maybe he did. My mobile doesn't work over here, and my mum doesn't have voicemail. I'll try him on his BlackBerry again, I suppose.'

'All right. He said he'd make an effort to get home early today so that Lydia could sleep in her own bed. I told him she's welcome to stay here.'

Again, Annie thought she heard strain in Heather's voice. 'Well, I hope it won't come to that,' she said. 'Thank you so, so much. For everything! I'll pay you back some day. I promise.'

After she'd hung up on Heather, Annie hesitated a moment and then dialled Simon's mobile number. Her mother would go through the roof when she saw the phone bill, but that couldn't be helped.

She'd tried him so many times since she left Norbury without managing to get through that she was momentarily speechless when he picked up after just one ring.

'Hello, Annie? Finally! What's going on? Are you OK? How's your mum?'

He sounded so normal that Annie couldn't help herself. She started making the 'ack-acking' noise that indicates to the person on the other end of a line that you're either choking on a chicken bone or trying not to sob.

'Hey, Annie? Are you still there? Oh God, how bad is it? Should I get on a plane?'

Annie managed to bring her vocal cords and tear ducts

under control. 'No, no. I'm sorry. Mum's fine, absolutely fine. They're discharging her tomorrow. I'm just a bit worried because the doctor said she ought to be watched very carefully for a while, and I'm not sure how ... I mean, I wonder if I should start advertising for someone to come in and look after her, or something? They're worried about her passing out again, I think. Something to do with her inner ear, plus she could break a hip if she has another fall. She's not fit to be alone. This is when I wish to God I wasn't an only child.'

'Annie, can she travel?'

'Travel?'

'Fly. Is she up to it? Because if she is, bring her here. We'll look after her here.'

'Really?'

'Of course! It's the only logical thing to do. Well – unless you don't want her to come?'

'Good grief! You're a genius! If I can force her onto that plane, she's coming! God, Simon, I can't believe I didn't even *think* of it.'

'Well, people don't think straight in an emergency. Ask the doctors when she can fly. She can sleep in the third spare room, downstairs. I knew we'd find a use for it one day.'

Annie was in her pyjamas, about to brush her teeth and turn in for the night after eating a desultory meal of toast and Marmite in front of the space heater in the living room, when the doorbell rang.

When she peered through her mother's little spy-glass, she saw the faces of Henny and Sarah, distorted so that their foreheads looked huge.

She threw open the door and both women rushed at her with open arms. A little scuffle ensued, during which Henny managed to air-kiss Annie's left cheek, but Sarah bested her by getting Annie in a bear hug and pounding her on the back.

'God, it's good to see you,' Sarah said over her shoulder. 'Both of us have been trying to reach you all day. In the end, I just got on the train from London. Henny picked me up and we came over to see for ourselves. When in God's name is Auntie Gladys going to get an answering machine? And why have you turned off your mobile phone? Wow, look at your hair!'

Annie drew back from the hug, grinning all over her face. 'This is so nice,' she said. 'I was feeling all lonely and sorry for myself. I've tried to get through to you lot, too, but you're never home, Henny. And Sarah, I didn't know your work number. As for my mobile, it seems to have died on me. No Service, it keeps telling me. I don't think it likes all this roaming around.'

'The hospital says your mum's doing really well,' Henny said. Dressed in baggy jeans and a long-sleeved T-shirt, her wavy blonde hair scraped back in a messy ponytail, Annie's oldest friend still managed to look glamorous despite the wear and tear of bringing up three unusually bouncy children. 'Thank God! I can't tell you how panicked I was when they rang me up. And they wouldn't let me see her yesterday, because I'm not family.'

Annie shook her head. 'What a nightmare for you, Hen. But thank God it wasn't serious. They're discharging her tomorrow, you know.' By now, they were in the chilly living room and Henny threw herself down on the sofa as if exhausted. Sarah took off her military-looking coat and draped it over the back of a chair, but within moments she was shrugging it back on again.

'It's like a morgue in here. Is the heating on the blink?' she asked.

Annie laughed. 'Mum asked me to turn the thermostat down. She was dead worried about the cost of heating the place with nobody in it. You know how she is about waste.'

'*You're* in it, mate,' Sarah said, nodding her red head emphatically. 'Here, I'll go and crank it up a bit. I mean, Auntie Gladys always kept the place cold, but this is ridiculous. I'll put the kettle on, too.'

'So,' said Henny. 'Look at you, all blonde.'

Annie patted at her hair. 'Yeah, I decided to go native,' she said. 'I'm letting it grow out, though – I think it was a mistake. Things are pretty good, otherwise.'

'Oh, don't grow it out. I like it! Tell me, have you figured out what to give Lydia for packed lunch?'

Annie grimaced. 'Still working on that one. She seems to live on air and lemonade.'

'But she's happy? And you're happy?'

Annie hesitated a moment. 'Oh yes,' she said. 'We're happy. Of course, it's not like Simon and I are still on honeymoon. It's not that kind of crazy happiness. We have a ton of, you know, daily things that come up. Little arguments and stuff. But that's so normal in a marriage, isn't it?'

Henny raised her eyebrows. 'What kind of arguments?'

'Oh, just ... stuff. Like I might decide to do something

with Lydia, and he might not think it's the right thing for her. That sort of thing.'

Henny was still frowning. 'Well, I suppose it's a little different if you start off with a kid already in the mix.'

Sarah came into the room with a tray and set it down heavily on the coffee table. 'I found oatcakes, water biscuits, and a tiny wedge of old Cheddar,' she said. 'It's going to be a feast!'

As they settled down to this spartan fare, Sarah suddenly looked over at Annie, winked salaciously, and asked, 'So, do you see much of the sexy cowboy bloke? He's a dead good kisser. You should try him some time.'

'Sarah!' Annie and Henny chorused in protest.

'Crikey, I forgot for a moment. You're married! Let's pretend I didn't say that.'

After Henny and Sarah had left that evening, Annie had a phone call from Simon. 'Annie, can I ask you a huge favour?' He sounded strangely tentative.

'Of course.'

'Can you ... can you possibly visit Lydia's grandparents?'

'Um, yes, sure, why not. I'd like to see your mum again. Would I go up by train? I wouldn't like to leave my mum for too long.'

'I don't mean Mum and Dad. I mean Beth's people. Wilma's been in touch. She knows you're over there and ... well, she says she'd like to meet you.'

Beth's parents had been invited to Annie and Simon's low-key wedding, but at the last minute they had decided not to come.

'Really? Gosh. I wonder why. OK, well, if you think I *should*.'

'I think you should,' he said.

With a sense of dread, Annie set off the next morning in her mother's Renault 5, listening to Classic FM and trying to navigate from an ancient map book that showed roads that didn't exist any more.

Wilma and Don Forsythe lived in a village about twelve miles south of Oxford – some sixty miles from Gladys's house as the crow flew, but quite a bit further by road. By the time Annie pulled up in front of their house – a substantial two-storey brick building with a green door – she was clammy with nerves. She thought she'd sit in the car a bit, just to give herself a break from the driving before rushing headlong into another stressful situation, but the green door opened almost the moment the engine died, and a woman stepped out onto the gravel.

At a glance, Annie could tell that this was Beth's mother. She bore a striking resemblance to the slender, blonde woman Annie had seen in Simon's photo albums. Wilma Forsythe was tall and slightly stooped, with sharp elbows and rather prominent teeth, but her eyes were just like Beth's – piercing blue and fringed with thick blonde lashes.

She was dressed with old-fashioned precision in a navy-blue woollen suit and flat shoes of the kind that Annie believed were called brogues.

As Annie straightened up out of the car, slightly flustered in her very casual jeans and woolly jumper, the woman held out her hand and gave her a firm handshake. 'Annie, we are so pleased you could come.' She had a slight foreign accent,

Annie noted. 'Come and meet my husband. He was having a little nap, but no doubt he is now awake.'

Annie followed her into the house, which was very dim owing to yards of heavy fabric at every window. In the living room they found Don Forsythe dozing in an armchair. He woke with a start and stared rather wild-eyed at the stranger in the room, while Wilma explained to him with great patience that this was the guest they'd been expecting.

'I have prepared a light lunch,' Wilma told Annie when Don had calmed down a bit. 'We have only to heat the soup and slice the baguette.'

'Very nice,' Annie replied with a placatory smile. This woman, with her unshakeable poise and steady decorum, made her feel wrong-footed, somehow. 'My mum is a big one for soup.'

The woman inclined her head graciously. 'Come, sit down,' she invited, gesturing at the kitchen table. 'You know, of course, that for some time I have looked forward to speaking with you.'

Annie gulped. 'Really?'

'But of course! I was disappointed when Don's health made it impossible to come to your wedding. It has been a matter of great interest to me, to converse with the woman who now has the care of my grandchild.'

'Oh. Right.'

'Lydia is prospering, I hope? Simon tells me he detects positive signs of spiritual healing since she went to America.'

'Um, oh yes. She's definitely prospering.'

Wilma ladled out soup, threw in some sprigs from a herb growing on her window sill, and crumbled goat's cheese into the bowls.

Then she gave Annie a smile. 'You have come a long way for a bowl of soup. I hope you will enjoy it.'

While they ate, they talked about the weather, the sad state of the global economy, and the kinds of plants that grew in Connecticut. After Wilma had cleared away their plates, she set a tray for Don and took it through to his chair. Then she came back, put the kettle on, sat down, and looked Annie in the eye.

'I will say only this, and then be done,' she said solemnly. 'Lydia has had much sadness to bear in her short life. She is not, how would you say, a charming child. Not these days. But she has need of a happy home.'

Annie felt her throat constrict. She put out a hand. 'Mrs Forsythe, I mean Wilma, I want you to know that I plan to do my very best for Lyddie. She's safe with me.'

Wilma nodded briskly. 'I think you will,' she said. 'I have looked in your eyes, and I think you will.'

# Chapter Nine

'I can walk, thank you,' Gladys Harleigh told the uniformed woman who was unfolding a wheelchair at the ticketing booth.

'Shhh, Mum,' Annie whispered. 'I'm counting on jumping all the queues with this thing. There's even a special fast track through security.'

Gladys's face lit up. 'Oh, I see. Good thinking.' Annie's mum had never asked for help in her life, and she wasn't about to start, even if she had a sore back and was covered in bruises. But she was always game to beat the system.

When they were ushered onto the plane, first in line with other wheelchair-bound travellers and a huddle of unhappy-looking parents of small children, Gladys was indignant to find that they were travelling first class.

'Simon booked the tickets,' Annie said in self-defence. 'I had nothing to do with it.'

'But it's outrageous! These seats cost as much as some people's annual salary!' She turned to an attendant. 'Excuse me, young lady, is there any way you can downgrade us to the economy section? We'd like to get refunds on these seats, if it's not too much trouble.'

The air hostess, eyes wide, shook her head. 'I'm sorry, madam,' she said. 'The seats are purchased now. It's too late to make any changes.'

'Mum! Relax,' Annie hissed in her ear. 'I'm pretty sure Simon used air miles to upgrade us. He travels so much for work that he has a ton. He's always trying to think of ways to use them up before they expire.'

'Really?'

'Really.'

'Well, all right then. I must say, it helps my back if I can put my feet up.'

Annie held her mother's elbow as she lowered herself into the seat, pretending not to notice her grimace of pain.

Simon hadn't been able to use his air miles. She knew that for a fact. They were travelling during some sort of black-out period. Despite the exorbitant price of these seats, he'd insisted that someone fresh out of a hospital bed couldn't travel with her knees in close proximity to her chin.

She must just remember to warn him not to spill the beans.

Simon was waiting at the airport, a tall, straight figure in a black trenchcoat, standing head and shoulders above the limo drivers with their scrawled handheld signs. His blue eyes crinkled as he smiled straight at her from across the room. They kissed briefly, aware of Gladys in her wheelchair, her string bag – bulging with newspapers, an umbrella, a scarf, cough sweets, and various oddments off the airline meal tray – balanced precariously on her lap.

Simon bent down to kiss his mother-in-law's powdery

cheek. 'Gladys, good to see you,' he said. 'The one silver lining in this whole business is that it got you to come and visit us.'

Annie watched her mother glow with pleasure. 'Well, I'd have come before if I'd been invited,' she said with a fake offended sniff. 'But a couple of newly-weds like you? No surprise you weren't begging me to come over.'

'Come on, you know we've been holding a room for you,' Simon replied. 'The day we looked at the house, Annie stuck her head into the downstairs bedroom and said, "This is Mum's room." You've been putting us off ever since we got here – admit it.'

He was helping her out of the wheelchair now, since the attendant seemed eager to be off.

She batted his hands away flirtatiously. 'Oh, don't fuss,' she said. 'Honestly. You'd think I was a complete invalid. Three days ago I was up a ladder pruning my standard wisteria.'

But in the end she allowed him to support her out into the mild day, across the busy road to the car park, while Annie brought up the rear, pushing the trolley. Watching them from behind – the wide-shouldered, upright figure modifying his long gait to accommodate his small, stooped companion – Annie's heart swelled again with gratitude. This was what it meant to be part of a family. You didn't have to shoulder your burdens alone.

She was brought down to earth with a rude shock a little later when she went to pick Lydia up from school. By then, her helpmeet was long gone (back into the city on the two-ten train) and she was waiting with Heather, who had come over to the house in the early afternoon to see if everything was all right, like the tried and trusted friend she had become.

As Lydia came out of the school building, frail body buckling under her large backpack, Annie smiled and waved – but couldn't catch her eye.

'She's been a bit quiet the last couple of days,' Heather had warned as they walked to school together, Annie hanging onto Patches' leash for dear life.

'Quiet?'

'OK, I didn't want to worry you, so I never said anything … but she, um, she stopped talking a day or so after you left.'

'Stopped – talking? At school, you mean? She's always been quiet at school.'

'No, not just at school. At our house too.'

'Oh, she probably felt shy with you. Just as long as she was talking to Hailey …'

'Sorry, nope, she wasn't even talking to Hailey. The only time she'd say a word was when she was over at your place throwing a ball for the dog.'

'But she was speaking to *Simon*, right?'

While Annie was in England, Lydia had spent her afternoons with the Gibsons, but Simon had made a superhuman effort to come home from work at around six so that she could spend the evenings and nights in her own home. Since the weather had been good, Patches had been able to stay at home for the most part, out in the backyard, restrained from wandering off by the new underground electric fence they'd had installed in the nick of time.

Heather shrugged. 'I don't know. You'll have to ask him. I do know he tried to take her trick or treating on Halloween, but she wouldn't go. Oh, and your house was tee-peed because he couldn't find the candy.'

'Shit. There wasn't any candy. I forgot to get it. What's tee-peed, anyway?'

'Toilet-papered. But Rob came over with a ladder and helped Simon get it down from the trees.'

Annie noticed for the first time that the normally vivacious Heather looked strained and subdued.

'Oh God, this has been a real trial for you,' she said with a guilty grimace, 'and all you got out of it was a bottle of perfume and a silk scarf from Duty Free. But I'll make it up to you somehow. I promise.'

But Heather shook her head and gave Annie's hand a quick squeeze. 'Don't get me wrong, Lydia was no trouble at *all*,' she said. 'I hardly even knew she was in the house. I've never known a kid who makes less of a rumpus. Sure, Hailey was a little bent out of shape when Lydia wouldn't play, but she understood when I explained that Lydia was probably just sad and scared. She was OK with it.'

Sad and scared. Yes, that sounded about right. Annie blinked quickly. She'd had her own sad and scared moments since that phone call from Henny.

'Anyway, I owed you one – remember?' Heather added. 'You took care of Pompom for me when you barely even knew me.'

'That's right – I did, didn't I? But then you got me the riding lessons.'

'Yes, but that doesn't count.'

'Well – OK. We'll call it even.'

Touched to hear that Lydia had missed her, Annie half expected her stepdaughter to come running out of the school building at full tilt, hair streaming out behind her and eyes full of happy tears, bent on throwing her arms around her stepmother in joyful reunion. But Lydia came out slowly, dragging her feet, eyes downcast, body ominously slumped, hair hanging limply down her back.

'Lydia, over here!' Annie called, thinking maybe she hadn't seen her. 'Here! Here!' Lydia (and most of the other kids pouring out of the building) finally looked at her.

Annie recoiled.

The resentment in Lydia's eyes could have stripped paint off walls, withered grapes on the vine, curdled milk in cows' udders.

It was a relief when the child dropped her eyes and walked over to greet Patches, who was as ecstatic to see her after six short hours of separation as he'd been to see Annie after six whole days.

Annie was beginning to think that people could learn a thing or two from dogs. Joyfulness, for example. Loyalty. Gusto. The ability not to bear grudges.

The short walk home was mostly silent, Lydia ignoring everybody, Hailey running ahead, Annie and Heather raising eyebrows at each other and shrugging.

Gladys was stationed at the sink when Annie and Lydia came into the house through the kitchen door. The old woman turned around stiffly, stripping off the washing-up gloves and holding her arms out. 'So, *there* you are, Lydia, goodness you've ...'

Lydia didn't even stop. She shrugged out of her backpack and jacket simultaneously, dropped them on the floor, kicked her shoes off without breaking her stride, and ran out of the kitchen. Annie and her mother stared at each other as they heard the child's feet pounding up the stairs, and then the distant slam of her bedroom door.

Gladys's eyebrows met above her nose. 'Don't tell me you're letting that child pick up American manners?'

Now, Annie hadn't minded when Gladys gazed around their minivan and said, 'Look at this *enormous* car! So these days a family of three needs, let me see, one, two, three ... *seven* seats?' Her mother knew nothing about car-pooling, after all.

Admittedly, when Gladys stood in the driveway looking up at their house and said, 'Oh, for heaven's sake! Look at the *size* of this place,' she'd begun to feel a prickle of annoyance.

But her own vehemence took her by surprise when Gladys piped up about Lydia's lack of etiquette.

'For God's sake, Mum. Give her a break. She's seven years old!'

Looking at her mother's startled face, she felt immediately contrite. 'I'm sorry, Mum. Turns out I'm a bit overprotective. Anyway, you're supposed to be in bed, aren't you? So for heaven's sake, leave the stuff in the sink and go and lie down. Please?'

Gladys gave one of her mock-offended sniffs and said, 'Well, it seems I was able to drum some manners into *you*, at any rate.'

Annie knocked steadily on Lydia's door for about five minutes before a voice burst out, 'Go away. I don't want to talk to you.'

'Rubbish,' said Annie. 'Of course you want to talk to me. I have a present for you.'

'I don't want your stupid presents.'

'Fair enough. I'll give it to Hailey. She likes horses too.'

A silence followed. Annie waited. She was just about to turn away when she heard the sound of feet moving over the floorboards. A moment later, Lydia's door opened a crack.

'All right, what did you get me?'

'You can come to my room and look.'

Lydia paused a moment, weighing the pros and cons. Then she sighed and inched out of her room, arms crossed over her chest.

Annie turned and walked to the master bedroom, her ears on stalks. She was just able to make out the shuffling sound of Lydia's socks.

Her suitcase was on the bed, half unpacked.

Lydia came reluctantly into the room. She was obviously finding it hard to maintain her air of bitter hostility alongside her eagerness to see what horse-related treasure Annie might have brought her.

'Dig around under the clothes,' Annie suggested.

Lydia approached the suitcase slowly and stood staring into it, her nose slightly wrinkled as if she smelled something unpleasant. But she could only hold the pose for a second or two. Soon, she was up to her elbows among Annie's jeans and T-shirts, bringing stray objects up for Annie's inspection. 'No, not that, that's my make-up bag. Not that, not that ... Ah, yes! You've found it.'

Lydia was holding an object wrapped in newspaper.

'Be careful,' Annie said, 'it's breakable.'

Lydia put it down on the bed and began to unwrap it, throwing crumpled pieces of paper over her shoulder with abandon. Patches jumped up from his basket in the corner and began tearing the paper to shreds. Annie didn't try to stop him.

At last, the present was revealed.

It was a ceramic Thelwell pony, comically rounded and sway-backed, with a whimsical expression in its eyes, and a wild, curling mane.

Lydia held it tight.

'Do you like it?' Annie asked.

Lydia nodded.

'Good.'

Lydia ran her fingers over the pony's mane. 'You missed the last soccer game,' she said out of the blue. 'And you weren't here for Halloween.'

'No, I'm sorry. I wish I could've been here. Did you score a goal?'

'I'll never score a goal. Everybody knows that.'

Annie gulped. 'You might, if you stick with it. You're getting better every time you go out. Do you know, I've never been trick or treating before?'

'I hate Halloween.'

'You do?'

'Duh! Of *course* I do. Stupid, dumb holiday. Who cares

about dead people and ghosts and skeletons! And – and I hate you too! You're not my mother. You can keep your stupid, ugly *pony*.'

So saying, she threw the little china horse at the floor where it smashed into several pieces. She didn't wait to see the damage, but ran out of the room, slamming the door behind her – much to the dismay of Patches, who had jumped up to run after her, confident that this was the start of some energetic new game.

Annie stood still a moment. Then she bent down to pick up the pieces of the pony. Perhaps she'd be able to glue them together. Moving too quickly, she managed to jab her finger straight onto the sharp end of a shard.

Annie watched the blood bubble up, then put it into her mouth and sucked it. 'Stupid, dumb *idiot*,' she said to herself, and felt almost triumphant to have made herself cry.

When Simon came home that evening, everybody was in bed, even Annie. Yes, it was only eight p.m., but Annie and her mother had lived through a day five hours longer than any day had a right to be – six hours of which had been spent on an aeroplane. What was more, they'd set out from a place where it was now one o'clock in the morning.

Nevertheless, Annie managed to raise her head and rasp, 'Why didn't you tell me Lydia was acting up?'

Simon, bundling shirts and his suit into a dry-cleaning bag, glanced up in surprise. 'Hey! You're awake!'

'Yes, I'm awake.' Annie sat up, rubbing her eyes. 'So why didn't you tell me?'

Simon shrugged. 'There wasn't much point, was there?

Nothing you could've done. Besides, you had enough on your hands.'

'Well, yes, but next time I'd like to be kept in the picture. I know nobody wanted to worry me because of Mum, but it was a shock to come home and find Lydia so ... so *angry* with me.' She was trying to sound calm, but she couldn't prevent a little wobble from creeping into her voice.

Simon dropped the dry-cleaning bag and came over to the bed. 'What happened?' he demanded.

Annie shrugged. 'Oh, nothing really.' She suddenly found herself reluctant to tell him about Lydia smashing the Thelwell pony. Just as he'd said earlier, there wasn't much point. 'It's OK. I'm just tired. We'll all feel better tomorrow.'

He bent down and kissed her chastely on the temple. 'You're right,' he said. 'Get some sleep.'


Annie took perverse pleasure in the impeccable manners of her new American friends as they went over to her mother's chair in ones and twos to introduce themselves, ask after her health, and tell her what a darling accent she had. Annie didn't think the ladies of the Women's Institute in Leatherhead could have outdone them.

They were at the home of Donna Knopf, who hosted an annual pre-festive-season coffee morning in early November. 'I'm sorry, I can't come,' Annie had said when Donna phoned to invite her. 'I have my mum over from England.'

'Oh, that's so cool. Bring her along too,' Donna insisted. 'I know everybody would just *love* to meet her.'

And sure enough, the ladies of Maple Tree Ridge all

behaved as if they'd been waiting their entire lives to meet an old-age pensioner from Surrey with firm opinions about the recycling of yoghurt cartons, jam jars and tea bags.

'You see, during the war,' Gladys told a rapt circle of admirers, 'we didn't throw a single thing away. Not a single thing. We found a use for everything that came into the house, and what was more, we bought almost nothing.' She shook her head sorrowfully. 'I'm telling you, there was no wastage back then. Not like you lot with your pumpkins. People would queue up for hours just to get their hands on one measly orange; fruit was that rare.'

'Good times,' Heather said to Annie out of the side of her mouth.

Annie laughed. 'Mum wasn't born until *after* the war,' she whispered back. 'But she likes to think she lived through it. Mind you, I think the rationing afterwards was pretty bad, too. Scarred the nation for a couple of generations. There are still people with entire garden sheds full of yoghurt cartons and jam jars.'

They both giggled.

But when Heather stopped laughing her face fell into haggard lines, and Annie couldn't help thinking, as she had so often recently, that Heather seemed distracted and vague.

'Heather – are you OK?' she asked.

Heather frowned and shot a furtive look around the room. 'Sure, I'm OK. How about you? How are things with Lydia? Looks like she's talking again, at least.'

Lydia was talking, all right – to Hailey, to Simon, to Gladys, even once or twice to her teacher, or so Annie heard. Just not to Annie herself.

Annie shrugged. 'Oh, she's fine.' She didn't feel like discussing Lydia, not in the middle of Donna Knopf's pre-festive season coffee.

The truth was, Lydia was behaving as if she wished Annie would simply disappear out of her life. If Annie entered a room, she walked out. If she asked her a question, she shrugged. If Annie tried to hug her, she held herself still and stiff as if waiting for the ordeal to be over.

'Do you need help with that?' Annie asked later that same day as Lydia pulled her homework folder out of her backpack.

Lydia shook her head as she spread her papers out on the kitchen table.

'What have you got there?' Gladys asked. 'I can probably help, as long as it's not fractions. I can't remember those for the life of me.'

'What are fractions?' Lydia asked.

'Halves and quarters and things.'

'Oh no, we haven't done those yet. It's spelling and word problems.'

Gladys hobbled to the table and lowered herself into a chair. 'Spelling,' she said. 'Annie was always good at spelling. I'll test you on the words, shall I?'

Lydia hesitated a moment. Then, 'OK,' she said. 'This is the list. I never do the bonus words at the bottom.'

'What's a bonus word?'

'Oh, it's just an extra word. You can get more than twenty out of twenty if you know your bonus words. But who needs more than twenty out of twenty?'

'Young lady, if there's one thing in life you've got to do

it's the extra things. If I'm helping you, you'll do the bonus words.'

Annie steeled herself. But Lydia didn't snatch the list out of Gladys's hands, or get up and storm out of the room. She simply sat very still for a moment, then shrugged and said, '*OK*, but it still seems kinda dumb to me.'

'Dumb means unable to speak,' said Gladys.

'No, it doesn't. It means stupid.' Lydia looked a little unsure as she said this.

'Do you have such a thing as a dictionary?' Gladys asked. 'We'll look it up.'

'My pocket *Oxford* is upstairs in the den,' Annie said. 'I'll get it, if you like.'

Gladys nodded briskly. 'That's a good idea.'

When Annie came back into the room with the book, she stood at the door watching the two of them for a moment. Neither of them knew she was there. Gladys was calling out words in her clipped, imperious accent, and Lydia was bent over her piece of paper, brows together, tongue between her teeth. Gladys peered at Lydia's paper and reached out to pat her hand.

'Well done,' she said.

Lydia looked up at Gladys and giggled. 'It's easy when you say the words 'cos I can hear all the letters. Except the r's. You don't say your r's.'

Annie felt a terrible pang, like heartburn only worse. Her mother did this so well. It was beautiful to see – the grey head next to the blonde one, bent together over the books. Gladys was such a natural. By contrast, Annie was a pitiful excuse for a mother figure. Anybody could see that.

Annie put the dictionary on the counter and walked soundlessly away.

'Isn't that a bit of a skimpy outfit?' Gladys asked one morning when Annie came down to the kitchen dressed for the first of her beginner tennis clinics. Tennis, Annie had decided, was definitely a lesser evil than either bridge or riding. 'You're not a teenager any more, you know. And won't you be cold?'

'I'm playing indoors, Mum,' Annie said, filling a plastic water bottle up at the fridge. 'The place is heated. If I went in a tracksuit, I'd be sweltering in five minutes.'

'I can't get over this whole tennis lark, I must say.' Gladys was standing beside the stove, boiling up Annie's kitchen cloths. (No matter how Annie begged, she simply wouldn't sit still and do nothing.) Gladys's sense of hygiene had intrigued Annie for years. It was a creed of hers that kitchen cloths needed regular boiling, but she couldn't see the point of dirtying two separate boards to chop up salad greens and raw chicken.

'I wish you wouldn't do that, Mum,' said Annie.

Gladys swirled the cloths with a fork. 'You were never any good at tennis at school,' she mused.

'It's never too late to learn something new.'

'Oh yes, it jolly well is. I don't know how to swim, and I never will. You can't teach an old dog new tricks.'

Patches, in the corner, thumped his tail. He thought his other name was 'dog'.

'Mum, people here think nothing of learning a new sport in their thirties. They do it all the time! That's one of the things I like about America. People really believe it's possible to change and improve.'

'Oh yes, I know all about that,' said Gladys darkly. 'Dale Carnegie. Oprah what's-her-name. But the truth is, *nobody* can make a silk purse out of a sow's ear.'

Annie took a deep breath. 'So anyway, Mum, I thought you could come along to the courts with me. I mean, if you're not feeling too stiff and sore? Maybe bring a book to read. They have comfortable sofas and you can even make yourself a cup of tea. There's an urn and everything.'

Although Gladys liked to play the curmudgeon, she was quite willing to try new things and visit new places. When they stepped into the club's reception area, expensively decorated in shades of chocolate brown and pink, Gladys lowered herself into a squishy armchair and looked around her with real pleasure.

Nervous, Annie found herself missing every second ball the pro hit at her. 'Sorry,' she kept shouting across the net. Eventually the pro beckoned her to the net.

'Don't move your racquet when I hit a ball to you,' he murmured. 'Just hold still. My aim is good.'

After that, things went better. Now and then, she even managed to hit a ball with reverberating force. Every few minutes, she found herself glancing through the plate glass window to see if her mother was paying attention. 'This is pathetic,' she muttered to one of the other women in the clinic. 'I'm in a tennis lesson and my mum's out there watching, so I've gone all butterfingers. I feel about ten years old again.'

On the drive home, Gladys surprised her by saying, 'You

looked very good out there, Annie. Never knew you could thump the ball like that.'

Annie glowed with simple pride.

When they arrived back, Annie found a message on her phone from Miss Scofield, Lydia's teacher. Her heart pumping with alarm, she dialled the school's number, wondering whether Lydia had been taken ill or perhaps fallen off the giant plastic 'spider' in the playground. That spider had always looked lethal, to her.

To her relief, she got through to the teacher directly. 'Oh no,' trilled Miss Scofield. 'Nothing's wrong. I just wanted to share something with you. We're all so proud of Lydia. She did it!'

'Um, did what?'

'You know – her class presentation.'

'Right, of course. The class presentation.' What class presentation? She'd never heard of it until this minute.

'She did so well! She said she'd been practising with her grandma.'

'Um, yes, that's right. My mum's been helping her a bit with her homework.'

'Well, your mom should be proud! Lydia did a fan-*tabulous* job! We gave her a standing ovation. Most of her classmates have never even heard her voice before, and she blew them away with this amazing speech about how dolphins communicate! I had tears in my eyes.'

Annie was delighted. She really was. This was a huge breakthrough for Lydia. Huge. And she wasn't small-minded enough to wish that she'd been the one coaching Lydia for her big moment. Of *course*, she wasn't. She was very grateful to her mum, very grateful indeed.

But she did wonder why Gladys had never let slip a single nugget of information about the whole project, from start to finish. Her mum, perhaps noticing an odd look in Annie's eyes, was quick to explain. 'We wanted to surprise you,' she said. 'And I thought Lyddie would do better without the pressure, to be frank. Even her teacher didn't know she was going to do it – not until the last minute.'

When Simon heard the news, he said he'd come home early and take them all out to dinner to celebrate. They went to Lydia's favourite restaurant, a local hibachi grill. Annie's grin was just as big as anybody else's when they all raised their glasses for a toast. Perhaps it faltered just a little when Simon said, 'Here's to you, Gladys, fantastic job with Lydia! And Lydia, here's to dolphins – and speaking up in class!' But she didn't think anybody noticed, because nobody was paying any attention to her.

Monday started innocuously enough with a visit to Costco. Annie didn't really need to go to Costco, but she was always looking for an outing for Gladys, who was constitutionally incapable of lolling about and doing nothing. That very morning, Annie had been forced to manhandle her away from Lydia's dressing table, which she had taken it upon herself to reorganise – even though, by the look on her face, all that stooping was pretty painful.

Besides, some inner devil kept urging Annie to take her mother to the giant warehouse store, just to goad her.

Back in Surrey, Gladys seldom ventured out of her own

village to go shopping. She was quite happy to patronise the local butcher, baker and candlestick maker, even though they were ruinously expensive. Since she didn't do any comparison shopping, and had a deep mistrust of mass-produced foods, she wasn't aware of how very extravagant her boutique shopping habits were. The concept of buying in bulk was completely foreign to her. This wasn't surprising, really. Her fridge was slightly smaller than Annie's cool box. Besides, grocery shopping provided a framework for her daily life.

Annie herself had been appalled when Heather first took her to Costco. In her flat in London, she'd never had much in her fridge beyond a pint of milk, an apple and a carton of leftover curry. Looking around in disbelief at the giant vats of mayonnaise and dill pickles, she had vowed to Heather that she would never shop at such a place, not if she suddenly found herself catering for an army. But mere days later, she was back, seduced by Heather's claim that one trip to Costco kept her family in 'bath tissue' for three to six months, depending. (Depending on what, she didn't like to ask.)

So she paid her joining fee, was issued with a card, and began her monthly bulk-buying pilgrimages. After her very first trip, she was a convert. How could she not be, when she'd found a revolving wooden stand housing twenty — yes, twenty! — pairs of scissors, each of which cut paper in a different pattern?

She wasn't disappointed by her mother's reaction to the place. As they walked in, Gladys fell silent. She remained silent as they pushed their super-sized shopping trolley past rows of digital cameras and monstrous flat-screen TVs. The silence persisted as they wheeled past tables piled high with leather jackets, cashmere sweaters and waffle-weave spa robes. The food department, with its three-pound cartons of cherries, forty-eight-count boxes of brownies and six-pound trays of minced sirloin, didn't elicit a single remark. Gladys had nothing to say as they passed beneath a garden shed, suspended from the ceiling above flat-packed boxes that you could load into your trolley in case the hanging shed caught your eye and you thought, 'what the heck, let's have one of those'. She didn't even comment when Annie showed her a bag of sixty frozen waffles.

It was the chewing gum that finally undid her. She stood in front of the towering display in dumbstruck wonder, then burst out, 'Who in God's name buys fifteen packs of spearmint gum at one time? I mean, that must be more than two hundred pieces of gum!'

'I don't know,' said Annie, 'but I know who buys those giant bags of pigs' ears. I do – for Patches.'

Gladys shook her head. 'I wouldn't have the heart to get a single thing from this place,' she said. 'I mean, look at that bottle of shampoo. I don't think I'd be able to lift it. And even if I could, I'm not sure I'd live long enough to get halfway through it.'

'Well, Mum,' said Annie a little defensively; she had that very same bottle of shampoo in her bathroom, 'most people do wash their hair every day, nowadays.'

Gladys rolled her eyes. 'I don't know. This modern mania about daily showering and clothes washing. Sign of an overly affluent society. A bath every third day is more than adequate unless you're working out in a potato field, and only *underwear* needs to be washed after every wear.'

'Mu-um!' Annie glanced around hastily, wondering if anybody had overheard. She felt uncannily like a teenager saddled with an embarrassing parent.

'Well, at least they get one thing right at this place,' Gladys said a little later, as they trundled off towards the car. 'No plastic shopping bags. Plastic shopping bags are the scourge of the earth. They should be banned. If people would just learn to keep a handy string bag with them at all times ...'

Annie was about to explain that Costco's no-bag policy was less about wastage and more about discouraging people from nicking things when she happened to glance into a parked car and spot a cloud of dark hair that reminded her of Heather.

She looked again, then rapped on the roof – because it was indeed Heather's cloud of hair.

Heather turned her head, and Annie gasped. Her friend's eyes were red and swollen, her nose was damp, and her lips were blotchy.

As Gladys loomed over Annie's shoulder, Heather made a desperate shooing gesture. Annie needed no second prompting. Taking her mother by the elbow, she steered her briskly towards their own car. Nobody wanted to draw a crowd when they were having a quiet cry in a car park.

'Wasn't that your friend, the one with the horse?' Gladys asked.

'Heather? It looked like her, didn't it? But it was somebody else.'

Gladys gave her a long look, and held her peace.

'I need to dash out for a bit,' Annie said after she'd unloaded the shopping from the boot of the car.

'Of course, you do,' said Gladys. 'Don't worry about me. I'm going to put my feet up after walking around that shop. I haven't had that much exercise since my car broke down and I had to walk a mile and a half to the garage in Croydon.'

Annie smiled. 'All right, Mum. Just keep the phone beside your bed. I'll be as quick as I can.'

'You tell her to keep her chin up,' Gladys said as Annie gathered her car keys and her bag.

After a quick reconnoitre of Heather's empty driveway and garage, Annie drove back to Costco. Sure enough, Heather's car was still there, and Heather was still inside it, not sobbing any more but staring into the middle distance.

Annie tapped on the window, and made a winding-down gesture. Heather seemed resigned but not surprised to see her back. She cracked the window open an inch or two and said, 'Sorry. This is dumb. I'll be OK in a moment. I don't need help. I'm OK.'

Annie didn't budge. 'Look, I'm not going anywhere, so you might as well let me in.'

Heather gave a shaky sigh and reluctantly pressed a button to unlock the car. Sliding into the passenger seat, Annie leaned over and squeezed Heather's shoulder.

'So what's it all about?'

Heather blew her nose and dabbed at her eyes. 'It's private,' she said.

Annie's stomach clenched painfully. 'Do you have breast cancer?' she blurted.

Heather's hand flew to her breast. 'God, I don't think so,' she said.

'Oh, thank goodness. You're not dying of something else, then?'

'No, of course I'm not freaking dying! I've had a miscarriage, that's all.'

'A ... miscarriage?'

'Yes, you know, when you're freaking pregnant one day, and then you're bleeding like Niagara Falls the next day, and then you're not freaking pregnant any more?'

'Oh, God. I'm sorry. Um, when did it happen? Not – surely not while you were watching Lydia for me?'

'Yes, it was around then. But don't worry, it was OK. I mean, having Lydia in the house didn't make it any worse. It wasn't painful or anything. I didn't need a D&C. There was nothing to it, really. It's just ... ten days ago I was having a baby. And now I'm not.' She blew her nose aggressively. 'I'm fine with it, I swear. I mean, I've always been pretty tough. I haven't cried at all, not until now. But ... going into Costco today and seeing those economy boxes of diapers ... I've been eyeing them out for the longest time. We've been trying for this baby ever since Hailey was three. Rob's sperm isn't at the top of its game, you see. Half of his little guys can't swim and the other half don't seem to know where to go. So I've been pricing those diapers for four freaking years. I nearly bought them outright the day I did the pregnancy test, but then I figured,' she blew her nose again, 'I figured I'd wait to get through the first trimester.'

'Oh, Heather! Do they know what went wrong?'

Heather shrugged. 'They couldn't pin it down. Advanced maternal age obviously doesn't help.'

Annie's mouth fell open. 'You're joking. Right?'

Heather shook her head. 'I'm thirty-eight, kiddo. If you're a minute over thirty-five when you conceive, they start reading you the riot act. The rule of thumb is, all risks go up fifty per cent once you pass the magic milestone. Down's syndrome. Cerebral palsy. Gestational diabetes. Miscarriage. You name it. It's all fifty per cent more likely.'

Annie was getting the picture. So. She herself had four more years, then. Oodles of time. She squeezed Heather's hand. 'I'm so sorry you had Lydia on your hands when you had all that going on.'

'You know, I was kind of glad she was there. It kept me civilised.' Heather looked out across the parking lot at the assorted shoppers pushing their groaning trolleys to their cars. 'Anyway, it's a bit of a relief. I wasn't looking forward to the sleepless nights.'

Out of respect, Annie averted her eyes from her friend's bleak face. 'I never even knew you wanted another baby,' she said. 'I thought Hailey was an only child by choice. So many people do that nowadays. It makes a lot of sense, in a way – only one lot of school fees, that sort of thing.'

Heather gave a hollow laugh. 'Not in this town. In this town, you're an under-achiever if you have just three. Four is the norm. Five shows ambition. Six is the height of chic, only attained by the chosen few.'

Annie had indeed noticed, when she glanced through the school directory, whole tribes of kids going by the same surname. 'That's weird,' she said. 'Sort of old-fashioned and traditional for a place like this; a place so close to New York.'

Heather shook her head. 'You still don't get the demographics, do you? Staying home with the kids these days is – well, it's unusual. It's a luxury. But you've probably noticed that most of the moms around here do it. That's because they can afford to. I'm telling you, half these women you meet on the PTO were captains of industry back in the day. They're all Type-A personalities, to a woman. And if they're going to do the mom thing, they're going to do it *right*. And they're going to do it *big*. They're going to do it with spreadsheets and clipboards and a full quota of kids. Oh, and a bunch of "help", of course.'

'But you don't care about all that! You don't give a damn about keeping up with the Joneses!'

'No, of course I don't. I just want another baby, that's all. Rob wants another baby too. To be honest,' she lowered her voice, 'we *need* this baby. We need more glue to hold us together.'

'Glue?'

Heather smoothed her eyebrows with her fingers. 'Rob likes to shake things up,' she said. 'He doesn't like more of the same every freaking day of his life. That's why we've moved so much. He likes new challenges, new people, big events. He doesn't like the day-to-day stuff so much.'

'Well, maybe, but—'

'He likes it when I'm pregnant. He's one of those weird men who gets turned on by the big belly.'

Annie coughed and shifted in her seat. She wasn't sure she wanted to hear all this.

'Believe me,' said Heather, 'we need the glue. But you know what? I'm not going to let a miscarriage slow me down. If I miscarried, it means I still have eggs.'

'Absolutely,' said Annie. 'Of course, you still have eggs.'

'And if Belinda Nielsen could squeeze out four nine-pound boys after her fortieth birthday, damn it, I can surely manage one measly baby while I'm still in my semi-fertile thirties!'

'Damn it, of course you can!' Annie agreed, punching the air.

It was hard to snatch a moment to talk to Simon, now that Gladys was in the house. But while they were getting ready for bed that night, Annie said, 'I was talking to Heather today. She wasn't going to tell us, but ... well, she had a miscarriage while I was in England.'

'What?' said Simon, pausing in the midst of emptying all the coins out of his pockets. 'Are you serious? Come to think of it, she looked a bit down while you were gone. I felt pretty bad; thought that maybe taking care of Lydia was wearing her out.'

'No, she says Lydia was no trouble. Anyway. She's pretty shaken up about it. Reckons that after the age of thirty-five, the whole pregnancy thing gets a lot harder.'

His fingers stopped stacking coins.

'So, well, we haven't really talked about it, but at some point I suppose we need to decide about ...' Somehow, she couldn't go on. Not without any encouragement. He must, after all, know what she meant. By now he should have chimed in with *something* – enthusiastic or otherwise.

He gave her a long look, then dropped his eyes. 'Yes, we'll have to talk about a lot of things,' he said. His expression was all wrong, somehow. 'But let's leave it until we know what's going on with your mum.'

# Chapter Ten

At Simon's urging, Annie took her mum to a highly recommended consultant in Greenwich who listened to Gladys's tale of dizziness, and diagnosed her with something called benign paroxysmal positional vertigo.

'Um – and what's it caused by?' Annie asked, trying to memorise the terminology. It didn't sound at all benign, especially the paroxysmal bit.

'Age,' said the doctor, a plump woman in a voluminous jumper. 'Age or injury. Basically, your mother has what we call ear rocks floating around in her canals. Now, I'm going to do a manoeuvre to see if we can settle them back where they belong.'

Annie watched as the woman got her mother to lie down on the examining table, then tilted her head this way and that.

'Ouch,' Gladys muttered.

'Watch it! She's got a bad back.'

The doctor helped Gladys back into a sitting position. 'She might be a bit dizzy now,' she told Annie. 'Drive her home and keep an eye on her today. Treatment of this kind of vertigo is about eighty per cent effective, so she shouldn't experience much dizziness after today.'

'What? You mean you think you've *cured* her by twisting her head around like that?'

'I am *here* you know,' Gladys interrupted testily.

'The treatment is eighty per cent effective,' the doctor repeated patiently, still talking to Annie. Then she looked at her watch. 'Did you have any more questions?'

Naturally, they didn't.

On the way home, Gladys said, 'What a lot of hocus-pocus. The woman was nothing but a quack. And she treated me as if I wasn't there.'

But when they got back home, Annie did a little internet research. To her surprise, she found there really *was* such a thing as benign paroxysmal positional vertigo, and it really *could* be effectively treated by twisting the head about in a certain way.

She leaned back in her chair, hand over her mouth, speculating. Her mum never talked much about her dizzy spells, but by a process of intense questioning, Annie gathered they'd been fairly regular for some time.

What if they went away?

Would Gladys be able to live on her own again? Did she want to live on her own again?

Obviously, Gladys couldn't live here for ever. Obviously, Annie didn't want her to. And yet – she had the feeling that she'd been given a bit of a reprieve, now that Gladys had joined their household; from what exactly, she didn't know.

'Is she driving you crazy?' Annie's neighbour Jennifer Miller asked in a low voice over the top of her skinny latte, watching Annie's mum browse through paperbacks.

Annie had bumped into Jennifer at the bookshop by chance.

Annie gave a wry shrug. 'Oh, she has her moments. She's a bit full of herself today because a woman she met at Donna Knopf's pre-festive-season coffee morning phoned up and asked her to be the guest speaker at some "New Frugality" thing she's hosting in honour of the recession.'

Jennifer's eyes widened. 'Wow. So what's she going to talk about?'

'Let's see, now.' Annie began counting things off on her fingers. 'Reusing wrapping paper. That's one of her favourites. I don't think she's bought a new roll of wrapping paper since 1979. The funny thing is, the patterns have come back into fashion! Recycling gifts. The idea is, you just keep the things people give you in a cupboard, and then pass them on again when the time is right. There's a glass jar of bath salts that's been doing the rounds of the Guildford WI since the late eighties. Hmm. What else? She wanted to talk about reusing tea bags, but I told her people here don't drink tea in the first place. Oh, and she's got a recipe for making soup out of a chicken carcass.'

Jennifer pulled a face. 'She's a real high roller, huh. It's kind of funny. Everybody round here has been living large for so long, they'll probably have to go back to school to learn how stay inside a budget. How are things with Simon on the work front?'

Annie's eyebrows shot up. 'He's fine, thanks. Working hard, as usual.'

Jennifer nodded. 'Drew's OK too. For the moment. A

bunch of people lost their jobs around him, but so far so good. He's feeling a bit more optimistic.'

'That's a relief,' said Annie. 'Let's just hope the economy stops tanking soon.' But she was really just mouthing the things she heard people saying around her. She didn't feel any personal anxiety. ChefPro was as sound as ever; she kept tabs on their share price on the internet. It was worrying, of course, to see that journalists had started referring to ChefPro's most direct competitor by the tag, 'ailing British food giant, William Tell'. If William Tell was ailing, it was possible that there would be rocky times ahead for ChefPro, too. But for the moment, all was well.

Gladys was making her way back to their table. She sat down heavily, dumping a book of slow-cooker recipes on the table.

'Anybody got a pen?' she asked. 'There're a couple of recipes in here I'd like to copy out.'

Annie looked over her shoulder nervously. 'Mum, I don't think you're supposed to do that.'

'Well, I'm not slapping fifteen dollars down on the table for this book,' Gladys declared. 'That's what went wrong with the economy the world over, you know. Impulse buying. Getting into debt. Paying for things you don't need.'

Jennifer stood up quickly, her mouth curling behind her cardboard mug. 'Well, got to run,' she trilled. 'Nice seeing you, Mrs Harleigh.'

Heather invited Annie and her family to Thanksgiving dinner because, as she privately told Annie, she couldn't bear to face the sympathy of her own family after her miscarriage, any more than she could bear to face the blissful ignorance of Rob's family, who knew nothing about her loss and never would. As her parents had retired to Florida, and Rob's family hailed from Chicago, avoiding family was relatively easy.

'Can I bring the mashed potatoes?' Annie asked – she was reasonable at mashing potatoes – but Heather graciously declined. Annie hoped she wasn't remembering the disastrous dinner party.

'I'm having everything catered,' Heather declared. 'I don't want to spend days thawing a freaking turkey in my tub. And I can't be messing around with basters. My hair would frizz.'

Gladys was shocked to the core when Annie told her about the caterers. 'What? You don't mean the woman can't even roast a bird and boil up some green beans? What else would you have – sweet potatoes? Just throw them in with the juices in the pan. Maybe you could buy the pumpkin pie – pastry can be tricky. But everything else – good Lord, even you could cook it, Annie.'

'I don't blame Heather at all,' Annie snapped back. 'Why spend a whole day sweating over the details when someone else could do it all for you, and so much better?'

Gladys shook her head in horror. 'You Americans are so extravagant!' she declared.

Heather's house on the day of Thanksgiving wasn't likely to dispel this view. It was all set about with hay bales, turkeys in various media, and cornucopias overflowing with fruit and flowers.

Simon met Annie's eye over Gladys's head as the older

233

woman stood frowning at a wreath on the front door made entirely of miniature winter squashes in different shades of green and orange.

'The *sheer waste*!' Simon mouthed at Annie. She grinned and winked at him.

But her mother surprised them with a different tack. 'Wreaths are for funerals,' she pronounced. 'I don't know where people get this odd idea of hanging them on doors. Mind you, don't go buying a wreath for me when I pop off. I'd rather you spent the money on a good, sturdy headstone, something that will last.'

'You're not going to die,' Lydia said loudly. 'Not until you're really, really old. And you're not old yet.'

'Of course, she's not going to die.' Annie glared at her mother. 'Right, Mum? She's probably going to live till she's a hundred.'

'Some days it feels as if I already have,' Gladys muttered, massaging her back.

At that moment, Heather threw the door open.

'Hi Heather. Wow! You're looking very ...' Annie trailed off, stumped for words. Heather was an astonishing sight in a deep purple wrap-around dress with a hem so high that Annie suspected it was really a blouse. A simple but stunning bead necklace slipped in and out of her generous cleavage and sparkled when she moved into the light. Her knees and thighs twinkled in luminescent tights above tall black boots.

'Thank you – I *think*,' Heather said with a wry smile. 'Come in, come in.' She graciously accepted the wine bottle Simon was proffering, and led the way to the living room.

Dan Morgan, wearing tassels, was standing over by the computer with Rob, downloading songs on iTunes.

Before anybody could speak, Hailey burst out from under the baby grand piano, brandishing a plastic horse. 'Come on, Lydia, let's go play upstairs,' she cried.

As the girls scampered off, the two men came forward to air-kiss Annie and shake Simon's hand.

'You must be Heather's husband?' Gladys was talking to Dan in her extra-high, socialising voice.

'No, that would be me.' Rob stepped up and treated an astonished Gladys to one of his scorching come-hither looks. Annie gave a nervous trill of laughter. Poor Heather, saddled with a husband who couldn't help giving the glad-eye to every female who came his way, including old-age pensioners. Well, just as long as he was all talk and no trousers.

'Good grief, I forgot the introductions,' said Heather. 'Gladys, this is my husband, Rob. And the guy in the cowboy boots is Dan.'

'And Dan is?' Gladys asked.

'He's a friend of the family,' said Heather. 'You've got to have a waif or stray over for Thanksgiving, and he's it, for us. He's from Texas, you see, so he doesn't have any family around here.'

Rob tore his gaze away from Gladys long enough to pour out several glasses of white wine, and began handing them around. When everybody had one, he raised his own glass. 'To waifs and strays!' he said – by which Annie understood that they, too, fell into this category. Then Rob turned to Gladys with a gallant air. 'And how are you liking Connecticut so far, Mrs— Gladys?'

Annie groaned inwardly.

'Come help me in the kitchen,' Heather muttered under her breath, and Annie needed no second bidding.

'Oh God, I bet Mum's telling Rob off about having the heating on too high,' Annie muttered. But Gladys, shaking Rob off with ease, had followed them into the kitchen.

'Right,' said Gladys, 'let's see what those catering people have fobbed us off with. I can always throw something together if it's too horrible. Do you have any Oxo?'

Annie caught Heather's eye and took a huge slug of wine.

'I like Thanksgiving,' Simon said later, when they were back in front of their own fireplace and Lydia and Gladys were in bed. 'Good to have a holiday about nothing in particular; just a taking stock kind of thing. Count your blessings, and all that. We should think about having a day like that back home.'

Annie screwed up her nose. 'What, two turkeys in two months? Englishwomen wouldn't stand for it.'

Simon laughed. 'Yeah, you're right. Funny sort of timing, really – just before Christmas.'

'Nowhere else to put it,' said Annie. She began to count off on her fingers. 'You've got Halloween in October, Christmas in December, New Year's Day in January, Valentine's Day in February, Easter in March or April, and then the weather starts warming up. You can't have a great big feast like that when it's sweltering. Plus you have to incorporate the whole harvest idea, don't you? No harvest in the spring.'

Simon sipped his coffee. 'That Dan chap was a bit cheeky, didn't you think?'

'In what sense?'

'Well, what kind of berk stands up and starts spouting about all the wonderful things going on in his life?'

Annie snorted with laughter. 'Darling, I think it's a tradition. I think that's what you're supposed to do at Thanksgiving: give thanks.'

'Well, nobody else did,' Simon pointed out.

'I don't think Heather and Rob are feeling very thankful at the moment,' Annie said quietly.

'Oh God, I was forgetting,' he said. 'It was good of them to have us over, considering.'

'What would *you* have said, if they'd put you on the spot?' Annie asked after a moment. 'You know, about what you're thankful for?'

He took a surprisingly long time to think about his answer. 'Well,' he began at last, but a loud cry from upstairs, followed by some bangs and crashes, stopped him in his tracks. Patches, blamelessly laid out at Annie's feet like a moth-eaten rug, leapt straight from a deep sleep into full-on, high-volume barking.

Annie and Simon jumped to their feet as one and stampeded for the stairs. Simon, in socks, skidded towards the rug in the hallway, tripped over a wrinkle in it and took a nosedive, breaking his fall with his elbows. Annie leapt over his body, barely breaking her stride, and raced up the stairs to Lydia's room.

She burst in and turned on the light. Lydia was lying on the floor, moaning, her hands over her head. Annie ran over and gathered her in her arms. 'Lydia, what happened? What's the matter?'

'The room is burning,' she said.

'The room ...? You must've had a bad dream. Nothing's burning. There's no fire.'

'Go away. I don't want you. I want Daddy.'

'You're very hot, sweetie. I think I need to take your temperature.'

Lydia was sobbing quietly now, her hair clumped wetly around her face. 'Go away. I want *Daddy*.'

'I'm here, Muffet.' Simon knelt down beside Annie, and Lydia scrambled into his arms.

'I'll get the thermometer.' Annie rushed to the spare bathroom where she kept a first-aid box. She found the brand new digital thermometer and ripped it out of its packaging with her teeth as she ran back to Lydia's bedroom.

'Open your mouth,' she told Lydia. 'Pop it under your tongue.'

The child was shivering now, and as she accepted the thermometer, Annie caught a whiff of her breath. It was sour and fetid.

Sure enough, Lydia's temperature was 103.

'Do we phone 911?' Annie asked, staring at the number in awe.

'Good grief, no.' Simon had lifted Lydia back into bed and was stroking her brow gently. 'Kids are always getting cricket-score temperatures. Just find something like Calpol and get her some water. I'll open the windows.'

Annie rushed back to the bathroom and returned with some ibuprofen.

'Go away, go *away*,' Lydia cried as Annie came at her with the teaspoon, like a contestant in an egg and spoon race.

'OK, but you need to swallow this first.'

Lydia flailed at Annie with a hand, and sent the teaspoon flying. Red syrup splattered over her white duvet.

'Oh, for God's sake,' Annie said.

'It's OK, she's always like this when she's ill,' Simon told her. 'Just pour out some more and I'll get it down her.'

Annie watched from the sidelines as Lydia accepted the medicine from her father, putting her small hand over his large one to steady the spoon.

'I'm going to sit with her for a while,' Simon murmured. 'She'll be fine once the medicine kicks in. You might as well go off to bed. No point both of us losing sleep.'

Feeling distinctly superfluous, Annie went downstairs to switch off lights, lock doors, and let the dog out for a last walkabout. Slamming shut the door of the dishwasher, she straightened up and rubbed her eyes briskly. There. She'd go off to bed now, and make a doctor's appointment first thing in the morning. Lydia would just have to make do with her stepmother tomorrow, because Daddy would be at work.

'Annie?'

At the sound of her mother's voice, she froze with her hand on the light switch.

'Annie? What's all the ruckus about?'

With a sigh, Annie walked through to the downstairs room where Gladys slept. 'It's OK, Mum. Lydia has a temperature, that's all.'

Gladys was sitting up in bed, magnificent in a lacy night-gown. 'Come closer, my dear, I can't see you out there.'

Annie advanced a step or two into the room.

Gladys stared hard at her. 'You've been crying,' she said.

'Rubbish.' Annie sniffed vigorously. 'It's allergies, that's all.'

'Come over here,' Gladys commanded. She patted the bed. Annie hesitated a moment, then went over and sat down.

To her astonishment, her mother leaned over and put an arm around her shoulders. 'Everything's going to be all right,' Gladys said, patting her hair.

Annie reared back, breaking out of Gladys's clasp. 'For heaven's sake, Mum,' she said. 'Everything *is* all right, thank you very much. Now, I'm going upstairs to get some sleep. Do you need anything before I go? A glass of water, maybe?'

'You need to loosen up and communicate better,' Gladys told her. 'We Brits are too reserved. Dr Phil reckons lack of communication is the root of all evil. You need to get real with yourself about your life before you can achieve anything.'

Annie's draw dropped. 'Get *real* ...?'

'That's right. Think about it.'

Stunned, Annie made her way up to bed.

'It's like a pregnancy test,' said the doctor, holding up a little tube containing some gunk from the back of Lydia's throat. Annie suppressed a shudder. 'Two lines and it's positive. One line and we *think* it's negative, but we send it out to be cultured, just to make sure.' Carefully, the doctor squeezed several drops out of the tube onto a white plastic strip.

'Yup,' she said with satisfaction a little while later. 'It's positive, all right. I always like a positive strep test, because – guess what? – she's going to be all better in about twenty-four hours.'

Looking at Lydia slumped over on the examining table, pale, thin and listless, Annie certainly hoped so.

As they left the offices, Annie said in an enticing voice, 'Do you want to press the buttons for the lift, Lydia?'

Lydia gave her a look that could have scorched a rain-forest.

'I'm guessing that's a no,' Annie said with a sigh.

'It's called an elevator,' Lydia replied in a voice of deep contempt. Lately, she'd been absorbing American colloqui-alisms like a sponge.

'Not where you and I come from, mate,' said Annie.

Lydia's face screwed up in confusion. 'But we live *here* now,' she said. 'We should talk the way everyone else talks. Otherwise people will think we're weird.'

'No, they won't. They'll think we're foreign and exotic and interesting.'

'They'll think we're *weird*,' Lydia repeated. And that was when Annie noticed, with a tiny jolt, that she sounded completely American.

Back home, Annie left Lydia and Gladys in front of the TV watching the frenzied advertising of Black Friday sales, and sneaked up to the den to make a phone call.

'Sarah? What a relief, you're actually home. Look, Sarah, I need your advice. It's about Mum.'

'How's she doing?'

'Very well. She's a *lot* better, actually. She hasn't had a dizzy spell in two weeks. The aches and pains from the fall are gone, too.'

'Is she enjoying Norbury?'

'Oh yes. She's having a fine old time. She's got herself involved with this "frugality" group, and they've had her to speak at one of their meetings. She came home cross as anything because the hostess had gone out and bought twelve jars of jam, then chucked the jam away so she could use the jars as vases for centrepieces. Oh, and she's doing a lot of cleaning and cooking, not to mention laundry. When she does consent to put her feet up, she watches Dr Phil and Oprah – and they seem to be giving her odd ideas.'

'Odd ideas? She's never been short of those.'

'No, I mean she's talking about how we should *communicate* more. Share our feelings. That sort of thing.'

Sarah gave a low whistle. 'Is she driving Lydia crazy?'

Annie drew in a sharp breath. 'Um, no. Actually, Lydia thinks she's great. They do homework together. She's teaching her to darn socks. They're really bonding.'

'What about Simon? Is she getting on his nerves?'

'Oh no! Far from it. He's fascinated by her Dig for Victory tales. He's gone and put it into her head that she should bring out a recipe book full of wartime horrors like crow pie and carrolade and squirrel-tail soup.'

'Good grief.'

'Yip, everybody loves her. All the women on my street

think she's such a character. She's always helping out around the house. She couldn't be making herself more useful.'

'But?'

'How do you know there's a "but"?'

'Well, isn't there?'

Annie sighed. 'But Simon's barely laid a finger on me since she's been here. And he says there are things we need to discuss, but we can only talk when Mum goes home. And sometimes she makes me feel about ten years old.'

'Sounds like it's time she came home.'

'Well, she can't, can she? She's not well. She might have another fall at any moment. She's not fit to live alone.'

'Annie, we'll think of something. She can't stay with you for ever, anyway. She doesn't have the right paperwork. We'll have to get a companion for her – or something. I'll look into it.'

Annie blew her nose. 'Thank you, Sarah. The weird thing is, in some ways I *want* her to stay here for ever. That's the truly scary thing.'

By Monday, Lydia was all recovered and ready to go back to school. The antibiotics had worked with almost magical speed. 'Just wait till she has pneumonia or Lyme disease,' Heather said as they walked home together. 'You'll be *really* happy we're not living in the dark ages.'

Annie stepped into the kitchen with a firm tread, determined to turn over a new leaf today and not be all nitpicky about her poor old mum. After all, in the spirit of Thanksgiving, she knew she should be very thankful for the extra pair of hands in the house. Nowadays, the dishwasher

243

seemed to unpack itself. (And there was even less for her to do than ever, a small voice pointed out. She quelled it imperiously.)

'I'm back, Mum,' she called into the house.

There was a silence, and then she heard her mum's footsteps on the stairs.

'Mum, I've told you not to go upstairs. What if you got dizzy on the staircase? What were you doing up there, anyway?'

'Oh, making beds. A bit of dusting. That cleaning team of yours doesn't always get to the window sills.'

Gladys came into view, wearing an apron and carrying a duster. 'By the way, my dear,' she lowered her voice and looked around quickly, as if casing the room for eavesdroppers, 'a word in your ear. With a child in the house, you need to be careful about leaving items of an, um, *intimate* nature lying around the place. I found *this* on your bedside table.'

In one latex-gloved hand, between thumb and forefinger, she held up a small, battery-operated gadget shaped a bit like a tumbleweed.

'Mu-um! For heaven's sake! That's a vibrating back massager.'

Gladys's eyebrows rose. 'I know it's a vibrating something,' she said. 'I suggest you stash it away somewhere. I'm surprised you leave it lying about.'

Annie yanked it out of her hand and stormed up to her room. She opened the bottom drawer of Simon's dresser and threw the back massager in among his socks.

'Annie!'

'*What?*'

'I've made you some tea.'

Annie caught sight of her own wild-eyed face in the mirror.

Right. That was it. She had to have a little word with Mum before she found herself pulling her hair out in chunks.

She marched downstairs, breathing deeply, and threw open the door to the kitchen.

'Mum,' she said, brushing aside the tea Gladys was proffering, 'we need to talk.'

'I know, my dear,' Gladys said, settling herself onto a stool at the counter. 'I've been meaning to have a word with you for a couple of days, now.'

Annie sank down into a stool, taken aback. 'You have? About *what*, exactly?'

'About going home.'

Annie's jaw dropped.

'That's right, love. I know it's time, as well as you do. So I've been writing some letters, making some arrangements. I've managed to persuade Flo Mitson to come and keep an eye on me.'

'Flo Mitson?'

'The nurse. You remember – my cousin Elvira's widowed daughter-in-law. Her varicose veins have been bothering her for years; all that walking around the wards. I told her she could put her feet up and watch TV most of the day at my place.'

'Mum! But ... but do you even like this woman?'

'Oh yes, Flo's all right. Addicted to lottery tickets, but otherwise quite sound. We'll get along just fine.'

'But how will you set things up? I mean, if she's giving up work to come and live with you, presumably you'll have to pay her something. How will——?'

Gladys raised a liver-spotted hand. 'Annie, I'm old, not senile. I've been managing my affairs quite nicely, thank you, since before you were born.'

'Well, yes, of course, Mum, but——'

'I've sorted it out, Annie. Let's leave it at that.'

So Annie did.

Annie wasn't prepared for the sense of panic she felt as she watched an attendant wheel her mother away through security. (Gladys had suggested the wheelchair herself, this time.) 'Come back,' Annie wanted to call. 'I can't handle all this without you! Who's going to help Lydia finish her crocheted frog? Who's going to boil the dishcloths?' But she stood firm and kept waving, her face fixed in a smile.

Simon, standing beside her, squeezed her hand. 'She'll be OK on the plane, and Sarah's meeting her on the other side,' he said.

'I know.' She blinked rapidly. 'I'm not worried about her, really. She's well able to look after herself.'

'She's going to miss everything,' Lydia piped up. 'The soccer party. The Christmas recital. Everything. She said I should write her a letter.'

Annie glanced down at the little girl. She looked dejected and wistful, and distinctly unkempt. Nobody had reminded her to brush her hair all day; Annie and Gladys had been too busy rounding up stray items and forcing them into Gladys's suitcase. In the end, Gladys had taken an extra bag to accommodate the waffle-weave spa robe and giant jar of cashew nuts from Costco.

'Of course you should write her a letter,' Annie enthused, working her fingers absent-mindedly through Lydia's hair.

'Ow,' yelped Lydia, jerking her head away. 'You're so *mean*, Annie.'

Simon frowned at his daughter. 'Lydia, don't talk to Annie that way.'

'Well, she's pulling my hair out by the *roots*.'

Annie gave a rueful laugh, showing Simon a strand or two of golden hair caught up in her rings. 'Look at that; she's right. Sorry, Lydia. I didn't mean to hurt you. Anyway, why don't you write a letter this evening? I'll find an airmail stamp for you and help you do the address.'

'I could draw her a picture of Patches so she doesn't forget what he looks like.'

The corner of Simon's mouth twitched. 'Oh yes, she'd never want to forget the noble features of the dog who ate her reading glasses,' he said.

Without Gladys clattering dishes and talking back to the TV, the house was Annie's own domain again. On the first morning of her repossession, Annie took care of her kitchen chores with grim satisfaction. But she suffered a little setback when, after turning on the kettle, she found herself automatically putting out two cups. She shook her head, then muttered to Patches, who was looking at her in concern, 'How do you take your tea, then, dog? Milk and two sugars?'

Patches cocked his head.

'Oh God, I hope I'm not going to turn into one of those mad people who talk to their dogs all the time.'

Patches thumped his tail.

To hear another human voice in the place, Annie turned on the radio – but turned it off again almost immediately when she found herself humming along: 'Everything is dust in the wind.'

'I know!' she told Patches suddenly. 'I'll phone Henny!'

'Well, I'm glad everything's back to normal,' Henny told her. 'You and Simon are still such newly-weds.'

'Well, not *such* newly-weds. To be honest, we're thinking of, you know, moving to the next stage. He said – he said we'd talk about the whole baby thing once Mum went home ...'

'The whole *baby* thing? Oh, Annie, you're not ...?'

'No, no, I'm not pregnant. We're just, sort of, thinking about it. Well, I am, anyway.'

Henny was whooping with joy on the other side of the phone. 'Oh my God, Annie – this is fantastic! I'll be able to give you so much advice. Like, did you know you shouldn't eat swordfish when you're pregnant because of the mercury?'

'Um, Henny? Slow down a moment, would you? You see, I'm not entirely sure about Simon's position on timing. Frankly, I'm not even sure if he wants a baby at all.'

'Oh.'

'So don't go getting too excited. And for God's sake, don't say anything to Mum if you happen to talk to her on the phone. I don't want her to get her hopes up.'

'Of course not. My lips are sealed. So your mum got home safely and everything?'

'Yes, I spoke to her first thing this morning. She's fine. Sarah took some time off work and drove her home. I bet she'll call you soon. She's staying with Mum for a few days until Flo Mitson shows up to take over.'

'Flo Mitson?'

'Some sort of relative. A nurse, apparently. Didn't know we had any nurses in the family. She's going to—' Suddenly, she was drowned out by a barrage of barking from Patches. 'Hang on, Henny, I'll have to go. Someone's knocking.'

# Chapter Eleven

The woman on the front porch was impeccably dressed in a black business suit and heels. What was more, she had a perfectly coiffed head of designer highlights. Patches, wagging his tail obsequiously, aimed a few squirts of wee at her shoes.

Luckily the woman, intent on rearranging a briefcase stuffed with papers, didn't notice this sycophantic gesture.

'Oh,' said Annie in surprise. 'Are you a Jehovah's witness?'

'A what?' Tinkling laugh. 'No, of course not. I'm Cindy Faig.'

'Cindy Faig?' The woman had said her name as if Annie was bound to recognise it. 'I'm sorry, I ... Wait, are you the room mum for Miss Scofield's class?'

The woman laughed. '*God* no. I'm not a mum at all. I work with Si, of course.'

'Oh, right. Of course!' She'd last seen this woman the day she'd fallen asleep in Simon's office. This was a member of his famous pie team! 'Good to see you! Would you like to come in?'

'If you don't mind. Did Si mention I might pop by?' She was staring at Annie quite hard.

'No, actually, he didn't. It must have slipped his mind.'
She ushered the woman through to the formal living room.
'Sit down, make yourself comfortable. I'll just put the kettle on. Would you like tea or coffee?'

'Thanks, I'll have tea.'

Annie hurried through to the kitchen to fill the kettle and
set a tea tray. Why hadn't Simon mentioned that Cindy Faig
would be popping in? she wondered.

Back in the living room, Annie asked, 'So you're still
enjoying New York?'

Her guest gave a wide smile. 'Oh my God, I just love living
in the city. It's fantastic. Don't you just adore Manhattan?'

'I do, actually,' Annie said a little wistfully. 'I wish I
could get down there more often, but it's hard with school
and everything. Simon never wants to go in over the weekends.'

'So how *is* Lydia? Si says she's doing well, settling in at
school, playing soccer.'

'Um, yes, that's right. So ... you know Lydia?'

The woman laughed. She wasn't pretty, exactly, but
her face was superbly made-up, her slightly slanted eyes
giving her a mysterious look. She didn't need to be pretty
because her body was magnificent. Never had a business
suit looked more like a Velcroed-on costume worn by an
exotic dancer.

In her jeans, T-shirt and cardigan, Annie felt every inch
the frumpy hausfrau.

'Oh, we go way back,' said Cindy. 'I've known Lydia since
she was a baby. Gosh, I remember the day Beth first brought
her into the London office. She was three weeks old.'

'Oh, wow. That is way back. We really should have you round for lunch or something!' Annie felt excited at the idea of an old friend, maybe a sort of aunt figure, for Lydia.

Cindy smiled. 'Sure, that would be great when things calm down. But as you know everybody's been under a lot of stress at the office. We've been working all hours God sends. Socialising hasn't really been on people's minds.'

'Well – quite. So, um, what brings you out here today?'

Cindy bent down to pick up her briefcase. 'I wanted to make sure he'd have this as soon as he gets in from Boston tonight,' she said, taking out a file. 'The Brewster focus group report. You know how desperate he's been to get his hands on these results. We didn't want to risk a messenger service, so I drove them up myself.'

'He's in *Boston* today?'

'You didn't know? He took the train – just a day trip. He's looking at the site.'

'The site?'

'You know, the site for the flagship restaurant. Head office finally agreed with us that Boston is the right place to start.'

'Of course.' She did have some vague memory now of Simon saying something about Boston, but she'd been too taken up with her mum to pay much attention. 'I'll make sure he gets that file. Hang on, I'll just go and pour the tea. Kettle should be boiling by now.'

As Annie entered the living room with the clinking tea tray, she found Cindy on her feet, peering at the titles of the books on the antique bookshelf. Good luck with that, Annie thought ironically. On the day they'd moved into this house, she'd discovered that the handsome, leather-bound library of classics was a façade. There were no actual books, just cardboard stage props.

'Oh God,' said Cindy, 'I hope you won't think I'm rude but I really mustn't stay for tea after all. I have a meeting in Stamford on my way back. You know how the traffic on the I-95 can be. Anyway, be sure to let him have those papers so he can read them before he comes in tomorrow.'

Annie set her tray down with a little thump. 'Of course,' she said, smiling with all her teeth but no conviction whatsoever. *To say you'd have a cup of tea, allow your hostess to make it, and then walk away from the steaming pot* — that would be letting slip the dogs of war, in her mother's book.

As she escorted Cindy Faig out, Annie couldn't help noticing that the woman stared into all the rooms with blatant curiosity as she went by.

She didn't have time to mention Cindy Faig's visit when Simon came home, because the moment he walked through the door they had to jump into the car and race off to an end-of-season soccer party at the coach's house. They arrived about fifteen minutes late.

The coach's wife directed them down to the family's 'media room' in the basement where they found the whole team plus parents sitting on the carpet, eating popcorn in the semi-darkness. The coach, a florid-faced man with curly dark hair, stood in front of the TV holding a handful of medals and a remote control. 'Ah, that's everybody now!' he said when Annie, Simon and Lydia slunk into the room. 'OK, as you know we've had another fabulous season, most of which was filmed by my lovely wife, Erin.'

There was a ragged round of applause. Annie exchanged an alarmed look with Simon.

'So, let's get this show rolling,' said the coach. 'First up, McKenna Trent.' He stepped to one side and pressed a button. The TV screen filled with an image of McKenna, easily the smallest girl on the team, stubbornly pursuing a ball, hampered by a T-shirt that hung down well below her knees. 'McKenna is one of our best defence players, and she did an excellent job keeping that ball away from the posts. McKenna, please come forward and get your medal.'

Huge applause broke out as the little girl stood up and picked her way through the audience to receive her medal.

And so it went, with the coach calling each girl by name, showing a piece of footage illustrating the high points of her game, and hanging a medal around her neck.

Annie felt an awful tension building in her stomach.

At last, there were only two girls left – Hailey and Lydia.

'And now,' said the coach, 'for our trophy of excellence. This goes to Hailey Gibson, for being our top goal scorer this season.' The screen jumped into life with an image of Hailey racing across a field, controlling the ball like a mini Beckham before smashing it into the undefended goal posts.

The media room rocked with cheers and clapping. Hailey, looking embarrassed and waggling her unibrow, went up for her trophy.

'Last of all,' said the coach, and Annie sucked her breath in sharply, 'I want to talk about a girl called Lydia Keeler. She came to us completely new to the sport of soccer, but we were happy to have her. I have to tell you, guys, I was excited. I mean, she had the right accent to play this game. Well, as most of us know, it took Lydia a little while to get warmed up.' On the screen, Lydia was shown squatting down to pick flowers as a ball whizzed by. 'But as the season progressed we saw her grow a little stronger every time she went out. And then, people, the very last game we played, we saw this.'

The TV screen flickered to life again, and Annie made out Lydia at the back of the picture, doing nothing much, as usual. But all of a sudden a girl on the opposing team kicked a long shot that went bouncing and bounding towards Lydia. Oh God, she probably scored another own goal, Annie thought.

But no, Lydia ran at the loose ball, stopped it with one foot, dribbled it up the field, dodged her own teammates as skilfully as she dodged the opposition, took the ball all the way to the other side of the field, then made a faultless pass to Hailey, who stood ready and waiting right in front of the goal posts. Hailey's quick, winning kick was a bit of an anticlimax compared to Lydia's long run.

'And that,' said the coach, 'is the beautiful game.'

People were clapping and cheering and standing on their feet. Lydia, as red as a tomato, was inching her way to the front of the room as people leaned in to pat her back and shake her hand.

'Without a doubt,' said the coach, holding up a trophy that matched Hailey's, 'this is our Most Improved Player of the season.'

'Why didn't you tell me?' Annie hissed at Simon, tears streaming down her cheeks.

'I missed it,' he said sheepishly. 'I had a conference call with a bloke in England, so Heather took them. She said Lydia played well, but I thought she was just being kind!'

Much later, when Lydia was asleep, her trophy perched on her bedside table, her medal slung over a post of her bed, Annie remembered the strange visit she'd had earlier that day.

'By the way,' she told Simon, handing him the file, 'Cindy Faig popped by today. She said to give you this.'

'Cindy Faig came here?' He looked amazed.

'Didn't you know? She said she had a meeting in Stamford, and that you'd need to look this paperwork over before tomorrow.'

He took the file from her, flicked through it, and stood up abruptly. 'I'll be up in the den,' he said, his whole body radiating tension.

For the next few days he was on edge and distracted, barely talking to her other than to thank her for the food she put in front of him.

'So, have you found a good pastry for the American market yet?' she asked brightly one evening as they were watching some programme about survival in the wilderness.

He didn't take his eyes off the screen, where a man was steeling himself to eat a handful of grubs. 'Please, Annie, when I come home I want to relax, not face a bloody inquisition.'

She didn't dare bring up the topic of babies.

Babies were not going to be in Patches' future, that was for sure. Annie was coming to agree with the vet that it was probably best for the environment if Patches was a one-off model.

Still she couldn't help feeling guilty as she loaded him in the car one morning to drive him to the 'animal hospital' to be neutered.

'But he's not broken,' Lydia had protested when Annie told her over the weekend that Patches had an appointment with the vet on Monday and would be there overnight, recuperating.

Ruffling Lydia's hair, Simon had explained, 'They call it fixing but it really means he'll be having an operation so that he can't have puppies.'

'Silly! He doesn't need to go. He's a *boy* dog. Boy dogs don't have puppies.'

Annie and Simon locked eyes. 'I'll just go and put the kettle on for tea,' Annie said with a devilish grin at Simon. 'Daddy can explain.'

She still hadn't asked him what he'd said to Lydia, but she'd noticed the child bending over with a creased brow to look at the dog's underbelly.

Patches was always happy to jump into the car, but he began to suspect foul play at the animal hospital when the receptionist took the leash out of Annie's hands and tugged him away towards a back room. Apparently he remembered the smell of the place, and he didn't like it one bit. Scrabbling fruitlessly at the slippery linoleum, he turned his head to give Annie a reproachful stare. As he was dragged off around the corner, she heard a high, despairing yowl, and then the thump of a door closing, and silence.

Feeling like a traitor, she turned to leave ... and walked

straight into somebody who seemed to have crept up sound-lessly behind her.

'Godammit, will you look where you're— *hey, Annie!*'

With a jolt, Annie recognised the drawl and the cowboy boots.

'Dan? What are you doing here?'

'I'm picking up a vitamin supplement for my horse,' Dan Morgan said, grinning down at her with such obvious pleasure that she couldn't help feeling pleased. 'And you? Did you bring the mutt in? Is he OK?'

Annie nodded. 'Yes, he's fine. Just going in to be fixed, that's all.'

At that moment the receptionist returned from the back rooms. 'Hey, Dan,' she called out. 'Good to see you. Your lick came in this morning.'

'Great,' he said, extracting a credit card from his wallet and tossing it onto the desk. 'Put it on that, will you?'

'Well, nice to bump into you,' Annie told him with a small wave, beginning to back out of the room.

'No, hang on! Let me finish up here, and then why don't we go grab a coffee? You look kinda shaken up.'

'I – I don't drink coffee, to be honest.'

'Well, you could have tea then. Or hot chocolate.'

Aware of the receptionist looking at them curiously, Annie shrugged and said, 'The thing is, I don't have much time. Got to get back home and, you know, do stuff.'

Dan shrugged. 'OK,' he said. 'Maybe another time. Have a good day.'

But when she got behind the wheel of her silver minivan, the damn thing wouldn't start. It wouldn't even make a noise. No matter how often she turned the key, all she got was a hopeless click. To make matters worse, it was beginning to rain.

'Having trouble?'

Dan was standing at her window in a sheepskin overcoat, his collar turned up against the drizzle.

'Bloody thing won't start.' She demonstrated the clicking noise.

'Sounds like a flat battery. Tell you what, if you come out for a coffee, I'll jump it for you afterwards.'

'You think you can get it going?'

'No problem,' he said. 'I have jump leads in my truck. So how about it?'

'Oh – all right.' She glanced at her watch. It was after eleven and she was suddenly aware that she hadn't eaten breakfast. 'Do you mind if we grab a quick bite to eat, too?'

Dan raised his eyebrows. 'Lunch? We-ell, it's kinda early – but what the hell. I know a Tex-Mex place nearby.'

As Annie got out of her car, the rain began to come down heavily. The two of them took off running across the parking lot. By the time they reached a massive red pick-up truck, Annie was laughing and breathless.

'Climb in,' he invited, opening the door. She looked up at the distant leather seat, feeling like Alice in Wonderland after she'd eaten the side of the mushroom that made her shrink.

'All right, but why do you have such a monster vehicle?'

He grinned at her, drops of rain caught in his eyelashes. 'Are you kidding? Because size matters.'

Annie chuckled to herself as she scrambled up to her seat. He was really playing the cheesy Texan to the hilt. She liked a man with a sense of humour.

Towering over other cars, they cruised down the road, made a couple of quick turns, and pulled up outside the seediest-looking establishment Annie had ever seen in Norbury. A fly-speckled sign, wedged between the plate glass window and the closed blinds, announced that this was, 'Bobby's'.

As they walked in, shaking rain from their clothes and hair, Annie felt the world darkening around her. Inside this place – bar, restaurant, whatever it was – no natural light penetrated. The windows were shrouded, and the room was lit by fluorescent signs shaped like cacti and sombreros. Five or six stainless-steel tables stood around, completely empty. There wasn't a soul in the place.

Annie's heart began to beat rather hard. She gulped. She hadn't bargained on anything quite so off the beaten track. Why couldn't they have gone to Friendly's where it was bright and clean and busy? Could it be that Dan didn't want to bump into anybody they both knew? The thought made her uneasy. After all, surely a woman could have a perfectly innocent bite to eat with a male friend who was about to jump-start her car without having to hide away in some hole-in-the-wall dive?

'Don't worry,' said Dan, following her gaze around the room, 'I won't make you drink sangria. What can I get you?'

'Um ... what are you having?'

'Scotch.'

'*Scotch?* What happened to the whole hot drink idea?' She glanced at her watch, feeling more nervous by the moment.

'Come on, have a shot to warm your bones.'

Annie pursed her lips. Well, she was here now. One drink wouldn't do her any harm. She was perfectly sure that when Simon went out to business lunches in the city he had a glass or two of wine. 'We-ell, all right, then. Just one drink. But I'm more of a vodka girl.'

'OK, one vodka coming up.'

He went over to the counter, which seemed to be completely unattended. By dint of banging and calling, he managed to flush somebody out of the back room. 'Hey, Juan, what's up?' he asked the thin, sad-looking individual who came in wiping his hands on an apron.

The man shrugged. 'Dan my man, how you doin'? What's it gonna be?' Then his eyes cut over to Annie and he gave a knowing smile.

'Give us a Scotch and a vodka.'

'On the rocks?'

'Sure. And how about you make us some chicken fajitas, medium spicy?'

Annie watched the drooping bartender extract a couple of bottles from a cupboard and dispense their drinks into two greasy-looking tumblers. Using his hands, he dumped in some ice cubes from the freezer. Then he disappeared again, no doubt to start grilling chicken.

Annie took the glass from Dan and sipped it gingerly. Her father, she found herself remembering, had always warned against allowing people to put ice in your glass in dodgy countries where the water could be bad. It was one of his cautionary tales, like not putting a plastic bag over your head, that seemed to have left an indelible impression on him, whereas he could never be persuaded that it wasn't safe to defrost meat by leaving it in the kitchen sink all day.

She felt the onset of sudden tears — thinking about her dad could still do that at odd moments — and hastily took another sip of her vodka.

'So,' said Dan Morgan, leaning back in his chair and squinting his eyes at her. 'That mutt doesn't know how lucky he is to have a woman like you going all teary-eyed over him getting his—'

'Right,' Annie said hastily. 'I'm not actually crying. I'm just having trouble with my contact lenses.'

'Oh, you can't kid me. It's funny, I didn't peg you for an animal lover the day we met at the barn.'

Annie grimaced, remembering Heather's mare going loopy over Dan's gelding. 'I don't *dislike* horses,' she said defensively. 'I'm just — well, a bit scared of them, to be honest. But I'm getting used to them. Sort of.'

'So you might just let that skinny kid of yours have one of her own some day?'

Annie took another sizeable sip of her vodka. 'She's not riding any more,' she said.

'You're kidding me. That little fall scared her off?'

'No, it wasn't the fall. It was … well, it's my husband. He doesn't want her to ride. He thinks it's too risky.'

'You don't say! Kid must be sick about it.'

Annie gulped more vodka. 'She's been really good about

it, actually. She sulked at bit at first. Called me – called me a few names. But she's resigned to it now.'

'Whoa,' he said, eyeing her all-but-empty glass. 'Easy does it, now.'

For some reason, this spurred her on to pick up her drink and drain it to the dregs. 'I think I'll have another, if you don't mind.' A strange recklessness was coming over her. She slid the glass towards him. 'We're going Dutch, of course.'

He gave her a long look, then stood up and called for Juan. When he came back with the drink he said, 'You seem kinda rattled. It's not just the mutt, I'm guessing. Want to talk about it?'

Annie took a slug of vodka. 'Not particularly. Not at all, really. Hey look, here comes our food.' Juan clanked over with a large tray and began arranging dishes of chicken, flour tortillas, salsa, sour cream and grated cheese on the table. Annie helped herself to a tortilla and began piling strips of chicken onto it.

'You homesick?' Dan asked, serving himself in a more leisurely fashion.

Annie slathered on the sour cream and began to roll the tortilla. 'I do miss home,' she admitted. 'But maybe not as much as you'd think. The weather's so much nicer here. Blue skies every day. And people are friendly. I mean, maybe they're only pretending to be friendly, maybe it's all just superficial, but it's nicer than people pretending that you're not actually there.' She paused and took a large bite of her fajita. Ah. Delicious.

He frowned. 'What do you mean?'

'Well, back home people tend to ignore each other in public. You know, on the street, on the train. I think it's because London is just so packed. If you started smiling at everybody who walked by, your cheeks would ache. I don't think I ever spoke more than two words to my neighbours back in Islington; it would've been an invasion of their privacy. But here – well, here they give you a street directory when you move in; even the dogs' names are on it.' She smiled and wiped cream off her lip. 'I like that.'

'I like it here too.'

'You don't miss Texas?'

He grinned into his whisky. 'I'm allergic to fire ants.'

'Fire ants?'

'Vicious sons of bitches. The day they marched into my house through the crack under the door, I swore I'd leave and never go back. Plus my ex-wife lives out there and she's more vicious than a whole army of ants.'

Annie burst out laughing. She laughed until her eyes watered, then pushed her glass towards Dan. 'Is there any more vodka in that bottle?'

'Don't you think you've had enough?'

'Just one more, if you don't mind?'

About twenty minutes later, Annie walked out of Bobby's, heavily supported by Dan, breathing garlic and feeling exhilarated. 'That's a good game,' she told him happily. 'Quarters. I don't know why, but I didn't play a lot of drinking games at uni.'

'Misspent youth,' said Dan.

''Zackly. Didn't know what I was missing. Whoa!' she

said as he clicked open his car. 'Your number plate says "STALLION"?'

He grinned. 'You didn't notice before? Climb on up.'

'No, hang on. You're in no shit fate ... fit state to drive.'

He shook his head. 'As soon as you knocked back that second vodka, I knew I was the designated driver. I've been drinking iced tea ever since. That's right, I was playing quarters with iced tea.'

Annie shook her head so hard she stumbled and had to clutch Dan for support. 'I just don't *get* this iced tea business,' she told him. 'Tea is a hot drink! *Hot*, I tell you! It's filthy when it's cold.'

'Easy now, Annie,' Dan said, steadying her. 'Nobody's gonna make you drink iced tea if you don't want to.'

Annie snorted theatrically. 'Ha! That's what you think. But they keeping bringing me the bloody stuff in restaurants when I ask for tea. And if they do bring the real thing, they screw that up too! I mean, along they come with a polystyrene mug of lukewarm water and a box of fancy herbal *infusions* that have about as much to do with tea as ... as storks have to do with making babies.'

'Whoa there, Annie. Just get in the truck and I'll drive you home.'

'Drive me ...? But what about my car? We have to go and jump-start it. We can't just *abandon* it in the vet's car park.'

'Annie, there's no way I'm going to let you drive. We can pick it up later. When you've sobered up a bit.'

She stopped in her tracks. 'You mean I'm that drunk?'

'I mean you're that drunk. Come on, let's get going. We need to pour some coffee into you before your kid comes home from school.'

Annie gave him a sideways look. 'You know what? I think you're enjoying this.' But she allowed him to help her up into the high leather seat.

She didn't say much on the way home, mainly because she was suddenly very sleepy. Dan's truck was warm and luxurious, just the place to curl up and close your eyes, and maybe nod off for a moment or two.

'Here we are,' Dan said directly into her ear. He seemed to be shaking her. 'Let's get you inside.'

Annie opened her eyes to find herself in her own drive-way. 'Ah! Home sweet home. Come along in, Dan.'

Smiling blearily, she allowed Dan to help her out and support her up the steps to the kitchen door. She scrabbled for her keys in her bag for what seemed like ages, located them at last, then fumbled at the keyhole. 'If the bloody door would just stay still a moment,' she found herself saying. Dan took the keys from her gently and opened the door.

'Can I put some coffee on for you?' he asked, shrugging off his jacket as he toured the countertops. 'Where's your coffee maker?'

'I don't like coffee much, but I suppose I'd better have some. It's in the corner near the fridge. Thanks so much. This is very good of you.'

He laughed. 'You've gone all polite on me,' he said. 'I kinda liked it when you were cussing me out about hot tea.'

'Was I? Gosh, I'm sorry. That's right, coffee's down there. Um, have you got the time on you?'

'It's just after noon,' he told her, glancing at his watch.

'Good. Three hours until the school run. I can have a little nap, maybe.'

'Coffee first,' Dan said firmly, following her into the family room.

She promptly collapsed onto a sofa. 'Come, sit down,' she said, grinning up at him and patting the cushion next to her. 'The coffee will take a while.'

He hesitated a moment, then sank down next to her. As he turned his head to look her in the eyes, she realised that they were very close to each other. Very close indeed. She could see his eyelashes. His shoulder, just inches away from hers, looked strangely inviting in its faded denim shirt.

Almost without volition, she found herself leaning towards him and resting her head on that handy shoulder. 'A shoulder to cry on,' she said with a tipsy giggle that turned into a sob. 'So this is what "maudlin" means,' she muttered, digging around in her pockets for a tissue.

When she thought about it afterwards, she realised Dan Morgan hadn't had much option. What could he have done, other than put his arms around her? Anything less would have seemed boorish.

The feel of those arms, warm even through their combined layers of clothing, was very comforting. Annie gave a sniff and settled in for a snooze.

That was when Dan lowered his mouth onto hers like a suction cap onto bathroom tiles.

Even in her woozy state his sudden onslaught gave her a nasty jolt and she reared away from him, pulling herself up into a kneeling position. He gazed up at her in surprise, his eyebrows raised, his hair ruffled, his shirt rucked up on his chest. 'What the hell?' he demanded.

'I think I'm going to be sick,' she said, hand over her mouth.

That got him moving. Few men, no matter how aroused, would linger downstream of a woman threatening to throw up on them.

As he jumped to his feet, she said, 'You'd better go, Dan. You'd better go now.' She was shivering with fright. God! She'd nearly gone and mucked up *everything*. And all because of a few terse words from Simon, a broken-down car, and too many vodkas.

'You asked me in,' he pointed out, tucking his shirt into his jeans.

'I know, I'm sorry,' she said, fingering her lips, which felt bruised. He was a bit of a vacuum cleaner. Still shivering, she gave a nervous snort of laughter, then tried to turn it into a cough. His eyebrows lowered. He was beginning to look distinctly peeved.

'I've had a tough morning, and the vodka went to my head in the worst way,' she explained hastily. 'Plus you're very attractive. Almost irresistible.' There, that should soothe his ruffles. 'But I *am* married, you know. *Happily* married. I'm very, very sorry if I misled you. So if you could please just go home now?'

'Look what you've gone and done to me,' he said morosely, gesturing towards his jeans. She wasn't going to look in that particular direction. 'You're nothing but a lousy tease. What the hell am I supposed to do now?'

'I don't know,' she shrugged. 'People seem to recommend

268

cold showers. Look, I really am terribly sorry.' She was herding him towards the kitchen and the back door. Who knows how many neighbours had already seen and recognised his truck in her driveway, with its distinctive vanity plates. 'You were so kind to me today. I don't know what came over me. Can you please just ... go?'

They were in the kitchen now and he was pulling on his jacket. 'Of course I'll go. But sheesh, talk about leading a guy on. Hold it!' He lifted a hand as if he were stopping traffic. 'Your car. It's still stuck over there at the animal hospital. Want me to give you a ride back a bit later? When you're feeling better?' His tone said he'd really rather not.

She shook her head. 'No, I'll sort myself out. I'll call a garage. Honestly, I don't want to be any more bother. Goodbye then. And ... and thanks again for a ... a lovely time.'

'Yeah, yeah,' he said, stomping down the steps in his heeled boots. 'Whatever.' All the cowboy charm was gone. But then, he hadn't had the benefit of years of manners training with Annie's mother.

Annie followed him out into a world washed clean by rain. The sky was a thin, high blue and the puddles were gilded with sunshine. Annie felt dazzled, like someone emerging, all disorientated, from an afternoon movie. As Dan climbed up behind the wheel of his truck, she breathed a ragged sigh of relief. God, what a morning. She couldn't wait to get into bed and pull the covers up over her head.

She was turning back towards the house when a voice hailed her.

'Annie!'

She froze.

'What was that cowboy bloke doing here?'

Slowly, inch by inch, she turned around.

# Chapter Twelve

Simon was standing in the driveway in his suit, his BlackBerry dangling at his side, gazing at Dan's enormous truck as it sped down the street. He must have walked up from the train station. Not surprisingly, Dan hadn't lingered to greet the master of the house.

'Simon! Good grief! Home at this hour? What's going on?' Time. She needed time to think.

He walked up and bent to plant a kiss, but she ducked down and fiddled with her shoe. She didn't want him getting a whiff of her breath.

'I had to come back for an overnight bag,' he told her, looking down at her with a puzzled frown. 'I have to go to Boston on the two o'clock train. I've been trying to reach you all morning. Did you forget to charge your phone or something?'

Annie's mobile phone was in the car, plugged into the cigarette lighter. In the vet's car park.

She looked up and gave a weak smile. 'Probably. Sorry.'

Since he was now walking briskly into the kitchen, she felt it was safe enough to straighten up and follow. You didn't kiss people hello after the hello moment had passed. At least, she hoped Simon wouldn't. Trying to breathe slowly, she pressed her icy hands to her face in the hope of cooling down her blazing cheeks.

Simon sniffed the air. 'Coffee? Since when do you drink coffee?' He walked over to the far corner of the kitchen and stared hard at the steaming coffee maker and the two mugs standing ready beside it.

Annie cleared her throat with a sudden, high squeak.

Simon's eyebrows snapped together. 'So. Looks like you were planning coffee for two. With Dan the Stallion, perhaps? But somehow you forgot to actually drink the coffee. Tell me, do you often entertain Mr Morgan in the mornings?' His voice was silky smooth, ominously polite.

Annie pressed her hands together to stop them from shaking. 'Um, no, never. He just dropped by. Out of the blue. He … he was trying to sell me a horse. For Lydia, obviously. He's some kind of horse broker in his spare time, you know. I told him we didn't want a horse.'

He gave her a long, searching look. In the end, she dropped her eyes.

'Where's Patches?' he asked at last. 'I haven't had my daily dose of fawning.'

Annie perked up. Here was a nice segue away from the dangerous topic. 'He's at the vet's. Remember? Today's the day he's being neutered, poor bloke. They're keeping him overnight and he'll come home wearing a thing like a clown's collar around his neck.'

Simon was pouring coffee. 'Here, would you like some, since it's made?'

'All right, then.' She took the mug he proffered and drank

it quickly, almost scalding her throat. Coffee had a strong smell. Perhaps it would mask the vodka and the garlic.

'I can give you your daily dose of fawning, if you like,' somebody suddenly said in a smoky, sultry, suggestive voice.

Good God. She clapped her hand over her mouth. It was *her* smoky, sultry, suggestive voice!

What on earth was the matter with her? She couldn't let him get close enough to smell her breath, and yet she seemed to be offering him sex! What if he took her up on it? She'd have to develop a sudden migraine.

He shot her a sideways look. 'Are you feeling OK, Annie?'

'Absolutely. Couldn't be better. Why do you ask?'

'I don't know. You don't seem yourself.' He moved a bit closer, still staring. 'If I didn't know better, I'd say you'd been drinking.'

Ah. Shit. Now what?

She gave a guilty laugh. 'Well, you're absolutely right,' she said. 'I have had a little drink. Um – over at Heather's.'

'At Heather's?'

'Yup. She was serving champers and orange juice. Her birthday. I went round to her house for a little party. Just a few friends.' She was improvising wildly now. 'I'd just got back from Heather's when Dan Morgan showed up on the doorstep. That's why I put on the coffee. To sober me up.'

The web was growing more tangled by the moment.

Annie could see the tension drain out of Simon's body. He relaxed visibly, all the hard lines in his face suddenly softening into a grin. 'So this is what you women do in the mornings,' he teased.

'Champers, tennis, tea parties, it's a high old life,' she agreed.

'I'm glad you're having some fun,' he said, suddenly serious. 'It's such a lifestyle change for you, stuck out here in the suburbs, after London.'

She shrugged. 'It's OK. I'm adaptable.'

'I've noticed. So anyway, could you to drive me to the station in about half an hour? I don't fancy the walk with my luggage.' Simon didn't have a car. It was his gesture towards the Green movement. Since they lived so close to the train station, he was rarely inconvenienced by his sacrifice.

Annie spluttered and began to cough. 'Drive you? Um, the thing is, the problem is, I had to take the car to the garage this morning. So, um, I don't actually have it today.'

'To the garage? Really? I didn't know it was playing up.'

'It's not really playing up. I just – well, I reckoned it was time for a service. You know. You can't be too careful when you're driving kids around.'

He shook his head. 'Annie, you're not supposed to get it serviced randomly, whenever you feel like it. There's a log book in the glove compartment. You're supposed to do it every so many thousand miles.'

'Well, *sorry*. Take me out and shoot me for being over-conscientious.'

He pursed his lips and drummed his fingers on the counter. 'OK, well I suppose I'll take a taxi then.'

'Good idea.' Annie felt quite weak with relief. 'I'll call one while you're getting ready.'

Walking home from dropping the girls at school the next day, Heather shook her head at Annie in amazement. 'So you're saying that for the rest of my life I'm going to have to pretend to your husband that my birthday is in *December*?' she asked. 'What if I want to have a big party when I turn forty?'

'I don't know. Maybe don't invite us?' Annie felt weak and wan, probably because of the after-effects of the vodka.

'It wouldn't be a party if I didn't invite you!'

'Thanks.' Annie gave a pale smile. 'Maybe you could have a girls' thing. A brunch or something. I mean, it's years away.'

Heather pulled a face. 'Not *that* many years. But men never remember birthdays, do they?'

Looking hard at her cuticles, Annie said: 'Um, Heather? Another thing. Could you possibly drive me over to the vet's to pick up my car? And do you happen to have jump leads?'

She hadn't told Heather everything that had happened yesterday. For example, she hadn't mentioned her wrestling match with Dan Morgan on the sofa. She'd only told her that she'd agreed to go to lunch with Dan after her car conked out at the vet's, and then ended up too tiddly to drive.

Tactfully, Heather didn't ask why on earth she'd been drinking at lunch time. She wouldn't really have known what to say, except that she'd been feeling out of sorts because of Simon's recent testiness.

'We'll have to step on it,' Heather said as they attached jump leads to the car batteries. 'We're supposed to be at school at eleven for the Happy Holidays recital.'

'Oh God, I forgot all about that!' Annie gasped. 'I'm a feeble excuse for a mummy, aren't I?'

'A mummy's a shrivelled-up corpse from an Egyptian tomb,' Heather said. 'You'll never be one of those, but you've got the makings of a first-class mommy.'

'Really? What are the makings?'

Heather grinned at her. 'You *give* a damn,' she said.

Half an hour later, Annie pulled up at her house in her own car again, inching along slowly so that Patches wouldn't be jostled too much. The dog was a shadow of his usual self, too humiliated by his Elizabethan collar even to jump up and greet people. As soon as she got him into the house, Annie unfastened the oversized plastic contraption around his neck and threw it recklessly into the recycling bin.

'Now,' she told him, 'if you can just resist licking yourself, you won't have to wear that thing ever again.'

He snorted derisively, then slumped onto the floor, closed his eyes, and fell heavily asleep.

Annie ran upstairs, threw open her wardrobe, and considered what she ought to wear for a Happy Holidays recital. Fifteen minutes later she was clicking down the street in her long boots, a figure-hugging black wool dress that she hadn't worn since her working days in London, and her red coat. Surely a bit of glamour wouldn't go amiss at a concert?

But the other mums were still in jeans, albeit designer ones. They had changed into jeans at some point in early October, when their Capri pants became too chilly around the ankles, and hadn't looked back since. In honour of the occasion today, most of them wore cashmere jumpers.

Perhaps to make up for the boredom imposed by the jeans regime, they all carried fabulous handbags.

Heather, who had gone straight to school from the vet's parking lot to secure a seat near the front of the hall, beckoned wildly to Annie from across the room.

'I had to fight off five women including the freaking head of the PTO to keep this seat for you,' Heather told her as she slipped into the vacant chair. 'Wow, you look fabulous.'

Annie pulled a face. 'Does anybody but me ever wear a skirt around here?'

'Sure, to weddings and funerals. Oh look, here they come!'

The children filed in, wearing Santa hats. If Annie had secretly hoped that Lydia would have a starring role, she was disappointed – unless playing the triangle qualified. All the same, Annie filmed away like mad, like any other mum in the room, capturing every flicker of Lydia's eyelids, every move of her hands, so that Simon could watch and admire when he came home.

But he didn't get home until after midnight. Patches heard the front door click and gave a muffled bark, but he wasn't up to his usual mad dash down the stairs. Hearing him moving around downstairs, Annie turned over in bed and tried to fall back asleep. Simon usually made himself a snack and sometimes even watched a little TV when he came home late, so she wasn't surprised that he didn't make his way upstairs immediately.

But when she woke up again, hours later, she felt a pang of alarm to see his side of the bed smooth and flat. She squinted at the green digital display on the radio-clock. It seemed to be four in the morning. Where on earth *was* the man?

Heaving herself out of bed, she found a dressing gown and shrugged it on, aware of the dog's wheezing breath as he slept heavily on. Simon had probably fallen asleep in front of the TV, she told herself. She'd better go downstairs and rouse him or he'd wake up stiff and cold in the morning.

When she shuffled out onto the landing, she thought she heard the low buzz of the TV, but as she approached the stairs, she realised the noise was coming from the den. A strip of light under the den door confirmed that Simon was holed up inside.

Curiosity propelled her forward.

Standing in the dark outside the closed door, she hesitated a moment. Who could he be talking to in the wee hours of the morning?

Probably somebody in England. It would be – what? – about nine a.m. over there. Something to do with the pies, no doubt.

What compelled her to put her ear to the keyhole, she never really knew.

'No, I disagree, I think we're beyond that now,' she heard Simon say quite vehemently. '... Can't keep putting off speaking to Annie ... Yes, I'm doing it tomorrow ... We're in crisis mode. Right, completely out of her depth ... I know all that ... I know, I *do* feel responsible ... Yes, it's true, she gave up a lot, coming over here. I don't deny it ... Yeah, a gamble for her, too ... Look, I *know* she's been trying – to be honest she's been bloody trying! – but she's just not cut out for it.'

Annie stood frozen, her ears burning.

'Well, exactly, and I wouldn't care ...' Simon went on. 'But the fact is she's in bed with someone else ... OK, maybe not in bed, but at least at the heavy petting stage ... I don't see why I should stand by ... Look, it's time for action ... Tomorrow ... Yes, try to make a clean break. To be honest, I think she might even be relieved to go home.'

Very slowly and quietly, Annie backed away from the door and crept to the bedroom.

Shit.

Had she really just heard that?

No, no, she couldn't have. She must be asleep and having a nightmare. Simon couldn't possibly have said ... He couldn't think ... He *couldn't* believe she was sleeping with Dan Morgan. He *couldn't* be about to ask her to go home to England. And yet that was what she thought she'd heard him say on the phone.

She climbed back into bed, shivering, still in the dressing gown. She would go back to sleep, and in the morning everything would be OK again. Because this was obviously, quite obviously, nothing but a very bad dream.

But in the morning, when she jolted awake, she found herself still in the dressing gown, the other side of the bed still flat and smooth. It seemed Simon had never even lain down on the bed! Jumping up, she ran to the den, half expecting to see him still sitting at the desk with the phone in his hand.

He wasn't there, of course – he was always out of the house by this time – but a mug of half-finished cold tea testified to the fact that he really had been sitting at the desk in the night.

Oh God. So it wasn't a nightmare after all.

OK. It couldn't be as bad as she thought it was. Things were never as bad as you thought they were.

So, what she'd do was, she'd get Lyddie ready for school, and then sit down and try to remember exactly what he'd said, and then work out exactly what the words meant. And she wouldn't think about any of it now, because Lyddie needed her to be normal.

She woke Lydia in the usual way, by opening her blinds and calling her name. As usual, Lyddie muttered and groaned and told her to go away.

She made Lyddie's usual breakfast – porridge. She packed Lyddie's usual lunch – a butter sandwich, some cheese, a yoghurt, an apple, a box of juice.

'Are you mad at me?' Lydia asked as the two of them set out for school. They were unusually early.

'Mad at you? No. Why would I be? I'm just . . . just thinking.'

'Are you still going to talk to Miss Scofield today?'

'To talk to—? Yes, yes, of course I am.' With a lurch, Annie remembered it was parent–teacher conference day.

'I thought maybe you'd forgotten.'

'Why?'

'Because you're wearing Daddy's dressing gown.'

In horror, Annie looked down to see the red terry-cloth sticking out between her black wool coat and her sheepskin boots. She turned her gasp into a careless laugh. 'Oh, for goodness sake, I'm not planning to wear *this* to the conference.'

'Good. I don't want Miss Scofield to think we're crazy people.'

Annie hurried home, showered, styled her hair and changed into something she might wear to a job interview: well-cut skirt, silk blouse, flattering little jacket, elegant heels. There, she thought, posing in the full-length mirror; even Lydia wouldn't be able to find fault.

Miss Scofield welcomed her into the classroom warmly. 'So good to see you, Mrs Keeler. I've been looking forward to showing you some of Lydia's work. Of all the children I've ever taught, I don't think I've seen such an improvement in a child over such a short space of time.'

'Really?' Annie tried to smile, willing her mind to focus on the woman in front of her.

'Oh yes! When Lydia came into this room, I had real concerns about her, as you know. The main issue of course was her choice not to use her voice in the classroom.'

'Yes, she was very shy in the beginning, wasn't she? I have my own theory about that. I think she was waiting until she figured out how to talk with an American accent.'

'What do you mean?'

'Well, now and then I catch her practising to herself. To-mah-to, to-may-do, that kind of thing.'

'Good grief, do you think that could be it?'

Annie nodded. 'I think it could be part of it.'

Miss Scofield thought for a moment, her head on one side. She looked a lot like a plump, speckled bird looking sideways at a worm.

'You know, you could be right,' she said at last. 'She really doesn't have much of an accent any more. But her written work has also progressed impressively. Here, take a look at this. It's something she wrote in class recently.'

Annie took the piece of paper the teacher handed to her.

The writing prompt at the top read, 'If you could wish for anything, what would it be?'

Annie drew in a sharp breath.

'If I could wish for anything I wood wish for a new poney statew,' she read. 'My mom gave me a statew of a poney when she came home from a trip. She went to Englnd to look aftr my granny in the hosptl. But sumthing bad happend and I broak the poney. My mom was sad. So I wish I had a new statew to give my mom.'

'Mrs Keeler? Are you OK? Can I get you a glass of water?'

Annie shook her head. 'Um, you know what, I *don't* actually feel that well.' She sniffed hard. 'I think I'd better ...' She stood up quickly. 'Thanks so much, but I think I'd better go home.'

Miss Scofield stood up too, the picture of concern. 'Yes, you look like you need to go lie down.' She held out a folder of papers. 'Here, take this with you. More of Lydia's work. You can look at it at your leisure.'

Sitting at her own kitchen table with a box of tissues at her elbow a few minutes later, Annie leafed through the small pile of Lydia's compositions. Her hands were shaking.

She blushed when she read, 'I ate porij for dinner last nite becos my mom didnt wont to cook bluddy mete again.'

And then she came to a page on which Lydia had written, in her cramped, slightly crooked hand:

'My mom is special because:

She is special becos she never had me in her tummy like ordnary moms. She is special becos there is no word for the color of her eyes. She is speciall becos she lisns to me. She is special becos she loves me. I love my mom becos she is specl.'

Patches jumped up against Annie's knee in concern. He had probably never seen a human howl before. After licking her face for a while, he wandered off and she could hear him lapping water from his bowl. The salt of her tears must have given him a thirst.

When Annie had recovered her composure, she went over to the sink and splashed cold water on her red eyes. Then she threw herself into the car and drove too fast over to Heather's house.

Without knocking or ringing, she crashed through the open door and went straight into the kitchen. Heather wasn't in it. 'Heather!' she yelled, walking into the family room.

A man with his jeans around his ankles was sprawled over Heather's sofa – and Heather was underneath him.

'God Almighty,' said Annie, and scurried to the safety of the kitchen, breathing in gulps, and struck by a terrible urge to laugh. She shoved her fist in her mouth, to be on the safe side.

She wished with all her might that she could simply leave the house altogether and go sprinting back up the street to the relative safety of her own kitchen, but she absolutely had to talk to Heather, even in these appalling circumstances.

Moments later, Heather appeared in the kitchen, still fiddling with buttons and zips. 'For God's sake, why didn't you *knock*?' she demanded.

'I don't know!' Annie tried to compose her twitching face. 'I'm sorry, Heather. Really, really sorry. I didn't mean to interrupt. I just – I have to tell you something.'

'It's not what you think,' Heather said, tossing her hair out of her face. 'I'm not cheating on Rob. Not really. You see, he's agreed we should try artificial insemination.'

'He— *what?*'

'That's right.'

'And that – that's how they do artificial insemination these days?' Again, an awful, inappropriate urge to guffaw was building up in Annie's mouth and nose area like an explosive sneeze that she had to quell, against all odds.

'No, of course not. But I don't like the idea of sperm from some complete stranger. I mean, what weirdo donates his sperm to a sperm bank, anyway? For indiscriminate use? You'd have to be some kind of megalomaniac trying to take over the whole freaking world with your gene pool, or something. And Dan just seemed like the best—'

Annie's hand flew to her mouth. 'That's *Dan* in there?'

'Oh shit. You didn't recognise him?'

'Well, I only saw his ... Heather, what the hell are you *doing*? You love Rob. I mean, don't you?'

Heather's eyes glittered. 'Yeah, I love him,' she said. 'That's why I'm freaking doing this. Oh God, Annie, you're making me second-guess myself now. I was so sure this was the way to go. I mean, Dan has the right body type and colouring and everything. He's smart too, under the cowboy act. And Rob's getting restless again. He's kind of like ... I don't know, like a half-tame wolf looking out into the woods at full moon. Sometimes I just get the feeling he wants to be released back into the wild real bad. You have *no idea* how much I need another baby.'

Annie shook her head. 'I think I'm beginning to have *some* idea. Look, don't listen to me, Heather. I mean, who am I to give advice about anybody's marriage?'

Heather narrowed her eyes. 'What do you mean? Nothing's up with your marriage ... *is* it?'

'I don't know! I mean, yes, everything's bloody falling apart, and I didn't even *know* it till last night. Simon's been tense, but I was such an idiot, I thought it was work related. See, at about four in the morning I heard him talking on the phone, and he – he was telling someone in England that he's planning to break things off with me. Probably his po-faced bloody brother. He seems to have this weird idea that I'm having an affair ...'

'What? With *who*, for Christ's sake?'

'Um, never mind. But the thing is, I've got to go into the city and talk to Simon.'

'Yeah, sounds like a good idea. Set the guy straight. Read him the riot act, Annie! What the hell does he think he's doing, talking about you to his freaking brother? Spreading vicious rumours?'

Annie felt her face puckering up. Heather strode over and folded her in a hug. 'Take it easy now,' she said, patting her shoulder.

'I'm fine, I'm fine,' Annie lied. 'I really just came over to ask if you could please pick Lydia up from school and have her over here this afternoon? I'm not sure how long I'll be.'

'Sure, no problem. She can come to the barn with us and watch Hailey ride.'

'Thanks a million. So sorry to burst in on you. I should've just called. I don't know why I didn't.'

'It's not the same over the phone,' Heather said.

'You're right,' said Annie. 'Anyway, bye, see you later. You'd better get back to . . . you know.' She jerked her head in the direction of the family room.

Heather grimaced. 'Are you kidding? I think the moment has passed.'

'I'm sort of glad to hear that,' Annie said. Then she squeezed Heather's shoulder and left.

# Chapter Thirteen

By the time Annie arrived at ChefPro's offices, her eyes were no longer red. She had found some powder in her bag and used it to tone down the shine on her nose and forehead. But she knew she still looked a bit wild and frenzied, especially after a small boy pointed her out to his mother and said, 'Mom, is *that* what you call a fruit-loop?'

When she burst into the office on the twenty-fourth floor, the woman behind the reception desk looked up with wide eyes. 'Mrs Keeler?' she gasped. 'Is . . . is your husband expecting you today? It's quite a big day for everybody, and he didn't say anything to me.'

'No, he jolly well isn't, but—'

She was stopped, mid-sentence, by the sudden appearance of Cindy Faig who erupted into the lobby carrying a briefcase and a large pie carton. She powered past Annie and the receptionist without a glance, striding through the room and out of the glass doors, towards the lifts.

'One moment,' said the receptionist, and scuttled off after Cindy.

Without hesitation, Annie seized the moment to sneak through the doors into the inner sanctum of ChefPro's

New York headquarters. From memory, she made her way down the corridor to Simon's corner office. Propelled by adrenalin, she threw the door open without knocking. But the room was as empty as it had been the first time she'd seen it, the throne-like chair behind the big desk pushed out at a crazy angle as if Simon had left the room in a hurry.

Undeterred by this minor setback, Annie went back out into the corridor, as determined as ever to track Simon down and confront him. She was thankful to be in her parent–teacher conference clothes as she hurried down the carpeted hallways. Jeans and sheepskin boots would probably have made her a bit conspicuous.

She passed two men in suits walking along, deep in conversation, and asked, 'Where can I find Simon Keeler?'

Both of them looked at her with wide eyes. 'Conference room,' one of them said, pointing down a corridor. 'But he's already started.'

Started what? she wondered. Never mind, whatever it was, he'd just have to stop.

As she rushed past doors, she noticed that they had numbers on them, and sometimes a discreet sign, such as 'Kitchen', or 'Restroom'. This was helpful, as it meant she didn't have to keep throwing open doors and startling people. She'd done that once or twice, and was now vaguely afraid that someone would call security.

When she reached a door labelled 'Conference Room', she paused for breath. It would probably be better if she composed herself before she went in. It was possible he wasn't alone in there.

She took out her make-up compact again and powdered

her nose. Finding an eye pencil, she quickly drew a line along her upper lids. It was her signature look, after all. The line turned out a little shaky so she smudged the kohl as best she could with one hand. There! She always felt more confident when she was wearing her war paint. Now if she could just find some lipstick ... She didn't seem to have any, so she made do with chap stick instead.

She took a last deep breath and opened the door.

About a dozen faces turned to stare at her.

Simon was standing at the far side of a round table, close to a screen, with a pointer in one hand. On the screen was a large photograph of a golden-brown pie divided into slices, with various facts and figures superimposed on the image. Seated around the table were several men and two women, all dressed in dark suits, all gaping at Annie.

'Um, hello.' Annie gave a tiny wave with the tips of her fingers.

Simon put his pointer down and inserted a finger between his collar and his throat. '*Annie?*' he breathed.

'Yes, hi, I, ah, I just thought I'd come in. For the, um, the presentation.'

'Everybody, this is my wife, Annie,' Simon said. 'How she got wind of this, I'm not sure. But I'm happy to, ah, have her support.'

A few people smiled and one man clapped – although, looking at his face, Annie couldn't help thinking it was an ironic kind of clapping.

Annie slipped into a seat quickly. She would just wait here until the presentation was finished, and then she'd be able to speak her mind to Simon. She could bide her time.

She was on a slow burn. As she settled in, somebody pushed a sheaf of papers across to her, but she didn't look at it.

At first, she didn't even try to listen to Simon's speech. She was too taken up with rehearsing in her head what she was going to say to him afterwards. But after a while, the words began to penetrate.

'. . . the results of the latest focus group,' he was saying. 'I think you'll find this new information quite surprising. I'm aware that some of you have already made up your minds, but I'd like you, just for the sake of argument, to pretend for the moment that you haven't.'

People were shuffling through papers, and Annie heard a collective intake of breath.

'These numbers can't be right,' said a man with jowls.

Simon was smiling now. 'Ladies and gentlemen, these numbers are not bogus. These numbers are one hundred per cent authentic. These numbers are based on genuine consumer reaction to our new line of products. So, just to take you through it: Pie One garnered a ninety-five per cent approval rating across a sample group of approximately three hundred tasters; the largest sample group we have ever run. Pie Two performed almost as well with an approval rating of eighty-seven per cent. And Pie Three was still a huge hit with an approval rating of seventy per cent.'

Annie glanced through the stapled presentation pack in front of her. She soon found the page everyone was look-ing at. It was divided in half horizontally, with the top half depicting three pies, labelled respectively 'Steak and Kidney', 'Chicken and Mushroom', and 'Pepper Steak'. A large number 66 was printed over the steak and kidney pie;

62 was printed over the chicken and mushroom one, and 59 was printed over the pepper steak one. Above the three pies was the title, 'Approval Rating from Large-Scale UK Sample Group'.

The lower half of the page showed three more pies, mysteriously labelled Pie One, Pie Two and Pie Three. These bore the numbers, 95, 87, 70. This graphic was titled, 'Approval Rating from Large-Scale US Sample Group'.

'What the research is telling us,' said Simon with absolute self-assurance, 'is that our new range of products has the potential to outsell – yes, to *outsell* – our top-selling pies in England. Think, ladies and gentlemen, of what this could mean to ChefPro in these tough financial times. And we're talking the *US* market here. The biggest – yes, the *biggest* – fast-food market in the world. The fast-food market that makes our fast-food market in the UK look like nothing but a . . . a cottage industry.'

A hand shot up. 'That's all very well,' said a woman with fierce eyebrows, 'but what about the cultural issues? Last time you had some of us convinced that we could sell our pies on the "Olde World Made New" platform – the whole Robin Hood and Sherwood Forest concept. But that idea has been shot down in flames pretty convincingly. How do we know your new ideas have any more stamina?'

'Yes,' shouted somebody else in a heckling tone, 'how do you make our pies competitive in a market that research – *your* research, I might add – has shown to be predisposed to be resistant?'

At that precise moment a knock sounded on the door.

'Come in,' Simon called. The door opened, and in walked

a nervous-looking young man in a suit and an apron, carrying a large round tray of pies. 'Put them in the middle of the table, please,' Simon instructed.

The delicious smell wafting up from the pies made Annie feel quite light-headed. She hadn't eaten breakfast, of course.

'Ta da!' said Simon with a small, ironic bow. 'Ladies and gentlemen, I give you Pie One. But before you sample it, I'd like to fill you in on our process here. The thing is, we've all been well aware of the cultural barriers. Americans are about as likely to eat steak and kidney pie as they are to eat … say, goat's scrotum.'

There was a burst of voices. Simon held up his hands.

'To the American market, pie is sweet. It doesn't involve meat. And pies are open, not closed. Plus, beef is generally consumed in the form of mince, or ground meat as it's known here. So how to address these issues? Well, I have to say, my wife was the one who gave me my first clue to a solution.'

'Me?' Annie mouthed, her face going red as people turned around to stare at her.

'We had a small dinner party at our house, and offered mini pies as hors d'ouevres,' Simon went on. 'Sadly, the pies went largely untouched. On the other hand, the shrimp cheese balls we were also offering went down a storm. That was when my wife made the incisive comment that we should have filled the pies with shrimp cheese balls.'

People were frowning and looking confused.

'Then it came to me,' said Simon with huge conviction. 'It's all about thinking outside the box. Why should we confine ourselves to traditional English fillings? So, before these pies on the table get cold, I'd like you to sample ...' he took a deep breath and flourished one arm in the air, 'the *hamburger* pie.'

A huge commotion broke out. 'Hamburger pie?' people were asking.

'It's a simple concept,' said Simon. 'Meat pie is unfamiliar to this market. Hamburger is tried and tested. So what do we do? Combine the two. It's a sort of entry-level meat pie for our American consumers. The idea is people then have enough faith in the product to try something less familiar. You can even make a cheeseburger pie – we've tried it. And guess, what? Our testers loved it. The only difference with this type of pie is its shape. The pastry is moulded around the burger, so you lose the traditional look – but that turns out to be a good thing. The traditional look seems to be associated with negative ideas about English cuisine. Gustav, would you please slice up the pies into bite-sized portions.'

The nervous young man brought a knife out of an apron pocket and sliced away.

Annie took a piece as soon as she could and popped it into her mouth. It was strangely delicious.

From the excited babble among the others at the table, Annie reckoned they thought so too – although some of the raised voices, she had to say, sounded faintly hostile.

'In the end we decided to stick with the original pastry recipe.' Simon was almost shouting to be heard, now. 'People don't seem to prioritise calorie counts when they buy fast food. Why should we be the chumps to force wholewheat on people?' Somebody cheered, but several people booed. Simon held up his hand. 'I'm not saying we won't have a healthy alternative line, but our main product will be the full monty. Gustav, you can bring in Pie Two and Pie Three.'

Gustav left the room and came back remarkably quickly with another tray.

'Pie Two and Pie Three are, respectively, pizza pie and All-American beef chilli pie.'

An even louder commotion broke out than before. Then a large man with a Scottish accent and quite a lot of crumbs around his mouth stood up, raised a hand for silence, and said, 'Simon Keeler, you're a bleeding genius.'

In spite of herself, Annie couldn't help swelling with pride. It was true – Simon was a genius! He'd presented the Americanised pie argument so persuasively that she was just about ready to cash out all her own savings and put them into the project herself. The only thing she didn't understand was why he'd had to make this presentation at all. Wasn't the American chain an established ChefPro venture already?

A thin woman raised her voice above the hubbub. 'This is all very well, but we can't make decisions on the spot,' she said coldly. 'We need to scrutinise all the facts and figures, look at all the research, go over all the backing documents before we say yay or nay to this.'

'You have those in front of you,' said Simon. 'Why don't I leave you to thrash it out? I'll be in my office when you need me. As I've already told you, I'm prepared to make considerable personal sacrifices to see this initiative go forward. My team is on the same page, too. Tough times call for tough measures.'

'Good plan,' said the Scot.

'Maybe, but will it be enough?' said the thin woman.

'Let's go, Annie.' Simon stood up and crossed to her side of the room, holding the door open for her to go out ahead of him.

# Chapter Fourteen

They walked down the corridor in utter silence.

When they reached Simon's office, he shut the door and leaned against it, closing his eyes for a moment. Annie noticed then that his face was pale and strained. And so it should be, given that he'd been up all night plotting to make a 'clean break' with his wife.

Outrage boiled up in her all over again.

'How did you know?' he asked, opening his eyes. 'It was supposed to be a secret meeting. Who leaked it to you?'

'*What?*'

'Don't get me wrong, I appreciate the support – but I was gobsmacked when you walked in. We've been under strict orders to keep a lid on this. Don't want to risk panicking our shareholders. Was it Cindy Faig? Did *she* tell you?'

'I have no clue what you're on about.'

'You . . . hang on. You *didn't* come specifically to sit in on the meeting with the executive committee?'

'Is that who those people are? I noticed they were all Brits.'

'Annie, they've been flying in all week for this. They're meeting to decide the fate of the whole American fast-food push.' He began to pace the room. 'People have been panicking and wanting to pull out. There's a lot of money involved, a lot of risk. I'm trying my damnedest to save the project.' He stopped and stared at her. 'So ... if you didn't come in for that, what on earth *are* you doing here? It's not another surprise lunch visit, is it?'

She threw her head back defiantly. 'I'm here to meet you halfway, mate,' she said. 'Were you planning to have it out with me this evening? On your own terms?'

He frowned. 'What the hell are you talking about now?'

'Oh, don't play innocent with me. I know you don't want a big scene with your precious executive committee sitting just a few doors down. But the point is, you've seriously underestimated me.'

'I've— *what?*'

'Yes, you bloody have. For one thing, I *am* Lydia's mother. Oh, maybe not biologically, maybe not genetically, maybe not even legally, but practically, emotionally, effectively – in all the bloody ways that really count – I *am* her mother. And I have documents to prove it.'

It was true. She felt like a lioness threatened with separation from her cub. Never again would she doubt she carried the maternal gene.

Fishing in her bag, she pulled out two pieces of paper and gave them to him. He took them, still looking puzzled, and read them swiftly.

'Lydia wrote this stuff?' he asked in wonder.

'Yes, she wrote it,' Annie said. 'So I'm here to tell you, mate, that I'm not budging. I'm here for the duration. I made a solemn promise to Wilma Forsythe that I would do my best for Lydia, and damn it, I will.'

'Wilma Forsythe?' Simon muttered. 'What on earth—'

'Don't interrupt. I've come all this way to have my say, and I'm going to have it. Whatever terms we have to work out, so be it. If you're fool enough to believe I'm cheating on you, then that's your problem, mate. But I'm not leaving that child. You saw what happened when I went away for just a few days. She pretty much went to pieces. If you reckon I'm ever going to walk away from her again, mate, you've got another think coming.'

Simon's eyebrows were close to his hairline now. 'Why in God's name do you keep calling me "mate" in that ... that *poisonous* way?'

She gave a bitter laugh. 'What's with all the backtracking? I heard you on the phone last night, mate. I *heard* you telling your brother that I was sleeping with Dan Morgan.'

'Sleeping with ...? Hey, hang on. This is just ... just crazy. I didn't even speak to my brother last night.'

'Well, maybe it wasn't him, but I heard you telling *somebody* that our marriage is in crisis and you were going to have to break the news to me today that you wanted me gone.'

Suddenly, Simon's face cleared and he sank down into a chair. 'Oh, God, I think I know what this is ...'

At that moment, there was a slight knock on the door and Gustav appeared, still wearing his apron.

'They want you,' he said to Simon. Then he noticed Annie, standing with her hands on her hips, chest heaving. 'Whoops! Didn't mean to interrupt.'

Simon stood up eagerly.

Annie felt pure fury flood through her body. He was about to walk out on her and go back to the executive meeting. His body language was unmistakable. If he walked out on her now, she didn't know what she would do – but it would be pretty spectacular, whatever it was.

'Does it look good?' Simon asked.

'Difficult to tell,' said Gustav. 'They're kind of quiet.'

'Quiet? Shit. That doesn't bode well.' Simon glanced at Annie, then back at Gustav. 'Can you go back and tell them they're going to have to wait a bit? I'll come as soon as I can. There's something really important I have to sort out first.'

Gustav's eyes widened. 'But Mr Abernathie says he has a plane to catch—'

'Tell them to *wait*.'

Gustav nodded mutely and left the room.

'Annie,' Simon said urgently, 'I had a conversation last night about sacking Cindy Faig. I think that's what you overheard.'

Annie shook her head. 'No, it definitely wasn't that. You mentioned my name. You said I was either in bed with someone else, or at the heavy petting stage. Why you would believe something like that on such minimal evidence is a mystery to me but if that's how little you think of me, well, it's your loss, mate. And don't try to fob me off with some bullshit story.'

Simon pressed a finger to the place between his eyebrows. 'Seriously, Annie. I know what I said. I said I thought *Cindy* was in bed with someone else. By that I meant I thought she was trying to sell our wholewheat crust recipe to our

299

direct bloody competitor. Which is exactly what she was threatening to do.'

Annie frowned. Something about Simon's tone was beginning to give her pause. He didn't sound like a man trying to blow smoke in his wife's eyes.

She shook her head. 'I don't understand.'

'Look, it's quite simple, really. Ever since we arrived here, I've been aware that Cindy wasn't performing at the same level as the rest of the team. She was responsible for researching locations for the restaurants, but she messed up. Repeatedly. When she screwed things up in Boston, she knew her job was on the line. Do you remember the day she came out to the house to give you that file?'

Annie nodded. She was still smarting over the way Cindy had walked away from a hot pot of tea.

'Well, she tucked a little note in there, along with the Brewster focus group report, letting me know that she was in talks with William Tell.'

Annie's eyes widened. William Tell had always been the Goliath among British baked goods companies.

'She let me know that she had access to our most successful wholewheat crust recipe. She said she wouldn't hesitate to pass it on, *if necessary*.'

'You mean, if you fired her?'

'Exactly.'

Annie suddenly thought of Cindy storming through the reception area that morning, holding her briefcase and a cardboard box.

'But you fired her anyway?' she asked with a flash of insight.

'Of course I bloody did. I was talking to our top personnel guy last night, over in the London office. He wanted me to hold onto her, to contain the damage, as he put it. But I wanted her gone. I don't give a damn about the wholewheat crust recipe. She can publish it in the *Sunday Times*, for all I care. I just didn't want her spilling the beans about the hamburger pie before I could speak to the committee. That's why I didn't give her the boot until this morning.'

Annie put her hands up to her face. 'This all sounds ... sort of convincing,' she said slowly, 'but you *were* talking about me. I know you were. You even said my name. You said you felt responsible for bringing me here. You said we were "in crisis". You said you were going to break the news to me today.'

'Well, dammit, that's because I *do* have news to break to you today. I was going to wait until after the committee's verdict on the pie project – but what the hell, I'll do it now. Annie, I'm sorry but it's bad news. Even if the committee agrees to go ahead with the American venture, they're going to cut our budget down to the bones. They told me that when I went over to London.'

Annie had an abrupt memory of him in the shower after that trip, his face turned up to the water in an attitude of despair.

'It's not surprising,' he went on. 'After all, most companies have frozen their development initiatives altogether. So, well, the thing is, I've offered to take a massive salary cut. We'd lose the ex-pat benefits. ChefPro wouldn't pay our rent or our health insurance, or anything. We'd have to move into a much smaller house and cut out all our discretionary spending. No more housekeepers, no more landscape gardeners, no more tennis lessons. We'd have to trade in the minivan for something smaller.'

Annie gaped at him. 'That's the crisis?'

'There's more, I'm afraid. If they don't go with the project, they're going to cut my job. They're going to fire me.'

Annie continued to gape for a moment. Then her face creased in an enormous smile. 'Oh, this is fantastic!' she said. 'This is wonderful!'

Simon looked baffled. 'Annie, did you understand what I just said? I'm on the brink of losing my job. Even if I don't, we're going to be in a tough situation.'

'Yes, yes, of course I understand. You think I care if you lose your job? You think I give a damn about moving to a smaller house? As long as we're together, I'll live in a bloody *tree*house, if we have to. We'll get my mum to come and give us lessons in frugality.'

'You mean it?' Simon still looked strained and pale. 'You're not just saying it to make me feel better?'

'Oh Simon, you're an idiot but I love you.'

All of a sudden the strain and anxiety left his face, and it lit up with relief. 'I am an idiot,' he said, shaking his head. 'I should have told you what was going on ages ago, but I wanted to shield you from the worry.'

'I don't need to be shielded,' Annie said fiercely. 'Never keep secrets from me again, OK?'

'Are you sure you're not keeping any secrets from me?' Simon looked at her searchingly.

She blushed scarlet. 'Of course I'm not.'

'Then why the hell mention that clown, Dan Morgan?'

'Because he's the only single man I know in this entire country,' she said quickly. 'And because you were jealous when I offered him coffee.'

'Good enough,' said Simon, and pulled her into his arms.

As his mouth came down on hers, a thunderous knock at the door caused them to leap apart.

Gustav poked his head into the room without waiting for permission to enter.

'You have to come right now,' he told Simon, his eyes wild. 'They're getting restless.'

'All right.' Simon smoothed down his shirt and rolled his shoulders like a prize fighter about to enter the ring. 'You'd better stay here, love,' he whispered to Annie. 'This could get ugly.'

'You've got to be joking,' she hissed back at him. 'I'm coming with you.' She grabbed his hand, which was cold and clammy, and hung on tight.

He shrugged in a resigned way and followed Gustav out of the room. As they reached the closed door of the conference room, he gave her fingers a quick and rather painful squeeze.

'This is it,' he said. 'Take a deep breath. Here we go.'

As they entered the room, the buzz of talk died abruptly and everybody turned to look at them. Nobody smiled, not even the jolly Scotsman. Annie almost wished she hadn't insisted on coming.

'So,' said the thin woman, 'you've found the time to pop back in and see us, have you?'

'To be honest, I thought you'd be deliberating for longer.' Simon's voice was pleasant. 'Something came up on my side that really couldn't wait.'

'Evidently. I'm sure there are dozens of things more important in your life right now than this committee meeting.' A small titter went round the room in tribute to the thin woman's wit.

'No, only one,' Simon murmured.

Then the stout Scot spoke up: 'Simon, lad, you did a fair job presenting your case to us today. But we all know the American market is a tough nut to crack. We all know the odds are stacked against you.'

Annie felt her throat constricting. She glanced at Simon. His face was an unreadable mask.

A mild-looking man in tweeds spoke up: 'Oh, for God's sake. Put the chap out of his misery.'

The thin woman sniffed. 'Very well. Simon, it was by no means unanimous, but I'm afraid the committee has decided to let you go ahead with this ill-advised venture.'

Annie's hand flew to her mouth. She felt dizzy with relief. Nauseous, even.

Simon, meanwhile, was taking the news with calm self-possession, walking around the room shaking people's hands and accepting their congratulations. But Annie could tell he was chock-full of bottled emotion because the tips of his ears were very red.

'Well done, lad,' said Mr Abernathie (for that was the Scotsman's name), 'you proved to everybody in this room that you have a fire in your belly. I just hope that the miserable state of the global economy isn't enough to souse it.'

'I'm not going to let a recession get in the way of my game plan,' Simon told him firmly.

'Well, since I've probably missed my plane by now, what say we go out and drink to that?' Mr Abernathie suggested, looking mightily pleased with Simon's rejoinder.

'I'm sorry, sir,' Simon said, 'but I can't do it. I'm taking my wife out to lunch.'

'He's a cool bloody customer,' Annie heard somebody mutter, 'turning down the CEO for his wife.'

Annie's heart thumped with fresh alarm. 'What if he's really annoyed that you wouldn't do drinks, and changes his mind about the entire project?' she hissed as she and Simon stepped into the lift together.

'On no, Abernathie admires a show of spirit,' Simon told her, grinning from ear to ear.

And so it came to pass that Annie and Simon finally did go out for lunch together in Manhattan.

Sitting in a dim room holding hands across the table, they stared into each other's eyes like honeymooners.

'You were magnificent,' Annie said. 'You blew them away.'

'You were pretty fabulous yourself,' Simon said. 'It was a stroke of genius, coming in on the meeting like that. Much harder to sack a man in front of his wife.'

She laughed. 'God, on the contrary, I think that woman would have enjoyed the drama.'

'You mean Skinny Bitch? That's what the team calls her. Thank God, here's the champagne at last!'

As the waiter moved to pour champagne for Annie, she put her hand over her glass. 'I'd better not,' she said.

He raised an eyebrow. 'Oh, surely you can have a glass? Plenty of time for it to wear off before you get back to Norbury.'

But she kept her hand over her glass. 'How come you're not asking me about Lydia?' she said suddenly. 'School gets out in just over an hour. I'll never make it back in time.'

'Well, I trust you've taken care of it,' he said.

'You mean, you think I've learned my lesson, since last time?'

'Annie, I never thought you needed to "learn a lesson". Last time, if you remember, you fell asleep. This time you're conscious, so I know you've done whatever needs to be done about Lydia – because, as you pointed out earlier – you *are* her mother.'

'You really believe that?'

His face was deadly serious. 'I really believe it.'

'Good,' she said. 'Because, well, I *have* actually been keeping a bit of a secret from you. From everybody, really. I wanted to wait for the right moment to say anything. I mean, I know the timing is terrible with this recession and everything, and I certainly would have liked us to, you know, discuss things first, but sometimes you don't have as much control over life as you think you do—'

'Annie. What are you saying?'

'I'm saying I seem to be, sort of, pregnant.'

She looked at Simon anxiously. For a moment his face was completely still. Then he took her hands in his and held on pretty tight, but still he didn't speak. He didn't need to, though; his face blazed with joy.

# Epilogue

It was May in Norbury, and the town was transformed by blossom. Drifts of crocuses and daffodils had appeared as if by magic under the beech and dogwood trees in Annie Keeler's tiny patch of garden.

Under one of these trees, Annie and Heather had set up a couple of folding tables and fifteen chairs. Heather was smoothing a tablecloth and Annie was tying balloons to the chairs when the school bus pulled up in front of the house and three girls came tumbling out into the street.

Patches, asleep under a folding table, woke instantly at the whoosh of the bus's brakes, and went hurtling across the lawn to jump all over the girls.

'Hi, girls. Go inside first and dump your backpacks!' Annie shouted across to them. 'Then you can play.'

But Lydia ran straight over to her and wrapped her arms around her waist. With a listening look, she pressed her ear against Annie's stomach. 'He's not moving,' she said after a moment, her brow buckling in worry. 'Is he OK?'

'Oh, he's sleeping,' Annie said. 'He sleeps all day and parties all night. You know that.'

'Come on, Lyddie,' Hailey called from the kitchen door. 'Let's get a snack.'

'Why don't we go in too; take a break,' Heather suggested. 'We're just about done out here. Plenty of time before the rest of them arrive, and you're supposed to be keeping your fluids up.'

'Yeah, I could do with a cup of tea,' Annie agreed.

In the tiny kitchen, Annie's mother, wearing a pink pin-striped apron, was cutting slices of bread and jam for Lydia, Hailey, and Courtney Phelps. 'Don't eat too much bread now, girls,' she was saying, 'you've got the birthday cake coming later.'

The children took their sandwiches and ran off outside to wolf them down in the treehouse, where there was a bit more space. Patches chased after them and positioned himself beneath the tree, watching for crusts.

As Annie put the kettle on, Heather squeezed herself along the wall to a seat at the kitchen table. 'What's this?' she asked, picking up a pile of papers.

'Oh, those are my notes for the frugality lecture at the library tomorrow,' said Gladys proudly.

'Wow.' Heather looked impressed. 'Listen to this, Annie! "Laundry: get over the idea that you have to wash every single item after just one wear. Instead, just give clothes in the hamper a good sniff. If something doesn't smell bad and hasn't got visible stains, fold it up and put it away for another outing." Eeew. That sounds gross.'

'I'm all for it,' said Annie, pouring out a cup of instant coffee for Heather. 'I've halved my laundry loads that way. Read out some more.'

'"Wash clothes in cold water unless they are badly soiled,"' Heather read. '"You will save on electricity and your clothes will last longer. String a washing line in your back garden and hang things out to dry. Again, you will save energy and your clothes will smell wonderful."'

'Oh God, that reminds me, I need to get the sheets off the line before the other kids arrive,' Annie said.

'Relax, it's taken care of.' Gladys nodded towards a basket of folded linens, visible through the kitchen door on the sofa in the living room.

'God, you're brave, hanging up your laundry in *this* town,' Heather said. 'I've never even laid eyes on a washing line around here.'

'On the contrary,' Annie told her, 'drive around a bit. It's catching on. You'll see.'

At that moment Courtney Phelps stuck her head through the door. 'Mrs Keeler, can we go on the trampoline now?'

'You can but you may not,' said Gladys.

'If you've finished chewing,' said Annie, shaking her head at her mum.

The trampoline was Lydia's birthday present, and it had been a huge hit ever since three men from the sports shop had set it up two days ago. Of course, it took up a good portion of the back garden, but Annie didn't mind the sacrifice. The grass would die in the shade beneath it, and there would be less lawn for Simon to mow.

'I still can't believe Simon got her a trampoline,' Heather said, shaking her head. 'I mean, weren't trampolines right up there with horses as waaaay too risky for Lydia?'

Annie smiled. 'Yeah, but Simon's making a huge effort

not to be paranoid about that sort of thing.'

'You mean he might let her ride?' Heather asked avidly.

Annie pulled a face. 'I didn't say that. For one thing, it costs an arm and a leg, doesn't it? But the pie places are doing pretty well. So you never know.'

Courtney Phelps poked her head in again. 'Mrs Keeler, can we take the bikes out?'

'Not now. There's no grown-up to watch you. Why don't you jump some more?'

'Short attention span, that one,' Heather muttered when Courtney had run off again. 'It's kind of surprising that she and Lyddie are so thick. Didn't they have a disastrous play date, ages ago?'

'Yeah, it was really bad,' Annie remembered, pulling a face. 'But Lyddie's sort of ... different, now. She likes Courtney's energy.'

'Darn right, she's different,' Heather said with a low whistle. 'Coach Matt tells me they're calling her The Assassin on the soccer field this season.'

'Why they can't play a nice game like netball, I don't know,' said Gladys, shaking her head. 'Whoever heard of little girls playing football?'

Heather met Annie's eye and gave a shadow of a wink. 'How long are you staying this time, Mrs Harleigh?' she asked.

'Oh, I don't know.' Gladys stopped wiping down surfaces and came over to sit with them at the table. It was a bit tight. 'This lecture tour Donna Knopf set up for me keeps getting extended. They want me to talk in libraries all over Connecticut, New York, Massachusetts and New

Jersey now. I might even be here when the baby comes. Flo will be getting a nice long break.'

'So it's working out with the companion?' Heather asked.

'Oh, she's all right but she's terribly hard on soap,' Gladys said. 'Goes through it like water.'

'Mum, should I tell her our plan?' Annie asked.

Gladys shrugged. 'I don't see why not.'

'Well, it's very hush-hush right now,' Annie told Heather, 'but I'm going to take Mum's frugality notes and make them into a book. *Bare-bones Living*. Something like that.'

'Hey! That's a *fantastic* idea! I mean, there's a huge market now for that sort of thing. Have you looked into finding a publisher, or is it too early for that?'

'Well, as a matter of fact, I've put out a few feelers,' Annie admitted. 'Just on the strength of my blog. Do you know, I have about five thousand followers now? So that gives me what they call a "platform". I already have a tentative—'

'MOM!' Lydia stood in the kitchen door, her eyes almost feverish with excitement. 'Mom! Come outside quick. People are coming! Samantha and McKenna are here! And Patches is knocking down chairs to get the balloons!'

So Annie and Heather and Gladys stood up and walked into the spring sunshine to throw a party.